Lecture Notes in Computer Science   6427

Commenced Publication in 1973
Founding and Former Series Editors:
Gerhard Goos, Juris Hartmanis, and Jan v

Robert Meersman   Tharam Dillon
Pilar Herrero (Eds.)

On the Move to
Meaningful Internet Systems:
OTM 2010

Confederated International Conferences:
CoopIS, IS, DOA and ODBASE
Hersonissos, Crete, Greece, October 25-29, 2010
Proceedings, Part II

 Springer

Volume Editors

Robert Meersman
Vrije Universiteit Brussel (VUB), STAR Lab
Bldg G/10, Pleinlaan 2, 1050 Brussel, Belgium
E-mail: meersman@vub.ac.be

Tharam Dillon
Curtin University, Digital Ecosystems and Business Intelligence
Institute (DEBII), EU4, De Laeter Way, Bentley, 6102 Australia
E-mail: t.dillon@curtin.edu.au

Pilar Herrero
Universidad Politécnica de Madrid, Facultad de Informática
Campus de Montegancedo S/N
28660 Boadilla del Monte, Madrid, Spain
E-mail: pherrero@fi.upm.es

Library of Congress Control Number: 2010938249

CR Subject Classification (1998): C.2, D.2, H.4, I.2, H.3, K.6.5

LNCS Sublibrary: SL 3 – Information Systems and Application, incl. Internet/Web
and HCI

ISSN	0302-9743
ISBN-10	3-642-16948-1 Springer Berlin Heidelberg New York
ISBN-13	978-3-642-16948-9 Springer Berlin Heidelberg New York

springer.com

© Springer-Verlag Berlin Heidelberg 2010
Printed in Germany

Typesetting: Camera-ready by author, data conversion by Scientific Publishing Services, Chennai, India
Printed on acid-free paper   06/3180

General Co-chairs' Message for OnTheMove 2010

The OnTheMove 2010 event in Hersonissos, Crete, during October 24–29, further consolidated the growth of the conference series that was started in Irvine, California, in 2002, and held in Catania, Sicily, in 2003, in Cyprus in 2004 and 2005, in Montpellier in 2006, in Vilamoura in 2007 and 2009, and in Monterrey, Mexico, in 2008. The event continues to attract a diversified and representative selection of today's worldwide research on the scientific concepts underlying new computing paradigms, which, of necessity, must be distributed, heterogeneous and autonomous yet meaningfully collaborative. Indeed, as such large, complex and networked intelligent information systems become the focus and norm for computing, there continues to be an acute and ever increasing need to address and discuss face to face in an integrated forum the implied software, system and enterprise issues as well as methodological, semantic, theoretical and application issues. As we all realize, e-mail, the Internet and even video conferences are not by themselves sufficient for effective and efficient scientific exchange.

The OnTheMove (OTM) Federated Conferences series has been created to cover the scientific exchange needs of the community/ies that work in the broad yet closely connected fundamental technological spectrum of Web-based distributed computing. The OTM program every year covers data and Web semantics, distributed objects, Web services, databases, information systems, enterprise workflow and collaboration, ubiquity, interoperability, mobility, grid and high-performance computing.

OTM does not consider itself a so-called multi-conference but instead is proud to give meaning to the "federated" aspect in its full title: it aspires to be a primary scientific meeting place where all aspects of research and development of Internet- and intranet-based systems in organizations and for e-business are discussed in a scientifically motivated way, in a forum of (loosely) interconnected workshops and conferences. This ninth edition of the OTM Federated Conferences event therefore once more provided an opportunity for researchers and practitioners to understand and publish these developments within their individual as well as within their broader contexts. To further promote synergy and coherence, the main conferences of OTM 2010 were conceived against a background of three interlocking global themes, namely, "Cloud Computing Infrastructures," "The Internet of Things, or Cyberphysical Systems," "(Semantic) Web 2.0 and Social Computing for the Enterprise."

Originally the federative structure of OTM was formed by the co-location of three related, complementary and successful main conference series: DOA (Distributed Objects and Applications, since 1999), covering the relevant infrastructure-enabling technologies, ODBASE (Ontologies, DataBases and Applications of SEmantics, since 2002), covering Web semantics, XML databases and ontologies, and CoopIS (Cooperative Information Systems, since 1993), covering the application of these technologies in an enterprise context through, for example, workflow systems and knowledge management. In 2007 the IS workshop (Information Security) was added to try cover also the specific issues of security in complex Internet-based information systems. Each of the main conferences specifically seeks high-quality contributions and encourages researchers to treat their respective topics within a framework that incorporates jointly (a) theory, (b) conceptual design and development, and (c) applications, in particular case studies and industrial solutions.

Following and expanding the model created in 2003, we again solicited and selected quality workshop proposals to complement the more "archival" nature of the main conferences with research results in a number of selected and more "avant-garde" areas related to the general topic of Web-based distributed computing. For instance, the so-called Semantic Web has given rise to several novel research areas combining linguistics, information systems technology and artificial intelligence, such as the modeling of (legal) regulatory systems and the ubiquitous nature of their usage. We were glad to see that seven of our successful earlier workshops (ADI, EI2N, SWWS, ORM, OnToContent, MONET, ISDE) re-appeared in 2010 with, in some cases, a fourth or even fifth edition, often in alliance with other older or newly emerging workshops, and that no fewer than four brand-new independent workshops could be selected from proposals and hosted: AVYTAT, DATAVIEW, P2PCDVE, SeDeS. Our OTM registration format ("one workshop buys all") actively intends to stimulate workshop audiences to productively mingle with each other and, optionally, with those of the main conferences.

We were also most happy to see that once more in 2010 the number of quality submissions for the OnTheMove Academy (OTMA, formerly called Doctoral Consortium Workshop), our "vision for the future" in research in the areas covered by OTM, took off again and with increasing success. We must thank the team of collaborators led by Peter Spyns and Anja Schanzenberger, and of course the OTMA Dean, Erich Neuhold, for their continued commitment and efforts in implementing our unique interactive formula to bring PhD students together. In OTMA, research proposals are submitted for evaluation; selected submissions and their approaches are (eventually) presented by the students in front of a wider audience at the conference, and are intended to be independently and are extensively analyzed and discussed in public by a panel of senior professors.

As said, all four main conferences and the associated workshops shared the distributed aspects of modern computing systems, and the resulting application pull created by the Internet and the so-called Semantic Web. For DOA 2010, the primary emphasis stayed on the distributed object infrastructure; for ODBASE 2010, it became the knowledge bases and methods required for enabling the use of formal semantics; for CoopIS 2010, the focus as usual was on the interaction of such technologies and methods with management issues, such as occur in networked organizations, and for IS 2010 the emphasis was on information security in the networked society. These subject areas overlap in a scientifically natural fashion and many submissions in fact also treated an envisaged mutual impact among them. As for the earlier editions, the organizers wanted to stimulate this cross-pollination by a "shared" program of famous keynote speakers around the chosen themes: we were quite proud to announce Wil van der Aalst, T.U. Eindhoven, The Netherlands, Beng Chin Ooi, National University of Singapore, Michael Brodie, Chief Scientist, Verizon, USA, and Michael Sobolewski, Polish-Japanese Institute of IT, Poland.

We received a total of 223 submissions for the four main conferences and 127 submissions in total for the workshops. The numbers are about 5% lower than for 2009. Not only may we indeed again claim success in attracting an increasingly representative volume of scientific papers, many from the USA and Asia, but these numbers of course allow the Program Committees to compose a high-quality cross-section of current research in the areas covered by OTM. In fact, the Program Chairs of the CoopIS 2010 conferences decided to accept only approximately one paper from every five submissions, while ODBASE 2010 and DOA 2010 accepted about the same number of papers for presentation and publication as in 2008 and 2009 (i.e., average one paper out of three to four submitted, not counting posters). For the workshops and IS 2010 the acceptance rate varied but the aim was to stay consistently at about one accepted paper for two to three submitted, and subordinated of course to scientific quality assessment. As usual we have separated the proceedings into three volumes with their own titles, two for the main conferences and one for the workshops, and we are most grateful to the Springer LNCS team in Heidelberg for their professional suggestions and meticulous collaboration in producing the files for downloading on the USB sticks.

The reviewing process by the respective Program Committees was again performed very professionally, and each paper in the main conferences was reviewed by at least three referees, with arbitrated e-mail discussions in the case of strongly diverging evaluations. It may be worthwhile to emphasize that it is an explicit OTM policy that all conference Program Committees and Chairs make their selections completely autonomously from the OTM organization itself. Like last year, paper proceedings were on separate request and order this year, and incurred an extra charge.

The General Chairs are once more especially grateful to the many people directly or indirectly involved in the set-up of these federated conferences. Few people realize what a large number of individuals have to be involved, and what a huge amount of work, and in 2010 certainly also financial risk, the organization of an event like OTM entails. Apart from the persons in their roles mentioned above, we therefore wish to thank in particular our eight main conference PC Co-chairs: CoopIS 2010: Herve Panetto, Jorge Cardoso, M. Brian Blake; ODBASE 2010: Alejandro Buchmann, Panos Chrysanthis, York Sure; DOA 2010: Ernesto Damiani, Kai Hwang. And similarly the 2010 IS, OTMA and Workshops PC (Co-)chairs: Javier Cámara, Carlos E. Cuesta, Howard Foster, Miguel Angel Pérez-Toledano, Stefan Jablonski, Olivier Curé, David Thau, Sara Comai, Moira Norrie, Alessandro Bozzon, Giuseppe Berio, Qing Li, Kemafor Anyanwu,

Hervé Panetto (again), Alok Mishra, Jürgen Münch, Deepti Mishra, Patrizia Gri-
foni, Fernando Ferri, Irina Kondratova, Arianna D'Ulizia, Paolo Ceravolo, Majed
Ayyad, Terry Halpin, Herman Balsters, Laura Ricci, Yan Tang, Jan Vanthienen,
Yannis Charalabidis, Ernesto Damiani (again), Elizabeth Chang, Gritzalis Ste-
fanos, Giles Hogben, Peter Spyns, Erich J. Neuhold and Anja Schanzenberger.
Most of them, together with their many PC members, performed a superb and
professional job in selecting the best papers from the harvest of submissions. We
are all grateful to our supremely competent and experienced Conference Secretariat and technical support staff in Antwerp, Daniel Meersman, Ana-Cecilia,
and Jan Demey, and last but certainly not least to our editorial team in Perth
(DEBII-Curtin University) chaired by Houwayda El Fawal Mansour. The General Co-chairs acknowledge with gratitude the academic freedom, logistic support and facilities they enjoy from their respective institutions, Vrije Universiteit
Brussel (VUB), Curtin University, Perth, Australia, and Universidad Politécnica
de Madrid (UPM), without which such an enterprise would not be feasible. We
do hope that the results of this federated scientific enterprise contribute to your
research and your place in the scientific network... We look forward to seeing
you again at next year's event!

August 2010   Robert Meersman
                                                               Tharam Dillon
                                                               Pilar Herrero

Organization

OTM (On The Move) is a federated event involving a series of major international conferences and workshops. These proceedings contain the papers presented at the OTM 2010 Federated conferences, consisting of four conferences, namely, CoopIS 2010 (Cooperative Information Systems), IS 2010 (Information Security), DOA 2010 (Distributed Objects and Applications) and ODBASE 2010 (Ontologies, Databases and Applications of Semantics).

Executive Commitee

General Co-chairs

Robert Meersman	VU Brussels, Belgium
Tharam Dillon	Curtin University of Technology, Australia
Pilar Herrero	Universidad Politécnica de Madrid, Spain

CoopIS 2010 PC Co-chairs

Hervé Panetto	Nancy University, France
Jorge Cardoso	Universidade de Coimbra, Portugal
Brian Blake	University of Notre Dame, USA

IS 2010 PC Co-chairs

Giles Hogben	European Network and Information Security Agency, Greece
Stefanos Gritzalis	University of the Aegean, Greece

DOA 2010 PC Co-chairs

Ernesto Damiani	Università degli Studi di Milano, Italy
Kai Hwang	University of Southern California, USA

ODBASE 2010 PC Co-chairs

Alejandro Buchmann	Technische Universität Darmstadt, Germany
Panos Chrysanthis	University of Pittsburgh, USA
York Sure	GESIS, Germany

Publication Chair

Houwayda Elfawal Mansour	DEBII, Australia

Publicity-Sponsorship Chair

Ana-Cecilia Martinez Barbosa	DOA Institute, Belgium

Logistics Team

Daniel Meersman   Head of Operations
Ana-Cecilia Martinez Barbosa
Jan Demey

CoopIS 2010 Program Committee

Marco Aiello	Leo Mark
Antonia Albani	Maristella Matera
Antonio Ruiz Cortés	Massimo Mecella
Kemafor Anyanwu	Ingo Melzer
Joonsoo Bae	Jan Mendling
Zohra Bellahsene	John Miller
Salima Benbernou	Arturo Molina
M. Brian Blake	Jörg Müller
Nacer Boudjlida	Nirmal Mukhi
Christoph Bussler	Miyuki Nakano
James Caverlee	Moira C. Norrie
Francisco Curbera	Werner Nutt
Vincenzo D'Andrea	Andreas Oberweis
Xiaoyong Du	Gerald Oster
Schahram Dustdar	Jin Woo Park
Johann Eder	Cesare Pautasso
Rik Eshuis	Barbara Pernici
Opher Etzion	Li Qing
Renato Fileto	Lakshmish Ramaswamy
Ted Goranson	Manfred Reichert
Paul Grefen	Stefanie Rinderle-Ma
Michael Grossniklaus	Duncan Ruiz
Amarnath Gupta	Paulo Rupino
Mohand-Said Hacid	Kai-Uwe Sattler
Geert-Jan Houben	Ralf Schenkel
Zhixing Huang	Jialie Shen
Stefan Jablonski	Aameek Singh
Paul Johannesson	Michael W. Sobolewski
Epaminondas Kapetanios	Xiaoping Sun
Dimka Karastoyanova	Susan Urban
Rania Khalaf	Willem-Jan Van den Heuvel
Hiroyuki Kitagawa	Irene Vanderfeesten
Akhil Kumar	François B. Vernadat
Frank Leymann	Maria Esther Vidal
ZongWei Luo	Mathias Weske
Sanjay K. Madria	Jian Yang
Tiziana Margaria	Aoying Zhou

IS 2010 Program Committee

Alessandro Acquisti
Vijay Atluri
Daniele Catteddu
Bruno Crispo
Gwenael Doerr
Josep Domingo Ferrer
Simone Fischer-Huebner
Clemente Galdi
Janusz Gorski
Jiankun Hu
Hai Jin
Maria Karyda
Stefan Katzenbeisser
Spyros Kokolakis
Wei-Shinn Ku
Evangelos Markatos
Sjouke Mauw

Chris Mitchell
Yi Mu
Nuno Ferreira Neves
Siani Pearson
Milan Petkovic
Andreas Pfitzmann
Frank Piessens
Norbert Pohlmann
Rodrigo Roman
Pierangela Samarati
Biplab K. Sarker
Aggeliki Tsochou
Luis Javier Garcia Villalba
Roman Yampolskiy
Alec Yasinsac
Andre Zuquete

DOA 2010 Program Committee

Subbu Allamaraju
Mark Baker
Boualem Benatallah
Elisa Bertino
Lionel Brunie
Athman Bouguettaya
Judith Bishop
Gordon Blair
Harold Carr
Geoffrey Coulson
Schahram Dustdar
Frank Eliassen
Pascal Felber
Benoit Garbinato
Niels Gruschka
Medhi Jazayeri
Eric Jul
Nick Kavantzas
Deyi Li

Ling Liu
Joe Loyall
Frank Manola
Gero Mühl
Nikola Milanovic
Graham Morgan
Lionel Ni
Rui Oliveira
Francois Pacull
Arno Puder
Michel Riveill
Luis Rodrigues
George Spanoudakis
Joerg Schwenk
Cyrus Shahabi
Azzel Taleb-Bendiab
Gaogang Xie
Kokou Yentongon
Albert Zomaya

ODBASE 2010 Program Committee

Karl Aberer
Harith Alani
María Auxilio Medina
Sonia Bergamaschi
Leopoldo Bertossi
Alex Borgida
Christof Bornhoevd
Mohand Boughanem
Paolo Bouquet
Silvana Castano
Tiziana Catarci
Paolo Ceravolo
Catherine Chronaki
Oscar Corcho
Ernesto Damiani
Irini Fundulaki
Aldo Gangemi
Benjamin Habegger
Mounira Harzallah
Manfred Hauswirth
Bin He
Prateek Jain
Vana Kalogeraki
Uladzimir Kharkevich
Manolis Koubarakis
Werner Kuhn
Maurizio Lenzerini

Li Ma
Vincenzo Maltese
Riichiro Mizoguchi
Peter Mork
Anne Ngu
Olga Papaemmanouil
Adrian Paschke
Ilia Petrov
Peter R. Pietzuch
Evaggelia Pitoura
Demetris Plexousakis
Wenny Rahayu
Rajugan Rajagopalapillai
Satya Sahoo
Pavel Shvaiko
Sergej Sizov
Veda C. Storey
Umberto Straccia
Heiner Stuckenschmidt
York Sure
Robert Tolksdorf
Susan Urban
Guido Vetere
Kevin Wilkinson
Baoshi Yan
Benjamin Zapilko
Demetris Zeinalipour

Supporting and Sponsoring Institutions

OTM 2010 was proudly supported or sponsored by Vrije Universiteit Brussel in Belgium, Curtin University of Technology in Australia, Universidad Politecnica de Madrid in Spain, Object Management Group, and Collibra.

Table of Contents – Part II

On the Move 2010 Keynotes

Distributed Objects and Applications (DOA) International Conference 2010

Data Storage and Processing

Transaction and Event Management

Virtualization Performance, Risk and Scalability

Cloud and Distributed System Security

Ontologies, DataBases, and Applications of Semantics (ODBASE) International Conference 2010

Invited Talks

Annotations

Inconsistencies

Reactivity and Semantic Data

Ontology Mapping and Semantic Similarity

Domain Specific Ontologies

Table of Contents – Part I

On the Move 2010 Keynotes

Cooperative Information Systems (CoopIS) International Conference 2010

Coopis Keynote Paper

Process Models and Management

Modeling of Cooperation

Services Computing

Information Processing and Management

Human-Based Cooperative Systems

Ontology and Workflow Challenges

International Symposium on Information Security (IS) International Conference 2010

Access Control, Authentication and Policies

Secure Architectures

Cryptography

OTM'10 Keynote

Beng Chin Ooi

National University of Singapore (NUS)

Short Bio

Beng Chin is Professor of Computer Science at School of Computing, at the National University of Singapore (NUS). He obtained his BSc (1st Class Honors) and PhD from Monash University, Australia, in 1985 and 1989 respectively. His research interests include database performance issues, indexing techniques, multimedia and spatio-temporal databases, P2P systems and advanced applications, and cloud computing. His current system projects include BestPeer, P2P based data management system, and epiC, a data-intensive cloud computing platform.

He has served as a PC member for international conferences including ACM SIGMOD, VLDB, IEEE ICDE, WWW, SIGKDD and Vice PC Chair for ICDE'00, 04,06, co-PC Chair for SSD'93 and DASFAA'05, PC Chair for ACM SIGMOD'07, and Core DB track PC chair for VLDB'08. He is the Editor-in-Chief of IEEE Transactions on Knowledge and Data Engineering (TKDE), and a trustee member of VLDB Endowment Board. He is the recipient of ACM SIGMOD 2009 Contributions award.

Talk

"Supporting OLTP and OLAP Queries on Cloud Platforms"

MapReduce-based systems have been widely used for large-scale data analysis. Although these systems achieve storage-system independence, high scalability, and fine-grained fault tolerance, their performance have been shown to be unsatisfactory.It has also been shown that MapReduce-based systems are significantly slower than Parallel Database systems in performing a variety of analytic tasks. Some attribute the performance gap between MapReduce-based and Parallel Database systems to architectural design. This speculation yields an interesting question: Must a system sacrifice performance to achieve flexibility and scalability? Consequently, we conducted an in-depth performance study of MapReduce in its open source implementation, Hadoop. We identified various factors that have significant performance effect on the system. Subsequently, based on what we have learned, we propose a new architectural design as an attempt to support both OLTP and OLAP queries on Cloud platforms. I shall describe some of our ongoing work in this talk.

R. Meersman et al. (Eds.): OTM 2010, Part II, LNCS 6427, p. 705, 2010.
© Springer-Verlag Berlin Heidelberg 2010

OTM'10 Keynote

Michael Brodie

Chief Scientist, Verizon, USA

Short Bio

Dr Michael Brodie is Chief Scientist of Verizon Services Operations in Verizon Communications, one of the world's leading providers of communications services. Dr Brodie works on large-scale strategic Information Technology opportunities and challenges to deliver business value from advanced and emerging technologies and practices. He is concerned with the Big Picture, core technologies and integration within a large scale, operational telecommunications environment.

Dr Brodie holds a PhD in Databases from the University of Toronto and has active interests in the Semantic Web, SOA, and other advanced technologies to address secure, interoperable web-scale information systems, databases, infrastructure and application architectures. Dr Brodie has authored over 150 books, chapters and articles and has presented over 100 keynotes or invited lectures in over 30 countries.

Dr Brodie is a member of the USA National Academies Committee on Technical and Privacy Dimensions of Information for Terrorism Prevention and other National Goals. He is an Adjunct Professor, National University of Ireland, Galway (2006-present) and Visiting Professor, Curtin University of Technology, Perth, Australia (2009). He chairs three Advisory Boards - Semantic Technology Institutes International, Vienna, Austria (January 2007 - present); Digital Enterprise Research Institute, National University of Ireland (2003-present); Semantic Technology Institute, Innsbrück, Austria (2003-present); and is a member of several advisory boards - The European Research Consortium for Informatics and Mathematics (2007 - present); School of Computer and Communication Sciences, École Polytechnique Fédérale de Lausanne, Switzerland (2001 - present); European Union's Information Society Technologies 5th, 6th and 7th Framework Programmes (2003-present); several European and Asian research projects; editorial board of several research journals; past Board member of research foundations including the VLDB Endowment (Very Large Data Bases, 1992 - 2004), and of the Advisory Board of Forrester Research, Inc. (2006-2008). He is on the Advisory Board of Chamberlain Studios (2006-present).

Talk

"Over The Moon: Data Integration's Essential Challenges".

R. Meersman et al. (Eds.): OTM 2010, Part II, LNCS 6427, pp. 706–707, 2010.

To understand and communicate reality, man simplifies his perception of reality by creating models that are necessarily simpler than reality. For an Information System and its supporting databases to fulfill their requirements, the databases are modeled by radical simplification of reality by identifying those aspects of reality that are essential to the intended perception, i.e., those that are relevant to the requirements, and eliminating all other aspects; and representing the essential properties of those aspects in terms that meet the requirements within the perceptual and modelling limits of the human modeler.

Data modelling involves human designers using a database design methodology together with data modelling tools, e.g., Entity-Relational (ER) and Relational, based on data models, e.g., ER and Relational, and implemented using a relational DBMS. To be more precise, data modelling is an integral component with Information Systems design and development that involves additional methodologies, models, e.g., workflow, and implementation information, e.g., workflow engines, application servers, and web servers. The design, development, and operation of an Information Systems and its databases in dependent on all of the methodologies, models, and tools. For simplicity, we limit this discussion to the design, development, and operation of databases; even though the requirements, loosely referred as the semantics, of the intended perception can be represented anywhere in the Information System - in the databases, the processes, or the application code.

Just as two or more human perceptions of the same or overlapping aspects of reality are unlikely to be identical, so are two or more databases representing overlapping aspects of reality unlikely to be identical. Different databases are designed and developed at different times, to meet different requirements, by different people with different understandings of reality, using different tools, and different methodologies. Hence, two or more different perceptions or databases are typically distinct and are relatively incomplete, inconsistent, and potentially conflicting.

Over time, business, legal, and other requirements have led to the need to represent the real world more precisely in Information Systems. Large-scale integration beyond the scale of most applications necessarily brings in real requirements that prevent the application of simplifying assumptions normally used to solve theses problems (as lower scale). It is likely that as modelling requirements become increasingly complex and as scale of integration grows, this complexity will arise for future Information Ecosystems and the conventional techniques will no longer work.

DOA'10 - PC Co-chairs Message

Welcome to the 12th International Symposium on Distributed Objects, Middleware and Applications (DOA 2010), held in Crete, Greece, October 2010. The DOA conference series has become a key forum for presenting and discussing new perspectives and exciting research results. Over the years, DOA topics have included new computing paradigms like Web Services and SOA, cloud computing, virtualization, and many others, dealing with new new problems and ideas as well as with the design and deployment of practical applications. DOA has always managed to reach the right balance between theoretical and practical aspects of IT research. Hopefully, this year is no exception. Much interest has focused on the emerging paradigm of Cloud Computing, with papers covering topics as diverse as virtualization management, cloud-based service environments and cloud encryption and security; but other key topics of distributed computing, especially the ones related to services, continued to be well represented among DOA submissions. Contributions based on experimental work have been particularly encouraged, with early results also accepted where they were considered to be sufficiently important to a wider audience. The quality of submissions this year has been very high, again following a well-established DOA tradition. All of the papers passed through a rigorous selection process, with at least three reviewers per paper and much discussion on the relative merits of accepting each paper throughout the process. At the end, we decided to accept 12 regular papers of the original 27 submissions. Two more submissions were accepted as posters. Putting together a conference like DOA is always a team effort, and many different contributions need to be acknowledged. First of all we would like to gratefully acknowledge the work of all of the authors, whether or not their paper was accepted. Thanks for choosing DOA to present your research work. Secondly, we are grateful to the dedicated work of the leading experts in the field from all over the world who served on the Program Committee and whose names appear in the proceedings. Thanks for helping us in putting together an excellent program. Finally, we would like to thank the whole OTM team for its support and guidance, including the general co-chairs Tharam Dillon and Robert Meersman, the publication chairs and the secretariat. The proceedings you hold in your hand are the result of the hard work that everyone has put into DOA. We hope you enjoy them and maybe consider submitting something in the future.

August 2010

Ernesto Damiani
Kai Hwang
DOA'10

R. Meersman et al. (Eds.): OTM 2010, Part II, LNCS 6427, p. 708, 2010.
© Springer-Verlag Berlin Heidelberg 2010

Data Stream Analytics as Cloud Service
for Mobile Applications

Qiming Chen and Meichun Hsu

HP Labs, Palo Alto, California, USA
Hewlett Packard Co.
{qiming.chen,meichun.hsu}@hp.com

Abstract. Many mobile applications are based on cloud services such as location service, messaging service, etc. Currently most cloud services are based on statically prepared information rather than the real-time analytics results of dynamically captured events. A paradigm shift is to take Continuous Stream Analytics (CSA) as a cloud service, which, however, poses several specific challenges in scalability, latency, time-window semantics and transaction control.

In this work we extend the SQL query engine to unify the processing of static relations and dynamic streams for providing the platform support of CSA service. This platform is significantly differentiated from the current generation of stream processing systems which are in general built separately from the database engine thus unable to take advantage of the functionalities already offered by the existing data management technology, and suffer from the overhead of inter-platform data access and movement.

To capture the window semantics in CSA, we introduce the *cycle-based query model* and support it in terms of the *cut-and-rewind* query execution mechanism. This mechanism allows a SQL query to run cycle by cycle for processing the unbounded stream data chunk by chunk, but without shutting the query instance down between chunks for continuously maintaining the application state across the execution cycles, as required by sliding-window oriented operations. We also propose the *cycle-based transaction model* with cycle-based isolation and visibility. To scale-up analytics computation, we introduce the parallel infrastructure with multi-engines cooperated and synchronized based the common data chunking criteria without centralized coordination. To scale-up service provisioning, we investigate how to stage the continuously generated analytics results efficiently through metadata manipulation without physical data moving and copying.

We have prototyped our approach by extending the PostgreSQL, resulting in a new kind of tightly integrated, highly efficient platform for providing CSA service. We tested the throughput and latency of this service using a well-known stream processing benchmark and with WebOS based Palm phones. The test results show that the proposed approach is highly competitive. Providing CSA cloud service using HP Neoview parallel database engine is currently explored.

R. Meersman et al. (Eds.): OTM 2010, Part II, LNCS 6427, pp. 709–726, 2010.
© Springer-Verlag Berlin Heidelberg 2010

1 Introduction

We are at the beginning of the age of planetary computing. Billions of people will be wirelessly interconnected, and the only way to achieve that kind of massive scale usage is by massive scale, brutally efficient cloud-based infrastructure where both the data storage and the data processing happen outside of the mobile device. Cloud computing is a model for enabling convenient, on-demand network access to a shared pool of configurable computing resources (e.g., networks, servers, storage, applications, and services) that can be rapidly provisioned and released with minimal management effort or service provider interaction. Today, there are already some good examples of mobile cloud computing applications including mobile Gmail, Google Maps, location service and some navigation applications. This trend will continue.

Further, mobile applications increasingly depend on the analytics results of real-time events, such as the traffic status based on the location, speed, accident involvement of many individual cars (Fig 1). To most of mobile device users, the interesting information is not the individual events such as each car's position and speed, but the statistically summarized information dictating the traffic status - the volume of cars, the average or moving average speed of a lane, etc, which are derived from the individual events through Continuous Stream Analytics (CSA). With the new technologies like HTML5, which does local caching, could help mobile cloud application to get past the internet access speed barrier in using the real-time information service. However, to the best of our knowledge, CSA as a Cloud Service has not yet been addressed properly.

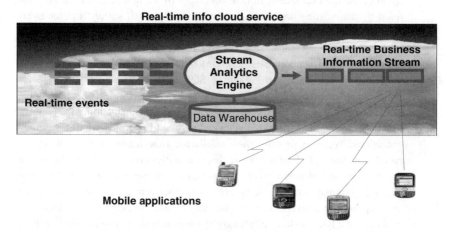

Fig. 1. Continuous stream analytics service for mobile applications

1.1 The Problem

There exist a number of common issues in cloud service provisioning which are not the focuses of this paper. Instead, we focus on combining data warehousing and stream processing technologies [3,8,9,12] to offer low-latency data-intensive CSA as a cloud service. We see the current generation of stream processing systems is not the candidates for the above purpose since they are in general built separately from the data warehouse and query engine, which can cause significant overhead in data access and data movement, and is unable to take advantage of the functionalities already offered by the existing data warehouse systems. In order to realize CSA as a Cloud Service, in this work we tackle the following hard problems.

- Converging stream processing and data management for lowering the latency of data-intensive CSA with fast data access and reduced data movement.
- Supporting continuous but granule-based query model for continuous and chunk-wise (e.g. on the data falling in apart or sliding time windows) stream analytics.
- Providing appropriate transaction semantics to allow the stream analytic results to be visible to the cloud clients in time while the continued query for generating them is still running.
- Scale-up the CSA through multi-engines cooperative parallel computing and efficiently staging the infinite, real-time stream analytics results.

1.2   The Solution

To support CSA as a Cloud Service, we propose the following approaches.

- We define a unified query model over both static relations and dynamic streaming data, and develop techniques to extend query engines to support the unified model. We propose the *cut-and-rewind* query execution mechanism to allow a SQL query to be executed cycle by cycle for processing the data stream chunk by chunk, but without shutting the query instance down between chunks for continuously maintaining the application context across the execution cycles as required by sliding-window oriented operations.
- We support the *cycle-based transaction model*, characterized by the cycle-based isolation and visibility, in delivering CSA results to the clients of cloud service in time while the query for generating these results is continuously running.
- We scale-out CSA by having multiple engines cooperated and synchronized with the common data chunking criteria without centralized coordination.
- In order to support fast access to the CSA results we develop the "table-ring" mechanism, and extended the query engine to support it, which allows the infinite, real-time analytics results to be kept in a list of small-sized tables based on time sequence, and staged through "switching labels" without actual data copying and moving, and without shutting down the continued query for generating them. As a result, these analytics results are easily manageable and downloadable to the mobile devices running WebOS and HTML 5.

We have implemented our approach by extending the PostgreSQL engine for supporting stream processing, and by using multiple extended PostgreSQL engines for parallelized CSA. In order to exam our platform, we tested it using the popular Linear Road benchmark designed for stream processing on the server side, and with WebOS based Palm phones on the client side. The test results show that the proposed approach is highly competitive. Providing CSA cloud service using HP Neoview parallel database engine is currently explored.

The rest of this paper is organized as follows: Section 2 deals with the convergence of stream analysis and data management for cloud service provisioning, including the cycle based query model and transaction model, the query engine extension, and the experiment results. Section 3 describes the CSA service architecture, the Map-Reduce based scheme for cooperating multiple engines in parallel and distributed CSA, as well as the specific data staging approach for efficiently handling real-time, continuous and infinite stream analytics results. Section 4 compares with the related work and concludes the paper.

2 Continuous Stream Analytics Engine for Cloud Service

Our CSA infrastructure unifies the capabilities of stream processing and query processing, with a set of core components as well as system support for providing cloud service. Mobile applications can use the real-time event analytics results generated by pre-defined continuous queries, or create specific continuous queries on the event streams. In this sense, our work actually covers SaaS (Cloud Software as a Service), PaaS (Cloud Platform as a Service), as well as IaaS (Infrastructure as a Service).

2.1 Extend Query Engine for Data-Intensive Stream Analytics

There exist some fundamental differences between the conventional query processing and the stream processing. First, a query is defined on bounded relations but stream data are unbounded; next, stream processing adopts window-based semantics, i.e. processing the incoming data chunk by chunk falling in consecutive time windows; however, the SQL operators are either based on one tuple (such as filter operators) or the entire relation; further, stream processing is also required to handle sliding window operations continuously across chunk based data processing; and finally, endless stream analytics results must be continuously accessible along their production, under specific transaction semantics.

In fact, the pipelined query processing is essentially a kind of streaming, and stream analytics is a data-intensive computation chain. With these in mind, we advocate an extended SQL model that unifies queries over both dynamic streams and static tables, and a new architecture for integrating stream processing and DBMS to support continuous, "just-in-time" analytics with granule-based query and transaction semantics.

Stream Source Function. We start with providing unbounded relation data to fuel queries continuously. The first step is to replace the database table, which contains a set of tuples on disk, by the special kind of table function, called Stream Source Function (SSF) that returns a sequence of tuples to feed queries without first storing on disk. A SSF can listen or read data/events sequence and generate stream elements tuple by tuple continuously. A SSF is called multiple, up to infinite, times during the execution of a continuous query, each call returns one tuple. When the end-of-cycle event or condition is seen, the SSF signals the query engine to terminate the current query execution cycle.

We rely on SSF and query engine for continuous querying on the basis that "as far as data do not end, the query does not end", rather than employing an extra scheduler to launch a sequence of one-time query instances. The SSF scan is supported at two levels, the SSF level and the query executor level. A data structure containing function call information, bridges these two levels; that is initiated by the query executor and passed in/out the SSF for exchanging function invocation related information. We use this mechanism for minimizing the code change, but maximize the extensibility, of the query engine.

Stream Analytics State. One important characteristics of stream processing is the use of stream-oriented history-sensitive analytic operators such as moving average or change point detection. This represents a different requirement from the regular query processing that only cares about the current state. While the standard SQL engine contains a number of built-in analytic operators, stream history-sensitive operators are not supported. Using User Defined Functions (UDFs) is the generally accepted mechanism to extend query operators in a DBMS. A UDF can be provided with a data buffer in its function closure, and for caching stream processing state (synopsis). Furthermore, it is also used to support one or more *emitters* for delivering the analytics results to interested clients in the middle of a cycle, which is critical in satisfying stream applications with low latency requirement.

We had extensive studies on UDFs [4,6]. We use UDFs to add window operators and other history sensitive operators, buffering required raw data or intermediate results within the UDF closures. A scalar UDF is called multiple times on the per-tuple basis, following the typical FIRST_CALL, NORMAL_CALL, FINAL_CALL skeleton. The data buffer structures are initiated in the FIRST_CALL and used in each NORMAL_CALL. A window function defined as a scalar UDF incrementally buffers the stream data, and manipulates the buffered data chunk for the required window operation. Since the query instance remains alive, as supported by our *cut-and-rewind* model, the UDF buffer is retained between cycles of execution and the data states are traceable continuously (we see otherwise if the stream query is made of multiple one-time instances, the buffered data cannot be traced continuously across cycle boundaries). As a further optimization, the static data retrieved from the database can be loaded in a window operation initially and then retained in the entire long-standing query, which removes much of the data access cost as seen in the multi-query-instances based stream processing.

2.2 Stream Analytics with Cycle-Based Continuous Query Model

We introduce the data granule-based query model for CSA: given a query Q over a set of relation tables $T_1,..,T_n$ and an infinite stream of relation tuples S with a criterion Φ for cutting S into an unbounded sequence of chunks, e.g. by every 1-minute time window,

$$<S_0, S_1, ..., S_i, ...>$$

where S_i denotes the *i-th* "chunk" of the stream according to the chunking-criterion Φ. S_i can be interpreted as a relation. The semantics of applying the query Q to the unbounded stream S plus the bounded relations $T_1,..,T_n$ lies in

$$Q(S, T_1,..,T_n) \rightarrow < Q(S_0, T_1,..,T_n), ... Q(S_i, T_1,..,T_n), ... >$$

which continuously generates an unbounded sequence of query results, one on each *chunk* of the stream data.

Our goal is to support the above semantics using a continuous query that runs cycle by cycle for processing the stream data chunks, each data chunk to be processed in each cycle, in a single, long-standing query instance. In this sense we also refer to the *data chunking criterion* Φ as the *query cycle specification*. The cycle specification can be based on time or a number of tuples, which can amount to as small as a single tuple, and as large as billions of tuples per cycle. The stream query may be terminated based on specification in the query (e.g. run for 60 cycles), user intervention, or a special end-of-stream signal received from the stream source. We also introduce the cycle-based transaction model with the *cycle-based isolation* mechanism, to support *continuous querying with continuous persisting*.

We introduce the *cut-and-rewind* query execution mechanism to support truly continuous query with the above semantics, namely, cut a query execution based on the cycle specification (e.g. by time), and then rewind the state of the query without shutting it down, for processing the next chunk of stream data in the next cycle.

- **Cut.** *Cutting* stream data into chunks is originated in the SSF at the bottom of the query tree. Upon detection of end-of-cycle condition, the SSF signals *end-of-data* to the query engine through setting a flag on the function call handle, that, after being interpreted by the query engine, results in the termination of the current query execution cycle. If the cut condition is detected by testing the newly received stream element, the *end-of-data* event of the current cycle would be captured upon receipt of the first tuple of the next cycle; in this case, that tuple will not be returned by the SSF in the current cycle, but buffered within the SSF and returned as the first tuple of the next cycle. Since the query instance is kept alive, that tuple can be kept across the cycle boundary.
- **Rewind.** Upon termination of an execution cycle, the query engine does not shut down the query instance but *rewinds* it for processing the next chunk of stream data. Rewinding a query is a top-down process along the query plan instance tree, with specific treatment on each node type. In general, the intermediate results of the standard SQL operators (associated with the current chunk of data) are discarded but the application context kept in UDFs (e.g. for handling sliding windows) are retained. The query will not be re-parsed, re-planned or re-initiated.

Note that rewinding the query plan instance aims to process the next chunk of data, rather than re-deliver the current query result; therefore it is different from "rewinding a query cursor" for re-delivering the current result set from the beginning.

Under this *cut-and-rewind* mechanism, a stream query execution is divided into a sequence of *cycles*, each for processing a chunk of data only; it, on one hand, allows applying a SQL query to unbounded stream data chunk by chunk within a single, long-standing query instance; on the other hand, allows the application context (e.g. data buffered associated with a UDF to be retained continuously across the execution cycles, which is required for supporting sliding-window oriented, history sensitive operations. Bringing these two capabilities together is the key in our approach.

Query Cycle based Transaction Model. One problem of the current generation of DSMSs is that they do not support transactions. Intuitively, as stream data are unbounded and the query for processing these data may never end, the conventional notion of transaction boundary is hard to apply. In fact, transaction notions have not been appropriately defined for stream processing, and the existing DSMSs typically make application specific, informal guarantees of correctness.

Conventionally a query is placed in a transaction boundary. In general, the query result and the possible update effect are made visible only after the commitment of the transaction (although weaker transaction semantics do exist). In order to allow the result of a long-running stream query to be incrementally accessible, we introduce the cycle-based transaction model incorporated with the *cut-and-rewind* query model, which we call *continuous querying with continuous persisting*. Under this model a stream query is committed one cycle at a time in a sequence of "micro-transactions". The transaction boundaries are consistent with the query cycles, thus synchronized with the chunk-wise stream processing. The per-cycle stream processing results are made visible as soon as the cycle ends. The isolation level is Cycle based Read Committed (CRC). To allow the cycle results to be continuously visible to external world, regardless of the table is under the subsequent cycle-based transactions, we enforce record level locking.

We extended both SELECT INTO and INSERT INTO facilities of the PostgreSQL to support the cycle-based transaction model. We also added an option to force the data to stay in memory, and an automatic space reclaiming utility should the data be written to the disk.

2.3 Experiment Results

We use the widely-accepted Linear-Road (LR) benchmark [11] to test our extended query engine. The LR benchmark models the traffic on express-ways for the 3-hour duration; each express-way has two directions and 100 segments. Cars may enter and exit any segment. The position of each car is read every 30 seconds and each reading constitutes an event, or stream element, for the system. A car position report has attributes *vid* (vehicle ID), *time* (seconds), *speed* (mph), *xway* (express-way), *dir* (direction), *seg* (segment), etc. The benchmark requires computing the traffic statistics for each highway segment, i.e. the number of active cars, their average speed per minute, and the past 5-minute moving average of vehicle speed. Based on these per-minute per-segment statistics, the application computes the tolls to be charged to a vehicle entering a segment any time during the next minute, and notifies the toll in real time (notification is to be sent to a vehicle within 5 seconds upon entering the segment). The application also includes accident detection; an accident occurring in one segment will impact the toll computation of that segment as well as a few downstream segments. An accident is flagged when multiple cars are found to have stopped in the same location. The graphical representation of our implementation of the LR stream processing requirement is shown in Fig. 2 together with its corresponding stream query.

```
INSERT INTO toll_table SELECT minute, xway, dir, seg, toll_comp(c.no_accident, c.cars_volume)
FROM ( SELECT minute, xway, dir, seg, cars_volume,
          5_minutes_moving_avg(xway, dir, seg, minute, avg_speed) as mv_avg, no_accident
       FROM ( SELECT floor(time/60)::integer AS minute, xway, dir, seg,
                 AVG(speed) AS avg_speed, COUNT(distinct Vid)-1) AS cars_volume,
                 MIN(no_accident) AS no_accident
              FROM ( SELECT xway, dir, seg, time, speed, vid,
                        accident_affected(vid,speed,xway,dir,seg,pos) AS no_accident
                        FROM STREAM_CYCLE_lr_data(60, 180) ) a
              GROUP BY minute, xway, dir, seg ) b
) c
WHERE c.mv_avg > 0 AND c.mv_avg < 40;
```

The features of this query can be explained by the following. The streaming tuples are generated by the Stream Source Function *STREAM_CYCLE_lr_data(time, cycles)*, from the LR data source file with timestamps, where parameter "*time*" is the time-window size in seconds; "*cycles*" is the number of cycles the query is supposed to run (setting cycle to 0 means running the query infinitely). For example, *STREAM_CYCLE_lr_data(60, 180)* delivers the position reports one-by-one until it detects the end of a cycle (60 seconds), and performs a "cut", then onto the next cycle, for a total of 180 cycles (for 3 hours). As illustrated by Fig. 2, the tolls are derived from the segment statistics, i.e. the number of active cars, average speed, and the 5-minute moving average speed, as well as from detected accidents, and dimensioned by express-way, direction and segment.

We leveraged the *minimum, average* and *count-distinct* aggregate-groupby operators built in the SQL engine, and provided the moving average (*5_minutes_moving_avg()*) operator and the accident detection (*accident_affected()*) operator in UDFs. Required by the LR benchmark, the segment tolls of every minute should be generated within 5 seconds after that minute. The toll of a segment calculated in the past minute is applied to the cars currently entering into that segment. The generated tolls are inserted into a *segment toll table* with the transaction committed per cycle (i.e., per minute). Therefore the tolls generated in the past minutes are visible to the current minute.

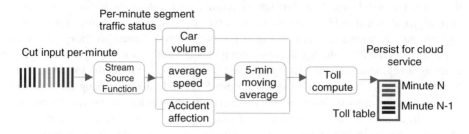

Fig. 2. Cycle based stream query for LR benchmark in generating per-minute tolls

The experimental results are measured on HP xw8600 with 2 x Intel Xeon E54102 2.33 Ghz CPUs and 4 GB RAM, running Windows XP (x86_32) and PostgreSQL 8.4.

The input data are downloaded from the benchmark's home page. The "L=1" setting was chosen for our experiment which means that the benchmark consists of 1 expressway (with 100 segments in each direction). The event arrival rate ranges from a few per second to peak at about 1,700 events per second towards the end of the 3-hour duration.

We have tested the performance of our approach under the stress test mode where the data are read by the SSF from a file continuously as fast as possible.

– The total computation time with L=1 setting is shown in Fig. 3, indicating that our system is able to generate the per-minute per-segments tolls for the total 3 hours of LR data (approx. 12 Million tuples) in a little over 2 minutes.
– *Performance of Persisting with Heap-Insert.* Unlike other reported DSMSs where the stream processing results are persisted by connecting to a separate database and issuing queries, with the proposed cycle-based approach, the continuous, minute-cycle based query results are stored through efficient heap-insert.

From Fig. 3 we can see that persisting the cycle based stream processing results either by inserting with logging (using INSERT INTO with extended support by the query engine) or by direct inserting (using SELECT INTO with extended support by the query engine – not shown in this query), does not add significant performance overhead compared to querying only. This is because we completely push stream processing down to the query engine and handle it in a long running query instance with direct heap operations, with negligible overhead for data movement and for setting up update queries.

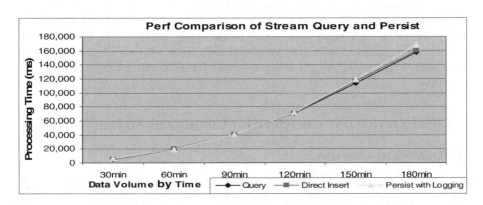

Fig. 3. Performance comparison of querying-only and query+persisting (with continuous input)

– *Post Cut Elapsed Time.* In cycle-based stream processing, the remaining time of query evaluation after the input data chunk is cut, called Post Cut Elapsed Time (PCET), is particularly important since it directly affects the delta time for the results to be accessible after the last tuple of the data chunk in the cycle has been received.

Fig 4 shows the query time, as well as the PCET, for processing each 1-minute data chunk. It can be seen that the PCET (the blue line) is well controlled around 0.2 second, meaning that the maximal response time for the segment toll results, as measured from the time a cycle (a minute) ends, is around 0.2 second.

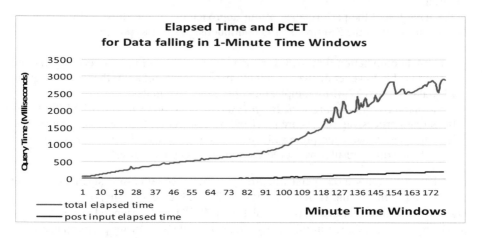

Fig. 4. Query time as well as PCET on the data chunk falling in each minute time window

As mentioned above, LR benchmark requires the segment tolls in each minute to be calculated within 5 second after the minute, and most reported results fall in the range from 1 second to 5 seconds. Our experimental result (0.2 second) indicates that our approach is highly competitive to any reported one. This is because we completely pushed stream processing down to the query engine with negligible data movement overhead and with efficient direct heap-insert. We eliminated the middleware layer, as provided by all other systems, for scheduling time-window based querying.

3   Cloud Service Infrastructure for Continuous Stream Analytics

3.1   Architecture Overview

The *cloud architecture* for delivering cloud computing service involves multiple cloud components communicating with each other over application programming interfaces, and in our case, includes the CSA engines integrated into the database engines as the core platforms. There exist several other components for managing connection, security, privacy, etc, which are not discussed in this report.

Our cloud service has the layering structure shown in Fig 5.

− Client: our *cloud clients* are typically smart phones such as HP Palm phones running WebOS applications. In these applications, SQL APIs are used to access the real-time results of continuous analytics.

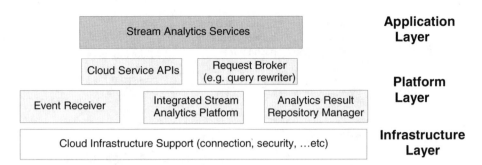

Fig. 5. Outline of stream analytics cloud service architecture

- Application: the CSA results are generated by the cycle-based continuous queries, in the context of "*Software as a Service (SaaS)*". These applications are managed from central locations rather than at each customer's site, enabling customers to access applications remotely via the Web.
- Platform: as every *SaaS* requires a *Paas* (*Platform as a Service*), we provide the cloud platform involving the CSA engines with both stream analytics capability and data management capability, allowing the privileged customers to run their own continuous queries for generating the CSA results of their interests.
- Infrastructure: we provide the proposed platforms as well as the common facilities for delivering cloud service. In this stage we exclude offering "*Infrastructure as a Service (IaaS)*".

Below we tackle two essential scalability issues.

3.2 Synchronize Distributed Streaming Processing through Cycle Based Query

With the massive data and low-latency requirement, it is unlikely that the single engine based stream analysis suffices; instead, parallel and distributed stream analytics is likely to offer better scalability. To provide parallel and distributed CSA service, multiple CSA Engines (CSAEs) are used, each takes a partition (e.g. partitioned by express-way, direction, segment) of the stream as its input; it performs a stream analysis process by executing the cycle-based Continuous Query (CQ), and therefore can run multiple stream analytics processes in terms of multiple CQs.

Network-Distributed Map-Reduce Scheme. CSAEs are logically organized in the Map-Reduce style [7, 8] illustrated in Fig. 6. The streams are partitioned and fed in multiple "Map" CSAEs; the resulting streams from the "Map" CSAEs are sent to and fused at multiple "Reduce" CSAEs based on certain grouping criteria specified in the network replicated hash-tables. The separation of "Map" CSAEs and "Reduce" CSAEs are logical, since a CSAE may act as a "Map" engine, a "Reduce" engine, or both.

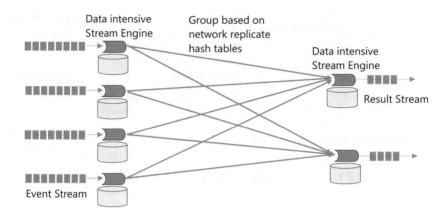

Fig. 6. Distributed stream analytics infrastructure for CQ based map-reduce style computation

Under the Map-Reduce model, a specific application is expressed in terms of two CQs – the CQ_{map} and the CQ_{reduce}. The same CQ_{map} is running at all the participating "Map" CSAEs, and the same CQ_{reduce} is running at all the participating "Reduce" CSAEs in parallel for the given application, such that each CQ_{map} is applied to a set of key-value tuples (k,v) and transforms it into a set of tuples of a different type (k',v'); then all the values v' are re-partitioned by k' and each CQ_{reduce} aggregates the set of values v' with the same k', as expressed below.

$$CQ_{map}: (k, v) => (k',v')*$$

$$CQ_{reduce}: (k', v')* => (k', v'*)$$

The aggregate-grouping criteria are specified in the network replicated hash-tables.

To benefit the LR computation on multiple express-ways and directions, we can so partition the stream data, assuming a vehicle reports its position to the event server designated to a particular direction of a particular express-way. For simplicity, we illustrate how to use the Map-Reduce model to parallelize the generation of traffic statistics – the volume of cars and their average speed in minute in each segment; for which the functionalities of Map query and Reduce query are outlined in Fig. 7 and explained as follows.

- We assume each vehicle reports its position to a specific event server; thus the stream data are hash partitioned by vehicle ID and the stream data corresponding to express- ways, directions and segments are crossing Map nodes. Note that the LR stream is not partitioned by time thus the time-window oriented cycle-based query processing are preserved and common to all partitions.
- The Map query covers partitioned stream processing, up to the local aggregation of car-volume, speed-sum, group-by time and location.
- The local aggregate results become the input streams to the Reduce queries running at the Reduce sites. Each Reduce query is again equipped with a SSF for receiving the local aggregates shuffled based on location, which is specified in the network-replicated hash tables. The local aggregations generated in different Map sites are fed in the Reduce query running on the designated Reduce site.

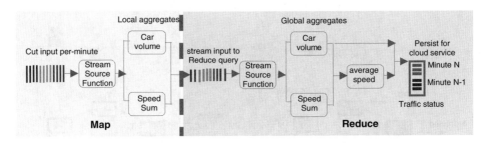

Fig. 7. The functionalities of Map query and Reduce query

- The Reduce query makes the global aggregation, including turning speed-sum and car-volume into average-speed for each segment of a direction of an express-way.

In this way, the Map results are treated as the input streams of the Reduce query at each reduce site, partitioned based on the network replicated hash tables, for the subsequent chunk-wise processing. Note that the SSF of the Reduce query reads the Map results for the designated express-ways, directions and segments, in the per-minute granule.

Synchronize Parallel CSA through Cycle based Query. In the presence of multiple distributed CSAEs running the same CQ for a given application, an important issue is how to have their work synchronized and collaborated. Our solution is fairly intuitive, i.e. let these engines process the stream data chunk by chunk based on the common window boundary, to allow them to cooperate without centralized scheduling.

3.3 Staging CSA Results without Data Movement

With the cloud service, the CSA results are accessed by many clients through PCs or smart phones. These results are time series data, stored in the read-sharable tables incrementally visible to users along their chunk-wise generation. As the CSA results are derived from infinite events, they are themselves infinite thus must be staged step by step along with their generation. Very often, only the latest data are "most wanted". For scaling up the CSA service, efficient data staging is the key.

Data staging is a common task of data warehouse management, aiming to keep latest data but avoid one table to grow too big. The general approach is to archive the older data from time to time. Such data archiving often involves data moving and copying, i.e. move the data from a table T holding the latest data to another table and continue using T to hold the new data. While this approach is acceptable for handling slowly-updated data in data warehousing, it is not efficient for supporting real-time stream analytics, due to the overhead of data move/copy and the service interruption during archiving.

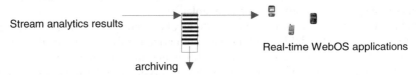

Fig. 8. Data staging of continuous stream analysis results

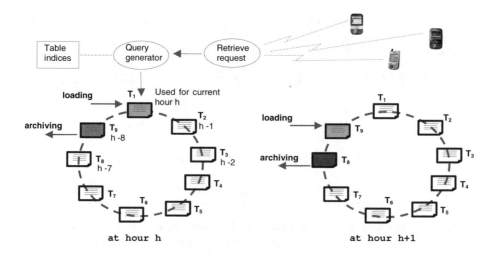

Fig. 9. Table-ring approach for staging continuously generated analytics data through metadata manipulation without physical data copying and moving

In order to support efficient data staging for real-time CSA service, we have developed a specific mechanism characterized by *staging through metadata manipulation without real data movement*. Below we explain this mechanism step by step using the above cycle based stream analytics for traffic management (Fig. 9).

- The stream analytics are made continuously but in per-minute cycles, resulting in the time series data expressing the traffic status in every minute, express-way, direction and segment.
- Assume that we keep the results of every hour (generated in 60 per-minute cycles) in a table, and keep the data for 8 hours "on-line" for the cloud service, then 9 tables on fast disk, flash or even memory buffer-pool, say T_1, T_2, ..., T_9, are used such that at a time, T_1 stores the results of the current hour, say h, T_2 stores the results of the hour $h-1$, ..., T_8 stores the results of the hour $h-8$, T_9 stores the oldest results beyond the 8-hours range thus is being archived asynchronously during the current hour; For data staging, our motivation is to change the "label" of a table for representing the time boundary (i.e. the hour) of its content, but without moving/copying the content to another table or file thus avoiding the read/write overhead.
- Specifically, when the hour changes, the archiving of T_9 has presumably finished and is used for storing the results of the new hour. Then, when that new hour becomes current, T_9 is for the current hour, T_1 for the last hour..., T_8 is being archived, etc, in the round-robin way. We refer to this arrangement as "table-ring".
- The hourly based timestamp of these tables are maintained either in the data dictionary or a specifically provided system table.
- A stable SQL interface is provided for both the client-side users and the server-side queries. Assuming the table holding the summarized traffic status in the current hour is named "*current_road_condition*", this name, in either the client-side query for retrieving, or the server-side query for receiving the CSA results, retains the same at all the times. This may be accomplished either by renaming or by

associating the table holding the latest results to *"current_road_condition"* through metadata manipulation.

- Conceptually we refer to the above meta-data manipulation as "changing labels" that is extremely efficient compared with data moving/copying.

For example, assume that the cloud service exposes to the clients with table named *"current_road_condition"*, but actually stores the CSA results in the tables internally identified by T_1, T_2, ..., T_9, for the traffic status of the current hour h and h-1,..., h-7, h-8. When a client connects to the cloud service and requests the current-hour traffic status using a SQL API for access the table *"current_road_condition"*, a cloud service provided query rewriter will change the table name from *"current_road_condition"* to, say T_9, should the analytics results of the current hour is stored in T_9. In this case, *"current_road_condition"* acts as a *virtual table name* although a table bearing this name must be created to comply the SQL parser. Alternatively, a system utility has altered the name of T_9 to *"current_road_condition"* in the data dictionary in the beginning of the current hour. These name substitution mechanisms apply to the tables keeping past hours data as well.

A deeper technical issue relates to the server-side support to table-ring, that is, how to switch the name of query destination while the query is still (actually always) running, in the context of *continuous* querying. This problem can be explained by the following example. Assume we have a cycle-based continuous query that runs in the per-minute (60 seconds) cycle, and persists its result in relation T_1 in hour 1, T_2 in hour 2, ... in the round-robin fashion described above. This query is specified as

INSERT INTO T SELECT .....;

but we expect the "into-relation" T is substituted by the actual relations T_1, T_2, ...from hour to hour. The key question consists in how to assign and switch the actual relations while the query is continuously running with a long-standing instance. Our solution is to extend the query engine to support the following.

- To have the query engine informed with the time boundary for switching the "into-relation" name, which can be accomplished either by extending SQL or by extending the query or SSF registration. For now we temporarily adopt the last approach. In this way the hourly boundary for table switch is turned to 60 per-minute cycles which is made recognizable by the query engine at run-time.
- The data dictionary or a specific system table maintains the metadata, such as name, ID, etc, of the set of actual "into-relations" as well as the order of them in the round-robin usage.
- A cycle based INSERT-INTO-SELECT... query commits each cycle, conceptually through the following call sequence:

        close_into_relation()
        complete_transaction()
        start_transaction()
        reopen_into_relation()

Between the *complete_transaction()* call and the *reopen_into_relation()* call, the number of execution cycles is checked, an if the number reaches 60, the switching of into-relations takes place.

– For switching into-relations, the above data dictionary or specific system table is looked up, and the "next" relation ID is obtained (before the first cycle, the initial relation ID is obtained) that is passed to the *reopen_into_relation()*. Thereafter another into-relation will act as the query destination.

This algorithm is outlined in Fig. 10.

Staging real-time analytics results with the above approach is particularly useful for supporting mobile applications. This is because due to the latency in connecting a mobile device to a cloud server, it is often more efficient to download a batch of information from the server for analytics purposes, and the HTML 5 enabled WebOS programs provide such data buffering capability (e.g. the *localStorage()* function). With the proposed server-side data staging approach, the tables containing the latest CSA results are kept small, thus downloading them is efficient and easily manageable.

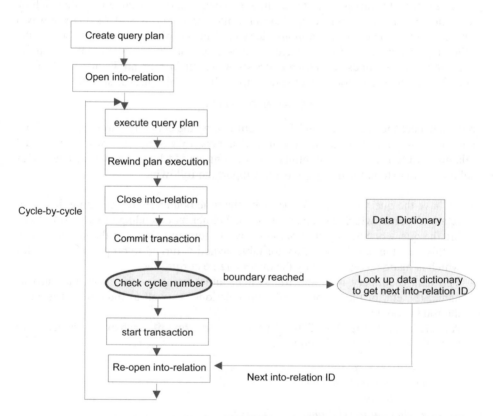

Fig. 10. Algorithm used by the extended query engine for switching into-relations

4   Conclusion and Comparison with Related Work

Providing cloud service for mobile applications is the new trend of computing, and more and more mobile applications depend on the analytics results of real-time events. As mentioned early in this report, to most of mobile device users, the interesting information is not the individual events such as each car's position and speed, but the summarized information such as the traffic status derived from the individual events through continuous stream analytics, i.e. CSA. However, the currently cloud services are generally based on pre-prepared information; providing CSA as a service, represents a paradigm shift and opens a new field in cloud computing. In this work we have addressed several specific challenges and reported our solutions.

We start with providing the platform that unifies dynamic stream processing and static data management for data intensive CSA. To capture the window semantics in CSA, we have introduced the cycle-based query model and transaction model which allows SQL queries to run cycle by cycle for analyzing unbounded stream data chunk by chunk, and for making the analysis results visible to the clients of cloud service timely while the continued query for generating them is still running. This model underlies truly continuous querying, but without shutting the query instance down between chunks for supporting sliding-window oriented operations across query cycles. Finally, we have developed the cloud service architecture, investigated the infrastructure for parallel and distributed CSA, and solved the problem of efficiently staging CSA results by metadata manipulation without physical data moving and copying in cloud service provisioning.

These features significantly differentiate the proposed platform from the current generation of DSMS which are built separately from the database systems [1,2,10]. As those systems lack the full SQL expressive power and DBMS functionalities, incur significant overhead in data access and movement [3,5,8], and do not have the appropriate transaction support for continuously persisting and sharing results, they fail to meet the requirements for providing high-throughput, low-latency stream analytics cloud service.

Our cycle-based query model also allows multiple CSA engines to synchronize and cooperation based on the common window boundaries. Such data-driven cooperation is very different from the workflow like centralized scheduling used in other DSMSs [9,12]. This feature allows us to applying Map-Reduce computation cycle by cycle continuously and incrementally for parallel and distributed CSA, in the way not seen previously.

Finally the table-ring based data staging is specifically efficient in coping with continuous information generation. This mechanism avoids the overhead of physical data copying and moving thus ensures low-latency data retrieval without being interrupted by data staging. For mobile applications such as those running on WebOS with HTML 5 caching capability, keeping CSA results in small sized tables makes them easily downloadable for batch usage with reduced internet connections. This approach ensures the stability of server APIs and client APIs, in the sense that in both server programs and client programs, the "representative" table names (as those specified in SQL queries) are kept stable regardless of data staging.

The proposed approach has been integrated into the PostgreSQL engine, resulting in a new kind of tightly integrated, highly efficient platform for CSA service provisioning. We tested the throughput and latency of this service using a popular stream processing benchmark and with WebOS based Palm phones. Our preliminary experiments reveal its merit in "CSA as a Service". Providing CSA cloud service using HP Neoview parallel database engine is currently explored.

References

1. Arasu, A., Babu, S., Widom, J.: The CQL Continuous Query Language: Semantic Foundations and Query Execution. VLDB Journal 15(2) (June 2006)
2. Chandrasekaran, S., et al.: TelegraphCQ: Continuous Dataflow Processing for an Uncertain World. In: CIDR 2003 (2003)
3. Chen, Q., Hsu, M.: Experience in Extending Query Engine for Continuous Analytics, Tech. Rep. HPL-2010-44 (2010)
4. Chen, Q., Hsu, M.: Cooperating SQL Dataflow Processes for In-DB Analytics. In: Proc. CoopIS 2009 (2009)
5. Chen, Q., Therber, A., Hsu, M., Zeller, H., Zhang, B., Wu, R.: Efficiently Support MapReduce alike Computation Models Inside Parallel DBMS. In: Proc. Thirteenth International Database Engineering & Applications Symposium (IDEAS 2009) (2009)
6. Chen, Q., Hsu, M., Liu, R.: Extend UDF Technology for Integrated Analytics. In: Proc. DaWaK 2009 (2009)
7. Dean, J.: Experiences with MapReduce, an abstraction for large-scale computation. In: Int. Conf. on Parallel Architecture and Compilation Techniques. ACM, New York (2006)
8. DeWitt, D.J., Paulson, E., Robinson, E., Naughton, J., Royalty, J., Shankar, S., Krioukov, A.: Clustera: An Integrated Computation And Data Management System. In: VLDB 2008 (2008)
9. Franklin, M.J., et al.: Continuous Analytics: Rethinking Query Processing in a Network-Effect World. In: CIDR 2009 (2009)
10. Gedik, B., Andrade, H., Wu, K.-L., Yu, P.S., Doo, M.C.: SPADE: The System S Declarative Stream Processing Engine. In: ACM SIGMOD 2008 (2008)
11. Jain, N., et al.: Design, Implementation, and Evaluation of the Linear Road Benchmark on the Stream Processing Core. In: SIGMOD (2006)
12. Liarou, E., et al.: Exploiting the Power of Relational Databases for Efficient Stream Processing. In: EDBT 2009 (2009)

On the Expressiveness and Trade-Offs of Large Scale Tuple Stores

Ricardo Vilaça, Francisco Cruz*, and Rui Oliveira

Computer Science and Technology Center
Universidade do Minho
Braga, Portugal
{rmvilaca,fmcruz,rco}@di.uminho.pt

Abstract. Massive-scale distributed computing is a challenge at our doorstep. The current exponential growth of data calls for massive-scale capabilities of storage and processing. This is being acknowledged by several major Internet players embracing the cloud computing model and offering first generation distributed tuple stores.

Having all started from similar requirements, these systems ended up providing a similar service: A simple tuple store interface, that allows applications to insert, query, and remove individual elements. Furthermore, while availability is commonly assumed to be sustained by the massive scale itself, data consistency and freshness is usually severely hindered. By doing so, these services focus on a specific narrow trade-off between consistency, availability, performance, scale, and migration cost, that is much less attractive to common business needs.

In this paper we introduce DataDroplets, a novel tuple store that shifts the current trade-off towards the needs of common business users, providing additional consistency guarantees and higher level data processing primitives smoothing the migration path for existing applications. We present a detailed comparison between DataDroplets and existing systems regarding their data model, architecture and trade-offs. Preliminary results of the system's performance under a realistic workload are also presented.

Keywords: Peer-to-Peer; DHT; Cloud Computing; Dependability.

1 Introduction

Storage of digital data has reached unprecedented levels with the ever increasing demand for information in electronic formats by individuals and organizations, ranging from the disposal of traditional storage media for music, photos and movies, to the rise of massive applications such as social networking platforms.

Until now, relational database management systems (RDBMS) have been the key technology to store and process structured data. However, these systems

---

* Partially funded by project Pastramy – Persistent and highly available software transactional memory (PTDC/EIA/72405/2006).

R. Meersman et al. (Eds.): OTM 2010, Part II, LNCS 6427, pp. 727–744, 2010.

based on highly centralized and rigid architectures are facing a conundrum: The volume of data currently quadruples every eighteen months while the available performance per processor only doubles in the same time period [22]. This is the breeding ground for a new generation of elastic data management solutions, that can scale both in the sheer volume of data that can be held but also in how required resources can be provisioned dynamically and incrementally[8,6,5,17]. Furthermore, the underlying business model supporting these efforts requires the ability to simultaneously serve and adapt to multiple tenants with diverse performance and dependability requirements, which add to the complexity of the whole system. These first generation remote storage services are built by major Internet players, like Google, Amazon, Microsoft, Facebook and Yahoo, by embracing the cloud computing model.

Cloud data management solutions rely on distributed systems designed from the beginning to be elastic and highly available. The CAP theorem [4] states that under network partitions it is impossible to achieve both strong consistency and availability. Cloud data management solutions acknowledge these difficulties and seek to establish reasonable trade-offs. Some focus on applications that have minor consistency requirements and can thus favor availability. They replace the traditional transactional serializability [2] or linearizability [14] strict criteria by eventual consistency (e.g. Basically Available Soft-state Eventual consistency [9]) or even explicit out of the system conflict resolution [8]. Furthermore, they provide only single tuple operations or at most range operations over tuples.

By doing so, these services focus on a specific narrow trade-off between consistency, availability, performance, scale, and migration cost, that fits tightly their motivating very large application scenarios. They focus on applications that have minor consistency requirements and can favor availability with an increasing complexity at the application logic. In most enterprises, in which there isn't a large in-house research development team for application customization and maintenance, it is hard to add this complex layer to the application. Moreover, these applications typically have queries that, in addition to single tuple and range operations, have the need for multi-tuple operations, and require the usual, standard, more consistent data management. As a result, it is hard to provide a smooth migration path for existing applications, even when using modern Web-based multi-tier architectures. This is a hurdle to the adoption of Cloud Computing by a wider potential market and thus a limitation to the long term profitability of businesses model.

In this paper we present DataDroplets that skews the current trade-off towards the needs of common business users. DataDroplets provides additional consistency guarantees and higher level data processing primitives that ease the migration from current RDBMS. In order to provide higher level data processing primitives, DataDroplets extends first generation remote storage services data models with tags and multi-tuple access that allow to efficiently store and retrieve large sets of related data at once. Multi-tuple operations leverage disclosed data relations to manipulate sets of comparable or arbitrarily related elements. Additionally we present a detailed comparison of existing solutions and DataDroplets regarding their data model and API, architecture, and trade-offs.

Finally, we have evaluated DataDroplets with a realistic environment and workload based on Twitter [26]. The results show the benefit of DataDroplets enhanced data model and API; the minimal cost of synchronous replication; and attest the scalability of DataDroplets.

The remainder of the paper is organized as follows. Section 2 presents emerging Cloud based tuple stores and DataDroplets. Sections 3, 4, and 5 present, respectively, a detailed comparison of existing solutions and DataDroplets regarding: data model and programming interface; architecture; and design trade-offs. Section 6 presents a evaluation of the performance of DataDroplets. Section 7 concludes the paper.

2   Tuple Stores

The need for elastic and scalable distributed data stores for managing very large volumes of structured data is leading to the emergence of several Cloud based tuple stores.

Major companies like Google, Amazon, Yahoo! and Facebook are competing for a lead in this model. In the following, we briefly present four available tuple stores and DataDroplets. The chosen tuple stores are the most representative and, although several open source projects exist, they are mostly implementations of some of the presented here.

Amazon's Dynamo [8] is a highly available key-value storage system. It has properties of both databases and distributed hash tables (DHTs). Although it isn't directly exposed externally as a web service, it is used as a building block of some of the Amazon Web Services [1], such as S3. Dynamo assembles several distributed systems concepts (data partitioning and replication, Merkle trees, load balancing, etc.) in a production system.

PNUTS [6] is a massively scalable, hosted data management service that allows multiple applications to concurrently store and query data. Its shared service model allows multiple Yahoo! applications to share the same resources and knowledge. PNUTS is a component of the Yahoo!'s Sherpa, an integrated suite of data services. Sherpa is composed of Yahoo!' Message Broker (YMB), a topic based publish-subscribe system and PNUTS.

Google's Bigtable [5] is a distributed storage system for structured data that was designed to manage massive quantities of data and run across thousands of servers. Besides being used internally at Google for web indexing, Google Earth and Google Finance, it is also used to store Google's App Engine Datastore entities. The Datastore API [13] defines an API for data management in the Google's App Engine (GAE) [12]. GAE is a toolkit that allows developers to build scalable applications in which the entire software and hardware stack is hosted at Google's own infrastructure.

Cassandra [17] is a distributed storage engine initially developed by Facebook to be used at the Facebook social network site and is now an Apache open source project. It is a highly scalable distributed database that uses most of the ideas of the Dynamo [8] architecture to offer a data model based on Bigtable's.

DataDroplets, is a key-value store targeted at supporting very large volumes of data leveraging the individual processing and storage capabilities of a large number of well connected computers. It offers a simple application interface providing the atomic manipulation of key-value tuples and the flexible establishment of arbitrary relations among tuples.

3   Data Model and API

The emergence of Cloud computing and the demand for scalable distributed tuple stores are leading to a revolution on data models. A common approach in all recent large scale tuple stores is the replacement of the relational data model by a more flexible one. The relational data model was designed to store very highly and statically structured data. However, most Cloud applications do not meet these criteria, which results in poorer maintainability than with a more flexible data model. Additionally, the cost of maintaining its normalized data model, by the enforcement of relations integrity, and the ability to run transactions across all data in the database make it difficult to scale.

Therefore, most of existing tuple stores use a simple key value store or at most variants of the entity-attribute-value (EAV) model [19]. In the EAV data model entities have a rough correspondence to relational tables, attributes to columns, tuples to rows and values to cells. Each tuple is of a particular entity and can have its own unique set of associated attributes. This data model allows to dynamically add new attributes that only apply to certain tuples. This flexibility of the EAV data model is helpful in domains where the problem is itself amenable to expansion or change over time. Other benefit of the EAV model, that may help in the conceptual data design, is the multi-value attributes in which each attribute can have more than one value.

Furthermore, cloud based tuple stores rather than using a global data model and operations across the entire universe define disjoint partitions of data that can't be queried together, making them easier to scale. The relational data model has no abstraction for partitions and the application designers must only later considering how it might be reasonably sharded. In the following we describe the data model and API of the tuple stores presented in Section 2 and then motivate and describe the data model and API of the proposed DataDroplets.

3.1   Current Tuple Stores

In this subsection we provide a detailed description of the data model and programming interface for each of the tuple stores. Dynamo uses a simple key-value data model while others use some variant EAV. Another design choice in the data models is either it leads to row-based or column-based storage. Bigtable and Cassandra are column based while the others are row based. In order to ease the comparison, for each tuple store we provide a standard representation of their data model and API. The notation has the following symbols: a) $A \times B$, product of A and B; b) $A + B$, union of A or B; c) A^*, sequence of A; d) $A \rightharpoonup B$, map of A to B; and e) $\mathcal{P}A$, set of A

Dynamo is modeled as:

$$K \rightharpoonup (V \times C) \ .$$

Each tuple has a key associated to it and a context, represented by C, which encodes system metadata such as the tuple's version and is opaque to the application. Dynamo treats both the key and the tuple, K and V, as opaque array of bytes.

$\mathcal{P}(V \times C)$ get(K key)
put(K key, C context,V value)

Fig. 1. Dynamo's API

Dynamo offers a simple interface, Figure 1. The `get` operation locates the tuple associated with the `key` and returns a single tuple or a list of tuples with conflicting versions. The `put` adds or updates a tuple also by `key`.

In PNUTS data is organized into tables, identified by a string, of tuples with dynamic typed attributes and tuples of the same table can have different attributes,

$$String \rightharpoonup (K \rightharpoonup \mathcal{P}(String \times V)) \ .$$

Each tuple can have more than one value for the same attribute. The type for the attributes, V, and for the key, K, can be typical data types, such as integer, string, or the "blob" data type for arbitrary data. The type for the attributes is dynamically defined per attribute.

```
𝒫(String × V) get-any(String tableName,K key)
𝒫(String × V) get-critical(String tableName,K key, Double version)
𝒫(String × V) get-latest(String tableName,K key)
put(String tableName,K key,𝒫(String × V) value)
delete(String tableName,K key)
test-and-set-put(String tableName,K key,𝒫(String × V) value, Double version)
K ⇀ 𝒫(String × V)  scan(String tableName,𝒫K selections,𝒫String projections)
K ⇀ 𝒫(String × V) rangeScan(String tableName,(K × K) rangeSelection,𝒫String projections)
String ⇀ (K ⇀ 𝒫(String × V)) multiget(𝒫(String × K) keys)
```

Fig. 2. PNUTS's API

In PNUTS as tables can be ordered or hashed the available operations per table differ, Figure 2. All tables support `get-*`, `put`, `delete`, and `scan` operations. However, only ordered tables support selections by range: `rangeScan` operation. While selections can be by tuple's key, `scan`, or specify a range, `rangeScan`, updates and deletes must specify the tuple's key. PNUTS supports a whole range of single tuple `get` and `put` operations with different levels of consistency guarantees, varying from a call where readers can request any version of the tuple, having highly reduced latency, to a call where writers can verify that the tuple is still at the expected version. Briefly, the `get-any` operation returns a possibly stale version of the tuple, `get-critical` returns a version of the tuple that is at least as fresh as the `version`, `get-latest` returns the most recent copy of the tuple, `test-and-set-put` performs the tuple modification if and only if the version of the tuple is the same as the requested `version`. Additionally, a `multiget` is provided to retrieve multiple tuples from one or more tables in parallel.

Bigtable is a multi-dimensional sorted map,

$$K \rightharpoonup (String \rightharpoonup (String \times Long \rightharpoonup V)) \ .$$

The index of the map is the row key, column name, and a timestamp. Column keys are grouped into *column families* and they must be created before data can be stored under any column key in that family. Data is maintained in lexicographic order by row key where each row range is dynamically partitioned. Each cell in BigTable can have multiple versions of the same data indexed by timestamp. The timestamps are integers and can be assigned by Bigtable, or by client applications. The type of the row key, K, and the value for columns V, is a string.

```
put(K key,String ⇀ (String × Long ⇀ V) rowMutation)
String ⇀ (String × Long ⇀ V) get(K key,String ⇀ String columns)
delete(K key,String ⇀ String columns)
K ⇀ (String ⇀ (String × Long ⇀ V)) scan(K startKey,K stopKey,String ⇀ String columns)
```

Fig. 3. Bigtable's API

The Bigtable API, Figure 3, provides operations to write or delete tuples (`put` and `delete`), look up for individual tuples (`get`) or iterate over a subset of tuples, `scan`. For all operations, the string representing the column name may be a regular expression. Clients can iterate over multiple column families and limit the rows, columns, and timestamps. The results for both `get` and `scan` operations are grouped per column family.

Cassandra data model, is an extension of the Bigtable data model,

$$K \rightharpoonup (String \rightharpoonup (String \rightharpoonup (String \times Long \rightharpoonup V))) \ .$$

It exposes two types of column families: simple and super. Simple column families are the same as column families in Bigtable and super column families are families of simple column families. Cassandra sorts columns either by time or name. In Cassandra the type for rows key, K, is also a string with no size restrictions.

```
put(K key,String ⇀ (String ⇀ (String × Long ⇀ V)) rowMutation)
String ⇀ (String ⇀ (String × Long ⇀ V)) get(K key,String ⇀ (String ⇀ String) columns)
K ⇀ (String ⇀ (String ⇀ (String × Long ⇀ V))) range(K startKey,K endKey,
        String ⇀ (String ⇀ String) columns)
delete(K key,String ⇀ (String ⇀ String) columns)
```

Fig. 4. Cassandra's API

The Cassandra API, Figure 4, is almost the same of Bigtable API except for the `scan` operation. The results of `get` are grouped both per super column family and column family and ordered per column. Additionally, the current version, 0.6, of the Cassandra open source project also supports an additional `range` operation.

None of the presented tuple stores distinguish between inserts and updates. The **put** operation stores the tuple with its unique key, and previous tuple that has that key gets overwritten.

3.2   DataDroplets

In very recent proposals, contrary to RDBMS, there is no standard API to query data in tuple stores. Most of existing Cloud based tuple stores offer a simple tuple store interface, that allows applications to insert, query, and remove individual tuples or at most range queries based on the primary key of the tuple. Regardless of using a simple key value interface or flavors of the EAV model, thus disclosing more details on the structure of the tuple, previous systems require that more ad-hoc and complex multi-tuple queries are done outside of the tuple store using some implementation of the Map Reduce[7] programming model: Yahoo's PigLatin [20], Google's Sawzall [21], Microsoft's LINQ [18].

Although this opens up the possibilities of what can be done with data, it has negative implications in terms of ease of use and in the migration from current RDBMS based applications. Even worse, if the tuple store API hasn't enough operations to efficiently retrieve multiple tuples for the ad-hoc queries they will have a high cost in performance. These ad-doc queries will mostly access a set of correlated tuples. Zhonk et al. have shown that the probability of a pair of tuples being requested together in a query is not uniform but often highly skewed [29]. They also have shown that correlation is mostly stable over time for real applications. Furthermore, it is known that when involving multiple tuples in a request to a distributed tuple store, it is desirable to restrict the number of nodes who actually must participate in the request. It is therefore more beneficial to couple related tuples tightly, and unrelated tuples loosely, so that the most common tuples to be queried by a request would be those that are already tightly coupled.

Therefore, an important aspect of our proposal, DataDroplets, is the multi-tuple access that allows to efficiently store and retrieve large sets of related data at once. Multi-tuple operations leverage disclosed data relations to manipulate sets of comparable or arbitrarily related elements. Therefore, DataDroplets extend the data model of previous tuple stores with tags that allow to establish arbitrary relations among tuples,

$$String \rightharpoonup (K \rightharpoonup (V \times \mathcal{P}String)) \,. \tag{1}$$

In DataDroplets, data is organized into disjoint *collections* of tuples identified by a string. Each tuple is a triple consisting of a unique key drawn from a partially ordered set, a value that is opaque to DataDroplets and a set of free form string tags. It is worth mentioning that the establishment of arbitrary relations among tuples can be done even if they are from different collections.[1]

---

[1] We are working on extending it to an EAV data model, by allowing each tuple to have dynamic typed attributes but allowing tuples of the same collection to have different attributes. Additionally, each tuple may have more than one value for the same attribute. Briefly, the current opaque value V will be replaced by $\mathcal{P}(String \times V)$.

```
put(String collection, K key, V value, PString tags)
V get(String collection, K key)
V delete(String collection, K key)
multiPut( K ⇀ (V × PString) mapItems)
K ⇀ V multiGet(P(String × K) keys)
K ⇀ V getByRange(K min, K max)
K ⇀ V getByTags(PString tags)
```

Fig. 5. DataDroplets' API

The system supports common single tuple operations such as `put`, `get` and `delete`, multi-tuple put and get operations (`multiPut` and `multiGet`), and set operations to retrieve ranges (`getByRange`) and equally tagged tuples (`getByTags`), Figure 5 .

4   Architecture

Tuple stores target settings of a distributed setting with hundreds or thousands of machines in a multi-tenant scenario and must be able to store and query massive quantities of structured data. At this scale, machines' failures are frequent and therefore tuple stores must replicate data to ensure dependability. Enabling distributed processing over this kind of massive-scale storage poses several new challenges: problems of data placement, dependability and distributed processing. Given these challenges and their different design requirements, all the systems under consideration came up with different architectures.

These architectures may be categorized in three types: fully decentralized, hierarchical and hybrid. In the fully decentralized type physical nodes are kept organized on a logical ring overlay, such as Chord [24]. Each node maintains complete information about the overlay membership, being therefore able to reach every other node. Dynamo and Cassandra fall in this category, Figures 6(c)) and 6(a).

In the hierarchical type, a small set of nodes is responsible for maintaining data partitions and coordinate processing and storage nodes. Both Bigtable and PNUTS (Figures 6(b) and 6(e)) follow this type and organize tuples into tablets, horizontal partitions of tuples. Bigtable is composed of three different types of servers: master, tablets, and lock servers. Master servers coordinate the tablets servers by assigning and mapping tablets to them, and redistributing tasks as needed. The architecture of PNUTS is composed of regions, tablets controllers, routers, and storage units. The system is divided into regions where each region has a complete copy of each table. Within each region, the tablets controllers coordinate the interval mapping that maps tablets to storage units.

DataDroplets uses a hybrid architecture [27] with two collaborating layers, a soft and a persistent state, of distinct structural and functional characteristics. At the top, a soft-state layer is responsible for 1) the client interface, 2) data partitioning, 3) caching, 4) concurrency control, and 5) high level processing. Nodes in the soft-state layer are organized in a logical ring overlay as nodes of the fully decentralized type. Stable storage is provided by the persistent-state layer. Nodes in this layer form an unstructured network overlay, in which nodes are not (a priori) structured but are probabilistically managed. Each layer tackles different aspects of the system, thus making specific assumptions over the computation model and exploiting different techniques to data management and propagation. With these two layers architecture we are able to clearly separate and address the concerns of, on one hand ensuring a strong consistent data storage and, on the other to leverage a massive and highly dynamic infrastructure.

Despite having different architectures, all of the presented tuple stores share common components like request routing and storage and use common dependable and distributed systems techniques such as partition and replication. Figure 6, shows the architecture of each system and highlights which layer is responsible for each component. In the following, we focus on those components highlighting the similarities and differences on how each component is realized in each data store.

The characterization of the architecture is directly related to the way each system realizes data partitioning, an aspect of major importance. While in tuples stores using a fully decentralized or hybrid architectures the data partition is done in a fully decentralized manner through consistent hashing, in the hierarchical based architectures a small set of nodes is responsible for maintaining the data partitions. In PNUTS data tables are partitioned into tablets - by the tablet controller - by dividing the key space in intervals. For ordered tables, the division is at the key-space level while in hashed tables it is at the hash space level. Each tablet is stored into a single storage unit within a region. In Bigtable the row range is dynamically partitioned into tablets distributed over different machines.

While existing tuple stores do data partitioning taking into account only a single tuple, randomly or in an ordered manner, DataDroplets also supports a data partition strategy that takes into account tuple correlations. Currently, it supports three data partition strategies: random placement, ordered placement, and tagged placement that handle dynamic multi-dimensional relationships of arbitrarily tagged tuples. The partition strategy is defined on a per collection basis.

Another mandatory aspect of these tuple stores is replication, which is used not only to improve performance of read operations by means of load balancing but also to ensure dependability. In Cassandra, Dynamo and DataDroplets replication is done by the node responsible for the data, as determined by consistent hashing, by replicating it to the R-1 successors - with a replication degree of R. However, while Cassandra and Dynamo use quorum replication, DataDroplets also allows the use of synchronous primary-backup offering stronger tuple consistency. In PNUTS the message broker assures inter-region replication, using asynchronous primary-backup, while in Bigtable it is done at the storage layer by GFS [11]. In DataDroplets, the replication in the synchronous primary-backup is complemented with replication at the persistent state layer. A tuple is assumed to be safely stored once it is stored in m nodes (which become the entry points

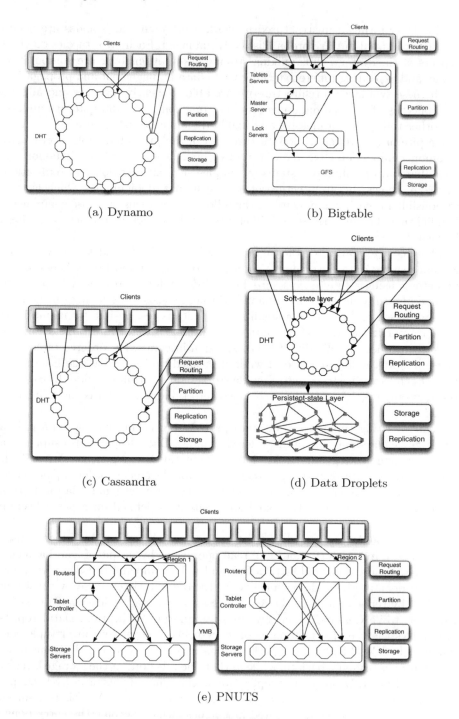

Fig. 6. Architectures

for the tuple at the soft-layer). For the sake of fault-tolerance more replicas of
the tuple are created.

Besides replication, all studied tuple stores use a persistency component to
ensure that writes are made durable. While Dynamo and Cassandra rely on local
disks for persistency, PNUTS, Bigtable and DataDroplets use a storage service.
However, while Bigtable uses it blindly, PNUTS and DataDroplets maintain
information about the mapping from tuples to storage nodes. PNUTS maintains the tablets to storage nodes mapping. In DataDroplets tuples stored in the
persistent-state layer are massively replicated through gossiping and each node
at the soft-state layer maintains a mapping of its tuples into a set of nodes in
the underlying persistent-state layer.

Due to the multiple nodes used and the partition of data, every time a request
is issued to the tuple store, that request has to be routed to the responsible node
for that piece of data. In DataDroplets and Cassandra any incoming request can
be issued to any node in the system. Then, the request is properly routed to
the responsible node. In PNUTS, when a request is received, the router determines which tablet contains the tuple and which storage node is responsible for
that tablet. Routers contain only a cached copy of the interval mapping that is
maintained by the tablet controller. In Dynamo, the routing is handled by the
client (i.e. the client library is partition aware) directly sending the request to
the proper node. Bigtable also needs a client library that caches tablet locations
and therefore clients send the requests directly to the proper tablet server.

5   Design and Implementation Trade-Offs

Cloud based tuple stores must adapt to multiple tenants with diverse performance, availability and dependability requirements. However, in face of the impossibility stated by the CAP theorem of providing at the same time: network
partitions tolerance, strong consistency and availability; cloud based tuple stores
must establish reasonable trade-offs.

Looking at the considered tuple stores, all provide two major trade-offs: no
table joins and single tuple consistency. The reason all share this first trade-off
is that making a relational join over data, which is spread across many nodes,
is unbearable, because every node would have to pull data from all nodes for
each tuple. Regarding the second trade-off, offering full database consistency
through global transactions would restrict scalability, because nodes would have
to achieve global agreement.

Although all tuple stores have in common those trade-offs, depending on the
internal design requirements each tuple store also establishes specific trade-offs.
As a result, in the following we present them and show how they focus on a
specific narrow regarding consistency, availability and migration cost. Then, we
describe how DataDroplets aims at shifting them towards the needs of common
business users. At the end, Table 1 presents a brief comparison of current tuples
stores and DataDroplets.

5.1   Trade-Offs of Current Tuple Stores

The data model type of a tuple store, in addition to determine its expressiveness, also impacts the way of storing data. In a row based (Dynamo and PNUTS) the tuples are stored contiguously on disk. While in a column oriented storage (Bigtable and Cassandra) columns may not be stored in a contiguously fashion. For that reason, column oriented storage is only advantageous if applications only access a subset of columns per request.

The API of tuple stores is not only highly coupled with their data model, but also with the supported data partition strategies. Single tuple operations are highly related to the data model, but the availability of a range operation is dependent on the existence of an ordered data partition strategy. Therefore, Dynamo doesn't offer a range operation like the other approaches.

Another important trade-off is the optimization either for read or write operations. A key aspect for this is how data is persistently stored. In write optimized storage, Bigtable and Cassandra, records on disk are never overwritten and multiple updates to the same tuple may be stored in different parts of the disk. Therefore, writes are sequential and thus, fast, while a read is slower because it may need multiple I/Os, to retrieve and combine several updates. Dynamo is also optimized for writes because the conflict resolution is done in reads ensuring that writes are never rejected.

As previously stated, all tuple stores offer only single tuple consistency. However, they differ from each other in the consistency given per tuple and how they achieve it through replication. Dynamo exposes data consistency and reconciliation logic issues to the application developers, which leads to a more complex application logic. Moreover, the application must tune the number of tuple replicas N, read quorum R and write quorum W. Therefore, stale data can be read and conflicts may occur, which must be tackled by the application. The conflict resolution can be syntactic or semantic based on the business logic. As multiple versions of the same data can coexist, the update of some tuple in Dynamo explicitly specifies which version of that tuple is being updated. PNUTS also chooses to sacrifice consistency. Its consistency model lays between single tuple atomicity and eventual consistency. Although every reader will always see some consistent version of a tuple, it may be outdated. The proper consistency guarantees depend on the specific calls made to the system. Therefore, the burden of strong consistency is left to the application that must reason about updates and cope with asynchrony. In Bigtable every read or write under a single tuple is atomic. However, every update on a given column of the tuple specifies a timestamp and therefore, creates a new version. Cassandra's consistency is similar to Dynamo with the value's timestamp defining its version.

More on replication, in order to tolerate data center outages, tuple stores must replicate tuples across data centers. Bigtable isn't data center aware. Dynamo is configured such that each tuple is replicated across multiple data centers. PNUTS's architecture was clearly designed as a geographically distributed service where each data center forms a region and a message broker provides replication across regions. Cassandra supports a replication strategy that is data center aware, using Zookeeper.

5.2 DataDroplets

As previously stated, current tuple stores focus on a specific narrow trade-off regarding consistency, availability and migration cost that fits tightly their internal very large application scenarios. Particularly, all current tuple store's API provide only single tuple operations or at most range operations over tuples of a particular collection. Moreover, while availability is commonly assumed, data consistency and freshness is usually severely hindered.

As explained in Section 3.2, for some applications single tuple and range operations are not enough. These applications have multi-tuple operations that access correlated tuples. Therefore, DataDroplets extends the data model of current tuple stores with tags, allowing to establish arbitrary relations between tuples, which allows to efficiently retrieve them through a tag based data partition strategy.

As previously shown, current tuple stores offer varying levels of tuple consistency but only PNUTS and Bigtable can offer tuple atomicity. However, in both the burden is left to the application that must deal with multiple tuple's versions. In DataDroplets if an application needs atomic guarantees per tuple, it simply configures synchronous replication and it will obtain it transparently without having to maintain and deal with multiple tuple' versions.

Table 1. Comparison of tuple spaces

	Dynamo	PNUTS	Bigtable	Cassandra	DataDroplets
Data Model	key value, row store	EAV, row store	column store	column store	key value + tags, row store
API	single tuple	single tuple and range	single tuple and range	single tuple and range	single tuple, range and correlated tuples
Data Partition	random	random and ordered	ordered	ordered	random and ordered; tuples correlation
Optimized for	writes	reads	writes	writes	reads
Consistency	eventual	atomic or stale reads	atomic	eventual	atomic or stale reads
Multiple Versions	version	version	timestamp	timestamp	none
Replication	quorum	async message broker	file system	quorum	sync or async
Data Center Aware	yes	no	yes	yes	no
Persistency	local and pluggable	storage service and custom/MySQL	replicated and distributed file system	local and custom	storage service and pluggable
Architecture	decentralized	hierarchical	hierarchical	decentralized	hybrid
Client Library	yes	no	yes	no	no

6   Experimental Results

We ran a series of experiments to evaluate the performance of DataDroplets, under a workload representative of applications currently exploiting the scalability of emerging tuple stores.

As there is neither an available version of most of considered tuple stores nor enough available machines to run them, in the following we present performance results for DataDroplets, in particular the enhanced data model and additional consistency guarantees. Moreover we present performance results for the effects of scale by substantially increasing the number of nodes.

6.1   Test Workload

For the evaluation of DataDroplets we have defined a workload that mimics the usage of the Twitter social network.

Twitter is an online social network application offering a simple micro-blogging service consisting of small user posts, the *tweets*. A user gets access to other user tweets by explicitly stating a *follow* relationship, building a social graph.

Our workload definition has been shaped by the results of recent studies on Twitter [15,16,3] and biased towards a read intensive workload based on discussions that took place during Twitter's Chirp conference (the Twitter official developers conference). In particular, we consider just the subset of the seven most used operations from the Twitter API [25] (Search and REST API as of March 2010): `statuses_user_timeline`, `statuses_friends_timeline`, `statuses_mentions`, `search_contains_hashtag`, `statuses_update`, `friendships_create` and `friendships_destroy`. Each run of the workload consists of a specified number of operations. The next operation is randomly chosen and, after it had finished, the system waits some pre configured time, think-time, and only afterwards sends the next operation. The probabilities of occurrence of each operation and a more detailed description of the workload can be found in [26].

6.2   Experimental Setting

We evaluate our implementation of DataDroplets using the ProtoPeer toolkit [10] to simulate 100 and 200 nodes networks. ProtoPeer is a toolkit for rapid distributed systems prototyping that allows switching between event-driven simulation and live network deployment without changing any of the application code.

From ProtoPeer we have used the network simulation model and extended it with simulation models for CPU as per [28]. The network model was configured to simulate a LAN with latency uniformly distributed between 1 ms and 2 ms. For the CPU simulation we have used a hybrid simulation approach as described in [23]. All data has been stored in memory, persistent storage was not considered. Briefly, the execution of an event is timed with a profiling timer and the result is used to mark the simulated CPU busy during the corresponding period, thus preventing other event to be attributed simultaneously to the same CPU. A simulation event is then scheduled with the execution delay to free the CPU. Further pending events are then considered. Each node was configured and calibrated to simulate one dual-core AMD Opteron processor running at 2.53GHz.

For all experiments presented bellow, the performance metric has been the average request latency as perceived by the clients. A total of 10000 concurrent users were simulated (uniformly distributed by the number of configured nodes) and 500000 operations were executed per run. Different request loads have been achieved by varying the clients think-time between operations. Throughout the experiments no failures were injected.

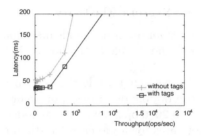

(a) 100 nodes configuration without replication

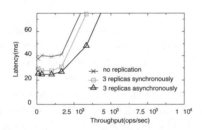

(b) 100 nodes with replication

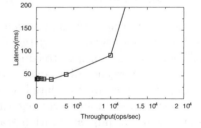

(c) 200 nodes configuration without replication

Fig. 7. System's response time

6.3 Evaluation of DataDroplets

Figure 7(a) depicts the response time for the combined workload. Overall, the use of tags in DataDroplets to establish arbitrary relations among tuples consistently outperforms the system without tags with responses 40% faster.

When using tags, DataDroplets may use the data partition strategy that takes into account tuple correlations and therefore, stores correlated tuples together. As the workload is composed of several operations that access correlated tuples, the access latency when using tags is lower than without tags, as only other data partition strategies that only take into account a single tuple may be used.

6.4   Evaluation of Node Replication

Data replication in DataDroplets is meant to provide fault tolerance to node crashes and improve read performance through load balancing. Figure 7(b) shows the results of the combined workload when data is replicated over three nodes.

Despite the impact replication inevitably has on write operations, the overall response time is improved by 27%. Moreover, we can see that despite the additional impact synchronous replication inevitably has on these operations, the overall gain of asynchronous replication is up to 14% which would not, per se, justify the increased complexity of the system. It is actually the dependability facet that matters most, allowing to provide seamless fail over of crashed nodes.

6.5   Evaluation of the System Elasticity

To assess the system's response to a significant scale change we carried the previous experiments over the double of the nodes, 200. Figure 7(c) depicts the results.

Here, it should be observed that while the system appears to scale up very well providing almost the double of throughput before getting into saturation, for a small workload, up to 2000 ops/sec with 200 nodes there is a slightly higher latency. This result motivates for a judicious elastic management of the system to maximize performance, let alone economical and environmental reasons.

7   Conclusion

Cloud computing and unprecedented large scale applications, most strikingly social networks such as Twitter, challenge tried and tested data management solutions. Their unfitness to cope with the demands of modern applications have led to the emergence of a novel approach: distributed tuple stores.

In this paper, we presented a detailed comparison of the most representative distributed tuple stores regarding their data model and API, architecture and design and implementation trade-offs. This comparison shows that despite having similar requirements each system offers different data modeling and operations' expressiveness and establish specific trade-offs regarding consistency, availability and migration cost.

Moreover, we introduce DataDroplets, a distributed tuple store, that aims at shifting the trade-offs established by current tuple stores towards the needs of common business users. It provides additional consistency guarantees and higher level data processing primitives smoothing the migration path for existing applications. Specifically, DataDroplets fits the access patterns required by most current applications, which arbitrarily relate and search data by means of free-form tags.

The results show the benefit, in request latency, of DataDroplets enhanced data model and API; the minimal cost of synchronous replication; and attest the scalability of DataDroplets. Our results are grounded on a simple but realistic benchmark for elastic tuple stores based on Twitter and currently known statistical data about its usage.

References

1. Amazon: Amazon WebServices (June 2010), http://aws.amazon.com/
2. Bernstein, P.A., Hadzilacos, V., Goodman, N.: Concurrency Control and Recovery in Database Systems. Addison-Wesley, Reading (1987)
3. Boyd, D., Golder, S., Lotan, G.: Tweet tweet retweet: Conversational aspects of retweeting on twitter. In: Society, I.C. (ed.) Proceedings of HICSS-43 (January 2010)
4. Brewer, E.A.: Towards robust distributed systems (abstract). In: Proceedings of the Nineteenth Annual ACM Symposium on Principles of Distributed Computing, PODC 2000, p. 7. ACM, New York (2000)
5. Chang, F., Dean, J., Ghemawat, S., Hsieh, W.C., Wallach, D.A., Burrows, M., Chandra, T., Fikes, A., Gruber, R.E.: Bigtable: a distributed storage system for structured data. In: Proceedings of the 7th Symposium on Operating Systems Design and Implementation, USENIX Association, OSDI 2006, Berkeley, CA, USA, pp. 205–218 (2006)
6. Cooper, B.F., Ramakrishnan, R., Srivastava, U., Silberstein, A., Bohannon, P., Jacobsen, H.A., Puz, N., Weaver, D., Yerneni, R.: Pnuts: Yahoo!'s hosted data serving platform. In: Proc. VLDB Endow, vol. 1(2), pp. 1277–1288 (2008)
7. Dean, J., Ghemawat, S.: Mapreduce: Simplified data processing on large clusters. In: Sixth Symposium on Operating System Design and Implementation, OSDI 2004, San Francisco, CA (December 2004)
8. DeCandia, G., Hastorun, D., Jampani, M., Kakulapati, G., Lakshman, A., Pilchin, A., Sivasubramanian, S., Vosshall, P., Vogels, W.: Dynamo: amazon's highly available key-value store. In: Proceedings of Twenty-First ACM SIGOPS Symposium on Operating Systems Principles, SOSP 2007, pp. 205–220. ACM, New York (2007)
9. Fox, A., Gribble, S.D., Chawathe, Y., Brewer, E.A., Gauthier, P.: Cluster-based scalable network services. SIGOPS Oper. Syst. Rev. 31(5), 78–91 (1997)
10. Galuba, W., Aberer, K., Despotovic, Z., Kellerer, W.: Protopeer: From simulation to live deployment in one step. In: Eighth International Conference on Peer-to-Peer Computing, 2008. P2P 2008, pp. 191–192 (September 2008)
11. Ghemawat, S., Gobioff, H., Leung, S.T.: The google file system. SIGOPS Oper. Syst. Rev. 37(5), 29–43 (2003)
12. Google: Google App Engine (June 2010), http://code.google.com/appengine/
13. Google: Google App Engine Datastore (June 2010), http://code.google.com/appengine/docs/datastore/
14. Herlihy, M.P., Wing, J.M.: Linearizability: a correctness condition for concurrent objects. ACM Trans. Program. Lang. Syst. 12(3), 463–492 (1990)
15. Java, A., Song, X., Finin, T., Tseng, B.: Why we twitter: understanding microblogging usage and communities. In: WebKDD/SNA-KDD 2007: Proceedings of the 9th WebKDD and 1st SNA-KDD 2007 workshop on Web mining and social network analysis, pp. 56–65. ACM, New York (2007)
16. Krishnamurthy, B., Gill, P., Arlitt, M.: A few chirps about twitter. In: WOSP 2008: Proceedings of the first workshop on Online social networks, pp. 19–24. ACM, New York (2008)
17. Lakshman, A., Malik, P.: Cassandra - A Decentralized Structured Storage System. In: SOSP Workshop on Large Scale Distributed Systems and Middleware (LADIS), Big Sky, MT (Ocotber 2009)

18. Meijer, E., Beckman, B., Bierman, G.: Linq: reconciling object, relations and xml in the.net framework. In: Proceedings of the 2006 ACM SIGMOD International Conference on Management of Data, SIGMOD 2006, pp. 706–706. ACM, New York (2006)

19. Nadkarni, P., Brandt, C.: Data extraction and ad hoc query of an entity-attribute-value database. Journal of the American Medical Informatics Association 5(6), 511–527 (1998)

20. Olston, C., Reed, B., Srivastava, U., Kumar, R., Tomkins, A.: Pig latin: a not-so-foreign language for data processing. In: Proceedings of the 2008 ACM SIGMOD International Conference on Management of Data, SIGMOD 2008, pp. 1099–1110. ACM, New York (2008)

21. Pike, R., Dorward, S., Griesemer, R., Quinlan, S.: Interpreting the data: Parallel analysis with sawzall. Sci. Program. 13(4), 277–298 (2005)

22. Skillicorn, D.: The case for datacentric grids. Tech. Rep. ISSN-0836-0227-2001-451, Department of Computing and Information Science, Queen's University (November 2001)

23. Sousa, A., Pereira, J., Soares, L., Jr., A.C., Rocha, L., Oliveira, R., Moura, F.: Testing the Dependability and Performance of Group Communication Based Database Replication Protocols. In: International Conference on Dependable Systems and Networks (DSN 2005) (June 2005)

24. Stoica, I., Morris, R., Karger, D., Kaashoek, F., Balakrishnan, H.: Chord: A scalable Peer-To-Peer lookup service for internet applications. In: Proceedings of the 2001 ACM SIGCOMM Conference, pp. 149–160 (2001)

25. Twitter.: Twitter API documentation (March 2010),
http://apiwiki.twitter.com/Twitter-API-Documentation

26. Vilaca, R., Oliveira, R., Pereira, J.: A correlation-aware data placement strategy for key-value stores. Tech. Rep. DI-CCTC-10-08, CCTC Research Centre, Universidade do Minho (2010),
http://gsd.di.uminho.pt/members/rmvilaca/papers/main.pdf

27. Vilaça, R., Oliveira, R.: Clouder: a flexible large scale decentralized object store: architecture overview. In: Proceedings of the Third Workshop on Dependable Distributed Data Management, WDDDM 2009, pp. 25–28. ACM, New York (2009)

28. Xiongpai, Q., Wei, C., Shan, W.: Simulation of main memory database parallel recovery. In: Proceedings of the 2009 Spring Simulation Multiconference, SpringSim 2009, San Diego, CA, USA, pp. 1–8 (2009)

29. Zhong, M., Shen, K., Seiferas, J.: Correlation-aware object placement for multi-object operations. In: The 28th International Conference on Distributed Computing Systems, ICDCS 2008, pp. 512–521. IEEE Computer Society, Washington (2008)

Context-Aware Tuples for the Ambient

Christophe Scholliers*, Elisa Gonzalez Boix**,
Wolfgang De Meuter, and Theo D'Hondt

Software Languages Lab
Vrije Universiteit Brussel, Belgium
{cfscholl,egonzale,wdmeuter,tjdhondt}@vub.ac.be

Abstract. In tuple space approaches to context-aware mobile systems, the notion of context is defined by the presence or absence of certain tuples in the tuple space. Existing approaches define such presence either by collocation of devices holding the tuples or by replication of those tuples across all devices. We show that both approaches can lead to an erroneous perception of context. The former ties the perception of context to network connectivity which does not always yield the expected result. The latter causes context to be perceived even if a device has left that context a long time ago. We propose a tuple space approach in which tuples themselves carry a predicate that determines whether they are in the right context or not. We present a practical API for our approach and show its use by means of the implementation of a mobile game.

1 Introduction

A growing body of research in pervasive computing deals with coordination in *mobile ad hoc networks*. Such networks are composed of mobile devices which spontaneously interact with other devices within communication range as they move about. This network topology is often used to convey context information to collocated devices [13]. Moreover, such context information can be used to optimize application behaviour given the scare resources of mobile devices [10]. In this paper, we focus on distributed programming abstractions to ease the development of context-aware applications deployed in a mobile environment.

Developing these applications is complicated because of two discriminating properties inherent to mobile ad hoc networks [18]: nodes in the network only have intermittent connectivity (due to the limited communication range of wireless technology combined with the mobility of the devices) and applications need to discover and collaborate without relying on a centralized coordination facility. Decoupled coordination models such as tuple spaces provide an appropriate paradigm for dealing with those properties [10]. Several adaptations of tuple spaces have been specially developed for the mobile environment (including LIME [13], L2imbo [2] and TOTA[9]). In those systems, processes communicate by reading from and writing tuples to collocated devices in the environment.

---

* Funded by a doctoral scholarship of the IWT-Flanders, Belgium.
** Funded by the Prospective Research for Brussels program of IWOIB-IRSIB, Belgium.

R. Meersman et al. (Eds.): OTM 2010, Part II, LNCS 6427, pp. 745–763, 2010.

Context information in such systems is thus represented by the ability to *read* certain tuples from the environment. In this paper we argue that this representation is inappropriate and can even lead to an erroneous perception of context. The main reason for this is that the ability to read a tuple from the environment does not give any guarantees that the context information carried by the tuple is appropriate for the reader. This forces programmers to manually verify that a tuple is valid for the application's context situation *after* the tuple is read.

In this paper, we propose a novel tuple space approach called *context-aware tuples* which decouples the concept of tuple perception from tuple reception. A context-aware tuple has an associated predicated called a *context rule* that determines when the receiving application is in the right context to perceive the tuple. Only when a tuple's context rule can be satisfied by the context of the receiving application, the tuple can be perceived by the application. Applications can also be notified when the tuple can no longer be perceived. The core contribution of this work lies in the introduction of a general programming concept under the form of a context rule to support development of context-aware applications in a mobile environment. Our contribution is validated by (1) a prototype implementation, (2) demonstrating the applicability of our model by using it in a non-trivial context-aware distributed application and (3) providing an operational semantics for our model.

2   Motivation

Tuple spaces were first introduced in the coordination language Linda [7]. Recently they have shown to provide a suitable coordination model for the mobile environment [10]. In the tuple space model, processes communicate by means of a globally shared virtual data structure (called a tuple space) by reading and writing tuples. A tuple is an ordered group of values (called the tuple content) and has an identifier (called the type name). Processes can post and read tuples using three basic operations: out to insert a tuple into the tuple space, in to remove a tuple from the tuple space and rd to check if a tuple is present in the tuple space (without removing it). Tuples are anonymous and are extracted from the tuple space by means of pattern matching on the tuple content.

In order to describe the main motivation behind context-aware tuples, we introduce a simple yet representative scenario and show the limitations of existing tuple space approaches. Consider a company building where each room is equipped with devices that act as *context providers* of different kinds of information. For example, information to help visitors to orient themselves in the building or information about the meeting schedule in a certain room. Employees and visitors are equipped with mobile devices which they use to plan meetings or to find their way through the building. Since each room is equipped with a context provider, a user located in one room will receive context information from a range of context providers. Only part of this context information which is broadcasted in the ambient is *valid* for the current context of the user.

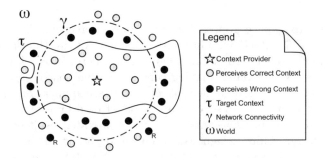

Fig. 1. Context perception in existing tuple space approaches

Figure 1 illustrates the scenario where ω represents the company building, τ a meeting room in the building, and γ the communication range of a device located in the meeting room. The star denotes a tuple space (acting as the context provider) which injects tuples into the ambient, i.e. all devices (depicted as dots) $\in \gamma$. Those tuples are aimed to be perceived by devices in the meeting room, i.e. in the target area τ. This device injects a tuple in the ambient to signal receivers that they are currently in the meeting room. Note that location is just one example of context, τ could involve more complex constraints, e.g. being located in the meeting room while there is a meeting.

A large body of tuple space systems targeting a mobile setting follows a *federated* tuple space model [13] in which the visibility of the tuples (and thus context perception) directly depends on collocation of devices holding these tuples. In this model, the perceived context of a device is equivalent to being in range of γ. The context delivery solely based on γ makes two groups of devices to perceive wrong context information (depicted as black dots). The first group consists of devices contained in the set $\gamma \setminus \tau$. In our example, these are all devices within communication range of the context provider but outside the meeting room. These devices will perceive to be in the meeting room while they are actually not. The second group consists of devices contained in the set $\tau \setminus \gamma$. In our example, these are all devices out of communication range of the context provider (possibly due to an intermittent disconnection) but in the meeting room. These devices will perceive not to be in the meeting room while they are actually.

Other tuple space systems have adopted a *replication* model where tuples are replicated amongst collocated devices in order to increase data availability in the face of intermittent connectivity [9,12]. In replication-based models, devices in $\tau \setminus \gamma$ will not perceive wrong context information. However, in these systems tuple perception is equivalent to have been once within reach of γ, possibly in the past. This means that devices which have been connected to the context provider once (τ) and are currently in $\omega \setminus \tau$ (depicted as black dots with a R) will perceive to be in the meeting room even though they are no longer there.

2.1   Summary

Using current tuple space approaches the context perception is correct in certain cases (the white dots) but, in many cases it is wrong (black dots). There are three main reasons for these erroneous context perceptions. First, there is a connectivity-context mismatch making context sharing based *solely* on connectivity unsuitable for the development of context-aware applications deployed in a mobile setting. Second, the observed context is affected by intermittent connectivity: temporal disconnections with the context provider result in an erroneous context perception. Third, when using replication-based models to deal with intermittent connectivity, a permanent disconnection leads devices to perceive that they are in the target area forever.

In order to solve these issues, programmers are forced to manually verify that every tuple (and thus context information) is valid for the application' context. More concretely, programmers have to manually determine tuple perception at the application level after a tuple is read from the tuple space. Manually determining the applications context and adapt accordingly leads to context-related conditionals (`if` statements) being scattered all over the program [1], hindering modularity. Additionally, the content of the tuples have to be polluted with meta data in order to infer tuple perception at application level, decreasing reusability of tuples. For example, a `Room` tuple indicating that a person is currently located in the meeting room should also contain the location information. Finally, programmers need to write application level code that deals with context-awareness in order to compensate for the lack of expressiveness of underlying model.

As the complexity of context-aware applications increases, manually computing tuple perception can no longer be solved using ad hoc solutions. Instead, the coordination model should be augmented with abstractions for context-awareness that allow developers to describe tuple perception in the coordination model itself. Context-aware tuples provides an alternative approach that keeps the simplicity of the tuple space model where interactions and context information are defined by means of tuples, while allowing tuples themselves to determine the context in which a receiving application should be in order to perceive a tuple.

3   Context-Aware Tuples

Context-aware tuples is a novel tuple space approach for mobile ad hoc networks tackling the tuple perception issues described. We introduce the notion of a *context rule* prescribing when a tuple should be perceived by the application, and a *rule engine* to infer when a tuple is perceivable and when it is not. Unlike existing tuple space approaches, *only* the subset of tuples which should be perceivable, is made accessible to applications.

The Core Model. The model underlying context-aware tuples gathers concepts from both federated and replication tuple spaces, and extends them with a declarative mechanism to express context information with tuples. Figure 2 depicts our model. A device in the network is abstracted as a virtual machine

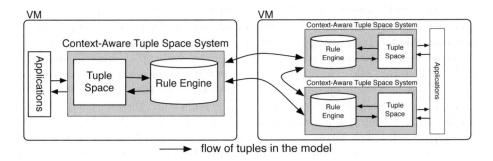

flow of tuples in the model

Fig. 2. Context-aware tuple space model

(VM) carrying one or more context-aware tuple space (CAT) systems. CAT systems are connected to other CAT systems by means of a mobile ad hoc network. Several interconnected CAT systems form a *CAT network*. The composition of a CAT network varies according to the changes on the network topology as the hosting device moves about with the user. A CAT system consists of a tuple space and a rule engine.

The tuple space serves as the interface between applications and the CAT system. It supports *non-blocking* Linda-like operations to insert, read and remove tuples. The main reason for the strict non-blocking operations is that it significantly reduces the impact of volatile connections on a distributed application[1]. As an alternative to blocking operations, we provide the notion of a *reaction* to a tuple (similar to a LIME reaction [13]): applications can register an observer that is asynchronously notified when a tuple matching a certain template is found in the tuple space.

The tuple space of a CAT system contains two types of tuples. *Public tuples* denote tuples that are shared with remote CAT systems, and *private tuples* denote tuples that remain local to the tuple space in which they were inserted and thus, will not be transmitted to other CAT systems. Applications can insert private and public tuples in the tuple space by means of the `out` and `inject` operation, respectively. As in LIME, applications can access tuples coming from the network without knowing the different collocated CAT systems explicitly.

The rule engine infers when a tuple should be perceived by applications (i.e. when its context rule is satisfied). Before further detailing the role of the rule engine, we describe how tuples are spread across the network.

Distribution of tuples in the network. When two CAT systems discover each other in the network, the public tuples contained in their tuple spaces are cloned and transmitted to the collocated CAT system. Hence, our model replicates tuples to remote CAT systems. Related work has shown that replication increases availability in such a highly disconnected environment allowing parties

---

[1] From previous work, we have found that a loosely-coupled communication model mitigates the effects of hardware characteristics inherent to mobile ad hoc networks [3].

not to have to be connected at the same time to communicate [12]. In this work, replication is used to support context-aware computation even though context providers and receivers are not connected at the same time. When a CAT system disconnects from the CAT network, the interchanged tuples are still stored in each CAT system allowing applications to perform some computation based on the stored context information despite being disconnected.

Tuples are propagated from CAT to CAT system when they see each other on the network according to a *propagation protocol* (similar to a TOTA propagation rule [9]). Tuples themselves carry a propagation protocol that allows a tuple itself to check whether it should be propagated to a certain CAT system. Such propagation protocol is triggered *before* a tuple is being physically transmitted to a new CAT system avoiding unnecessary exchange of tuples. In this work, the propagation protocol is limited to one-hop neighbours. A description of this scoped propagation mechanism can be found in [16]. Note that other replication techniques could be used [12], and the mechanism for replication is orthogonal to the abstractions for context-awareness introduced in this work.

Managing Tuple Perception. The rule engine is a central component in our model which ensures that applications can only see those tuples that they should perceive. Each tuple inserted in a CAT system carries a *context rule*. A context rule defines the conditions that need to be fulfilled for a tuple to be perceivable. Such context rule is defined by the creator of the tuple and gets transmitted together with the tuple when the tuple is injected in the network.

When a tuple is inserted at a certain CAT system, the tuple is first handed in to the rule engine which installs the necessary machinery to evaluate the tuple's context rule. When the rule engine infers that the conditions on a context rule are satisfied, the tuple's context rule is triggered and said to be *satisfied*. Only when the context rule of a tuple is satisfied, the tuple is inserted in the tuple space of the CAT system. At that moment, the applications are able to read the tuple. The rule engine takes care of reflecting the changes to the receiver' context so that applications cannot perceive those tuples whose context rule is not satisfied. The rule engine combined with the context rule solve the erroneous context perception problems from which replication-based approaches suffer.

As explained in the introduction, context information in tuple space approaches is represented by the ability to read certain tuples from the tuple space. These tuples can be either received from the environment or inserted locally. An example of a locally inserted tuple is a tuple which indicates the user location (e.g. GPS coordinates). As this information is always true, the associated context rule of such a tuple is always satisfied independently of the context. In contrast, a tuple received from the ambient indicating that a user is located in the meeting room needs a custom rule. The rule could specify that, e.g., there should be a location tuple in the receiving tuple space whose coordinates are within the boundaries of the meeting room. Our model conceives a context rule as a set of conditions defined in terms of the presence of certain tuples in the receiving tuple space. The rule engine thus observes the insertion and removal of the tuples in the tuple space to infer which context rules are satisfied. Defining context rules in terms of tuples allows the application to abstract away from the underlying hardware while keeping the simplicity of the tuple space model.

The rule engine incorporates a truth maintenance system built on top of a RETE network [5]. A RETE network optimizes the matching phase of the inference engine providing an efficient derivation of context rule activation and deactivation. The network has also been optimized to allow constant time deletions by applying a *scaffolding* technique [15]. A full description of the engine and its performance is out of the scope of this paper and can be found in [17].

The lifespan of a context-aware tuple. Context rules introduce a new dimension in the lifespan of a tuple. Not only can a tuple be inserted or removed from the tuple space, but it can also be perceivable or not for the application. Figure 3 shows a UML-state diagram of the lifespan of a context-aware tuple. When an application inserts a tuple in a CAT system[2], the tuple is not perceivable and its context rule is asserted in the rule engine. The rule engine then starts listening for the activation of that context rule (CR activation in the figure).

A tuple will become perceivable depending on whether the context rule is satisfied. If the context rule is satisfied, the tuple is perceivable and it is subject to tuple space operations (and thus becomes accessible to the application). If the tuple is not perceivable, the tuple is not subject to tuple space operations but its context rule remains in the rule engine. Every time a tuple's context rule is not satisfied, the out of context listeners for a tuple (OC listeners in the figure) are triggered. Applications can install listeners to be notified when a tuple moves out of context and react to it.

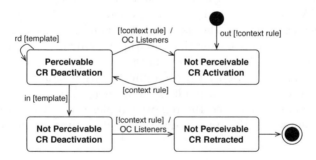

Fig. 3. Lifespan of a context-aware tuple

Upon performing an `in` operation, the tuple is removed from the tuple space but its context is not modified. As such, the tuple is considered not to be perceivable (as it is out of the tuple space) and its context rule remains in the rule engine. Once out of the tuple space, the rule engine listens for the deactivation of the context rule. Once the context rule is no longer satisfied, the context rule is retracted from the rule engine, and the tuple will be eventually garbage collected (once it is no longer referenced by the application).

---

[2] To keep the figure concise `out` denotes the insertion of a private or a public tuple.

Coordination. Our model combines replication of tuples for read operations while guaranteeing atomicity for remove operations. Atomicity for remove operations is an essential feature to support synchronization between applications. In our model, applications cannot remove tuples coming from a remote CAT system which is no longer connected. In order for a remove operation to succeed, the CAT system which created and injected the tuple in the network (called the *originator* system) needs to be connected. This means that a remove operation in our approach is executed *atomically* as defined in Linda [7]: if two processes perform a remove operation for a tuple, only one removes the tuple. When an originator is asked to remove one of its (stored) tuples by another CAT system, it removes the tuple and injects an *antituple* in the network for the removed tuple. For every tuple there is (conceptually) a unique antituple with the same format and content, but with a different sign. All tuples injected by an application have positive sign while their antituples have a negative sign. Whenever a tuple and its antituple are stored in the same tuple space, they immediately *annihilate* one another, i.e. they both get removed from the tuple space. By means of antituples, CAT systems can "unsend" tuples injected to the network.

Garbage Collection of Tuples. In our model, a public tuple gets replicated to collocated CAT systems. Some of these tuples may not be used by the receiving CAT system, resulting in accumulation of obsolete tuples. We use two mechanisms to garbage collect tuples in the CAT network. First, all tuples are injected in the network with an associated timeout. Such a timeout denotes the total lifespan of a tuple and it is determined by the application that creates and injects the tuple to the network. A tuple is transmitted together with its timeout to another CAT system. When the time period has elapsed, independently of the state in which a tuple is, the tuple becomes candidate for garbage collection in the CAT system. This means that the tuple context' rule is retracted from the engine, and the tuple is removed from the tuple space if necessary. The transitions for garbage collection have been omitted from figure 3 to keep it clear and concise. Secondly, when a public tuple gets removed, an antituple is sent to those systems that received the removed tuple. If a CAT system cannot be reached, the removal of the tuple is delayed until its timeout elapses.

3.1   Operations

In this section we describe context-aware tuples from a programmer's perspective. Context-aware tuples have been implemented as part of AmbientTalk[3], a distributed object-oriented programming language specifically designed for mobile ad hoc networks [18]. We introduce the necessary syntax and features of the language along with our explanation.

In order to create a CAT system programmers can call the `makeCatSystem` operation as follows:

---

[3] Context-aware tuples is available with AmbientTalk at
`http://soft.vub.ac.be/amop`

```
def cat := makeCatSystem();
```

This operation initializes a CAT system (including the rule engine and the tuple space) and publishes it to the *ambient*, i.e. the CAT network. It returns the tuple space of the newly created CAT system. Variables are defined with the keyword def and assigned to a value with the assignment symbol (:=).

As mentioned before, all operations for interacting with the tuple space of a CAT system are non-blocking. We provide the rdp(template) operation to check if a tuple matching the template is present in the tuple space(without removing it), and the out(tuple) operation to insert a private tuple in the tuple space. In order for applications to insert a public tuple, thereby making it available to other collocated CAT systems, the inject: operation is provided:

```
cat.inject: tuple   inContext: contextRule timeout: timeInterval;
```

This operation takes as parameter a tuple and its context rule and a time interval denoting the timeout value for the tuple. A context rule is defined by an array containing the set of templates and constraints that need to be satisfied for the tuple to be perceivable. Constraints are conceived as logical conditions on the variables used in a template. As a concrete usage example, consider again the scenario sketched in the motivation. In order to model that a device is within the meeting room, the context provider could inject a public tuple as follows:

```
cat.inject: tuple(inRoom, meetingRoom)
    inContext: [tuple(location,?loc), withinBoundary(roomArea,?loc)];
```

A tuple is created by means of the tuple operation which takes as parameter a list of fields. As usual, the first field of a tuple is its type name. In this case, we create a inRoom tuple for the meeting room whose context rule consists of two terms that need to match. First, there must be a tuple in the tuple space matching the tuple(location,?loc) template[4]. The ? operator indicates a variable in a template, i.e. the template matches *any* location tuple in the tuple space. Secondly, the location tuple needs to satisfy a constraint: its coordinates have to be within the area of the meeting room. The withinBoundary function returns such a constraint given the coordinates stored in the ?loc variable and the meeting room area stored in roomArea variable.

Programmers can use reactions to register a block of code that is executed when a tuple matching a template is inserted in the tuple space. Our approach extends a LIME reaction with the notion of *context*: a reaction can only be triggered when the tuple matching the pattern is perceivable. Programmers can also react to a tuple moving out of context by installing an outOfContext listener. In what follows, we describe the different kinds of reactions supported.

```
cat.when: template read: closureIn outOfContext: closureOut;
```

---

[4] A template is created by means of the tuple operation as well. However, only templates can take variables as fields.

The `when:read:` operation takes as parameter a template to observe in the tuple space, and two closures that serve as event handlers to call when the tuple is perceivable and when it is not, respectively. When a perceivable tuple matches the template, the `closureIn` handler is called binding all variables of the template to the values of the matching tuple. As this operation performs a reaction to a `rd` operation, the tuple is not removed from the tuple space. When the context rule of the matching tuple is not satisfied, the `closureOut` handler is called. The `when:read:` operation only triggers the event handlers once for a matching tuple. If several perceivable tuples match the template, one is chosen non-deterministically. The `whenever:read:` operation works analogously but it triggers the event handlers for *every* perceivable tuple matching the template. The code snippet below shows the usage of this operation in our scenario.

```
cat.whenever: tuple(inRoom,?name) read: {
   display("You are in room" + name);
} outOfContext: {
   display("You moved out of room" + name);
};
```

In the example, each time an `inRoom` tuple is matched, the application notifies that the user moved in a certain room. Once the user moves out of the boundaries of that room, the `inRoom`'s context rule is not satisfied and the `outOfContext` closure is applied notifying the user that he moved out of the room.

The following two operations work analogously to the previous ones but, they perform a reaction to an `in` operation rather than a `rd` operation.

```
cat.when: template in: closureIn outOfContext: closureOut;
cat.whenever: template in: closureIn outOfContext: closureOut;
```

Those operations remove the tuple from the tuple space before calling the `closureIn` handler. Note that if the tuple to be removed comes from another CAT system, the underlying CAT system contacts the originator CAT system to atomically remove the original tuple. If that removal fails, the replicated tuple is not removed from the local tuple space and `closureIn` is simply not triggered.

4   Semantics

We now formalize the context-aware tuples model by means of a calculus with operational semantics based on prior works in coordination [19,20]. The syntax of our model is defined by the grammar shown in table 1. k identifies the type of the tuple: + for a public tuple, $\oplus$ for a private tuple and $-$ for an antituple. A context-aware tuple c is specified as a first order term τ. $\tau^k_{x,t}\langle r \rangle$ indicates that the tuple with content τ, type k and timeout t, originates from a tuple space with identifier x and is only perceivable when its context rule r is satisfied. The context rule is considered optional and the notation $\tau^k_{x,t}$ should be read as $\tau^k_{x,t}\langle 1 \rangle$, i.e. the context rule is always true. The antituple of a tuple $\tau^k_{x,t}$ is denoted by $\tau^-_{x,t}\langle 0 \rangle$, i.e. its context rule is always false.

Table 1. Context-Aware Tuples: Grammar

$k ::= + \mid \oplus \mid -$	Tuple Types
$c ::= \tau_{x,t}^{k} \langle r \rangle$	Context-Aware Tuple
$S ::= \emptyset \mid c, S$	Tuple Set
$P ::= \emptyset \mid A.P$	Process
$C ::= \emptyset \mid ([\![S]\!]_x \mid C) \mid (P \mid C)$	Configuration
$A ::= out(x,\tau,r,t) \mid inject(x,\tau,r,t) \mid rd(x,\nu) \mid in(x,\nu) \mid$	
$outC(x,\nu) \mid whenRead(x,\nu,P_a,P_d).P \mid whenIn(x,\nu,P_a,P_d).P$	Actions

A process P consists of a sequence of tuple space operations A. Tuples are stored in S which is defined as a set of tuples composed by the operator $(,)$. A tuple space with content S and identifier x is denoted by $[\![S]\!]_x$. A system configuration C is modeled as a *set* of processes P and collocated tuple spaces $[\![S]\!]_x$ composed by the operator $|$. An application consists of all $P \in C$.

Next to the grammar, we assume the existence of a matching function $\mu(\nu,\tau)$ that takes a template ν and a tuple content τ, and returns θ. θ is a substitution map of variable identifiers from the template ν to the actual values from τ. A concrete value in this map can be accessed by θ_z that returns the actual value for z. The matched tuple can be accessed by θ_τ. We also assume the existence of a function *time* which returns a numeric comparable value indicating the current time. $r(S)$ indicates that the context rule r is satisfied in the tuple set S.

The semantics of the context-aware tuples model is defined by the transition rules shown in table 2. Every transition $C \xrightarrow{\lambda} C'$ indicates that a configuration C can be transformed into a configuration C' under the condition λ.

Table 2. Operational Semantics

$$out(x,\tau,r,t).P \mid [\![S]\!]_x \mid C \xrightarrow{t'=time()+t} P \mid [\![\tau_{x,t'}^{\oplus} \langle r \rangle, S]\!]_x \mid C \qquad (OUT)$$

$$inject(x,\tau,r,t).P \mid [\![S]\!]_x \mid C \xrightarrow{t'=time()+t} P \mid [\![\tau_{x,t'}^{+} \langle r \rangle, S]\!]_x \mid C \qquad (INJ)$$

$$[\![\tau_{x,t}^{k} \langle r \rangle, S]\!]_x \mid [\![S']\!]_y \mid C \xrightarrow[\substack{(x \neq y)}]{\tau \notin S' \wedge (k \neq \oplus) \wedge} [\![\tau_{x,t}^{k} \langle r \rangle, S]\!]_x \mid [\![\tau_{x,t}^{k} \langle r \rangle, S']\!]_y \mid C \qquad (RPL)$$

$$rd(x,\nu).P \mid [\![\tau_{y,t}^{k} \langle r \rangle, S]\!]_x \mid C \xrightarrow[\substack{r(S)}]{\mu(\nu,\tau)=\theta \wedge (k \neq -) \wedge} P\theta \mid [\![\tau_{y,t}^{k} \langle r \rangle, S]\!]_x \mid C \qquad (RD)$$

$$[\![\tau_{y,t}^{-} \langle 0 \rangle, \tau_{y,t}^{k} \langle r \rangle, S]\!]_x \mid C \xrightarrow{(k \neq -)} [\![\tau_{y,t}^{-} \langle 0 \rangle, S]\!]_x \mid C \qquad (KILL)$$

$$[\![\tau_{y,t}^{k} \langle r \rangle, S]\!]_x \mid C \xrightarrow{t \leq time() \wedge (k \neq -)} [\![\tau_{y,t}^{-} \langle 0 \rangle, S]\!]_x \mid C \qquad (TIM)$$

$$in(x,\nu).P \mid [\![\tau_{x,t}^{k} \langle r \rangle, S]\!]_x \mid C \xrightarrow{\mu(\nu,\tau)=\theta \wedge r(S) \wedge} P\theta \mid [\![\tau_{x,t}^{-} \langle 0 \rangle, S]\!]_x \mid C \qquad (INL)$$

$$in(x,\nu).P \mid [\![\tau_{y,t}^{+} \langle r \rangle, S]\!]_x \mid [\![\tau_{y,t}^{+} \langle r \rangle, S']\!]_y \mid C \xrightarrow[\substack{(x \neq y)}]{\mu(\nu,\tau)=\theta \wedge r(S) \wedge} P\theta \mid [\![S]\!]_x \mid [\![\tau_{y,t}^{-} \langle 0 \rangle, S']\!]_y \mid C \qquad (INR)$$

$$outC(x,\tau).P \mid [\![\tau_{y,t}^{k} \langle r \rangle, S]\!]_x \mid C \xrightarrow{!r(S)} P \mid [\![\tau_{y,t}^{k} \langle r \rangle, S]\!]_x \mid C \qquad (OC)$$

$$whenRead(x,\nu,P_a,P_d).P \mid [\![S]\!]_x \mid C \xrightarrow{1} rd(x,\nu).P_a.outC(x,\theta_\tau).P_d \mid P \mid [\![S]\!]_x \mid C \qquad (WR)$$

$$whenIn(x,\nu,P_a,P_d).P \mid [\![S]\!]_x \mid C \xrightarrow{1} in(x,\nu).P_a.outC(x,\theta_\tau).P_d \mid P \mid [\![S]\!]_x \mid C \qquad (WI)$$

The (OUT) rule states that when a process performs an out operation over a local tuple space x, the tuple is immediately inserted in x as a private tuple with context rule r and timeout t'. The process continuation P is executed immediately. When a tuple is inserted in the tuple space x with an inject operation as specified by (INJ), the tuple is inserted in x as a public tuple and is replicated to other tuple spaces as specified by (RPL). This rule states that when a tuple space y moves in communication range of a tuple space x, all tuples $\tau_{x,t}^{k}$ which are not private and are not already in y will be replicated to y. The (RD) rule states that to read a template ν from a tuple space x, x has to contain a matching $\tau_{y,t}^{k}$ and the context rule of τ is satisfied in S. (RD) blocks if one of these conditions is not satisfied. When (RD) does apply, the continuation P is invoked with substitution map θ. Note that we do not disallow x to be equal to y in this rule. The (KILL) rule specifies that when both a tuple τ and its unique antituple τ^{-} are stored in the same tuple space, τ is removed immediately. The (TIM) rule specifies that when the timeout of a tuple τ elapses, its antituple τ^{-} is inserted in the tuple space. The **in** operation is *guaranteed* to be atomically executed. In the semantics, it has been split into a local rule (INL) and a remote rule (INR). (INL) works similarly to (RD), but it removes the tuple $\tau_{x,t}^{k}$ originated by the local tuple space x and inserts its antituple $\tau_{x,t}^{-}$. (INR) states that when the **in** operation is matched with a tuple published by another tuple space y, y must be one of the collocated tuple spaces (i.e. be in the configuration). Analogously to (INL), the tuple is removed and its antituple is inserted. The (OC) rule states that to move out of context a tuple τ from a local tuple space x, x has to contain τ (possibly its antituple) and its context rule is *not* satisfied. The WR rule states that a **whenRead** operation performed on the local tuple space x with template ν and processes P_a and P_d, is immediately translated into a new parallel process and the continuation P will be executed. The newly spawned parallel process is specified in terms of performing a **rd** operation followed by an **outC** operation. A **rd** operation blocks until there is a tuple matching ν in the local tuple space. The continuation P_a is then executed to subsequently perform an **outC** which blocks until the tuple is no longer perceivable. Finally, the continuation P_d is invoked whereafter the process dies. The WI is specified analogously but as it models a **whenIn** operation, it performs a **in** operation rather than a **rd** one. The **wheneverRead** and **wheneverIn** operations have been omitted as they are trivial recursive extensions of **whenRead** and **whenIn**, respectively.

Note that $(KILL)$ does not remove antituples. This has been omitted to keep the semantics simple and concise. By means of (RPL), the antituple of a tuple τ is only replicated to those systems that received τ. In our concrete implementation if a system cannot be reached, the removal of the antituple is delayed until the timeout of its tuple elapses (which inserts an antituple as specified by (TIM)). An antituple can only be removed once there are no processes in the configuration which registered an **outC** operation on the original tuple.

5   Flikken: Programming with Context-Aware Tuples

We demonstrate the applicability of context-aware tuples by means of the implementation of *Flikken*[5]: a game in which players equipped with mobile devices

---

[5] Flikken (which means *cops* in Dutch) is also included in the AmbientTalk distribution.

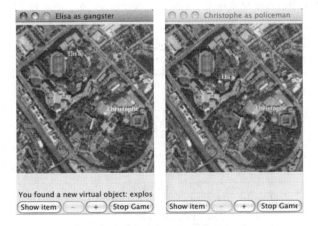

Fig. 4. Flikken GUI on the gangster device (left) and a policeman device (right)

interact in a physical environment augmented with virtual objects. The game consists of a dangerous gangster on the loose with the goal of earning 1 million euro by committing crimes. In order to commit crimes a gangster needs to collect burgling equipment around the city (knives, detonators, etc). Policemen work together to shoot the gangster down before he achieves his goal. Figure 4 shows the gangster's and a policeman's mobile device at the time the gangster has burgled the local casino. The gangster knows the location of the places with big amounts of money (banks, casinos, etc). When a gangster commits a crime, policemen are informed of the location and the amount of money stolen. Policemen can see the position of all nearby policemen and send messages to each other to coordinate their movements. The gangster and policemen are frequently informed of each other positions and can shoot at each other.

Flikken is an ideal case study for context-aware tuples as it epitomizes a mobile networking application that has to react to context changes on the environment such as changes on player's location, appearance and disappearance of players, and the discovery of virtual objects while moving about. Moreover, how to react to these changes highly depends on the receivers of the context information, e.g. virtual objects representing burgling items should only be perceived by the gangster when he is nearby their location while they should not be perceived at all by policemen. In what follows we describe the coordination and interaction between policemen and the gangster which is fully specified by means of context-aware tuples.

5.1   Implementation

Every player has a CAT system in his mobile device. Once the game starts, policemen and the gangster communicate player to player by means of the CAT network. Throughout the city various context providers (i.e. CAT systems) are

Table 3. Overview of the Context-Aware Tuples used in Flikken

Tuple Content	Tuple Context Rule	Tuple Description
All Players		
τ(TeamInfo, uid, gip)	[true]	Private tuple denoting the player's team.
τ(PlayerInfo, uid, gip, location)	[τ(TeamInfo, ?u, ?team), ?team $\neq$ gip]	Injected to opposite team members every 6 minutes to notify the position of a player. Location is a 2-tuple indicating the (GPS) coordinates of the player.
τ(OwnsVirtualObject, GUN, bullets)	[true]	Private tuple inserted by players when they pick up their gun at their HQ.
Only The Gangster		
τ(CrimeCommitted, name,location,reward)	[τ(TeamInfo, ?u, POLICEMAN)]	Notifies policemen that the gangster committed a crime.
τ(OwnsVirtualObject, type, properties)	[true]	Private tuple inserted when the gangster picks up a virtual object in the game area.
Only Policemen		
τ(PlayerInfo, uid, gip, location)	[τ(TeamInfo, ?u, gip)]	Notifies the position of a policemen to his colleagues every time he moves.
HeadQuarters		
τ(InHeadquarters, location)	[τ(PlayerInfo,?u,?team,?loc), inRange(location, ?loc)]	Notifies that the player entered his HQ. Used to start the chase (when this tuple moves out of context for the gangster's HQ) and to reload policemen's guns.
τ(CrimeTarget, name, location)	[τ(TeamInfo, ?u, GANGSTER)]	Notifies the gangster of the position of crime targets.
τ(CommitCrime,name, location,reward, vobj)	[τ(TeamInfo, ?u, GANGSTER), τ(PlayerInfo,?u, GANGSTER,?loc), inRange(location,?loc), hasVirtualObjects(vobj)]	Notifies the gangster of the possibility of committing a crime. hasVirtualObjects takes an array of virtual object ids and checks that the gangster has the required OwnsVirtualObject tuples.
City Context Providers		
τ(VirtualObject, id, location)	[τ(TeamInfo, ?u, GANGSTER), τ(PlayerInfo,?u, GANGSTER,?loc), inRange(location, ?loc)]	Notifies the gangster of the nearby presence of a virtual object. inRange is a helper function to check that two locations are in euclidian distance.
τ(Rechargeable-VirtualObject,GUN, BULLETS)	[τ(InHeadQuarters,?loc), τ(OwnsWeaponVO,GUN,?bullets), ?bullets < BULLETS]	Represents the player's gun. The gangster gets only one charge at the start of the game, while policemen's guns are recharged each time they go back to their HQ.

placed to inform players about virtual objects or crime locations by injecting the necessary tuples. A special type of context provider is the headquarter (HQ) of the players which signals the start of the chase.

Due to space limitations, this section only describes the set of tuples coordinating the core functionality. Table 3 shows an overview of the tuples used in the game and its context rule. The tuples are divided in five categories depending on the entity that injects them in the environment, i.e. all players, only gangster, only policemen, headquarters and city context providers. As used in the semantics, a tuple is denoted by the term τ and the first element of a tuple indicates its type name. We use capitals for constant values.

The CAT system on the player's device carries a vital private tuple τ(TeamInfo, uid, gip) indicating to which team he belongs. Every player transmits its location to the CAT network by means of the tuple τ(PlayerInfo, uid, gip, location). These tuples are often used in other tuple's context rules to identify the current whereabouts of a player and his team. For example, the tuple implementing a grenade uses them as follows.

```
cat.inject: tuple(VirtualObject, grenade, location)
inContext: [tuple(TeamInfo, ?u, GANGSTER),
            tuple(PlayerInfo, ?u, GANGSTER, ?loc),
            inRange(location, ?loc) ]
```

The tuple τ(VirtualObject, grenade, location) should be only perceived if the receiver is a gangster whose location (given by ?loc in the PlayerInfo tuple) is physically proximate to the virtual object. The inRange function returns the constraint that checks if the gangster location is in euclidian distance with the location of the grenade (stored in location). Upon removal of a VirtualObject tuple, a private tuple τ(OwnsVirtualObject, object) is inserted in his CAT system. OwnsVirtualObject tuples are used in the context rule of CommitCrime tuples which notify the gangster of a crime that can be committed. As crimes can only be committed when the gangster has certain burgling items, the context rule of the CommitCrime tuple requires that certain OwnsVirtualObject tuples are present in the tuple space. For example, in order for the gangster to perceive the CommitCrime tuple for the grandCasino, a τ(OwnsVirtualObject,grenade) tuple is needed as shown below.

```
cat.inject: tuple(CommitCrime, grandCasino, location, reward)
inContext: [tuple(TeamInfo, ?u, GANGSTER),
            tuple(PlayerInfo, ?u, GANGSTER, ?loc),
            inRange(location, ?loc),
            tuple(OwnsVirtualObject,grenade)];
```

Each player also registers several reactions to (1) update his GUI (e.g. to show the OwnsVirtualObject tuples collected), and (2) inject new tuples in response to the perceived ones, e.g. when a gangster commits a crime, he injects a tuple τ(CrimeCommitted, name,location,reward) to notify policemen. The code below shows the reaction on PlayerInfo tuples installed by the application.

```
cat.whenever: tuple(PlayerInfo, ?uid, ?tid, ?location) read: {
    GUI.displayPlayerPosition(tid, uid, location);
} outOfContext: {
    //grey out a player if there exists no update of his coordinates.
    def tuple := cat.rdp(tuple(PlayerInfo, uid, tid, ?loc));
    if: (nil == tuple) then: { GUI.showOffline(uid) };
};
```

Whenever a PlayerInfo tuple is read, the player updates his GUI with the new location of that player. As PlayerInfo tuples are injected with a timeout, they are automatically removed from the tuple space after its timeout elapses triggering the outOfContext: handler. In the example, this handle greys out the GUI representation of a player if no other PlayerInfo tuple for that player is in the CAT system. If the rdp operation does not return a tuple, the player is considered to be offline as he did not transmit his coordinates for a while.

5.2   Discussion

Flikken demonstrates how context-aware tuples aid the development of context-aware applications running on mobile ad hoc networks and address the tuple perception issues described in section 2 by introducing two key abstractions: (i) the context rule of a tuple which determines the context in which a receiving CAT system should find itself in order to perceive the tuple, and (ii) the rule engine which takes care of inferring tuple perception before applications are exposed to the tuple. A tuple space model with such abstractions has the following benefits:

1. Decomposing a tuple into content and context rule leads to separation of concerns, increasing modularity.
2. Since context rules can be developed separately, it enables programers to reuse the rules to build different kinds of tuples, increasing reusability. For example, in Flikken, we used a `inRangeOfGangster(?loc)` function to build the rule for the different `VirtualObject` tuples which was also reused to build the three first conditions of `CommitCrime` tuples.
3. Programmers do not need to add computational code to infer tuple perception as the rule engine takes care of it in an efficient way, making the code easier to understand and maintain.

Flikken is a significant subset of an augmented reality game inspired by the industrial game The Target[6]. The game functionality counts 11 tuples (8 of which carry a custom context rule) and 7 reactions. Currently, the game only provides one kind of virtual object for the player's defense, namely a gun. As future work, we would like to extend it with more complex virtual objects like mines, bombs, bulletproof vests, and radio jammers (to disrupt the communication with nearby players). We would also like to enhance the game interaction by incorporating compass data from the mobile device to be able to aim and kill players in a certain trajectory rather than using a certain radius of action.

The AmbientTalk language and context-aware tuples run on J2SE, J2ME under the connected device configuration (CDC), and Android 1.6 Platform. The current discovery mechanism is based on multicast messaging using UDP. Our current experimental setup for Flikken is a set of HTC P3650 Touch Cruise phones communicating by means of TCP broadcasting on a wireless ad hoc WiFi network. As future work, we aim to port the current Java AWT GUI of Flikken to the Android platform to deploy the game on HTC Hero phones.

6   Related Work

In this section, we discuss related systems modeled for context-awareness and show how context-aware tuples differs from them. Most of the tuple space systems designed for a mobile environment can be divided into federated and replication tuple space models. Both suffer from the problems shown in Section 2.

In TOTA, tuples themselves decide how to replicate from node to node in the network. As tuples can execute code when they arrive at a node, they can be exploited to achieve context-awareness in an adaptive way. But, programming such tuples has proven to be difficult [9]. TOTA, therefore, provides several basic

---

[6] http://www.lamosca.be/en/the-target

tuple propagation strategies. None of these propagation strategies addresses the perception problem tackled by our approach. Writing context-aware tuples in TOTA would require a considerable programming effort to react on the presence of an arbitrary combination of tuples as it only allows reactions on a single tuple.

GeoLinda [14] augments federated tuple spaces with a geometrical read operation `read(s,p)`. Every tuple has an associated shape and the `rd` operation only matches those tuples whose shape intersects the addressing shape `s`. GeoLinda has been designed to overcome the shortcomings of federated tuple spaces for a small subset of potential context information, namely the physical location of devices. As such, it does not offer a general solution for context-aware applications. In contrast, we propose a general solution based on context rules, which allows programmers to write application-specific rules for their tuples. Moreover, in GeoLinda the collocation of devices still plays a central role for tuple perception which can lead to erroneous context perception.

EgoSpaces provides the concept of a *view*, a declarative specification of a subset of the ambient tuples which should be perceived. Such views are defined by the *receiver* of tuples while in context-aware tuples it is the other way around. Context-aware tuples allow the *sender* of a tuple to attach a context rule dictating the system in which state the receiver should be in order to perceive the tuple. EgoSpaces suffers from the same limitations as federated tuple spaces since at any given time the available data depends on connectivity [8].

Publish/subscribe systems are closely related to tuple spaces as they provide similar decoupling properties [4]. Context-aware publish subscribe (CAPS) [6] is the closest work as it allows certain events to be filtered depending on the context of the receiver. More concretely, the publisher can associate an event with a *context of relevance*. However, CAPS is significantly different from context-aware tuples. First, CAPS does not allow reactions on the removal of events, i.e. there is no dedicated operation to react when an event moves out of context. Moreover, it is not a coordination abstraction, i.e. atomic removal of events is not supported. And last, their context of relevance are always associated to physical space.

The Fact Space Model [11] is a LIME-like federated tuple space model that provides applications with a distributed knowledge base containing logic facts shared among collocated devices. Unlike context-aware tuples, rules in the Fact Space Model are not exchanged between collocated devices and are not bound to facts to limit the perception of context information.

7   Conclusion

We have introduced a novel tuple space approach in which a tuple itself carries a predicate, called a *context rule*, that determines when the receiving application is in the right context to perceive the tuple. The novelty of our approach lies in the use of context rules combined with the introduction of a rule engine in the tuple space system which takes care of inferring when a context rule is satisfied, to control which tuples present in the tuple space should be actually accessible by applications. This decouples tuple reception from tuple perception solving the context perception problems exhibited by existing tuple space systems. By decomposing a tuple into content and context rule we allow the programmer to separate concerns. Since context rules can be developed separately, it enables programers to reuse the rules to build different kinds of tuples. Programmers do not longer need to infer tuple perception manually as the rule engine takes care of it in an efficient way, making the code easier to understand and maintain.

Acknowledgments. The authors would like to thank Amy L. Murphy for her helpful comments on earlier versions of the paper, and Bruno De Fraine for his invaluable help with the formal semantics of our model.

References

1. Costanza, P., Hirschfeld, R.: Language constructs for context-oriented programming: an overview of contextl. In: DLS 2005, pp. 1–10. ACM, NY (2005)
2. Davies, N., Friday, A., Wade, S.P., Blair, G.S.: L2imbo: a distributed systems platform for mobile computing. ACM Mob. Netw. and Appl. 3(2), 143–156 (1998)
3. Dedecker, J., Van Cutsem, T., Mostinckx, S., D'Hondt, T., De Meuter, W.: Ambient-oriented Programming in Ambienttalk. In: Thomas, D. (ed.) ECOOP 2006. LNCS, vol. 4067, pp. 230–254. Springer, Heidelberg (2006)
4. Eugster, P.T., Felber, P.A., Guerraoui, R., Kermarrec, A.: The many faces of publish/subscribe. ACM Computing Survey 35(2), 114–131 (2003)
5. Forgy, C.L.: Rete: A fast algorithm for the many pattern/many object pattern match problem. In: Mylopoulos, J., Brodie, M.L. (eds.) Artificial Intelligence & Databases, pp. 547–557. Kaufmann Publishers, INC., San Mateo (1989)
6. Frey, D., Roman, G.-C.: Context-aware publish subscribe in mobile ad hoc networks. In: Murphy, A.L., Vitek, J. (eds.) COORDINATION 2007. LNCS, vol. 4467, pp. 37–55. Springer, Heidelberg (2007)
7. Gelernter, D.: Generative communication in Linda. ACM Transactions on Programming Languages and Systems 7(1), 80–112 (1985)
8. Julien, C., Roman, G.-C.: Active coordination in ad hoc networks. In: De Nicola, R., Ferrari, G.-L., Meredith, G. (eds.) COORDINATION 2004. LNCS, vol. 2949, pp. 199–215. Springer, Heidelberg (2004)
9. Mamei, M., Zambonelli, F.: Programming pervasive and mobile computing applications with the TOTA middleware. In: IEEE Int. Conf. on Pervasive Computing and Communications (PERCOM), p. 263. IEEE Computer Society, Los Alamitos (2004)
10. Mascolo, C., Capra, L., Emmerich, W.: Mobile Computing Middleware. In: Gregori, E., Anastasi, G., Basagni, S. (eds.) NETWORKING 2002. LNCS, vol. 2497, pp. 20–58. Springer, Heidelberg (2002)
11. Mostinckx, S., Scholliers, C., Philips, E., Herzeel, C., De Meuter, W.: Fact spaces: Coordination in the face of disconnection. In: Murphy, A.L., Vitek, J. (eds.) COORDINATION 2007. LNCS, vol. 4467, pp. 268–285. Springer, Heidelberg (2007)
12. Murphy, A.L., Picco, G.P.: Using lime to support replication for availability in mobile ad hoc networks. In: Ciancarini, P., Wiklicky, H. (eds.) COORDINATION 2006. LNCS, vol. 4038, pp. 194–211. Springer, Heidelberg (2006)

13. Murphy, A.L., Picco, G.P., Roman, G.-C.: LIME: A middleware for physical and logical mobility. In: Proceedings of the The 21st International Conference on Distributed Computing Systems, pp. 524–536. IEEE Computer Society, Los Alamitos (2001)
14. Pauty, J., Couderc, P., Banatre, M., Berbers, Y.: Geo-linda: a geometry aware distributed tuple space. In: Proc. of the 21st Inter. Conf. on Advanced Networking and Applications (AINA), pp. 370–377. IEEE Computer Society, Los Alamitos (2007)
15. Perlin, M.: Scaffolding the RETE network. In: International Conference on Tools for Artificial Intelligence, pp. 378–385. IEEE Computer Society, Los Alamitos (1990)
16. Scholliers, C., Gonzalez Boix, E., De Meuter, W.: TOTAM: Scoped Tuples for the Ambient. In: Workshop on Context-aware Adaptation Mechanisms for Perv. and Ubiquitous Services, vol. 19, pp. 19–34. EASST (2009)
17. Scholliers, C., Philips, E.: Coordination in volatile networks. Master's thesis, Vrije Universiteit Brussels (2007)
18. Cutsem, T.V., Mostinckx, S., Gonzalez Boix, E., Dedecker, J., De Meuter, W.: Ambienttalk: object-oriented event-driven programming in mobile ad hoc networks. In: Int. Conf. of the Chilean Comp. Science Society, pp. 3–12. IEEE C. S., Los Alamitos (2007)
19. Viroli, M., Casadei, M.: Biochemical tuple spaces for self-organising coordination. In: Field, J., Vasconcelos, V.T. (eds.) COORDINATION 2009. LNCS, vol. 5521, pp. 143–162. Springer, Heidelberg (2009)
20. Viroli, M., Omicini, A.: Coordination as a service. Fundamenta Informaticae 73(4), 507–534 (2006)

Overlay Routing under Geographically Correlated Failures in Distributed Event-Based Systems

Kyriakos Karenos[1], Dimitrios Pendarakis[1], Vana Kalogeraki[2],
Hao Yang[3], and Zhen Liu[3]

[1] IBM, T.J. Watson Research Center
{kkarenos,dimitris}@us.ibm.com
[2] Athens University of Economics and Business
vana@aueb.gr
[3] Nokia Research
{hao.2.yang,zhen.38.liu}@nokia.com

Abstract. In this paper we study the problem of enabling uninterrupted delivery of messages between endpoints, subject to spatially correlated failures in addition to independent failures. We developed a failure
model-independent algorithm for computing routing paths based on failure correlations using both a-priory failure statistics together with available real-time monitoring information. The algorithm provides the most
cost-efficient message routes that are potentially comprised of multiple simultaneous paths. We also designed and implemented an Internet-based
overlay routing service that allows applications to construct and maintain highly resilient end-to-end paths. We have deployed our system over
a set of geographically distributed Planetlab nodes. Our experimental
results illustrate the feasibility and performance of our approach.

1 Introduction

Over the past few years, many critical infrastructures such as energy distribution
networks, aviation information systems and electrical power grids have been
incorporating event-driven systems which combine computational systems with
the *physical* process. A central characteristic of such applications is the fact that
they are being deployed across large geographic areas. The level of availability
and responsiveness that is expected from these infrastructures raises considerable
challenges in delivering messages from producers to consumers in a continuous
and uninterrupted manner.

Consider, for example, an electrical power grid that transmits electricity flows
through multiple paths from the power plant to a number of substations interconnected over an Internet-based wide-area network, which then distribute the
power to end-consumers. Such systems are vulnerable to hardware and/or software component failures in the control computer systems as well as external
events such as earthquakes, hurricanes and fires. Although these latter events
are rare, their impact on the application can be dramatic [1].

R. Meersman et al. (Eds.): OTM 2010, Part II, LNCS 6427, pp. 764–784, 2010.

In order to meet the objective of maintaining *uninterrupted* message communication path under node/link failures, a common approach is to deploy a *disjoint* backup path in addition to the primary communication path and either divert to the backup path at the onset of detecting a failure or propagate all the packets along both paths [2,3]. However, it is not always clear whether a pair of primary-backup paths suffices to provide uninterrupted service. In fact, these techniques assume independent single link or node failures, i.e., when a failure occurs, it will only affect one of the paths. In large geographic areas, failures can also be caused by external phenomena which affect *a group* of nodes. These types of failures are referred to as *geographically correlated* failures wherein nodes that are in relative proximity with respect to each other have higher probability of failing together. Example causes of such failures are natural disasters (earthquakes, hurricanes) as well as power outages and malicious attacks.

Correlated failures may cause multiple paths to fail simultaneously even if the sets of links comprising the paths are disjoint. A solution to this problem would be to increase the number of paths established in an attempt to increase the probability that at least one of the paths survives a correlated failure. Arbitrarily increasing the number of concurrent paths, however, increases the resource consumption overhead (i.e., the *cost* of the path), due to the utilization of additional forwarding nodes and links. Consequently, an important challenge is to make sure that the resiliency level of the communication path, and the corresponding event flow supported by this path, is reached with minimal additional resource cost.

In this paper we describe an *overlay-based* routing technique that addresses the challenge of efficiently meeting the resiliency expectations for distributed event driven systems under large geographical correlated and independent failures. Our objective in this work in particular, is stated as follows: Given the node locations, interconnection topology, failure statistics and resiliency requirements, our goal is to construct an end-to-end path (potentially consisting of one or more sub-paths) between the source and the destination end-points, that jointly (i) satisfy availability constraints, *i.e.* maintain high *resiliency*, defined as the probability of a data packet (event) being delivered via any active path at any time under the above combined failures, (ii) optimize resource utilization (cost).

We propose a framework that addresses this problem. We first motivate the need for addressing geographically correlated failures via real-world examples and observations. We then utilize a tractable model for mapping correlated failures to geographic locations and affected network nodes and links. Then, to efficiently solve the resiliency/cost optimization problem, we adopt a two-step decomposition approach that first constraints the set of eligible paths and then employs a branch-and-cut-based heuristic toward computing the least-cost, potentially non-disjoint, multi-path. Our deployment on a geographically distributed network of PlanetLab [4] testbed nodes demonstrates the feasibility and benefits our approach over traditional primary/backup path approaches in the presence of geographically correlated failures.

2   Geographic Failures

The challenge with large scale spatially correlated failures is that they are hard to characterize and model. One important reason is that correlated failures can be very difficult to distinguish from independent failures. Second, in many cases, nodes are not dense enough to reveal the actual geographic span of a failure event. Below we present examples of area failures that we consider as well as some observations that motivate our design and solution.

Fig. 1. Cascading area failures. From left to right, a time-lapse of the geographic span of the failures (within the periphery indicated by black lines) is shown. (Extracted from the "Final Report on the August 14, 2003 Blackout in the United States and Canada: Causes and Recommendations". Available at www.nerc.com)

Blackouts: Energy distribution grids are interconnected in a network to stations located in proximity forming service sub-regions. When a failure occurs, it will propagate from the geographical start point toward near-by locations due to load redistribution, potentially overloading those locations and causing cascading effect. Observe that at different points in time, different failures will occur in different regions due to a failures in different stations (centers). These failures eventually manifest themselves as a single, continuous, cascading failure. An illustrative example of a series of area failures can be seen in Figure 1 which shows the correlation as revealed by the investigation of a large scale blackout conducted by the North American Electric Reliability Corporation (NERC).

Seismic data studies: Recent seismological studies [5], found that the spatial correlations of observed intensities (described by ground accelerations and ground velocities) of earthquakes are described by *exponential functions* with respect to the geographical distance between two points of interest. More specifically, given the epicenter of the earthquake, the earthquakes catastrophic effect will decay exponentially in the distance to the epicenter. This fits the "center and radius" model, where centers are decided based on the epicenter location and the historic probability of an earthquakes happening, and a exponentially decaying radius that reflects the intensity of the earthquake.

Planetlab Data: We also performed extensive studies of Planetlab node failures using data from the all-pairs-pings service[1]. For this dataset, at the end of each time slot (with duration of 20 minutes) all nodes attempt to ping all other nodes

---

[1] http://ping.ececs.uc.edu/ping/ by Jeremy Stribling at Massachusetts Institute of Technology.

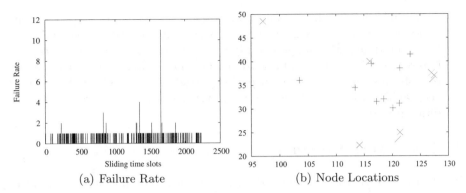

Fig. 2. An example area failure extracted from PlanetLab dataset. The visible spike in (a) indicates a large-scale failure. The node locations are shown in (b); X-axis is longitude, Y-axis is latitude. + sign shows locations of failed nodes and × shows operational nodes.

in a finite set and report the ping time to a central logger. Our goal was to identify failures of nodes that are in geographical proximity by associating each node with its actual location (longitude and latitude). This study turns out to be tedious due to the fact that geographic regions are not always of fixed sizes while the scarceness of nodes hinders the task of uncovering area failures. We first, analyzed the data and extract all the time slots where nodes have failed. Using the ping information, we deem a node as down when a large percentage of other nodes cannot ping it. This identifies a hop failure (i.e. node and/or link). In Figure 2(a), pertaining to a dataset for July of 2006, large failures are easily distinguishable by the spike in the *failure rate*, i.e. the total number of failures in that time slot. We then restrict the failures by proximity based on the longitude and latitude. In Figure 2(b) the X and Y axis show longitude and latitude, representing an area in China where all nodes marked with symbol + have failed almost simultaneously. In this case-study, most failed nodes belonged to the same educational institution which suggests a possible failure at the institution's core IP infrastructure (e.g. one or more IP gateway routers). Therefore, such failure resulted in unreachable nodes in geographical proximity.

The key observation is that due to the inherent proximity-based nature of the effects of such failures, it is possible to devise a topology and a framework that can produce informed decisions on how to route events across large areas, however introducing additional challenges. In particular:

- Geographical failures happen at the physical level and may be hard to capture, however their effects are manifested at the application layer. Therefore, in order to facilitate routing of events across these areas, one can superimpose a routing layer on top of the physical layer to divert traffic away from failure prone regions.
- Routing events using a single path diverted away from one failure region, does not necessarily guarantee a high degree of availability (or equivalently, the *resiliency* formally defined in Section 4); this is true also because path

nodes/links can fail independently regardless of area failures. Previous studies an real-world deployments also support such observations e.g. [6,7].

– Using multiple paths can potentially increase resiliency. Since a geographical failure can affect multiple forwarding path nodes/links in a region simultaneously (potentially in different paths), a tradeoff is introduced between the geographical diversity of the paths and the overhead cost introduced by additional routes.

3   Framework Design

In this section we discuss the network architecture and components of our routing framework. In particular, our frameworks comprises of: (a) a network of routing nodes with known geographical locations deployed on top of the physical network in a logical network in the form of an *overlay*, (b) a failure model used for mapping *failures in the physical network to failures in the logical, overlay network* (c) a *model-independent* path computation algorithm that uses as input the failure model, the overlay network and the resiliency level required by the event-based application and computes the route (potentially consisting of multiple paths) on which messages should be forwarded that meets the requested resiliency and (d) an implementation of a monitoring component that is used at run-time to reconfigure the paths as failures occur and update the model.

3.1   Network Architecture

We consider *overlay* networks comprised of a group of connected nodes built *over* the physical network. In particular, our work targets applications pertaining to event-driven corporate networks with geographically distributed nodes or distributed event processing infrastructures. As an example, consider currently deployed *Aviation Information Systems* that are utilized to deliver streams of flight tracks status to subscribing Internet-based endpoints[2]. The receiving sites are connected via Virtual private Network links (VPN). Thus, such systems can take advantage of the presence of multiple connected sites to deploy redundant delivery paths and maximize the probability of uninterrupted delivery which is a critical requirement. Note that for such applications, distributed deployment with *centralized* (but resilient) control suffices, thus we will focus on solving the joint resiliency-cost optimization problem and how to utilize our solution in real-world geographical deployments.

Why overlays: Routing using overlays has been well motivated in previous works [2,3,8]. In particular, the use of an overlay allows for diverting from the single, fixed IP-defined route, bypassing congested or unavailable IP routers and enhancing applications with quality of service (QoS) support. Furthermore, using Internet-based best-effort techniques (such as TCP/IP) to detect and repair route failures might take arbitrary and unpredictable time to reconstruct a new route. In many cases, even when an IP-based path is established, a single path

---

[2] www.faa.gov/airports_airtraffic/air_traffic/

might not suffice to provide the resiliency level required by the application and thus additional parallel source-destination paths may need to be constructed; a feature not currently supported by TCP.

Two types of nodes can be distinguished in our network model: (i) end nodes and (ii) forwarding nodes. End nodes represent the physical sources of the event flows (such as sensors and actuators) as well as the destinations or consumers of the flows (such as stream processing centers and event sinks). We currently make the simplifying assumption that there is no processing performed at forwarding nodes. We also assume that nodes are distributed within a bounded, two-dimensional geographic area. Within this area, each node is associated with two-dimensional location coordinates. In addition to the locations, we assume that the node connectivity graph is given. In our model, the connectivity graph does not necessarily reflect a particular underlying structure; it could be a mapping of the actual IP-layer's physical connectivity or, alternatively, links may comprise an overlay network where nodes are interconnected in a topology determined by some overlay routing scheme (e.g., ALMI [9], Pastry [10] or topology-aware schemes [11]).

3.2   Pluggable Failure Model

We will consider two types of failures; independent and geographically correlated failures. Independent failures are associated with overlay forwarding segments N_i (e.g. nodes and links) with a failure probability $Pr_{ind}(N_i)$. For the modeling used, an assumption we make is that time comprises of *distinct time slots* and at each timeslot, a node or link N_i fails with the aforementioned probability. Also, at any timeslot, one or more nodes or links may fail concurrently and independently. For the geographically correlated failure model we consider a fault area A within which geographic failures may occur. Furthermore, we assume that at any one time slot only *a single* correlated failure may occur.

Due to the inherent distance-based nature of the effects of geographically correlated failures, such failures can be approximated by a *failure center* and a probability to affect *other areas (and components within that area) that are in the proximity of the center*. In particular, given a two-dimensional geographical area A, the failure distribution can be described by two probability functions: (i) the probability that a failure will occur at a point v in that area (i.e. the failure center) and (ii) the probability that a failure event that pertains to the failure at v will occur. Thus, a correlated geographic failure model can be defined as follows:

$$Pr_v(event) \equiv Pr(event \mid correlated\ failure\ at\ v) \qquad (1)$$

This model returns the probability of an *event* occurring at the logical routing topology given that a failure has occurred at the physical level at center v. The key observation here is that an event includes one or more failures at the logical topology. For example, a geographical failure at v may have cause the failure of all nodes within a fixed distance of v. This modeling allows for generic incorporation of different failure models with potentially little adaptation overhead, assuming that the locations of the various failure generation centers in the physical network are known or can be approximated. For example, we may be able to collect IP layer connectivity (underlay) and use the information of the underlaying IP paths to map the correlation to the overlay using a methods such as in [8] and the geographical correlations such as the ones studied in [12]. These methods can provide 2-way correlation between the various components (such as links comprising Internet routes) based on the distance, thus has n^2 complexity for mapping correlations for n components. Physical proximity is achieved by considering a node failed (or unreachable) by the proximity of failed IP routers. Another example could be to use historical data to map the spread of a failure over time. In [1] the authors use a Markov model to compute cascading failures in a power outage scenario. Finally, a third example is using a disk area failure model as in [13] where a failure span is characterized by its center and a radius. This type of failures pertain, for example, a seismic scenario.

Note that the failure probability can be computed for any given point in A. Such point can represent the location of a node or a list of points that represent the location of a link. The addition of points in the computation does not affect the complexity of the algorithm since *all* points need to be considered in integrating the probability across A.

3.3 Routing and Adaptation

Once we are provided with a failure model, we need to compute appropriate routes on top of the overlay structure to meet the application QoS requirements. We first define more carefully the term path *resiliency*.

Definition of resiliency: We define resiliency as the probability of a data packet (event) being delivered via any active path at any time. Equivalently, consider the event "all paths fail"; if the probability of the event of all paths in the multipath have failed is $Pr(all\ paths\ fail)$ then the resiliency is the probability at least one multiplath is up, i.e., $1 - Pr(all\ paths\ fail)$. The problem is then defined as follows: Given the interconnection topology and locations, the physical layer failure mapping and resiliency requirements, construct an end-to-end path (potentially consisting of one or more sub-paths) between the source and the destination end-points, that jointly (i) satisfy resiliency constraints, *i.e.* maintain high *availability*, under the above combined failures, (ii) optimize resource utilization (cost). We will provide details into the route computation and algorithm in Section 4.

Once paths are computed, our concern is to *maintain* the application QoS. Although the failure model may provide historical statistics, these may not always provide long-term accuracy as was also observed in [14]. Thus, if a failure does occur, we should be able to restore the routes and update the failure models. There exist few techniques for identifying overlay node failures [15]. In our work, we implemented a *monitoring* component at each overlay node which effectively provides continuous statistics on the state of overlay nodes and links. Once a failure is detected, the route computation is re-initiated. Furthermore, even-based applications usually associate a flow with a delay requirement, therefore, monitoring is necessary to ensure that the end-to-end paths are timeliness-aware by providing statistics on the individual overlay link delays.

4 Path Computation

In this section we will discuss the analytical extraction of the failure probability under combined independent and correlated failures given a logical routing graph and a general failure model. We will then provide an algorithm to compute the multipath that meets the application constraints as described in the problem definition in Section 3.3.

Due to possible non-convexity of the resiliency function, traditional flow optimization and linear/convex programming techniques cannot be directly applied. Thus, we decompose the problem into two basic steps. First, the selection of multiple paths may potentially increase the availability level of delivery, however it may lack responsiveness. Thus, we follow a path selection process that additionally incorporates delay awareness. In this way we consider the shortest delay paths first in computing the multipath routes. We call the first K paths that are considered in the process, the "search depth". In the second step, we provide a heuristic (branch-and-cut-based) algorithm that calculates the most cost-efficient combination of the selected paths.

4.1 Resiliency Computation under Combined Failures

We now derive the resiliency metrics under the assumption of both correlated and independent failures. We consider k paths in multipath route Q. The failure probability of Q can be broken down into the summation of the probabilities of cases which are mutually exclusive. The failure event to be considered is clearly *"all paths fail"*. This event can be broken down to the following mutually exclusive, conditional probability events:

- The event where all paths have failed, given that no correlated failure appeared. This implies that exactly k paths (i.e., all) have failed due to independent failures.
- The events where all paths have failed, given that a correlated failure appeared at some center v. There is some n, $0 \leq n \leq k$, such that exactly n paths have failed due to the correlated failure at v and the remaining $k - n$ paths failed due to independent failures. Note that this case includes the event of no paths being affected by the correlated failure at center v.

$Pr(all\ paths\ fail) =$
$Pr(all\ paths\ fail \mid no\ correlated\ failure) \cdot Pr(no\ correlated\ failure)+$
$\int_v \langle Pr(all\ paths\ fail \mid correlated\ failure\ at\ v) \cdot Pr(correlated\ failure\ at\ v) \rangle$ (2)

The first term of the integral can be extracted using the provided correlated failure model in Equation 1. In Appendix 1, we show an example instance of the computation for the above Equation 2, pertaining a seismic failure model where all paths will fail when the radius of the failure affects all paths simultaneously or a subset of the paths have failed due to independent failures.

For the computation of independent failures only, previous studies have tackled the problem in the area of network reliability. Define E_i as the event that all nodes in path p_i are operational. Since the combined probabilities are not independent, we will use the *inclusion-exclusion* technique to compute the reliability of the multi-path of k sub-paths, i.e:

$$Pr_{ind}(Q) = \sum_{j=1}^{k}(-1)^{j+1}\sum_{I\subseteq\{1...k\}|I|=j}Pr(E_I) \tag{3}$$

where, $Pr(E_I)$ is the probability that all paths p_i, $i \in I$, are operational. Using (3) we can compute $Pr_{ind}(all\ paths)$. The first term of the summation in Equation (2) can be simply rewritten as below:

$Pr(all\ paths\ fail \mid no\ correlated\ failure) \cdot Pr(no\ correlated\ failure) =$
$Pr_{ind}(all\ paths) \cdot (1 - Pr_{corr})$ \hfill (4)

The above computation is intensive due to the need of calculating the integral to be done using numerical methods. It is required that at least one integration calculation takes place per multipath failure probability computation. In the next section our goal is to find the least cost multipath that satisfies the resiliency requirement which suggests that the resiliency computation will be used extensively. However, we might need to search through multiple possible combinations of paths. More specifically, the number of calculations (combination) is exponential with the number of paths. In the next section we investigate methods to reduce the number of required computations.

4.2   Path Computation Algorithm

The first step of the algorithm is the computation of the k *ranked, non-disjoint,* (loopless) shortest paths, ordered based on their respective delays. A non-disjoint path is a path that may overlap with a previously computed path. The ranking of paths is based on an additive metric such as the delay.

Why non-disjoint paths: One important issue is whether paths should be disjoint or not. Our argument is, that, the paths we consider are non-disjoint because it minimizes the cost: in particular, consider a path that partly traverses an area with very small probability of being affected by a failure, and partly an area with high probability of failure. In this scenario, if the paths are non-disjoint, we need only to "extend" the path with an additional path only along the most failure-prone area. The alternative, of creating two disjpoint paths, would result in higher resource cost.

For k-shortest paths step, we have implemented a modified version of the algorithm proposed in [16] based on the *deviation* technique. In brief, the computation of the k-shortest paths starts with the shortest path and "expands" it to the next highest delay non-disjoint path. If the event-driven application requires a deadline to be achieved, say D_f, then we can immediately stop the computation when the delay of the next path returned by the rankings process is found to be higher than D_f without additional overhead. We will term this the D_f-shortest paths algorithm.

Algorithm 1. Forward Bound Step

1: INPUT: Level l, Cost C^*, Bound Set B, Optimal P^*
2: OUTPUT: Update B, C^*, P^*
3: $P_h = $ set of multipaths of h-path combination
4: Sort P_h by increasing $cost$
5: $P_n = P_h[1]$
6: **if** $P_n.cost \geq C^*$ **then**
7:     Eliminate all multipaths in P_h
8: **else**
9:     **if** $P_n.resiliency \leq R_t$ **then**
10:         $P^* = P_n$; $C^* = P_n.cost$
11:     **else**
12:         $B = B \cup P_n$

Algorithm 2. Backward Elimination

1: Cost $C^* = \infty$, Bounding set $B = \varnothing$, $l = 1$
2: Compute the path set $P_{all} \equiv D_f$ shortest paths (Sec. 4.2)
3: Sort P_{all} by increasing $cost$
4: **while** $l \leq |P_{all}|$ **do**
5:     $P_l = l$-path combinations of P_{all}
6:     **if** $C^* == \infty$ **then**
7:         **Execute Algorithm 1 for level $h > l$**
8:     **while** $P_l \neq \varnothing$ **do**
9:         $P_n = $ next in P_l
10:        **if** $P_n.cost \geq C^*$ **then**
11:            Eliminate remaining elements in P_l; $l = l + 1$
12:        **if** $P_n \subset P_m$ for any $P_m \in B$ **then**
13:            Eliminate P_n;
14:        **else**
15:            **if** $P_n.resiliency \leq R_t$ **then**
16:                $P^* = P_n$; $C^* = P_n.cost$; Eliminate P_n

---

A first brute-force approach would be to simply produce all possible combination of a single path (1-combinations), of any two paths (2-combinations), ..., l-combinations among the paths selected (in essence, executing a Breadth-First-Search).

One optimization would be, at each step, to additionally sort the path combinations and compute the reliability in order of increasing cost. When a multipath is found to satisfy the reliability constraint it is set as the temporary solution and the next l-combination can be considered. The cost of the temporary solution C^* is stored and the reach process among the l-combinations can be interrupted when the cost of a multipath is found to be higher than C^*. This guarantees that the optimal cost path found cannot have cost higher than any other path in the sorted order thus we do not need to compute the reliability values of the remaining multipaths.

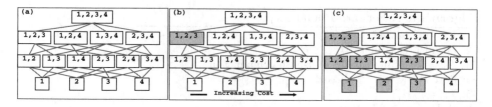

Fig. 3. Simple Example of the algorithm execution forward step; each node represents a multipath comprised of the union of some subset of a total of 4 paths. (a) shows the complete computation tree. In (b) the algorithm jumps to the 3-path combination level. Here, multipath (1,2,3) does not meet the resiliency. Therefore, in (c) all sub-multipaths can be eliminated. Otherwise, all 3-path right siblings of (1,2,3) can be eliminated due to having higher cost than the optimal so far. Then, the next path combination can be considered.

Another observation is that when adding an additional path P to a multipath MP the failure probability of the new multipath $MP \cup P$ is in at most equal to MP. This observation motivates the utilization of a branch-and-cut-based search. We can construct a tree, the root of which is the complete set of paths as shown in Figure 3. Each node of the tree represents a multipath. For each node of the tree, its children are associated to all its sub-paths. Clearly, when a node does not satisfy the resiliency level, none of its children will; thus it can be safely eliminated.

The latter technique requires the reliability computation of multipaths with a larger number of paths which is computationally expensive due to the computation of all the combinations of paths is exponential on the number of paths. We introduce a heuristic approach which combines *both the above techniques*. Our approach is based on the premise that a small number of paths have generally lower cost but lower resiliency than the required, while a larger number of paths will probably satisfy the resiliency constraint but will have a non-optimal (greater) cost. Therefore, we can eliminate computations of the resiliency for lower number of paths by finding a bound on the optimal multipath's resiliency and also eliminate computations of the resiliency for higher number of paths by finding a bound on the optimal multipath's cost. We do this by injecting one **forward** computation of a higher path number and then revert (**backwards**) to the normal BFS execution. These two steps are illustrated in Figure 3. If the computed resiliency is higher than R_t then the cost of the multipath provides us with an upper cost bound. If the computed resiliency is lower than R_t, then all the sub-paths of the multipaths can be safely eliminated from the computation search tree. The two steps are outlined in Algorithms 1 and 2.

Analysis: The above algorithm will, in the worst theoretical case, run as slow as a naive BFS.

$$\binom{N}{1} + \binom{N}{2} + \cdots + \binom{N}{N-1} + \binom{N}{N}$$

which results to

$$N + \frac{(N-1)N}{2} + .. + N + 1$$

Thus, the worst running time is $O(N^{\frac{N}{2}})$. Note, however, that for small number of paths (3-4), the computation is, in practice, *polynomial*. Also, note that unless the resiliency level is very close to the maximum possible, there is rarely a need to compute very large combinations of paths. this is because as we add paths to a multipath, the resiliency converges *exponentially* towards is maximum value. In other words, the resiliency increase is less significant as we add additional paths. Therefore, after employing the elimination step, in most cases, the result is reached within the first few combination levels. We present a comparison of the heuristic approach versus the naive BFS approach in the experimental section.

5 Implementation

In this section we discuss our system's architectural and communication components.

5.1 Architectural Components

Controller: The multi-path computation is done in a centralized manner via the use of a *controller*. An event publisher node contacts the controller to construct and return a multipath on its behalf. More particularly, a controller is responsible for (i) managing the node membership and connectivity graph, (ii) maintaining the static failure statistics (Failure Model), (iii) collecting the dynamic delay changes among the overlay nodes, (iv) utilize the statistics and delay measurements to control the admission of new flows and (v) perform on-line computation and dynamic adjustment in the events of delay fluctuations and node failures. Typically, we deploy multiple controllers for a specific overlay to address possible failures. Controllers exchange node participation updates to synchronize the topology amongst themselves. Currently we are concerned with networks that comprise of a few tens of overlay nodes such as typical corporate networks with offices in a moderate number of cities or a number of distribution substation in a power grids. To incorporate larger networks, nodes can be grouped into domains and resilient paths can be constructed between domains, in a much similar way as between overlay nodes. However, we will reserve extending our approach to multiple domains for future work.

Messaging middleware: The middleware infrastructure comprises a group of interconnected overlay processing nodes. Overlay nodes are implemented on different physical machines and locations and are connected over the public Internet. These nodes have two main tasks: (i) Monitoring links that connect them to other overlay nodes for delay statistics as well as availability maintenance and (ii) event packet forwarding as part of a multipath.

Initially, in order for the nodes to be considered in the path computation, the nodes must register with the controller of their domain, *i.e.* advertise their availability. Secure authentication and authorization is implemented as part of the overall system but it is an orthogonal issue. When a node becomes available it is instructed by the controller to *monitor* a subgroup of other nodes in the overlay. More specifically, each node monitors all its *downstream* neighbors as these are defined in the connectivity graph. Monitoring includes periodically reporting the measured link delay and availability of the downstream node to the controller. Delay is measured using periodic pings. Nodes set a ping timeout to assess cases of node unavailability. Upstream or downstream pings are utilized to verify the availability of an upstream or downstream node respectively. To compute the link delay measurements, the nodes utilize Exponentially Weighted Moving Averaging (EWMA) to avoid sudden spikes and drops in the measurements. We note that with this practical monitoring assignment, the update process is scalable and efficient while link losses can be effectively detected.

Application Programming Interface (API): We provide two basic constructs to facilitate the usage of the routing middleware by various application endpoints. These are *Agents* and *Ports*. An Agent is almost equivalent to a messaging middleware node, however it does not forward any traffic, i.e. it is associated with some specific application requesting the routing service. An application can construct an Agent by providing an application level unique name. Upon initialization, the Agent logs into the overlay via communicating with the controller similar to overlay nodes. Using the Agents, an application can then construct application *Ports* which associate individual application sending and receiving end-points (in essence an IP/port pair known to and maintained by our routing overlay). A Port defines an event handling interface which allows the application developer to implement specific responds to packet receive events and path notification (availability and unavailability) events. An application requiring to use the overlay, constructs a Port via the local Agent and submits to the Controller its resiliency, delay requirements and a destination application Agent name. The Controller receives the request and performs admission control. Upon accepting the application and constructing the best multi-path via the mechanisms described in Section 4, a new Port is constructed automatically by the destination Agent. On success, the application is then notified and can start transmitting packets letting the overlay transparently maintain the end-to-end path. Transparency is achieved via the use of *Sessions* that effectively implement the link between two individual Ports. Sessions are described in more detail next.

5.2 Communication Components

Sessions: A session is our central communication structure. Sessions are, in essence, UDP connection threads which attach themselves to a specific port and IP address. Each session has a unique ID and is associated with a set of *Connections*; a list of other sessions to which communication is established.

We have implemented four types of a Session: (i) A *Controller session*, i.e. the session that facilitates node registration at the Controller, as well as collections and propagation of resiliency and delay statistics. The Controller Session's Connection structure is populated with a list of *Node Sessions*, described next.

(ii) A *Node Session* is used to assign corresponding monitoring duties by the Controller. Thus, its Connection list contains only the node's upstream and downstream (registered) nodes as reflected in the network graph. (iii) A *Controller Flow Session* is created as a new thread by the Controller at each incoming flow request and is responsible for constructing and reconstructing broken paths by autonomously monitoring the delay changes and availability along the multipath. (iv) A *Node Flow Session* is created locally at a node with the only functionality of forwarding event packets as instructed by the path construction signaling which we describe in the next paragraph. Additionally, it is responsible for path tear–down. Our goal is to allow these different sessions to function almost completely independently by decoupling dependencies among concurrent flows in order to provide low complexity and self management.

Path Construction Signaling: We implemented a simple *distributed* and fast process for constructing and reconstructing multipaths. When the multipath is computed, the controller sends a message to all participating nodes that simply contains its upstream nodes' IDs and the total number of downstream nodes. Each node creates a new node session with the unique ID provided by the controller and waits to receive 'READY' messages from *all* the downstream nodes to, in turn, notify its own upstream nodes. The destination has zero downstream nodes, thus it sends the message immediately. This process ensures that when the source starts transmitting on its path, all nodes are available for forwarding. Note that a failure can be similarly signaled among sessions along a multipath and the failed nodes removed. A path reconstruction is almost identical except from the fact that no new session ID is issued. A source node session simply adds the new downstream nodes of the new paths, as in the case of the initial construction, almost completely transparently.

Implementation of the Failure Model: We have implemented a generic component for geographic failure mappings, able to accommodate a wide range of failure distributions. The geographic failure model is mapped to a rectangular *failure grid*. Real world geographic failures can be mapped by regulating the resolution of the grid. Each cell of the grid is assigned a failure probability and a set of cells the failure affects. Remember that the set of cells can be returned as fixed set or a function.

6   Evaluation

6.1   Network Setup

We deployed a set of 40 middleware Node Sessions on the Planetlab platform [4]. While our system will generally be deployed in a more constrained geographical region (such as within the bounds of a US state), Planetlab is still an extremely attractive platform since it is able to provide a large number of test nodes located in *different* geographical locations, which might not be the case in on-campus experimentation. The node locations are shown in Figure 4. We have produced random connections between nodes, ensuring however a fully connected network.

In particular, nodes have at least 2 outgoing connections to different nodes both geographically adjacent as well as nodes in larger distances to realize a generic overlay network structure. In our tests, as many as 15 non-disjoint paths may be available between each source–destination pair.

Fig. 4. Planetlab Network of Nodes Used in the Experiments

One of the nodes takes the role of the controller. In fact, any of the nodes can be employed as a controller, given that the node is not heavily loaded. A new controller session may be initiated and perform path computation and construction independent of the existence of other controller sessions. While we currently assume that the controller does not generally fail, a controller failure can be quickly restored by requesting the nodes to test their current controller and login on a new controller session periodically. State information only pertain to active sessions which can be reconstructed locally using the session IDs (the connections can be deducted from the network graph).

We also note that since correlated failures are rather infrequent, we decided to perform experiments where we assume that the correlated failure happens within a bounded time period (i.e., we isolate the timespan within which correlated failure may appear). Our goal is to test the effect of failure on a real setup, actual response times and multipath performance and reconstruction feasibility. Effectively, we emulate the failures in the real network by injecting them via manually "killing" the listening functionality at a forwarding node. More system parameters are summarized in Table 1.

Table 1. Runtime Parameters

Number of Nodes	40
Number of flows	40
Time slot length	1sec
Total Time slots	1000≈17min
Independent failure probability.	0.05
Resiliency Constraint	0.97
Geographic Failure Radius	50 units
Event Rate	10 kbps (10 p/s)
Ping Interval/Timeout	10/22 sec

6.2   Experimental Results

In the following set of results our main goal is to evaluate the quantitative effect of large correlated area failures on a set of source–destination event flows. For this reason, a number of system parameters remained fixed while we increase the impact of the correlated failures by increasing the rate with which an area failure appears. We compare our *multipath, correlated failure aware* approach construction and reconstruction technique against the following variations:

- A *Primary-Backup* path approach, where at any given time a *single* path is available for event forwarding. The active path is the primary path and selected to be the one with the lowest failure probability among all source destination paths. Upon failure, the immediately next least failure-prone path is constructed. For this technique, the failure probability computation *does consider correlated failures*. A critical point here, however, is that the single path approach may *not* satisfy the resiliency level of the application. Thus this is our baseline comparison protocol.

- A *Path-disjoint, Correlated Failure Agnostic* technique wherein, multiple disjoint paths are selected to forward messages in parallel, however, *without* considering correlated failures, *i.e.* correlated failures are subsumed by the independent failure probabilities. In this technique, disjoint paths are added to the multipath until the resiliency level is met. Upon failure, a reconstruction takes place as in the non-disjoint path approach.

We construct 10 random scenarios of node failures. We replay the same scenario for each of the algorithms and report the average values. For the following results we set the deadline requirement to infinity to study the multipath availability performance. In these results, however, we do consider the delay metric to study the potential effect of each algorithm on the deadline bound. We have used equal share budgeting for these experiments; a comparison of the budgeting techniques is provided later in this section.

Downtime: Our first critical metric is downtime. This reflects the total time that *all paths of a specific flow* were unavailable throughout a complete run. This is, in effect, the total time to identify and report a failure as well as to fully reconstruct the downstream multipath. We measure this time as the time between undelivered packets; a source continues to generate packets with increasing sequence number even when the path is down. Upon reconstruction, we measure the time between two non-consecutive packet receptions, i.e., the partial downtime that all paths were unavailable. The sum of all partial downtimes is the total downtime.

In Figure 5 we report the average downtimes as the correlated failure rate increases. Due to the fact that the Primary-Backup approach does not take advantage of multiple paths, it performed the worst. At each failure, a source needs to wait for failure identification and path reconstruction. During that period, no packet can be delivered. An important result is observed for the correlated failure agnostic algorithm, which performs worse than the multipath correlated failure aware algorithm. While both techniques allow for the parallel

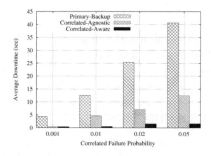 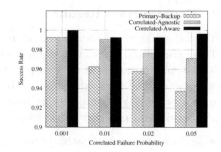

Fig. 5. Downtime Vs Correlated Failures Impact

Fig. 6. Percentage of Received Event Packets Vs Correlated Failure Impact

paths to continue delivering packets, as the impact of the correlated failures grows, the distribution of the failures changes from uniform to a more skewed form. This effect causes the correlation unaware algorithm to overestimate the resilience of its disjoint multipath which may, in fact, be prone to a correlated failure. Thus, the case is observed where all parallel paths fail simultaneously and the downtime increases. By considering correlated failures, our approach achieves the resiliency level set by the application.

1–Success Rate: A critical measure in resiliency-critical applications is uninterrupted operation which suggests that success rates must be extremely high. The 1-success rate metric indicates that from all packets sent, none was lost. Due to the variability of flow activities, in Figure 6 we plot the average success rate of the flows (i.e the percentage of packets successfully delivered over the total number of packets attempted to be sent over all paths.) All three techniques achieve rates above 90%, however, in event-based applications, uninterrupted operation is a critical requirement as stated above. The reduced success rate of the single path technique is attributed to the fact that some small amount of time is required to detect a failure and reconstruct the new path. Similarly, not considering the effects of correlated failures may cause the selection of ineffective parallel paths, even if these are disjoint.

Delay: In Figure 7, we illustrate the responsiveness benefits of utilizing multipaths versus single path approach. We measure the end-to-end delay for each delivered packet of all flows. As expected, we find that using multiple paths, either disjoint or having common nodes, can potentially be beneficial in terms of supporting lower delays. This is because it is more probable that at a given time either of the multipaths may be less loaded and thus have lower per hop delays. Failures do not critically affect the end-to-end delay, although they reduce the search space of eligible paths. In our tests, we ensured that the flow requirements will ensure the existence of at least one end-to-end path availability while in general, as many as 15 non-disjoint paths could be found. We can increase the number of paths to further improve the application QoS (*i.e.*, end-to-end delay).

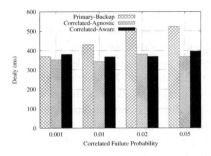

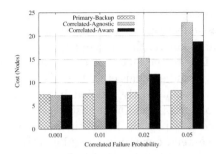

Fig. 7. End-to-end Delay (Deadline Sensitivity) Vs Correlated Failures Impact   **Fig. 8.** Cost as Number of Nodes Used in Multipaths Vs Correlated Failure Impact

Cost: A final critical metric is the multipath cost. Our goal is to minimize the overall path cost while maintaining the reliability level. We present the comparisons of the three techniques in Figure 8. Here our cost function pertains to the total number of nodes used for the multipath construction. This is an indication of the resources required to implement each alternative technique. Clearly, the Primary-Backup approach is less costly in terms of nodes required, but as shown previously, it might not achieve the application required reliability level. When the failure impact is low, all techniques can choose a single path to establish the resiliency level. However, as the correlated failure rate increases, more paths need to be concatenated together to reach the reliability goal. We illustrate that, disjoint paths may be an overkill when simply a non-disjoint extension of the initial path may be sufficient to achieve the target.

7   Related Work

Resilient routing involving multiple paths has initially been studied as a theoretic network combinatorics problem. The cost-optimization requirement in conjunction with both independent and correlated failures, considerably differentiates our problem from classic two-terminal reliability problem formulations [17]. Multipath resiliency was studied extensively in the context of *path protection* in MPLS networks [18,19]. These techniques are based on a two-path strategy, either a Primary-Backup approach or intelligent parallel paths utilization. An effort to understand the performance and resilience of large-scale multi-hop wireless networks was made in [20]. Sustaining resiliency via overlays was implemented in RON [3], illustrating its benefits over traditional IP routing. In our work instead we consider an extended multipath approach without necessarily disjoint paths. Finally, [21] proposes a DHT-based a routing approach that can rebound from node failures but does not provide guarantees on either delay or uninterrupted operation.

In the P2P community, overlay forwarding has taken the form of efficient reliable multicasting such as [22] [23] [24] and event-driven middleware [25]. IrisNet utilizes overlay routing for providing application layer assurances for multimedia streams [26]. In our work we instead attempt to consider resilience as well as cost-effectiveness, in concert while taking into consideration the delay metric. Furthermore, the aforementioned works did not consider correlated failures.

Due to the fact that correlated failures are hard to model, real-world studies have studied characteristics of correlated failures such as [7]. Correlated failures have been mostly studied in the context of reliable storage systems were the problem of deciding a cost effective and resilient set of backup nodes is considered [27] [28] [6]. In continuation of previous work in [13] on resilient storage, we extend our study a significantly different problem – that of routing and uninterrupted delivery. Routing under correlated failures has not been addressed extensively. Link correlation models as in [8] may suffer from the problem of having to define the correlation between each pair of links or nodes directly. Our geographic failure model instead, avoids this problem by defining the correlation of multiple nodes simultaneously with respect to a common point of reference, i.e. the failure center.

8   Conclusions

We provide an algorithm to support resilient and cost-effective overlay routing for event-driven applications in the presence of both independent and geographically correlated failures. We present a model for spatially correlated failures and compute the combined failure probabilities. We then design a two-step decomposition algorithm based on a branch-and-cut heuristic approach to solve our optimization problem. We show, via real end-to-end flow initiations over multiple, geographically distributed Planetlab nodes that our approach is both feasible and effective. We provide improvements over basic Primary-Backup and Disjoint path approaches under geographical failures.

Acknowledgments. This research has been supported by the European Union through the Marie-Curie RTD (IRG-231038) Project.

References

1. Nedic, D.P., Dobson, I., Kirschen, D.S., Carreras, B.A., Lynch, V.E.: Criticality in a cascading failure blackout model. Int'l. Journal of Electrical Power & Energy Systems 28, 627–633 (2006)
2. Andersen, D.G., Balakrishnan, H., Kaashoek, M.F., Morris, R.: Resilient overlay networks. In: Proc. 18th ACM SOSP, pp. 131–145 (2001)
3. Andersen, D.G., Snoeren, A.C., Balakrishnan, H.: Best-path vs. multi-path overlay routing. In: Proc. of ACM IMC, pp. 91–100 (2003)
4. PlanetLab, http://www.planet-lab.org
5. Wang, M., Takada, T.: Macrospatial correlation model of seismic ground motions. Earthquake spectra 21, 1137–1156 (2005)
6. Haeberlen, A., Mislove, A., Druschel, P.: Glacier: Highly durable, decentralized storage despite massive correlated failures. In: Proc.of NSDI, vol. 75 (2005)
7. Nath, S., Yu, H., Gibbons, P.B., Seshan, S.: Subtleties in tolerating correlated failures in wide-area storage systems. In: Proc. USENIX NSDI, pp. 225–238 (2006)

8. Cui, W., Stoica, I., Katz, R.H.: Backup path allocation based on a correlated link failure probability model in overlay networks. In: IEEE ICNP, p. 236 (2002)
9. Pendarakis, D.E., Shi, S., Verma, D.C., Waldvogel, M.: ALMI: An application level multicast infrastructure. In: Proc. of USENIX USITS, pp. 49–60 (2000)
10. Rowstron, A., Druschel, P.: Pastry: Scalable, decentralized object location and routing for large-scale peer-to-peer systems. In: IFIP/ACM Middleware, pp. 329–350 (2001)
11. Ratnasamy, S., Handley, M., Karp, R.M., Shenker, S.: Topologically-aware overlay construction and server selection. In: INFOCOM (2002)
12. Subramanian, L., Padmanabhan, V.N., Katz, R.H.: Geographic properties of internet routing. In: USENIX Annual Technical Conference, pp. 243–259 (2002)
13. Fan, J., Chang, T., Pendarakis, D., Liu, Z.: Cost-effective configuration of content resiliency services under correlated failures. In: Proc. of DSN, pp. 536–548 (2006)
14. Rowstron, A., Druschel, P., Yalagandula, P., Nath, S., Yu, H., Gibbons, P.B., Sesha, S.: Beyond availability: Towards a deeper understanding of machine failure characteristics in large distributed systems. In: WORLDS (2004)
15. Dennis, S.Z., Geels, D., Stoica, I., Katz, R.H.: On failure detection algorithms in overlay networks. In: IEEE INFOCOM (2003)
16. de Queirós Vieira Martins, E., Marta, M.: A new implementation of yen's ranking loopless paths algorithm. 4OR-Q J. Oper. Res. 1(2), 121–133 (2003)
17. Colbourn, J.: The Combinatorics of Network Reliability. Oxford University Press, New York (1987)
18. Gupta, A., Jain, B.N., Tripathi, S.: QoS aware path protection schemes for MPLS networks. In: Proc. of ICCC, pp. 103–118 (2002)
19. Han, S., Shin, K.G.: A primary-backup channel approach to dependable real-time communication in multihop networks. IEEE Trans. Computers 47(1), 46–61 (1998)
20. Xu, Y.: Understanding the performance and resilience of large-scale multi-hop wireless networks. In: NCSU PhD thesis (2010)
21. Gupta, A., Liskov, B., Rodrigues, R.: Efficient routing for peer-to-peer overlays. In: NSDI, San Francisco, CA (March 2004)
22. Banerjee, S., Lee, S., Bhattacharjee, B., Srinivasan, A.: Resilient multicast using overlays. In: Proc. of SIGMETRICS, pp. 102–113 (2003)
23. Mittra, S.: Lolus: A framework for scalable secure multicasting. In: SIGCOMM, pp. 277–288 (1997)
24. Pappas, V., Zhang, B., Terzis, A., Zhang, L.: Fault-tolerant data delivery for multicast overlay networks. In: Proc. of ICDCS, pp. 670–679 (2004)
25. Mahambre, S., Bellur, U.: Reliable routing of event notifications over p2p overlay routing substrate in event based middleware. In: IPDPS, pp. 1–8 (2007)
26. Campbell, J., Gibbons, P.B., Nath, S., Pillai, P., Seshan, S., Sukthankar, R.: Irisnet: an internet-scale architecture for multimedia sensors. In: Proc. of ACM MULTI-MEDIA, pp. 81–88 (2005)
27. Bakkaloglu, M., Wylie, J.J., Wang, C., Ganger, G.R.: Modeling correlated failures in survivable storage systems. In: Proc. of DSN (2002)
28. Kotla, R., Alvisi, L., Dahlin, M.: Safestore: A durable and practical storage system. In: USENIX (2007)

A Exponentially Decaying Seismic Failure Probability Computation

The range of the failure is represented as r. To simplify the calculation and without loss of generality, we assume that the distances $\{d_f(p_1), d_f(p_2), ..., d_f(p_k)\}$

are sorted in increasing order. For this sorted set $d_f[i]$ represents the distance to the $i - th$ furthest path and $p[i]$ represents the corresponding path. Denote the set of paths $Q_j \equiv \{p[1], p[2], ..., p[j]\}$.

$Pr_f(all\ paths\ fail) =$
$Pr_f(all\ paths\ fail\ |\ r < d_f[0])+$
$Pr_f(all\ paths\ fail\ |\ d_f[0] \leqslant r < d_f[1])+$
$... +$
$Pr_f(all\ paths\ fail\ |\ r > d_f[k]) =$

$Pr_{ind}(Q_k) \cdot Pr(r < d_f[0])+$
$\sum_{n=0}^{k-1}\langle Pr_{ind}(Q_k - Q_n) \cdot Pr(d_f[n] \leqslant r < d_f[n+1])\rangle+$
$Pr(r \geqslant d_f[k])$ $\hspace{4cm}$ (4)

Correlated Failure Probability of a single point/node: The probability of a point/node N_i failing due to a geographically correlated failure $Pr_{corr}(N_i, v)$ for a specific failure center v, depends on its distance from the failure center which we will denote as $d(N_i, v)$. The probability of a node failing is equal to the probability that the failure radius is *greater* than the euclidean distance between the failure center and the node. For example, in the case of the exponentially decaying radius, denoting the probability that a correlated failure occurs at point v, as $Pr_f(v)$, then $Pr_{corr}(N_i, v) = Pr_f(v) \cdot (e^{-c \cdot d(N_i, v)})$. Here, $Pr_f(v)$ is the probability that the failure center is v computed from its given distribution over the failure area A and the exponential distribution formula denotes that the impact of the failure event is exponentially decaying. Finally, the probability should be integrated over *all possible failure centers* in A, i.e., $Pr_{corr}(N_i) = \int_v Pr_{corr}(N_i, v)dv$.

Correlated Failure Probability of a single path: For a given source-destination path P, the path fails if at least one node in P has failed. We define the distance of a path to a failure point as the minimum distance between the failure center and a node in P, i.e. $d(P, v) = min\{distance(N_i, v), N_i \in P\}$. As an example – and similarly to the case of a single node – for exponential decaying function, the probability of a path failing due to a geographically correlated failure is $Pr_{corr}(P, v) = Pr_f(v) \cdot (e^{-c \cdot d(P, v)})$. To compute the failure probability, we must then integrate this result over *all possible failure points*.

Correlated Failure Probability of a Multi-path: The general case is when a path consists of multiple subpaths (that are either disjoint or non-disjoint). For a given source-destination multipath MP the multipath fails if at least one node in each of its subpaths P_i has failed. The *distance* between a multipath and a failure center is defined as $d(MP, v) = max\{distance(P_i, v), P_i \in MP\}$ and the failure probability can be calculated as above.

Scalable Transactions in the Cloud: Partitioning Revisited*

Francisco Maia[1], José Enrique Armendáriz-Iñigo[2],
M. Idoia Ruiz-Fuertes[3], and Rui Oliveira[1]

[1] Computer Science and Technology Center, University of Minho,
Braga, Portugal
{fmaia,rco}@di.uminho.pt
[2] Departamento de Ingeniería Matemática e Informática,
Universidad Pública de Navarra, Pamplona, Spain
enrique.armendariz@unavarra.es
[3] Instituto Tecnológico de Informática
Universidad Politécnica de Valencia, Camino de Vera s/n,
46022 Valencia, Spain
miruifue@iti.upv.es

Abstract. Cloud computing is becoming one of the most used
paradigms to deploy highly available and scalable systems. These systems usually demand the management of huge amounts of data, which
cannot be solved with traditional nor replicated database systems as we
know them. Recent solutions store data in special key-value structures,
in an approach that commonly lacks the consistency provided by transactional guarantees, as it is traded for high scalability and availability.
In order to ensure consistent access to the information, the use of transactions is required. However, it is well-known that traditional replication
protocols do not scale well for a cloud environment. Here we take a look
at current proposals to deploy transactional systems in the cloud and we
propose a new system aiming at being a step forward in achieving this
goal. We proceed to focus on data partitioning and describe the key role
it plays in achieving high scalability.

Keywords: Distributed Systems, Cloud computing, Transactional
support.

1   Introduction

Nowadays, the most common service architecture to build enterprise web applications is based on a multi-tier approach. We can identify three different layers.
The web server layer, the application server layer and the data layer. Typically,
when the application load increases we can scale the web and application layers

---

* This work has been partially supported by the Spanish Government under grant
  TIN2009-14460-C03-02 and by the Spanish MEC under grant BES-2007-17362 and
  by project ReD – Resilient Database Clusters (PDTC/EIA-EIA/109044/2008).

R. Meersman et al. (Eds.): OTM 2010, Part II, LNCS 6427, pp. 785–797, 2010.

horizontally. This means we can add web servers and application servers and the system will be able to cope with more client requests. This is not the case at the data layer. To scale the data layer and still provide consistency and persistency guarantees, a replication mechanism must be implemented. However, traditional database replication techniques do not scale well after a few tens of replicas [1].

Following the CAP (Consistency, Availability and Partition Tolerance) theorem [2][3] it is clear that we cannot provide a data management system which is at the same time always available, partition tolerant and providing consistent data. On traditional relational database management systems (RDBMS), availability is often compromised in order to guarantee data consistency. These systems will not accept client requests if they cannot serve consistent data as a consequence of failures. Guaranteeing consistency is also the main reason why these systems do not scale well, as the replication mechanisms are costly and heavily depend on synchronization.

Recently, cloud computing has emerged as a promising computing paradigm aimed at developing highly scalable distributed systems. Cloud computing comes from the idea that computing should be seen as an utility with a model of use similar to that of the electric network. Concepts such as *Infrastructure as a Service, Platform as a Service* or *Software as a Service* then became very common. Each resource should be seen as a service and all the implementation details hidden from the client. To provide this level of abstraction to the client, properties such as elasticity and high availability became crucial to the implementation of these services. Elasticity denotes the capacity of a system to adjust its resource consumption according to the load, while availability typically represents revenue to the service provider.

Cloud computing impelled a number of companies (Amazon, Microsoft, Google or Hadoop) to provide a new set of data management services with elasticity, availability and cost effectiveness as their core features. The elasticity property of these systems required them to scale really well and thus these data management systems became a building block for applications with incredible fast growth, such as social network applications [4]. Examples of these systems are Google Bigtable [5], Amazon's Dynamo [6] or PNUTS from Yahoo! [7] just to mention a few. To provide high scalability and availability, these systems often compromise consistency guarantees, in contrast to the traditional approach described above. These data storage services often provide a key-value data model and lack transactional guarantees even for a single row access. Given the data model and the fact they do not support SQL, these systems are often grouped under the name of *NoSQL* systems.

In between the traditional RDBMS and the NoSQL systems, a third kind of data management systems is being proposed. Namely, there have been several attempts to provide transactional support in the cloud [8,9,10,11,12]. These systems aim at providing high scalability and availability and yet still provide data consistency guarantees by supporting some types of transactions. The key idea behind these systems is to simplify as much as possible all kind of interaction among replicas to decide the outcome of a transaction. These systems also rely heavily on data partitioning to provide the desired scalability properties.

Along this paper we look at data partitioning as a key to scalability. In order to better illustrate our idea we take a look at one of the existing systems that provides simple transactional support in the cloud. We propose an architecture of our own aimed at solving some issues the previous system may exhibit. In Section 3, we highlight the role partitioning plays in scalability. We discuss some related work in Section 4. In Section 5, we take a look to the next step forward in all the ideas covered in the paper and their implementation in a real system. Finally, conclusions end the paper.

2 Transactional Support in the Cloud

Alongside transactional RDBMS and the more recent NoSQL databases a novel approach is being made regarding data management. In the pursuit of the strong consistency guarantees made by RDBMS and the high scalability and availability of the NoSQL databases, some proposals have been made representing a compromise between the two worlds. *ElasTraS* [10] is an elastic, scalable and self managing transactional database for the cloud. The ElasTraS system provides some basic transactional support while still providing high scalability.

2.1 *ElasTraS*

ElasTras allows the management of both large single tenant databases and the small independent databases commonly observed in a multi-tenant DBMS. In any case, data is partitioned (small databases may fit into a single partition) and transactions are only allowed to access data on a single partition. ElasTraS offers full transactional RDBMS functionality to small single-partition databases and still a rich functionality for the multiple-partition case, relaying on a judicious schema partitioning.

The architecture of ElasTraS is depicted in Figure 1. The system has four main components. We succinctly describe each one of these components and the relations between them in order to understand how ElasTraS works.

The *Owning Transaction Manager (OTM)* component has a set of partitions for which is responsible. A certain OTM is responsible for (owns) a partition when that partition is assigned to it by the system. Each partition is owned by a single OTM at a time. The OTM executes transactions guaranteeing *ACID* properties at the partition level. It is important to remember that, even if each OTM can own more than one partition, each partition is independent from each other and there is no support for inter partition transactions. ElasTraS was designed in a way that clearly separates system data from application data. This separation makes it possible to remove system data and system management from the application data path thus favoring scalability. This feature led to two key components of the system: the *TM Master* and the *Metadata Manager*.

The TM Master monitors the system and is responsible for failure recovery and for making the necessary adjustments in partition assignment to tune the

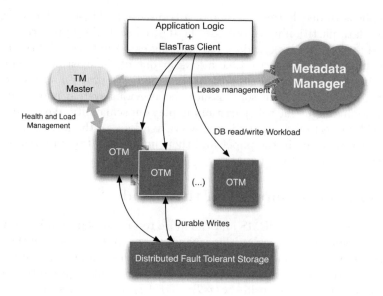

Fig. 1. ElasTraS architecture

system according to its load. In a sense, it is the component that governs system elasticity.

The Metadata Manager stores the system state. This includes the mapping of partitions to OTMs (the partition ownership). By partition ownership we mean information about the nodes responsible for a certain partition of the data. The Metadata Manager is the component that guarantees that a certain partition is owned by a single OTM. This is done by recurring to a lease mechanism. Detailed information on these mechanisms can be found in [10] and is beyond the focus of this paper.

The Metadata Manager component is similar to the Chubby [13] system used at Google. This component is not in the data path and, as the information it stores is not expected to grow nor change very often, it does not represent a scalability bottleneck. However, this is a critical component of the system and downtime of the Metadata Manager represents downtime of the system as a whole. To avoid this from happening the Metadata Manager is, like Chubby, replicated using an implementation of the Paxos algorithm[14].

The last component is a *Distributed Fault-tolerant Storage* which persistently stores application data and a commit log which will allow recovery in the presence of OTM failures.

As stated before, ElasTraS can be used as a single large database where data is partitioned across the OTMs and as a multi-tenant database where each partition is an independent small database. Data partition assumes a key role in this design and will influence the system's performance. Further on we will devote a section of this paper on this topic.

2.2   What Can Be Improved in ElasTraS

ElasTraS represents a pragmatic approach to the design of a transactional data store for the cloud. However, there are some aspects of the system's design we believe can be improved. The first observation we can make is that ElasTraS will scale really well if we have several small databases and we can fit each one into a single partition or if we have a large database that we can split into several independent partitions. If this is not the case the system's bottleneck will be the OTM. The system would be able to cope with as many requests as the single OTM. To improve the system's performance in this case we would have to scale up the OTM which is not the best solution and hinders elasticity.

Moreover, recovery of the OTMs in ElasTraS implies downtime of the partitions the OTM owns. In the case of OTM failure the TM Master detects the failure and launches a new OTM. This new OTM will have exclusive ownership over the same set of partitions as its predecessor and will have access to the commit log. With log information it will be able to recover the state and start to service that set of partitions. During this OTM recovery process the set partitions it owns will be unaccessible. This might not be desirable specially when a database is entirely assigned to a single partition as it will mean downtime of the entire database, no matter how fast the recovery process is.

2.3   Possible Solution and Our Proposed System

We propose a new system evolved from ElasTraS that aims at solving the problems stated in the previous section. The main change we introduce is at the OTM level and in the way transactions are executed. The TM Master and Metadata Manager components remain with similar functions. With availability in mind, instead of assigning a partition to a single OTM, we assign it to a *OTM group*. This OTM group is a set of OTMs under a replication mechanism. Specifically, we apply a Database State Machine (DBSM) approach [15][16]. The failure of a single OTM does not represent unavailable partitions on an OTM group, thus improving the overall availability of the system at the cost of adding the new replication layer. The system elasticity is also guaranteed as we can create new OTM groups when load increases or reassign partitions when the load decreases. Each OTM group can also be assigned more than one partition and at the limit we can have an OTM group per partition.

As we mentioned earlier, a strong consistent replication mechanism does not scale well. However, in our design we only consider a small number of OTMs per OTM group which will not make the replication mechanism the system's bottleneck. Moreover, the DBSM approach uses a single atomic broadcast message to perform the certification protocol over the replicas avoiding blocking protocols such as the modified 2PC in ElasTraS.

Another change is on the Distributed Fault-tolerant Storage component. In ElasTraS the DFS is common to all the OTMs. All the persistent writes to the DFS are expensive and if we have a high number of OTMs this component can become a performance bottleneck. In our design there is no need for the DFS to

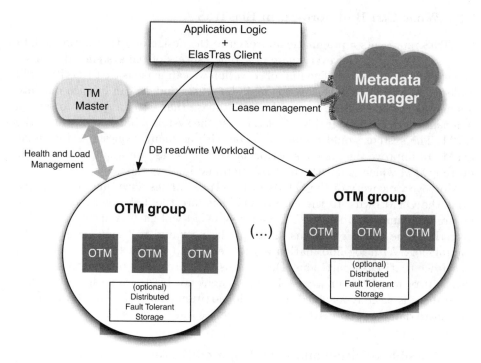

Fig. 2. Our system architecture

be common to all the OTMs. In fact, the persistency guarantees given by the DFS can now be ensured by the replication mechanism itself. Furthermore, when an OTM crashes, another one is launched and the current state is passed by the existing replicas. This also represents an enhancement in system performance as we avoid expensive DFS writes.

ElasTraS was designed to fit two different scenarios. The changes we are introducing will improve the ElasTraS system in both scenarios when considering a read intensive workload. In the first one, where we have several small databases sharing the same data management system resources, ElasTraS assigns each of these small databases to an OTM. The size of the database is therefore limited according to the ability of the single OTM to handle requests on that database. In our design we have each database assigned to a replicated system (OTM group) which leads to performance comparable to that of a replicated RDBMS, which is still the common and effective solution to data management. The second scenario, where a large database is divided into independent partitions, we have a similar situation as the performance per partition is improved. Our system design is depicted in Figure 2.

Although ElasTraS is suitable to the case where we have several small databases or a partitioned large database, there is no solution when we have a database large enough to exceed the single node capacity and which cannot be partitioned. When this is the case, in our system, we can extend the group

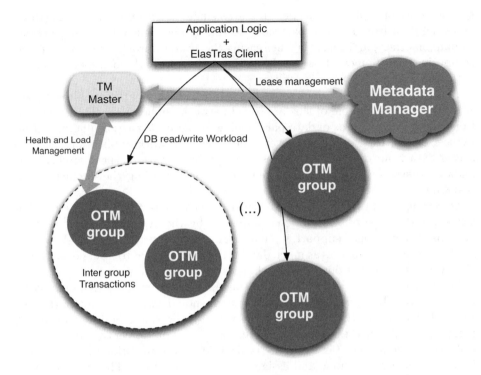

Fig. 3. Our system architecture with the notion of inter partition transactions

abstraction and create groups of groups. This allows inter group transactions which means inter partition transactions. The downside is that this has a performance cost. Namely, running a certification protocol over OTM groups can be expensive. However, this empowers the system to accommodate another set of databases. These databases are characterized by having a workload which allows partitioning but still has a small percentage of global transactions, i.e., those that access more than one partition. The architecture of the system incorporating the notion of groups of OTM groups is depicted in Figure 3. In this design, a certain OTM group plays the role of the coordinator and aggregates results from all the different OTM groups as well as guarantees data consistency. This feature is not trivial to implement and definitely requires the OTM groups to support a special transactional call to ensure consistency. Failures of the coordinator must be considered although, in this case, as the coordinator is an OTM group, it is, by definition, already replicated.

3   Partitioning, the Key to Scalability

Data partitioning is a common method used for improving the performance and the scalability properties of data management systems. The database is divided into smaller pieces called partitions. Partitions are then managed by different system nodes or replicas. This design allows single-partition transactions (those accessing data from a single partition) to run independently from transactions running in other partitions, thus increasing the system throughput. In the cloud computing environment this has been the main approach to provide services with high scalability and availability.

Recently, many applications proved to exhibit a highly partitionable data set. A characteristic example of this are social network applications. These applications allow a high degree of data partitioning (geographic partitioning, partition by user or interests, etc.). Moreover, when social network applications need to access data from different partitions, the specific nature of these applications allows the system to relax consistency guarantees avoiding the impairment of scalability.

Observing the systems described earlier, one can note that data partitioning influences the type of transactions supported by the system. In fact, in these systems, transactional support is guaranteed at the partition level. A certain transaction can only access as much data as the one assigned to a single partition. The way data is partitioned defines the system's ability to scale.

Starting with a single database in a single node how would a dynamic partitioning system be implemented? Such system should have as an input the live value of the load of the system and the value of the single node's capacity to handle load. When the system's load reaches a certain percentage of the total capacity of the system (let's say the typical 70%), the partitioning system will have to launch a new node and assign data partitions to it. The system has to make a decision on how data should be partitioned. The simple case would be ignoring the workload and simply divide data into two partitions. The problem with this approach is that it requires those inter partition transactions that do not scale. Thus this is not a proper approach. The solution is to look at the workload and partition the data according to which data transactions are accessing. The problem is that if we have a transaction accessing all the data in the database the system will not be able to scale.

Data partitioning is crucial to scalability and some proposals have already been made, such as *Schema Level Partitioning* [10], but new partitioning schemas should be studied. Moreover, each data set has its own optimum partitioning schema and we can easily predict it will be hard to find a solution applicable to every case.

Data partition should be also part of data schema design in modern applications with scale requirements. Design techniques should be investigated in order to facilitate the design of database schemas which are inherently scalable.

Finally, it is important to notice that not all applications coexist well with relaxed consistency guarantees. Applications designed for banking, travel agencies, insurance companies, etc., still require data to be strongly consistent. Considering an application with these requirements, it is clear that transactions accessing data on more than one partition (global transactions) will require some kind of synchronization mechanism in order to guarantee data consistency. Synchronization mechanisms weaken the scalability of a system, and thus represent an obstacle to the move of such applications to the cloud. The system we propose in this paper follows the pragmatic approach of assuming a scalability and performance cost when providing inter partition transactions. This enables a new set of applications, those with a high partitioning degree but that require (but not frequently) inter partition transactions, to move to the cloud. Nonetheless, this does not apply to all kinds of applications and there is still work to do in this area.

4   Related Work

Management of distributed transactions [17] has been thoroughly studied in the literature ranging from distributed databases to the particular case of replicated databases [18,19]. The latter one aims to hide all aspects of data replication from the user. Hence, the replicated database should behave as if it were a stand-alone database system managing all user transactions. This way, when considering serializability, an extended criteria has been proposed, called one-copy serializability (1CS) [18]. It ensures that the interleaved execution of all transactions in the replicated system is equivalent to a serial execution of those transactions on a single database. With the advent of Snapshot Isolation (SI) databases [20] a similar correctness criterion was formalized as 1CSI [19]. It is clear that some kind of coordination is needed to the decide the outcome of a transaction; this is done by a replication protocol. Nevertheless, the scaling factor of these protocols [1] is very limited. On one hand, we have that primary copy solutions [21] do not scale well for update intensive scenarios, apart from the single point of failure, because the maximum throughput is limited by the primary. On the other hand, update everywhere solutions [22,23] use a total order broadcast facility [24] to generate the one copy history (i.e., update transactions are delivered to all replicas in the same order). It is well-known that total order broadcast does not scale well after a few tens of replicas have been added [25]. Hence, partial database replication protocols seem a good approach to cope with scalability issues [26].

As already mentioned, partitioning means that all replicas do not necessarily store the whole database but part of it. Hence, if transactions can be executed only in one replica, without any kind of interaction with the rest of replicas or keeping it to a minimum, the system may scale up better than full replicated systems. This is specially useful in cloud computing where we want to deploy highly scalable systems while supporting transaction mechanisms. Replicas are owners of one or several partitions, whose assignment can be changed on the fly by a data repository manager, and are entirely responsible for the execution of transactions over that partition. Actually, if the partition can be stored in main memory and the workload consists of transactions whose content can be known in advance (e.g., stored procedures) then transactions can be executed serially in each partition without wasting resources [11,12]. Nevertheless, if transactions can potentially access several partitions then we have network stalls that have to be reduced to the maximum. One solution is to use *minitransactions* as in

Sinfonia [8] or ElasTraS [9], where a modification of the two-phase-commit protocol [18] is proposed in order to make it scalable. In our case, we have taken a more scalable and originally non-blocking solution based on certification protocols for replicated databases [26]. This is the idea behind the notion of an OTM group to increase the performance and fault-tolerance without incurring in the high cost of delivering a total order message outside the cluster or having a number more than reasonable that compromise the scalability inside the cluster.

Another way of overcoming stalls is through the speculative execution of transactions, which is an optimistic approach shown to be useful in [11]. If transactions are decomposed into smaller actions, each one accessing to a different partition, then these actions can be forwarded to the corresponding partitions, where they are serially executed, along with actions coming from other transactions, by a single thread assigned to that partition [12]. The coordination of actions belonging to the same transaction is done with a rendezvous point that decides the outcome of transactions. As we have already mentioned, we prefer to rely on a single total-order delivered message rather than a shared object which can be a single point of failure or storing the set of executed speculative actions to undo them. We believe our approach does not block the execution of transactions in the system and can take all the benefits of these approaches [11,12].

Finally, the kind of consistency obtained in these cloud environments is a general one-copy multiversion scheduler, since transactions reading from several partitions can have a time (version) wrap. This is due to the fact that there is no guarantee as in 1CSI that transactions get a consistent snapshot of the database. Nevertheless, this is an eventually consistent model [27] as updates will eventually get propagated to all replicas, reaching a consistent state in all of them.

5   Work in Progress

This paper reports on our ongoing implementation of a system that leverages from ElasTraS. The objective is to test it against RDBMS and, if possible, against ElasTraS. Some of the performance measures should help us to compare, for example, the OTM recovery time in ElasTraS with the time our replicated system takes to move transactions from a crashed replica to another one. Another measure would be the time overhead our replication system imposes over transaction execution and try to conclude if the changes we propose behave as expected.

These previous tests should be carried out using different replication mechanisms at the OTM groups. For instance, we are designing and implementing an hybrid replication approach in an OTM group where we can distinguish two subsets of OTMs: primaries and secondaries. The primary OTMs will be in charge of performing certification on behalf of update transactions. Apart from that, they are responsible for asynchronously propagating the updates to a subgroup of secondary OTMs (not all secondary ones), pretty much like in traditional primary copy replication, so that all primary OTMs will cover the whole set of secondary OTMs. The role of secondary OTMs will be to execute read-only transactions; the benefit of this is the elasticity when the system needs to take over new (primary) OTMs for a given OTM group or partition since it already stores most of the up-to-date state of that partition.

We also expect that varying the workload leads to different performances of each of all the different replication mechanisms we have proposed so far in this paper. Alongside the implementation we expect to study suitable workloads and benchmarks in order to be able to fairly compare the different systems [28]. Namely, we expect to use those workloads to research new data partitioning methods and data schema design tools. With these methods and tools designing a scalable system becomes a more straightforward task.

6   Conclusion

Along this paper we described a novel approach to offer transactional support in the cloud environment. Namely, we propose a system aimed at high availability and scalability and still guaranteeing transactional support. The system we proposed is inspired by ElasTraS [10] and presents several enhancements that overcome the problems detected in the original system.

Our system is also elastic and self-managed, characteristics most desirable in a cloud computing scenario. Moreover, the ability to accommodate various independent databases allows the system to be used as a platform service. A client of such a service can deploy their database with a *pay per use* model and without an initial high investment. This aspect has also been regarded as one of the main stimulus to the success of cloud computing [29].

With this paper we also point out the fundamental role partitioning plays in system scalability. In fact, to provide transactional support it is necessary some kind of coordination between partitions or replicas. This coordination can be achieved with many different mechanisms, but it always represents a performance cost and an impairment to scalability. The scalability of a system thus depends on how it will handle data. If we define the size of a transaction based on the number of different tables, relations or partitions it accesses, then the system's scalability will be the maximum when the size of the largest transaction is reduced to the minimum.

We believe that for data management systems it is difficult to provide a system aimed at the famous *one size fits all* model. To achieve maximum system performance and scalability the data set must be studied to find the specific partition schema most appropriate to each case.

Data partitioning, although proved to be crucial to the scalability of a system, must be complemented with novel approaches to providing transactional support in the cloud. There is still plenty of work to be done and we expect our system to be a step forward in this area.

References

1. Gray, J., Helland, P., O'Neil, P.E., Shasha, D.: The dangers of replication and a solution. In: Jagadish, H.V., Mumick, I.S. (eds.) SIGMOD Conference, pp. 173–182. ACM Press, New York (1996)

2. Brewer, E.A.: Towards robust distributed systems (abstract). In: Proceedings of the Nineteenth Annual ACM Symposium on Principles of Distributed Computing, PODC 2000, p. 7. ACM, New York (2000)
3. Gilbert, S., Lynch, N.A.: Brewer's conjecture and the feasibility of consistent, available, partition-tolerant web services. SIGACT News 33(2), 51–59 (2002)
4. von Eicken, T.: Right scale blog: Animoto's facebook scale-up (2010), http://blog.rightscale.com/2008/04/23/animoto-facebook-scale-up/
5. Chang, F., Dean, J., Ghemawat, S., Hsieh, W.C., Wallach, D.A., Burrows, M., Chandra, T., Fikes, A., Gruber, R.E.: Bigtable: A distributed storage system for structured data. ACM Trans. Comput. Syst. 26(2) (2008)
6. DeCandia, G., Hastorun, D., Jampani, M., Kakulapati, G., Lakshman, A., Pilchin, A., Sivasubramanian, S., Vosshall, P., Vogels, W.: Dynamo: amazon's highly available key-value store. In: Bressoud, T.C., Kaashoek, M.F. (eds.) SOSP, pp. 205–220. ACM, New York (2007)
7. Cooper, B.F., Ramakrishnan, R., Srivastava, U., Silberstein, A., Bohannon, P., Jacobsen, H.A., Puz, N., Weaver, D., Yerneni, R.: Pnuts: Yahoo!'s hosted data serving platform. PVLDB 1(2), 1277–1288 (2008)
8. Aguilera, M.K., Merchant, A., Shah, M.A., Veitch, A.C., Karamanolis, C.T.: Sinfonia: A new paradigm for building scalable distributed systems. ACM Trans. Comput. Syst. 27(3) (2009)
9. Das, S., Agrawal, D., Abbadi, A.E.: Elastras: An elastic transactional data store in the cloud. In: HotCloud 2009 Workshop at USENIX (2009)
10. Das, S., Agarwal, S., Agrawal, D., Abbadi, A.E.: Elastras: An elastic, scalable, and self managing transactional database for the cloud. Technical Report UCSB-CS-2010-04, University of California, Santa Barbara (2010)
11. Jones, E.P.C., Abadi, D.J., Madden, S.: Low overhead concurrency control for partitioned main memory databases. In: Elmagarmid, A.K., Agrawal, D. (eds.) SIGMOD Conference, pp. 603–614. ACM, New York (2010)
12. Pandis, I., Johnson, R., Hardavellas, N., Ailamaki, A.: Data-oriented transaction execution. Technical Report CMU-CS-10-101, Carnegie Mellon University (2010)
13. Burrows, M.: The chubby lock service for loosely-coupled distributed systems. In: OSDI, USENIX Association, pp. 335–350 (2006)
14. Lamport, L.: The part-time parliament. ACM Trans. Comput. Syst. 16(2), 133–169 (1998)
15. Pedone, F.: The Database State Machine and Group Communication Issues. PhD thesis, École Polytechnique Fédérale de Lausanne, Switzerland (1999)
16. Schneider, F.B.: Implementing fault-tolerant services using the state machine approach: A tutorial. ACM Comput. Surv. 22(4), 299–319 (1990)
17. Gray, J., Reuter, A.: Transaction Processing: Concepts and Techniques. Morgan Kaufmann, San Francisco (1993)
18. Bernstein, P.A., Hadzilacos, V., Goodman, N.: Concurrency Control and Recovery in Database Systems. Addison-Wesley, Reading (1987)
19. Lin, Y., Kemme, B., Jiménez-Peris, R., Patiño-Martínez, M., Armendáriz-Iñigo, J.E.: Snapshot isolation and integrity constraints in replicated databases. ACM Trans. Database Syst. 34(2) (2009)
20. Berenson, H., Bernstein, P.A., Gray, J., Melton, J., O'Neil, E.J., O'Neil, P.E.: A critique of ANSI SQL isolation levels. In: Carey, M.J., Schneider, D.A. (eds.) SIGMOD Conference, pp. 1–10. ACM Press, New York (1995)
21. Plattner, C., Alonso, G., Özsu, M.T.: Extending DBMSs with satellite databases. VLDB J. 17(4), 657–682 (2008)

22. Lin, Y., Kemme, B., Patiño-Martínez, M., Jiménez-Peris, R.: Middleware based data replication providing snapshot isolation. In: Özcan, F. (ed.) SIGMOD Conference, pp. 419–430. ACM, New York (2005)

23. Elnikety, S., Zwaenepoel, W., Pedone, F.: Database replication using generalized snapshot isolation. In: SRDS, pp. 73–84. IEEE Computer Society, Los Alamitos (2005)

24. Chockler, G., Keidar, I., Vitenberg, R.: Group communication specifications: a comprehensive study. ACM Comput. Surv. 33(4), 427–469 (2001)

25. Jiménez-Peris, R., Patiño-Martínez, M., Alonso, G., Kemme, B.: Are quorums an alternative for data replication? ACM Trans. Database Syst. 28(3), 257–294 (2003)

26. Serrano, D., Patiño-Martínez, M., Jiménez-Peris, R., Kemme, B.: Boosting database replication scalability through partial replication and 1-copy-snapshot-isolation. In: PRDC, pp. 290–297. IEEE Computer Society, Los Alamitos (2007)

27. Vogels, W.: Eventually consistent. Commun. ACM 52(1), 40–44 (2009)

28. Sobel, W., Subramanyam, S., Sucharitakul, A., Nguyen, J., Wong, H., Patil, S., Fox, A., Patterson, D.: Cloudstone: Multi-platform, multi-language benchmark and measurement tools for web 2.0. In: 1st Workshop on Cloud Computing (CCA 2008) (2008)

29. Gartner:: Gartner identifies top ten disruptive technologies for 2008 to 2012 (2010), http://www.gartner.com/it/page.jsp?id=681107

Fadip: Lightweight Publish/Subscribe for Mobile Ad Hoc Networks

Koosha Paridel, Yves Vanrompay, and Yolande Berbers

K.U. Leuven, Department of Computer Science
Celestijnenlaan 200A, Heverlee, Belgium
{koosha.paridel,yves.vanrompay,yolande.berbers}@cs.kuleuven.be
http://www.cs.kuleuven.be

Abstract. Publish/Subscribe is an interesting communication paradigm because it fosters a high degree of decoupling between the communicating parties and provides the ability to communicate in an asynchronous way. Publish/Subscribe systems have been extensively studied for wired networks but designing a Publish/Subscribe system for mobile ad hoc networks is still a challenge. In this paper we propose a lightweight Publish/ Subscribe system for mobile ad hoc networks which uses a limited gossip mechanism to match the published messages with the subscriptions. The goal of this work is to reduce the number of exchanged messages used for communication and maintenance while keeping an acceptable delivery ratio. Experimental results show that Fadip achieves an acceptable delivery ratio even in high mobility rates.

Keywords: Publish/Subscribe, MANET.

1 Introduction

Publish/Subscribe is an asynchronous communication model in a network. It has been a popular model because of its decoupling and asynchronous communication properties. The decoupling property allows the communicating parties to exchange information without knowing each other. The asynchronous communication property also allows them to communicate even though they are not online at the same time.

Mobile ad hoc networks (MANETs) on the other hand are networks of mobile nodes which can move freely and arbitrarily. MANETs have several characteristics[5]: (i) dynamic topologies, (ii) bandwidth-constrained, variable capacity links, (iii) energy-constrained operation and (iv) limited physical security. The need for mobile ad hoc networking technology is increasing and consequently there is a growing need for scalable and robust communication mechanism for MANETs.

Publish/Subscribe systems have been intensively studied for wired networks and infrastructured mobile networks. However, there are not many solutions for Publish/Subscribe systems in mobile ad hoc networks and all of these solutions suffer from scalability issues. These scalability issues can be categorized into:

R. Meersman et al. (Eds.): OTM 2010, Part II, LNCS 6427, pp. 798–810, 2010.

(i) large number of nodes, (ii) large network area, (iii) high mobility rates and (iv) large number of messages. In this paper, our focus is on the number of nodes and on mobility rate which all the current solutions are struggling with.

We propose a lightweight Publish/Subscribe systems for MANET called Fadip (Publish/Subscribe using FADing GossIP). In designing Fadip our goal is to make it lightweight in terms of the logical network structure (i.e repairing and maintenance needed) and the number of messages exchanged for communication. Meanwhile, we want to achieve a reasonable deliver ratio of the messages. We also aim to make a system suitable for high mobility rates and extremely volatile networks.

To achieve these goals, we propose to use a hybrid model by using bounded subscription propagation and publication propagation at the same time. The idea is to propagate subscriptions and publications as bounded as possible and make matchings in the intermediary nodes. This approach is to some extent similar to the idea of having rendezvous points which is used in Publish/Subscribe systems for wired network because the matching is done in some intermediary nodes which can be assumed as a kind of a rendezvous point. However, the difference is that unlike wired networks we cannot rely on any node as a dedicated rendezvous point. Thus, neither the publishers nor the subscribers have any information about where their publications and subscription might be matched. In this paper we describe the basic protocol which includes subscription propagation, publication propagation, matching and delivery. Subsequently, we introduce Fadip or *fading gossip* technique to further limit the number of messages. We also did extensive simulation studies to determine the effectiveness of the basic protocol and the effect of applying the Fadip technique.

The rest of this paper is structured as follows: We present the Fadip protocol in Section 2, then we describe the results of simulation in Section 3. Next, we discuss the related work in Section 4 and finally we conclude in Section 5.

2 The Fadip Protocol

The idea of this work is to use bounded propagation of both publish and subscribe messages and match them in intermediary nodes between a publisher and a subscriber. The goal is to increase the delivery ratio of the publications and decrease the number of multicasts. Although there are other important factors for a publish/subscribe system such as matching techniques and event expressiveness, we do not deal with them in this paper.

We propose a content-based publish/subscribe system for mobile ad hoc networks called Fadip. It is a light-weight protocol in the sense that it does not maintain any kind of logical structure for the mobile nodes such as a routing tree[10] or grouping clusters[14]. Fadip is content-based because it routes the publications to the subscribers by matching their content with the subscriptions. Because we are not dealing with expressiveness here we choose the publications to be in a range of integers specified by $value_{min}$ and $value_{max}$.

The network is considered to be an ad hoc network of homogeneous mobile nodes that are moving freely in a 2-dimensional playground with an area of $size_x$

by $size_y$. Every node has a transmission range and when a broadcast message is sent, all the nodes in the transmission range can receive that message. All nodes can have the roles of a publisher and a subscriber.

2.1   The Basic Protocol

The Fadip protocol consists of four operations: (i) subscription propagation, (ii) publication propagation, (iii) matching, and (iv) delivering. In the following we describe these operations but first we describe the properties of a message and basic propagation rules.

Messages and Maximum Hop Count: Each subscription is propagated up to a certain hop count which is called $hcMax_{subscribe}$. On the other hand, each publication is published up to hop count limit which is called $hcMax_{publish}$. We name these two parameters *Subscribe Penetration* and *Publish Penetration* recpectively. Depending on the number of nodes and the size of the playground these hop count limits should be chosen in a way to provide an acceptable probability for publications to be matched with subscriptions. As we show in Section 3 a proper hop count can be easily calculated after a few runs of the protocol. Each message (publish or subscribe message) has a variable which indicates the number of hops that this message is away from its producer. This variable is called hc. Each node, upon receiving a publish or subscribe message checks the value of hc with $hcMax_{publish}$ or $hcMax_{subscribe}$ respectively. If the value is smaller than the limit the node forwards the message by broadcasting it to the neighbors. This node also remembers forwarding this special message to avoid forwarding it again and make forwarding loops.

Subscription Propagation: If the forwarding message is a subscription, an intermediary node $node_i$ checks if it already received this subscription or not. Suppose that the originating node of this subscription is $node_a$. $node_i$ can receive a subscription earlier from $node_a$ or it can receive a similar subscription but from another node $node_b$ sooner. In this case $node_i$ checks the hc variable of the message which shows the number of hops that this message has been forwarded. If hc of the message is lower than the minimum hc value that $node_i$ has seen until this moment for this specific subscription, $node_i$ will replace his old value for this subscription with the newer and smaller value. For example if $node_i$ has a hc value of 5 for a subscription S and it receives a new subscription with hc value of 4, it will change the value of hc_S from 5 to 4. Finally $node_i$ will increase hc value of the forwarding messages and sends it to the neighbors.

Publication Propagation: If the forwarding message is a publication $node_i$ checks if it has already forwarded the same publication originating from the same publisher $node_a$. It prevents unnecessary and redundant forwarding of publications. If it is the first time that $node_i$ is receiving this message it increases the hc value of the messages and forwards it to the neighbors.

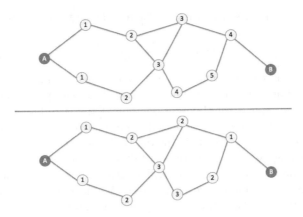

Fig. 1. Subscription Forwarding in Fadip. The upper figure shows hop count values for the intermediary nodes after a subscription propagation by Node A. The lower figure shows the same network after the propagation of the same subscription by Node B.

Matching and Delivering: Upon receiving a publication message m_p, $node_i$ checks if it has already received a subscription S which matches m_p[1]. If a match is found, m_p will be forwarded to the neighbors even if it has hc value more than $hcMax_{publish}$. However, it is still necessary to control the propagation depth to avoid unnecessary forwarding. Thus, for a matched publication, instead of limiting hc value to $hcMax_{publish}$ we limit it to $hcMax_{publish}+hcMax_{subscribe}$ so that it can have enough steps to reach the subscriber. Note that if for a message hc is exceeding $hcMax_{publish} + hcMax_{subscribe}$, it means that it is going on a wrong direction, because m_p should be able to reach from $node_i$ to the subscriber using the same path that the subscription was routed which is shorter or equal to $hcMax_{subscribe}$. When m_p is matched at the subscriber node it will not be forwarded anymore.

2.2 Fading Gossip

In addition to limiting data dissemination to a certain hop limit, to decrease the number of broadcasts we use another technique which we call it *fading gossip*. In fading gossip we decrease the fanout of each broadcast (which makes it a multicast) at every hop level. For example, the fanout for the message sender is 100% of its neighbors, while for the next level the fanout is 80% of neighbors, for the next level 60% and so on. This means that the message will be forwarded to a random fraction of neighbors and this fraction is equal to the fanout percentage. On the other hand we do not want to decrease fanout less than a certain threshold such as 50% of the neighbors. Hence, we define a formula to adjust the fanout

---

[1] As mentioned earlier we are not dealing with expressiveness in our Publish/Subscribe system. Thus, subscriptions and publication are positive integers ranging from $value_{min}$ and $value_{max}$.

at each hop level which starts from 100% and leans towards 50%. We use the formula:

$$fanout = \frac{1}{2} + \frac{1}{2}e^{-c.hc} \tag{1}$$

In this formula c is the coefficient used to speed up the fanout decrement and hc is the hop count of the forwarding message. For example, when $c = 1$ which means that we are using normal fanout decrement speed and $hc = 1$ which means a message is on first hop level (immediate neighbor of the message's source) we have a fanout equal to 0.684. This means that the second level neighbors will receive this message with a probability of 68.4%. Using similar calculation, the second level fanout is 0.568 and it will continue decreasing each level down to 0.5. However, in sparse networks where nodes do not have many neighbors, it is possible that a forwarding message gets eliminated in the early stages. For example, suppose a subscriber in a sparse network where it has only one neighbor. There is a good probability that using the fading gossip technique the subscription get stopped at the first neighbor and never reaches the other nodes in network. Therefore, there is a need to change the proposed formula so that it can adapt itself with sparse networks. In order to do that, we can suspend the formula from acting until a certain hop limit (e.g. first or second level of neighbors) and apply it after that limit. Thus, the adjusted formula becomes:

$$fanout = \begin{cases} 1 & \text{if } hc \leq \text{limit} \\ \frac{1}{2} + \frac{1}{2}e^{-c.hc} & \text{if } hc > \text{limit} \end{cases} \tag{2}$$

Using this formula to compute fanout, we can avoid the forwarding message to get eliminated in the beginning levels. For example, by setting limit to 1 we can make sure that the message will be broadcasted to all the second level neighbors and after that fading gossip technique takes effect.

In the following section we show the performance of basic protocol and the effect of fading gossip through extensive simulations.

3   Simulation

Fadip is simulated in OMNeT++ [13], an open source discrete event simulator, and using a mobility framework for OMNeT++ called MiXiM [9]. The nodes move in a playground with an area of 1500 meters by 1000 meters which resembles a campus area. The movement model used is the Random Waypoint model [3] which is considered as a benchmark mobility model to evaluate routing protocols in MANET [1]. The speed and the number of nodes changes in different simulations and will be given for each case.

Figure 2 illustrates the simulation environment with mobile nodes and the wireless links between the nodes represented by the images of laptops and black arrows respectively. In this example, there are 75 nodes in a playground of 1500 meters by 1000 meters. The mobile nodes move in the playground according to the movement model. When two nodes enter each other's wireless communication range a wireless link is established, and when they go out of this range the

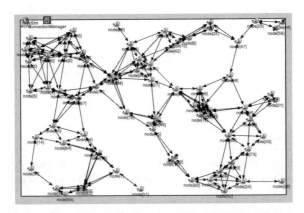

Fig. 2. Simulation in OMNeT++ using MiXiM. Each laptop icon represents a mobile node and arrows show direct wireless links between nodes. A link is established when two nodes are in each others wireless communication range. A link is broken when the two nodes are not in each other's wireless communication range anymore.

wireless link is broken. In the following, we describe the different simulating experiments that we have done to evaluate Fadip.

Propagation Limit: The goal of this simulation is to see the effect of propagation limit in terms of hop counts on delivery ratio of the messages and to observe the costs of it in terms of the number of sent messages. In this setup we use 75 nodes in the same playground of 1500 by 1000 meters. There is one random subscriber and 20 random publishers which each publisher publishes only one message. Figure 3 shows the effect of different values of $hcMax_{publish}$ and $hcMax_{subscribe}$ on delivery ratio and number of broadcasts. We did the same experiment with 150 nodes and 49 random publishers too (randomly chosen by 20% chance which is our simulation turned out to be 49). Figure 4 shows the result of using different publish and subscription penetration for a network of 150 nodes in the same playground which we used for the network of 75 nodes. However, this time we used multiple subscribers (5% of total nodes) instead of a single subscriber. The results show that increasing the penetration after a certain limit has a neutral or even negative effect on delivery ratio and at same time it increases the number of broadcasts rapidly. For example for the network of 75 nodes and value of 4 and 4 for $hcMax_{publish}$ and $hcMax_{subscribe}$ respectively gives about 65% delivery ratio and uses fewer broadcasts comparing to larger penetration (hop count limit) values. Also for the network of 150 nodes a penetration value of around 5, 5 or 6, 6 perform very well in term of delivery ratio and number of broadcasts. These results suggest that for every network, based on the size of playground and the number of nodes there is an efficient setting for the penetration limit which can be calculated easily. Next we see the effect of publish and subscribe penetration separately.

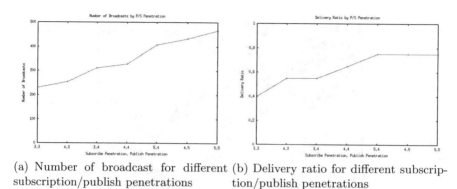

(a) Number of broadcast for different subscription/publish penetrations

(b) Delivery ratio for different subscription/publish penetrations

Fig. 3. The effect of subscription and publish penetration on number of broadcasts and on delivery ratio for a single subscriber and a network of 75 nodes

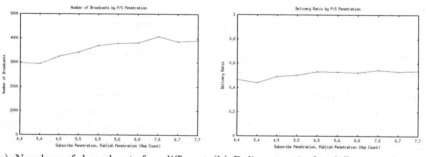

(a) Number of broadcast for different subscription/publish penetrations

(b) Delivery ratio for different subscription/publish penetrations

Fig. 4. The effect of subscription and publish penetration on number of broadcasts and on delivery ratio for a multiple subscribers and publishers in a network of 150 nodes

Subscribe Penetration: We did simulations having a constant publish penetration and a varying subscription penetration. The reason is to see the effect of changing a subscription penetration alone. Again we use a single subscriber and 49 random publishers. The network consists of 150 nodes and the playground size is the same as previous setups. Figure 5 shows the result of changing subscription propagation from 3 to 8 hops. The results suggest that increasing the subscription penetration after a certain limit does not have a positive effect on delivery ratio but increases the number of broadcast rapidly. Hence, there is an efficient threshold for subscription penetration that can be determined for a network easily through simulations or experiments.

Publish Penetration: We also did simulations having a constant subscription penetration and a varying publish penetration. Figure 6 shows the result of changing publish propagation from 3 to 8 hops. The results again suggest that increasing the subscription penetration after a certain limit increases the number of broadcast sharply but does not provide more delivery ratio.

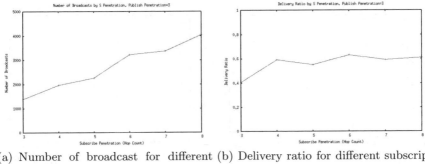

(a) Number of broadcast for different (b) Delivery ratio for different subscrip-
subscription penetrations   tion penetrations

Fig. 5. The effect of subscription penetration on number of broadcasts and on delivery
ratio for a single subscriber and a network of 150 nodes

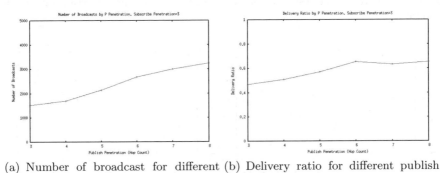

(a) Number of broadcast for different (b) Delivery ratio for different publish
publish penetrations   penetrations

Fig. 6. The effect of publish penetration on number of broadcasts and on delivery ratio
for a single subscriber and a network of 150 nodes

Multiple Subscribers: In order to verify the results we showed earlier with a
single subscriber we also did simulations with multiple subscribers. In this setup
we randomly chose 5% of nodes as subscribers and 15% of nodes as publishers
in a network of 150 nodes. We ran 3 simulations for each publish/subscribe
penetration setting and computed the average and a 95% confidence interval for
the results. Figure 7 shows the results of running Fadip with multiple subscribers
with the calculated confidence interval. The results show a similar trend with
the single subscriber scenario.

Fading Gossip: As described in section 2.2, we use the fading gossip technique
to control the number of broadcasts. We did simulation to compare the basic
protocol and fading gossip and to see the effects on the number of broadcasts
and delivery ratio. Figure 8 compares the basic protocol and fading gossip in
terms of the two mentioned parameters. The results show that using fading
gossip technique limits the number of broadcasts considerably while loosing a

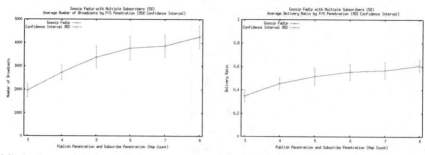

(a) Average number of broadcast by publish and subscribe penetration Fadip with multiple subscribers

(b) Average delivery ratio by publish and subscribe penetration for Fadip with multiple subscribers.

Fig. 7. Fadip with multiple subscribers (5% of total nodes) and multiple publishers (15% of total nodes). The results are shown with 95% confidence interval. Network size is 150 nodes.

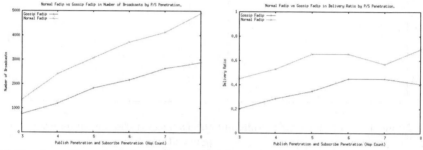

(a) Number of broadcast for basic protocol vs. Fadip with different publish and subscribe penetrations

(b) Delivery ratio for basic protocol vs. Fadip with different publish and subscribe penetrations

Fig. 8. Basic protocol vs. Fadip with different publish and subscribe penetrations for a network of 150 nodes

small percentage of delivery ratio, specially for higher publish and subscribe penetration values.

Mobility Ratio: An important factor for a Publish/Subscribe system for MANET is its behavior as mobility ratio increases. Higher mobility ratio invalidates routing information and logical network structures (e.g. clusters, routing trees) more rapidly. Therefore, as mobility ratio increases we expect to have a decrement in delivery ratio. In our simulations, we use a network of 150 nodes and change the mobility speed of nodes from 1 meter per second up to 10 meters per second. We a have 5% of nodes as subscribers and 15% of nodes as publishers. We ran each experiment 3 times and calculated the average with a confidence interval of 95% for the number of broadcasts and average delivery ratio. Figure 9 shows the effect of mobility ratio on number of broadcasts and

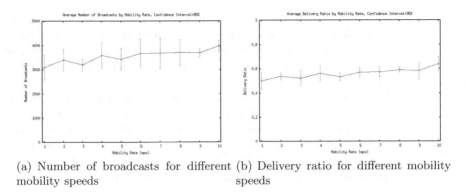

(a) Number of broadcasts for different mobility speeds

(b) Delivery ratio for different mobility speeds

Fig. 9. The effect of mobility ratio on number of broadcasts and on delivery ratio for a network of 150 nodes. (5% Subscriber, 15% Publisher).

on delivery ratio. Interestingly, there is no negative effect on delivery ratio. The reason for such a good behavior towards high mobility ratio is the fact that Fadip is not dependent on any logical network structure which can be damaged quickly by high mobility ratios. On the other hand, because of not relying on logical structures there is no need for maintenance communication and therefore there is no bad effect on the number of exchanged messages. That is an important result because Publish/Subscribe systems for MANET suffer heavily from the negative effects of increasing the mobility ratio.

4   Related Work

There are already many decent solutions for Publish/Subscribe systems in wired networks [2] and infrastructured mobile networks[4][7][8]. Recently, several pub/sub systems have been proposed for mobile ad hoc networks. In this section we describe several Publish/Subscribe systems for mobile ad hoc networks and we discuss their scalability in terms of network size and mobility ratio.

In Yuan et al. [15], the authors propose a pub/sub protocol for mobile ad hoc networks involving the construction of dynamic Voronoi regions. All nodes are divided into broker and non-broker categories, and each region is represented by a broker node. The authors propose mechanisms for constructing these Voronoi regions and for message deliveries.

Yoo et al. [14] also propose a pub/sub system for mobile ad hoc networks involving a hybrid model which uses flooding and content-based routing techniques hierarchically. They divide the network into clusters of nodes and use the event flooding technique for inter-cluster communication and content-based routing for intra-cluster communication. They try to utilize the advantages of content-based routing to achieve more efficient subscription propagation and maintenance and also reduce the costs of document delivery, while avoiding the high topology maintenance costs of content-based routing by using clusters and using flooding techniques for inter-cluster communication.

Also in Mottola et al. [10], the authors propose a protocol to organize the nodes of a mobile ad hoc network in a single, self-repairing tree structure which can be used for efficient content-based routing in the network. Their idea of maintaining the tree topology is inspired by a protocol for multicast over mobile ad hoc networks called MAODV.

Costa et al. [6] present a semi-probabilistic content-based pub/sub system in which the authors propose to use deterministic decision for event routing when there exists subscription information and to use probabilistic decisions when lacking subscription information. To do this, they propagate the subscription in the surrounding area of a subscriber. Upon receiving a forwarding event if subscription information is available, the event will be routed along the link that the subscription was received. If no subscription information is available, the event will be routed to a randomly chosen set of neighbors. The authors argue that their technique performs better than a fully deterministic and a fully probabilistic approach.

In Rezende et al. [12] the authors propose a pub/sub system for mobile ad hoc networks which does not build routing trees or other logical structures that need to be maintained. However, their goal is just to deliver publications using the minimum amount of broadcasts and they do not assume any time constraints for that. As they state in their paper their system is only suitable for applications that can tolerate delays of dozens of minutes. They also assume that mobile devices move and stop continuously and they are able to know if they are moving or not.

While [14] and [10] provide some analysis based on mobility ratio, [6], [15] and [12] do not deal with mobility ratio in their evaluations. In [6] the authors do simulation with a single moving speed of 2 m/s. In [12] nodes move with a randomly chosen speed of 1.5 to 4.0 m/s. It is also a similar case with [15] in which the range of randomly chosen speeds is between 10 to 20 m/s. In [14] the authors study the effect of mobility ratio on delivery ratio by changing the maximum speed of nodes from 1 m/s to 10 m/s. However, their results show a rapid decrement in delivery ratio as nodes move faster. In [10] the authors do not evaluate the performance of their system based on mobility rate. They only state that because the results of their simulations for nodes moving at 1 m/s and nodes moving at 10 m/s are not much different, their system is reasonably independent of node speed.

The routing mechanism used in Fadip is to some extent similar to Gradient Routing which is presented in [11]. In Gradient Routing each node maintains a cost table which keeps the estimated cost of sending a message to a target node. When a node forwards a message, only those neighbors which can deliver the message with a lower cost will participate in forwarding it. The concept of maintaining a cost table based on hop count is somehow similar to what we do in Fadip by keeping the distance of intermediary nodes in terms of hop count from a subscriber. Gradient Routing is a routing mechanism and it routes a message to a particular destination, and the originator is aware of the existence of the destination and its identification information. However, in Fadip a publisher is not aware of the subscribers. A publisher propagates its message in the network up to certain limit and hopes that its message would be matched in some places in the network with subscriptions. Moreover, for each publication in Fadip multiple destinations can exist. Thus, a publication can be forwarded in several branches to reach different subscribers, in contrast with Gradient Routing in which a message only follows the shortest route to its single destination. After the first matching, we forward a publication through all neighbors which have received a matching subscription and not only through those that have a shorter distance.

5   Conclusion

In this paper we presented Fadip, a light-weight Publish/Subscribe system for mobile ad hoc networks. Fadip uses controlled propagation of both publications and subscriptions and does the matching in the intermediary nodes. First, we described the basic protocol in which the propagation is done to all neighboring nodes at each level and next we introduced the fading gossip technique to further limit the number of broadcasts. Results show that Fadip tolerates high mobility rates without loosing any considerable delivery ratio.

References

1. Bai, F., Helmy, A.: A survey of mobility models in wireless adhoc networks. In: Wireless Ad Hoc and Sensor Networks. Kluwer Academic Publishers, Dordrecht (2004)
2. Baldoni, R., Virgillito, A.: Distributed event routing in publish/subscribe communication systems: a survey. DIS, Universita di Roma" La Sapienza", Tech. Rep. (2005)
3. Broch, J., Maltz, D.A., Johnson, D.B., Hu, Y.C., Jetcheva, J.: A performance comparison of multi-hop wireless ad hoc network routing protocols. In: Proceedings of the 4th annual ACM/IEEE international conference on Mobile computing and networking, p. 97. ACM, New York (1998)
4. Burcea, I., Jacobsen, H.A., De Lara, E., Muthusamy, V., Petrovic, M.: Disconnected operation in publish/subscribe middleware. In: 2004 IEEE International Conference on Mobile Data Management, Citeseer
5. Corson, S., Macker, J.: Mobile ad hoc networking (manet): Routing protocol performance issues and evaluation considerations. Request for comments 2501 (1999)
6. Costa, P., Picco, G.: Semi-probabilistic content-based publish-subscribe. In: International Conference on Distributed Computing Systems, vol. 25, p. 575. Citeseer (2005)
7. Fiege, L., Gartner, F.C., Kasten, O., Zeidler, A.: Supporting mobility in content-based publish/subscribe middleware. LNCS, pp. 103–122. Springer, Heidelberg (2003)
8. Huang, Y., Garcia-Molina, H.: Publish/subscribe in a mobile environment. Wireless Networks 10(6), 643–652 (2004)
9. Köpke, A., Swigulski, M., Wessel, K., Willkomm, D., Haneveld, P.T., Parker, T.E.V., Visser, O.W., Lichte, H.S., Valentin, S.: Simulating wireless and mobile networks in omnet++ the mixim vision. In: Proceedings of the 1st international conference on Simulation tools and techniques for communications, networks and systems & workshops. ICST (Institute for Computer Sciences, Social-Informatics and Telecommunications Engineering), p. 71 (2008)

10. Mottola, L., Cugola, G., Picco, G.P.: A self-repairing tree topology enabling content-based routing in mobile ad hoc networks. IEEE Transactions on Mobile Computing, 946–960 (2008)
11. Poor, R.D.: Gradient routing in ad hoc networks (2000)
12. Rezende, C.G., Rocha, B.P.S., Loureiro, A.A.F.: Publish/subscribe architecture for mobile ad hoc networks. In: Proceedings of the 2008 ACM symposium on Applied computing, pp. 1913–1917. ACM, New York (2008)
13. Varga, A., et al.: The omnet++ discrete event simulation system. In: Proceedings of the European Simulation Multiconference (ESM 2001), pp. 319–324 (2001)
14. Yoo, S., Son, J.H., Kim, M.H.: A scalable publish/subscribe system for large mobile ad hoc networks. The Journal of Systems & Software 82(7), 1152–1162 (2009)
15. Yuan, Q., Wu, J.: Drip: A dynamic voronoi regions-based publish/subscribe protocol in mobile networks. In: IEEE INFOCOM, Citeseer (2008)

Analysis of the Performance-Influencing Factors of Virtualization Platforms*

Nikolaus Huber, Marcel von Quast, Fabian Brosig, and Samuel Kounev

Karlsruhe Institute of Technology
Chair for Software Design and Quality
Am Fasanengarten 5
76131 Karlsruhe, Germany
{nikolaus.huber,fabian.brosig,samuel.kounev}@kit.edu
marcel.quast@student.kit.edu
http://descartes.ipd.kit.edu

Abstract. Nowadays, virtualization solutions are gaining increasing importance. By enabling the sharing of physical resources, thus making resource usage more efficient, they promise energy and cost savings. Additionally, virtualization is the key enabling technology for Cloud Computing and server consolidation. However, the effects of sharing resources on system performance are not yet well-understood. This makes performance prediction and performance management of services deployed in such dynamic systems very challenging. Because of the large variety of virtualization solutions, a generic approach to predict the performance influences of virtualization platforms is highly desirable. In this paper, we present a hierarchical model capturing the major performance-relevant factors of virtualization platforms. We then propose a general methodology to quantify the influence of the identified factors based on an empirical approach using benchmarks. Finally, we present a case study of Citrix XenServer 5.5, a state-of-the-art virtualization platform.

Keywords: Virtualization, Modeling, Benchmarking, Performance.

1 Introduction

In recent years, advances in virtualization technologies promise cost and energy savings for enterprise data centers. Server consolidation, i.e., running multiple virtual servers on a single shared infrastructure, increases resource utilization, centralizes administration, and introduces flexibility. Virtualization allows sharing server resources on-demand, thus creating new business opportunities by providing a new delivery model for a broad set of enterprise services. Therefore, it can be considered as a key technology enabler for Cloud Computing. According to the International Data Corporation (IDC), 18% of all new servers shipped in the fourth quarter of 2009 were virtualized, an increase from 15% compared

---

* This work was funded by the German Research Foundation (DFG) under grant No. KO 3445/6-1.

R. Meersman et al. (Eds.): OTM 2010, Part II, LNCS 6427, pp. 811–828, 2010.

to 2008 [6]. The server virtualization market is expected to grow 30% a year through 2013 [7]. However, the adoption of server virtualization comes at the cost of increased system complexity and dynamics. The increased complexity is caused by the introduction of virtual resources and the resulting gap between logical and physical resource allocations. The increased dynamics is caused by the lack of direct control over the underlying physical hardware and by the complex interactions between the applications and workloads sharing the physical infrastructure introducing new challenges in systems management.

Hosting enterprise services requires an efficient performance management at the application level. Service-Level Agreements (SLAs), e.g., performance guarantees such as service response time objectives, have to be respected. On the other hand, it is important to use server resources efficiently in order to save administration and energy costs. Thus, service providers are faced with questions such as: What performance would a new service deployed on the virtualized infrastructure exhibit and how much resources should be allocated to it? How should the system configuration be adapted to avoid performance problems arising from changing customer workloads? Answering such questions for distributed, non-virtualized execution environments is already a complex task [11]. In virtualized environments, this task is complicated by the sharing of resources. Moreover, since changes in the usage profiles of services may affect the entire infrastructure, capacity planning has to be performed continuously during operation. Proactive performance management, i.e., avoiding penalties by acting *before* performance SLAs are violated, requires predictions of the application-level performance under varying service workloads. Given that computation details are abstracted by an increasingly deep virtualization layer, the following research questions arise: i) What is the performance overhead when virtualizing execution environments? ii) Which are the most relevant factors that affect the performance of a virtual machine? iii) How can the performance influence of the identified factors be quantified?

Related work concerning the characterization of virtualization platforms focuses mainly on comparisons of specific virtualization solutions and techniques, e.g., container-based virtualization versus full virtualization [3,12,16,14]. Other work like [2,17,8] investigates core and cache contention effects, but the focus there is on reducing the virtualization overhead by introducing shared caches. To the best of our knowledge, an explicit characterization of the major performance-relevant factors of virtualization platforms does not exist.

In this paper, we classify and evaluate the major factors that affect the performance of virtualization platforms. We capture those factors that have to be considered for performance prediction at the application level, i.e., which have an impact on the application-level performance. We abstract from all possible configuration options of the currently available virtualization solutions with the goal to provide a compact hierarchical model capturing the most important performance-relevant factors and their dependencies. In addition, we propose a general methodology to quantify the performance influence of the identified factors. The methodology is based on an empirical approach using benchmarks executed in an automated manner in several predefined configuration scenarios. We applied the methodology to Citrix XenServer 5.5, the most popular freely available and state-of-the-art solution [6]. The conducted experiments involved a series of benchmark runs on different hardware platforms. We evaluated the overhead of full virtualization for CPU-intensive and memory-intensive workloads, respectively. Following this, we evaluated how different core affinity properties affect the performance of individual virtual machines (VMs). Furthermore, we evaluated how different orders of overcommitment (when the logical resources allocated to all VMs exceed the available physical resources) influence the performance of the overall system and the individual VMs. The contributions of this paper are: 1) a generic model of the most relevant performance-influencing factors of virtualization platforms, 2) a benchmark-based methodology for quantifying the effect of the identified factors and 3) a case study applying the methodology to the state-of-the-art Citrix XenServer 5.5 virtualization platform.

The remainder of this paper is organized as follows. Section 2 provides an overview and classification of current virtualization technologies. A model characterizing the major performance-relevant factors of virtualization platforms is introduced in Section 3. In Section 4, we present our automated approach to quantify the effect of the identified factors. Section 5 presents the case study of Citrix XenServer 5.5 on two representative hardware platforms. Section 6 discusses related work, followed by a conclusion and an outlook on future work.

2   Background

Virtualization technology enables consolidating multiple systems on a shared infrastructure by running multiple *virtual machines* (VMs) on a single physical machine. Each VM is completely separated from the other VMs and hence, it can be moved to other machines. This simplifies load balancing, dealing with hardware failures and eases system scaling. In addition, sharing resources promises a more efficient usage of the available hardware. However, as all VMs share the same physical resources, they also mutually influence each others performance.

Over the last years, different types of virtualization were introduced and sometimes terms related to virtualization are used with a different meaning. In this paper, virtualization always refers to *native virtualization* (or system virtualization, see Figure 1). In this case, the virtualization layer provides the native instruction set architecture (ISA) to its guests. This is in contrast to *emulation* (or non-native virtualization) where the virtualization layer can provide a different ISA. The latter allows software applications or operating systems (OS) written for a special purpose computer processor architecture to be executed on a different platform. The rest of this paper focuses on system virtualization. The core of each virtualization platform is the *virtual machine monitor* (VMM, also called hypervisor). Basically, a VMM is an abstraction layer added on top of the bare metal hardware [10]. It provides a uniform interface to access the underlying hardware. A VM is an execution environment created by a VMM and is similar to the underlying physical machine, but usually with different or reduced hardware resource configuration (e.g., less memory).

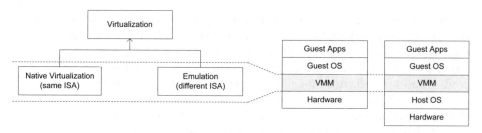

Fig. 1. Native Virtualization vs. Emulation and the VMM as an abstraction layer between hardware and guest (type-I) and between Host OS and guest (type-II)

Vallee et al. distinguish between two different types of system virtualization [18]. The first is *type-I virtualization* where the VMM runs directly on the physical hardware (see Figure 1), e.g., the Xen hypervisor. On the other hand, if the VMM runs within a host operating system, it is called *type-II virtualization*. An example is the VMware Server. The VMM provides an abstraction of the underlying machine's hardware and transparent hardware access to all VMs. This implies that software, e.g., an operating system, can be executed without changes or adjustments. An example of such a VMM is the z/VM hypervisor [13]. Unfortunately, not all architectures were designed to support virtualization, e.g., the x86 architecture [10,15]. Not all instructions of the standard x86 architecture can be virtualized and hence, standard x86 processors do not support direct execution. There are several approaches to address this issue.

Para-virtualization (PV) is a software solution that addresses the above mentioned problem. Here, the VMM provides an "almost" identical abstraction of the underlying ISA. Any operating system running in a para-virtualized VM must be adapted to support the changed instruction set which limits the set of possible guest OSs. On the other hand, para-virtualization provides better performance since guest systems can be further optimized for their virtualized execution. An example of a VMM that uses para-virtualization is the Xen hypervisor. Another software solution is direct execution with *binary translation*, introduced by VMware [1]. The advantage of binary translation is that any unmodified x86 OS can be executed in VMware's virtual machines. Binary translation basically translates kernel code by replacing non-virtualizable instructions with new sequences of instructions that have the intended effect on the virtualized hardware. Recently, a hardware approach to address the challenge of virtualizing the x86 architecture has been developed by Intel and AMD, enabling *full virtualization* (FV) and the execution of unmodified guest operating systems.

3   Modeling Performance-Influencing Factors of Virtualization Platforms

Ongoing trends show that virtualization technologies are gaining increasing importance. VMware ESX continues to be the most popular virtualization platform followed by VMware Server and Microsoft Hyper-V. Citrix XenServer showed

Table 1. Common virtualization platforms

Name	Type	Executed As	License	Since	Latest Ver. (06-2010)
Xen	PV/FV	type-I	GPL	10-2003	4.0.0
KVM	FV	type-I	(L)GPL (v2+)	02-2007	kvm-88
VirtualBox	FV	type-II	GPL	02-2007	3.2.4
VMware ESXi	FV/PV	type-I	comm. (free)	12-2007	4
VMware Server	FV/PV	type-II	comm. (free)	07-2006	2
OpenVZ	container-based		GPL v2	12-2005	vzctl_3.0.23
Linux-VServer	container-based		GNU FDL 1.2	2003	2.2stable

year-over-year growth of 290% and hence is among the top 5 [6]. Table 1 gives a quick overview of the most common, currently available virtualization solutions. This overview is not complete but shows the diversity of existing solutions and their maturity. It shows several open source implementations like Xen, KVM, VirtualBox and OpenVZ covering all types of virtualization. Other commercial but also free alternatives are, e.g., VMware Server or VMware ESXi. Also important to note is that parts of the open source solutions like Xen or KVM are also used in commercial products like Citrix XenServer or RedHat Enterprise Server, respectively.

In this section, we summarize the performance-influencing factors of the presented virtualization platforms. The goal is to provide a compact hierarchical model of performance-relevant properties and their dependencies. To this end, we abstract from all possible configurations of the currently available virtualization platforms presented in Table 1. We capture those factors that have to be considered for performance predictions at the application level, i.e., that have a considerable impact on the virtualization platform's performance, and we structure them in a so-called *feature model*. Feature models, used in the context of the engineering of software product lines [4], capture variabilities of software products. They define all valid combinations of the software product's property values, called features. One feature defines a certain set of options in the considered domain. In our context, a feature corresponds to a performance-relevant property or a configuration option of a virtualization platform. The goal of the feature model is to reflect the options that have an influence on the performance of the virtualization platform in a hierarchical structure. The feature model should also consider external influencing factors such as workload or type of hardware (with or without hardware support).

We now discuss the different influencing factors included in the feature model depicted in Figure 2. The first performance-influencing factor is the *virtualization type*. Different techniques might cause different performance overhead, e.g., full virtualization performs better than other alternatives because of the hardware support. In our feature model, we distinguish between the three types of virtualization: i) full virtualization, ii) para-virtualization and iii) binary translation.

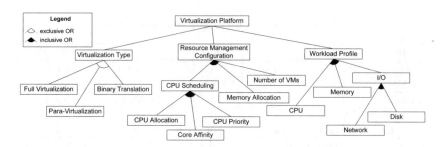

Fig. 2. Major performance-influencing factors of virtualization platforms

Several influencing factors are grouped under *resource management configuration*. First, CPU scheduling has a significant influence on the virtualization platform's performance. In turn, it is influenced by several factors. The first factor CPU allocation reflects the number of virtual CPUs allocated to a VM. Most of the performance loss of CPU intensive workloads comes from core and cache inferences [2]. Hence, the second factor that has a significant performance influence is core affinity, specifying if a virtual CPU of a VM is assigned to a dedicated physical core (core-pinning). The third parameter reflects the capability of assigning different CPU priorities to the VMs. For example, the Xen hypervisor's weight and cap parameters or VMware's limits and fixed reservations parameters are represented by these CPU priority configurations. Finally, the memory allocation and the number of VMs influence the resource management configuration, too. Managing memory requires an additional management layer in the hypervisor. The number of VMs has a direct effect on how the available resources are shared among all VMs.

Last but not least, an important influencing factor is the *type of workload* executed on the virtualization platform. Virtualizing different types of resources causes different performance overheads. For example, CPU virtualization is supported very well whereas I/O and memory virtualization currently suffer from significant performance overheads. In our model we distinguish CPU, memory and I/O intensive workloads. In the case of I/O workload, we further distinguish between disk and network intensive I/O workloads. Of course, one can also imagine a workload mixture consisting of all three workload types.

4   Automated Experimental Analysis

We now present a generic approach based on an automated experimental analysis to quantify the performance-influence of the factors captured in our feature model. First, we give an overview of the experimental setup and describe the general process that is followed when conducting experiments. We then describe the different sets of experiments and how to structure them to assess the performance influence of a given factor. We assume that in each set of experiments a selected benchmark is executed multiple times in different scenarios to characterize the impact of the considered factor. The process is completely automated using a set of scripts for each experiment type. In Section 4.3, we provide an overview of several benchmarks that provide a basis for evaluating the various influence factors.

4.1 Experimental Setup

Static view: As a first step, the virtualization platform to be evaluated is installed on the target hardware platform. In case of type-II virtualization, one would have to install a host OS first. Then, we create a *MasterVM* (see Figure 3) which serves as a template for creating multiple VM clones executing the selected benchmark as part of the considered set of experiments described in Section 4.2. To this end, the respective benchmark is installed on the MasterVM together with scripts to control the benchmark execution (e.g., to schedule benchmark runs). The MasterVM is the only VM with an external network connection. All other VMs and the MasterVM are connected via an internal network. The second major part of our framework is the *controller* which runs on a separate machine. It adjusts the configuration (e.g., amount of virtual CPUs) of the MasterVM and the created clones as required by the considered type of experiments. The controller also clones, deletes, starts, and stops VMs via the virtualization layer's API. Furthermore, it is responsible for collecting, processing and visualizing the results. In this generic approach, the benchmark choice is left open and one can use any available benchmark stressing the considered influencing factor.

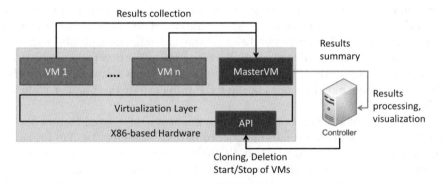

Fig. 3. Static view of the experimental setup

Dynamic view: Figure 4 shows the process of automated execution of experiments from the controller's point of view. At first, the controller starts and configures the MasterVM by configuring the benchmark to be executed and scheduling the experiment runs. After that, the MasterVM is replicated according to the requirements of the respective set of experiments described in Section 4.2. After the VM cloning, the controller undertakes further VM-specific configuration for each created clone as required, e.g., assigning the VMs' virtual CPUs to physical cores. Finally, the VMs are started and the benchmarks are executed at the scheduled starting time. The controller is responsible to detect

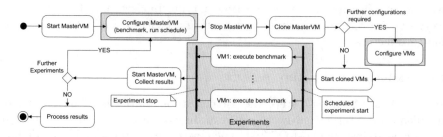

Fig. 4. Automated execution of experiments from the controller's point of view

the end of the benchmark runs and after the experiments are finished, it triggers the MasterVM to collect the results of all VMs. This is done by the MasterVM because it is the only connection between the VM subnet and the controller. If there are further experiments to be executed, the MasterVM is reconfigured and the whole process starts from the beginning, continuing until all experiments are completed. Finally, the controller processes and stores the results from the experiments. The grey boxes of Figure 4 depict the parts of the process where configuration is applied depending on the specific set of experiments considered.

4.2   Experiment Types

We distinguish between the following categories of influencing factors according to Section 3: (a) virtualization type, (b) resource management configuration, and (c) workload profile. For category (a), an initial set of experiments is executed to quantify the performance overhead of the virtualization platform, possibly varying the hardware environment and/or the virtualization type if multiple alternatives are supported . This initial set of experiments quantifies the overhead of the hypervisor but does not consider the influence of the number co-located VMs.

The number of VMs and other resource management-related factors like core affinity or CPU scheduling parameters are part of category (b). We investigate the influence of these factors in two different scenarios. The first one focuses on *scalability* (in terms of number of co-located VMs), the second focuses on *overcommitment* (in terms of allocating more resources than are actually available). For scalability, we increase the number of VMs until the all available physical resources are used. For overcommitment, the number of VMs is increased beyond the amount of available resources. The process is illustrated in Figure 5. As the example resource type, we use the number of available physical cores c. In the first case, the number of VMs is increased step-by-step up to c, whereas in the second case the number of VMs is increased by a factor $x \in \{1, \ldots, n\}$ multiplied with the number of cores c. As an example, to determine the influence of core affinity on scalability and overcommitment, the experiment series depicted in Figure 5 is executed one time with and one time without core affinity comparing the results. In the latter case, each virtual core is automatically pinned to a dedicated physical core.

Fig. 5. Benchmark execution in scalability and overcommitment scenarios

Finally, for category (c) we execute a set of benchmarks focusing on the different types of workloads as described in the next section.

4.3 Benchmark Selection

We now briefly discuss a set of benchmarks representing different types of workloads that can be used in the experiments described in the previous section. For CPU and memory-intensive workloads, we recommend two alternative benchmarks: Passmark PerformanceTest v7.0[1] (a benchmark used by VMware [19]) and SPEC CPU2006[2] (an industry standard CPU benchmark).

Passmark PerformanceTest is a benchmark focused on CPU and memory performance. The benchmark rating is a weighted average of several single benchmark categories (CPU, memory, I/O, etc.). In this paper, we focus on the CPU mark and memory mark rating and are not interested in the overall Passmark rating. SPEC CPU2006 is an industry standard benchmark for evaluating CPU performance. It is structured in a similar fashion and consists of CINT2006 integer benchmarks and CFP2006 floating point benchmarks. However, unlike Passmark, SPEC CPU2006 does not distinguish between CPU and memory performance.

The Passmark benchmark has the advantage that it explicitly distinguishes between CPU and memory, and its benchmark runs are much shorter. Given the short benchmark runs, in our experiments with Passmark we repeat each benchmark run 200 times to obtain a more confident overall rating and to gain a picture of the variability of the results.

In the scalability scenario, multiple instances of the benchmark are executed in separate identical VMs simultaneously. In the end, the results of all benchmark instances are aggregated into one set to compute the overall mean rating. For example, when executing 200 benchmark runs on one machine, we would get 4800 separate benchmark results when scaling up to 24 VMs.

In addition to the above, the Passmark benchmark offers a separate workload focusing on I/O performance, however, for I/O intensive workloads we recommend to use the *Iometer* benchmark[3] which measures the performance of disk and network controllers as well as system-level hard drive performance. Furthermore, for network performance measurements, the *Iperf* benchmark[4] can be

---

[1] Passmark PerformanceTest: http://www.passmark.com/products/pt.htm
[2] SPEC CPU2006: http://www.spec.org/cpu2006/
[3] Iometer: http://www.iometer.org/
[4] Iperf: http://iperf.sourceforge.net/

used. It is based on a client-server model and supports the throughput measurement of TCP and UDP data connections between both endpoints.

Finally, further workloads that can be used in our experiments are provided by SPEC standard benchmarks such as SPECjbb2005 (stressing CPU and memory performance), SPECmail2009 (stressing I/O performance) and SPEC-jEnterprise2010 (emulating a complex three tier e-business application). These benchmarks are partly used together with others in the new SPECvirt benchmark which is currently under development. However, this benchmark is out-of-scope of this work as it calculates an overall metric to compare servers and different virtualization option. It is not designed to analyze the influence of specific factors on the system performance.

5   Case Study: Citrix XenServer 5.5

We now present a case study with the Citrix XenServer 5.5 virtualization platform. We apply our automated experimental analysis to evaluate the influence of the major performance-influencing factors. We chose Citrix XenServer 5.5 as the representative virtualization platform because it is a free solution with a significant market share and implementing current virtualization technologies based on the open source hypervisor Xen. We consider full virtualization because it is the most common type used in practice. As workload types, we investigate CPU, memory and network intensive workloads. Concerning the resource management configuration, we investigate the influences of the memory management and the credit-based CPU scheduler implemented in the Xen hypervisor. We also put a special focus on varying the number of co-located VMs.

5.1   Experimental Environment

We conducted experiments in two different hardware environments described below. In each considered scenario, unless stated otherwise, we used Windows 2003 Server as the native and guest OS hosting the benchmark application.

Environment 1: The purpose of the initial experiments was to evaluate the overhead of the virtualization layer. To this end, we used a standard desktop *HP Compaq dc5750* machine with an Athlon64 dual-core 4600+, 2.4 GHz. It has 4 GB DDR2-5300 of main memory, a 250 GB SATA HDD and a 10/100/1000-BaseT-Ethernet connection. We also used this hardware to run experiments on a single core of the CPU by deactivating the second core in the OS.

Environment 2: To evaluate the performance when scaling the number of VMs, we used a *SunFire* X4440 x64 Server. It has 4*2.4 GHz AMD Opteron 6 core processors with 3MB L2, 6MB L3 cache each, 128 GB DDR2-667 main memory, 8*300 GB of serial attached SCSI storage and 4*10/100/1000-BaseT-Ethernet connections.

5.2   Experimental Results

We now describe the different experiments we conducted. We consider three different scenarios. The target of the first scenario is to quantify the performance overhead of the Xen hypervisor for CPU and memory intensive workloads. The second scenario addresses the influences of core affinity. The third scenario analyses the influence of the number of VMs and specifically addresses the scalability of the virtualization platform.

Scenario 1 – Native vs. Virtualization: The purpose of this scenario is to compare the performance of the native system with a virtualized platform for CPU, memory and network intensive workloads. To this end, we executed Passmark, SPEC CPU2006 and Iperf benchmarks in native and virtualized environments. In the virtualized environment, we used only one VM executing the benchmark. The results of these experiments are depicted in Table 2. The relative delta is the ratio of absolute delta and native system performance. As one can see, the performance overhead of CPU intensive workloads is almost negligible. For both the Passmark and SPEC CPU2006 benchmark, the performance degradation when switching from a native to a virtualized system remains below 4%. The results from the two benchmarks are very similar in terms of the measured overhead and lead to the same conclusion. Moreover, the boxplots of the Passmark measurements in Figure 6 show a relatively low scattering. Please note the different y-axis scales in the sub-figures. Also consider that for the SPEC benchmark results we can only publish the relative delta because of licensing reasons.

When comparing the performance of a memory-intensive workload (Table 2), one can observe a much higher performance degradation, i.e., about 40%. The reason for this is the fact that CPU virtualization is well-understood and hardware supported, whereas memory virtualization is still rather immature and currently lacks hardware support [15].

Table 2. CPU, memory and network benchmark ratings for native and virtualized system on the HP Compaq dc5750

CPU Benchmark Ratings	native	virtualized	delta (abs.)	delta (rel.)
Passmark CPU, 1 core	639.3	634.0	5.3	0.83%
Passmark CPU, 2 cores	1232.0	1223.0	9.0	0.97%
SPECint(R)_base2006				3.61%
SPECfp(R)_base2006				3.15%
Memory Benchmark Ratings	**native**	**virtualized**	**delta (abs.)**	**delta (rel.)**
Passmark Memory, 1 core	492.9	297.0	195.9	39.74%
Passmark Memory, 2 cores	501.7	317.5	184.2	36.72%
Network Benchmark Ratings	**native**	**virtualized**	**delta (abs.)**	**delta (rel.)**
Iperf, Client to Server	527.0	393.0	134.0	25.43%
Iperf, Server to Client	528.0	370.0	158.0	29.92%

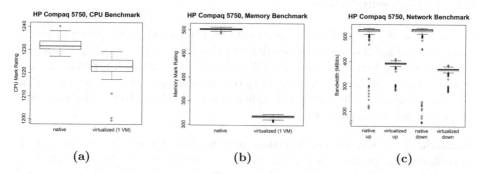

Fig. 6. Native vs. virtualized Passmark CPU and memory mark results and the Iperf benchmark results

Table 2 and Figure 6c depict the results of the network performance measurements with Iperf. In our experiment setup, client and server were connected with a DLink 1Gbit Switch and we used Windows2003 Server for both machines. We observe a performance decrease for TCP connections in both directions, upstream (Client to Server) 25% and downstream (Server to Client) 30%. This shows that like for memory virtualization there is still a relatively high performance loss because of lacking hardware support. Also interesting is that performance degradation of up- and downstream differs by 5%. Hence, it is important to consider the type of network traffic (up- or downstream)when modeling the workload.

As a preliminary result, we consider the performance overhead of CPU, memory and I/O virtualization to be 5% and 40% and 30%, respectively (in the case of full virtualization).

Scenario 2 – Core Affinity and Scalability: In a virtualized environment, the way VMs are scheduled to cores has a significant influence on the VMs' performance [2]. For example, imagine a machine with 24 cores, each core having its own cache. If a VM is re-scheduled from one core to another, its performance will suffer from cache misses because the benefit of a warm cache is lost. To avoid this, current virtualization platforms provide means to assign cores to VMs. In this scenario, we quantify the performance influence of core affinity considering the effect of scaling the number of co-located VMs. Core affinity denotes the assignment of virtual CPU(s) of VMs to dedicated physical cores, also called core pinning. In this case, the VM is executed only on the assigned core(s) which in turn has a significant influence on the cache and core contention and hence on performance. We also investigate the performance overhead when scaling the number of VMs up to the limit of available resources, i.e., CPU cores.

We tested the effect of core pinning using several experiments on the 24 core SunFire X4440 (see Table 3 and Figure 7). First, we compare the CPU and memory mark rating of one VM running with no affinity and one VM pinned to a dedicated core. In this case, performance changes about 0.80% for the CPU mark and 0.10% for the memory mark, so there is no measurable performance

Table 3. CPU and memory benchmark results for different core affinity experiments. The values shown are the median over all benchmark runs (200 for one VM, 200 ∗ 24 for 24 VMs) on the SunFire X4440.

	CPU Mark			Memory Mark		
	no affinity	with affinity	rel. delta	no affinity	with affinity	rel. delta
one VM	953.60	961.30	0.80%	339.95	339.60	0.10%
24 VMs	832.90	921.00	9.56%	198.40	244.40	18.82%
rel. delta	12.66%	4.19%	-	41.64%	28.03%	-

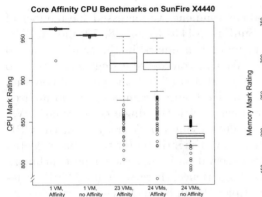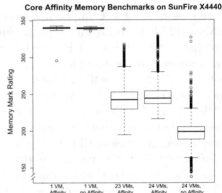

Fig. 7. Performance influence of core affinity in different experiments. The boxplots for multiple VMs contain the measurements over all VMs.

influence. However, when comparing the benchmark results of the same experiment for 24 VMs (each VM has one virtual CPU), performance increases by 88.1 (9.56%) and 46 (18.82%) for the CPU and memory mark, respectively.

The performance loss comparing one VM without affinity and 24 VMs without affinity is 120.7 (12.66%) and 141.55 (41.64%) for CPU and memory mark, respectively. However, when increasing the amount of VMs from one VM with core affinity to 24 VMs with core affinity, performance drops only by 40.3 (4.19%) and 95.2 (28.03%), respectively. Hence, on average 8.47% of the performance penalty for the CPU mark and 13.61% for the memory mark can be avoided when using core pinning. Also interesting is that the variability of the measurements increases with the number of co-located VMs. This leads to performance degradations of up to 10% in the worst case. Nonetheless, the difference between the median and mean values is negligible.

Another interesting fact observable in Figure 7 is that there is little difference in performance between 23 VMs and 24 VMs both with affinity. In the former case one core is left free for the hypervisor. The median of both measurements deviates only by 0.12% for the CPU mark and 0.83% for the memory mark.

Hence, leaving one core for the hypervisor has no significant effect on reducing the performance degradation introduced by virtualization.

From the above results we conclude that core affinity has a significant effect on virtualization platform's performance. We model this factor in such way that for predictions consider performance gains up to 20% relative to the ratio of executed virtual machines and available resources.

Scenario 3 – Overcommitment: In this scenario, we investigate the performance degradation when systematically overcommitting shared resources. In this scenario, we scale the amount of VMs (each VM is configured with one virtual CPU) above the amount of physically available CPUs by a factor x ranging between 1 and 4.

In case of the HP Compaq dc5750 environment, we increased the number of VMs to 2, 4, 6 and 8 and for the SunFire X4440 to 24, 48, 72 and 96. The absolute results for the CPU and memory benchmark in the SunFire X4440 environment are depicted in Figure 8. We also considered a single core scenario with the SunFire X4440 in which we deactivated all but one physical core and increased the number of VMs to 1, 2, 3 and 4. Figure 9 compares the normalized CPU rating of both hardware environments with the single core scenario. We observe that performance decreases roughly about $1/x$. Moreover, for the CPU benchmark, the measured performance is even slightly better than this expected theoretical value. The reason for this observation is that the single benchmark cannot utilize the CPU at completely 100%. Hence, there are unused CPU cycles which are utilized when executing multiple VMs in parallel. When increasing the number of VMs up to 72, we observed a CPU utilization of all cores at 100%. This effect however does not apply to the memory-intensive workload. Therefore the memory mark rating is slightly worse than the expected theoretical value. The single core performs better than the HP Compaq which in turn is better than the SunFire.

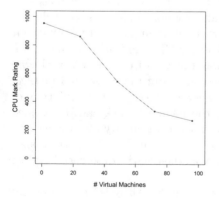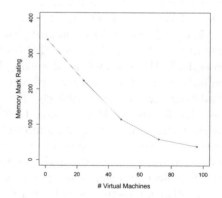

Fig. 8. Absolute scalability and overcommitment experiment results of the CPU and memory benchmark on SunFire X4440

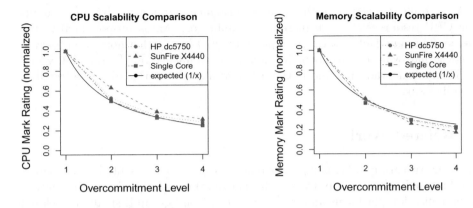

Fig. 9. Normalized scalability comparison of the HP dc5750, the SunFire X4440 and a single core for CPU and memory benchmark compared to the expected value of $1/x$

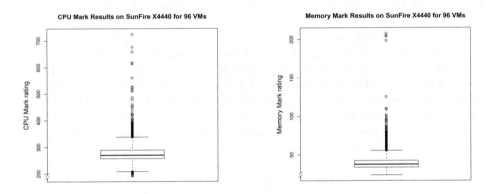

Fig. 10. Boxplots of CPU mark and memory mark results over all 96 VMs (overcommitment factor of 4)

From the results we see that the performance degradation can be approximated by $1/x$ which is the expected theoretical value. Intuitively, one might assume that performance decreases faster or even suddenly drops when overcommitting system resources. Moreover, one can see that performance degradation is very similar in both hardware environments (max. 10% deviation). This is remarkable because one would intuitively assume that the SunFire would perform significantly better because of the more resources it has available. Additionally, the boxplots in Figure 10 show the CPU and memory mark measurements over all 96 VMs. Although there is a relative huge positive deviation of the outliers from the median, the scattering around the median is low, indicating a fair resource sharing and good performance isolation.

As a result, we conclude that the performance degradation by overcommitting CPU resources through increasing number of VMs is proportional to the overcommitment factor with an upper limit of $1/x$. Furthermore, we observed that the hardware environment has almost no influence on the scalability and performance degradation and both CPU and memory workloads are affected in a similar way.

6   Related Work

There are two groups of existing work related to the work presented in this paper. The first and bigger group deals with benchmarking and performance analysis of virtualization platforms and solutions. The second group is small and related to this work in terms of modeling the performance-influencing factors.

In [3], Barham et al. present the Xen hypervisor and compare its performance to a native system, the VMware workstation 3.2 and a User-Mode Linux (comparable to container-based virtualization) on a high level of abstraction. They show that the performance is practically equivalent to a native Linux system and state that Xen is able to run up to 100 operating systems on a single server. Quétier et al. [14] follow a similar approach by benchmarking and analyzing the overhead, linearity and isolation for Linux-VServer 1.29, Xen 2.0, User-Mode Linux kernel 2.6.7 and VMware Workstation 3.2. Soltesz et al. propose an alternative to the Xen hypervisor, the container-based virtualization Linux-VServer [16]. In their work they evaluate the Linux-VServer with Xen3 performance with system benchmarks and compare performance in scalability scenarios. Similar is the work by Padala et al., where the authors compare Xen 3.0.3 unstable with OpenVZ, another container-based virtualization solution [12]. Both approaches conclude that a container-based virtualization performs better than the hypervisor solution, especially for I/O intensive workloads. In [2], Apparao et al. analyze the performance characteristic of a server consolidation workload. They study the performance slowdown of each workload due to consolidation. Their results show that most of the performance loss of CPU intensive workloads is caused by cache and core interferences. They also show that core affinity can mitigate this problem. However, they do not consider the virtualization overhead due to consolidation. Moreover, the considered virtualization solutions have changed a lot since the above results were published (e.g., hardware support was introduced) which renders them outdated. For example, meanwhile Xen 4.0 has been released, introducing a lot of new features. Hence the results of these works must be revised especially to evaluate the influences of hardware support. Moreover, all the work presented do not come up with a model of the performance-influencing factors nor do they propose a systematic approach to quantify their impact.

The second area of related work is the modeling of virtualization platforms or shared resources. Tickoo et al. identify three challenges of VM modeling, namely modeling the contention of the visible and invisible resources and the hypervisor [17]. In their consecutive work based on [2] and [17], Iyer et al. measure and model the influences of VM shared resources. The concept they present is a virtual platform architecture (VPA) with a transparent shared resource management [8]. They show the importance of shared resource contention on virtual machine performance. However, their model only focuses on cache and core effects and does not consider other performance-influencing factors. There is still a lot of work to do on measuring, benchmarking and analyzing different virtualization solutions and their performance-relevant factors. Particularly because virtualization is a technology improving and changing very quickly, it is difficult to keep benchmark results and models up-to-date.

7   Conclusion and Future Work

In this paper, we presented a generic feature model of the performance-influencing factors of virtualization platforms. We proposed a benchmark-based methodology for quantifying the effect of the identified factors and applied the methodology to analyze and quantify the performance-influencing factors and properties of the Citrix XenServer 5.5. The results showed that performance degradation for CPU intensive workloads on full virtualized platforms is below 5% and for network workloads below 30%, and memory intensive workloads suffer from performance degradation of up to 40%. We also showed that core affinity has a considerable influence on reducing the performance degradation. Our scalability experiments revealed that performance degradation is independent of the hardware environment and is roughly proportional to the overcommitment factor. Moreover, it is remarkable that performance converges to the reciprocal of the overcommitment-factor and does not suddenly drop when overcommitting resources.

As a next step, we plan to study further performance influencing factors considering other virtualization platforms such as VMware. In addition, we plan to use the results of this work as input in the Descartes research project to predict the performance of services deployed in dynamic virtualized environments, e.g., Cloud Computing [5,9].

References

1. Adams, K., Agesen, O.: A comparison of software and hardware techniques for x86 virtualization. In: Proceedings of ASPLOS (2006)
2. Apparao, P., Iyer, R., Zhang, X., Newell, D., Adelmeyer, T.: Characterization & Analysis of a Server Consolidation Benchmark. In: VEE 2008: Proceedings of the 4th Int. Conference on Virtual Execution Environments (2008)
3. Barham, P., Dragovic, B., Fraser, K., Hand, S., Harris, T., Ho, A., Neugebauer, R., Pratt, I., Warfield, A.: Xen and the Art of Virtualization. In: SOSP 2003: Proceedings of the 19th Symposium on Operating Systems Principle (2003)
4. Czarnecki, K., Eisenecker, U.W.: Generative Programming. Addison-Wesley, Reading (2000)
5. Descartes Research Group (June 2010), http://www.descartes-research.net
6. IDC. Virtualization Market Accelerates Out of the Recession as Users Adopt "Virtualize First" Mentality, According to IDC (April 2010)

7. IT world, The IDG Network. Gartner's data on energy consumption, virtualization, cloud (2008),
http://www.itworld.com/green-it/59328/
gartners-data-energy-consumption-virtualization-cloud
8. Iyer, R., Illikkal, R., Tickoo, O., Zhao, L., Apparao, P., Newell, D.: VM3: Measuring, modeling and managing VM shared resources. Computer Networks 53(17), 2873–2887 (2009)
9. Kounev, S., Brosig, F., Huber, N., Reussner, R.: Towards self-aware performance and resource management in modern service-oriented systems. In: Proceedings of the 7th IEEE International Conference on Services Computing (2010)
10. Menascé, D.A.: Virtualization: Concepts, applications, and performance modeling. In: Int. CMG Conference, pp. 407–414 (2005)
11. Menascé, D.A., Almeida, V.A.F., Dowdy, L.W.: Capacity Planning and Performance Modeling - From Mainframes to Client-Server Systems. P.-H. (1994)
12. Padala, P., Zhu, X., Wang, Z., Singhal, S., Shin, K.G.: Performance evaluation of virtualization technologies for server consolidation. HP Labs Tec. Report (2007)
13. Parziale, L., Alves, E.L., Dow, E.M., Egeler, K., Herne, J.J., Jordan, C., Naveen, E.P., Pattabhiraman, M.S., Smith, K.: Introduction to the New Mainframe: z/VM Basics. IBM Redbooks (2007)
14. Quétier, B., Néri, V., Cappello, F.: Scalability Comparison of Four Host Virtualization Tools. Jounal on Grid Computing 5(1), 83–98 (2007)
15. Rosenblum, M., Garfinkel, T.: Virtual machine monitors: current technology and future trends. Computer 38(5), 39–47 (2005)
16. Soltesz, S., Pötzl, H., Fiuczynski, M.E., Bavier, A., Peterson, L.: Container-based operating system virtualization: a scalable, high-performance alternative to hypervisors. SIGOPS Oper. Syst. Rev. 41(3), 275–287 (2007)
17. Tickoo, O., Iyer, R., Illikkal, R., Newell, D.: Modeling virtual machine performance: Challenges and approaches. In: HotMetrics (2009)
18. Vallee, G., Naughton, T., Ong, C.E.H., Scott, S.L.: System-level virtualization for high performance computing. In: Proc. of PDP (2008)
19. VMware. A Performance Comparison of Hypervisors (2007)

Measuring Software Systems Scalability for Proactive Data Center Management*

Nuno A. Carvalho and José Pereira

Computer Science and Technology Center
Universidade do Minho
Braga, Portugal
{nuno,jop}@di.uminho.pt

Abstract. The current trend of increasingly larger Web-based applications makes scalability the key challenge when developing, deploying, and maintaining data centers. At the same time, the migration to the cloud computing paradigm means that each data center hosts an increasingly complex mix of applications, from multiple owners and in constant evolution. Unfortunately, managing such data centers in a cost-effective manner requires that the scalability properties of the hosted workloads to be accurately known, namely, to proactively provision adequate resources and to plan the most economical placement of applications. Obviously, stopping each of them and running a custom benchmark to asses its scalability properties is not an option. In this paper we address this challenge with a tool to measure the software scalability regarding CPU availability, to predict system behavior in face of varying resources and an increasing workload. This tool does not depend on a particular application and relies only on Linux's SystemTap probing infrastructure. We validate the approach first using simulation and then in an actual system. The resulting better prediction of scalability properties should allow improved (self-)management practices.

Keywords: Scalability, Self-management, Monitoring, Provisioning.

1 Introduction

Managing current data-centers is an increasingly challenging task. On one hand, virtualization and cloud computing mean that there is more flexibility and more opportunities to act upon systems to optimize their performance. On the other hand, the sheer size and complexity of applications, along with the pace of change, means that chances of eventually getting to know their behavior are slim. As a consequence, there is a growing call for self-management[1], in which such complexity is managed by the system itself, and more recently, in applying systematic methods to enable informed management decisions[2].

Consider first the impact of virtualization and cloud computing in provisioning hardware resources. Traditionally, allocating server hardware was a lengthy process leading to acquisition of expensive systems that would last for quite some time. Moreover, each system would typically be dedicated to a fixed task throughout its useful life, until it

---

* Partially funded by PT Inovação S.A.

R. Meersman et al. (Eds.): OTM 2010, Part II, LNCS 6427, pp. 829–842, 2010.

became obsolete. Currently, one can perform such provisioning decision multiple times everyday and then be able to smoothly migrate application components, housed in virtual machines, between servers or even between multiple data centers. This flexibility can be used to closely match application demands with hardware characteristics. Consider the following example: An organization that has a diversity of hardware ranging from low end servers, with a small number of cores and a small amount memory to some large servers, with tens of cores and several hundred gigabytes of memory. A large application can be run on a cluster of independent servers or on a large partition of a powerful server. On the other hand, several small applications can take one small server each, or a number of smaller partitions of the larger server. The same must then be considered for other resources, such as network bandwidth and placement, storage bandwidth, and so on.

Consider then the impact of continuous change in applications. For instance, a telecom operator is often proposing novel and more complex services, or the "eternal beta" approach to Web applications and on-line businesses. This means that the performance characteristics of an application can change frequently and often in ways that were unforeseen by developers, namely, by introducing dependencies on new resources or external services, or by intrinsically changing the processing complexity of common operations or the amount of time some mutual exclusion lock is held. Note that these changes can be subtle, but invalidate the basis on which provisioning decisions were made and lead to the disruption of service when, during peak periods, the system fails to scale as expected.

Most self-management proposals that have been prototyped and can be applied in a real setting, reduce to a simple feedback control loops to adapt system parameters or structure [3], thus failing to properly address continuous change. The adaptation policy is defined explicitly by administrators for the system as a whole and the ability to foresee and cope with the impact of design and development decisions is thus limited. Therefore, such proposals are mostly useless for large scale systems since the ad-hoc definition and maintenance of the management component is not feasible. On the other hand, the most encouraging proposals focus on adaptation policies that can be derived from an abstract model of the system and high level goals. However, the effectiveness is only as good as the underlying understanding of the system as a whole and ability to keep the model current with system evolution. Unfortunately, a large portion of the effort is in accurately modeling specific systems [4].

In this paper we address this challenge with a contribution focused on the key issue of CPU scalability. In detail, we propose a method and a tool for assessing the CPU scalability curve of an application. In contrast to previous approaches [5], we rely only on passive monitoring of production systems and not on a set of benchmarks performed off-line. This allows us to continuously assess the impact of each change to the system and, using the scalability curve, derive at each time the most promising resource provisioning solution to cope with increasing traffic *proactively*.

The rest of the paper is structured as follows. In Section 2 we briefly survey existing scalability assessment methods and the key scalability facts. In Section 3 we derive the main scalability formula from a queuing model of a computing system. Section 4 then shows the validation of the formula using simulation. Section 5 shows how passive monitoring can be implemented in real systems. Finally, Section 6 concludes the paper.

2   Related Work

Scalability assessment is a key enabler for effectively managing Web applications that are able to cope with workload spikes and thus must be be built in at an early stage of design and development. The most common method to assess it is to use synthetic benchmarks such as TPC-W [6], where representative operations are tested and apportioned a weight to faithfully reproduce typical use. The benchmark is then scaled up until the maximum capacity of the system is determined. Besides requiring potentially a lot of resources to discover system capacity this method is only as reliable as the knowledge of the target system which causes the original benchmarks to lose their representativeness. If the benchmark does not adequately capture actual usage its result is hopelessly compromised, because all conclusions are supported on false assumptions.

In fact, the scalability of computing systems is described by a simple equation known as Amdahl's law [7], that models the relationship between the increase in the number of processors and the speedup of an parallel algorithm, while the implementation remains constant. More precisely the speedup is modeled as Eq. 1, where $(1 - P)$ represents the sequential portion of the algorithm, P the parallel one and N the number of processors, i.e., as N increases, the sequential part is being increasingly significant limiting scalability, as shown in Fig. 1.

$$speedup = \frac{1}{(1 - P) + \frac{P}{N}} .\qquad(1)$$

This simple equation give us the maximum speedup, or scalability, that a system can achieve without software modifications, thus giving us a simple and deterministic way

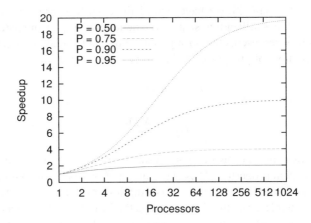

Fig. 1. The speedup of a program using multiple processors in parallel computing is limited by the sequential fraction of the program

of classifying systems. This relation has since been extended to model also shared resources and been called the Universal Law of Computational Scalability [8]. The number of benchmark runs can thus be reduced by fitting the expected curve to a small set of
results using linear regression [5]. Nonetheless, this still shares the problems of standard
synthetic benchmarks: The validity of results is directly proportional to the knowledge
of the system and representativeness of the workload; it is necessary to stop the system
to run the benchmark, which often is simply impossible; beyond that does not work for
varying workloads, i.e., only works for constant workloads, because any reduction in
throughput is interpreted as a loss of scalability and not workload variation.

The same approach can be used for software scalability [9], in which the number
of processors is a constant and the independent variable is the number of concurrent
clients. This benchmark gives us, once again limited by the assumptions, the expected
behavior of the system to increase the number of concurrent clients, in particular the
point at which the system goes into thrashing.

3   Passive Observation

As stated in Section 2, benchmarks are impractical to use in production systems, due the
constant evolution that makes very hard to effectively know all the system components
and the lack of representativeness of the workload over time. Furthermore, we need to
stop the system to run the benchmark, which in most cases is not an option.

To solve this problem we present a tool to measure the software scalability regarding
CPU availability, without stop or disturbing the system. It is based on passive observation, only depending on Linux's SystemTap probing infrastructure and current CPU
load. Our tool is a mix of three techniques: Amdahl's law, operational laws [10] and
queueing models [11].

3.1   Relations between Measurements

Recalling Amdahl's law [7], we have two distinct types of processing, and therefore
two types of resources utilization: sequential, denoted by Eq. 2; and parallel denoted by
Eq. 3. In which X represents the throughput, D the CPU delay (time spent to perform
a job), N the number of processors and p the parallel portion.

$$Us = XD(1-p) . \tag{2}$$

$$Up = \frac{XDp}{N_p} . \tag{3}$$

As our tool allows direct measurements, we can use the operational laws to extract relations of the system properties. These laws are relations based on assumptions that can
be proved by measurements, unlike the assumptions of the queuing models supported
on statistical principles. The first law we use is the Little's law [12], denoted by Eq. 4 in
which Q is mean queue length, that includes the jobs being served, λ is the arrival rate
and R is the mean time of jobs in the system.

$$Q = \lambda R . \tag{4}$$

Since the systems we analyse have a balanced job flow [10], i.e., the number of jobs served equals the number of jobs submitted, we can use the variation denoted by Eq. 5, because the arrival rate is equal to the throughput.

$$Q = XR.$$
(5)

From Queueing Models we know that in the case of M/M/1 queues, those used to model the sequential utilization, represented by Eq. 2, the average number of jobs in the system is given by Eq. 6, where in turn traffic intensity (ρ) is given by Eq. 7. Since the systems analyzed here adhere to the balanced job flow principle, once again, the arrival rate can be replaced by the throughput. The service rate in jobs per unit time can be calculated by the CPU delay, as we are in the case of sequential utilization, i.e., only one job can be done at a time, just divide that by the time necessary to execute the sequential portion of each job Eq. 8. Through these equivalences, Eq. 9, we can infer that the traffic intensity (ρ) for the sequential resources is equal to its utilization, causing the average number of jobs in system be equal to Eq. 10.

$$E[n] = \frac{\rho}{1 - \rho}.$$
(6)

$$\rho = \frac{\lambda}{\mu}.$$
(7)

$$\mu = \frac{1}{D_s}$$
(8)

$$\rho = \frac{\lambda}{\mu} = \frac{X}{\frac{1}{D_s}} = XD_s = XD(1 - p) = U_s.$$
(9)

$$E[n] = \frac{U_s}{1 - U_s}.$$
(10)

Applying the same reasoning to parallel utilization, using M/M/m queuing models, we know that the average number of jobs in the system is given by Eq. 11, where ρ is given by Eq. 12, where m represents the number of resources that can be used simultaneously. Again, given the balanced job flow principle, arrival rate can be replaced by the throughput. But now the aggregate service rate ($m\mu$) is equivalent to the number of CPU resources over the delay Eq. 13, but in this case, the time spent by the parallel tasks. This means that the traffic intensity is given by Eq. 14, i.e., again given by the utilization, now parallel. This means that the average number of jobs in system is given by Eq. 15.

$$E[n] = m\rho + \frac{\rho\varrho}{1 - \rho}.$$
(11)

$$\rho = \frac{\lambda}{m\mu}.$$
(12)

$$m\mu = \frac{N_p}{D_p}$$
(13)

$$\rho = \frac{\lambda}{m\mu} = \frac{X}{\frac{N_p}{D_p}} = \frac{X D_p}{N_p} = \frac{X Dp}{N_p} = U_p \; . \tag{14}$$

$$E[n] = mU_p + \frac{U_p \varrho}{1 - U_p} \; . \tag{15}$$

Recalling the Little's law on Eq. 5, with which we calculate the mean queue length, a value also achievable through queueing models with Eq. 10, for the sequential utilization we can say that this two formulas are equivalent, Eq. 16, and that the mean response time of jobs in the system is given by Eq. 17.

$$E[n] = Q_s \Leftrightarrow Q_s = \frac{U_s}{1 - U_s} \; . \tag{16}$$

$$R_s = \frac{Q_s}{X} \; . \tag{17}$$

3.2   Asymptotic Bounds

With these relations we can estimate the typical asymptotic bounds of the systems under consideration, good indicators of the performance of a system, they indicate the factor that is limiting performance. The throughput bounds are Eq. 18; i) the case of sequential utilization, only limited by the sequential part of the job, because only one job can use the resource; ii) the parallel utilization, which is now limited not only by the service time of the system but also by the number of processors; iii) the case limited by clients N_c, which also depends on the CPU delay and clients interval between requests Z.

$$X \le min\{\frac{1}{D(1 - p)}, \frac{N_p}{D_p}, \frac{N_c}{D + Z}\} \; . \tag{18}$$

But despite good indicators, these values are just that, what we want are real values and current performance of the system, ideally without having to stop or disrupt the system.

3.3   System Scalability

Lets recall once more the Amdhal's law Eq. 1, in which the utilization of a system is modeled by Eq. 19, i.e., composed by sequential and parallel utilization. To measure the scalability of a system, besides being necessary to have precise measurements, the time at which they are obtained is also of extreme importance, to the point of if the moment is badly chosen is quite impossible to distinguish between bad scalability or a slow down in workload.

$$U = \frac{U_s + U_p}{N} \; . \tag{19}$$

Our solution is based on the choice of times when the system is limited by the sequential part Eq. 20, which belongs to the first interval of the system asymptotic bounds. This makes that the system utilization, in this critical moment, is represented by Eq. 21, that through Eq. 3 can be written like Eq. 22. The throughput X is calculated by Eq. 23, in which the measure throughput of the system U_x is given by the ratio of the number of CPUs and CPU delay multiplied by the utilization of CPUs that are conducting parallel tasks. So, this makes that utilization is given by Eq. 24. Solving this equation in the order to p means that we can measure the scalability of the system by the Eq. 25, that only depends on processors number and measured utilization.

$$U_s = 1 . \tag{20}$$

$$U = \frac{1 + U_p}{N} . \tag{21}$$

$$U = \frac{1 + X D_p}{N} . \tag{22}$$

$$X = \frac{N}{D} U_x . \tag{23}$$

$$U = \frac{1 + \frac{N}{D} U_x D p}{N} = \frac{1 + N U_x p}{N} . \tag{24}$$

$$p = -\frac{1 - N U_x}{N U_x} . \tag{25}$$

For example, if a node with 4 processors at the time that the sequential utilization is equal to 1, i.e., we have requests waiting to be able to use the sequential resource, and the measured utilization is 0.33, that means that its p is 0.24, which is really bad, because many of its processors are stalled waiting for sequential tasks, which means that this node does not scale out.

$$p = -\frac{1 - 4 * 0.33}{4 * 0.33} = 0.24(24) .$$

4   Validation

We validate the applicability of our approach through simulation, using the architecture on Fig. 2, in which there is one sequential resource for which the requests sequential portion is directed and resources that can be used in parallel, in this case 4, to handle the requests parallel portion. Sequential portions, once inserted in a queue, are sent one by one to the parallel resources in order to faithfully mimic what happens in reality, including the dependency between sequential ans parallel portions. The queues contain requests that have been accepted but not yet been done due to lack of available resources. Being a simulation, usage of sequential and parallel resources can easily be accounted for.

In Fig. 3 we see the accuracy of our approach, in this case we have a node with 4 processors that receives the load of 10 clients. The proportion of the parallel portion is 0.4, and hence the sequential part is 0.6. The points where the p value is calculated

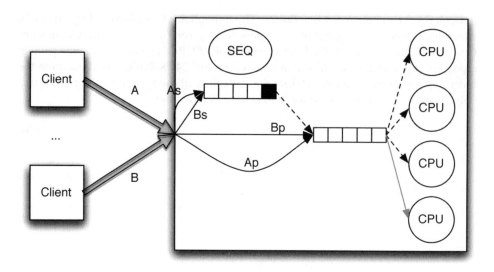

Fig. 2. Simulation architecture

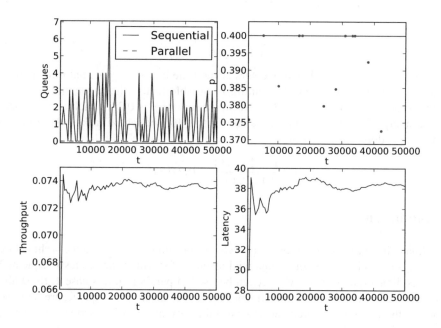

Fig. 3. Simulation for $p = 0.4$ with 4 CPUs and 10 clients

(green dots on the second chart) correspond to samples when there is contention on the sequential resource, i.e., there is queueing. Our tool has an error of only hundredths in the estimation of the value of p, due to the measurements being performed in the precise moments in which there is contention.

Our tool only loses accuracy when the p value is high, above 0.6, which is supposed because all resources are suffering from contention, making the formula ineffective, since it assumes the only resource that suffers contention is the sequential. This is evident in Fig. 4, on which are shown the estimate p values, where the injected p goes from 0.1 to 0.9. Being in the x-axis the value of injected p and in the y-axis the estimated value, where the node contains 4 processors and receives requests from 10 clients.

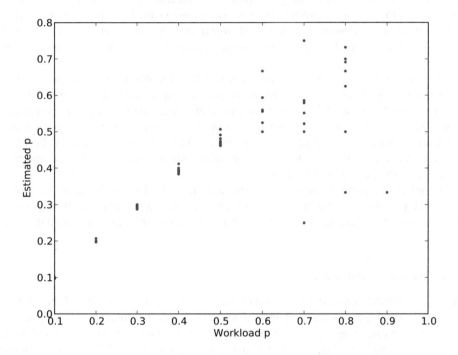

Fig. 4. Simulations for p between 0.1 and 0.9

5   Implementation

5.1   Challenges

After validating the approach, the implementation of the scalability assessment tool must address the challenge of measuring sequential and parallel resource utilization. The problem is that general purpose instrumentation and monitoring interfaces such as SNMP [13] or JMX [14] (the latter only for Java Virtual Machines) are not enough to estimate the scalability of a system. These provide real time access to statistical measurements such as resource usage occupancy or event counts, as well as notifications of exceptions and faults, but without knowing in which asymptotic bound the system is (Eq. 18), making its measurements uninteresting for this problem. The same problem occurs in the use of the Unix load average number, the average system load over a period of time, that despite being an interesting measure remains indifferent to critical areas.

So, the more complicated challenge is the identification of the contention moments in sequential resources, which itself leads to another question "What resources are sequential?", since in real environments there are no centralized points of contention. We resolve this matter considering the sequential resources areas of code protected by locks in concurrent tasks, but the problem to measure the contention still remains.

In Linux in particular, locking is done using the kernel *futex* primitive. As this is invoked for contended cases only it provides the ideal triggering mechanism. The invocation of this primitive can be observed using the SystemTap infrastructure [15,16], which allows us to activate and use in real-time traces and probes directly on the kernel. SystemTap eliminates the need to instrument, recompile, install, and reboot applications or system to collect data.

As we evaluate the scalability in terms of CPU, the points of contention will be synchronized accesses to areas protected by locks in concurrent tasks, i.e., areas of code that can only be executed by a process or thread at a time. To identify these competition areas we use the SystemTap infrastructure, that allows insight on the contention zones, without having to know and/or edit the application that is running, allowing to be aware when is requested exclusive access to a given resource, when it is released and how many requests are waiting for access.

To accurately estimate the scalability we need the CPU load in the same timeline as SystemTap probes, to do that we are continuously calculating the contention windows in order to obtain the lowest possible error, in most cases negligible, as we shall see in Sec. 5.4.

5.2 Hardware and Software

The experimental evaluation described in this paper was performed using three HP Proliant dual Dual-Core Opteron processor machines with the configuration outlined in Table 1. The operating system used is Linux, kernel version 2.6.24-28, from Ubuntu. Both clients and servers are programed in C and compiled with GCC 4.2.4 without any special flags.

Table 1. System specifications

Resource	Properties
Processor	$2 \times$ Dual-Core AMD Opteron Processor (64 bits)
RAM	12 GBytes
Operating System	Linux 2.6.24-28 (Ubuntu Kernel)
Network	Gigabit

5.3 Measurements

A run consists in having one multi-thread server, or several servers, deployed in one node that handles the workload generated by 12 clients that are located in another two nodes, as shown in Fig. 5. Clients submit requests to the server that need access to restricted areas to perform their operations, the portion of access to restricted areas depends on the value of parameter p. Although experiments have been reproduced with

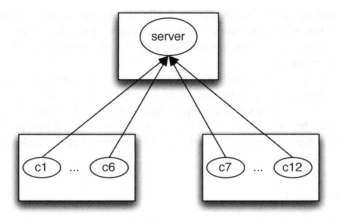

Fig. 5. Real system deployed

different workloads, this paper includes only results obtained by using the lightest workload that have a few points of contention on sequential resources, each request without
concurrency takes on average 403ms to be executed (on server side, this time does not
include network usage) and the clients think time is on average 100ms. We choose this
workload because it is the more interesting one, if we choose a heavy workload, the sequential resources will be always suffering from queuing making the estimation trivial,
on the other hand, if the workload was too light would be impossible to estimate the
value of p, since any resources will be a bottleneck.

CPU load is measured concurrently by running Dstat [17] every second. Dstat is a
standard resource statistics tool, which collects memory, disk I/O, network, and CPU usage information available from the operating system kernel. All measurements therefore

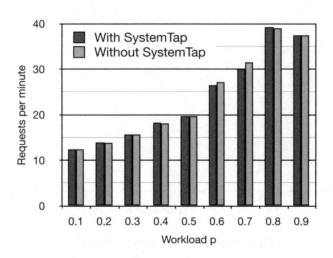

Fig. 6. Request rate per minute with and without SystemTap probes for the different p values

include all load on each of the machines. Locks measurements are also made concurrently by SystemTap probes, both CPUs and locks measurements are read continuously in order to discover the contention windows to allow the estimation of the p value for the running applications.

The SystemTap probes adds a little latency to the system calls observed, however in this case specifically, as the two probes used only insert and remove the entry and exit timestamps of the several mutexes, being these information dumped through a periodic event, the added latency is almost negligible, as shown in Fig. 6 that plots the request rate per minute for the different p values with and without probes, allowing its use in production systems.

5.4   Results

In real environment our tool is even more precise than in simulation, due to SystemTap precision and real CPU load, in real environment it only loses accuracy when the p value is higher than 0.7, but once more, this is supposed to happens due the assumption that only the sequential resources are suffering from contention. The p estimations are plotted on Fig. 7, on which the injected p goes from 0.1 to 0.9, with a configuration of 4 CPUs and 12 clients.

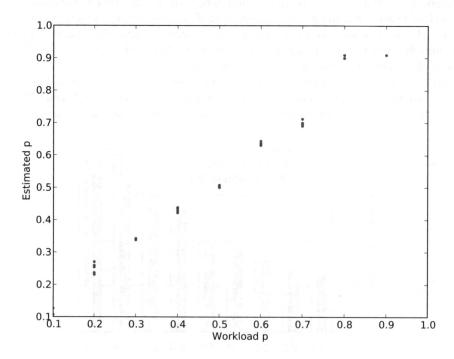

Fig. 7. Real results for p between 0.1 and 0.9

6 Conclusions and Future Work

In this paper we present a novel solution to calculate the scalability of a system, in which is not necessary to know or change the applications that are running. This tool runs concurrently with the deployed system without the need to stop, interrupt or change settings thus respecting one of the major requirements of a production system. As it runs concurrently, it produces results that are calculated on live data and not just projections of possible behaviors, such as those offered by other solutions [5,9].

As the scalability estimation is only carried out at critical moments of the system, more specifically when there is contention on sequential resources, these values are extremely accurate, especially for small values of p, where it is most meaningful to perform this analysis, because any small improvement will have a major impact on the scalability of the system, reducing the weight of the sequential portion in the aggregate performance.

The simulation module in addition to provide a proof of concept, also works as a workbench capable of answer questions like "What if?". The parameters of the systems components under consideration are customizable, allowing to experience how the system behave, for example, with more processors and/or clients, or even with different architectures, simply by changing the way the components are connected together. Whether the scalability analysis itself or the chance to experience different settings allow improved proactive (self-) management practices.

These key features pave the way for future development in several directions. First, it is interesting perform this same analysis for other types of resources, such as disk I/O, memory or network, ideally with the interference that each one causes to the others. Second, conducting analysis of multi-tier systems, being able to relate, for example, that the latency of component X is due to poor scalability of a resource located in another node or instance. Finally, estimate the system scalability taking all these factors into account, allowing the system classification as a whole.

References

1. Middleware: ACM/IFIP/USENIX 9th International Middleware Conference (2008), http://middleware2008.cs.kuleuven.be/keynotes.php
2. Spector, A.: Distributed computing at multidimensional scale (2008), http://middleware2008.cs.kuleuven.be/AZSMiddleware08Keynote-Shared.pdf
3. Bouchenak, S., Palma, N.D., Hagimont, D., Taton, C.: Autonomic management of clustered applications. In: IEEE International Conference on Cluster Computing, Barcelona, Spain (September 2006)
4. Jung, G., Joshi, K.R., Hiltunen, M.A., Schlichting, R.D., Pu, C.: Generating adaptation policies for multi-tier applications in consolidated server environments. In: International Conference on Autonomic Computing, pp. 23–32 (2008)
5. Gunther, N.J.: Evaluating Scalability Parameters. In: Guerrilla Capacity Planning: A Tactical Approach to Planning for Highly Scalable Applications and Services, ch. 5. Springer, New York (2006)
6. Transaction Processing Performance Council (TPC): TPC benchmark W (Web Commerce) Specification Version 1.7 (2001)

7. Amdahl, G.M.: Validity of the single processor approach to achieving large scale computing capabilities. In: Proceedings of the Spring Joint Computer Conference, AFIPS 1967 (Spring), April 18-20, pp. 483–485. ACM, New York (1967)
8. Gunther, N.J.: Scalability - A Quantitative Approach. In: Guerrilla Capacity Planning: A Tactical Approach to Planning for Highly Scalable Applications and Services, USA, ch. 4. Springer, New York (2006)
9. Gunther, N.J.: Software Scalability. In: Guerrilla Capacity Planning: A Tactical Approach to Planning for Highly Scalable Applications and Services, ch. 6. Springer, New York (2006)
10. Jain, R.: Operational Laws. In: The Art of Computer Systems Performance Analysis: Techniques for Experimental Design, Measurement, Simulation and Modeling, ch. 33. John Wiley & Sons, Inc., New York (1991)
11. Jain, R.: Analysis of a Single Queue. In: The Art of Computer Systems Performance Analysis: Techniques for Experimental Design, Measurement, Simulation and Modeling, ch. 31. John Wiley & Sons, Inc., New York (1991)
12. Jain, R.: Introduction to Queueing Theory. In: The Art of Computer Systems Performance Analysis: Techniques for Experimental Design, Measurement, Simulation and Modeling, ch. 30. John Wiley & Sons, Inc., New York (1991)
13. A simple network management protocol (SNMP). RFC 1157 (1990)
14. Java management extensions (JMX) (2004), http://java.sun.com/developer/technicalArticles/J2SE/jmx.html
15. Prasad, V., Cohen, W., Hunt, M., Keniston, J., Chen, B.: Architecture of systemtap: a linux trace/probe tool (2005), http://sourceware.org/systemtap/archpaper.pdf
16. Red Hat, IBM, Intel, Hitachi, Oracle and others: Systemtap (2010), http://sourceware.org/systemtap/
17. Wieërs, D.: Dstat (2009), http://dag.wieers.com/home-made/dstat/

Semantic Similarity Model for Risk Assessment in Forming Cloud Computing SLAs

Omar Hussain, Hai Dong, and Jaipal Singh

Digital Ecosystems and Business Intelligence Institute
Curtin University of Technology, GPO Box U1987
Perth, Australia
{O.Hussain,Hai.Dong,J.Singh}@cbs.curtin.edu.au

Abstract. Cloud computing has enabled users to access various resources and applications as a service and in return pay the provider only for the time for which they are used. Service Level Agreements (SLA) are formed between the user and provider to ensure that the required services and applications are delivered as expected. With the increase of public cloud providers, challenges such as availability, reliability, security, privacy and transactional risk demand detailed assessment during the formation of SLAs. This paper focuses on one subcategory of transactional risk while forming SLAs: namely, performance risk. We argue that performance risk assessment should be done by the user before entering into an SLA with a service provider. We propose to measure performance risk according to the specific context and assessment criteria with the aid of a semantic similarity model for the SLA requirement being negotiated in a cloud computing environment. We show through simulations that the performance risk analysis is more accurate using semantic similarity matching compared with analysis without semantic similarity matching.

Keywords: Performance Risk, Service Level Agreement, Cloud Computing, Context, Assessment Criteria, Semantic Similarity Model.

1 Introduction

Cloud Computing means different things to different people. To some, cloud computing is similar to thin-client Web-based applications, while others consider it as a computing utility that charges metered rates for every service. Some regard it as a means of efficiently processing scalability through highly distributed or parallel computing. However people look at cloud computing, it is an enabler for a new paradigm in computing.

In this paper, we define cloud computing as a model that commoditises resources, software and information as services, and delivers them in a manner similar to traditional utilities such as electricity and water. In such a model, users access services based on their requirements at a particular point in time regardless of where the services are hosted or how they are delivered.

Previous work in cloud computing focussed on technological frameworks for implementation and deployment of user services on the cloud, such as software as a

R. Meersman et al. (Eds.): OTM 2010, Part II, LNCS 6427, pp. 843–860, 2010.
© Springer-Verlag Berlin Heidelberg 2010

service (SaaS), infrastructure as a service (IaaS), platform as a service (PaaS), etc. While these cloud computing resources are controlled and provided by the service provider, the cloud consumer needs to ensure that the quality, availability, reliability and performance of these resources meets their business functionality requirements. The consumers need to obtain guarantees from providers on service delivery to ensure that their business functions smoothly, and a means for recovery or compensation if these guarantees are not met. These are provided through Service Level Agreements (SLAs) negotiated between the providers and consumers.

An SLA is an extremely important document, as it (1) identifies and defines customer needs and expectations, (2) provides a mechanism to weight, verify, evaluate and enforce the agreed criteria, and (3) provides an appropriate level of granularity to trade-off between expressiveness and complexity. A typical SLA should contain a definition of required services, the methods for monitoring and measuring service performance, methods for compensation or indemnity for services provided, processes to manage unplanned incidents, customer duties and responsibilities to support the service delivery, security policies and procedures, disaster recovery, and termination of SLA.

Thus, a well-defined SLA will provide a framework for understanding, reduce areas of conflict, encourage dialogue in the event of disputes, and eliminate unrealistic expectations between provider and consumer [1]. As cloud computing provides different cloud offerings (IaaS, PaaS, and SaaS), there is a need to define different SLA meta-specifications. Some work has been done in defining cloud SLA models, performance criteria and measurement [2], and development of a standardised Web SLA language [3]. However, this work cannot be directly applied to every type of cloud service [4].

The cloud provider must monitor any changes in the cloud environment in order to make real-time evaluation and adjustment for SLA fulfilment. Fast and effective decision models and optimisation algorithms are needed for this. Providers may also need to reject resource requests when SLAs cannot be met. These operations need to be carried out in a nearly automatic fashion due to the promise of "self-service" in cloud computing [5]. Once a business association has been established, this real-time information is also used by consumers to measure the quality of cloud service provided and calculate the probability of an SLA violation occurring [6, 7].

While this is important, we believe it is far more beneficial for a consumer to assess and manage this risk before an SLA is formalized. This is achieved through transactional risk assessment before entering into an SLA with a service provider. This assists the consumer to make an informed decision when selecting the most appropriate service provider with which to form an SLA from a given set of possible cloud service providers.

Therefore, we propose a transactional risk framework to aid consumers in pre-selecting an IaaS cloud service provider. We will highlight the importance of risk in decision-making when forming an SLA and existing approaches for providing risk-based decision making in Section 2. In Section 3, we propose a new transactional risk assessment framework to model risk criteria and identify the similarity between different risk criteria faced by other agents. The risk assessment models for making a decision in selecting a cloud service provider are defined in Section 4. The results are shown in Section 5. Finally, we conclude the paper in Section 6.

2 Related Work

2.1 Assessing Transactional Risk

SLA negotiations are carried out between the consumer and service provider so the consumer can decide which provider can provide services that maximises the successful achievement of the consumer's desired outcomes and minimises any losses. To do this, the consumer will make a decision by analysing criteria that it considers to be important, such as reliability, availability, security, privacy, trust and risk in the business interaction.

These concepts assess and address all the factors which have the potential to affect the interaction negatively. The assessment criteria will be used by the consumers to form a business contract (SLA) with the service provider. The notion of risk will inform the consumer of the consequences of failure of its collaboration with the provider. An interaction between a provider and consumer is dynamic, and the risk is likewise dynamic. Therefore, the analysis of each of these SLA criteria concepts is important at different time periods during the collaboration for making an informed interaction-based decision.

Various approaches have been proposed in the literature that analyse each of these concepts in forming an SLA. However, these approaches consider the notion of risk as a subset of trust, security and privacy which can be mitigated by analysis of these concepts. In reality, this is not the case. Risk expresses the occurrence of those events that will lead to experiencing a negative outcome along with the level and magnitude of possible loss that an interacting buyer can experience. Both these representations play an important part in decision making and are not determined by the analysis of trust, security or privacy in the collaboration. Thus, any decision taken in a cloud service interaction cannot be considered as being fully informed without the analysis of risk.

ISO/IEC Guide 73 defines risk as the combination of the probability of an event and its consequences (whether positive or negative) [8]. The process of how risk is analysed is termed as risk analysis, which is a combination of various sub-steps like Risk Identification, Risk Assessment, Risk Evaluation and Risk Management. Risk Management is the process of treating risk in a methodical way to obtain benefits and sustainable values from each activity [9]. But for this process to occur, a risk assessment must be carried out. Risk assessment determines the probability of a risk event occurring along with its associated threats or consequences. There are three primary methods for assessing risk [6]: qualitative, for classifying risk without determining numerical values of all assets at risk and threat frequencies; quantitative, which calculates the magnitude and probability of risk occurring; and semi-quantitative (or hybrid), which is less numerically intensive than the quantitative method and classifies (prioritises) risks according to consequences and foreseen probabilities.

Risk will have different representations according to the area in which it is being determined. For example, if the risk being determined relates to the security aspects while forming the business association, then its analysis represents security risks. Previous work in risk assessment decision making generally considers the probability of an agent cheating [10] and the costs associated with an interaction [11]. Some other works consider risk to be a component of trust [12-15] but do not quantify the negative consequences in their model or consider it in decision making.

When risk is being determined during the decision-making stage of forming an SLA contract, its analysis represents the transactional risk. Measuring the loss or its impact by analysing the level and degree of transactional risk in the interaction is very important when making an informed interaction-based decision. The sub-categories of transactional risk to be assessed when forming an SLA are 'performance risk' and 'financial risk'.

In this paper, our focus is on performance risk. Performance risk represents the probability to which the risk assessing agent (service consumer) will not achieve the expectations of its business interaction. This is mainly due to the incapability or non-cooperation of the risk assessed agent (service provider) in committing to the expectations of the business interaction as decided initially. These agents may be an individual user, small and medium enterprises (SME) or businesses that want to achieve certain aims or desired outcomes. An agent can also be a software or web service. In our previous work, we proposed an approach by which the risk assessing agent determines the performance risk of a risk assessed agent in a business interaction [16] as explained below.

In any business interaction, the level of failure is not just two extremes, High or Low, but different levels of possible failures. We used a Failure Scale to capture those varying levels, with six different severities of failures as shown in Table 1. Each FailureLevel (FL) value on the scale quantifies and represents a different magnitude or severity of failure in the interaction.

The association of a consumer with a service provider on which the SLA is being formed may be either limited to the current period of time or may extend to a point of time in the future. To determine the performance risk of a service provider, the consumer should determine its ability to commit to the expectations at that point in time. This is achieved by determining the FL of the service provider to commit to the expectations of the SLA at that point in time. If the time period extends to a point of time in future, then the service consumer has to predict the FL of the service provider in committing to the expectations at that future period of time.

To consider the time-specific nature of transactional risk while doing so, we adopt the methodology proposed by Chang et al. [17] and determine the time space of the interaction, then divide it into different non-overlapping, mutually exclusive time slots, and identify the time spot of the interaction. Time spot represents the point in time where the service consumer initiates its association with the service provider as illustrated in Figure 1. The time space is divided into two broad phases, namely:

Table 1. The Failure Scale

Semantics of Failure Level	Probability of Failure	FailureLevel
Total Failure	91-100 %	0
Extremely High	71-90 %	1
Largely High	51-70 %	2
High	26-50 %	3
Significantly Low	11-25 %	4
Extremely Low	0-10 %	5

a) pre-interaction start time phase, representing the period before the consumer starts its association with the provider, and b) post-interaction start time phase, representing the period after the initiation of the association. Our method enables the consumer to utilize the impression or capability of the service provider in the pre-interaction time period and utilize it to predict its FL in the post-interaction time period.

To consider the dynamic and variable property of time related with transactional risk assessment, the service consumer should ascertain the FL of a service provider in each pre-interaction start time slot [16]. Some important characteristics of transactional risk that need to be considered are its:

• Context specific nature, which represents the purpose for which the business association is being carried out. Performance risk cannot be quantified successfully without taking into consideration the context in which the interaction is being formed.
• Assessment criteria specific nature, which represents the specific outcomes which the risk assessing agent wants to achieve in its interaction. Based on the context, the assessing agent will measure only the desired assessment criteria instead of all possible criteria.

There are two ways by which the consumer determines the FL of a service provider in committing to the expectations:

• By utilizing its own past interaction history and/or
• By utilizing the recommendations from other users.

We proposed that the risk assessing agent gives first preference to its own past interaction history (if it is in the expectations of its future association) to determine the FL of the risk assessed agent in a pre-interaction time slot. If it does not have any past interaction history in the specific expectations of its business interaction, then it solicits recommendations from other users and assimilates it to determine its FL value in the pre-interaction start time slot. Once the FL of each assessment criterion in a time slot has been determined, they should be combined according to their significance to ascertain the combined FL of the risk assessed agent in that pre-interaction start time slot. The determined FL of each assessment criterion in a time slot will be a value in the range of 0-5. But scenarios may arise where for a given assessment criterion in a pre-interaction start time slot, the risk assessing agent may not have either its own past interaction history or obtains recommendations from other users. In such scenarios, due to the incomplete information present, we consider that the assessing agent will err on the side of caution (assuming the worst scenario) and considers an FL value of zero (0) for that assessment criterion in that time slot.

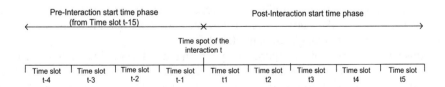

Fig. 1. Division of Time Space of the Interaction

2.2 Problem Definition

The absence of past interaction history for assessment criteria has led to very conservative outcomes when analysing performance risk. However, such outcomes might not be the best result as the risk assessed agent could still meet the assessed criteria even though the risk assessing agent has no prior knowledge of such. It is important to note that an FL value assigned for an assessment criterion will be propagated further as:

a) The FL of risk assessed agent in a pre-interaction start time slot is dependent on its FL for each assessment criterion in that time slot.

b) The performance risk of the risk assessed agent in the post-interaction start time phase is dependent on the FL values in the pre-interaction start time phase.

c) The sub-category of Financial Risk is dependent on the performance risk determined in the post-interaction start time phase, and

d) The level of transactional risk is dependent on the performance risk and financial risk determined in the post-interaction start time phase.

So it is important to make an informed decision about the FL of an assessment criterion in a pre-interaction start time slot. In this paper, we address this problem by proposing an approach where, in the absence of both direct past interaction history and recommendations from other agents, the FL of an assessment criterion can be determined by utilizing its level of similarity with the assessment criteria present. We achieve this by utilizing an ontology-based semantic similarity model.

2.3 Ontology-Based Semantic Similarity Models

Traditional semantic similarity models focus on measuring semantic similarity between nodes in semantic networks. Semantic networks refer to the graphic notations comprising arcs and nodes, in which nodes represent concepts and arcs represent relations between concepts [18]. Semantic networks can be used to represent simple knowledge in specific domains and a typical example is WordNet. However, limitations of semantic networks include: 1) nodes are usually single words and cannot be defined by properties; and 2) arcs are cannot be defined by restrictions and characteristics [19]. Compared with semantic networks, ontologies are a form of knowledge representation with more complex attributes. Ontologies consist of concepts and relations between concepts [20]. The advantages of ontologies include: 1) concepts can be defined by both datatype and object properties (relations); 2) object properties (relations) can be defined by multiple restrictions and characteristics. In terms of the comparison, it is not difficult to observe that ontologies can be employed to represent knowledge with more complex structures. Meanwhile, with the emergence of ontologies, new forms of semantic similarity models were developed in order to measure concept similarity in the ontology environment, known as ontology-based semantic similarity models, e.g., Dong et al.'s model [21].

In this paper, we propose an approach by which the risk assessing agent determines the level of similarity between the assessment criterion of its expectations and the other similar assessment criteria to accurately determine the FailureLevel (FL) of the risk assessed agent. The proposed approach is explained in the next sections.

3   Ontology-Based Risk Assessment Criteria Similarity Matching Framework

If an assessing agent (cloud service consumer) is unable to find a matching assessment criteria from the past cloud service interaction history of an assessed agent (cloud service provider), it will assume the worst case scenario and subsequently assign the worst FL weight of zero (0) for that criterion for any future interaction. This will influence the assessment in a negative manner, giving a high risk assessment due to uncertainty that might not accurately model the future interaction with an assessed agent.

In order to obtain more accurate values for the FL, we have extended our previous work by developing an ontology-based semantic similarity model that will measure the similarity of the current assessment criteria to the assessing agent or other cloud service consumers' previous interactions with the assessed agent. We propose to design a knowledge base which stores generic ontologies representing relationships between context-specific risk assessment criteria (figure 2). In terms of those generic ontologies, the similarity between the risk assessment criteria in the current interaction and the criteria in previous interactions can be calculated. Due to space constraints, the design of such ontologies is not discussed in this paper. This paper will explain the framework and its use in providing a failure level for a cloud service interaction between an assessing agent (cloud service consumer) and an assessed agent (cloud service provider).

In this framework, the assessing agent will store the assessment criteria of its previous interactions with the assessed agent in a database repository. The assessing

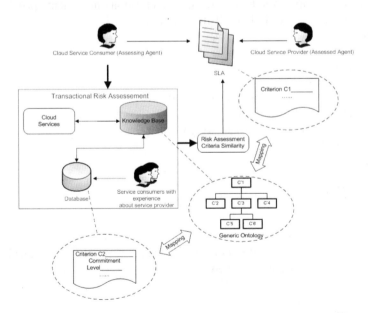

Fig. 2. Cloud Service Transaction Risk Assessment Criteria Similarity Measure Framework

agent will further acquire the assessment criteria of previous interaction history from other service consumers that interacted with the assessed agent. There are no guarantees that these historical interactions would have used the same assessment criteria since each on-demand cloud service interaction is different for each service consumer and at different points of time. The other cloud service consumers might have used assessment criteria that are not recognised by the assessing agent's cloud service. Therefore, in our proposed framework, the assessing agent will use those generic ontologies from the knowledge base to match the assessment criteria in the current interaction with the criteria used in historical interactions with the assessed agent.

Assessing the risk for a cloud service interaction should be multi-dimensional (e.g. availability, price, latency, etc.). We maintain that each generic ontology should provide a shared representation of context-specific concepts in a cloud service risk assessment dimension. With the purpose of simplifying computation, we regard each generic ontology as a hierarchical structure of concepts linked by is-a relations. Therefore, an assessment criterion can be annotated by one or more concepts from a relevant generic ontology.

Here, we propose a semantic similarity model to measure the similarity between the current assessment criteria and the historical assessment criteria. This similarity model is designed based on the theory of Rada et al. [22]'s distance-based metric, which calculates the semantic distance between two concepts in terms of the shortest distance between the two concepts in a semantic network. In terms of the instances in Figure 2, our semantic similarity model for measuring two assessment criteria can be presented as follows:

Input: c1, c2 are two assessment criteria, O is an e-business ontology which consists of concepts (c'1...c'n) linked by *is-a* relations and its maximum depth is d.
Output: sim(c1, c2) – the similarity between c1 and c2.
Algorithm:
  begin
  for i = 1 to n
          if c'[i] ∈ c1 **then**
                  Put c'[i] into an array C1;
          else if c'[i] ∈ c2 **then**
                  Put c'[i] into an array C2;
          end if
  end for
  k = count (C1);
  l = count (C2);
  for i = 1 to k
      s = 2d;
      for j = 1 to l
          A[i][j] = the shortest distance between C1[i] and C2[j] in O;
          if A[i][j] < s **then**
                  s = A[i][j];
          end if
      end for
      d' = d' + s;

```
end for
for j = 1 to l
        t = 2d;
        for i = 1 to k
                if A[i][j] < t then
                        t = A[i][j];
                end if
        end for
        d' = d' + t;
end for
```

$$sim(c1,c2) = 1 - \frac{d'}{(k+l)x2d'};$$

```
end
```

The scope of the similarity value is between the interval [0, 1], where 0 stands for nothing similar and 1 stands for completely similar. It needs to be noted that each ontology should represent an assessment dimension in a disjoint cloud service context. Therefore, this semantic similarity model cannot measure the similarity between two assessment criteria in different contexts, and we consider the similarity value should be 0 in that case. For example, the similarity value between the criterion of latency in a video service and that in an audio service should be 0, since there is no direct relationship between the two service contexts and a service provider's performance in the audio service cannot affect his/her performance in the video service.

In order to clearly explain the proposed semantic similarity model, we provide a case study to describe the application of this model in the domain of cloud computing. With the purpose of revealing the feasibility of the proposed semantic similarity model in the cloud computing environment, we make use of a real-use scenario adopted from Amazon Web Services[TM] (http://aws.amazon.com).

We premise that a consumer in Virginia wants to use an Amazon Elastic Compute Cloud (EC2) service (http://aws.amazon.com/ec2/). According to the actual demand of the consumer, s/he wants to use a small instance of the EC2 service (Windows). The consumer intends to obtain the risk performance of the small instance on the criterion of price. However, the consumer does not have any previous transaction with Amazon on the usage of the small instance. In contrast, s/he has the transaction history with Amazon on the usage of the large instance (Windows) and the usage of the high CPU medium instance (Windows). Here we define a price ontology in the context of the Amazon EC2 services (figure 3). Therefore, in terms of the price ontology and the proposed semantic similarity model, the similarity between the price for the small instance (S) and the price for the large instance (L) can be obtained by

$$sim(S,L)=0.667$$

Subsequently, the similarity between the price for the small instance (S) and the price for the high CPU medium instance (CM) can be calculated by

$$sim(S,CM)=0.333$$

Once our framework has measured the similarity between the current assessment criteria and the historical assessment criteria, the degree of similarities are used as weights to determine the FailureLevel (FL) of the assessment criteria.

4 Performance Risk Assessment Model

A series of further computations have to be carried out to determine the FL of the service provider in an assessment criterion. There might be different scenarios according to different factors and these are achieved as follows.

Step 1: Determine the Commitment Level of Agent 'B' in Assessment Criterion C_n.

Case 1: The risk assessing agent has previous interactions with the risk assessed agent in partly similar assessment criteria as compared to the current expectations of the SLA of its future interaction.

If the risk assessing agent 'A' has a past interaction history with the risk assessed agent 'B' in not exactly, but in partly similar assessment criteria (C_{ns}) as compared to the required assessment criteria (C_n) of the SLAs of its future interaction (termed as expectations), then we propose that the Commitment Level of agent 'B' in assessment criteria (C_1) is ascertained by:

(a) Determining the level of similarity of the assessment criteria (C_n) of the expectations and other similar assessment criteria, and

(b) Weighing the Commitment Level of agent 'B' in assessment criterion C_{ns} with the level of similarity between (a) assessment criteria and (b) the weight 'w' applied to the commitment level of the risk assessed agent to adjust and consider its status in the time slot 't-z'.

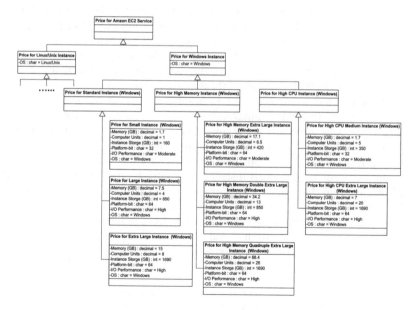

Fig. 3. Abbreviated view of a price ontology in the context of Amazon EC2 services

If there is more than one assessment criteria in the risk assessing agent's past interaction history with the risk assessed agent which partly matches the expectations of its future interaction with it, then agent 'A' should capture the similarity between each of them and accordingly weigh it to determine the commitment level of the risk assessed agent in criterion C_n. The mathematical representation of the commitment level of agent 'B' in assessment criteria C_n by utilizing its similarity to the other contexts is:

$$\text{CommLevel }_{BCn\ t\text{-}z} = (w * \frac{1}{m} (\sum_{i=1}^{m} (\text{Sim }_{Cn\text{->}Cnsi} (\text{CommLevel }^{i}_{BCns})))) \tag{1}$$

where:

'B' represents the risk assessed agent, 'C' represents the context of the SLA; 'C_n' represents the assessment criterion, in which the commitment level of the risk assessed agent 'B' is being determined; 'C_s' represents a context that is partly similar to context 'C' in which the SLA is being formed; 'C_{ns}' represents the assessment criterion which is partly similar to assessment criteria 'C_n' of the SLA; 'CommLevel $_{Cns}$' represents the level of commitment of the risk assessed agent for assessment criterion 'C_{ns}'; 'm' represents the number of similar context and assessment criteria to context 'C' and assessment criteria 'C_n'; Sim $_{Cn\text{->}Cnsi}$ represents the level of similarity between assessment criteria C_n and C_{nsi}, 'w' is the weight applied to the commitment level of the risk assessed agent to consider its status in the time slot 't-z'.

The variable 'w' is used to consider the recency of the time slot 't-z' in question with respect to the time spot of the current association. It is important to take into consideration the dynamic nature of transactional risk during its assessment. This can be explained by an interaction scenario of agent 'A' forming an association with agent 'B' for one year from 25/07/2010. To elucidate, let us consider that agent 'A' had a previous association with agent 'B' in partly similar assessment criteria that completed on 15/07/2009. Assuming that:

a) agent 'A' does not have any past interaction experience with agent 'B' in the current context and assessment criteria of its business association;
b) its past interaction history matches partly with one of the assessment criteria (C_n) of its current interaction; and
c) the time period of its previous association is within the pre-interaction start time slot (PFL) of its current interaction in which it does not have any past interaction history

then agent 'A' can utilize its past interaction history to determine the commitment level of agent 'B' in C_n. But due to the dynamic nature of risk, agent 'A' cannot consider the impression of agent 'B' that it had in that previous period of time as it is quite possible that its capability to act according to the expectations may have changed during that time. So in order to consider the dynamic nature of transactional risk, it is important for agent 'A' to accordingly adjust the commitment level of agent 'B' according to the time delay factor (w) to consider its fresh status. We determine the weight (w) to be given to each time slot of the pre-interaction start time phase by:

$$w = \begin{cases} 1 & \text{if } m \leq \Delta t \\ e^{\frac{-(\Delta t - m)}{N}} & \text{if } m > \Delta t \end{cases} \tag{2}$$

where:

'w' is the weight or the time delaying factor to be given to the status of the risk assessed agent; 'm' represents the time slot for which the weight of adjustment is determined; 'Δt' represents the number of time slots from the time spot in which the risk assessing agent will give more importance to the freshness of the status of the risk assessed agent; 'N' is the term which characterizes the rate of decay.

The adjustment factor 'w' adjusts the commitment level values of the risk assessed agent in the recent time slots from the time spot of the current interaction more heavily as compared to those in the far recent time slots, progressively adjusting the effect of the older values in order to take into consideration its fresh status. We consider that the risk assessing agent among the 15 time slots of the pre-interaction start time phase, does not weigh the commitment level values in the five time slots previous to the time spot of its interaction (time slot t-1 till t-5, that is characterized by Δt in Eq 2) as they are near to the time spot of its future interaction. For the importance to be given to the commitment level of the risk assessed agent in the other time slots of the pre-interaction start time phase (from t-6 till t-n), the weight according to which they have to be adjusted is a progressively declining value determined by using eq. 2.

Another advantage of adjusting the values according to their time weight avoids modelling the behaviour of agent 'B' in the future that may no longer be relevant according to the expectations of its future interaction. This is particularly important while ascertaining the FailureLevel of agent 'B' at a future period of time by utilizing its impression in the pre-interaction start time slots.

In cases when the risk assessing agent does not have its own past-interaction history in the part assessment criteria of its current business association, then it can utilize the recommendation-based method to ascertain the level of commitment of agent 'B' in the assessment criteria of its SLA. We explain the process of achieving this in the next sub-section.

Case 2: The risk assessing agent receives recommendations from other agents that are in partly similar assessment criteria as compared to the current expectations of the SLA of its future interaction.

When agent 'A' receives recommendations from other agents about agent 'B' that are in partly similar assessment criteria as compared to the current expectations of the SLA of its future interaction, then we propose that the Commitment Level of agent 'B' that assessment criteria is determined by:

a)   *Classifying the recommendations according to their credibility.*

There are two broad types of groups in such classification. They are *Known* and *Unknown* recommendations. Known recommendations are the feedback from agents with whom the risk assessing agent has previous experience in soliciting and considering recommendations. Unknown recommendations are the feedback from those agents with whom the risk assessing agent does not have previous experience in considering recommendations. The known recommendations are further classified into two types, which are either *Trustworthy* or *Untrustworthy* recommendations. Trustworthy recommendations are those which the risk assessing agent considers to be correct opinions. On the other hand, untrustworthy recommendations are those which the risk assessing agent does not believe to be totally correct. We consider that that the risk assessing agent considers only recommendations that are either trustworthy or unknown when it aggregates them to determine the commitment level of the risk assessed agent. It omits taking into consideration the untrustworthy recommendations as they do not provide with the correct representation of the risk assessed agent. Further details on how the risk assessing agent considers the recommendations according to their trustworthiness are explained later.

b)   Combining the recommendations to determine the Commitment Level:

From the trustworthy and unknown recommendations in the particular assessment criterion of its interest, consider the 'Commitment Level' value and adjust it according to the:

- level of similarity between the assessment criteria (C_n -> C_{ns}),
- credibility of the recommendation,
- time decay weight factor to be given according to the status of the risk assessed agent in that time slot.

Represented mathematically, the commitment level of agent 'B' in assessment criteria C_n by utilizing its similarity from the recommendations of other users is determined by:

$$\text{CommLevel}_{BC_n\,t\text{-}z} =$$

$$(\alpha * (w * \frac{1}{K} (\overset{K}{\underset{i=1}{\Sigma}} \; \text{Sim}_{C_n\text{->}C_{nsi}} (RCV_i \oplus \text{CommLevel}_{BC_{nsi}})))) +$$

$$(\beta * (w * \frac{1}{J} (\sum_{o=1}^{J} \text{Sim}_{C_n\text{->}C_{nso}} (\text{CommLevel}_{BC_{nso}})))) \qquad (3)$$

where:
    'B' represents the risk assessed agent, 'C_n' represents the assessment criterion, in which the commitment level of the risk assessed agent 'B' is being determined, 'C_{ns}' represents the assessment criterion which is partly similar to assessment criteria 'C_n' of the SLA, 'RCV_i' is the credibility value of the trustworthy recommending agent 'i', 'K' is the number of trustworthy recommendations that the risk assessing agent obtains for the risk assessed agent in similar assessment criterion to 'C_{ns}' in time slot 't-z', 'J' is the number of unknown recommendations that the risk assessing agent gets for the risk assessed agent in similar assessment criterion to 'C_{ns}' in time slot 't-z', 'α and β' are the variables attached to the parts of the equation which will give more weight to the recommendation from the trustworthy known recommending agents as compared to those from the unknown recommending agents. In general $\alpha > \beta$ and $\alpha + \beta = 1$, 'w' is the weight applied to consider the status of the risk assessed agent in time slot 't-z'.

    As shown in equation 3, the commitment level value of agent 'B' for an assessment criterion 'C_n' is determined in two parts. The first part of the equation calculates the commitment level value of agent 'B' for the assessment criterion 'C_n' by taking the recommendations of the trustworthy known recommending agents whereas the second part of the equation calculates the commitment level value of agent 'B' in the same assessment criterion 'C_n' by taking the recommendations of the unknown recommending agents. The recommendations from the untrustworthy known recommending agents are omitted and not considered. In order to give more importance to the recommendations from the trustworthy known recommending agents as compared to ones from the unknown recommending agents, variables are attached to the two parts of the equation. These variables are represented by α and β respectively. It depends upon the risk assessing agent how much weight it wants to assign to each type of recommendation. Furthermore, as explained in the previous sub-section, each recommendation for the risk assessed agent in a time slot is adjusted according to the weight to be given to the status of the risk assessed agent in that time slot.

The RCV of the trustworthy known recommending agent is also considered with the adjustment operator '$\oplus$' while assimilating its recommendation. This takes into consideration the accurate recommendation from the trustworthy recommending agent according to the credibility and accuracy by which it communicates its recommendations. The rules for the adjustment operator '$\oplus$' are:

$$a \oplus b = \begin{cases} a + b, & \text{if } 0 \leq (a+b) \leq 1 \\ 1, & \text{if } (a+b) > 1 \\ 0, & \text{if } (a+b) < 0 \end{cases}$$

Step 2: Determine the FailureLevel of agent 'B' in Assessment Criterion C_n.

Once the commitment level of a risk assessed agent for an assessment criterion has been determined then it should be mapped on the Failure Scale to determine its FailureLevel value (PFL) to complete that SLA in that time slot. The commitment level of agent 'B' for an assessment criterion shows its level of capability to meet the particular criterion according to the expectations. To determine the FailureLevel of agent 'B' for that criterion, the extent of its inability to complete the given assessment criterion has to be determined. To achieve this, the risk assessing agent should:

(a) *Map the commitment level of that assessment criterion on the Failure Scale (FS).*

Doing so, agent 'A' determines the capability of agent 'B' to meet that assessment criterion on the Failure Scale. As mentioned earlier, the levels on the Failure Scale between 0 and 5 represent varying degrees and magnitudes of failure. Hence, for ascertaining the FailureLevel of the risk assessed agent in an assessment criterion, its commitment level for that criterion should be mapped on the range of (0, 5) on the Failure Scale, as it is within these levels that its capability to complete the assessment criterion has to be ascertained on the Failure Scale. The trustworthiness or the reputation of the risk assessed agent in an assessment criterion can be represented on the Failure Scale (FS) by:

$$\text{CommLevel}_{BCn\,t\text{-}z\,FS} = \text{ROUND}(\text{CommLevel}_{BCn\,t\text{-}z} * 5) \qquad (4)$$

where:

'$\text{CommLevel}_{BCn\,t\text{-}z\,FS}$' represents the commitment level of agent 'B' in time slot 't-z' and in assessment criterion 'C_n' on the Failure Scale; '$\text{CommLevel}_{BCn\,t\text{-}z}$' represents the commitment level of agent 'B' in assessment criterion 'C_n' and in time slot 't-z'.

(b) *Determine the probability of failure of agent 'B' in committing to that assessment criterion according to its expectations.*

By ascertaining the difference between what agent 'A' expects in an assessment criterion and how far agent 'B' can fulfil it according to its commitment level for that criterion, agent 'A' should determine the probability of failure to achieve that assessment criterion in that time slot. The FailureLevel of the assessment criterion in that time slot is then achieved by mapping the probability of failure of that assessment criterion to the Failure Scale (which is between 0 and 5).

Agent 'A' expects agent 'B' to complete the assessment criterion according to its expectations. This expectation of agent 'A' can be quantified with a value of 5 on the Failure Scale, as it represents the lowest probability of failure of the assessment criterion and expresses the maximum commitment by agent 'B' to its expectations. The probability of failure to achieve an assessment criterion 'C_n' according to the expectations in interacting with the risk assessed agent 'B' in a time slot 't-z', according to its trustworthiness or reputation in this can be determined by:

$$\text{Probability of Failure }_{BCn\,t\text{-}z} = (\frac{5 - \text{CommLevel }_{BCn\,t\text{-}z\,FS}}{5}) * 100 \tag{5}$$

The determined probability of failure to achieve assessment criterion 'Cn' according to the expectations, in interacting with the risk assessed agent 'B' and in time slot 't-z' will be on a scale of 0-100 %. The risk assessing agent from this can determine the FailureLevel (PFL) of the risk assessed agent 'B' in assessment criterion 'C_n' and in time slot 't-z' on the Failure Scale (PFL $_{BCn\,t\text{-}z}$) by:

$$\text{PFL }_{BCn\,t\text{-}z} = \text{LEVEL (Probability of Failure }_{BCn\,t\text{-}z}) \tag{6}$$

Once agent 'A' determines the FailureLevel of each assessment criteria of its expectations, either by utilizing its own past interaction history or recommendations in those assessment criteria (proposed in) or in the absence of those by utilizing the similarity of other assessment criteria in its own past interaction history or recommendations (proposed in this paper) then the next step is to combine then to ascertain the FailureLevel of the risk assessed agent 'B' in a pre-interaction start time slot 't-z' (PFL $_{Pt\text{-}z}$). This is shown in the next step.

Step 3: Determine the FailureLevel of agent 'B' in time slot 't-z'.

The FailureLevel of agent 'B' in time slot 't-z' is determined by weighing its FailureLevel to complete each assessment criterion of the expectations in that time slot, with the significance of the assessment criteria as shown in Equation 7.

$$\text{PFL }_{Bt\text{-}z} = \text{ROUND } (\sum_{n=1}^{y} S_{Cn} * \text{PFL }_{BCn\,t\text{-}z}) \tag{7}$$

where:

'S_{Cn}' is the significance of the assessment criterion 'C_n'; 'PFL $_{PCn\,t\text{-}z}$' represents the FailureLevel of the risk assessed agent 'P' in assessment criterion 'C_n' in time slot 't-z'; and 'y' is the number of assessment criteria in the expectations.

5 Discussion

We simulated the case study discussed in Section 3 in order to determine the performance risk in the pre-interaction timeslot using our original model [16] and our proposed semantic similarity matching framework. We considered that when the consumer is forming the SLA with Amazon for using the small instance of EC2 service (Windows); (a) there are 5 assessment criteria, and (b) the time space is formed such that there are 15 timeslots (ts) in the pre-interaction time phase and 10 timeslots in the post-interaction time phase. We determine the performance risk (PFL) of Amazon in committing to those criteria (C1 to C5) in timeslots t-15 to t-1. Due to space limitations, we show only the determined PFL value of Amazon in timeslots t-1 to t-5 in table 2. The shaded rows of each timeslot show the PFL using the proposed method while the unshaded rows use the original model. As can be seen in t-4, the PFL determined using the original method is 0 on the failure scale as the consumer did not have any past interaction history or receive any recommendations about Amazon in C1-C5. But by using semantic similarity matching, we used those assessment criteria that are similar to C1-C5 for determining the PFL as 2 in the failure scale. Figure 4 shows the improvement in the PFL value of Amazon in timeslots t-15 to t-1.

Table 2. Calculation of PFL in Timeslots t-5 to t-1

TS	AssCrit C1	AssCrit C2	AssCrit C3	AssCrit C4	AssCrit C5	PFL
t-5	CommLevel: 1 Source: OWN	CommLevel: 0 Source: OWN	CommLevel: 1 Source: OWN	CommLevel: 1 Source: OWN	CommLevel: 0 Source: OWN	3
	-	-	-	-	-	3
t-4	CommLevel: 0 Source: NONE	CommLevel: 0 Source: NONE	CommLevel: 0 Source: NONE	CommLevel: 0 Source: NONE	CommLevel: 0 Source: NONE	0
	CommLevel: 0 $Sim_{Cn \rightarrow Cnsi}$: 0.9 Source: OWN	CommLevel: 1 $Sim_{Cn \rightarrow Cnsi}$: 0.4 Source: OWN	CommLevel: 1 $Sim_{Cn \rightarrow Cnsi}$: 0.8 Source: OWN	CommLevel: 1 $Sim_{Cn \rightarrow Cnsi}$: 0.6 Source: OWN	CommLevel: 1 $Sim_{Cn \rightarrow Cnsi}$: 0.75 Source: OWN	2
t-3	CommLevel: 0 Source: NONE	CommLevel: 0 Source: NONE	CommLevel: 0 Source: NONE	CommLevel: 0 Source: NONE	CommLevel: 0 Source: NONE	0
	CommLevel: 1 $Sim_{Cn \rightarrow Cnsi}$: 0.8 Source: OWN	CommLevel: 1 $Sim_{Cn \rightarrow Cnsi}$: 0.4 Source: REC-K RCV: 1	CommLevel: 1 $Sim_{Cn \rightarrow Cnsi}$: 0.5 Source: REC-U	CommLevel: 1 $Sim_{Cn \rightarrow Cnsi}$: 0.3 Source: REC-U	CommLevel: 1 $Sim_{Cn \rightarrow Cnsi}$: 0.6 Source: OWN	2
t-2	CommLevel: 1 Source: OWN	CommLevel: 1 Source: REC-K RCV: 0.87	CommLevel: 1 Source: REC-U	CommLevel: 1 Source: REC-U	CommLevel: 1 Source: REC-K RCV: 0.74	4
	-	-	-	-	-	4
t-1	CommLevel: 0 Source: OWN	CommLevel: 0 Source: NONE	CommLevel: 0 Source: NONE	CommLevel: 0 Source: NONE	CommLevel: 0 Source: NONE	0
	-	CommLevel: 1 $Sim_{Cn \rightarrow Cnsi}$: 0.4 Source: OWN	CommLevel: 1 $Sim_{Cn \rightarrow Cnsi}$: 0.4 Source: REC-K RCV: 0.6 CommLevel: 1 $Sim_{Cn \rightarrow Cnsi}$: 0.4 Source: REC-U	CommLevel: 1 $Sim_{Cn \rightarrow Cnsi}$: 0.9 Source: OWN	CommLevel: 1 $Sim_{Cn \rightarrow Cnsi}$: 0.8 Source: OWN	3

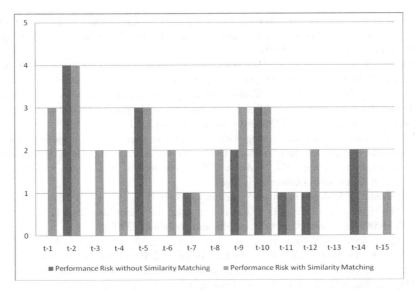

Fig. 4. Comparison of PFL using semantic similarity matching and original model over timeslots t-15 to t-1

6 Conclusion

In this paper, we proposed an improved approach for performance risk assessment that is used by a consumer to choose a cloud service provider that can meet its SLA requirements in the cloud environment. In order to determine risk, the consumer will base its decisions on the past capability of the provider. However, if there is no information that matches the capability of the provider according to the current assessment criteria, it will assume that the risk is very high for those criteria. Our proposed approach addresses this by utilizing a semantic similarity model that incorporates similar criteria from the provider's past interaction history into its performance risk assessment of the current interaction. This will help the consumer to make more informed decisions about (a) the performance risk of the provider in the post-interaction time phase, and (b) the financial risk and transactional risk in forming a SLA with the provider. We have shown that the use of semantic similarity matching improves the performance risk analysis. As part of our future work, we will extend our framework to assess the performance risk of a provider in providing multiple services to a consumer over the cloud environment, such as IaaS, SaaS and PaaS.

References

1. Kandukuri, B.R., Paturi, V.R., Rakshit, A.: Cloud Security Issues. In: Proceedings of the 2009 IEEE International Conference on Services Computing, pp. 517–520. IEEE Computer Society, Bangalore (2009)
2. Comellas, J.O.F., Presa, I.G., Fernández, J.G.: SLA-driven Elastic Cloud Hosting Provider. In: Proceedings of the 18th Euromicro Conference on Parallel, Distributed and Network-based Processing, pp. 111–118. IEEE Computer Society, Pisa (2010)

3. Nurmela, T., Kutvonen, L.: Service Level Agreement Management in Federated Virtual Organizations. In: Indulska, J., Raymond, K. (eds.) DAIS 2007. LNCS, vol. 4531, pp. 62–75. Springer, Heidelberg (2007)
4. Pearson, S., Charlesworth, A.: Accountability as a Way Forward for Privacy Protection in the Cloud. In: Cloud Computing, pp. 131–144. Springer, Heidelberg (2009)
5. Dillon, T., Wu, C., Chang, E.: Cloud Computing: Issues and Challenges. In: Proceedings on the 24th IEEE International Conference on Advanced Information Networking and Applications, pp. 27–33. IEEE Computer Society, Perth (2010)
6. Fitó, J.O., Guitart, J.: Introducing Risk Management into Cloud Computing. Barcelona Supercomputing Center and Technical University of Catalonia, Barcelona, Spain (2010)
7. AssessGrid Consortium.: D4.1 Advanced Risk Assessment. In: Carlsson, C., Weissmann, O. (eds.): Assess Grid Deliverable (2008)
8. ISO Guide 73: Risk Management Vocabulary (2009),
   http://www.iso.org/iso/cataloguedetail?csnumber=44651
9. ISO 31000: Risk management - Principles and guidelines (2009),
   http://www.iso.org/iso/cataloguedetail?csnumber=43170
10. Aberer, K., Despotovic, Z.: Managing trust in a Peer-2-Peer Information System. In: ACM (ed.): Proceedings of the Tenth International Conference on Information and Knowledge Management (CIKM 2001), Atlanta, Georgia, USA, pp. 310–317 (2001)
11. Zheng, X., Wu, Z., Chen, H., Mao, Y.: A Scalable Probabilistic Approach to Trust Evaluation. In: Stølen, K., Winsborough, W.H., Martinelli, F., Massacci, F. (eds.) iTrust 2006. LNCS, vol. 3986, pp. 423–438. Springer, Heidelberg (2006)
12. Jøsang, A., Keser, C., Dimitrakos, T.: Can We Manage Trust? In: Herrmann, P., Issarny, V., Shiu, S.C.K. (eds.) iTrust 2005. LNCS, vol. 3477, pp. 93–107. Springer, Heidelberg (2005)
13. Hassell, L.: Affect and Trust. In: Herrmann, P., Issarny, V., Shiu, S.C.K. (eds.) iTrust 2005. LNCS, vol. 3477, pp. 131–145. Springer, Heidelberg (2005)
14. Pearson, S., Mont, M.C., Crane, S.: Persistent and Dynamic Trust: Analysis and the Related Impact of Trusted Platforms. In: Herrmann, P., Issarny, V., Shiu, S.C.K. (eds.) iTrust 2005. LNCS, vol. 3477, pp. 355–363. Springer, Heidelberg (2005)
15. Wang, Y., Wong, D.S., Lin, K.-J., Varadharajan, V.: Evaluating transaction trust and risk levels in peer-to-peer e-commerce environments. Information Systems and E-Business Management 6, 25–48 (2008)
16. Hussain, O.K., Chang, E., Hussain, F.K., Dillon, T.S.: A methodology to quantify failure for risk-based decision support system in digital business ecosystems. Data & Knowledge Engineering 63, 597–621 (2007)
17. Chang, E., Dillon, T., Hussain, F.K.: Trust and Reputation for Service-Oriented Environments. John Wiley & Sons, Ltd., West Sussex (2006)
18. Sowa, J.F.: Semantic Networks. In: Shapiro, S.C. (ed.) Encyclopaedia of Artificial Intelligence. Wiley, Chichester (1992)
19. Dong, H., Hussain, F.K., Chang, E.: A hybrid concept similarity measure model for ontology environment. In: Meersman, R., Herrero, P., Dillon, T. (eds.) OTM 2009, pp. 848–857. Springer, Vilamoura (2009)
20. Gruber, T.: A translation approach to portable ontology specifications. Knowledge Acquisition 5, 199–220 (1995)
21. Dong, H., Hussain, F.K., Chang, E.: A context-aware semantic similarity model for ontology environments. Concurrency and Computation: Practice and Experience (in Press)
22. Rada, R., Mili, H., Bicknell, E., Blettner, M.: Development and application of a metric on Semantic Nets. IEEE Transactions on Systems, Man and Cybernetics 19, 17–30 (1989)

A Distributed and Privacy-Preserving Method for Network Intrusion Detection

Fatiha Benali[1], Nadia Bennani[2], Gabriele Gianini[3], and Stelvio Cimato[3]

[1] CITI, INSA-Lyon, F-69621, France
[2] Université de Lyon, CNRS, INSA-Lyon, LIRIS, UMR5205, F-69621, France
[3] Universitá degli Studi di Milano, Milano, Italy
fatiha.benali@insa-lyon.fr, nadia.bennani@liris.cnrs.fr,
{gabriele.gianini,stelvio.cimato}@unimi.it

Abstract. Organizations security becomes increasingly more difficult to obtain due to the fact that information technology and networking resources are dispersed across organizations. Network intrusion attacks are more and more difficult to detect even if the most sophisticated security tools are used. To address this problem, researchers and vendors have proposed alert correlation, an analysis process that takes the events produced by the monitoring components and produces compact reports on the security status of the organization under monitoring. Centralized solutions imply to gather from distributed resources by a third party the global state of the network in order to evaluate risks of attacks but neglect the *honest but curious* behaviors. In this paper, we focus on this issue and propose a set of solutions able to give a coarse or a fine grain global state depending on the system needs and on the privacy level requested by the involved organizations.

1 Introduction

Today, information technology and networking resources are dispersed across an organization. Threats are similarly distributed across many organization resources. Therefore, the Security of information systems (IS) is becoming a crucial part of business processes. Companies must deal with open systems on the one hand and ensure a high protection on the other hand. As a common task, an administrator starts with the identification of threats related to business assets, and applies a security product on each asset to protect an IS. Then, administrators tend to combine and multiply security products and protection techniques such as firewalls, anti-virus, Virtual Private Network (VPN), Intrusion Detection System (IDS) and security audits. Usually attacks against open and or distributed systems are difficult to detect as attackers acts independently on different resources to accomplish a full attack scenario. On a previous work, Saraydaryan and al [29] propose an efficient solution to detect Abnormal Users Behavior. In this solution, users' behaviors are modeled through a Bayesian network. The

R. Meersman et al. (Eds.): OTM 2010, Part II, LNCS 6427, pp. 861–875, 2010.
© Springer-Verlag Berlin Heidelberg 2010

Bayesian Network modeling allows a great detection effectiveness by injecting incoming events inside the centralized model and computing all the associated conditional probabilities.

Collaboration between organizations to detect security threats allow organizations to enforce the organization's security policies, to stop attacks in progression and to react at the right time in order to prevent information, financial or reputation losses. However, when several organizations decide to collaborate in order to detect intrusive activities, every organization resource manager is requested to send the events log to a central unit that analyses them and calculates the Bayesian graph. In this case, the central unit is supposed to act as a trusted entity. Indeed, when the analyzer receives the event description from the participant, a lot of private information about resources, IP addresses, is communicated. Moreover, it could be embarrassing for a participant to be pointed out by the third party as a particular weak participant. In this paper, different solutions to preserve local privacy while detecting an overall intrusion attempt are proposed. The solutions assume still the existence of the central node starting the distributed probability calculations, which are done locally, and whose result is obtained by executing a privacy preserving protocol. At the end, the central node will be able to recover the global state of the network, and take the appropriate countermeasures, but the information on the state of each single node will be obfuscated according to the starting assumptions and the requested privacy level.

The paper is outlined as follows: section 2 reminds the centralized solution. Section 3 covers some related work and preliminary information on the cryptographic solutions adopted. Section 4 describes the solutions offering a distributed intrusion detection protocol with different privacy-preserving techniques. Section 5 concludes and presents future work.

2   The Centralized Intrusion Detection System

As more security products (such as intrusion detection systems, antivirus, firewall,etc.), security mechanisms (such as access control, authentication, etc.), and critical assets (such as web server, mail server, etc.) are deployed in an organization, security administrators are faced with the hard task of analyzing an increasing number of events trigged by these monitoring components.

To address this problem, researchers and vendors have proposed alert correlation or more generally events correlation, an analysis process that takes the events produced by the monitoring components and produces compact reports on the security status of the organization under monitoring. Several alert correlation techniques have been proposed to facilitate the analysis of these events. A probabilistic method [16,20,32,33] was used to correlate alerts based on feature similarity between some selected events attributes such as source IP address, login name and/or port number. Events with higher degree of overall feature similarity will be linked. Several work propose event correlation based on prerequisites and consequences of known attacks [17,28]. The prerequisite of an attack is the necessary condition for the attack to be successful, the consequence of an attack is the possible outcome of the attack. The correlation method uses logical formulas, which are logical combinations of predicates, to represent the prerequisites and the consequences of attacks. Ning et al. [27] integrate these two types of correlation in order to improve the performance of intrusion alert correlation and reduce the impact of missed attacks. Another correlation technique proposed to correlate events based on the known attacks scenarios [26,?]. An attack scenario is specified by an attack language or learned from training datasets using data mining approaches. New approaches have emerged recently to learn event correlation models by applying machine learning techniques to training data sets with known intrusion scenarios [19,30]. This approach can automatically build models for alert correlation, but a training in every deployment is required to learn the new behavior of the system.

Event correlation methods need that the information security are normalized. There is a high number of alerts classification proposed for use in intrusion detection research. Three approaches were used to describe security information: list of terms, taxonomies and ontologies. The easiest classification proposes a list of single terms [15] covering various aspects of attacks. A variant of such an approach is listing of categories that regroup many terms under a common definition [14,31]. To avoid ambiguity between categories, a lot of taxonomies were developed to describe attacks. Lindqvist and Jonson [25] have proposed the intrusion results and the intrusion techniques as dimension for classification. John Howard [23] This process-driven taxonomy consists in five dimensions: attackers, tools, access, results and objectives. Howard extends his work by refining some of the dimensions [22]. Undercoffer and al [24] describe attacks providing an ontology as a new effort for describing attacks in intrusion detection field. Initially, they developed a taxonomy defined by the target, means, consequences of an attack and the attacker. The taxonomy was extended to an ontology, by defining the various classes, their attributes and their relations. A recent work [13] uses an ontology which describes in a uniform way all the actions that can be performed by users of an IS based on the action theory [21]. The ontology is based on four concepts: the intention, the movement, the target and the gain. The intention is the objective for which the user carries out his action, the movement is the means used to carry out the objective of the user, the target is the resource in the IS to which the action is directed to, the gains is the effect produced by the action on the system. This modeling is validated by a correlation of events trigged in a real organization [29].

2.1   Architecture

Cooperation between multiple monitoring product in an organization in term of security is achieved by means of cooperation modules in an architecture. A centralized architecture for the analysis of distributive knowledge in the IS relies on one central point for the collection and the analysis of the collected information. The architecture is composed of three modules as presented on figure 1: a collect, an analysis, and a response module. First an agent is installed on each asset. An

Asset can be a security product (IDS, Firewall, etc.), a management product (router, switch, etc.) or a sensitive service (web server, mail server, etc.). The security administrator assigns names to the sensitive assets. The collect module uses installed agents on each asset. The agent collects information from the target system on the activities performed on each asset and stores them as raw data in the asset log file. The agent maps the collected event in the same representation in order to give the same syntax to all the events, and the same security information semantics modeling. Once the data are unified, they are saved in the same database. The analysis module implements the processes to perform the collected such as the correlation methods that construct scenarios and classify them as normal or intrusive, reports generation of activities which were undertaken in the system and risk-value quantization of behaviors that exceeds a certain threshold. The response module takes care of the alarms or labeled events from the analysis module and decides how to respond to them.

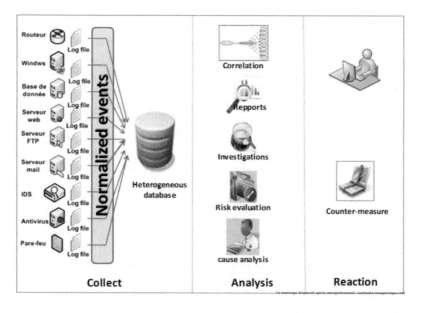

Fig. 1. Centralized analysis for distributive security information

2.2 Attack Scenario in Centralized Analysis

This section present an example of events correlation based on normalized events in centralized architecture. We dispose of a corpus of events generated by a company activities during 11 days (To preserve confidentiality, the details on the company are not published). These events are heterogeneous. The corpus consists of 6351565 raw events generated by the deployed products in the company.

IETF have proposed the Intrusion Detection Message Exchange Format (ID-MEF) [18] as a way to set a standard representation for the syntax of intrusion alerts. IDMEF became a standard format with the RFC 47652[1]. We use the IDMEF as data model for security information. This format dispose of a class named *Classification text* to put the name of the detected event. We redefine the classification text class by a category of the ontology developped in [13] in order to describe the security information semantics. In this way, all events are normalized: same semantics using the ontology, and same syntax using the IDMEF data model. Then, we apply the behavioral correlation engine of autors [30] on normalized data. This behavioral correlation aims to learn a normal profile of the IS and to detect all deviances from this profile. This correlation method allows the automatic discovery of relations between the collected events on the IS. The proposed approach by the author is a supervised approach. The relations between the events are discovered from prior knowledge, and are presented by a graph of events which defines normal behaviors scenarios. To complete this model, the author transformed the events graph into a Bayesian network [30] in order to represent all the conditional probabilities of the graph events. This model allows comparison of future events to the normal behavior models and detect abnormal behaviors like user errors or intrusive activities.

We present here an attack scenario, a variant of website defacement (is usually the substitution of the original home page by a system attacker). We used the ontology developed in [13] to normalize the raw events.The different steps of this attack are represented by the following categories of events:

- E1-System_Attack.InformationGathering.Web. Detected (Information gathering on the website)
- E2- Rights_Vulnerability.Gain.web.Detected (vulnerability exploitation)
- E3-Authentication_Activity.Session.Admin.Success (acces to the website as the admin)
- E4-Rights_Activity.WEB_Command.Executed (have more rights on the web)
- E5- Rights_Activity.Modify.Web_Homepage.Success (modification oh the home page)

The engine has generated graphs of events performed on the IS use. The figure 2 illustrates a graph of events among the graphs which were detected by the behavioral correlation.

When multiple organizations decide to collaborate for intrusion analysis, they do not reveal some sensitive information contained in some attributes of events like attacks name or IP destination address because of privacy concerns. Alert correlation methods will be affected due to the lack of precise data provided by other organizations. In distributed secure intrusion detection, we can use the same approaches already presented in literature for centralized intrusion detection to normalize events and the same correlation methods but it is necessary to have techniques to perform privacy preserving alert correlation such that the privacy of participating organizations is preserved, and at the same time, alert correlation can provide correct results.

---

[1] http://www.rfc-editor.org/rfc/rfc4765.txt

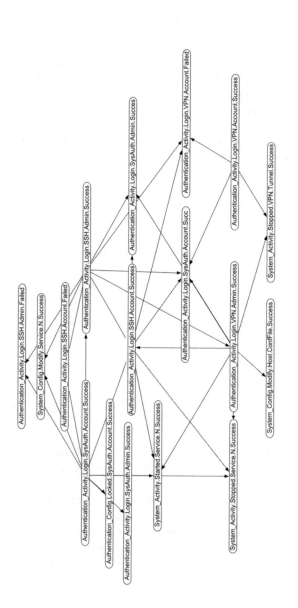

Fig. 2. A graph of events on the IS use

3   Background

3.1   Secure Multi Participants Computation(SMC)

The paradigm of secure two party computation was introduced by Yao [12], and successively generalized to include multi participants [5]. The resulting protocol assumes the representation of the function F to be computed via a boolean circuit and enable the parties to engage in a protocol to securely compute the output of each gate till the completion of the result. While the theoretical result is strong (any function can be computed in a secure way), the resulting protocol is not very practical, since its complexity depends on both the number of the inputs and the size of the combinatorial circuit representing the function F. Different applications of SMC have been presented in the literature, however in many cases, the main results in this area remain of theoretical interests, since even simple computations involving few parties still require several rounds of interaction. Much of the research work in this area is devoted to the design of efficient SMC protocols for the computation of particular functions (such as set operations, or scalar product, and so on) in different application scenarios.

3.2   Privacy Preserving Computation of Bayesian Network

Privacy preserving computation of Bayesian Network (BN) has been previously addressed in literature. The focus of previous work has been the computation of the parameters of the BN when the data are partitioned in different databases. In [9,4] the problem of distributed Bayesian network learning has been addressed for both the cases of horizontally and vertically partitioned data. The solution however, do not really preserves the privacy of the data, since the parts are required to share some information with the other parties. A more complete solution for learning both the structure of the BN and the parameters on vertically partitioned data has been presented in [10,11] which improves on another solution presented in [8]. The computation of the structure of the BN is obtained by modifying the learning algorithm widely used to extract the BN form a set of data (the K2 algorithm) in a privacy preserving way. At the same time the BN parameters are computed using a secure two party computation protocol between the owners of the database.

3.3   Preliminaries

We assume that the nodes are *honest but curious* parties, meaning that they will follow the steps of the protocol in which they are engaged, but could be motivated to access information they observe on the communication channel. We also assume that an ordering is imposed among the nodes and each node is able to communicate with the successive node in the list of all the participants to the protocol. The notion of an one-way accumulator has been introduced by Benaloh and de Mare in [1]. Basically a *one way accumulator* is a cryptographic primitive giving the capability of accumulating a set of values into a unique output value.

It has been defined as a family of one way hash functions $h : X.Y \rightarrow X$ with the additional property of quasi-commutativity, meaning that if the initial value x is selected, for any values y_1, y_2, it holds $h(h(x, y_1), y_2) = h(h(x, y_2), y_1)$. The basic functionality of an accumulator is that of constructing a compact representation of a set of values, providing at the same time method for constructing a proof that an element has been accumulated into the set. In [1], a time stamping and a membership testing application have been proposed exploiting such a primitive. Successively, dynamic accumulators have been proposed, providing the capability of adding and deleting elements from the set [2]. Accumulators have also been used to propose authenticated dictionaries, where untrusted directories mirror source contents, providing verifiable answers to membership queries [7]. An example of accumulator function is the RSA accumulator defined as

$$f(y, x) = y^x mod\ N$$

Such function is quasi commutative and is also one-way if some conditions on the domain and the choice of the modulus are met.

4   The Distributed Intrusion Detection System

The privacy properties of secure multi party computation require that the participants learn no more about other parties' input at the end of the protocol than it would if they get the computed result. Security in this context is often defined with respect to an ideal model [6], where a Trusted Third Party (TTP) is requested to do all the computation needed to return the requested result.

In this work, we are proposing a privacy preserving protocol for the computation of the global state of the network. The scenario we are considering is that of a network composed of n nodes, $P_1, \ldots, P_n$, collaborating in intrusion detection system. A querying node Q, is evaluating the probability of an attack state for the network, by analyzing the Bayesian model of the network. The attack probability is computed , Q assigns different probability values to the possible configurations of the network. Then the knowledge of the actual state of the network, is needed to compute correctly the attack probability. In a centralized scenario where a TTP is enabled to collect all the information about the collaborating nodes, the computation is an easy task, since the TTP could return the state of each node of the network and the querying node could correctly compute all the associated probability value in the Bayesian graph.

As regards the state representation, we assume that the state can be associated to a k-bit binary string. In the simplest scenario $k = 1$, i.e. the state of each node is represented by 1 bit, where 0 means *normal* status, and 1 means *attack*.

Referring to the sample network configuration and the attack scenario given in section 2.2, each node has a 3-bits state (0 is equivalent to a normal state, 1, to E1 state, ...,5 to the E5 state and lastly state 6 and state 7 are not assigned configurations).

4.1 Privacy Requirements

A distributed computation that does not rely on a TTP is secure if the involved parties do not learn anything more that they would during the execution of the protocol in the ideal model. In particular, the privacy requirements are the following:

- The querying node should be able to retrieve the associated probability value with the returned state from the protocol, without knowing the local state of each node;
- During the protocol, each node should not be able to compute the state of other nodes involved in the computation;

To better clarify the scenario we are considering, here we briefly discuss the notion of state of the network, and the level of requested privacy w.r.t. the previous requirements.

The privacy requirements above listed seem to contrast somehow with the knowledge the querying node needs to collect. Indeed the intrusion detection system, should be able to recognize the current status of the network in the most detailed way, in order to take the most appropriate countermeasures. For example, the recognition of a corrupted node inside the network could lead the network manager to isolate the node and move critical activities away from the node. Such kind of actions, can only be taken when the network manager knows exactly the topology of the network and the current condition of each node. In this work, we are concerned with privacy preserving techniques for the recognition of the network status, where the nodes are collaborating in the intrusion detection mechanism. According to the amount of information that the nodes want to release to the querying node, the kind of analysis that can be performed on the network and the corresponding countermeasures change. We take into account three basic scenarios, distinguishing on the basis of the information that the querying node can retrieve after the execution of the protocol and the corresponding privacy level requested:

- *centralized knowledge*: The state of the network depends on the condition of each individual node;
- *topology dependent knowledge*: The state of the network depends on the number and the position of the nodes;
- *summary knowledge*: The state of the network depends on the number of nodes in a given condition;

We do not deal here with the first scenario, where nodes collaborate with the intrusion detection system releasing all their private information. In the second case, the computation of the global state of the network takes into account the positions of the nodes within the network graph, but a certain degree of obfuscation is guaranteed, since the querying node will know the state of the network up to a permutation of the nodes. To this purpose we assume that all the information collected by the querying node is not directly linkable to a node.

In the last scenario, the computation of the global state returns the number of nodes in a given condition. The IDS system will trigger some reactions based on the occurrence of some threshold condition on the nodes, independently by their positions in the network graph.

4.2   The Privacy Preserving Protocol

The aim of a distributed privacy preserving protocol for the computation of the global state of the network is to let the querying node correctly compute the attack probability values in the BN. In this section, we discuss different solutions all returning a state string representing the global status of the distributed network under different assumptions. All the proposals preserve in some degree the privacy of the involved nodes, and are applicable in one of the above presented scenarios.

4.3   Counting the Corrupted Nodes

In this setting, we assume that the state of each node is represented by a single bit and the computation aims to return the number of nodes in attack conditions. The solution is offered by the execution of a secure sum protocol, assuming that more than three nodes are collaborating and that they do not collude [3]. The querying node computes a random number r in the range $[1, \ldots, n]$, and sends it to P_1. Each node will simply add its state value ($s_i = 0$ or $s_i = 1$) and forward it to the next node in the network, till the result $r + \sum_{j=1}^{n} s_i$ is sent from the last node P_n to Q. Q can now retrieve the number of corrupted nodes by subtracting r from the received summation. Notice also that each node can't learn anything on the state of the previous nodes, since she does not know the random value r and cannot know if the previous node changed the received value. A collusion however between nodes P_{i-1} and P_{i+1} could determine the state of node P_i. To this purpose the basic protocol can be extended to work if a majority of honest nodes exists in the network.

4.4   Collecting the State String

In this scenario we assume that the state of each node is represented by k bits and the returned state string is obfuscated (second scenario above discussed). The distributed protocol simply consist in retrieving the state of each node in the network, by accumulating the encryption of the k-bit strings. To this purpose, we assume that nodes know the public key of the querying node and use a semantically secure asymmetric encryption system. Each node simply forwards to the successive node the encrypted state string, adding its own local status to the string previously received. The querying node, will retrieve the global status of the network, by decrypting with the private key the state string. Also in this case, each node cannot retrieve any information on the previous nodes, and the querying node can only reason on the returned obfuscated information about the nodes in the network. Let us illustrate this method by mean of the example in section 2.2: Node P_1 calculates S_1 as $E_Q(e_i)$ and sends it to P_2 having state e_j. Node P_2 calculates the state string $S_{1,2} = S_1||S_2$, where $S_2 = E_Q(e_j)$ and $||$ is the concatenation operation. The protocol goes on till P_n returns the computed global state string to Q.

4.5   Traversing the State Tree

We present here a very simple protocol, which enables the querying node to retrieve the state string, by intelligently traversing the state tree, still preserving the privacy of each node. For the sake of clarity, we assume that the state of each node is represented by 1 bit (but the reasoning can be easily extended to k bits). The global state of the network is retrieved by traversing the binary state tree. Starting from the root associated to the first node P_1, it is possible to descend on the left or on the right subtree, according to its state. Each nodes behaves in the same way, till one of the 2^n leaves is reached. Then the state of the system is described by the associated n-bits long string.

The traversing of the tree is simulated by privacy aware distributed protocol by asking each node to propagate the state string, starting from the $n \cdot 2^n$ bit long sequence, composed by the sequence of all the leaves of the state tree. To preserve the privacy of each node and of its local choice, we assume that the string is encrypted with a private key, known only to Q. Each node will split the string and pass to the successive the node the right or the left half of the string, according to its own state. At the end, the last node will return to the querying node the leaf state string, n-bits long, corresponding to the actual state of the system. Figure 3 illustrates the traversing tree state protocol for the configuration of section 2.2.

Notice that, the privacy of each node is maintained, since the local choice does not disclose the state to the successive node, which cannot read the state string and know the state of the previous nodes. The propagation of the string, however could cause some problem, since for a large number of nodes, i.e. if n is great, the communication costs are high.

In a variant of the protocol the network could circulate not the string with the state of the network, but rather a string with the probabilities of attack corresponding to each state. The querying node Q can pre-compute locally all probabilities of attack corresponding to all the possible states of the network, then each probability value can be approximated by a representation using only r bits. At this point, the querying node transmits the probability string consisting in $r \cdot 2^n$ bits, and each node will drop the left or the right half of the string depending on her state being 0 or 1. In the end, the querying node will receive a string of r bits representing a single probability value, the one corresponding to the state of the network. This protocol has the advantage of keeping the state of the network private also to the querying node, furthermore the number of circulating bits can be reduced with respect to the previous protocol if $r < nk$.

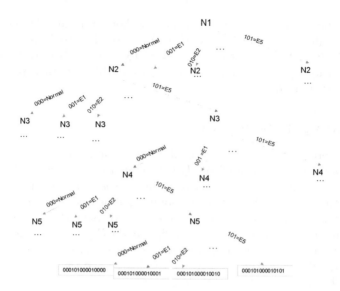

Fig. 3. Illustration of the traversingtree state method on the example of section 2.2

4.6   Accumulator-Based Protocol

Finally we present two privacy preserving protocols based on the use of a cryptographic accumulator A. In the first version, each node is simply requested to add to the received value, the value corresponding to its own state, and forward the obtained value to the successive node. In particular, let Q select random values q, r, and pass to P_1 the value $A_0 = A(q, r)$. Each node P_i is requested to compute the value $A_i = A(s_i, A_{i-1})$, and forward it to the successive node, where s_i is the k-bit string representing its state. At the end of the protocol, Q will obtain the value A_n returning the global status of the network. Due to the commutative property of the accumulator, Q will be able to determine the number of nodes in a given state, independently of the topology of the network, and match the returned value with the one obtained during the construction of the BN.

In a second version, it is possible to add topological information, by adding the encryption of the state string. Here we assume the existence of a semantically secure symmetric encryption scheme E, and the possibility of using the accumulated value received during the execution of the protocol as key. In particular during the execution of the protocol, each node P_i

- Uses the value A_{i-1} to encrypt its state, obtaining $S_i = E_{A_{i-1}}(s_i)$;
- Accumulates its own state computing $A_i = A(s_i, A_{i-1})$;
- Forwards A_i to the successive node and concatenates S_i to the state string.

At the end of the protocol, Q gets A_n, representing the global status of the network, and the global state string $S = S_1, \ldots, S_n$. Notice that in this case no secret information or key is assumed to be known by the participants to the protocol. Each node is able to add her status to the global status, but cannot compute the state of the previous node.

5   Discussion

The solutions presented above are efficient methods for preserving nodes privacy, while ensuring that the network manager is able to collect information enough on the state of the network and react to abnormal situations. Some solutions rely on the exploitation of secure computing protocols while others use cryptographic primitives for achieving the requested privacy level.

If the IDS needs only to know the number of nodes under a given attack condition, both solutions illustrated in sections 4.3 and 4.6 can be used. Notice that the second solution improves on the first one, since it is possible to count nodes laying in different kinds of attack conditions. Due to the commutativity property of the accumulator, each node is able to add its local state to the global count, letting Q able to distinguish how many nodes stay in a given condition.

If on the other side, the IDS needs to retrieve more detailed knowledge on the network state, Q can adopt one of the solutions presented in 4.4, 4.5, or 4.6. The solution presented in 4.4 relies on the basic assumption that some shared knowledge is owned by all the nodes in the network; in particular all the nodes should know the updated public key of the querying node. The other two solutions release also this assumption. For the solution presented in sec. 4.5, however, it is requested that Q pre-computes all the possible network states, and assign a probability value to each of them. The solution presented in 4.6, finally, returns a very compact representation of the network state, computing the accumulated value that can be matched with some of values that Q can compute and associate to potential dangerous situations. Such values will trigger the reaction from the network manager, who can adopt the requested countermeasures.

6   Conclusions and Perspectives

The recognition of attack scenarios in open and or distributed systems is a complex and difficult task since attackers acts independently on different resources to accomplish a full attack scenario. Collaboration between organizations to detect security threats often relies on a central entity that analyses logged data and computes a Bayesian graph, where probabilities are assigned to the possible different configurations of the system under monitoring. In this work we discussed some efficient solutions for computing the state of network in which nodes collaborate with an intrusion detection system, but would like to avoid disclosing all private information to a trusted entity, and would like to retain a given privacy level. In future, we would like to evaluate the performance and the effectiveness of the proposed protocols in practical situations involving a given number of nodes. Furthermore, in the proposed solutions we have to consider situations where several abnormal behaviors could be detected simultaneously on

874 F. Benali et al.

the same node. Finally, in the proposed solutions, a common assumption is that all the nodes adopt the same behavior. An interesting investigation challenge is to consider different types of participants with different kinds of requested privacy level. In this case, the computation of the network state should be adapted in order to collect the maximum amount of information that nodes are willing to disclose.

References

1. Benaloh, J., de Mare, M.: One-way accumulators: A decentralized alternative to digital signatures. In: Helleseth, T. (ed.) EUROCRYPT 1993. LNCS, vol. 765, pp. 274–285. Springer, Heidelberg (1994)
2. Camenisch, J., Lysyanskaya, A.: Dynamic accumulators and application to efficient revocation of anonymous credentials. In: Yung, M. (ed.) CRYPTO 2002. LNCS, vol. 2442, p. 61. Springer, Heidelberg (2002)
3. Clifton, C., Kantarcioglu, M., Vaidya, J., Lin, X., Zhu, M.Y.: Tools for privacy preserving distributed data mining. SIGKDD Explor. Newsl. 4(2), 28–34 (2002)
4. Chen, R., Sivakumar, K., Kargupta, H.: Learning Bayesian Network Structure from Distributed Data. In: Proc. SIAM Int'l Data Mining Conf., pp. 284–288 (2003)
5. Goldreich, O., Micali, S., Wigderson, A.: How to Play ANY Mental Game. In: Proc. 19th Ann. ACM Conf. Theory of Computing, pp. 218–229 (1987)
6. Goldreich, O.: Foundations of Cryptography, vol. II: Basic Applications. Cambridge Univ. Press, Cambridge (2004)
7. Goodrich, M.T., Tamassia, R., Hasic, J.: An efficient dynamic and distributed cryptographic accumulator. In: Chan, A.H., Gligor, V.D. (eds.) ISC 2002. LNCS, vol. 2433, pp. 372–388. Springer, Heidelberg (2002)
8. Meng, D., Sivakumar, K., Kargupta, H.: Privacy-Sensitive Bayesian Network Parameter Learning. In: Proc. Fourth IEEE Int'l Conf. Data Mining, pp. 487–490 (2004)
9. Yamanishi, K.: Distributed cooperative Bayesian Learning strategies. Information and Computation 150(1), 22–56 (1999)
10. Wright, R.N., Yang, Z.: Privacy-Preserving Bayesian Network Structure Computation on Distributed Heterogeneous Data. In: Proc. 10th ACM SIGKDD Int'l Conf. Knowledge Discovery and Data Mining, pp. 713–718 (2004)
11. Yang, Z., Wright, R.N.: Privacy-Preserving Computation of Bayesian Networks on Vertically Partitioned Data. IEEE Transactions on Knowledge and Data Engineering, 1253–1264 (September 2006)
12. Yao, A.: How to Generate and Exchange Secrets. In: Proc. 27th IEEE Symp. Foundations of Computer Science, pp. 162–167 (1986)
13. Benali, F., Legrand, V., Ubéda, S.: An ontology for the management of heterogenous alerts of information system. In: The 2007 International Conference on Security and Management (SAM 2007), Las Vegas, USA, pp. 374–380 (June 2007)
14. Cheswick, W.R., Bellovin, S.M.: Firewalls and Internet Security Repelling the Wily Hacker. Addison-Wesley, Reading (1994)
15. Cohen, F.B.: Information system attacks: A preliminary classification scheme. Computers and Security 16(1), 29–46 (1997)
16. Cuppens, F.: Managing alerts in a multi-intrusion detection environment. In: ACSAC 2001: Proceedings of the 17th Annual Computer Security Applications Conference, Washington, DC, USA, p. 22. IEEE Computer Society, Los Alamitos (2001)

17. Cuppens, F., Miège, A.: Alert correlation in a cooperative intrusion detection framework. In: SP 2002: Proceedings of the 2002 IEEE Symposium on Security and Privacy, Washington, DC, USA, p. 202. IEEE Computer Society, Los Alamitos (2002)
18. Curry, D., Debar, H.: Intrusion detection message exchange format
19. Dain, O., Cunningham, R.K.: Fusing a heterogeneous alert stream into scenarios. In: Proceedings of the 2001 ACM Workshop on Data Mining for Security Applications, pp. 1–13 (2001)
20. Dain, O.M., Cunningham, R.K.: Building scenarios from a heterogeneous alert stream. In: IEEE Workshop on Information Assurance and Security, pp. 231–235 (June 2001)
21. Davidson: Actions, reasons, and causes. Journal of Philosophy 685–700 (1963) (Reprinted in Davidson 1980, pp. 3–19)
22. Howard, J., Longstaff, T.: A common language for computer security incidents. Sand98-8667, Sandia International Laboratories (1998)
23. Howard, J.D.: An Analysis of Security Incidents on the Internet -normalement phd dissertation. PhD thesis, Carnegie Mellon University, Pittsburgh, Pennsylvania 15213 USA (April 1997)
24. Johi, A., Pinkston, J., Undercoffer, J.: Modeling computer attacks: an ontology for intrusion detection. In: Vigna, G., Krügel, C., Jonsson, E. (eds.) RAID 2003. LNCS, vol. 2820, pp. 113–135. Springer, Heidelberg (2003)
25. Lindqvist, U., Jonsson, E.: How to systematically classify computer security intrusions. In: Proceeding of the IEEE Symposium on Security and Privacy, pp. 154–163 (1997)
26. Lindqvist, U., Porras, P.A.: Detecting computer and network misuse through the production-based expert system toolset(p-best). In: Proceeding of the 1999 Symposium of Security and Privacy, Oakland, CA, USA. IEEE Computer Society, Los Alamitos (May 1999)
27. Ning, P., Xu, D., Healey, C.G., Amant, R.S.: Building attack scenarios through integration of complementary alert correlation methods. In: Proceedings of The 11th Annual Network And Distributed System Security Symposium (NDSS 2004), pp. 97–111 (2004)
28. Peng, N., Yun, C., Reeves Douglas, S.: Constructing attack scenarios through correlation of intrusion alerts. In: Proceedings of the 9th ACM Conference on Computer and Communications Security, CCS 2002, pp. 245–254. ACM, New York (2002)
29. Saraydaryan, J., Benali, F., Ubéda, S., Legrand, V.: Comprehensive security framework for global threads analysis. International Journal of Computer Science Issues IJCSI 2, 18–32 (2009)
30. Saraydaryan, J., Legrand, V., Ubéda, S.: Behavioral anomaly detection using bayesian modelization based on a global vision of the system. In: NOTERE (2007)
31. Stallings, W.: Network and internetwork security: principles and practice. Prentice-Hall, Inc., Upper Saddle River (1995)
32. Staniford, S., Hoagland, J.A., McAlerney, J.M.: Practical automated detection of stealthy portscans. J. Comput. Secur. 10(1-2), 105–136 (2002)
33. Valdes, A., Skinner, K.: Probabilistic alert correlation. In: Proceedings of the 4th International Symposium on Recent Advances in Intrusion Detection, RAID 2000, London, UK, pp. 54–68. Springer, Heidelberg (2001)

Enforcing UCON Policies on the Enterprise Service Bus

Gabriela Gheorghe[1], Paolo Mori[2], Bruno Crispo[1], and Fabio Martinelli[2]

[1] University of Trento, Italy
first.last@disi.unitn.it
[2] IIT CNR Pisa, Italy
first.last@iit.cnr.it

Abstract. In enterprise applications, regulatory and business policies are shifting their semantic from access to usage control requirements. The aim of such policies is to constrain the usage of groups of resources based on complex conditions that require not only state-keeping but also automatic reaction to state changes. We argue that these policies instantiate usage control requirements that can be enforced at the infrastructure layer. Extending a policy language that we prove equivalent to an enhanced version of the UCON model, we build on an instrumented message bus to enact these policies.

Keywords: Usage control model, message bus, policy, enforcement, SOA.

1 Introduction

Modern organizations need to face business conditions that change much more frequently than ever before. Two main drivers for such changes are first, the pressure to reduce costs and the time to market for new services and applications; and second, the need to comply with regulatory requirements that, in recent years, have grown very rapidly in terms of both numbers and complexity.

To support such organizational dynamism, IT systems had to go through a profound transformation. The software-as-a-service paradigm started to be adopted together with SOAs. Among the several potential advantages of SOA, interoperability, modularity and scalability are the first ones organizations are already experiencing. While existing SOA technologies address the first of the two drivers we mentioned (i.e. by supporting standard service interfaces that make outsourcing much easier to implement), not much work as been done until now to address the problem of regulatory compliance. To be suitable, any solution must be: 1) integrated with SOAs, 2) able to easily adapt to regulatory changes (i.e. due to a department relocation in a new country or simply due to the new version of the current regulations) since often the same regulatory requirements apply to many services and departments of the organizations; 3) inclusive of a wide range of policies that may control not only who accesses some services but also how these services are used.

This paper proposes a novel solution that apart from meeting these three requirements, extends the role of reference monitors in enforcing the applicable policies. We build on an existing reference monitor at the *message bus* level [4], which is a common requirement in all service-oriented architectures. By positioning the policy enforcement

R. Meersman et al. (Eds.): OTM 2010, Part II, LNCS 6427, pp. 876–893, 2010.

within the message bus, the security logic is decoupled from the business logic, making it simpler to enforce new regulations that have as scope several services of the organization. Furthermore, different from existing SOA solutions, our extension to the reference monitor supports the UCON model along with classic access control models (i.e. RBAC). This is achieved by using an extended version of the POLPA [10,11] policy language, that we prove able to express any UCON policy.

Overall, to make use of all the properties of the message bus as mediator of all service invocations, we extended the semantics of traditional reference monitors. We propose a first step towards the possibility to design reference monitors which act proactively on service invocations that do not comply with the policy. These actions consist of applying a set of predefined transformations to try to make the invocations compliant rather than resulting in service rejection. Our contributions are:

- A language for expressing SOA message-level requirements and the proof of its equivalence with the UCON model. In this way, we can correctly express any constraint on the usage of the enterprise infrastructure (Sect. 5).
- An extended UCON semantics to a reference monitor for large scale applications. The usability of the concept resides in separating policy specification, enforcement mechanism and enforcement semantics (Sect. 6).
- A prototype for message-flow enforcement that considers cross-service UCON-related policies. Existing message-level security solutions do not consider this kind of restrictions (Sect. 4).

The remainder of this paper is organized as follows: after presenting the need of message-level policy enforcement in a real-world scenario (Sect. 2), we give an overview of the UCON model and the enterprise bus (Sect. 3). Then we describe our proposal of a three-step enforcement process (Sect. 4), and introduce a UCON language that we prove is able to express the policies we aim to enforce (Sect. 5). We present the implementation of the model within the enhanced service bus (Sect. 6), and conclude by discussing the advantages and limitations of our approach (Sect. 8).

2 Motivating Example

Our work is motivated by a case study provided by the Hong Kong Red Cross organization, which manages blood donations for a number of public hospitals. The Red Cross works as an intermediary between several actors: the blood donors, blood receivers, and public hospitals. We concentrate on several of Red Cross's components that relate to data gathering and processing (see Figure 1): a Data Collector Service (DC), a Data Submitter service (DS), a Notification Service (NS), a Logger Service (LS) and a Donation Processing Service (PD). The data collector service is shared between the Red Cross (who gets donor data) and public hospitals. The service can be deployed on several locations, and we assume there is metadata to specify these locations. This service will wrap a standard electronic form and will send it to the DS. The data submitter service DS inserts data into a database. For the Red Cross, this database contains the donor data. This service has a public operation called submit_donor_data(). PD is a service for processing possible donation cases, that wraps a business process that decides to allow

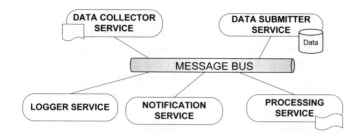

Fig. 1. Web Services used by the Hong Kong Red Cross

or deny the blood donation. The notification service NS sends an email to the Red Cross security administrator. Blood donation data is subject to the internal or even regulatory policies:

(P1). New electronic entries of blood donor data can *only* be issued from the Red Cross branches throughout Hong Kong. This requires the DS to record an entry to the donor database only if the DC has some metadata certifying its location.

(P2). Once a potential donor fills in a paper form, the donation volunteering case will be processed for approval by a nurse within 3 days. This requires a mechanism to monitor any incoming requests to the PD service that contain a reference to a recent donor_id. If such requests are not reported within the given time frame, a notification will be sent to the NS.

(P3). The Red Cross must keep record of all data and operations onto the system. This is both for statistical purposes and for controlling what happens to the data once it reaches its points of interest. This constraint requires an additional logging action (invoking the Logger Service) every time a message to a data-processing service is received.

(P4). Donor data can be kept in the hospital data base for a maximum of 300 days. After this period, a service that deletes the expired donor data will be invoked.

The Red Cross is trusted by all actors in the system to provide assurance that such constraints are complied with. Hence the Red Cross needs a centric view over the general application design, data release and usage. In order to manage a common infrastructure to which the hospitals and government organizations connect, the Red Cross employs the Enterprise Service Bus (ESB) to integrate application components. Using the ESB helps to enact restrictions as P1-P4, as the ESB can distinguish between types of services – data sources and data consumers, as well as map actual endpoints to business logic endpoints. With the help of the ESB, the Red Cross can ensure that what reaches these services is only the *right data*, used on the *right terms*. However, since the restrictions can change depending on external organizational requirements, the Red Cross system needs to offer flexibility and assurance in dealing with the issues described above.

3   Background

This section overviews the two building blocks of our approach. Firstly, UCON comes as a promising way of modeling security concerns in realistic distributed applications.

Secondly, the enterprise service bus has been a well-established vehicle of application integration. The model we use, xESB [4], combines these two concepts and can give guarantees in enforcing policies such as those described above.

3.1 The UCON Model

The Usage Control (UCON) model is a next generation access control model designed for modern and distributed environments. The main novelties of UCON are that attributes of subjects and objects are mutable over time, and hence the decision process and the enforcement of the security policy is performed continuously during access time. This means that an access that has been authorized and that is currently in progress could be revoked because some factors have changed and the access right does not hold any more. The UCON core components are subjects, objects and their attributes, rights and authorizations, conditions and obligations, as described in [12,19].

3.2 The ESB in SOA

The ESB is a middleware placed between the various services of an SOA application. It offers a layer of communication and integration logic in order to mitigate technology disparities between communication parties, ranging from intelligent routing to XML data transformation. For example, if the communication partners use different communication protocols, the ESB mediator will perform the protocol conversion; the same if a business consumer needs to aggregate data from several providers, to change the format of its data, or to route it to different services. The ESB increases connectivity by facilitating application integration.

Java Business Integration (JBI) [16] standardizes deployment and management of services deployed on an ESB. It describes how applications need to be built in order to be integrated easily. The generic JBI architecture is shown in Fig. 2 (top). Since the primary function of the ESB is message mediation, the Normalized Message Router (NMR) is the core of the JBI-ESB and provides the infrastructure for all message exchanges once they are transformed into a normalized form (an example is shown in Fig. 2 (bottom)). Components deployed onto the bus can be either service engines, which encapsulate business logic and transformation services; or binding components, which connect external services to the JBI environment.

4   The Enforcement Model

This section examines in more detail the prerequisites of enforcing the policies previously described. Motivating the connection with the usage control model, we argue that enacting these requirements is separate from application logic and can be best performed at the mediation layer provided by the ESB. To that end, we present the enhanced semantics of a message-level reference monitor that enforces Red Cross's usage control constraints.

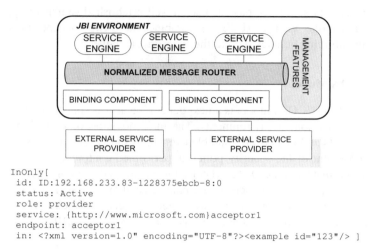

```
InOnly[
  id: ID:192.168.233.83-1228375ebcb-8:0
  status: Active
  role: provider
  service: {http://www.microsoft.com}acceptor1
  endpoint: acceptor1
  in: <?xml version=1.0" encoding="UTF-8"?><example id="123"/> ]
```

Fig. 2. The architecture of the JBI system (top) and example of a normalized message in an InOnly exchange (bottom)

4.1   A New Vision of Enforcement

Policies such as Red Cross's P1-P4 require an enforcement layer that is independent from any data processing or data management logic. The Red Cross *mediates* all interactions between individual users and the system, and between the system and hospital or government applications. This mediation controls *how* the data is used and how the different actors use the system. We argue that this mediation logic can be naturally integrated with the mediation framework presented by Gheorghe et al. [4]. Note here that no matter the Web services concerned, their states and life cycle are transparent to the messages they use to communicate; the service bus and any extra logic would only handle these messages.

The policies that the Red Cross wants enforced pertain to usage control. They respectively relate to: (P1) location-based usage of a piece of code, (P2) and (P4) time-bound obligations of certain roles or entities, (P3) a system-wide obligation to log application events. P1 refers to a pre-authorization that evaluates an environment condition – the code can only be invoked if the location attribute is a Red Cross branch. P2 is an attribute-based authorization for groups of subjects. P3 is an ongoing obligation that may require management of data or system states.

Designing a *versatile* enforcer of usage control policies at the ESB level requires some refinement and additions to the original UCON model. First, UCON enforcement is binary: it either allows or disallows the usage of an object by a subject. This might be a draconic solution in most applications, when the impossibility to execute an application step might have side-effects over an entire flow of actions. To bridge this gap, a solution is to allow the system to interfere with the original invocation or with any other connected state. This interference has several aspects: what entity performs it, when it should happen, how can it happen. First, we envision two possibilities of what trusted

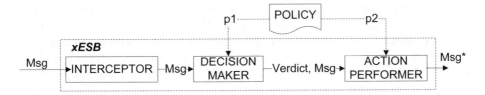

Fig. 3. The enforcement process behind xESB. The interceptor captures a message, the decision maker decides if the message complies with the p1 part of a policy; if not, the action performer enacts the p2 part of a policy, that describes the action to be taken.

entity can interfere with the enforcement process: the system or a trusted third-party (designated in advance). Second, this interference can be performed in two ways: *preventively* or *reactively*, that is before or after the UCON authorization decision. Third, once settled that a usage policy may specify an action to be performed when a condition holds, this action can either be delegated to a subsystem or performed on the fly. These three aspects lead to the following *additional semantics of a UCON-based enforcer*: separation between system and subject obligations as well as between pre- and post-obligations (also noticed in [7]), an active mechanism that can both execute an action or delegate it and observe the results (termed *executor*), the separation between subject actions and consequences of those actions onto the system.

4.2   The Three Steps in Enforcement

As shown in Fig. 3, the enforcement process has three basic steps [4]. **Interception** refers to capturing a usage request as specified by a policy. This assumes the existence of a filtering mechanism that can separate between requests that are interesting from those that are not. The second is the **decision** phase, where based on the same policy, the request just captured is deemed allowable or forbidden by the system, based on its internal state keeping. Making this evaluation implies reasoning about previous actions and obligations. The result is a decision seconded by a set of actions to be executed before of after allowing or forbidding the usage request. Thirdly, the **action performing** means the actions provided in the decision phase will be performed either by the system, or by a trusted third-party entity. In the case of a fault occuring anytime along these steps of the process, a fault message is sent back to the requesting entity and the default action is performed on the original message. In case an external actor performs these actions, the evidence of these actions will be sent back to the usage control enforcer, and they will have to be trusted. Having this split design of the enforcement process helps in achieving good flexibility: if a mechanism implementing any of these steps changes, the others can remain unmodified.

5   Policy Language

The language we use to express security policies is POLPA, an operational *PO*licy *L*anguage based on *P*rocess *A*lgebra [10,11]. This language represents the allowed behaviour of users by defining the sequences of actions that are allowed on the system, and which authorizations, conditions and obligations must hold before, during and after the execution of each action. Compared to XACML, POLPA ensures continuous usage control: resource accesses can be interrupted if the factors that authorized them before are not valid any more. Let us suppose that $\alpha(x)$ is an action and $p(x)$ is a predicate whose evaluation returns a boolean result; a security policy P is obtained by composing actions according to the following grammar:

$$P ::= \perp \parallel \top \parallel \alpha(x).P \parallel p(x).P \parallel x := e.P \parallel P_1 or P_2 \parallel P_1 par_{\alpha_1,...,\alpha_n} P_2 \parallel \{P\} \parallel Z$$

The informal semantics is the following:

- $\perp$ and $\top$ are the *deny-All* and *allow-All* operators;
- $\alpha(x).P$ is the *sequential operator*, and represents the possibility of performing an action $\alpha(x)$ and then to behave as P;
- $p(x).P$ behaves as P in the case the predicate $p(x)$ is true;
- $x := e.P$ assigns the values of expressions e to variables x and then behaves as P;
- $P_1 or P_2$ is the *alternative operator*, and represents the nondeterministic choice between P_1 and P_2;
- $P_1 par_{\alpha_1,...,\alpha_n} P_2$ is the *synchronous parallel operator*. It expresses that both P_1 and P_2 policies must be simultaneously satisfied. This is used when the two policies deal with actions (in $\alpha_1, \ldots, \alpha_n$);
- $\{P\}$ is the *atomic evaluation*, and represents the fact that P is evaluated in an atomic manner, that once started must be completed. P here is assumed to have at most one action, along with predicates and assignments. It allows the testing or update of variables prior or after an action;
- Z is the constant process. We assume that there is a specification for the process $Z \doteq P$ and Z behaves as P.

As usual for (process) description languages, derived operators may be defined. For instance, $P_1 par P_2$ is the *parallel operator*, and represents the interleaved execution of P_1 and P_2. It is used when the policies P_1 and P_2 deal with disjoint actions. The policy sequence operator $P_1; P_2$ may be implemented using the policy language's operators and control variables; see [6]. It allows to put two process behaviours in sequence. By using the constant definition, the sequence and the parallel operators, the iteration and replication operators, $i\,(P)$ and $r\,(P)$ resp., can be derived. Informally, $i\,(P)$ behaves as the iteration of P zero or more times, while $r\,(P)$ is the parallel composition of the same process an unbounded number of times.

This language is able to naturally represent even complex execution patterns. As an example, given that α, β and γ represent actions and p, q and r represent predicates, the following policy:

$$(p\,(x)\,.\,\alpha\,(x)\,.\,q\,(y)\,.\,\beta\,(y))\ \ \mathrm{par}\ \ (r\,(z)\,.\,\gamma\,(z))$$

allows the execution of the action α when its parameters x satisfy predicate p, followed by the execution of the action β when its parameters y satisfy the predicate q. Hence, this rule defines an ordering among the actions α and β, because β can be executed only after α. Even if the sequential operator determines the precedence between the two actions α and β, it does not require that β is executed immediately after α. As a matter of fact, after the execution of α and before the execution of β, the policy allows the execution of γ, provided that z satisfies the predicate r.

As in [10,11], the set of actions of the policy has been defined following an approach inspired by Zhang et al.[19]. However, here we introduce a further action: *execute(c)*. Given that the triple (s, o, r) represents the access performed by a user s to execute the operation r on the object o, the following is the list of the actions that can be used in the policy:

- *tryaccess(s,o,r)*: performed when the subject s requests the access (s, o, r).
- *endaccess(s,o,r)*: performed when the access (s, o, r) ends.
- *permitaccess(s,o,r)*: performed by the system to grant the access (s, o, r).
- *denyaccess(s,o,r)*: performed by the system to reject the access (s, o, r).
- *revokeaccess(s,o,r)*: performed by the system to revoke the access (s, o, r) previously granted while it is in progress.
- *update(s,a)*: performed by the system to update the attribute a of subject or object s.
- *execute(c)*: performed by the system to execute the command c. This action is an addition to the approach in [19] and extends the original POLPA obligations model. In our implementation, it piggybacks the command that the decision component delegates to the action performer.

For example, the following policy allows the user to access the web site *www.siteA.it*, but before this access the system requires that he should wait some time.

1 *tryaccess*(user, net, get_site(url)).
2 [(url == "www.siteA.it")].
3 *execute*(delay).
4 *permitaccess*(user, net, get_site(url)).
5 *endaccess*(user, net, get_site(url)).

In particular, line 1 of the policy refers to the access request for the A web site, and line 2 includes the authorization predicate that checks whether the URL of the site is *www.siteA.it*. In line 3 the policy asks the system to execute a command that generates a delay before actually allowing the access with the *permitaccess* action in line 4.

5.1   The Correspondence of POLPA to UCON Model

The authors of UCON defined a set of several core models that differ by the temporal position of the UCON components with respect to the execution of the access. As an example, in the $preA_3$ authorization model, the authorization phase is executed before the access, while the update of the attributes is performed after the usage. Since the POLPA language is able to define complex sequences of actions by exploiting its composition operators (i.e. sequential, alternative, parallel, iterative and replication), it is natural to encode the UCON core models in POLPA policies. It was showed [10] that POLPA's expressiveness is sufficient to model the basic features of UCON model by encoding all the basic UCON core models. In what follows we will show the example of the preAuthorization with preUpdate because is very general, as well as two widely used onAuthorizations models.

PreAuthorization with preUpdate ($PreA_1$). The preAuthorization model with preUpdate of the attribute a of the subject s is represented by the following policy.

$$tryaccess(s,o,r).$$
$$p_A(s,o,r).$$
$$update(s,a).$$
$$permitaccess(s,o,r).$$
$$endaccess(s,o,r)$$

In this policy we can see that both the evaluation of the authorization predicate $p_A(s,o,r)$ and the $update(s,a)$ action are executed by the system before issuing the $permitaccess(s,o,r)$ action, i.e. before the actual execution of the required operation.

OnAuthorization without Update (OnA_0). The following policy represents the ongoing authorization model without update. Here the predicate $\overline{p_A}$ denotes the negation of the predicate p_A, expressing the authorization condition. This policy states that after granting the permission to execute an access, if the authorization condition does not hold any more this permission is revoked even if the access is still in progress.

$$tryaccess(s,o,r).$$
$$permitaccess(s,o,r).$$
$$(endaccess(s,o,r) \text{ or } (\overline{p_A}(s,o,r).revokeaccess(s,o,r)))$$

In this case, the system authorizes the access as soon as it receives the request, because the $permitaccess(s,o,r)$ action immediately follows the $tryaccess(s,o,r)$ one. However, while the access is in progress, i.e. before the $endaccess(s,o,r)$ action has been received by the system, the predicate $\overline{p_A}(s,o,r)$ is repeatedly tested, and if it is satisfied the $revokeaccess(s,o,r)$ action is executed by the system, i.e. the access is interrupted before it naturally ends.

OnAuthorization with preUpdate (OnA_1). The following policy encodes the onAuthorization model with preUpdate.

$$tryaccess(s,o,r).$$
$$update(s,a).$$
$$permitaccess(s,o,r).$$
$$(endaccess(s,o,r) \text{ or } (\overline{p_A}(s,o,r).revokeaccess(s,o,r)))$$

In this policy the $update(s,a)$ action follows the $tryaccess(s,o,r)$ action and precedes the $permitaccess(s,o,r)$ action in the policy. Hence, the update is executed as soon as the access request is received, i.e. before granting the access to the resource and before evaluating the authorization predicate.

5.2   Expressing Usage Control Policies

Policies P1-P4 are expressed in POLPA in Table 1. Lines from 2 to 6 allow the execution of the security relevant action *submit_donor_data()* that requests the registration of the donor *name* in the data base, only if the predicate in line 3 is satisfied. This predicate checks that the location of the remote service that sent the message to the Data Submitter (DS) service is equal to "Hong Kong". If it is satisfied, the registration request is allowed by the *permitaccess(source,DS,submit_donor_data())* control action in line 4, and the *execute(writelog(submit_donor_data()))* command in line 5 asks the PEP to add an entry in the "shadow" log service for this action (P3). Hence, the PEP implements the *writelog* command by invoking the log service and communicating it the data about the action received by the PDP. After the registration of the donor data has been executed (line 6), the policy either allows the request for the confirmation of the previous registration, or asks the PEP to execute the *send_notification(donor_id)* command. Lines from 10 to 14 of the policy allow the execution of the confirmation action only if the donor id paired with the confirmation request is the same of the registration action previously allowed, as stated by the predicate in line 10. If the confirmation of the registration is allowed, the *execute* command in line 13 asks the PEP to invoke the log service to add a new entry in the log file for the current action (P3). However, if the confirmation request is not received within 3 days, the predicate in line 7 of the policy, that checks the elapsed time from the registration request arrival, is satisfied and the *send_notification(donor_id)* command is sent to the PEP. The PEP implements this command by invoking the Notification Service (NS) and communicating it the id of the donor whose registration has not been confirmed. The registration request arrival time is saved in the variable *req_date*, while the current time is stored in the *system.cur_date* system attribute. Since the alternative operator (or) in line 9 allows only one between the two previous actions, if the confirmation request is not received within 3 days from the registration, the system executes the notification command, and the confirmation action is not allowed any more.

If the confirmation action has been executed (line 14), the policy waits for 300 days before requesting the cancellation of the donor data from the data base (P4). In fact, line 15 of the policy includes a predicate that is satisfied when the time elapsed from the registration action is greater than 300 days. In this case, line 16 of the policy asks the PEP to execute the command *clean(donor_id)* that invokes the data cancellation service to delete the data of the donor *donor_id* from the data base.

Finally, the *rep* operator in line 1 of the policy allows the parallel execution of any number of instances of the policy from line 2 to line 17. This means that the policy can handle any number of registration and confirmation requests in parallel.

5.3 Extending POLPA

The reason why the original language had to be extended was the need for more verdicts. As mentioned before, all current access control and usage control monitors produce a binary decision: a service request can either be allowed, because the policy does not forbit it, or can be blocked, because it is a violation of the policy. We argued that these two options are no longer sufficient in a real system - it may be that *the bad thing* cannot be prevented. If the policy writer is astute to refer to the visible effects of a violation, then there is a chance of correction. The original POLPA had only allow/deny verdicts, hence we needed to extend it with the possibility to *execute* an external trusted action. We can support the features described by Gheorghe et al. [4], by allowing

Table 1. POLPA policy showing policies P1-P4

```
01 rep(
02    tryaccess(source, DS, submit_donor_data(location,req_date,name,donor_id)).
03    [(location = "Hong Kong")].
04    permitaccess(source, DS, submit_donor_data(location,req_date,name,donor_id)).
05    execute(writelog(submit_donor_data(location,req_date,name,donor_id))).
06    endaccess(source, DS, submit_donor_data(location,req_date,name,donor_id)).
07    (  (  [(system.cur_date - req_date > 3days)].
08          execute(send_notification(donor_id)))
09    or
10       (  tryaccess(source, PD, confirm_donor_data(confirm_id)).
11          [(donor_id = confirm_id)].
12          permitaccess(source, PD, confirm_donor_data(confirm_id)).
13          execute(writelog(confirm_donor_data(confirm_id)).
14          endaccess(source, PD, confirm_donor_data(confirm_id)).
15          [(system.cur_date - req_date > 300days)].
16          execute(clean(donor_id)))
17    )
18 );
```

variable granularity to this action: it can be an atomic action (delay a message, modify message payload or metadata, etc.) or a set of ordered actions. For modularity, these actions can be expressed in a language that the PDP is agnostic of. Overall, this POLPA extension preserves its capabilities to encode the UCON model.

6 Design and Implementation

6.1 Design

The design of xESB merges the enforcement process described above with the capabilities of POLPA. As shown in Fig. 4, xESB consists of an instrumented message router that mediates the interactions between service (or resource) clients and providers. These interactions are governed by POLPA policies that are enforced by the modified NMR. For the implementation, we chose Apache Service Mix 3.3[1] as an open-source ESB platform and instrumented its NMR by adding three modules corresponding to the three basic enforcement steps.

The interceptor captures XML messages within the ESB. The POLPA policies dictate what message types and parameters to look at: message destination, source, size, or metadata like annotation information. In xESB, this functionality is implemented by extending a listener interface immediately after an XML message is fired – this allows pre-updating, pre-authorization, pre-obligation enforcement – and immediately before a message is received by a client or provider – this allows for post-updating and post-obligation management. Our implementation captures every message on the ESB, but we are aware a prefiltering mechanism is important. Figure 2 (right) shows the format of a message on the NMR; because of the normalized format, split into structured metadata and payload, the message destination and the direction of the message can be easily extracted and compared against a filter. This mechanism would separate between policy relevant and non-relevant messages.

---

[1] http://servicemix.apache.org/home.html

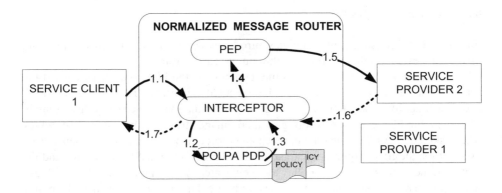

Fig. 4. The xESB design

The POLPA PDP makes the enforcement decision. It gets a message from the interceptor and evaluates it against the applicable policy (see Fig.3). In our implementation the PDP examines all policies in the policy base (or policy repository) against the current message, until the first one applies, but we are aware there is room for optimization. Once the applicable policy is found, evaluation is done by comparing message context and actual parameters (e.g., destination service, source service, message type, etc) with the conditions required by the POLPA policy. The output of the decision phase is called the *verdict* and zero or more actions. The enforcement decision is binary: the request is either allowed or rejected. While the first case implies no consequences onto the message flow, the second case calls for one or more enforcement actions that the PEP must perform. These actions are a form of *execute(c)* as expressed above. In our implementation, the PDP cannot interpret and execute these actions.

The PEP interprets and enacts the actions specified in the previous phase. At the ESB level, we envision several custom mechanisms for usage control enforcement: **The acceptor** accepts whole messages. If the verdict does not indicate any policy violation, then the acceptor is invoked, with the effect that the message is allowed without any modification. No effective action is supplied. **The blocker** rejects whole messages. The blocker mechanism is invoked to react to a policy violation by rejecting the entire message and sending back an error message. In xESB it is implemented by routing the XML message to an internal endpoint while sending back an error message. **The executor** describes enforcement actions other than accept or block. The reaction to a violation can be either modifying, duplicating or postponing a message. *Modifying* a message acts on the fly so that it conforms to the given policy. The action specifies the pairs of field-new values. In this way, a policy like "anonymize patient id when calling a statistics service" can be enacted automatically. *Duplicating* creates a clone of each intercepted message and forwards it to a predefined logging endpoint. *Delaying* is postponing a message until a condition is satisfied. This mechanism maps to the idea of obligation enforcement, where an actor would only be allowed to perform an action only after a condition has been verified. A policy like "delay patient data deletion for 10 days" can be implemented by delaying the deletion of call traces until the arrival of a message that signals the end of the tenth day.

6.2   Experimental Results

Enforcing POLPA usage control policies introduces a delay in message forwarding, and this section evaluates this overhead within our research prototype.

As depicted in Figure 4, the xESB interceptor calls the PDP to determine the if the action included in every message can be executed. Then the PEP enforces the PDP decision either by forwarding the message to the destination service or by discarding it. Moreover, the PEP executes the obligation commands triggered by the security policy when asked by the PDP. The time to reach an enforcement decision mainly depends on two factors: the time required to exchange data between the xESB interceptor and the PDP, and the complexity of the policy to be evaluated, since complex policies will take more time to be checked than simple ones. In particular, the time to evaluate the policy to determine the right to forward the message that requests the execution of given action α, depends on the number of *tryaccess* commands concerning α in the policy, and on the number and complexity of predicates in-between these tryaccesses and the related permitaccess commands.

In fact, the PDP searches in the security policy for all the *tryaccess* commands that refer to α, and for each of them evaluates all the following conditions in the policy until the related permitaccess is reached. For example, take the policy in Appendix A. To determine whether to allow the forwarding to the Data Submitter (DS) service of the message concerning the action *submit_donor_data*, the PDP evaluates the *tryaccess* command in line 2 of the policy, and the related *permitaccess* command is in line 4. Hence, the PDP evaluates one predicate only (line 3) for *submit_donor_data*, that compares the value of a parameter of this action with a constant string. The obligations that the PDP asks the PEP to execute may cause additional delays. For example, the *writelog(..)* function in line 5 of the policy represents an obligation that is triggered by the PDP but is executed by the PEP.

In order to evaluate the overhead, we set up a number of experiments against our research prototype. Table 2 reports the results. In our tests, we let xESB forward two messages originating from the Data Collector (DC) service. The first message invokes the *submit_donor_data* method on the Data Submitter (DS) service, the second invokes the *confirm_donor_data* method on the Process Donor service (see the first and second lines of Table 2, respectively).

To show how the complexity of the security policy impacts on the overhead introduced by the UCON authorization system, for the messages previously described, we measured the decision time enforcing three distinct policies: the policy shown in Table 1 (Policy 1), and two other derived policies (Policies 2 and 3, respectively). Policy 2 is shown in Appendix A, and it has been obtained adding two new clauses to Policy 1 for the actions *submit_donor_data* (lines 21 to 25 and lines 40 to 44) and *confirm_donor_data*, (lines 10 to 14 and lines 48 to 52). The purpose of Policy 2 is to increase the complexity of Policy 1 by increasing the number of tryaccess commands that the PDP has to evaluate to decide whether to allow the *submit_donor_data* and *confirm_donor_data* actions. In fact, to decide whether to allow the forwarding of the message including the *submit_donor_data* action, the PDP should evaluate three tryaccess commands, that are in lines 2, 21 and 40, and hence the related predicates in lines 3, 22 and 41.

The purpose of policy 3, instead, is to show that the time required to evaluate the security policy for an action α depends only on the tryaccess commands that refer to α, and it is not affected by the number of tryaccess commands related to other actions. Hence, policy 3 is obtained by adding to policy 1 ten tryaccess commands that concern other actions than *submit_donor_data* and *confirm_donor_data*. For the sake of brevity we don't show policy 3 here.

Table 2. Average round-trip time for message forwarding (μs)

action name	policy 1	policy 2	policy 3
submit_donor_data	5205 (22)	5166 (24)	4939 (22)
confirm_donor_data	4036 (29)	4108 (31)	4104 (29)

We obtained the figures in Table 2 by installing the PDP on a dedicated machine on the same local network as xESB. We measured both the average decision time with network delay including time for serialization and deserialization (the first figure), and without network delay (the second figure, in parentheses). Hence the second figure measures the average authorization system overhead due to the decision process only.

We observe that the maximum delay introduced by the authorization system is around 5000 μs, and this delay is greater for the *submit_donor_data* message than for the *confirm_donor_data* message, because the first message needs the transmission of four parameters compared to only one parameter for the second message.

We also observe that the PDP decision time is negligible when compared to the delay introduced by the local network. In fact, in the case of the *submit_donor_data*, Policy 1 is evaluated in about 22 μs, while the overhead including the network delay is about 5205 μs. Hence, placing the PDP on the same machine as xESB considerably reduces the overhead.

The experimental results also confirm that the PDP decision time depends on the complexity of the security policy to be enforced. As a matter of fact, the evaluation of Policy 2 takes more time than the evaluation of Policy 1 for the two messages because for each of them, policy 2 requires the evaluation of three tryaccess commands, while Policy 1 requires the evaluation of 1 tryaccess command only. Finally, we observe that the evaluation of Policy 3 takes the same time of Policy 1. This confirms that, to authorize a given action, the PDP does not evaluate all the tryaccess commands in the policy, but it only evaluates the tryaccess commands that concern that action.

7 Related Work

Usage Control. The complexity of usage control over access control makes elaborate access control languages (e.g., Ponder [2], EPAL [1], SPL [15]) unable to express obligations as per usage control, nor decisions other than allow or block. The work of Pretschner et al. [13,14] describes a formalized usage control language and the mechanisms to enforce it, but do not cover an enforcement model for SOA. Our solution reuses these enforcement mechanisms but applies them for the first time to the ESB level. Another related approach is that of Minsky [8], but just as [2], they consider generic distributed dedicated entities to realize the law. Our approach uses the ESB as a centralized mechanism that either performs runtime enforcement or delegates it.

Message-level standards. There are several XML security standards for message authentication, authorization, encryption and confidentiality: OASIS's WS-Security, SAML, and other WS-* specifications. They deal with narrow issues of SOA communication, and are orthogonal to our solution: they can bring generic guarantees on the security of the payload of the message and of the communicating ends. Our solution uses the message metadata for enforcing requirements on message mediation (and not only communication ends), which are adapted to the business logic.

Message-level enforcement language. Research in policy language capabilities for message-level enforcement retains open problems. Svirskas et al. suggest an XACML architecture for role-based access control enforcement [17]. Their solution employs ESB capabilities, but there is no stress on interception or mediation. Likewise, languages like Ponder2 [3] focus on authorizations without ongoing conditions, but Ponder2's obligations cannot update subject and target attributes. xDUCON tries to solve that problem with a shared data space model, but the solution remains purely abstract and stays away from a concrete policy language. Other approaches that discuss message-level enforcement do not discuss policy language capabilities [9,18,5]. Our solution uses POLPA, a process algebra policy language, within an instrumented ESB, and is shown to support ongoing usage control and obligations that affect attributes of any system user or asset. Our work is based on an existing approach [4], but while Gheorghe et al. use a customized policy language, we focus on formal enforcement capabilities, and prove the usefulness of POLPA when enforcing UCON policies.

8   Discussion and Conclusions

With the need of enforcing usage control policies at the enterprise message level, we model and implement an enterprise reference monitor enacting an extended semantics of the UCON concepts. An important contribution is to use a formally proved usage control language to express and enforce usage policies. This language allows for a set of *enforcement primitives* on secure messaging (the blocker, the modifier, the delayer, the executor). Because implementing these primitives might have different semantics from application to application, we argue that our design caters for a *customizable* ESB enforcement framework because it offers a semantic-independent wiring between the components.

As future work we plan to further extend obligations in POLPA and refine the subclasses of UCON policies enforced at the message bus level. In terms of our prototype, we plan to evaluate our implementation against different policy languages to the extend of their expressivity and against different policy complexities. Also, we plan to investigate if the extension of POLPA, initially unable to fully model all the Red Cross policies, warrants a conceptual extension of the UCON model.

Acknowledgement

The work published in this article has partially received funding from the European Community's 7th Framework Programme Information Society Technologies Objective under the MASTER project[2] contract no. FP7-216917.

References

1. Backes, M., Pfitzmann, B., Schunter, M.: A toolkit for managing enterprise privacy policies. In: Snekkenes, E., Gollmann, D. (eds.) ESORICS 2003. LNCS, vol. 2808, pp. 162–180. Springer, Heidelberg (2003)
2. Damianou, N., Dulay, N., Lupu, E., Sloman, M.: The ponder policy specification language. In: Sloman, M., Lobo, J., Lupu, E.C. (eds.) POLICY 2001. LNCS, vol. 1995, pp. 18–38. Springer, Heidelberg (2001)
3. Damianou, N., Dulay, N., Lupu, E., Sloman, M., Tonouchi, T.: Tools for domain-based policy management of distributed systems. In: NOMS, pp. 203–217 (2002)
4. Gheorghe, G., Neuhaus, S., Crispo, B.: xESB: An Enterprise Service Bus for access and usage control policy enforcement. In: 4th IFIP WG 11.11 International Conference on Trust Management (2010)
5. Goovaerts, T., Win, B.D., Joosen, W.: A flexible architecture for enforcing and composing policies in a service-oriented environment. In: Indulska, J., Raymond, K. (eds.) DAIS 2007. LNCS, vol. 4531, pp. 253–266. Springer, Heidelberg (2007)
6. Hoare, C.: Communicating sequential processes. Communications of the ACM 21(8), 666–677 (1978)
7. Katt, B., Zhang, X., Breu, R., Hafner, M., Seifert, J.: A general obligation model and continuity: enhanced policy enforcement engine for usage control. In: Proc. 13th ACM Symposium on Access Control Models and Technologies, SACMAT 2008, pp. 123–132. ACM, New York (2008)
8. Lam, T., Minsky, N.: A collaborative framework for enforcing server commitments, and for regulating server interactive behavior in soa-based systems. In: Proc. 5th Intl. Conf. on Collaborative Computing: Networking, Applications and Worksharing, pp. 1–10 (2009)
9. Maierhofer, A., Dimitrakos, T., Titkov, L., Brossard, D.: Extendable and adaptive message-level security enforcement framework. In: ICNS 2006, p. 72 (2006)
10. Martinelli, F., Mori, P.: On usage control for grid systems. In: Future Generation Computer Systems (to appear 2010)
11. Martinelli, F., Mori, P., Vaccarelli, A.: Towards continuous usage control on grid computational services. In: Proc. Intl. Conf. Autonomic and Autonomous Systems and International Conference on Networking and Services 2005, p. 82. IEEE Computer Society, Los Alamitos (2005)
12. Park, J., Sandhu, R.: The UCON$_{ABC}$ usage control model. ACM Trans. Inf. Syst. Secur. 7(1), 128–174 (2004)
13. Pretschner, A., Hilty, M., Basin, D., Schaefer, C., Walter, T.: Mechanisms for usage control. In: Proc. of 2008 ACM Symposium on Information, Computer and Comm. Sec., ASIACCS 2008, pp. 240–244. ACM, New York (2008)
14. Pretschner, A., Schütz, F., Schaefer, C., Walter, T.: Policy evolution in distributed usage control. In: 4th Intl. Workshop on Security and Trust Management (June 2008)

---

[2] http://www.master-fp7.eu

15. Ribeiro, C., Zúquete, A., Ferreira, P., Guedes, P.: Spl: An access control language for security policies with complex constraints. In: Proceedings of the Network and Distributed System Security Symposium, pp. 89–107 (1999)
16. Sun, Java Community Process Program: Sun JSR-000208 Java Business Integration,
    `http://jcp.org/aboutJava/communityprocess/final/`
    `jsr208/index.html`
17. Svirskas, A., Isachenkova, J., Molva, R.: Towards secure and trusted collaboration environment for european public sector. In: Intl. Conf. on Collaborative Computing: Networking, Applications and Worksharing, pp. 49–56 (November 2007)
18. Verhanneman, T., Piessens, F., Win, B.D., Joosen, W.: Uniform application-level access control enforcement of organizationwide policies. In: ACSAC 2005, pp. 431–440. IEEE Computer Society, Los Alamitos (2005)
19. Zhang, X., Parisi-Presicce, F., Sandhu, R., Park, J.: Formal model and policy specification of usage control. ACM Trans. on Information and System Security, 351–387 (2005)

A   Appendix: Policy P2 Expressed in POLPA

```
01rep(
02    (  tryaccess(source, DS, submit_donor_data(location,req_date,name,donor_id)).
03       [(location = "Hong Kong")].
04       permitaccess(source, DS, submit_donor_data(location,req_date,name,donor_id)).
05       execute(writelog(submit_donor_data(location,req_date,name,donor_id))).
06       endaccess(source, DS, submit_donor_data(location,req_date,name,donor_id)).
07       (  (  [(system.cur_date - req_date > 3days)].
08             execute(send_notification(donor_id)))
09       or
10          (  tryaccess(source, PD, confirm_donor_data(confirm_id)).
11             [(donor_id = confirm_id)].
12             permitaccess(source, PD, confirm_donor_data(confirm_id)).
13             execute(writelog(confirm_donor_data(confirm_id)).
14             endaccess(source, PD, confirm_donor_data(confirm_id)).
15             [(system.cur_date - req_date > 300days)].
16             execute(clean(donor_id))
17          )
18       )
19    )
20    or
21    (  tryaccess(source, DS, submit_donor_data(location,req_date,name,donor_id)).
22       [(location = "Italy")].
23       permitaccess(source, DS, submit_donor_data(location,req_date,name,donor_id)).
24       execute(writelog(submit_donor_data(location,req_date,name,donor_id))).
25       endaccess(source, DS, submit_donor_data(location,req_date,name,donor_id)).
26       (  (  [(system.cur_date - req_date > 3days)].
27             execute(send_notification(donor_id)))
28       or
29          (  tryaccess(source, PD, confirm_donor_data(confirm_id)).
30             [(donor_id = confirm_id)].
31             permitaccess(source, PD, confirm_donor_data(confirm_id)).
32             execute(writelog(confirm_donor_data(confirm_id)).
33             endaccess(source, PD, confirm_donor_data(confirm_id)).
34             [(system.cur_date - req_date > 600days)].
35             execute(clean(donor_id))
36          )
37       )
38    )
39    or
40    (  tryaccess(source, DS, submit_donor_data(location,req_date,name,donor_id)).
41       [(location = "UK")].
42       permitaccess(source, DS, submit_donor_data(location,req_date,name,donor_id)).
43       execute(writelog(submit_donor_data(location,req_date,name,donor_id))).
44       endaccess(source, DS, submit_donor_data(location,req_date,name,donor_id)).
45       (  (  [(system.cur_date - req_date > 3days)].
46             execute(send_notification(donor_id)))
47       or
48          (  tryaccess(source, PD, confirm_donor_data(confirm_id)).
49             [(donor_id = confirm_id)].
50             permitaccess(source, PD, confirm_donor_data(confirm_id)).
51             execute(writelog(confirm_donor_data(confirm_id)).
52             endaccess(source, PD, confirm_donor_data(confirm_id)).
53          )
54       )
55    )
56);
```

Detecting Sybil Nodes in Static and Dynamic Networks

José Antonio Cárdenas-Haro* and Goran Konjevod

School of Computing, Informatics and Decision Systems Engineering
Arizona State University
Tempe, AZ 85287-9309
{jose.cardenasharo,goran.konjevod}@asu.edu

Abstract. Peer-to-peer systems are known to be vulnerable to the Sybil attack. The lack of a central authority allows a malicious user to create many fake identities (called Sybil nodes) pretending to be independent honest nodes. The goal of the malicious user is to influence the system on his/her behalf. In order to detect the Sybil nodes and prevent the attack, we use here a reputation system for every node, built through observing its interactions with its peers. The construction makes every node a part of a distributed authority that keeps records on the reputation and behavior of the nodes. Records of interactions between nodes are broadcast by the interacting nodes and honest reporting proves to be a Nash Equilibrium for correct (non-Sybil) nodes. We argue that in realistic communication schedule scenarios, simple graph-theoretic queries help in exposing those nodes most likely to be Sybil.

Keywords: Distributed Systems, Sybil attack, Network security.

1 Introduction

In a large distributed network system, many types of security threats arise. A number of these are due to weaknesses in cryptographic protocols and concern the detection of malicious users trying to access data they do not have the rights to access, or forging another user's identity. Unlike those problems, Sybil attack is closely linked to the level of anonymity allowed by the system. Many security mechanisms, voting and recommendation systems base their protocols in the assumption of a one-to-one correspondence between entities and identities. If this basic assumption is broken, those systems are compromised. Sybil attack denotes the creation of many (fake) identities by a single entity in a distributed system, for the purpose of influencing and disrupting the normal behavior of the system.

1.1 Existing Work

Sybil attack was first named and studied by Douceur [8]. Douceur used the "communication cloud" model of communication, where a node "submits" a (possibly

---

* Research supported by the Fulbright-LASPAU and CONACyT Fellowships.

R. Meersman et al. (Eds.): OTM 2010, Part II, LNCS 6427, pp. 894–917, 2010.

encrypted) message into the cloud, and any node capable of reading the message may do so by simply "plucking it out" of the cloud and decrypting it if necessary. The point of stating the model this way was not so much the broadcast nature of it, but the fact that the origin of a message may only be determined from the message contents, and not from any network-provided information on the message (headers, or the actual host/router from which the message was received). In other words, the identity of a message sender cannot be determined from any external information about the message, only from the message contents. Douceur proved that Sybil attack cannot be prevented in such a model, and its severity only depends on the computational power of the malicious user relative to the computational power of honest users. Basically, as long as there is no centralized authority that would certify identities of users accepted into the network, the number of identities an entity may create is only limited by the amount of work the entity puts into this activity. (The removal of typical communication infrastructure from the model may also be motivated by thinking of this infrastructure as equivalent to a centralized identity-verification authority.)

Since the paper of Douceur [8], many others papers have been published on various forms of the Sybil attack problem [11] [13] [15] [2] [4] [5] [17] [16] [9].

Newsome et al. [11] studied the problem in the context of sensor networks and their methods were designed to work with the specific properties of radio resources, for example, they assumed that a node may not listen simultaneously on more than one frequency. Sastry et al. [13] presented an early version of a protocol that verifies node locations and bases node identities on their location information. Similar ideas were also proposed by Waters and Felten [15], Bazzi and Konjevod [2] and Čapkun and Hubaux [4,5]. In the most general form, these works are based on measuring the delays incurred by communications between nodes and imposing a geometric structure on the "distance space" to determine node locations. In particular, Bazzi and Konjevod show that, assuming the triangle inequality and a geometry close to Euclidean, even in the presence of colluding malicious users, one can design distributed protocols to localize nodes and thus help prevent Sybil attack. The common fundamental assumption here is that each real entity has the additional property of physical location within the distributed system, and that this property will influence the communication by the entity sufficiently that a powerful enough observer may distinguish it from the communication by any other entity. (Even if it is not always the case that every pair of entities may be distinguished, if the groups of indistinguishable entities are small enough, most of the repercussions of a Sybil attack may be prevented.)

The disadvantage of relying on the geometry of roundtrip delays is that it applies only to systems with honest routers. Also, due to the variability of network load and delays it is not always possible to have accurate measurements of roundtrip delays and clock synchronizations between routers that can be far apart physically. Another inconvenience is when a malicious user controls several network positions. In such condition the attacker can fabricate arbitrary network coordinates between those positions breaking totally the security system proposed. Furthermore, this system would not work at all in a dynamic network. On the other hand, this work does describe remotely issued certificates that can be used to test the distinctness of identities, and that idea may be of use combined with some facets of our approach.

More recently, Yu et al. [17,16] gave protocols that use a different restriction: they assume the existence of "secure" links between, say, pairs of friends in the network. Thus, any message coming directly through such a link comes with a known origin. In other words, one recognizes that the message was sent by a good friend (although, if the message is only relayed by the friend, no more is known about its origin). This may be seen as a step towards allowing centralized infrastructure, but the local nature of the edges encourages us to think about them as "local authorities". In order to "set up" these edges, Yu et al. assume prior "out-of-band" communication. They also assume that the network formed by these edges is fast-mixing, which they claim seems to be the case for most social networks. Finally, they notice a different type of restriction that is naturally present at Sybil nodes. Since a malicious node that creates many Sybil identities is only one node, not only is its computational power limited, but so is its bandwidth. In short, Yu et al. require a node applying for acceptance to the system to send a message that performs an "almost random" walk. The node receiving the application ("the verifier") does the same. Then, if two messages cross paths, the node is accepted. The idea behind their argument is that Sybil regions are bandwidth-limited and a message sent from within one will rarely "escape".

In both of SybilGuard and SybilLimit [17][16], the protocol is based on the "social network" among user identities, where an edge between two identities indicates a human established trust relationship. The edge key distribution is done out of band which is a disadvantage in most cases. The protocols will not work if the adversary compromises a large fraction of the nodes in the system. An assumption on which both SybilGuard and SybilLimit rely is that malicious users may create many nodes but relatively few attack edges. This is partially true since these protocols are more effective defending against malicious users than defending against compromised honest users that belong to the system. This is because a malicious user must make real friends in order to increase the number of attack edges, while compromised honest users already have friends. These protocols also break the anonymity of users, which is impractical in most cases since anonymity for many peer-to-peer users is a high priority. Taking away anonymity will prevent many users from participation.

Chris Lesniewski-Laas [9] assumes a one hop distributed hash table which uses the social links between users to resist the Sybil attack. As in the case of SybilGuard and SybilLimit he bases his protocols in human established trust relationships breaking the anonymity of users. This is similarly difficult to apply to real-life networks since many users in peer-to-peer systems prioritize anonymity as a condition of participation. Furthermore, a one-hop distributed hash table (DHT) is not a realistic approach for the world wide web. Users many hops apart, breaking the protocol proposed in[9].

Piro et al. [12] study Sybil attack in mobile ad-hoc networks, and propose some protocols we find interesting. The simple observation made by them (that we are not aware of having appeared in the literature before) is that in a mobile network, Sybil nodes are tied to their "maker". That is, identities from a Sybil group that was constructed by a single malicious user will never appear simultaneously in different regions of the network. So, if nodes have limited capabilities of observation and if two nodes who know they are far apart observe two identities roughly simultaneously, then these two identities are certainly not part of the same Sybil group. On the flip side, if two identities are always seen together over a long period of time, then there should be a reason for that. Unless they are linked by some other mechanism, they are very likely Sybil identities. Remarkably, this intuition, while it appears key in the mobile setting, is of little use in the static case. Thus, it forms a complement to the location- and delay-based certification mechanisms of [2] which were limited to the static setting. In fact, the basic observation is that a pair of independent users of a mobile ad-hoc network will frequently be seen simultaneously in different locations in the network, while a Sybil node is never seen far from its "master", forms the foundation for this research as well. However, we believe our approach is simpler and at the same time requires fewer additional assumptions.

[12] also propose monitoring of the network traffic and the collisions at the MAC level. The limitation in this case is that this only works for mobile Ad hoc networks. Others propose resource testing [1] to discourage rather than prevent Sybil attacks.

1.2 Discussion

What all of these existing approaches have in common is that they restrict the original problem formulation by making assumptions that allow the distributed system to enforce stronger limitations on the creation of fake identities. Usually, these assumptions are justified by arguments about physical properties of any real peer-to-peer network that restrict the communication cloud model by requiring some form of cost to be associated with each interaction between peers, either time taken by a message to reach its recipient(s), or bandwidth required for the message, or cost paid by an entity to have the message processed. This observation motivates our work by indicating that a distributed mechanism (in which all correct nodes participate) that imposes a certain type of cost on each communication step may in fact sufficiently emulate the implications of the existence of a centralized authority that Sybil attack becomes much harder in the system that employs such a mechanism.

2   Model and Assumptions

In most of this paper, we assume the setting is a network whose topology changes over time as nodes join and leave, and move within the network. However, the topology of the network ends up being mostly abstracted away by the communication cloud assumption mentioned earlier: we assume that each message sent by any node is broadcast into the communication cloud and the only information about the origin of a message a node observes in the communication cloud (or, equivalently, hears, by listening) is contained within the contents of the message. For example, a node cannot tell the source or even a single network router from which the message comes from a header, or by examining the message without reading its contents. Thus, a message may be signed by a node, but the identity claimed by the signing node cannot be verified directly unless we already know that node. On the other hand, we do assume standard cryptographic protocols such as digital signatures and public-key cryptography work.

One assumption we do make about the communication cloud, and the reason for saying that the network is only "mostly abstracted away," is that any message broadcast in the network has limited range: only the nodes in the general vicinity of the sender receive the message. We use this instead of any specific assumptions about the geometry (a metric and in particular Euclidean space was the key to the design of Sybil attack detection protocols in [2]) or the topology (a fast-mixing network was crucial to the protocols in [17,16]). Note that, similar to [2], we make an assumption that identifies a property of a Sybil attacker and its collection of fake identities that, to an observer capable of surveying all the events in the network, would make it obvious that there is something strange going on here. In the static setting of [2], the observer would notice many identities at the exact same physical location in the network. In our current dynamic setting, the image would be even more blatant: not only would many identities be located very close to each other, but whenever visible at all, they would be visible all in the same location. In other words, the observer would notice many identities always moving together through the network and never separating.

However, we avoid specific details beyond this general assumption. We are more interested in the fundamental consequences of anonymity in distributed systems and in the fundamental obstacles to secure identity management than in special cases, and so our goal is to study what can be achieved with a minimum set of assumptions rather than to provide a complete practically working solution for a very specific existing real world system.

The basic observation made in [12] is instrumental in our work as well, although we use it in a fundamentally simpler way. We also address a few variants of the more general problem that were left open until now, where a Sybil attacker attempts to thwart the detection process, and uses different subsets of its identities at different times, or even exchanges its identities with another attacker.

3   General Observations

We begin by noting that Sybil nodes by themselves may not be bad, but the major reason to create them in the first place is to affect the system at some point in time. All those nodes under the control of an individual can be used to negatively affect the system. For example, they can change the outcome of a ballot or influence the reputation of others. On the other hand, when a Sybil node is not actively used, it doesn't really change the system behavior, and so its bare existence is not necessarily a threat.

We consider the network as evolving over a period of time, and, for simplicity, divide the timeline into discrete intervals. Then, we consider a set of nodes assigned the role of network "observers". An observer simply keeps track of nodes it sees in its vicinity over a sequence of time intervals. Aggregating the data from multiple observers allows us to list, for every time interval, nodes observed in various parts of the system. Since the range of a message is limited, observers that are far away from each other will observe disjoint subsets of nodes during any given time interval. Thus we notice and claim the basic fact that underlies our approach: *two identities observed during a single time interval by observers that are far away from each other belong to two independent entities.* In other words, if an entity and any of its Sybil nodes are observed simultaneously, they will be observed in regions of the system that are close-by. We avoid a strict definition of "close-by" or "far away" for the exact purpose of keeping the discussion as general and the applicability of the approach as broad as possible. In fact, in any real implementation of these ideas, there will be a trade-off between the properties (the range) of communication, the duration of a time interval, and the region an observer is in charge of.

Let us consider the conclusions that can be attempted by (a group of) observers.

1. Node A is observed by o_1 and node B by o_2 during the same time interval. The observers o_1 and o_2 are far away from each other.

   In this situation, it is immediately clear that A and B are identities that belong to distinct entities, since a single entity could not be visible simultaneously in several network locations. This events implies that A and B are distinguishable entities, and the distributed system should in the future be able to rely on this knowledge. (The only situation in which this observation may be dangerous is if a malicious node exchanges some of its identities with another one through exchanging private keys or certificates. We later outline an approach to some versions of this problem.)

2. Node A is observed simultaneously with node B by observer o_1.

   We cannot conclude much from a single such observation. On the other hand, it may be reasonable to assume that distinct entities will in fact not constantly move together and be located near each other. If this is true, then each time two nodes are observed together, the likelihood that they are not independent, and that one is a fake identity created by the other, becomes higher. For maximum generality, we do not rely heavily on such assumptions in this paper.

3. Node A is observed during a time period when node B is not seen anywhere.

   As in the previous case, we cannot conclude with certainty anything about these two nodes from a single observation. The two nodes may be independent, but this event may also be a consequence of a malicious node trying to hide its tracks by selectively activating subsets of nodes it controls. If one could assume that distinct entities operate so that the periods in which the entities in a subset are active are not highly correlated, or are even statistically independent, then the laws of probability would imply that two

identities such that at any given time at most one is seen anywhere really
are two identities associated with the same entity, and so that at least one
of them is a Sybil identity.

However, in some cases, this situation is not as severe: since at most one
of the two identities is seen at any given moment, even if one or both are
fake identities, the damage to the distributed system is likely not very large.
Depending on the actual purpose of the distributed system, this situation
may not be of grave concern.

4   Distinguishability Errors

How can a protocol based on the ideas described above fail? The main action
performed is to conclude that two identities are distinguishable when they are
reported to be present in two different locations simultaneously. Now, suppose
two identities A and B are pronounced distinguishable when they are in fact two
Sybil identities controlled by the same entity. First, the mode in which nodes of
the network lie is not such that nodes simply lie about having seen one of the two
identities. For if the reports about having seen A and B really do come from two
regions of the network that are sufficiently far away, then the nodes reporting
about this cannot be controlled by a single entity. In fact, thus we see that if A
and B are falsely pronounced distinguishable, then some node participating in
this must be lying about its location in the network: only if a node claims to be
farther away from its Sybil siblings can its claim of having seen A at the same
time as the rest of the nodes saw B be taken as evidence of distinguishability
for A and B. Suppose X claims to have seen A and Y to have seen B, while X
and Y were far away from each other. Now, either X or Y is lying about its own
location. Since the Sybil siblings of X and Y are restricted to one of the two
locations, say the location of X, we may conclude that Y's lie will be exposed
as soon as one consults any node who really was where Y claims to have been
at the time.

If we refer to an error such as described above as a false positive (two identities
falsely distinguished), what about a false negative? This means two identities are
never pronounced distinguishable while they are actually two separate entities.
As argued above, except for special circumstances, this should be a very rare
event. In [12], it is suggested that one may detect this by examining the amount
of traffic within such a group of mutually indistinguishable nodes. Namely, the
amount of traffic should be proportional to the square of the number of nodes
in the group if these are distinct entities, while it will be much smaller in a
Sybil group: whenever Sybil node A communicates with Sybil node B, the Sybil
master is the one actually working the communication channel on both ends.

4.1   Collusion Among Sybil Groups

We've argued that a false positive is not easy to achieve for a single malicious
adversary. However, if two entities controlling Sybil groups collude, the detection

problem becomes more difficult. Consider two nodes A and B, each controlling a Sybil group. In order to help A cheat and pass off its Sybil nodes a_1 and a_2 as distinguishable, B (located sufficiently far away from A) claims (through any of its Sybil nodes) to have seen a_2 at the same time that A claims (through any of its Sybil nodes) to have seen a_1. Now, if there are no honest nodes located close enough to B's position to be able to observe a_2 where B claims to have seen it, there is not much that can be done. However, if there are, there will be a discrepancy between their reports and those of B.

In this situation, in fact, it appears that one must require that more honest nodes than the Sybil nodes controlled by B are in the area where they would observe a_2. Then when it comes to examining their reports on observed nodes, more nodes will vote not to have seen a_2 than to have seen it, and the system will correctly conclude that a_2 could not have been in the area.

4.2   Formal Observers

Having sketched out the generalities, we describe more precisely a possible approach to more precise implementation of the ideas. As in some other proposed strategies to defeat Sybil attack, one could maintain a set of nodes formally authorized to work as a group and issue credentials for accessing the network. Of course, there will be a need to enforce the correctness of their behavior, for example, to prevent them from defection and sudden turn to working with a Sybil group. This can be achieved, for example, by duplicating the system and thus reducing the chance of corruption.

But let us describe the role of these "observers". They are relatively static in the network and they relinquish their roles when they move, handing off to new members of the group. They cover all the regions of the network and maintain a connected overlay that has members close enough to "every corner" so they can observe and confirm any claimed location of a node in the network. Then, they may work similarly to "beacons" in [2], establishing protocols by which new applicants to the network and those who have just moved are issued and reissued access credentials.

A few corrupt observers will not break the system in general, but strategically selected ones may cause some serious damage and so we envision these nodes as running distributed protocols resilient to failure of a small subset of nodes.

5   Goals

To summarize our discussion so far, here is a list of desirable properties for an approach to the Sybil attack problem that would improve on the current state of knowledge.

5.1   Anonymity

Design a self-policing peer-to-peer system that allows users to keep their anonymity. At issue is anonymity of users (which is endangered in the presence of a central certificate authority) versus safety against Sybil attacks.

It is not always possible to use certificate authorities to guarantee that each person has only one identity. Good certifying agencies are expensive and may discourage the participation of many users. In other cases the users would prioritize anonymity like in forums about religion, sex, politics, family violence, etc. In other words the system has to be self-policing and users should be allowed to maintain anonymity.

5.2 Static and Dynamic Settings

Existing solutions against Sybil attack work in special network models. Furthermore, each of them assumes either a completely static or a very dynamic topology. Is there a unified solution?

Another issue here is that in the real world the users are a mixture of mobile and static nodes. So far the proposed approaches work only exclusively in static or mobile networks but not in both. There is a lack of an algorithm that works to validate static and mobile users as well. In the absence of a certifying authority, the rules and policy used have to be defined and enforced by the peers themselves.

5.3 Dealing with Multiple Sybil Groups

The existence of multiple of malicious users is a major unsolved problem related to Sybil attack. By unsolved, we mean here that in practically no proposed approach to dealing with Sybil attack offers any relief in the situation where several malicious users create independent Sybil groups, even if they act independently and do not collude to make each other's behavior more difficult to detect.

We argue that our solution works well even in the presence of multiple malicious users, as long as they are not colluding. With several or many attackers working as a team handling together the same group of Sybil nodes, they can camouflage even more the Sybil nodes making them appear "more normal" in their behavior and making their detection harder.

6 Our Algorithm

Our basic solution has two major components: a reputation system based on the outcomes of interactions between peers in the network, and a separate analysis of interactions according to their participants' locations in time and space.

We consider the Sybil nodes as under the control of an adversary which may be one or more malicious users, colluding or not. Honest nodes participate in the system to provide and receive service as peers. Honest nodes need a mechanism to detect Sybil nodes and protect themselves against the Sybil attack. Ideally, the mechanism of detection should be efficient enough to detect the Sybil nodes before they gain enough reputation as trustable. The nodes are not restricted in any way to participate in P2P operations and they can build a reputation over time that will make them trustable. The nodes earn reputation points using a game-theoretic mechanism. In some of our approaches, after interacting with a peer, each node must (locally) broadcast a report on the outcome of such interaction. Any nearby authority nodes are always listening for those reports and collecting information on the fly. Such information is later used to infer Sybil relations between nodes.

At a high level, every interaction between two nodes results in summary reports of the interaction made by both participants. These reports contribute to reputation scores, but they are also used to create a graph (where the edges link nodes who are rating other nodes) whose connectivity structure is analyzed. Since a pair of reports is created solely by the pair of nodes reporting on their interaction, two Sybil nodes might falsify a large number of reports in order to boost each other's reputation. However, if overused, this will become obvious through an analysis of the rating graph.

The third mechanism we use to detect Sybil candidates is based on the observation that independent nodes tend to behave independently, both in terms of where they are located, and in terms of when they communicate.

It is worth noticing here that we never restrict in any way a node in participating and interacting with its peers (unlike some earlier systems where a node would have to be certified before it was admitted to the network). We consider each node honest until proven otherwise; however, if a node has not enough reputation points, it will not be considered trustable enough and subsequently it cannot cause much damage. When the interaction between any two peers is over, both nodes perform a (local) broadcast of their reports on that interaction. These two reports must match, otherwise those nodes are marked as suspicious. From the reports that have been broadcast and their timing, every node over time builds three data sets as explained in section 6.3. There is always the possibility of pairs of Sybil nodes simulating an interaction and broadcasting false reports, in order to increase their reputations as trustable nodes. It is possible they may do this infrequently, however if this is abused, they will expose themselves since after a large number of "interactions" such as these, there will be enough information to explore the graph induced by such interactions and identify active Sybil groups as its strongly connected components. For details, see section 6.5.

Furthermore, from the timing on the broadcasts of the reports we can learn useful information too. For this we discretize time into slots or *time buckets* that we use as observation periods. Just after an interaction between any two peers is finished, they have to broadcast their reports with the results of such interaction. Several or many pairs of nodes might be broadcasting their information within the same *time bucket*. Analyzing this information, we can identify nodes that are more likely to be cheating as they will appear as *densest subgraphs* of a different graph. In this part, we take advantage of the fact that a group of Sybil nodes are under the control of a single malicious user, which limits the capacity of the Sybil nodes in appearing as all broadcasting simultaneously.

6.1 Temporal Coincidences

Our first observation here is that if two nodes never broadcast within the same bucket, then it is very unlikely they are independent. Indeed, if we model the communication pattern of a node by a stochastic process, then the probability of two independent nodes behaving in a coordinated fashion for a long period of time will naturally tend to zero.

To be more specific, consider a family of stochastic processes that describe the behavior of nodes in the peer-to-peer network. Suppose each independent node randomly decides whether to interact with another node in each time step. Suppose the probability of each node's participation in a time step is lower-bounded by a positive constant ϵ. Then the probability that two nodes never or rarely both broadcast in the same time step tends to 0 as time passes.

This observation may be used by observers collecting broadcast interaction report data to find likely groups of nodes whose behavior is correlated. Since the particular type of correlation mentioned here is simultaneous broadcast, and each broadcast consumes considerable bandwidth resources, it seems reasonable to assume that Sybil groups will have overall relatively low coincidence of broadcast reports.

Nevertheless, there is the possibility that some non-Sybil nodes show strong relation between them; and because of that appear connected and suspicious of being Sybil. In order to differentiate regular nodes from Sybil nodes, a set of tests have to be run on them. So as to avoid saturating the suspected nodes with tests coming from many other peers (such action would cause false positives), from the set of nonsuspicious nodes some nodes are chosen randomly and agree to run the tests on the suspected peers and inform the others about the results. The suspected nodes have to answer the tests within a short timeframe. If the nodes are independent, they will reply simultaneously or close to it. There may even be many collisions on the replies if the nodes are in fact independent. On the other hand, the replies from Sybil nodes are more sequential and most of them outside of the timeframe.

6.2 Game Theory and the Reputation System

Incentives and keeping a record of the behavior of peers provide a method to promote healthy systems and cooperation [3]. This is widely used in online shopping, by Amazon and eBay among others. Problems arise in systems where there is no central authority and they are open to Sybil attack. In our model every node keeps track of his/her peers' reputations. When two peers interact they earn or lose points based on the cooperation or defection between them. Every node reports its good and bad points earned as well as the points of the peer it has interacted with.

After two nodes finish an interaction they have to submit (broadcast) a report independently. These reports contain the reputation points earned by them, the index numbers of the two nodes, the time they started and finished the interaction and a key (for example, containing a digital signature of each of the two nodes that cannot be forged by other nodes). The reports are sent individually, so the key may be used to establish a correspondence. The two reports must match. The reputation points earned could be different for each node (asymmetric).

We assume that all interactions between two peers follows the payout rules indicated below, where "C" states for cooperation and "D" for defection.

	C	D
C	(1,1)	(2,-3)
D	(-3,2)	(0,0)

All the other peers in the network, once they receive both reports and if they match, they will add those points in the *reputation* matrix (defined in section 6.3). Honest reporting for the cases of online sellers and buyers proves to be a Nash Equilibrium [10]. In our model this is the case as well.

Proposition 1. *In the reporting game, truthful reporting is a strict Nash Equilibrium.*

Under some different initial conditions, Miller et al. [10] prove that honest reporting is a strict Nash Equilibrium. In their model buyers gain points by rating sellers under the control of a central authority (like in Amazon, eBay, etc). They consider each rater's signal as private information and if a rater believes that other raters will announce their information truthfully, then transfers based on a strictly proper scoring rule induce the rater to truthfully announce his/her own information. That is, according to Miller et al., truthful reporting is a strict Nash Equilibrium.

In our case, we have a distributed authority which will evaluate the truthfulness of the reports based on their counterparts. Reputations points from no matching reports are not counted and will put the reporting peers in the list of suspicious peers. Thus the best bet for peers is truthful reporting.

The proposition can be proved analogously to [10]. What follows is basically the same as their proof. For each peer, choose another peer $r(i)$, the playing peer for i, whose report i will be asked to match. Let

$$\tau_i^* \left(a^i, a^{r(i)} \right) = R \left(a^{r(i)} | a^i \right), \tag{1}$$

where $a_m^i m$ is the announcement of rater i when the rater signals s_m, $a^i = (a_m^i)_m$ and $R \left(a^{r(i)} | a^i \right)$ is a strictly proper scoring rule [7].

Assume that peer $r(i)$ reports honestly: $a^{r(i)}(s_m) = s_m$ for all m. Since S^i (the random signal received by i) is stochastically relevant for $S^{r(i)}$, and $r(i)$ reports honestly, S^i is also stochastically relevant for $r(i)$'s report as well. Given that $S^i = s^*$, player i chooses $a^i \in S$ in order to maximize:

$$\sum_{n=1}^{M} R \left(s_n^{r(i)} | a^i \right) g \left(s_n^{r(i)} | s^* \right) \tag{2}$$

Since $R(\cdot|\cdot)$ is a strictly proper scoring rule, (2) is uniquely maximized by announcing $a^i = s^*$, i.e., truthful announcement is a strict best response. Thus, given that player $r(i)$ announces truthfully, player i's best response is to announce truthfully as well.   □

6.3 Matrices Built

From the information provided by the broadcast reports and the time slots (see section 6.4), every node is able to fill up three square matrices on the fly of size $N \times N$, where N is the total number of nodes participating. Next are described those matrices.

- The *reputation* matrix is to keep track of all the points earned by every node from every interaction. Here we add the points earned by node i from node j in the row i column j of this matrix.
- The *counter* matrix, as its name suggests, is used to count the nodes appearing in every time bucket. This matrix is filled up by increments of one for every node that appears in the time bucket. Suppose we have the next vector of pairs of nodes reporting in the same *time bucket*, this is $\{(n_3, n_7), (n_{21}, n_{77}), (n_{53}, n_{27}), (n_{33}, n_{10})\}$. Then in the matrix, for the first pair of reporting nodes, **all** the values in column 3 and 7 are incremented by one, excepting the intersections with row 3 and row 7. Ditto for the other three pairs of reporting nodes.
- Last but not least we have the *inbucket* matrix, which is to detect what nodes never (or seldom) appear in the same *time bucket* in different reporting pairs. For the same vector of pairs of nodes $\{(n_3, n_7), (n_{21}, n_{77}), (n_{53}, n_{27}), (n_{33}, n_{10})\}$, in this case here the matrix is filled up in a similar way that the *counter* matrix, but now incrementing the values only in the rows corresponding to the nodes in the vector, excepting the rows of the reporting pair. By example, the values for column 3 and 7 in this matrix are incremented by one only at the rows 21, 77, 53, 27, 33 and 10. Columns 21 and 77 are incremented by one only at the rows 3, 7, 53, 27, 33 and 10. The same for the other pairs of reporting nodes. The matrix resulting here is symmetric (a more detailed example of this matrix is in section 6.4).

6.4 Report Broadcasting and the Time Buckets

Peers interact through an encrypted channel. Every pair of nodes interacting (according to the rules in section 6.2) have to broadcast independently their reports just after their interaction is over. The reports that they broadcast contain the next information:

- The ID of itself and the ID of its interacting peer.
- The reputation points earned by it and by its interacting peer.

- 10 character hexadecimal key generated randomly by both at the end of the interaction.

The random key reported independently by the interacting pair of peers, have to be exactly the same. The other information in the reports need to be a match as well. In order to keep track of all those independent nodes able to broadcast their reports simultaneously (non Sybil), we monitor them through *time buckets*. Let us explain this through figure 1 where the black dots represent the regular nodes and the red circles represent the Sybil nodes. The links indicate interaction between two nodes. In the case of Sybil nodes that is not necessarily a real interaction, since a malicious user can just broadcast the two reports almost simultaneously trying to make them appear as independent nodes.

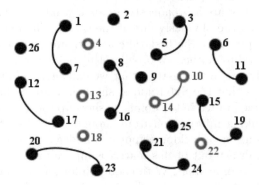

Fig. 1. A Sybil couple (η_{10} and η_{14}) broadcasting reports along with regular couples within the same *time bucket*

Imagine that all the interacting nodes of figure 1 broadcast their reports within the same *time bucket* or slot of time. Any node is able to read all the broadcast reports from every *time bucket*, and keep a record on every node not only on its reputation points but also on which nodes broadcast their reports within the same *time bucket*. As an example, assume that η_3 represents node 3 from figure 1, then all the nodes will register that the nodes showing up simultaneously (in the same *time bucket*) with η_3 are $\eta_1, \eta_6, \eta_7, \eta_8, \eta_{10}, \eta_{11}, \eta_{12}, \eta_{14}, \eta_{15}, \eta_{16}, \eta_{17}, \eta_{19}, \eta_{20}, \eta_{21}, \eta_{23}$ and η_{24}. As you can see $\eta_2, \eta_4, \eta_5, \eta_9, \eta_{13}, \eta_{18}, \eta_{22}, \eta_{25}$ and η_{26} are not in the register.

The reason for omitting η_5 is because it is the partner or interacting peer of η_3. The others are omitted just because they are not broadcasting any reports. It means that the nodes registered for η_5 will be exactly the same nodes registered for η_3. This same method is applied on every broadcasting pair and all this is repeated in all the *time buckets*. With all the information provided by this means, every node can fill up a matrix on the fly. Next we show a matrix with the output values corresponding to the first fourteen nodes, according to the interactions and broadcast shown in the example of figure 1.

	η_1	η_2	η_3	η_4	η_5	η_6	η_7	η_8	η_9	η_{10}	η_{11}	η_{12}	η_{13}	η_{14}	η_{15}	η_{16}	η_{17}	η_{18}	η_{19}	η_{20}	η_{21}	η_{22}	η_{23}	η_{24}	η_{25}	η_{26}
η_1	0	0	1	0	1	1	0	1	0	1	1	1	0	1	1	1	1	0	1	1	1	0	1	1	0	0
η_2	0	0	0	0	0	0	0	0	0	0	0	0	0	0	0	0	0	0	0	0	0	0	0	0	0	0
η_3	1	0	0	0	0	1	1	1	0	1	1	1	0	1	1	1	1	0	1	1	1	0	1	1	0	0
η_4	0	0	0	0	0	0	0	0	0	0	0	0	0	0	0	0	0	0	0	0	0	0	0	0	0	0
η_5	1	0	0	0	0	1	1	1	0	1	1	1	0	1	1	1	1	0	1	1	1	0	1	1	0	0
η_6	1	0	1	0	1	0	1	1	0	1	0	1	0	1	1	1	1	0	1	1	1	0	1	1	0	0
η_7	0	0	1	0	1	1	0	1	0	1	1	1	0	1	1	1	1	0	1	1	1	0	1	1	0	0
η_8	1	0	1	0	1	1	1	0	0	1	1	1	0	1	1	0	1	0	1	1	1	0	1	1	0	0
η_9	0	0	0	0	0	0	0	0	0	0	0	0	0	0	0	0	0	0	0	0	0	0	0	0	0	0
η_{10}	1	0	1	0	1	1	1	1	0	0	1	1	0	0	1	1	1	0	1	1	1	0	1	1	0	0
η_{11}	1	0	1	0	1	0	1	1	0	1	0	1	0	1	1	1	1	0	1	1	1	0	1	1	0	0
η_{12}	1	0	1	0	1	1	1	1	0	1	1	0	0	1	1	1	0	0	1	1	1	0	1	1	0	0
η_{13}	0	0	0	0	0	0	0	0	0	0	0	0	0	0	0	0	0	0	0	0	0	0	0	0	0	0
η_{14}	1	0	1	0	1	1	1	1	0	0	1	1	0	0	1	1	1	0	1	1	1	0	1	1	0	0

As can be seen, nodes η_1 and η_7 are not counted neither in the first nor the seventh row since they are a broadcasting pair in that *time bucket*. Nodes that are not broadcasting are obviously out of the count. The matrix shown in this example is the output after the first *time bucket*, subsequently under the same procedure and according to the new broadcasting pairs, the corresponding values are incremented by one in this matrix that we call *inbucket* matrix.

The point here is that the Sybil nodes, since they are under the control of a malicious user, are so limited in the ability to show up together [8] as independent nodes do. After taking information from enough *time buckets* the matrix will show which nodes never (or seldom) appear broadcasting within the same *time bucket*. The graph drawn out of this matrix is an undirected one, and the Sybil nodes here tend to form a *clique*. With enough information in this matrix, every listener node is able to look out for *densest subgraphs* which represent a Sybil behavior. The Sybil nodes will be then exposed. However, we still do not consider them Sybil. We tag all the nodes in the densest subgraph just as highly suspicious of being Sybil. The next step to confirm this, is the phase of testing as described in section 6.7.

6.5   Finding the Strongly Connected Components

Here we need the information from the *reputation* and *counter* matrices in order to find the *strongly connected components*. The reputation points earned by node A from node B are not necessarily the same quantity that the points earned by node B from node A. That is why we get *strongly connected components*. We set the affinity between nodes depending on the reputation points earned and on the number of interactions. We use the following expression to describe the *affinity* between two nodes:

$$A_{ij} = \frac{P_{ij}}{\Psi_i} + \frac{I_{ij}}{\iota_i} \qquad (3)$$

Where A_{ij} is defined to be the affinity of node i for node j. We use P_{ij} to represent the total of points earned by node i from the interaction with node j, and Ψ_i is the total of points earned by node i in its lifetime. The value of I_{ij} is the number of interactions between the nodes i and j, and ι_i is the total of interactions performed by the node i in its lifetime. Obviously, the values for A_{ij} are rational in the range from 0 to 2. All the other variables have integer values. From the *reputation* matrix we can have the value of P_{ij} directly from the intersection of row i and column j. The value of Ψ_i is obtained from this same matrix by the summation of all the reputation points in the respective row. We have then:

$$\Psi_i = \sum_{j=0}^{n-1} P_{ij}$$

Where n is the total of nodes participating and being screened. The values of I_{ij} and ι_i are taken from the *counter* matrix. The value of ι_i is equal to the summation of all the values in column i divided by $n-2$. This is:

$$\iota_i = \frac{\sum_{i=0}^{n-1} \delta_{ij}}{n-2}$$

Where δ_{ij} represent the value in row i and column j from the *counter* matrix. The value I_{ij} is just the remainder of ι_i minus δ_{ij}.

$$I_{ij} = \iota_i - \delta_{ij}$$

Once we have all the required values we can apply the formula 3 to find A_{ij} which is a rational number. We set here a threshold value or lower cap σ, if the value $A_{ij} > \sigma$ we say that node i is strongly connected to node j. Then we can apply the Tarjan's algorithm [14] to find the *strongly connected components*. The pseudocode for this is shown in Algorithm 1.

Observation 1. *When peers from a group of nodes earn too many reputation points between them, that group can be detected through the strongly connected components method.*

Indeed, the reputation points earned between nodes are asymmetric. According to our formula (3) for affinity, the more a node earn reputation points from a peer, the higher its affinity for it. There is a trigger point to consider that one node is connected to another. If a group of nodes earn between them reputation points beyond the trigger point, all of them will appear as a *strongly connected component*.

6.6   Finding the Densest Subgraphs

For this we use the *inbucket* matrix as explained in subsections 6.3 and 6.4. We can find relations among nodes based on the timing of their broadcastings (Section 6). A group of Sybil nodes under the control of a malicious user are limited in their capacity of showing up simultaneously. After we have enough information in the *inbucket* matrix, we will be able to find connections among the nodes that will put in evidence that they belong to a Sybil group. The quantity of samples or *time buckets* that we need depends on the percentage of Sybil nodes in the network.

Algorithm 1. Detecting the Sybil groups by the Strongly Connected Components

---

Require: *Reputation Matrix, Counter Matrix, N, σ;*
Ensure: *SCC {Strongly Connected Components (Sybil groups)};*
1: **for** $i := 0$ to $N - 1$ **do**
2:     **for** $j := 0$ to $N - 1$ **do**
3:         $\Psi_i \Leftarrow \Psi_i + P_{ij}$
4:     **end for**
5: **end for**
6: **for** $j := 0$ to $N - 1$ **do**
7:     **for** $i := 0$ to $N - 1$ **do**
8:         $\iota_i \Leftarrow \iota_i + \delta_{ij}$
9:     **end for**
10: **end for**
11: **for** $i := 0$ to $N - 1$ **do**
12:     $\iota_i \Leftarrow \frac{\iota_i}{N-2}$
13: **end for**
14: **for** $i := 0$ to $N - 1$ **do**
15:     **for** $j := 0$ to $N - 1$ **do**
16:         $I_{ij} \Leftarrow \iota_i - \delta_{ij}$
17:     **end for**
18: **end for**
19: **for** $i := 0$ to $N - 1$ **do**
20:     **for** $j := 0$ to $N - 1$ **do**
21:         $A_{ij} \Leftarrow \frac{P_{ij}}{\Psi_i} + \frac{I_{ij}}{\iota_i}$
22:     **end for**
23: **end for**
24: **for** $i := 0$ to $N - 1$ **do**
25:     **for** $j := 0$ to $N - 1$ **do**
26:         **if** $A_{ij} \geqslant \sigma$ **then**
27:             $dedge_{ij} \Leftarrow True$
28:         **end if**
29:     **end for**
30: **end for**
31: *Apply Tarjan's algorithm on the graph;*
32: *SCC $\Leftarrow$ results from Tarjan's algorithm;*

Observation 2. *When peers from a group of nodes never (or seldom) appear broadcasting within the same time bucket, then that group of nodes can be detected as a densest subgraph.*

Without loss of generality suppose that we have n nodes and that all of them broadcast randomly with the same probability; and that at every *time bucket* $\lceil \frac{n}{10} \rceil$ nodes broadcast. After τ samples we will see that the appearance of the nodes show a uniform distribution; where τ is the minimum number of samples needed to detect that the distribution is uniform. A group of Sybil nodes is limited in showing up together, the larger the group the more the limitation. The distribution of Sybil node appearances will thus not come out uniform with respect to the other nodes.

Observation 3. *The more the Sybil nodes, the sooner they can be detected as a densest subgraph by the data collected from the time buckets.*

The bigger the group of Sybil nodes the harder for a malicious user on making them appear as an independent entities, and the less of *time buckets* needed to discover the connections among them. In other words, the non uniform distribution of the Sybil nodes with respect to the others will be accentuated and noticeable in fewer samples.

We can build an undirected graph from the information we have at the *in-bucket* matrix. A Sybil group will have few or no links among its Sybil nodes. We need to invert this situation in order to spot the Sybil groups through the densest subgraph method. For that purpose we set M as the maximum number of edges between any two nodes in the graph, and ε_{ij} as the number of edges between nodes a_i and a_j; the value ε_{ij} is taken directly from the *inbucket* matrix, then:

$$e_{ij} = M - \varepsilon_{ij} \ , \forall \ i \neq j \qquad (4)$$

Where e_{ij} is the new number of edges between nodes a_i and a_j. So, we can now spot the Sybil groups in a polynomial time through Linear Programming by the the Densest Subgraph algorithm of Charikar [6]. The Densest Subgraphs represent the groups of nodes we are looking for, the Sybil ones. The pseudocode for this is shown in Algorithm 2.

Algorithm 2. Detecting the Sybil groups by the Densest Subgraphs

---

Require: *Inbucket Matrix, N;*
Ensure: *DS {Densest Subgraphs (Sybil groups)};*
 1: $M \Leftarrow 0$
 2: **for** $i := 0$ to $N - 1$ **do**
 3:     **for** $j := 0$ to i **do**
 4:         **if** $\varepsilon_{ij} > M$ **then**
 5:             $M \Leftarrow \varepsilon_{ij}$
 6:         **end if**
 7:     **end for**
 8: **end for**
 9: **for** $i := 0$ to $N - 1$ **do**
10:     **for** $j := 0$ to $N - 1$ **do**
11:         **if** $i \neq j$ **then**
12:             $e_{ij} \Leftarrow M - \varepsilon_{ij}$
13:         **end if**
14:     **end for**
15: **end for**
16: *Apply Charikar's algorithm on the new graph;*
17: $DS \Leftarrow$ *results from Charikar's algorithm;*

6.7 The Tests on Suspicious Nodes

It is necessary to run some tests on all those nodes detected through the Algorithms 1 and 2, in order to avoid any false positive. For that matter we need to choose some nodes among those not in the $SCC \cup DS$ group and with at least γ reputation points to form a group of testers. We refer to the size of the tester group as ϱ, the size depends on the redundancy we might need. Those chosen nodes now coordinate the testing on their suspected peers. The one with the lowest index broadcast first the test to all the suspected nodes and it waits for their replies within a time frame. Then that tester node sends a ready signal to the next tester. After that, the second tester node starts the testing phase and goes through the same method; and so on. Then from most of the matches on the test reports, we have the Sybil nodes. The pseudocode for the complete method is listed in Algorithm 3.

Algorithm 3. Detecting the Sybil nodes

Require: *Reputation Matrix, Counter Matrix, Inbucket Matrix, N, α, γ, ϱ, σ, τ;*
Ensure: *SN {Sybil nodes};*
 1: **for** $i := 0$ to $\alpha - 1$ **do**
 2:    Read reports from *time bucket$_i$*
 3: **end for**
 4: Call algorithm 1 (Input:*Reputation Matrix, Counter Matrix, N, σ;* Returns: *SCC;*)
 5: Call algorithm 2 (Input:*Inbucket Matrix, N;* Returns: *DS;*)
 6: $x \Leftarrow |SCC \cup DS|$
 7: **for** $i := 0$ to $\varrho - 1$ **do**
 8:    Select *tester$_i$*
       Where: *tester$_i$* $\notin \{SCC, DS\}$ and *tester$_i$* reputation $\geqslant \gamma$;
 9: **end for**
10: **for** $i := 0$ to $\varrho - 1$ **do**
11:    *tester$_i$* broadcast the test to the $\{SCC \cup DS\}$ nodes;
12:    **while** time $\geqslant 2\tau$ **do**
13:       *tester$_i$* listen
14:       **if** $node_{x_j}$ does not reply within τ **then**
15:          $K_{ix_j} \Leftarrow 1$
16:       **end if**
17:    **end while**
18:    Ready signal for *tester$_{i+1}$*
19: **end for**
20: **for** $j := 0$ to $x - 1$ **do**
21:    $y \Leftarrow 0$
22:    **for** $i := 0$ to $\varrho - 1$ **do**
23:       $y \Leftarrow y + K_{ix_j}$
24:    **end for**
25:    **if** $y \geqslant \frac{3}{4}\varrho$ **then**
26:       $node_{x_j} \in SN$
27:    **end if**
28: **end for**
29: Return *SN*

6.8   Some Experimental Results

We modeled a network environment with different percentages of Sybil nodes under the control of a malicious user. Those Sybil nodes pretend to interact between them in order to build a false reputation claiming to be independent and trustable nodes which is the foundation for the Sybil attack. We got some interesting results that we show next.

The point in coordinates {1800,50} of figure 2 tells that in a network with 10% of Sybil nodes and after one thousand eight hundred *time buckets* of information, in one hundred experiments we had fifty with at least one of the nodes detected through the *strongly connected components* not being Sybil (i.e. false positive).

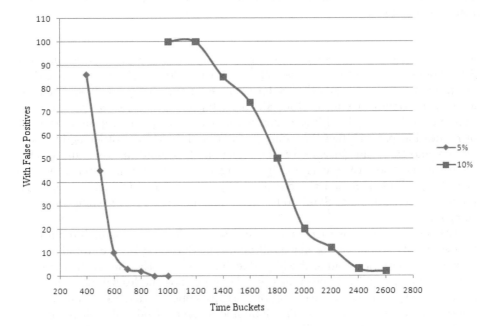

Fig. 2. Detection results through the *strongly connected components* for every one hundred experiments with 5% and 10% of Sybil nodes respectively

In all the experiments, at every *time bucket*, there were always ten percent of the nodes interacting and broadcasting. Those nodes were chosen randomly every time. In figures 2 and 4 we see that the less the percentage of Sybil nodes the sooner they are detected. This is because the more the Sybil nodes, the reputation points earned among them become more diffused and consequently their Sybil connections appear weaker.

Furthermore, the Sybil nodes could be many enough and their reputation points and interactions so widely dispersed that they would avoid appearing

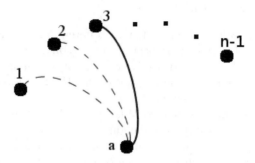

Fig. 3. Sybil nodes simulating an interaction with their Sybil peer a, in order to boost their reputation points

as a *strongly connected component*. This is not an easy task, in a group of n Sybil nodes, it would take at least $\Omega(n)$ operations for a Sybil node to simulate an interaction with every other Sybil peer (see figure 3). So, it would take at least $\Omega(n^2)$ operations in total for all the Sybil nodes to interact with all their Sybil peers. If every Sybil interaction is reported with about the same amount of reputation points, then the affinity of one node with any other node would be $\approx \frac{2}{n}$ and this value just need to be under the threshold to avoid this specific detection method. All that is nothing straightforward for a malicious user who needs big values of n and the costly $\Omega(n^2)$ interactions in order to give high reputation to all his/her Sybil nodes without appearing as a *strongly connected component*.

Although, a malicious user can concentrate the effort in giving high reputation to few or only to one of his/her Sybil nodes, in that case he/she would require only $\Theta(n)$ interactions but still a big value of n. On the other hand, the more the Sybil nodes created by a malicious user, the more those nodes will be exposed in our other detection method (see section 6.6) and appear as a densest subgraph by the timing of their broadcasts. The Sybil nodes can also gain all their reputation points honestly and they will not appear as a *strongly connected component*, avoiding this way just one of our detection methods. In this case our algorithm prevents the nodes from cheating on the reputation points.

In figure 5 we show the results of some experiments. As we can see, the fewer the Sybil nodes the more the *time buckets* (or information in the *inbucket* matrix) that we need to detect the *densest subgraphs*. In figure 5 the point in coordinates {1400,53} means that in one hundred experiments in a network with 10% of Sybil nodes and using only one thousand and four hundred *time buckets*, fifty three of the experiments had at least one false positive in the Sybil nodes detected through the *densest subgraphs*. As we have more information in the *inbucket* matrix the false positives tend to be zero. It is easier to detect a group of Sybil nodes in a network with high percentage of them. Since they are limited in their capacity of broadcasting together, the bigger the group, the more they are exposed and fewer the time buckets required to spot them.

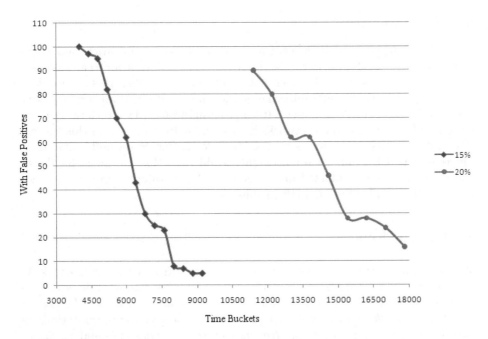

Fig. 4. Detection results through the *strongly connected components* for every one hundred experiments with 15% and 20% of Sybil nodes respectively

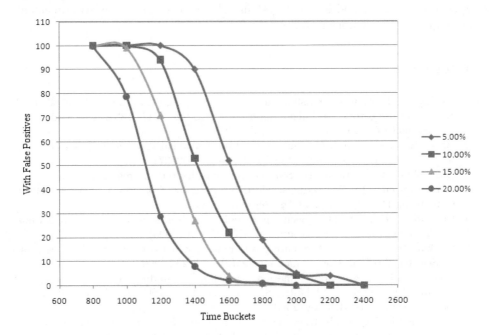

Fig. 5. Detection results through the *Densest Subgraph* method for every one hundred experiments with different percentages of Sybil nodes

6.9 Some Remarks

Our algorithm works well in local area networks, communication and timing problems arise as the network size increases. The solution for that case is to divide big networks in smaller ones and create clusters of observers or *distributed authority* groups that would interchange their information. However, new issues and coordination problems appear. It is not straightforward to track the behavior of nodes of several different networks interacting between them. In this last case it would be easier for a malicious user to hide his/her Sybil nodes among the different networks, and to some extent, avoid detection through the *densest subgraph* method as explained in section 6.6. This is an open problem yet as in the case of several colluding malicious users.

7 Conclusions

We show a novel system to detect Sybil nodes and prevent the Sybil attack. We combine ingredients from earlier work, but as far as we know, this is the first approach that addresses both the static and the dynamic networks. We use here a *distributed authority* to keep track of the nodes' behavior and reputation, and detect the Sybil nodes through *strongly connected components* and/or *densest subgraphs*. After that, tests are run on the suspected nodes in order to eliminate false any positives. Our algorithm is effective even in the presence of a high percentage of Sybil nodes in the system. This algorithm is easy to implement and requires few memory resources.

References

1. Aspnes, J., Jackson, C., Krishnamurthy, A.: Exposing computationally-challenged Byzantine impostors. Technical Report YALEU/DCS/TR-1332, Yale University Department of Computer Science (July 2005)
2. Bazzi, R.A., Konjevod, G.: On the establishment of distinct identities in overlay networks. Distributed Computing 19(4), 267–287 (2007)
3. Buragohain, C., Agrawal, D., Suri, S.: A game theoretic framework for incentives in p2p systems. In: Proceedings. Third International Conference on Peer-to-Peer Computing P2P 2003, pp. 48–56 (September 2003)
4. Čapkun, S., Hubaux, J.-P.: Secure positioning of wireless devices with applications to sensor networks. In: Proceedings of INFOCOM (2005)
5. Čapkun, S., Hubaux, J.P.: Secure positioning in wireless networks. IEEE Journal on Selected Areas in Communications 24(2), 221–232 (2006)
6. Charikar, M.: Greedy approximation algorithms for finding dense components in a graph. In: Jansen, K., Khuller, S. (eds.) APPROX 2000. LNCS, vol. 1913, pp. 84–95. Springer, Heidelberg (2000)
7. Cooke, R.M.: Experts in Uncertainty: Opinion and Subjective Probability in Science (Environmental Ethics and Science Policy). Oxford University Press, Oxford (October 1991)
8. Douceur, J.R.: The sybil attack. In: IPTPS, pp. 251–260. Springer, London (2002)

9. Lesniewski-Laas, C.: A sybil-proof one-hop dht. In: SocialNets 2008: Proceedings of the 1st Workshop on Social Network Systems, pp. 19–24. ACM, New York (2008)
10. Miller, N., Resnick, P., Zeckhauser, R.: Eliciting informative feedback: The peer-prediction method. Manage. Sci. 51(9), 1359–1373 (2005)
11. Newsome, J., Shi, E., Song, D., Perrig, A.: The Sybil attack in sensor networks: analysis and defenses. In: Proc. of IPSN (2004)
12. Piro, C., Shields, C., Levine, B.N.: Detecting the sybil attack in mobile ad hoc networks. In: Securecomm and Workshops, September 1-28, pp. 1–11 (2006)
13. Sastry, N., Shankar, U., Wagner, D.: Secure verification of location claims. In: Proc. of ACM WiSe (2003)
14. Tarjan, R.E.: Depth-first search and linear graph algorithms. SIAM J. Comput. 1(2), 146–160 (1972)
15. Waters, B.R., Felten, E.W.: Secure, private proofs of location. Technical Report TR-667-03, Princeton (2003)
16. Yu, H., Gibbons, P.B., Kaminsky, M., Xiao, F.: Sybillimit: A near-optimal social network defense against sybil attacks. In: IEEE Symposium on Security and Privacy (Oakland 2008) (2008)
17. Yu, H., Kaminsky, M., Gibbons, P.B., Flaxman, A.: Sybilguard: defending against sybil attacks via social networks. In: SIGCOMM, pp. 267–278 (2006)

ODBASE'10 - PC Co-chairs Message

Welcome to the proceedings of the 9th International Conference on Ontologies, Databases, and Applications of Semantics (ODBASE 2010) held in Crete, Greece, October 26-28, 2010.

The ODBASE conferences provide a forum for the sharing of original research results and practical experiences on the use of ontologies and data semantics in novel applications. Of particular relevance to ODBASE 2010 are papers that bridge traditional boundaries between disciplines such as databases, networking, mobile systems, artificial intelligence, information retrieval, and computational linguistics.

We have received 41 submissions, out of which we have selected 11 full papers, 7 short papers, and 5 posters. The main topics of this year are: ontology management, ontology applications, annotations, and heterogeneity and inconsistency management.

This year we have two special invited speakers. Our first invited speaker is Prof. Iryna Gurevych, who is one of the leading researchers in the area of Semantic Information Management, and Natural Language Processing for Wikis. Prof. Gurevych's talk is titled "Wikabularies and the Like - Community-Based Knowledge Resources on the Web". Our second invited speaker is Prof. Yannis Ioannidis who is internationally recognized for his contributions to query optimization and his extensive research in Data Visualization and Personalization, Heterogeneous Information Systems, Intelligent Databases and Digital Libraries. Prof Yannis Ioannidis' talk has the title "Personalization, Socialization, Contextualization: Preferences and Attitudes for Advanced Information Provision".

We would like to thank all the authors of the submitted papers, the program committee members and reviewers for their thoughtful reviews and the session chairs. We are grateful to the OTM team, the general co-chairs Robert Meersman, Tharam Dillon and Pilar Herrero, the publication chair Houwayda Elfawal and the OTM secretariat Daniel Meersman, Ana- Cecilia Martinez Barbosa, and Jan Demey.

We hope that you enjoyed ODBASE 2010 and had a wonderful stay in the beautiful Greek island of Crete.

August 2010

Alejandro Buchmann
Panos K. Chrysanthis
ODBASE'10

R. Meersman et al. (Eds.): OTM 2010, Part II, LNCS 6427, p. 918, 2010.
© Springer-Verlag Berlin Heidelberg 2010

Wikabularies and the Like - Community-Based Knowledge Resources on the Web

Iryna Gurevych

UKP Lab, Computer Science Department
Technical University of Darmstadt, Germany

In recent years, community-based knowledge resources on the Web have gained increasing popularity. Resources, such as the community-based encyclopedia Wikipedia or the community-based dictionary Wiktionary, have been employed as background knowledge sources in processing unstructured textual information in multiple languages. They yielded excellent results comparable to or better than the manually constructed resources by experts.

In the talk, we will discuss the major properties of already established and emerging community-based knowledge resources, whose most prominent examples are Wikipedia http://www.wikipedia.org and its dictionary spin-offs Wiktionary http://www.wiktionary.org and OmegaWiki http://www.omegawiki.org. We will analyze how they represent word senses and synonyms, which are fundamental units of knowledge about the words for processing human languages. Finally, we will conclude by outlining some promising application areas and future research directions.

We expect that the results of this research will have clear impact beyond natural language processing. They can also inspire related fields concerned with unstructured information management, knowledge representation and data integration.

R. Meersman et al. (Eds.): OTM 2010, Part II, LNCS 6427, p. 919, 2010.
© Springer-Verlag Berlin Heidelberg 2010

Personalization, Socialization, Contextualization: Preferences and Attitudes for Advanced Information Provision

Yannis Ioannidis

Dept. of Informatics and Telecommunications
National and Kapodistrian University of Athens

Human actions in real life are often influenced by several characteristics of the individual human involved in the actions. These characteristics can be broadly classified into three categories: those that are unique to the individual, those of the social environment of the individual, and those of the overall context or situation in which the individual is found while performing the actions. Usability of various types of information systems, e.g., database systems, digital libraries, or the Web, increases dramatically if the information they provide and their overall behavior is customized to these characteristics. Such personalization, socialization, and contextualization of information provision touches upon a broad spectrum of technical and other challenges.

This talk describes the general problem and its associated challenges, hints upon a general framework for modeling a large number of cases, and offers some examples of systems and techniques that have been developed by the Univ. of Athens to address related challenges in various application environments.

R. Meersman et al. (Eds.): OTM 2010, Part II, LNCS 6427, p. 920, 2010.
© Springer-Verlag Berlin Heidelberg 2010

Integrating Keywords and Semantics on Document Annotation and Search

Nikos Bikakis[1,2], Giorgos Giannopoulos[1,2],
Theodore Dalamagas[2], and Timos Sellis[1,2]

[1] Knowledge & Database Systems Lab, National Technical University of Athens, Greece
[2] Institute for the Management of Information Systems, "Athena" Research Center, Greece
bikakis@dblab.ntua.gr, giann@dblab.ntua.gr
dalamag@imis.athena-innovation.gr,
timos@imis.athena-innovation.gr

Abstract. This paper describes GoNTogle, a framework for document annotation and retrieval, built on top of Semantic Web and IR technologies. GoNTogle supports ontology-based annotation for documents of several formats, in a fully collaborative environment. It provides both manual and automatic annotation mechanisms. Automatic annotation is based on a learning method that exploits user annotation history and textual information to automatically suggest annotations for new documents. GoNTogle also provides search facilities beyond the traditional keyword-based search. A flexible combination of keyword-based and semantic-based search over documents is proposed in conjunction with advanced ontology-based search operations. The proposed methods are implemented in a fully functional tool and their effectiveness is experimentally validated.

Keywords: GoNTogle, Semantic Annotation, Document Annotations, Ontology based Retrieval, Hybrid Search, Semantic Search, Keyword Search.

1 Introduction

Document annotation and search have received tremendous attention by the Semantic Web [2] and the Digital Libraries [3] communities. Semantic annotation involves tagging documents with concepts (e.g., ontology classes) so that content becomes meaningful. Annotations help users to easily organize their documents. Also, they can help in providing better search facilities: users can search for information not only using keywords, but also using well-defined general concepts that describe the domain of their information need.

Although traditional Information Retrieval (IR) techniques are well-established, they are not effective when problems of concept ambiguity or synonymity appear. On the other hand, neither search based only on semantic information may be effective, since: a) it does not take into account the actual document content, b) semantic information may not be available for all documents and c) semantic annotations may cover only a few parts of the document.

R. Meersman et al. (Eds.): OTM 2010, Part II, LNCS 6427, pp. 921–938, 2010.

Hybrid solutions that combine keyword-based with semantic-based search deal with the above problems. Developing methodologies and tools that integrate document annotation and search is of high importance. For example, researchers need to be able to organize, categorize and search scientific material (e.g., papers) in an efficient and effective way. Similarly, a press clipping department needs to track news documents, annotating specific important topics and searching for information.

This paper describes GoNTogle, a framework for document annotation and retrieval, built on top of Semantic Web and IR technologies. GoNTogle provides both manual and automatic ontology-based annotations, supporting documents of several formats (doc, pdf, txt, rtf, odt, sxw, etc.). Annotation is based on standard Semantic Web technologies like, OWL and RDF/S. All annotations are stored in a centralized server, providing a collaborative environment. A learning method, exploiting textual information and user annotation history, is proposed to support the automatic annotation mechanism.

GoNTogle also provides three search types: a) *Keyword-based*, b) *Semantic-based* and c) *Hybrid*. Experimental evaluation validates the effectiveness of the proposed hybrid method, compared to the other two. Finally, several advanced ontology-based searching operations are provided, including the capability to expand or shrink the result list using ontology information, in order to retrieve higher quality results.

Regarding the design principles of our framework, they are based on the requirements set in previous works [4, 5, 7]. In contrast with the existing approaches, our aim was to design an easy-to-use document annotation and search framework that supports (a) viewing and annotating popular document types while maintaining their initial format, (b) offering a collaborative environment by sharing those annotations (c) supporting Semantic Web standards, (d) integrating textual information with semantics and (e) supporting a flexible combination of keyword-based and semantic-based search in conjunction with advanced ontology-base search operations.

Contributions. The main contributions of this work are summarized as follows:

1. We have designed and implemented an easy-to-use document annotation framework that supports the most widely used document formats, providing also advanced search facilities.

2. The framework is based on a server-based architecture, where document annotations are stored in a central repository, separately from the original document. This offers a collaborative environment where users can annotate and search documents.

3. We propose a learning method for automatic annotation of documents based on models trained from user annotation history and textual information, so that annotation suggestions are tailored to user behavior.

4. We introduce a hybrid search method that provides a flexible combination of traditional keyword-based and semantic-based search for effective document retrieval.

5. We present a user-based evaluation to demonstrate the effectiveness of the automatic annotation method. Moreover, we demonstrate a comparative evaluation to validate that the proposed hybrid search outperforms keyword-based and semantic-based search in terms of precision and recall.

Paper Outline. The rest of the paper is organized as follows. The semantic annotation mechanism is presented in Section 2, while Section 3 describes the search facilities. Section 4 presents the system architecture and provides technical information about the implementation. Section 5 presents the evaluation of our proposed methods. Section 6 discusses the related work and, finally, Section 7 concludes our work.

2 Semantic Annotation

GoNTogle framework supports semantic, ontology-based annotations, for widely used document formats (doc, pdf, txt, rtf, odt, sxw, etc.). It allows annotating the whole document or parts of it. GoNTogle framework supports both manual and automatic annotations. For automatic annotation we propose a learning method that exploits user annotation history and textual information to automatically suggest annotations for new incoming documents.

GoNTogle provides a common ontology-based annotation model (Figure 1) for all supported document formats. Annotations are stored on a centralized ontology server, separately from the original document. Annotations from different document formats are defined and stored in exactly the same way. Each annotation is stored as an ontology class instance, along with information about the annotated document. We define a set of ontology properties that are used to store the minimum essential information needed to provide a bidirectional connection between documents and ontologies. These properties contain information like: document URL, annotation offsets, page number, extent of annotation over the document, etc.

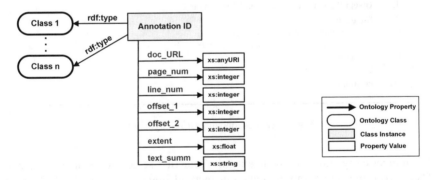

Fig. 1. Ontology-based annotation model

Figure 1 shows the ontology-based annotation model we developed in the context of the GoNTogle framework. Annotations are represented as class instances that can belong to one or more ontology classes. Using ontology properties, all the essential annotation information is attached to these instances. Property *doc_URL*, corresponds to the document's URL (including document's file name) of represented annotation. *page_num* and *line_num* properties, correspond to the number of the page and line respectively where the annotation begins. The property *offset_1* corresponds to a number that indicates the offset from the beginning of the document until the beginning of the annotation. As the same, property *offset_2* corresponds to the offset from the end of annotation until the end of the document. The property *extent* represents the extent of the annotation over the document. Finally, *text_summ* used for storing the summary of the annotated text (i.e., 1-3 tokens from the begin and the end) required for the GUI functionality.

2.1 Automatic Semantic Annotation

In this section, we present the learning method used for automatic document annotation. We propose a method based on *weighted kNN* classification [1] that exploits user annotation history and textual information to automatically suggest annotations for new documents. Next, we describe our approach in detail.

The training data of our method include document annotations provided manually by the users. When a document is manually annotated, the annotation text is extracted and indexed using an inverted index. Along with the textual information, the index also stores information about the annotation classes for each annotated document (or part of document).

Annotation Suggestion Algorithm

Input: *selected text st, index I*

Output: *suggested class cl_i, suggested class score Scr_{cli}*

    1.   **for each** annotated text *at* **in** *I*
    2.   **calculate** $ts_{st,at}$
    3.   **end for**
    4.   **Insert** the *k* most similar annotated texts in *S*
    5.   **for each** *at* in *S*
    6.   **for each** class *cl* annotate *at*
    7. $Scr_{cl} = Scr_{cl} + (w_1 * ts_{st,at}) * (w_2 * e_{cl,at})$
    8.   **end for**
    9.   **end for**
    10.   **return** cl_i, Scr_{cli}

Fig. 2. Annotation suggestion algorithm

To automatically annotate documents, the user first selects a document or a part of it. Then, given the set of training data, our method suggests a ranked list of ontology concepts (classes) to annotate the document (or its part). Figure 2 presents our method. It takes as input the selected text *st* and the inverted index *I*. Based on textual similarity $ts_{st,at}$ between *st* and each indexed annotated text *at*, the *k* most similar annotated texts are considered for further processing, and included in set *S* (*lines 1-4*). Then for each *at* in *S*, we retrieve the ontology classes used to annotate *at*. Each class *cl* is given a score Scr_{cl} that combines (a) the textual similarity (based on Lucene similarity model[1]) score $ts_{st,at}$ between *st* and *at* and (b) a score $e_{cl,at}$ representing the

---

[1] http://lucene.apache.org/java/3_0_1/api/core/org/apache/lucene/search/Similarity.html

extent to which each *at* in *S* is annotated with class *cl* (*line 7*). As $e_{cl,at}$ we define, the number of tokens of the *cl* annotations in *at* divided by the number of tokens in *at*.

$$e_{cl,at} = \frac{number\ of\ tokens\ of\ cl\ annotations\ over\ at}{number\ of\ tokens\ in\ at}$$

The w_1 and w_2 weights are used to quantify the preference of textual similarity against semantic similarity (or vice versa). Finally, a ranked list of suggested annotation classes cl_i and their score Scr_{cli} is presented to the user (*line 10*). The user may choose one or more suggested classes to conclude the automatic annotation process.

3 Search

In this section, we present the search facilities proposed in the context of GoNTogle framework. We formally define the supported search types (Section 3.1) and we analyze the ontology-based advanced search operations (Section 3.2). Moreover, we introduce the hybrid search method, which combines keyword-based and semantic-based search. Below we introduce the notation used in the following paragraphs.

Symbol	Notation
q_{key}	Keyword query, consisting of search term $\{t_1, t_2,...t_m\}$
$S_{key}(q_{key})$	Keyword-based search
RS_{key}	Keyword-based search result set
$Scr_{key}(q_{key},d)$	Keyword-based similarity score
q_{sem}	Semantic query, consisting of search classes $\{cl_1, cl_2,...cl_n\}$
$S_{sem}(q_{sem})$	Semantic-based search
RS_{sem}	Semantic-based search result set
$Scr_{sem}(q_{sem},d)$	Semantic-based similarity score
$S_{hybr}(q_{sem},q_{key})$	Hybrid search
RS_{hybr}	Hybrid search result set
$Scr_{hybr}(q_{sem},q_{key},d)$	Hybrid similarity score

3.1 Search Types

We categorize the basic search facilities of our framework into three types: a) *Keyword-based* search, b)*Semantic-based* search *and c) Hybrid* search.

Keyword-based search. This is the traditional search model. The user provides keywords and the system retrieves relevant documents based on textual similarity. We adopted the text similarity metric used in Lucene IR engine.

Keyword-based search is denoted as $S_{key}(q_{key})$, where $q_{key}=\{t_1, t_2,...t_m\}$ and t_i are the search terms with $m \geq 1$.

Keyword-based search returns an ordered *Result Set RS_{key}* of tuples $<d, Scr_{key}(q_{key},d)>$, containing all the documents *d* matched with terms q_{key}. $Scr_{key}(q_{key},d)$ is the similarity score of document *d* for the searching terms q_{key}. This score is based on document textual similarity with the searching terms.

Semantic-based search. This search facility allows the user to navigate through the classes of an ontology and focus their search on one or more of them.

Semantic-based search is denoted as $S_{sem}(q_{sem})$, where $q_{sem}=\{cl_1, cl_2,...cl_n\}$ and cl_i are the searching classes with $n \geq 1$.

It return an ordered *Result Set* RS_{sem} of tuples $<d, Scr_{sem}(q_{sem}, d)>$, containing all the documents d that have been annotated with one or more of the search classes q_{sem}. $Scr_{sem}(q_{sem}, d)$ is the similarity score of document d for the searching classes q_{sem}. This score is based on semantic similarity between the searching classes q_{sem} and document d. To define semantic similarity $ss_{cl_i,d}$ between a class cl_i and a document d, we consider the *extent* of the class annotations over the document: that is the number of tokens used to define the class annotations in d divided by the number of tokens in d.

The final similarity score is defined as follows:

$$Scr_{sem}(q_{sem}, d) = \sum_{i=1}^{n} ss_{cl_i,d} / n$$

$$ss_{cl_i,d} = \frac{number\ of\ tokens\ of\ cl_i\ annotations\ over\ d}{number\ of\ tokens\ in\ d}$$

where n is the number of ontology classes used during the semantic-based search, and $ss_{cl_i,d}$ is a score representing the *extent* to which document d is annotated with class cl_i.

Hybrid search. The user may search for documents using keywords and ontology classes. She can, also, determine whether the results of her search will be the intersection or the union of the two searches.

Hybrid search is denoted as $S_{hybr}(q_{sem}, q_{key}) = S_{sem}(q_{sem})\ Op\ S_{key}(q_{key})$, where $q_{sem}=\{cl_1, cl_2,...cl_n\}$ and cl_i are the searching classes with $n \geq 1$, $q_{key}=\{t_1, t_2,...t_m\}$ and t_i are the searching terms with $m \geq 1$ and Op the Boolean operators *OR* or *AND*.

Hybrid search returns an ordered *Result Set* RS_{hybr} of tuples $<d, Scr_{hybr}(q_{sem}, q_{key}, d)>$, the contents and the order of the result set depend on Op value:

- *Op=AND.* The *Result Set* contains all the documents d that have been annotated with one or more of the search classes q_{sem} and match with terms q_{key}.

$$RS_{hybr} = RS_{key} \bigcap_{over\ d} RS_{sem}$$

The final similarity score is defined as:

$$Scr_{hybr}(q_{sem}, q_{key}, d) = Scr_{sem}(q_{sem}, d) * w_3 + Scr_{key}(q_{key}, d) * w_4$$

where $Scr_{sem}(q_{sem}, d)$ is the similarity score from semantic-based search, and $Scr_{key}(q_{key}, d)$ is the similarity score from keyword-based search. The w_3 and w_4 weights are used to quantify the relative importance of the semantic-based and keyword-based scores, when both keyword and semantic queries must be satisfied.

- *Op=OR.* The *Result Set* contains all the documents d that have been annotated with one or more of the searching classes q_{sem} and all the documents d matched with terms q_{key}.

$$RS_{hybr} = RS_{key} \bigcup RS_{sem}$$

The final similarity score is defined as:

$$Scr_{hybr}(q_{sem}, q_{key}, d) = Scr_{sem}(q_{sem}, d) * w_5 + Scr_{key}(q_{key}, d) * w_6$$

where $Scr_{sem}(q_{sem}, d)$ is the similarity score from semantic-based search, and $Scr_{key}(q_{key}, d)$ is the similarity score from keyword-based search. The w_5 and w_6 weights are used to quantify the relative importance of the semantic-based and keyword-based scores, when either keyword or semantic queries must be satisfied.

3.2   Advanced Search Operations

Here we present a set of advanced search operations that can be used after an initial search has been completed.

Find related documents. Starting from a result document d, the user may search for all documents that have been annotated with a class cl that also annotates d. For example, if a user had initially searched with class *H.2[DATABASE MANAGEMENT]*[2] and selected one of the results that is also annotated with class *H.2.5[Heterogeneous Databases]*, then *"Find related documents"* would return all documents annotated with both classes.

Find similar documents. This is a variation of the previous search facility. Starting from a result document d, the user may search for all documents that are already in the result list and have been annotated with a class cl that also annotates d. For example, if a user had initially searched with keyword *"XML"* AND class *H.2[DATABASE MANAGEMENT]* and selected one of the results that is also annotated with class *H.2.5[Heterogeneous Databases]*, then *"Find similar documents"* would return all documents annotated with both classes and contained the keyword *"XML"*.

Get Next Generation. The resulting list from a semantic-based (or hybrid) search can be confined by propagating the search on lower levels in the ontology (i.e., if class cl has been used, then search is propagated only in direct subclasses of cl). This is the case when the search topic is too general. For example, if a user had initially searched with *H.2[DATABASE MANAGEMENT]*, then *"Get Next Generation"* would return all documents annotated with at least one of its subclasses (*H.2.5[Heterogeneous Databases]*, *H.2.3[Languages]*, etc.).

Get Previous Generation. This offers the inverse functionality of the previous option. The resulting list from a semantic-based (or hybrid) search can be expanded by propagating the search on higher levels in the ontology (i.e., if class cl has been used, then search is propagated only in direct superclasses of cl). This is the case when a search topic is too narrow. For example, if a user had initially searched with

---

[2] We turned the ACM Computing Classification (http://www.acm.org/about/class/) into an OWL ontology.

H.2[DATABASE MANAGEMENT], then "*Get Previous Generation*" would return all documents annotated with its superclass (*H.[Information Systems]*).

Proximity Search. This search option allows the user to search for documents that belong to all subclasses of a selected class, by applying a ranking model based on ontology hierarchy. That is, if class *cl* is the initial class, then search is propagated in all direct and indirect subclasses of *cl*. The resulting documents gathered from all levels of the ontology hierarchy are weighted properly (i.e., documents from the selected class *cl* get higher score than 1st level subclasses and even higher than 2nd level subclasses).

4 System Overview

4.1 System Architecture

Due to its centralized server-based annotation storage and management architecture, GoNTogle offers a collaborative user environment. Annotations are stored separately from the original document and may be shared by several user groups. GoNTogle's architecture is presented in Figure 3. The system is divided into 4 basic components:

a) *Semantic Annotation Component* provides facilities regarding the semantic annotation of documents. It consists of 3 modules: (i) Document Viewer, (ii) Ontology Viewer and (iii) Annotation Editor.

b) *Ontology Server Component* stores the semantic annotations of documents in the form of class instances. It consists of 2 modules: (i) an Ontology Manager and (ii) an Ontology Knowledge Base.

c) *Indexing Component* is responsible for indexing the documents using inverted indexes.

d) *Search Component* allows users to search for documents using a flexible combination of textual (keyword-based search) and ontology (semantic-based search) information.

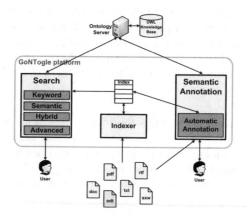

Fig. 3. GoNTogle architecture

4.2   Semantic Annotation In-Use

Semantic Annotation Component offers 2 primary functionalities: (a) annotation of whole document and (b) annotation of parts of a document. Also, a user may choose between manual and automatic annotation.

Figure 4 shows the Semantic Annotation window of our application. The user may open a document in the Document Viewer, maintaining its original format. Moreover, she can load and view the hierarchy of an ontology through the Ontology Viewer. In the specific example, the loaded ontology corresponds to the ACM Computing Classi-fication hierarchy. The user can, then, select one or more ontology classes and manually annotate the whole document or part of it. The annotation is stored as an ontology class instance in the Ontology Server, along with information about the annotated document. At the same time, an annotation instance is added in the Annota-tion Editor list. Each record of this list corresponds to an annotation stored in the Ontology Server. For example (Figure 4), the abstract of the document is annotated with class *H.2.3 [Languages]:Query Languages*, while the whole document is anno-tated with class *H.2[DATABASE MANAGEMENT]*. The user can manage those anno-tation instances, adding or removing ontology classes, or completely remove them. Also, when she selects an annotation from the list (regarding a part of a document), the document scrolls to the corresponding part, which is highlighted with the same color as the annotation instance.

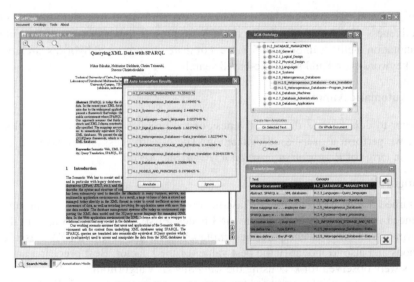

Fig. 4. Semantic annotation example

4.3   Implementation

In what follows we provide technical information about the implementation of our system. All annotation and search facilities presented in this paper have been imple-mented in a Java prototype. Application screenshots, as well as the application itself and installation instructions can be found in http://web.imis.athena-innovation.gr/ ~dalamag/gontogle. A demonstration of GoNTogle tools is presented in [23].

To develop our system, we used several open source tools and libraries. For indexing and keyword searching we used the Lucene search engine library. Lucene modules participate in several components of our system: a) Document text indexing for search purposes (*Indexing Component*). b) Document retrieval and scoring regarding textual similarity (*Search Component*). c) Indexing and querying documents for automatic annotation purposes (*Semantic Annotation Component*).

We used the Protégé[3] server and MySQL database for the *Ontology Server Component*, so that document annotations are stored as class instances. Through Protégé API, for each annotation, we store information that is required for processes such as retrieval of the specific annotation, ontology search scoring for a specific class-document pair, etc.

OpenOffice API[4] was essential in incorporating in our system a viewer that could maintain the exact format of *.doc* documents, which is a very common filetype. The same applies for Multivalent[5], a generalized document viewer that was integrated in our system so that *.pdf* files could also maintain their format when being viewed and annotated.

5 Evaluation

In this section, we present the experiments we performed in order to evaluate the effectiveness of our methods. In Section 5.1 we present the evaluation of the automatic annotation method. In Section 5.2, we compare our proposed hybrid search method with keyword-based and semantic-based search.

5.1 Automatic Annotation

In order to demonstrate the effectiveness of the proposed automatic annotation method, we perform a user-based evaluation. The effectiveness of our method is validated in terms of *Precision at position n (P@n)* and *Recall*.

Configuration

We turned the ACM Computing Classification into an OWL ontology. The ontology produced is a 4-level structure with 1463 nodes. First, we performed an initial set of experiments in order to compare the simple *kNN* and the *weighted kNN* classification methods and also to indentify the best value for the *k* factor. Best precision and recall values were observed for *k=7* using the *weighted kNN* algorithm.

Moreover, the weights used for the automatic annotation method (Section 2.1), w_1 and w_2 are calculated at *0.6* and *0.4* respectively after tuning. Intuitively, these values suggest that, in our problem setting, textual similarity is slightly more important than semantic similarity in case of automatic annotation.

---

[3] http://protege.stanford.edu/
[4] http://api.openoffice.org/
[5] http://multivalent.sourceforge.net/

Evaluation Scenario

We asked from 15 users (PhD students and researchers in various areas of computer science) to participate in our experimental evaluation. Each user selected 2 areas of her research interests and for each area she collected 10 research papers that she was familiar with. In order to train our system, we asked from each user to annotate (parts or/and the whole of) 12 out of her 20 papers with at least one ACM class, using the GoNTogle framework.

After every user had performed the training task, we asked each of them to evaluate the automatic annotation suggestions provided by GoNTogle, for the remaining 8 papers of each user (test set). Note that, before reviewing the system suggestions, each user was asked which annotation classes she expected to be given by the system. The system presented a ranked list of annotation classes and each user was required to check the valid ones. Also, each user should point out valid classes that were not found between the system suggestions, as well as valid classes that, even they had not thought of, the system correctly suggested them.

Based on the data collected, we calculated the *Precision at position n (P@n)* and *Recall* values for each user separately, as well as the mean average values for all users. Also, for correctly suggested annotation classes that the user had not initially thought of using them, we introduce the measure of *Unexpected Valid Class Suggestion (UVCS)*, defined as follows:

$$UVCS = \#Correctly\ suggested\ and\ not\ initially\ though\ classes$$

P@n and *Recall* are defined as follows: $P@n = \frac{\#relevant\ results\ in\ top\ n\ suggestions}{n}$ and $Recall = \frac{\#relevant\ results\ in\ suggestions}{\#relevant\ results}$, where we count as *relevant results*, the ACM classes considered valid by the user.

Evaluation Results

Table 1 presents, for each user, the average *P@n* values, for her 8 automatically annotated papers. In addition, the average *Recall* (regarding the top-5 results) and the average *UVCS* values are presented at Table 2.

Note that, due to our annotation scenario (annotating research papers with ACM classes), it is rational to regard only the top-5 results during the *P@n* computation. That is, because the majority of the research papers under consideration do not handle more than 5 ACM hierarchy topics.

As we can observe, our method achieves high values both for *Precision* and *Recall* metrics. Moreover high *Recall* values have been achieved, with an average *Recall* value equal to 0.93. We should note that the relatively low *P@4 and P@5* are justified from the fact that, for a respectable amount of test documents, the users expected (and thus validated) no more than 1-3 classes, that were found in the top 3 positions of the system's ranked suggestion list. Finally, it is obvious from the *UVCS* metric, that the automatic annotation mechanism supports and guides users during the annotation process, by suggesting correct classes that users had not previously thought of.

Table 1. The average *Precision at position n* (*P@n*) for each user

User	P@1	P@2	P@3	P@4	P@5
1	0.82	0.79	0.79	0.75	0.68
2	1.00	0.94	0.80	0.65	0.60
3	0.80	0.80	0.70	0.70	0.76
4	1.00	1.00	0.80	0.84	0.80
5	1.00	0.90	0.90	0.82	0.81
6	0.80	0.90	0.73	0.70	0.64
7	1.00	1.00	0.93	0.85	0.84
8	0.93	1.00	0.73	0.71	0.69
9	0.90	0.90	0.87	0.80	0.76
10	0.91	0.87	0.80	0.75	0.71
11	1.00	1.00	0.87	0.84	0.78
12	0.80	0.77	0.72	0.70	0.66
13	0.95	0.92	0.83	0.75	0.68
14	1.00	0.90	0.87	0.80	0.76
15	0.80	0.80	0.73	0.65	0.56
Avg	0.91	0.90	0.81	0.75	0.72

Table 2. The average *Recall* and the average *UVCS* for each user

User	Recall	UVCS
1	0.80	0.40
2	0.92	0.20
3	0.98	0.20
4	0.97	0.40
5	0.98	0.40
6	1.00	1.20
7	0.97	0.20
8	0.82	0.20
9	1.00	0.20
10	0.89	1.00
11	0.88	0.80
12	0.95	0.65
13	0.87	0.40
14	0.95	1.60
15	1.00	0.00
Avg	0.93	0.52

5.2 Search

In this section, we present an evaluation comparing the effectiveness of the search types provided by our framework. The comparison is performed in terms of *Precision at position n, Recall, F-measure* and *Precision-Recall curve*. In all cases, the proposed hybrid search method delivers higher quality results than traditional keyword-based or semantic-based search methods.

Configuration

The weights used for the hybrid search method (Section 3.1) are assigned the following values: $w_3=0.7$, $w_4=0.3$ and $w_5=0.6$, $w_6=0.4$ after tuning. Intuitively, these values suggest that, in our problem setting, semantic-based score is slightly more important than keyword-based score in hybrid search.

Evaluation Scenario

Our corpus consists of the 300 manually and automatically annotated research papers from the previous experiment (Section 5.1). First, we collect all the keywords defined in these papers and we randomly choose 10 keywords to be used as queries. Note that, keywords queries may contain one or more tokens.

Also, we map the selected keyword queries to semantic queries, using the ontology classes. That is, to construct semantic queries that correspond to the keyword ones, we select the ontology classes that are most similar to the keyword content. In this way, we are able to perform both keyword, and ontology search, as well as hybrid search, comparing the effectiveness of each approach.

Table 3 presents the 10 keyword queries (q_{key}) which are used for this experiment. Table 4, presents the corresponding semantic queries (q_{sem}) expressed using the classes from ACM ontology. Hybrid queries are expressed by the combination of a keyword query and its corresponded semantic query. For hybrid search we apply booth (*OR, AND*) Boolean operators. The hybrid queries applying *AND* and *OR* operators are denoted respectively as q_{hybrA} and q_{hybrO}.

<table>
<tr><td colspan="2">Table 3. Keyword Queries</td><td colspan="2">Table 4. Semantic Queries</td></tr>
</table>

ID	Keywords
$q_{key}1$	knowledge discovery and privacy
$q_{key}2$	stream mining
$q_{key}3$	RDF indexing
$q_{key}4$	spatial databases
$q_{key}5$	clustering
$q_{key}6$	spatial access
$q_{key}7$	query language
$q_{key}8$	data model
$q_{key}9$	XML interoperability
$q_{key}10$	information integration

ID	Classes
$q_{sem}1$	K.4.1 [Public Policy Issues]: Privacy
$q_{sem}2$	H.2.8 [Database Applications]: Data mining
$q_{sem}3$	H.3.1 [Content Analysis and Indexing]: Indexing methods
$q_{sem}4$	H.2.8 [Database Applications]: Spatial databases and GIS
$q_{sem}5$	H.3.3 [Information Search and Retrieval]: Clustering
$q_{sem}6$	H.2.2 [Physical Design]: Access Methods
$q_{sem}7$	H.2.3 [Languages]: Query languages
$q_{sem}8$	H.2.1 [Logical Design]: Data models
$q_{sem}9$	D.2.12 [Interoperability]
$q_{sem}10$	H.2.5 [Heterogeneous Databases]

For each query we measure the quality of retrieval method using the *Precision at position n at position n,* for *n* [1 to10] and *Recall*. Based on these measures, we compare the various search types offered by our system: a) *Keyword-based* search, b) *Semantic-based* search, c) *Hybrid* search using *AND* operator (*hybrA*) and d) *Hybrid* search using *OR* operator (*hybrO*). Finally, for each search type, we compute the average *Precision* at positions 1 to 10, *Recall, F-measure* and *Precision-Recall curves* for all queries.

Average Evaluation Results for All Queries

Table 5 presents the average *P@n* for *n* [1 to 10] and the average *Recall* and *F-measure* values for all queries. Note that, most queries in hybrid search using the *AND* operator, do not retrieve more than 5-6 documents (as we can see from Figure 6). As a consequence, the precision, for this search type is calculated only at positions 1 to 5.

Precision. As we can observe from Table 5, the hybrid search (for both operators) outperforms the keyword-based and semantic-based search at every position, with *hybrA* achieving slightly higher values at positions 4 and 5. Moreover, we can see that keyword-based search radically decreases after position 4, where semantic-based and hybrid search start decreasing progressively after the 6th position.

Hybrid search compared to keyword-based search, achieves a maximum increase of 100% at position 7 and a minimum increase of 33.3% at position 2. Comparing hybrid with semantic-based search, hybrid, achieves a maximum increase of 17.2% at position 10 and a minimum increase of 0% at position 1.

Recall. As we can see, the *hybrO* outperforms the keyword-based and semantic-based search, achieving recall value close to 1 (0.98). Moreover, *hybrA* achieves slightly lower recall values than semantic-based search. This is due to the fact that *hybrA* search is very restrictive. So, too few documents are returned for each query with negative influence on the recall values.

Comparing *hybrO* with keyword-based search, *hybrO*, achieves an increase of 78.2%. Moreover, despite the low recall values of *hybrA* method, in comparison with keyword-based search, it increases the recall value at 20%. In comparison with semantic-based search, *hybrO* achieves a increase of 16.7%. Finally, *hybrA* achieves lower recall values than semantic-based search, having a decrease of 21.4%.

F-measure. As we can see, the hybrid search outperforms the other methods in F-measure value. Comparing *hybrO* with keyword-based and semantic-based search, *hybrO* achieves an increase of 77% and 16.4% respectively. Moreover, comparing *hybrA* with keyword-based and semantic-based search, *hybrA* achieves an increase of 52% and 0% respectively.

Table 5. The average *Precision at position n (P@n)*, *Recall* and *F-measure* for all queries

	P@1	P@2	P@3	P@4	P@5	P@6	P@7	P@8	P@9	P@10	Recall	F-measure
q_{key}	0.70	0.75	0.70	0.70	0.60	0.52	0.47	0.48	0.44	0.43	0.55	0.48
q_{sem}	1.00	0.95	0.90	0.88	0.90	0.87	0.81	0.76	0.70	0.64	0.84	0.73
q_{hybrA}	1.00	1.00	1.00	1.00	0.98	-	-	-	-	-	0.66	0.73
q_{hybrO}	1.00	1.00	0.97	0.98	0.96	0.95	0.94	0.89	0.81	0.75	0.98	0.85

Precision vs. Recall. Figure 5 shows the average precision-recall curve for all queries. As we can see, hybrid search has a very stable performance, achieving high precision (close to 1) even for recall values greater than 0.8. *hybrO* precision starts to decrease noticeably only after recall values are greater than 0.9. For recall values lower than 0.6, *hybrA* achieves precision values higher than *hybrO*. Semantic-based search precision, progressively decreases from the beginning while recall increases. Finally, keyword-based search precision values rapidly decrease for recall values greater than 0.4.

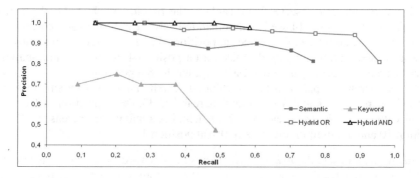

Fig. 5. The average precision-recall curve for all queries

Evaluation Results for Each Query

Figure 6 presents for each query, the *P@n* for *n*[1 to 10] and *Recall* values.

As we can see, in all queries, the hybrid search (for both boolean operators) outperforms the keyword-based and semantic-based search in precision values at every position. Moreover, regarding the recall measures, the *hybrO* search outperforms the other search methods in every query, with 9 out of 10 queries achieving recall values equal to 1.

As far as $P@n$ is concerned, hybrid search achieves the highest precision values for all queries in every position. Hybrid search using *AND* and *OR* operators achieve similar precision values. However in many cases *AND* operator returns less than 10 documents. Semantic-based search achieves lower precision values (except *hybrA* for Query 6) than hybrid search, and higher values than keyword-based search (with 3 exceptions, Queries 4,5,6). Finally, keyword-based search achieves, in general, the lowest precision values.

As far as *recall* is concerned, hybrid search using *OR* operator achieves the highest recall values in all queries, with 9 out of 10 queries achieving recall values equal to 1. Semantic-based search achieves lower recall values than the former and higher or equal than rest methods, with two exceptions (Queries 6,8). Moreover, hybrid search using *AND* operator achieves lower or equal recall values than semantic-based search and higher than keyword-based search (with one exception, Query 2). Finally, keyword-based search achieves, in general, lowest recall values.

	Query 1				Query 2				Query 3				Query 4			
	$q_{key}1$	$q_{sem}1$	$q_{hybrA}1$	$q_{hybrO}1$	$q_{key}2$	$q_{sem}2$	$q_{hybrA}2$	$q_{hybrO}2$	$q_{key}3$	$q_{sem}3$	$q_{hybrA}3$	$q_{hybrO}3$	$q_{key}4$	$q_{sem}4$	$q_{hybrA}4$	$q_{hybrO}4$
P@1	1.00	1.00	1.00	1.00	0	1.00	1.00	1.00	1.00	1.00	1.00	1.00	1.00	1.00	1.00	1.00
P@2	1.00	1.00	1.00	1.00	0.50	0.50	1.00	1.00	1.00	1.00	1.00	1.00	1.00	1.00	1.00	1.00
P@3	1.00	1.00	1.00	1.00	0.33	0.67	1.00	0.67	0.67	0.67	1.00	1.00	1.00	0.67	1.00	1.00
P@4	1.00	1.00	1.00	1.00	0.50	0.50	-	0.75	0.75	0.75	1.00	1.00	1.00	0.75	1.00	1.00
P@5	1.00	1.00	1.00	1.00	0.40	0.60	-	0.60	0.60	0.80	1.00	1.00	1.00	0.80	1.00	1.00
P@6	0.83	1.00	-	1.00	0.33	0.67	-	0.67	0.50	0.67	-	0.83	0.83	0.83	1.00	1.00
P@7	0.71	1.00	-	1.00	0.29	0.57	-	0.57	0.43	0.71	-	0.86	0.71	0.71	-	1.00
P@8	0.63	1.00	-	1.00	0.25	0.50	-	0.50	0.38	0.63	-	0.75	0.75	0.75	-	1.00
P@9	0.56	1.00	-	1.00	0.22	0.44	-	0.44	0.33	0.56	-	0.67	0.67	0.78	-	0.89
P@10	0.50	0.90	-	1.00	0.20	0.40	-	0.40	0.40	0.50	-	0.60	0.60	0.80	-	0.80
Recall	0.45	0.82	0.45	0.91	0.50	1.00	0.25	1.00	0.67	0.83	0.83	1.00	0.75	1.00	0.75	1.00

	Query 5				Query 6				Query 7				Query 8			
	$q_{key}5$	$q_{sem}5$	$q_{hybrA}5$	$q_{hybrO}5$	$q_{key}6$	$q_{sem}6$	$q_{hybrA}6$	$q_{hybrO}6$	$q_{key}7$	$q_{sem}7$	$q_{hybrA}7$	$q_{hybrO}7$	$q_{key}8$	$q_{sem}8$	$q_{hybrA}8$	$q_{hybrO}8$
P@1	1.00	1.00	1.00	1.00	1.00	1.00	1.00	1.00	0	1.00	1.00	1.00	0	1.00	1.00	1.00
P@2	1.00	1.00	1.00	1.00	1.00	1.00	1.00	1.00	0	1.00	1.00	1.00	0	1.00	1.00	1.00
P@3	1.00	1.00	1.00	1.00	1.00	1.00	1.00	1.00	0.33	1.00	1.00	1.00	0	1.00	1.00	1.00
P@4	1.00	0.75	1.00	1.00	1.00	1.00	1.00	1.00	0.25	1.00	1.00	1.00	0	1.00	1.00	1.00
P@5	0.80	0.80	1.00	1.00	0.80	1.00	0.80	1.00	0.20	1.00	1.00	1.00	0	1.00	1.00	1.00
P@6	0.67	0.83	-	1.00	0.67	0.83	0.67	1.00	0.33	1.00	1.00	1.00	0	1.00	1.00	1.00
P@7	0.57	0.71	-	1.00	0.71	0.71	0.57	1.00	0.29	1.00	1.00	1.00	0.14	1.00	-	1.00
P@8	0.63	0.63	-	0.88	0.75	0.63	0.50	1.00	0.38	1.00	1.00	1.00	0.13	0.88	-	0.88
P@9	0.56	0.56	-	0.78	0.67	0.56	0.44	0.89	0.44	0.89	1.00	1.00	0.11	0.78	-	0.78
P@10	0.50	0.50	-	0.70	0.60	0.50	0.40	0.80	0.50	0.80	0.90	1.00	0.10	0.70	-	0.70
Recall	0.63	0.63	0.63	0.88	0.67	0.63	0.50	1.00	0.50	0.80	0.90	1.00	0.14	0.70	0.89	1.00

	Query 9				Query 10			
	$q_{key}9$	$q_{sem}9$	$q_{hybrA}9$	$q_{hybrO}9$	$q_{key}10$	$q_{sem}10$	$q_{hybrA}10$	$q_{hybrO}10$
P@1	1.00	1.00	1.00	1.00	1.00	1.00	1.00	1.00
P@2	1.00	1.00	1.00	1.00	1.00	1.00	1.00	1.00
P@3	1.00	1.00	1.00	1.00	0.67	1.00	1.00	1.00
P@4	0.75	1.00	1.00	1.00	0.75	1.00	1.00	1.00
P@5	0.60	1.00	1.00	1.00	0.60	1.00	1.00	1.00
P@6	0.50	1.00	-	1.00	0.50	0.83	1.00	1.00
P@7	0.43	0.86	-	1.00	0.43	0.86	-	1.00
P@8	0.38	0.75	-	0.88	0.50	0.88	-	1.00
P@9	0.33	0.67	-	0.78	0.56	0.78	-	0.89
P@10	0.30	0.60	-	0.70	0.60	0.70	-	0.80
Recall	0.43	0.86	0.71	1.00	0.75	0.88	0.75	1.00

Fig. 6. The *Precision at position n* ($P@n$) and the *Recall* for each query

6 Related Work

A great number of approaches on semantic annotation have been proposed in the literature [6, 7]. Most of them are focused on annotating web resources such as HTML pages [8, 9, 10, 11, 12, 13, 14].

As far as plain text (or HTML) annotation is concerned, there are approaches that differ in the annotation and search facilities they offer. GATE [15] is a platform that offers an architecture, a framework and a graphical tool for language processing. Tools and resources are offered to perform textual annotation both manually and automatically using information extraction (IE) techniques.

KIM [16] provides an infrastructure for semantic annotation of documents (text or HTML), restricted, however, to its own ontology, called KIMO. The information extraction, document management and annotation part is based on GATE. The aim of the IE engine is the recognition of named entities with respect to the KIMO ontology. Compared to the above approaches, GoNTogle provides advanced searching facilities using a flexible combination of keyword-based and semantic-based search over documents. Also, it provides automatic annotation facilities based on models trained from user annotation history, so that annotation suggestions are tailored to user behavior.

AKTiveMedia [17] supports the annotation of text, images and HTML documents using both ontology-based and free-text annotations. For the automatic annotation task an underlying information extraction (IE) system has been integrated, learning from previous annotations and suggests annotations to the user. However, AKTive-Media does not provide search facilities. Furthermore, the supported automatic annotation mechanism provides very low performance, when annotations concerns more than one tokens (due to the IE system). In addition, a serious limitation of the automatic annotation mechanism is that it takes into consideration only one class per annotation. In case of annotations with multiples classes, the rest of the classes are skipped.

The above tools support annotations on HTML or plain text. As far as popular document formats are concerned, PDFTab [18] is a Protégé plug-in for annotating PDF documents with OWL ontologies classes. Annotations are stored in the internal document representation, with the document structure remaining unchanged. Compared to GoNTogle, PDFTab has several limitations: it does not provide any search facilities or automatic annotation method. SemanticWord [19] is a MS Word plug-in which offers MS Word annotations with DAML+OIL ontologies. Compared to GoNTogle, SemanticWord integrates an information extraction system with no learning support to suggest annotations. Also, SemanticWord does not provide search facilities and does not support OWL and RDF/S ontologies.

Regarding the semantic search, in the recent years, numerous systems and approaches have been proposed in the literature [20]. An approach close to our, is introduced at [21], where a combination of keyword and semantic search over web sources is supported, on top of the AKTiveMedia framework [17]. A noticeable drawback of this approach is that the ranking of hybrid search, is relying only at keyword search where the semantic part is utilized only to exclude or include a result and not to rank it. Moreover, [21] does not support advanced search operations related to ontology semantics. Additionally, an interesting but less relative approach [22], analyzes the meaning of words and phrases, to define semantic relations between lexicalized concepts. In that case, syntactic search is extended with semantics, by converting words into concepts and exploiting the arisen semantics.

7 Conclusion and Future Work

In this paper we presented GoNTogle, a framework for document annotation and retrieval, built on top of Semantic Web and IR technologies. GoNTogle supports both manual and automatic document annotation using ontologies. A learning mechanism is implemented, providing automatic document annotation facilities based on textual information and user annotation history.

In order to overcome the drawbacks of traditional keyword-based (like concept polysemy and synonymy) and semantic-based search (like partial or not existing annotations) we propose a hybrid search method. Hybrid search provides a flexible combination of keyword-based and semantic-based search. Moreover, several advanced ontology-based search operations are provided. Ontology information is exploited, to help the user expand or shrink the resulting list in order retrieve high quality results.

A user-based evaluation is performed, in order to demonstrate the effectiveness of the automatic annotation method. Moreover, a comparative evaluation validates that, the proposed hybrid search, outperforms in all cases the keyword-based and semantic-based search in terms of precision and recall.

Finally, all the proposed methods are implemented as a fully functional tool.

Our future work involves: a) Supporting more knowledge representation forms (e.g. Mind maps). b) Adding advanced search facilities exploiting ontology reasoning techniques. c) Integrating several semantic-based natural language techniques. d) Studying how tagging techniques can be integrated to GoNTogle framework. e) Using GoNTogle framework to support the clipping department of an organization or a company in order to perform extended experiments in large corpora. f) Adapting the framework to commercial document viewers (MS Word and Adobe Reader).

Acknowledgments. We would like to thank the all the PhD students and the research staff from *IMIS R.C. "Athena"* and *KDBS Lab (NTUA)* for their contribution in the evaluation part of this work. Finally, we would also like to thank Dimitris Sacharidis from *IMIS/R.C. "Athena"* for many helpful comments on earlier versions of this article.

References

1. Mitchell, T.M.: Machine Learning. WCB/McGraw-Hill (1997)
2. Handschuh, S., Staab, S. (eds.): Annotation for the Semantic Web. IOS Press, Amsterdam (2003)
3. Agosti, M., Ferro, N.: A Formal Model of Annotations of Digital Content. ACM Transactions on Information Systems (TOIS) 26(1), 3:1–3:57 (2008)
4. Agosti, M., Albrechtsen, H., Ferro, N., Frommholz, I., Hansen, P., et al.: DiLAS: a digital library annotation service. In: Proc. of IWAC 2005 (2005)

5. Haslhofer, B., Jochum, W., King, R., Sadilek, C., Schellner, K.: The LEMO annotation framework: weaving multimedia annotations with the web. JODL 10(1), 15–32 (2009)
6. Reeve, L., Han, H.: Survey of semantic annotation platforms. In: Proc. of the ACM Symposium on Applied Computing 2005 (2005)
7. Uren, V.S., Cimiano, P., Iria, J., Handschuh, S., Vargas-Vera, M., Motta, E., Ciravegna, F.: Semantic annotation for knowledge management: Requirements and a survey of the state of the art. Journal of Web Semantics 4 (2006)
8. Kiyavitskaya, N., Zeni, N., Cordy, J.R., Mich, L., Mylopoulos, J.: Cerno: Light-weight tool support for semantic annotation of textual documents. Data Knowl. Eng. (DKE) 68(12) (2009)
9. Hogue, A., Karger, D.: Thresher: automating the unwrapping of semantic content from the World Wide Web. In: Proc. of WWW 2005 (2005)
10. Cimiano, P., Handschuh, S., Staab, S.: Towards the self-annotating web. In: Proc. of WWW 2004 (2004)
11. Dill, S., Eiron, N., Gibson, D., Gruhl, D., Guha, R., Jhingran, A., Kanungo, T., McCurley, K.S., Rajagopalan, S., Tomkins, A., Tomlin, J.A., Zien, J.Y.: A Case for Automated Large-Scale Semantic Annotation. Journal of Web Semantics 1(1) (2003)
12. SMORE: Create OWL Markup for HTML Web Pages, http://www.mindswap.org/2005/SMORE/
13. Handschuh, S., Staab, S., Ciravegna, F.: S-CREAM: Semi-automatic CREAtion of Metadata. In: Gómez-Pérez, A., Benjamins, V.R. (eds.) EKAW 2002. LNCS (LNAI), vol. 2473, p. 358. Springer, Heidelberg (2002)
14. Vargas-Vera, M., Motta, E., Domingue, J., Lanzoni, M., et al.: MnM: Ontology Driven Semi-automatic and Automatic Support for Semantic Markup. In: Gómez-Pérez, A., Benjamins, V.R. (eds.) EKAW 2002. LNCS (LNAI), vol. 2473, p. 379. Springer, Heidelberg (2002)
15. Cunningham, H., Maynard, D., Bontcheva, K., Tablan, V.: GATE: A Framework and Graphical Development Environment for Robust NLP Tools and Applications. In: Proc. of the ACL 2002 (2002)
16. Kiryakov, A., Popov, B., Terziev, I., Manov, D., Ognyanoff, D.: Semantic annotation, indexing, and retrieval. Journal of Web Semantics 2(1) (2004)
17. Chakravarthy, A., Lanfranchi, V., Ciravegna, F.: Cross-media document annotation and enrichment. In: 1st Semantic Authoring and Annotation Workshop 2006 (2006)
18. Eriksson, H.: An annotation tool for semantic documents. In: Franconi, E., Kifer, M., May, W. (eds.) ESWC 2007. LNCS, vol. 4519, pp. 759–768. Springer, Heidelberg (2007)
19. Tallis, M.: SemanticWord processing for content authors. In: Proc. of the Knowledge Markup and Semantic Annotation Workshop 2003 (2003)
20. Mangold, C.: A survey and classification of semantic search approaches. Int. J. Metadata Semantics and Ontology 2(1) (2007)
21. Bhagdev, R., Chapman, S., Ciravegna, F., Lanfranchi, V., Petrelli, D.: Hybrid search: Effectively combining keywords and semantic searches. In: Bechhofer, S., Hauswirth, M., Hoffmann, J., Koubarakis, M. (eds.) ESWC 2008. LNCS, vol. 5021, pp. 554–568. Springer, Heidelberg (2008)
22. Giunchiglia, F., Kharkevich, U., Zaihrayeu, I.: Concept search. In: Aroyo, L., Traverso, P., Ciravegna, F., Cimiano, P., Heath, T., Hyvönen, E., Mizoguchi, R., Oren, E., Sabou, M., Simperl, E. (eds.) ESWC 2009. LNCS, vol. 5554, pp. 429–444. Springer, Heidelberg (2009)
23. Giannopoulos, G., Bikakis, N., Dalamagas, T., Sellis, T.: GoNTogle: A Tool for Semantic Annotation and Search. In: Proc. of the ESWC 2010 (Demo)

A Context-Based Model for the Interpretation of Polysemous Terms

Chrisa Tsinaraki, Yannis Velegrakis,
Nadzeya Kiyavitskaya, and John Mylopoulos

Department of Information Engineering and Computer Science (DISI),
University of Trento, Via Sommarive 14, Povo (TN), 38100, Italy
{chrisa,velgias,nadzeya,jm}@disi.unitn.eu

Abstract. The problem of polysemy involves having terms, such as "truck", that refer to multiple concepts in different contexts; and conversely, having the same concept referred to with different names in different contexts. Contexts may be defined along different dimensions, such as language (Italian, English, French, ...), domain (Philosophy, Computer Science, Physics, ...), time (Ancient Greece, 20th century, ...) etc. Given a conceptual model M (aka ontology), a context C and a query Q we motivate and propose algorithms for interpreting all the terms of the query with respect to M and C. We also define and solve the inverse problem: given a set of concepts S which are part of the answer to query Q and a context C, we propose algorithms for choosing terms for all the concepts in S. To illustrate the framework, we use a case study involving a history ontology whose elements are named differently depending on the time period and language of the query.

Keywords: Polysemy, Context, Ontology, Multilingualism.

1 Introduction

The advent of the Internet and the World Wide Web (WWW) have made vast amounts of information – including conceptual models, i.e. ontologies in the Semantic Web jargon – available to all the people of the world. This has brought to the foreground in Information Technology (IT) research an old problem: people of the world speak different languages and, due to this, information needs to be made available to them accordingly.

The general problem of multilingual information sources, such as digital libraries, is an active area of research in Computational Linguistics and Computer Science. We focus in this paper on a smaller problem: polysemy in conceptual models, such as ontologies. A word (or more generally, sign) is polysemous if it means different things in different contexts. Polysemy includes the dual phenomenon of having a concept referred to by different names in different contexts, such as the concept of "ontology" in Philosophy being referred to as "ontology" in English, "ontologia" in Italian and "ontologie" in French and German. Polysemy in the Social Sciences is not just a problem of multilingualism. Terms

R. Meersman et al. (Eds.): OTM 2010, Part II, LNCS 6427, pp. 939–956, 2010.

change meaning over time, topic, and dialect. Again, the term "ontology" means different things in Philosophy and Computer Science (topic) and meant different things in Ancient Greece and the 20th century. These issues are of great concern to historians, for example, who need to take into account all these dimensions that affect polysemy as they analyze a given collection of documents. Unfortunately, polysemy is treated only at the level of locating the synonyms (while working with only one language) and/or the translations (while working with more than one languages) of the terms, taking into account only the spoken language factor [1]; thus, the term context is essentially ignored.

The main objective of this paper is to propose a general mechanism for the interpretation of polysemous terms in environments where a given concept is referred to by different names depending on context. Contexts are defined along several dimensions, consistently with [2]. Given a polysemous conceptual model, a context and a query, we propose algorithms for identifying possible interpretations for the query and also for naming the concepts that are included in the query response.

This research was motivated by, and uses as key case study, a project involving a history ontology used by historians to express queries such as "show me the evolution of the semantics of the term 'biotechnology' in the 20th century". This query can be formalized as: "given a modern name of a concept, identify all the documents related to it in a multilingual archive". The challenge arising from this task is posed by the fact that the terminology changes with time. The users of the history ontology are not aware of the obsolete terms used for the concept in the past in their language; they also have no clue of the possible equivalent terms used for this concept in other languages. For instance, biotechnology was referred at different periods of its development as "biontotechnology", "zymotechnology", "biotechnics", and "biological engineering". Moreover, the history of biotechnology in different countries is very diverse. For example, the translation of this word was equivalent at some point to "biotechnical chemistry" (literal translation from Danish "biotechnisk kemi"). As a result, the lexical translation of the term "biotechnology" is not enough to discover relevant documents written in other languages and in different time periods.

The remainder of the paper is structured as follows: The motivation for our work and the proposed solution are discussed in Section 2, the context-based framework that we have developed for the interpretation of polysemous terms is described in Section 3, a case study that focuses on the formation of biotechnology in the perspective of the History of Science and Technology is provided in Section 4, the related work is presented in Section 5 and the paper concludes in Section 6, where our future research directions are also outlined.

2   Motivation and Solution

Consider the English term "ontology", which has the Italian translation "ontologia". This term was introduced by the ancient Greek philosophers in order to describe a subdomain of metaphysics that was dealing with the philosophical

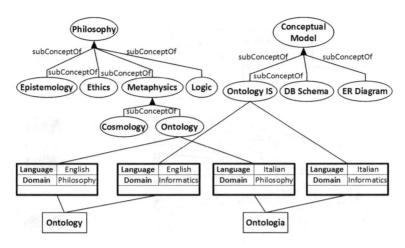

Fig. 1. Context-based associations of the terms "Ontology" and "Ontologia" with the appropriate concepts

study of the nature of being, existence or reality in general, as well as the basic categories of beings and their relations [3]. In addition to its use in Philosophy, the "ontology" term has been recently used in Computer Science in order to describe a formal, explicit specification of a shared conceptualization [4]. Thus, the interpretation of the term "ontology" is highly context-dependent, with the context including both the language and the application domain, as is shown in Fig. 1.

Consider now a digital library that contains material from several different disciplines. This material may be written in any spoken language. In this setting, consider an Italian-speaking informatics researcher that poses a query containing the term "ontologia". The lexical translation of the term in English is not sufficient for retrieving only the relevant material written in English; the user query context, and in particular the application domain, should be specified in order to interpret the query correctly.

In order to satisfy this requirement, we have developed a novel model in which we differentiate between *terms* (i.e. string values used in the data) and *concepts* (i.e. constructs modeling real world concepts and artifacts).

We associate terms to concepts. Each association comes with some confidence and is valid only under certain conditions that are determined through sets of parameters representing *contexts*. For the context representation we use the traditional definition of a vector of N values, the context dimensions [2]. In our application we have chosen 8 dimensions, which we found broadly applicable in real-world scenarios.

The queries are expressed using terms. Based on the query terms, we find the concepts related to them. This is done by taking into account the association context, From the concepts found, we select the terms related to them, again based on the context. Then we retrieve the data that contain these terms.

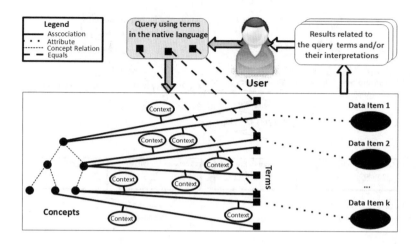

Fig. 2. Generic Cross-lingual Retrieval Use Case

The generic use case supported by our framework is outlined in Fig. 2. As shown, the user poses her queries using terms from her native language. These terms are associated with language-neutral concepts. Since the concepts may be associated with other terms through concept-term associations, the query results may contain any interpretation of the original query terms. Notice that the users may specify (explicitly or implicitly) in their queries some context and receive results related to the query terms under the respective context. This way, the query terms are not interpreted in isolation, but only relative to the query they appear in. Accordingly, if the user in our example specifies the "Informatics" domain in the context of a query containing the "ontologia" term, the documents returned from the digital library are those containing the term "ontologia" as it is used in Informatics or any of its valid interpretations. Our approach is consistent with Gottlob Frege's *Context Principle* [5], a form of semantic holism from Philosophy of Language holding that a philosopher should *"never ... ask for the meaning of a word in isolation, but only in the context of a proposition"*.

3   Context-Based Interpretation Model

We present here the context-based framework that we have developed for the interpretation of polysemous terms. The fundamental concepts of the framework are defined in Section 3.1, the query term interpretation is described in Section 3.2, the model implementation is presented in Section 3.3 and the implementation of the query term interpretation is presented in Section 3.4.

3.1   Fundamental Concepts

Let $Q(t_1, t_2, \cdots, t_n)$ be a query that involves n terms $t_1, t_2, \cdots, t_n$ and $R(t_1, t_2, \cdots, t_n)$ be the query results of $Q(t_1, t_2, \cdots, t_n)$. If there exist valid interpretations of the query terms, then $\forall\, t_i, i = 1 \cdots n, \exists\, \mathbb{IT}(t_i)$, where $\mathbb{IT}(t_i)$ is the set of the valid interpretations of t_i. If these interpretations should be taken into account, then $R(t_1, t_2, \cdots, t_n)$ should include the results $R'(t'_1, t'_2, \cdots, t'_n)$ of every query $Q'(t'_1, t'_2, \cdots, t'_n)$ with $t'_i \in \mathbb{IT}(t_i)$. If there exist m combinations of the valid interpretations of $t_1, t_2, \cdots, t_n$ and $R'_j(t'_{j1}, t'_{j2}, \cdots, t'_{jn})$ is the query containing the j_{th} combination, then (1) holds.

$$R(t_1, t_2, \cdots, t_n) = R'_1(t'_{11}, t'_{12}, \cdots, t'_{1n}) \cup \cdots \cup R'_m(t'_{m1}, t'_{m2}, \cdots, t'_{mn}) \qquad (1)$$

Let s be a concept, t a term and c a context, such that s is associated with t under the context c through an association $a(s, t, c, w)$, where w is a numeric value in the range $[0, 1]$ and describes the strength of the association.

A context c, formally described in (2), is used in order to localize the term-concept associations, while it preserves the compatibility of the reasoning that can be performed in different contexts [6]. According to (2), a context c essentially is a vector of name-value pairs, the *context dimensions*.

$$c\langle d_1 : v_1, \ldots, d_k : v_k\rangle \qquad (2)$$

Thus, in the example of Section 2 the term "ontologia" is associated with the "Ontology" concept through an association $a_1('Ontology', 'ontologia', c_1\langle language : 'Italian', domain : 'Philosophy'\rangle, 1)$ and with the concept "Ontology IS" through an association $a_2('OntologyIS', 'ontologia', c_2\langle language : 'Italian', domain : 'Informatics'\rangle, 1)$.

A *top* value is defined for every context dimension $d_i, (i = 1 \ldots k)$, which includes all the values of the domain of the dimension and is denoted by the $\top$ symbol. If the value v_i of the context dimension d_i of c is not specified, this dimension is assumed to have the $\top$ value. A context $c\langle d_1 : v_1, \ldots, d_k : v_k\rangle$ has the top context value (denoted by $\top$) if it has the $\top$ value in all the dimensions.

A *null* value is also defined for every context dimension $d_i, (i = 1 \ldots k)$, which has the "no value" sense and is denoted by the $\perp$ symbol. A context $c\langle d_1 : v_1, \ldots, d_k : v_k\rangle$ has the null context value (denoted by $\perp$) if it has the $\perp$ value at least in one of its dimensions. For example, the context $c\langle language : 'Italian', domain : \perp\rangle$ has the $\perp$ value.

A partial order is defined for each of the context dimensions, so that their values can be effectively compared. The $\prec$ operator allows detecting if the value v_{ai} of the ith dimension $(i = 1 \ldots k)$ of a context $c_a\langle d_{a1} : v_{a1}, \ldots, d_{ak} : v_{ak}\rangle$ is lower than the value v_{bi} of the ith dimension of a context $c_b\langle d_{b1} : v_{b1}, \ldots, d_{bk} : v_{bk}\rangle$, denoted as $v_{ai} \prec v_{bi}$. For example, '$1821 - 1936$' $\prec$ '$1789 - 1940$'.

Based on the partial order of the context values, a context $c_b\langle d_{b1} : v_{b1}, \ldots, d_{bk} : v_{bk}\rangle$ is more abstract than a context $c_a\langle d_{a1} : v_{a1}, \ldots, d_{ak} : v_{ak}\rangle$, denoted as $c_a \prec c_b$, iff $\forall\, i, (i = 1 \ldots k), v_{ai} \preceq v_{bi}$ and $\exists\, m, (m = 1 \ldots k)$ such that $v_{am} \prec v_{bm}$. As an example, consider two contexts $c_a\langle t : '1821 - 1936'\rangle$ and $c_b\langle t : '1789 - 1940'\rangle$, where t is the name of the time dimension of the contexts c_a and c_b. According to the context partial order definition, $c_a \prec c_b$.

The *Greatest Lower Bound* of the values v_{ai} and v_{bi} of the ith dimension of two contexts $c_a\langle d_{a1} : v_{a1}, \ldots, d_{ak} : v_{ak}\rangle$ and $c_b\langle d_{b1} : v_{b1}, \ldots, d_{bk} : v_{bk}\rangle$, denoted as $\mathfrak{glb}(v_{ai}, v_{bi})$, is formally defined in (3).

$$\mathfrak{glb}(v_{ai}, v_{bi}) = g, ((g \preceq v_{ai}) \wedge (g \preceq v_{bi}) \wedge$$
$$\nexists\, g'((g \prec g') \wedge (g' \preceq v_{ai}) \wedge (g' \preceq v_{bi}))) \tag{3}$$

For example, according to the definition of $\mathfrak{glb}$, we have for the time dimension of the previously defined contexts c_a and c_b that $\mathfrak{glb}('1821 - 1940', '1789 - 1936') = '1821 - 1936'$.

The *Least Upper Bound* of the values of the ith dimension of two contexts $c_a \langle d_{a1} : v_{a1}, \ldots, d_{ak} : v_{ak} \rangle$ and $c_b \langle d_{b1} : v_{b1}, \ldots, d_{bk} : v_{bk} \rangle$, denoted as $\mathfrak{lub}(v_{ai}, v_{bi})$, is formally defined in (4). For example, for the time dimension of the contexts $c_a \langle t : '1821 - 1940' \rangle$ and $c_b \langle t : '1789 - 1936' \rangle$ we have $\mathfrak{lub}('1821 - 1940', '1789 - 1936') = '1789 - 1940'$.

$$\mathfrak{lub}(v_{ai}, v_{bi}) = l, (v_{ai} \preceq l) \wedge (v_{bi} \preceq l) \wedge \nexists\, l'((l' \prec l) \wedge (v_{ai} \preceq l') \wedge (v_{bi} \preceq l')) \tag{4}$$

The *Greatest Lower Bound* $\mathfrak{GLB}(c_a \langle d_{a1} : v_{a1}, \ldots, d_{ak} : v_{ak} \rangle$, $c_b \langle d_{b1} : v_{b1}, \ldots, d_{bk} : v_{bk} \rangle)$ of two contexts $c_a \langle d_{a1} : v_{a1}, \ldots, d_{ak} : v_{ak} \rangle$ and $c_b \langle d_{b1} : v_{b1}, \ldots, d_{bk} : v_{bk} \rangle$ is a context c', formally defined in (5).

$$\mathfrak{GLB}(c_a \langle d_{a1} : v_{a1}, \ldots, d_{ak} : v_{ak} \rangle, c_b \langle d_{b1} : v_{b1}, \ldots, d_{bk} : v_{bk} \rangle) =$$
$$c' \langle \mathfrak{glb}(v_{a1}, v_{b1}), \ldots, \mathfrak{glb}(v_{ak}, v_{bk}) \rangle \tag{5}$$

For example, assume that t and p are, respectively, the names of the time and place context dimensions. Then, $\mathfrak{GLB}(c_a \langle t : '1821 - 1940', p : 'Greece' \rangle, c_b \langle t : '1789 - 1936', p : 'Europe' \rangle) = c' \langle t : '1821 - 1936', p : 'Greece' \rangle$. Also, $\mathfrak{GLB}(c_a \langle t : '1821 - 1940', p : 'Greece' \rangle, c_b \langle t : '1789 - 1936', p : 'Canada' \rangle) = c' \langle t : '1821 - 1936', p : \bot \rangle = \bot$.

The *Least Upper Bound* $\mathfrak{LUB}(c_a \langle d_{a1} : v_{a1}, \ldots, d_{ak} : v_{ak} \rangle, c_b \langle d_{b1} : v_{b1}, \ldots, d_{bk} : v_{bk} \rangle)$ of two contexts $c_a \langle d_{a1} : v_{a1}, \ldots, d_{ak} : v_{ak} \rangle$ and $c_b \langle d_{b1} : v_{b1}, \ldots, d_{bk} : v_{bk} \rangle$ is a context c', formally defined in (6). For example, $\mathfrak{LUB}(c_a \langle t : '1821 - 1940', p : 'Greece' \rangle, c_b \langle t : '1789 - 1936', p : 'Europe' \rangle) = c' \langle t : '1789 - 1940', p : 'Europe' \rangle$.

$$\mathfrak{LUB}(c_a \langle d_{a1} : v_{a1}, \ldots, d_{ak} : v_{ak} \rangle, c_b \langle d_{b1} : v_{b1}, \ldots, d_{bk} : v_{bk} \rangle) =$$
$$c' \langle \mathfrak{lub}(v_{a1}, v_{b1}), \ldots, \mathfrak{lub}(v_{ak}, v_{bk}) \rangle \tag{6}$$

The framework that we have developed is generic and it does not depend neither on the number of the context dimensions nor on the parameter described by each dimension. From our studies on real-world problems, we suggest that a context c for the interpretation of polysemous query terms comprises of the following $k = 8$ dimensions:

- $d_1 = l$, which represents the language of c;
- $d_2 = p$, which represents the place of c;
- $d_3 = t$, which represents the time period(s) covered by c;
- $d_4 = d$, which represents the application domain of c;
- $d_5 = h$, which represents the historiographical issues (i.e. social conditions, economical issues etc.) that should hold for c to be valid;
- $d_6 = dl$, which represents the dialect of c;

- $d_7 = dt$, which represents the diatype of c (i.e. a language variation, determined by its social purpose [7] like, for example, the specialized language of an academic journal); and
- $d_8 = f$, which represents the formality of c and may take one of the values "Very formal", "Formal", "Neutral", "Informal", "Very informal").

The above listed context dimensions have been identified in our case studies. We selected these dimensions in order to cover: *(a)* The variations of the term semantics in terms of language (d_1), dialect (d_6), social purpose, i.e. diatype, (d_7), formality (d_8) and place (d_2); *(b)* The evolution of the term semantics in time (d_3); and *(c)* The influence of the application domain (d_4) and the historiographical issues (d_5) in the interpretation of polysemous terms.

3.2 Query Term Interpretation

Let $\mathbb{T}$ be the set of all the terms, $\mathbb{S}$ the set of all the concepts, $\mathbb{C}$ the set of all the contexts and $\mathbb{A}$ the set of all the associations. $\mathbb{T}(s) \subseteq \mathbb{T}$ is the set of the terms associated with a concept s and $\mathbb{T}(s,c) \subseteq \mathbb{T}(s)$ is the set of the terms related to s under the c context through an association $a(s,t,c,w)$ with $w \geq w_0$, where $w_0 > 0$ is a threshold value for the strength. For instance, in the example of Section 2, $\mathbb{T}(\text{``Ontology''}) = \{\text{``Ontologia''}, \text{``Ontology''}\}$ and $\mathbb{T}(\text{``Ontology''}, c\langle l : \text{`Italian'}\rangle) = \{\text{``Ontologia''}\}$.

Let also $\mathbb{S}(t) \subseteq \mathbb{S}$ be the set of the concepts associated with a term t. Then, for every pair $\langle t, c \rangle$ exists a (possibly empty) set $\mathbb{S}(t,c)$, comprised of concepts associated with t under c through an association with $w \geq w_0$, as in (7). In addition, for every $s_i \in \mathbb{S}(t,c)$ exists a (possibly empty) set $\mathbb{T}_i(s_i, c_i)$, comprised of terms associated with s_i through an association $a_i(s_i, t, c_i, w_i)$ with $w_i \geq w_0$, as in (8). Notice that $|\mathbb{P}|$ is the cardinality of a set $\mathbb{P}$. In our example, for instance, we have $\mathbb{S}(\text{``Ontologia''}) = \{\text{``Ontology''}, \text{``OntologyIS''}\}$ and $\mathbb{S}(\text{``Ontologia''}, c\langle l : \text{`Italian'}, d : \text{`Informatics'}\rangle) = \{\text{``OntologyIS''}\}$.

$$\forall \langle t, c \rangle, t \in \mathbb{T}, c \in \mathbb{C}, \exists \, \mathbb{S}(t, c') \subseteq \mathbb{S}, c' \in \mathbb{C}, c' \preceq c \tag{7}$$

$$\forall \, s_i \in \mathbb{S}(t, c), \exists \, \mathbb{T}_i(s_i, c_i) \subseteq \mathbb{T}, c_i \in \mathbb{C}, c_i \preceq c, i = 1 \ldots M, M = |\mathbb{S}| \tag{8}$$

Let $Q(t_1, t_2, \ldots, t_h, c)$ be a generic query that involves, under the c context, h terms $t_1, \ldots, t_h$ and $R(t_1, \ldots, t_h, c)$ be the results of $Q(t_1, \ldots, t_h, c)$. Let also $Q'(s_1, \ldots, s_p, c')$ be a generic query that involves, under the c' context, p concepts $s_1, \ldots, s_p$ and $R'(s_1, \ldots, s_p, c')$ be the results of $Q'(s_1, \ldots, s_p, c')$. Then (9) and (10) hold and $R(t_1, \ldots, t_h, c)$ is calculated as in (11).

$$\forall \langle t_i, c \rangle, t_i \in \mathbb{T}, c \in \mathbb{C}, \exists \, \mathbb{S}_i(t_i, c_i) \subseteq \mathbb{S}, c_i \in \mathbb{C}, c_i \preceq c, i = 1 \ldots h \tag{9}$$

$$\forall \, s_{ij} \in \mathbb{S}_i(t_i, c_i), \exists \, \mathbb{T}_{ij}(s_{ij}, c_{ij}) \subseteq \mathbb{T}, c_{ij} \in \mathbb{C}_i, c_{ij} \preceq c_i, \\ i = 1 \ldots h, j = 1 \ldots M_i, M_i = |\mathbb{S}_i| \tag{10}$$

$$R(t_1, \ldots, t_h, c) = R'_1(s_{11}, \ldots, s_{1h}, c'_1) \cup \ldots \cup R'_T(s_{T1}, \ldots, s_{Th}, c'_h),$$
$$s_{ij} \in \mathbb{S}_i(t_i, c_i), c'_i = \mathbf{\mathfrak{GLB}}(c_{i1}, \ldots, c_{ih}), c'_i \neq \bot \qquad (11)$$
$$i = 1 \ldots h, T \leq h \cdot max(M_1, M_2, \ldots M_h)$$

Finally, $R'_i(s_{i1}, \ldots, s_{ih}, c'_i)$ is calculated as in (12).

$$R'_i(s_{i1}, \ldots, s_{ih}, c'_i) = R_{i1}(t_{11}, \ldots, t_{1h}, c_{i1}) \cup \ldots \cup R_{ih}(t_{h1}, \ldots, t_{hh}, c_{ih})$$
$$t_{ij} \in \mathbb{T}_i(s_{ij}, c'_i), c'_{ij} = \mathbf{\mathfrak{GLB}}(c_{11}, \ldots, c_{hh}), c'_{ij} \neq \bot \qquad (12)$$
$$i = 1 \ldots h, j = 1 \ldots h$$

For instance, using the above notation the query of our example is expressed as $Q(\text{"}Ontologia\text{"}, c\langle l : \text{'}Italian\text{'}, d : \text{'}Informatics\text{'}\rangle)$ and the query results are $R(\text{"}Ontologia\text{"}, c\langle l : \text{'}Italian\text{'}, d : \text{'}Informatics\text{'}\rangle)$. From (11) we have (13) and from (12) we have (14). Thus, (15) holds.

$$R(\text{"}Ontologia\text{"}, c\langle l : \text{'}Italian\text{'}, d : \text{'}Informatics\text{'}\rangle) =$$
$$R'(\text{"}Ontology\text{"}, c\langle l : \text{'}Italian\text{'}, d : \text{'}Informatics\text{'}\rangle) \qquad (13)$$

$$R'(\text{"}Ontology\text{"}, c\langle l : \text{'}Italian\text{'}, d : \text{'}Informatics\text{'}\rangle) =$$
$$R(\text{"}Ontologia\text{"}, c\langle l : \text{'}Italian\text{'}, d : \text{'}Informatics\text{'}\rangle) \cup \qquad (14)$$
$$R(\text{"}Ontology\text{"}, c\langle l : \text{'}English\text{'}, d : \text{'}Informatics\text{'}\rangle)$$

$$R(\text{"}Ontologia\text{"}, c\langle l : \text{'}Italian\text{'}, d : \text{'}Informatics\text{'}\rangle) =$$
$$R(\text{"}Ontologia\text{"}, c\langle l : \text{'}Italian\text{'}, d : \text{'}Informatics\text{'}\rangle) \cup \qquad (15)$$
$$R(\text{"}Ontology\text{"}, c\langle l : \text{'}English\text{'}, d : \text{'}Informatics\text{'}\rangle)$$

3.3   Model Implementation

The proposed model has been realized in a dataspace in the context of the TRENDS system [8]. The dataspace data model is flexible enough to consider data of different types, such as semi-structured, relational or RDF. In contrast to data models like the relational that are based on some structural notion, e.g., the notion of a tuple, the dataspace model is centered around the notion of *entity*, which is used to model any real-world object (web document, relational tuple, image, spreadsheet record). As it is typically the case in real world scenarios, despite the fact that entities can be clustered into groups with similar characteristics, it is rarely the case that all the entities in the same group will fully conform to the same strict specification. As such, the basic model imposes no restrictions on the structure and characteristics of the entities [9]. Only a unique identifier is stored for every object regardless of the object type.

We assume the existence of an infinite set of entities $\mathcal{E}$, of names $\mathcal{N}$ and of atomic values $\mathcal{V}$ containing values such as integers, strings, reals, etc.

Definition 1. *A* dataspace *is a tuple* $\langle E, G \rangle$ *where E and G are finite sets with $E \subseteq \mathcal{E}$ and $G \subseteq E \times \mathcal{N} \times \{E \cup \mathcal{V}\}$. An* attribute *is a pair* $\langle n, v \rangle$ *with the $n \in \mathcal{N}$ being referred to as the* attribute name *and the $v \in \mathcal{E} \cup \mathcal{V}$ as the* attribute value. *The attributes of an entity e in a dataspace $\langle E, G \rangle$ is the set $A(e) = \{\langle n, v \rangle \mid \langle e, n, v \rangle \in G\}$.*

The data model contains constructs to support schema information when this is required. In particular, certain entities in the dataspace can be used to describe the structure of a set of entities. These entities are called *classes*. To declare that the structure of an element e is described by a class c, an attribute *type* with value c is added in e. To identify the entities that can serve as classes, we assume by default in every dataspace the existence of a special entity *Class* and we require that every class entity has an attribute *type* with value *Class*. Furthermore, hierarchies among classes can be defined using a predefined attribute *subtype*.

The implementation of the context-based model for the interpretation of polysemous query terms is built upon three types of special entities: The *concepts*, the *terms* and the *concept-term associations*.

Definition 2. *A concept is a dataspace entity* s, *which belongs to the* Concept *class and has the* $A(s)$ *set of attributes.*

$$A(s) = \{\langle type : `Concept'\rangle, \langle id : sid\rangle, \langle name : sn\rangle, \langle concept\_relation : r\rangle\} \quad (16)$$

The *type* attribute associates s with the *Concept* class to which s belongs, the *id* attribute identifies s, the *name* attribute represents the name of s and the *concept_relation* attribute represents a relationship between concepts (like, for example, sub_concept_of, refines, generalizes ...) in which s participates.

The value of the *concept_relation* attribute is a dataspace entity r of *ConceptRelation* type, which has the $A(r)$ set of attributes formally described in (17). The *type* attribute associates r with the *ConceptRelation* class to which r belongs, the *id* attribute identifies r, the *source* attribute represents the source of the relationship, the *target* attribute represents the target of the relationship and the *concept_relation_type* attribute specifies the relationship type.

$$\begin{aligned} A(r) = \{&\langle type : `ConceptRelation'\rangle, \langle id : rid\rangle, \langle source : src\rangle, \langle target : trg\rangle, \\ &\langle concept\_relation\_type : t\rangle\} \end{aligned} \quad (17)$$

For instance, the "Ontology IS" concept in the example of Section 2 is represented by a dataspace entity s_1 that has the $A(s_1)$ set of attributes.

$$\begin{aligned} A(s_1) = \{&\langle type : `Concept'\rangle, \langle id : `OntologyIS'\rangle, \langle name : `OntologyIS'\rangle, \\ &\langle concept\_relation : `r_1'\rangle\} \end{aligned} \quad (18)$$

Notice that the "Ontology IS" concept in our example is associated with the "Conceptual Model" concept through a relation of type "subConceptOf". This relation is represented by the dataspace entity r_1 that has the $A(r_1)$ set of attributes.

$$\begin{aligned} A(r_1) = \{&\langle type : `ConceptRelation'\rangle, \langle concept\_relation\_type : `subConceptOf'\rangle, \\ &\langle id : `r_1'\rangle, \langle source : `OntologyIS'\rangle, \langle target : `ConceptualModel'\rangle\} \end{aligned} \quad (19)$$

Definition 3. *A term is a dataspace entity* t, *which belongs to the* Term *class and has the* $A(t)$ *set of attributes.*

$$A(t) = \{\langle type : `Term'\rangle, \langle id : tid\rangle, \langle name : tn\rangle\} \quad (20)$$

The *type* attribute associates t with the *Term* class to which t belongs, the *id* attribute identifies t and the *name* attribute represents the name of t.

For instance, the "Ontologia" term in our example is represented by a dataspace entity t_1 that has the $A(t_1)$ set of attributes.

$$A(t_1) = \{\langle type : 'Term' \rangle, \langle id : "Ontologia" \rangle, \langle name : "Ontologia" \rangle\} \qquad (21)$$

Definition 4. *A concept-term association is a dataspace entity* cta, *which belongs to the* CTAssociation *class and has the* $A(cta)$ *set of attributes.*

$$A(cta) = \{\langle type : 'CTAssociation' \rangle, \langle id : ctaid \rangle, \langle concept : s \rangle, \langle term : t \rangle,$$
$$\langle confidence : w \rangle, \langle definition : d \rangle, \langle context : c \rangle\} \qquad (22)$$

The *type* attribute associates *cta* with the *CTAssociation* class to which *cta* belongs, the *id* attribute identifies *cta*, the *concept* attribute links *cta* to the participating concept *s* and the *term* attribute links *cta* to the participating term *t*. The confidence of *cta* is represented by the *confidence* attribute, the textual definition of *t* under *cta* is represented by the *definition* attribute and the *context* attribute specifies the association context of *cta*.

For instance, the "Ontology IS" concept in our example is associated with the "Ontologia" term through a concept-term association. This association is represented by a dataspace entity cta_1 that has the $A(cta_1)$ set of attributes.

$$A(cta_1) = \{\langle type : 'CTAssociation' \rangle, \langle id : 'cta_1' \rangle, \langle concept : 's_1' \rangle,$$
$$\langle term : 't_1' \rangle, \langle confidence : '1' \rangle, \langle definition : '...' \rangle, \langle context : 'c_1' \rangle\} \qquad (23)$$

The value of the *context* attribute is a dataspace entity *c* of *Context* type, which has the $A(c)$ set of attributes, formally described in (24).

$$A(c) = \{\langle type : 'Context' \rangle, \langle id : cid \rangle, \langle language : l \rangle, \langle place : p \rangle, \langle time : t \rangle,$$
$$\langle domain : d \rangle, \langle historiographical\_issues : h \rangle, \langle dialect : dl \rangle, \langle diatype : dt \rangle, \qquad (24)$$
$$\langle formality : f \rangle\}$$

The *type* attribute associates *c* with the *Context* class to which *c* belongs, the *id* attribute identifies *c* and the rest of the (optional) attributes essentially are the context dimensions; In particular, the *language* attribute specifies the language of *c*, the *place* attribute specifies the place of *c*, the *time* attribute specifies the time of *c*, the *domain* attribute specifies the domain of *c*, the *historiographical_issues* attribute specifies the historiographical issues of *c*, the *dialect* attribute specifies the dialect of *c*, the *diatype* attribute specifies the diatype of *c* and the *formality* attribute specifies the formality of *c*.

For example, the context of the cta_1 concept-term association is represented by a dataspace entity c_1 that has the $A(c_1)$ set of attributes.

$$A(c_1) = \{\langle type : 'Context' \rangle, \langle id : 'c_1' \rangle, \langle language : 'Italian' \rangle,$$
$$\langle domain : 'Informatics' \rangle\} \qquad (25)$$

3.4   Implementation of Query Term Interpretation

In our working environment [10][11], a query is described by a rule. A rule consists of two parts: the *head* and the *body*. Each part is a conjunction of atoms (or subgoals). There are two kinds of atoms: the arithmetic and the entity atoms. An arithmetic atom is a Boolean condition that involves variables and constant values, i.e., $x \leq 10$ or $x=y$. Arithmetic atoms can appear in the body of the rule but not in the head. An entity atom is of the form $e(n_1:v_1, n_2:v_2, \ldots, n_k:v_k)$, where e, n_i and v_i are variables or constants. Variables appearing outside the parenthesis in an atom, like the variable e, are called entity variables and can be bound only to dataspace entities. Variables like the n_1, n_2, ... can be bound only to attribute names, and variables like the v_1, v_2, ... can be bound either to atomic values or to entities. Given a binding of the variables e, n_i, v_i to e^b, n_i^b and v_i^b, respectively, for every $i=1..k$, the entity atom $e(n_1:v_1, n_2:v_2, \ldots, n_k:v_k)$ is said to be true if there is an entity e^b in the dataspace that has attributes $\langle n_i^b:v_i^b \rangle$, for every $i=1..k$.

The atoms in the head of a query are true, if the all the atoms in the body of the query are true. When the body of the query is evaluated to true, a set of entities and attributes as described by the head of the query are returned. Thus, the result of a query in our model is itself a dataspace which makes the query language closed over the set of all possible dataspaces and allowing the composition of queries. For readability purposes and to reduce the number of arithmetic operations, variables may be shared across atoms or be replaced by constants. Furthermore, atoms may be used in attributes as values to simulate nesting.

In order to perform the context-based query term interpretation in our dataspace working environment, the original queries should be rewritten in such a way that the required attribute values and/or names can also be matched by their interpretations in a given context.

Let Q be a generic dataspace query, of the form shown in expression (26), where a_i ($i = 1 \ldots n$) are attribute names and v_i are attribute values. The query context is $c(language : l, place : p, time : t, domain : d, dialect : dl, diatype : dt, formality : f, historiographical\_issues : h)$. The semantics of the query Q is that the results should include all the entities having the value v_i in the attribute a_i. If v_i is a literal value, the results should also include all the entities having an interpretation v_i as value of the a_i attribute. In addition, if a_i is a literal value, the results should also include all the entities with the desired value in an attribute having as name an interpretation of a_i. For every query result x, the context c' under which x is valid is also specified.

$$\$\mathbf{x}(context : \$c') : - \$\mathbf{x}(a_1 : v_1, a_2 : v_2, \cdots, a_n : v_n), \$\mathbf{c}(language : l,$$
$$place : p, time : t, domain : d, dialect : dl, \qquad (26)$$
$$diatype : dt, formality : f, historiographical\_issues : h)$$

In our implementation, Q is rewritten in a way that exploits the concept-term associations in order to allow the required attribute values and names to be matched by their interpretations. The equivalent query Q' is shown in expression (27). A weight w is also specified for every result of Q', which is calculated on the basis of the strengths of the concept-term associations.

$x(\$w : \$w_{sv1} \cdot \$w_{sk1} \cdot \$w_{av1} \cdot \$w_{ak1} \cdot \ldots \cdot \$w_{svn} \cdot \$w_{skn} \cdot \$w_{avn} \cdot \$w_{akn},$
$context : \$c') : - \$x(\$key_{a1} : \$key_{v1}, \ldots, \$key_{an} : \$key_{vn}),$
$\$y_{v1}(concept : \$s_{v1}, type : 'CTAssociation', term : v_1, confidence : \$w_{sv1},$
$context : \$c_{sv1}), \ldots, \$y_{vn}(concept : \$s_{vn}, type : 'CTAssociation',$
$term : v_n, confidence : \$w_{svn}, context : \$c_{svn}),$
$\$z_{v1}(concept : \$s_{v1}, type : 'CTAssociation', term : \$key_{v1},$
$confidence : \$w_{sk1}, context : \$c_{sk1}), \ldots, \$z_{vn}(concept : \$s_{vn},$
$type : 'CTAssociation', term : \$key_{vn}, confidence : \$w_{skn}, context : \$c_{skn}),$
$\$y_{a1}(concept : \$s_{a1}, type : 'CTAssociation', term : a_1, confidence : \$w_{av1},$
$context : \$c_{av1}), \ldots, \$y_{an}(concept : \$s_{a1}, type : 'CTAssociation',$ $\qquad(27)$
$term : a_n, confidence : \$w_{avn}, context : \$c_{avn})$
$\$z_{a1}(type : 'CTAssociation', term : \$key_{a1}, concept : \$s_{a1},$
$confidence : \$w_{ak1}, context : \$c_{ak1}), \ldots, \$z_{an}(type : 'CTAssociation',$
$term : \$key_{an}, concept : \$s_{an}, confidence : \$w_{akn}, context : \$c_{akn}),$
$\$c(language : l, place : p, time : t, domain : d, dialect : dl, diatype : dt,$
$formality : f, historiographical\_issues : h)$
WITH $(\$c_{sv1} \preceq c) \wedge \ldots \wedge (\$c_{svn} \preceq c) \wedge (\$c_{av1} \preceq c) \wedge \ldots \wedge (\$c_{avn} \preceq c)$
$\wedge (\$c' \neq \bot) \wedge (\$c' = \mathfrak{GLB}(\$c_{sv1}, \ldots, \$c_{svn}, \$c_{av1}, \ldots, \$c_{avn},$
$\$c_{sk1}, \ldots, \$c_{skn}, \$c_{ak1}, \ldots, \$c_{akn}))$

Consider, as an example, the query of our motivating example, which should retrieve all the objects that contain the keyword "ontologia", assuming that: (a) The entity keywords are stored in the *keyword* attribute; (b) The user specifies the Italian term "ontologia"; and (c) The user is interested only in the entities that are referring to the term "ontologia" as it is used in the informatics domain. The query has the form Q_a shown in expression (28), which will retrieve all the entities having "ontologia" as value of the *keyword* attribute, in a context $c(language : 'Italian', domain : 'informatics')$. In our implementation, Q_a is rewritten in the form of Q'_a shown in expression (29).

$\$x(context : \$c') : - \$x(keyword : 'ontologia'),$
$\$c(language : 'Italian', domain : 'informatics')$ $\qquad(28)$

$\$x(\$w : \$w_v \cdot \$w_k, context : \$c') : - \$x(keyword : \$key),$
$\$y(type : 'CTAssociation', concept : \$s, term : 'ontologia',$
$confidence : \$w_v, context : \$c_v), \$z(type : 'CTAssociation', concept : \$s,$
$term : \$key, confidence : \$w_k, context : \$c_k), \$c(language : 'Italian',$ $\qquad(29)$
$domain : 'informatics')$
WITH $(\$c_v \preceq c) \wedge (\$c' = \mathfrak{GLB}(\$c_v, \$c_k)) \wedge (\$c' \neq \bot)$

Consider now a query Q_b, which assumes that: (a) The entity keywords are stored in an attribute that has as name an interpretation of "keyword"; (b) The user specifies the English term "ontology"; and (c) The user is interested only in the entities that are referring to the term "ontology" as it is used in the informatics domain. Q_b has the form of (30) and it is rewritten as in expression (31).

$$\$\mathbf{x}(context : \$c') : - \$\mathbf{x}(`keyword' : `ontology'),$$
$$\$\mathbf{c}(language : `English', domain : `informatics') \quad (30)$$

$$\$\mathbf{x}(\$w : \$w_{sv} \cdot \$w_{sk} \cdot \$w_{av} \cdot \$w_{ak}, context : \$c') : - \$\mathbf{x}(\$key_a : \$key_v),$$
$$\$\mathbf{y_v}(type : `CTAssociation', concept : \$s_v, term : `ontology',$$
$$confidence : \$w_{sv}, context : \$c_{sv}), \$\mathbf{z_v}(type : `CTAssociation',$$
$$concept : \$s_v, term : \$key_v, confidence : \$w_{sk}, context : \$c_{sk}),$$
$$\$\mathbf{y_a}(type : `CTAssociation', concept : \$s_a, term : `keyword',$$
$$confidence : \$w_{av}, context : \$c_{av}), \quad (31)$$
$$\$\mathbf{z_a}(type : `CTAssociation', concept : \$s_a, term : \$key_a, confidence : \$w_{ak},$$
$$context : \$c_{ak}), \$\mathbf{c}(language : `English', domain : `informatics')$$
$$\mathbf{WITH} \ (\$c_{sv} \preceq c) \wedge (\$c_{av} \preceq c) \wedge (\$c' \neq \perp) \wedge$$
$$(\$c' = \mathfrak{GLB}(\$c_{sv}, \$c_{av}, \$c_{sk}, \$c_{ak}))$$

4 Use Case

To illustrate the application of our approach, we present a case study which focuses on the formation of biotechnology from the perspective of History of Science and Technology, introduced earlier in section 1. In order to answer a user query on biotechnology, we need to identify all the documents related to the term of interest in the underlying archive. This is not a trivial task, given that during the 20th century the notion of biotechnology has undergone many terminological and conceptual changes, as discussed in the seminal essay of Robert Bud [12]. Those changes must be modeled appropriately in order to be able to identify the documents related to the term "biotechnology" in a given query context that may include the time period, country etc.

In particular, the word "biotechnology" was first introduced in 1917 by a Hungarian agricultural engineer, Karl Ereky, to cover the area of technology associated with the living beings.

However, the origins of biotechnology as a field of study go back to the late 19th century in relation to the field of zymotechnology that concerns industrial fermentation and brewing techniques. In different countries different terms were used with a similar meaning, e.g., "biontotechnik", "biotechnik", "biotechnics" and others. In the 1960s, biotechnology came to connote the environment friendly technological orientation rather than a specific technology. Thus, the definition of biotechnology had been very fluid till the 1970s, when it finally obtained its current meaning based on its links to microbiology and genetics. In this setting, conventional query answering mechanisms would return the documents explicitly mentioning the "biotechnology" keyword, while leaving out the rest of the relevant resources which might use, for instance, the obsolete term "zymotechnology" instead.

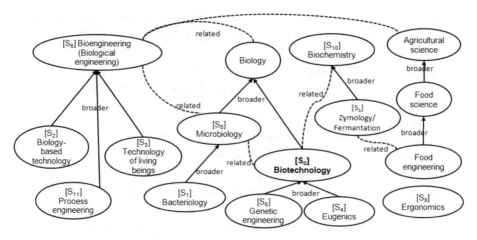

Fig. 3. An approximate model of biotechnology-related fields

See a fragment of the ontology representing the contemporary understanding of the relevant scientific fields in Fig. 3 and the record of the main historical milestones in Table 1.

If we consider our initial query "show me the evolution of the semantics of the term 'biotechnology' in the 20th century" (see Section 1), the proposed context-based model for the interpretation of polysemous terms comes in handy to comprehensively answer such historical queries. In particular, the query is initially expressed, using the term 'biotechnology' in English, as in (32) and is then rewritten as shown in (33). The later will return any valid interpretation of the term 'biotechnology' that was used during the 20th century in any language together with the context in which this interpretation is valid.

$$\$x(context : \$c') : - \$x(keyword : 'biotechnology'),$$
$$\$c(language : 'English', time = '20^{th} century') \tag{32}$$

$$\$x(\$w : \$w_v \cdot \$w_k, context : \$c') : - \$x(keyword : \$key),$$
$$\$y(type : 'CTAssociation', concept : \$s, term : 'biotechnology',$$
$$confidence : \$w_v, context : \$c_v),$$
$$\$z(type : 'CTAssociation', concept : \$s, term : \$key, confidence : \$w_k, \tag{33}$$
$$context : \$c_k), \$c(language : 'English', time = '20^{th} century')$$
$$\textbf{WITH } (\$c_v \preceq c) \wedge (\$c' = \mathfrak{GLB}(\$c_v, \$c_k)) \wedge (\$c' \neq \bot)$$

Consider now that the initial query is modified in order to show the recent (after 1970) evolution of the term "biotechnology". The new query is initially expressed as in (34) and is then rewritten as shown in (35). The later will return only the valid interpretations of the term 'biotechnology' used during from 1970 together with the context in which this interpretation is valid.

$$\$x(context : \$c') : - \$x(keyword : 'biotechnology'),$$
$$\$c(language : 'English', time = '1970 - now') \tag{34}$$

Table 1. Terms and related concepts in the history of biotechnology

Term	Concepts	Concept IDs	Context		
			Language	Place	Time (uncertain dates in parentheses)
Bioteknisk kemi	Fermentation physiology (industrial fermentation, agruculture)	S_1	Danish	Denmark	1915-1945
Biotechnologie	Biology-based technology	S_2	Hungarian	Hungary	1917-1945
Biotechnologie	Biology-based technology	S_2	German	Germany	1920-1945
Biontotechnik	Technology of living beings	S_3	German	Germany	1901-1945
Biotechnik	Technology for human improvement (eugenics, social biology)	S_4	German	Germany	1911-1945
Zymotechnology	Brewing technique (industrial fermentation)	S_1	English	UK	1900-1918
Biotechnology	Applied microbiology, brewing	S_1, S_5	English	UK	1918-1939
Biotechnology	Applied microbiology, brewing	S_1, S_5	English	USA	1918-1939
Biotechnology	Biological technology for human improvement (eugenics, social biology)	S_4	English	UK	1936-(1945)
Biotechnics	Technology based on biology	S_2	English	UK	1915-(1962)
Biotechnics	(Bio)engineering	S_6	English	USA	1934-1945
Biological Engineering	(Bio)engineering	S_6	English	USA	1936-(1945)
Biotechnology	Ergonomics (Biologically compatible technology)	S_9	English	USA	1946-1972
Biotechnology	Modern definition	S_0={S_1, S_4, S_5, S_6, S_8}	English	USA	1975-Now
Biotechnik	Biology-based technologies, brewing	S_1, S_2	Swedish	Sweden	1943 - late 1950s
Biotechnik	Biology-based technologies, brewing, bacteriology, eugenics, microbiology	S_1, S_2, S_4, S_5, S_7	Swedish	Sweden	late 1950s - Now
Biotechnologi	Ergonomics	S_9	Swedish	Sweden	1950-(1975)
Biotechnologi	Modern definition	S_0={S_1, S_4, S_5, S_6, S_8}	Swedish	Sweden	(1975)-Now
Biotechnologie	Microbiology, biochemistry, biotechnical chemistry/fermentation, process engineering	S_1, S_5, S_{10}, S_{11}	German	Germany	1974-1980
Biotechnologie	Modern definition	S_0={S_1, S_4, S_5, S_6, S_8}	German	Germany	1980-Now

$$\$\mathbf{x}(\$w : \$w_v \cdot \$w_k, context : \$c') : - \$\mathbf{x}(keyword : \$key),$$
$$\$\mathbf{y}(type : 'CTAssociation', concept : \$s, term : 'biotechnology',$$
$$confidence : \$w_v, context : \$c_v),$$
$$\$\mathbf{z}(type : 'CTAssociation', concept : \$s, term : \$key, confidence : \$w_k,$$
$$context : \$c_k), \$\mathbf{c}(language : 'English', time = '1970 - now')$$
$$\mathbf{WITH}\ (\$c_v \preceq c) \wedge (\$c' = \mathfrak{GLB}(\$c_v, \$c_k)) \wedge (\$c' \neq \bot)$$

(35)

5 Related Work

The context-based query term interpretation framework that we have presented in this paper relates with two main research disciplines: *(a)* Systems that support multilingualism; and *(b)* Context-based systems.

Multilingualism. The research works that support multilingualism are usually based on the association of the conceptual model elements (i.e. entities, classes, ...) with terms describing them in different languages. This may be done either by keeping the multilingual labels inside the conceptual model elements [13] or by mapping them to sets of synonym terms [1][14][15]. This approach does not usually allow the association of the conceptual model elements to more than one sets of synonyms. There exist, though, some variations of this approach, based on the alignment of conceptual models built using terms from different spoken languages [16][17][18]. If the alignment involves more than two languages, a pivot language is utilized (usually English), in which all the concepts of the application domain are represented [19].

An important disadvantage of the aforementioned approaches is the limited (or even altogether lack of) context utilization for the disambiguation of the terms used in different languages; only the dubbed context is used in some research works for the disambiguation of the text-translation process [20][21]. In this sense, our context-based framework proposes a new research direction in the multilingualism domain that allows for the more reliable interpretation of the query terms in cross-lingual retrieval. The only approaches that have some similarities with our work are: (a) [22], where the context is used in order to associate terms with concepts, is the approach of the ontological engineering framework DOGMA. In that work, though, the context is not structured and is intended to be used by human readers; and (b) [23], where a domain is associated with every term in the Wordnet lexical database. This is a special case in our context-based model, where the domain is just one of the context dimensions.

Context. The notion of context plays a central role in the framework that we have developed for the interpretation of polysemous query terms. The context model used in our framework is compatible with well-accepted general purpose context models [2], [24], while it is applied in a domain that has not yet benefited from the utilization of context. In particular, both our approach and the aforementioned ones model the context as a set of values, the context dimensions. In addition, we adopt the idea of the partial order of the values of the context dimensions from [2], while we also specify a null context value and the $\mathcal{LUB}$ and $\mathcal{GLB}$ context operations, that are compatible, respectively, with the empty context value and the union and intersection context operations that were proposed in [24]. Moreover, our context management approach has similarities with [25], where the context is also handled as a first-class entity (concept or instance). Last, but not least, our use of weights for associations is adopted from Computational Linguistics [26], where has been research on the selection among synonyms in different contexts.

6   Conclusions and Future Work

We have proposed a general-purpose mechanism for dealing with the interpretation of polysemous terms. Our proposal adopts ideas from a number of sources, including multilingual ontologies, contexts and Computational Linguistics. The mechanism has been implemented and is used in a special-purpose digital library founded on a history ontology for renewable energy and biotechnology in the context of the EU project PAPYRUS.

Our future research includes the extensive evaluation of our framework in cross-lingual retrieval. We also intend to explore other potential applications of the proposed framework, both in digital libraries and apart from the digital library domain, that need to correctly interpret polysemous terms in a multi-contextual setting.

Acknowledgement

We acknowledge funding for this research from the PAPYRUS project (ICT-215874). The authors would like to thank our colleagues working on the project, especially our historian colleagues, for introducing us to the complexities of historical research.

References

1. Dong, X., Halevy, A.: Indexing dataspaces. In: Proc. of the 2007 ACM SIGMOD International Conference on Management of Data, pp. 43–54 (June 11- 14, 2007)
2. Bolchini, C., Schreiber, F.A., Tanca, L.: A methodology for a very small data base design. Information Systems 32(1), 61–82 (2007)
3. The Wikipedia Free Encyclopedia, http://www.wikipedia.org
4. Gruber, T.R.: A translation approach to portable ontology specifications. Knowledge Acquisition 5/2, 199–220 (1993)
5. Frege, G.: The Foundations of Arithmetic (EN Transl. by J.L.Austin), 2nd revised edn. (1884/1980)
6. Ghidini, C., Giunchiglia, F.: Local models semantics, or contextual reasoning=locality+compatibility. Artificial Intelligence 127(2), 221–259 (2001)
7. Gregory, M.: Aspects of varieties differentiation. Journal of Linguistics 3, 177–197 (1967)
8. Bykau, S., Kiyavitskaya, N., Tsinaraki, C., Velegrakis, Y.: Bridging the gap between heterogeneous and semantically diverse content of different disciplines. In: Proc. of the 2010 DEXA Workshop (FlexDBIST) (August 30 - September 4, 2010)
9. Dong, X., Halevy, A., Madhavan, J.: Reference reconciliation in complex information spaces. In: Proc. of the 2005 ACM SIGMOD Int. Conf. on Management of Data, pp. 85–96. ACM, New York (2005)
10. Rizzolo, F., Velegrakis, Y., Mylopoulos, J., Bykau, S.: Modeling concept evolution: A historical perspective. In: Laender, A.H.F. (ed.) ER 2009. LNCS, vol. 5829, pp. 331–345. Springer, Heidelberg (2009)
11. Presa, A., Velegrakis, Y., Rizzolo, F., Bykau, S.: Modeling associations through intensional attributes. In: Laender, A.H.F. (ed.) ER 2009. LNCS, vol. 5829, pp. 315–330. Springer, Heidelberg (2009)

12. Bud, R.: Biotechnology in the twentieth century. Social Studies of Science 21, 415–457 (1991)
13. Segev, A., Gal, A.: Egovernment policy evaluation support using multilingual ontologies. In: Proc. of 1st Int. Conf. on Interoperability of eGovernment Services (eGovInterop 2005) (February 23-24, 2005)
14. Kerremans, K., Temmerman, R.: Towards multilingual, termontological support in ontology engineering. In: Proc. of Termino 2004, Workshop on Terminology (2004)
15. Nichols, E., Bond, F., Tanaka, T., Sanae, F., Flickinger, D.: Multilingual ontology acquisition from multiple mrds. In: Proc. of 2nd Workshop on Ontology Learning and Population (OLP2), pp. 10–17 (2006)
16. Yeh, J.F., Wu, C.H., Chen, M.J., Yu, L.C.: Automated alignment and extraction of bilingual ontology for cross-language domain-specific applications. International Journal of Computational Linguistics & Chinese Language Processing 10(1), 35–52 (2005)
17. Ajani, G., Boella, G., Lesmo, L., Mazzei, A., Rossi, P.: Multilingual conceptual dictionaries based on ontologies. In: Proc. of V Legislative XML Workshop, pp. 1–14. European Press, Academic Publishing (June 2006)
18. Trojahn, C., Quaresma, P., Vieira, R.: Framework for multilingual ontology mapping. In: Proc. 6th Edition of the Language Resources and Evaluation Conference (LREC 2008). European Language Resources Association (ELRA) (2008)
19. Almeida, J.J., Simoes, A.: T2o recycling thesauri into a multilingual ontology. In: Calzolari, N., Choukri, K., Gangemi, A., Maegaard, B., Mariani, J., Odjik, J., Tapias, D. (eds.) Proc. of the 5th Int. Conf. on Language Resources and Evaluation (LREC 2006), pp. 1466–1471 (May 22-28, 2006)
20. Pazienza, M.T., Stellato, A.: An environment for semi-automatic annotation of ontological knowledge with linguistic content. In: Sure, Y., Domingue, J. (eds.) ESWC 2006. LNCS, vol. 4011, pp. 11–14. Springer, Heidelberg (2006)
21. Espinoza, M., Perez, A.G., Mena, E.: Enriching an ontology with multilingual information. In: Proc. of 5th European Semantic Web Conference (ECSW 2008), pp. 333–347 (2008)
22. De Leenheer, P., de Moor, A., Meersman, R.: Context dependency management in ontology engineering: a formal approach. Journal on Data Semantics VIII, 26–56 (2007)
23. Magnini, B., Cavagli, G.: Integrating subject field codes into wordnet. In: Proceedings of LREC 2000, 2nd International Conference on Language Resources and Evaluation, pp. 1413–1418 (2000)
24. Stavrakas, Y., Gergatsoulis, M.: Multidimensional semistructured data: Representing context-dependent information on the web. In: Pidduck, A.B., Mylopoulos, J., Woo, C.C., Ozsu, M.T. (eds.) CAiSE 2002. LNCS, vol. 2348, pp. 183–199. Springer, Heidelberg (2002)
25. Ram, S., Park, J.: Semantic conflict resolution ontology (scrol): An ontology for detecting and resolving data and schema-level semantic conflicts. Transactions on Knowledge and Data Engineering (TKDE) 16(21), 189–202 (2004)
26. Marcu, D.: The rhetorical parsing of unrestricted texts: A surface-based approach. Computational Linguistics 26(3), 395–448 (2000)

Automatic Web Page Annotation with Google *Rich Snippets*

Walter Hop[1], Stephan Lachner[1], Flavius Frasincar[1], and Roberto De Virgilio[2]

[1] Erasmus University Rotterdam
Erasmus School of Economics
PO Box 1738, NL-3000 DR, Rotterdam, The Netherlands
{w.w.hop,s.lachner}@student.eur.nl, frasincar@ese.eur.nl
[2] Dipartimento di Informatica e Automazione
Universitá Roma Tre, Rome, Italy
devirgilio@dia.uniroma3.it

Abstract. Web pages are designed to be read by people, not machines. Consequently, searching and reusing information on the Web is a difficult task without human participation. Adding semantics (i.e meaning) to a Web page would help machines to understand Web contents and better support the Web search process. One of the latest developments in this field is Google's *Rich Snippets*, a service for Web site owners to add semantics to their Web pages. In this paper we provide an approach to automatically annotate a Web page with Rich Snippets RDFa tags. Exploiting several heuristics and a named entity recognition technique, our method is capable of recognizing and annotating a subset of Rich Snippets' vocabulary, i.e., all attributes of its *Review* concept, and the names of *Person* and *Organization* concepts. We implemented an on-line service and evaluated the accuracy of the approach on real E-commerce Web sites.

1 Introduction

The World Wide Web provides a huge amount of information that humans can comprehend. Computers on the other hand have almost no understanding of the information contained in a Web page. To this aim, the *Semantic Web* [1], an extension to the World Wide Web in which information is defined semantically (as concepts with meaning) instead of presented visually, tries to close this gap. It will allow the Web to match requests of people and machines to Web content in a more accurate way. Although it may unfold in interesting new functionality involving finding, sharing, and combining information on the Web, wide adoption of the Semantic Web is yet to be waited for.

One of the latest developments in this field is Google's *Rich Snippets* [2], a service for Web site owners to add semantics to their (existing) Web pages using the Google's vocabulary [3] (i.e. a list of concepts and their attributes). Although the existing vocabulary is limited to a small number of simple concepts (i.e *Person, Review, Review Aggregate, Product,* and *Organization*) it is likely

R. Meersman et al. (Eds.): OTM 2010, Part II, LNCS 6427, pp. 957–974, 2010.

only a matter of time before new concepts will be introduced. Fig. 1 shows an example of a Rich Snippet in Google's search results. When a Web site uses Rich Snippets on its pages, recognized concepts will be highlighted in Google's search results using visual cues and a brief display of the concepts' attributes.

Drooling Dog Bar B Q - Colfax, CA
★★★★☆ 15 reviews - Price range: $$
Drooling Dog has some really good BBQ. I had the pulled pork sandwich, ... **Drooling Dog** BBQ is a great place to stop at on your way up the hill to Tahoe ...
www.yelp.com/biz/**drooling-dog**-bar-b-q-colfax - 75k - Cached - Similar pages

Fig. 1. An example of a *Review Aggregate* Rich Snippet in Google search results

Since a highlighted and more explanatory result will stand out in long uniform lists of search results, it is hoped that this feature will incentivize Web site owners to start using Rich Snippets on their Web sites. Future usage of annotated Web pages is not limited to displaying Rich Snippets in search results. It is only a small step to introduce more advanced search capabilities. For example, you might search for Web pages about the company "Philip Morris" or the programming language "Java", while ignoring Web pages about unrelated entity types (such as persons and geographical regions) with the same name. Another example would be to query Google for products sold in a certain price range with positive reviews.

The success of Rich Snippets depends on the support of search engines on one hand, and the coordinated adoption by a loosely-knit community of Web site owners and software companies on the other hand. Although Rich Snippets were introduced quite recently (i.e. May 12, 2009), it appears that Google seriously commits itself to a future of semantic search. For Web site owners however, adopting Rich Snippets still requires a considerable effort. If a Web site owner retrieves their information as structured data from a database, annotating pages with Rich Snippets is a simple exercise, as it is sufficient to identify its concepts in generated pages and add attributes to the generated HTML output. Fig. 2 shows an example of semantic annotation of a *Review* entity in a Web page. It is supported by the RDFa [4] format.

```
<span xmlns:v="http://rdf.data-vocabulary.org/#" typeof="v:Review">
    <span property="v:itemreviewed">Komala Vilas</span>
    <span property="v:reviewer">Meenakshi Ammal</span>
    <span property="v:rating">3.7</span>
    <span property="v:dtreviewed">1st April 2005</span>
    <span property="v:summary">Best south Indian vegetarian food in South Bay</span>
</span>
```

Fig. 2. A Rich Snippets annotation of a *Review* entity, using the RDFa format

Nevertheless, automatic pre-generation of annotations is not always possible. Problems appear for instance when information is not available in structured database form, or when the Web site owner does not have full control over the Web page generation process. Other problem instances arise if the site owner must start from static documents such as those originating from legacy software systems or OCR methods. Semantically annotating these Web pages may then become a matter of time-consuming manual labor.

In this paper, we introduce a method to read existing Web pages and automatically annotate them with the necessary RDFa attributes defined by Google Rich Snippets. We have explored recognizing the Rich Snippets concepts *Reviews*, *People* and *Organizations*. Using algorithms based on heuristics and Named Entity Recognition techniques, we have implemented a tool that takes a URL as an input, and outputs a Google Rich Snippets-compliant Web page. A Web-based version of the tool is available on-line[1].

The remainder of this paper is organized as follows. Section 2 introduces the state of the art. Section 3 illustrates an architecture of reference to provide a functional global view of the approach. Section 4 describes in detail the adopted heuristics and step-by-step the annotation process. Section 5 discusses the implementation of our framework and evaluates the performance of our algorithm. Finally, in Section 6 we sketch conclusions and future work.

2   State of the Art

Named Entity Recognition. Our work is related to a research field called Named Entity Recognition (NER). NER aims at processing natural text and identifying certain occurrences of words or expressions as belonging to particular categories of named entities [5]. These named entities belong to predefined entity types (categories) such as persons, organizations, locations, expressions of time, et cetera. Although most techniques rely on gazetteers (lists of names of people, organizations, locations, and other named entities), NER is not simply a matter of searching text for known words. Such a word list would be enormously long and unfeasible to compose. Moreover, certain words can belong to multiple concepts of different entity types. The text "Philip Morris" might be in the list of names as well in the list of companies, leading to an ambiguity issue. Therefore, NER involves more advanced techniques.

Most approaches to NER problems can be classified as statistical, grammar-based, or hybrids of these two approaches. Statistical systems typically make use of annotated training data from which word lists are generated and features are selected. The classifier then uses a statistical model to compute the probability of a word belonging to one of the output classes based on its context. As mentioned above, NER usually depends on extensive gazetteers. However, there are researchers that argue against the use of large gazetteers. Participants in the Named Entity recognition competition (part of MUC-6) report that gazetteers did not make a significant difference to their systems [6,7]. In [5] the authors

---

[1] http://annotator.lfms.nl/

avoid large gazetteers by combining rule-based grammars with statistical (maximum entropy) models. They show that it is sufficient to use relatively small gazetteers of well-known names, rather than large gazetteers of low-frequency names.

Source code analysis. Our project makes use of NER techniques to recognize and label the names of *Person* and *Organization* entities, two basic concepts from Google's Rich Snippets vocabulary. However, not the recognition of every entity that is in the Google vocabulary can be reduced to a NER problem. Review text bodies for example won't let themselves be captured by applying NER. To be able to automatically recognize reviews on a Web page, a set of rules or patterns to extract a review has to be found. This so-called 'pattern-matching' on a Web page can be done either by inspecting the source code of the page or by analyzing linguistic properties.

Ranking text sections on a Web page in terms of importance is an important topic, popularized by search engines like Google, which uses HTML tags such as h1, h2, et cetera to determine the relevance of information found on a Web page. This simple heuristic is also useful to find summaries and titles of text bodies. While actual algorithms used by search engine companies remain unpublished, we have implemented a tag ranking heuristic based on current assumptions by search engine specialists [8]. An example of more extensive source code analysis is the work of De Virgilio and Torlone [9]. In this study, the authors reverse engineer data that is contained in (data-intensive) Web pages by analyzing the structure of that page and how it would be visually formatted on a screen. The underlying idea is that semantically identical data is mostly displayed in visually grouped object blocks. Another example in this field is recognizing a postal address from a Web page. An interesting algorithm, based on first assessing visual similarity of Web page elements and then using a grammar-based approach, is sketched in [10]. This method could be helpful in detecting postal addresses of *Person* and *Organization* entities.

Search engines. Google Rich Snippets is not the only service aimed at integrating semantic information into search engines. A similar initiative is Yahoo! SearchMonkey, a service that also traverses Web sites to find RDFa or Microformats annotations for concepts such as Reviews, Persons and Organizations. Additionally, it allows Web site owners to create applications that build "enhanced results" using this information [11]. Fortunately, Google Rich Snippets and Yahoo! SearchMonkey have overlapping vocabularies which both include the entities recognized by our method, which means that the resulting annotated Web pages can be interpreted by both search engines.

3   An Architecture of Reference

Google Rich Snippets supports a vocabulary concerning Reviews on different Products, as shown in Fig. 3.

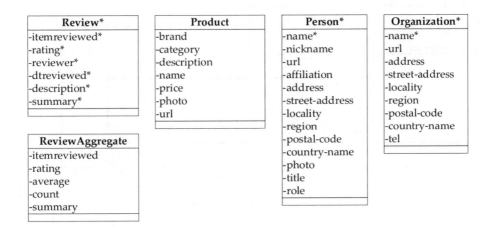

Review*
-itemreviewed*
-rating*
-reviewer*
-dtreviewed*
-description*
-summary*

ReviewAggregate
-itemreviewed
-rating
-average
-count
-summary

Product
-brand
-category
-description
-name
-price
-photo
-url

Person*
-name*
-nickname
-url
-affiliation
-address
-street-address
-locality
-region
-postal-code
-country-name
-photo
-title
-role

Organization*
-name*
-url
-address
-street-address
-locality
-region
-postal-code
-country-name
-tel

Fig. 3. Vocabulary supported by Google Rich Snippets. Entities and attributes marked with an asterisk (*) will be annotated by our method.

Our main focus is on recognizing Review entities and their attributes. In particular our framework is able to annotate the following entities and attributes. In particular in detail we extract the following subset of entities and attributes from the vocabulary

$$\text{REVIEW} = (itemreviewed, rating, reviewer, dtreviewed, description, summary)$$
$$\text{PERSON} = (name)$$
$$\text{ORGANIZATION} = (name)$$

Our framework for automatically adding Google Rich Snippets annotations to a Web page is composed of a number of stages. Fig. 4 sketches an architecture of reference showing the main steps of our framework and their interdependencies.

The process starts with a *Preprocessing step* to clean and to make uniform the (X)HTML code of Web pages. Unfortunately, currently a large number of Web pages are invalid (more than 50% in some survey [12]) which may not pose a problem for the human user but makes automatic processing harder. Further, Web pages can be transmitted in various encodings. All encodings should be converted to a common format, i.e. UTF-8, in order to allow uniform processing.

Requirements to the algorithm are a high sensitivity (low false negative rate), good specificity (low false positive rate), and reasonable robustness (i.e. the ability to be used on a variety of Web pages that do not match the trained set). Of high importance therefore is the task to choose the parts of a Web page to investigate. We use the term *"hotspot"* to identify an area of a page that is — before intensive analysis — most likely to be a place of interest (e.g a document section containing a product review to annotate). To this aim an *Identification* step provides heuristics to identify the most relevant hotspots and to filter false positive portions of page. Then the *Entity Recognition* phase exploits a named

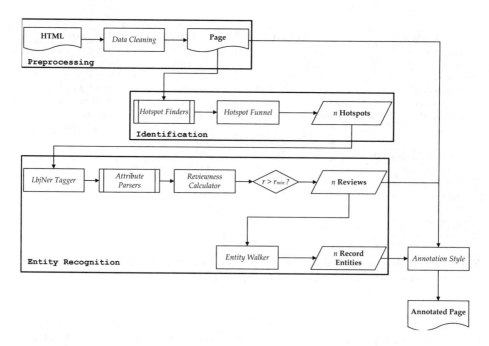

Fig. 4. Stages of our recognition algorithm, their interdependencies and intermediate products

entity recognition algorithm to extract entities and attributes of pages matching the portion of Review vocabulary discussed above. Finally the *Annotation* takes place supported by RDFa format to model the annotations in the page.

In the following section we will describe in detail the entire process in terms of both identification of hotspots and entity recognition.

4   Automatic Annotation of Web Pages

4.1   Hotspot Identification

Our need to identify hotspots on a Web page starts first from the necessity to demarcate recognized entities. A recognized review must have a start and end location that together span over all its properties. Also, we may want to perform transformations or computationally expensive analyses on texts. It is not necessary to know for sure if a hotspot definitely corresponds to a review: it is not problematic if we are too eager in recognizing an element, but it is unrecoverable if we now skip an element for further processing.

What then, should be considered a hotspot? First and foremost, any page element that contains a reasonable amount of natural text qualifies as a hotspot. However, this might miss very short or long elements; therefore we can also use cues such as HTML *name, id* and *class* attributes of elements, or their textual contents. It is simple to realize that an instance of the concept *Review* will most likely have a visual cue to the reader indicating this, or a descriptive element name on the part of the Web page designer. We can match these naively with a word list. To discover reviews we look for the terms `review` and `rating`. Other heuristics that can be used to find hotspots are the presence of repeating element structures, which are an indication of automatically generated content in a page, or similarity of HTML element *id* attributes (for instance, a common prefix or Levenshtein distance). However, we have not pursued these heuristics in our implementation because the first two tests already gave a very good coverage. After that, we must remove duplicates, as multiple hotspot finders will likely trigger on the same hotspots. Every hotspot finding measure increments the "hotness" of a hotspot. This measure is retained for subsequent filtering of hotspots before further processing.

A large portion of a Web page is limited to non-visual and non-textual items such as navigation sections, styling information, advertisements, et cetera. To the human user, these are immediately distinct from textual content, but to automated systems this may not be so clear. For instance, navigations certainly contain many terms that turn up in our cue word lists. We therefore introduce the measure *tag ratio* for a DOM node, which we define in Equation 1:

$$t = \frac{L_H - L_N}{L_H} \tag{1}$$

where L_H is the total character length of the DOM node and its descendants including all the HTML tags; and L_N is the character length of all natural text contained within the node. L_H is directly taken from the HTML document, while L_N is constructed by removing all the HTML tags, normalizing whitespace characters such as newlines and tabs to single spaces, and then trimming the output. An example of these measures is presented in Fig. 5.

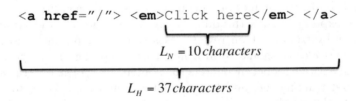

Fig. 5. Example of L_H and L_N measures of an HTML fragment

If a hotspot has a high (near 1) value of t, then the element consists almost entirely of HTML tags. This is uncommon for textual content, so we should disqualify the element for further processing. A reasonable threshold value t_{max} must be determined empirically from test data. At the same time, we want to stop false positive recognition of too short texts that stand on their own in the page. For instance, a page title or caption may contain some very on-topic terms, causing it to be recognized as a hotspot. We will disqualify hotspots that contain less than a minimum amount of natural text, L_{min} (number of characters). In a similar fashion we will be throwing away hotspots that are displayed as *inline* (with respect to text) by a browser, i.e., they are part of a natural sentence flow. Examples of these are a or b tags. A hotspot demarcated by these elements is part of a larger *block*-level element and is not a distinct page area in its own right. In these cases, we expect the outer element to be recognized as a hotspot as well. Since we have multiple methods to find hotspots, we filter next on "best hotness". Different Web pages may conform more or less to our different hotspot-finding heuristics, but within a *single* Web page, different entities of the same type generally have the same hotness measures, especially when the Web pages are generated automatically. When additional hotspot finders would be added, this filter step could be changed to require for instance 75% of the maximum hotness found on the whole page, in order to make this step more robust. An important property of hotspots for a certain entity type is finally that they are disjunct. Only one review entity can be an "active" hotspot at any location in the document. As a Web page document is a tree, this means that hotspots cannot be contained in each other. For instance, it is thinkable that we would consider two consecutive page elements to be hotspots, but at the same time consider their combined parent element a hotspot as well, as it certainly matches most of the criteria that hold for its descendants. In these cases, we should throw away all the "super-hotspots" that contain other hotspots, so that only the most minimal valid hotspots remain. After this stage ends, we have identified a number of hotspot page elements that may correspond to review entities. We will now inspect these elements more closely.

4.2   Named Entity Recognition

In the context of Google Rich Snippets' vocabulary, NER appears mostly useful in discovering the names of reviewed items and review authors. Similarly, NER can be used to discover names of person and organization entities.

We have experimented with adding more knowledge to an existing named-entity tagger by training it on review texts containing product names. These product names ideally should form a new entity type for the tagger. Merging them into an existing model encounters the nontrivial problem of "transfer learning", i.e., first training the model on one dataset and then trying to add more knowledge to the existing model. To update the models of the tagger, we would have to retrain the tagger from scratch using its original datasets in order to retain its original usefulness. A complicating feature is that product names are often not mentioned in natural text portions of Web pages, but rather in separate page sections, which prohibits using natural language-based methods. From our testing data, it appears that named entity recognition alone is often not successful to determine names of reviewed items and review authors. The nature of review texts on the Web is such that often the name of the reviewed item is not mentioned at all. Therefore, additional heuristics are needed to provide better coverage for detection of the name of the reviewed item and the review author.

Table 1. Relative tag importance. When ranking two tags, only the *order* of the tags' scores is considered. The *absolute* values are not significant, but are chosen in a way that more tag rankings can later be added.

Tag name	Importance
h1	100
h2	90
h3	80
h4	70
h5	60
h6	50
strong	10
b	10

These heuristics may use data from the NER phase, the review text itself, the Web page source code and its properties such as the page title.

As defined in the Google Rich Snippets summary, reviews have some predefined attributes, such as the *reviewed item, summary, rating, date* and *review author*. In our approach, each of these attributes has a separate attribute parser which follows its own heuristics.

Summary attribute. *Tag ranking* is a method that we use to discern the document element containing the most important title, heading, or summary of a page section. We rank element tags first according to their relative importance, which is modeled as shown in Table 1. If two elements are tied, we rank them using their position on the page, where higher positioned items have a better rank. This strategy corresponds to the approach that Google is currently assumed to use when it ranks the importance of information in a Web page for inclusion in its search index [8].

Author attribute. The author of a review is often supplied on the page within the review element. We employ two strategies for finding the author's name. First, we walk through the DOM subtree of the review to find any elements that most likely contain a name or nickname of the review author. We look for tags with HTML *class, id* and *name* attributes matching one of the following strings:

- author
- username
- reviewer

If this approach does not yield a positive result, we inspect the review text for named entities of type *Person*. This entity type has been recognized by the Named Entity Recognition stage earlier. We expect this approach to be more error-prone, as for instance other person entities may become incorrectly recognized as the author.

Product name attribute. The product name attribute contains the name of the reviewed item. During development of the methodology, we found that reviews on Web sites generally do not contain the name of the reviewed item. Often, a review Web page contains a variable number of reviews, while the product name is only mentioned once. As discussed earlier, training a NER tool to recognize product names as a proper entity class is outside the scope of this work. Therefore we derive the product name from the Web page title. The page title often contains unnecessary extra information, such as the name of the Web site and a descriptor text like "Product reviews". These texts should not be present in the product name. Therefore, we remove some strings from the result:

- variants of the name and the domain name of the Web URL of the Page (e.g., *amazon, amazon.com, www.amazon.com*);
- stop words such as `reviews` and `product`;
- separator characters such as `: - |`

Rating attribute. A pattern matching approach is used to discover the rating of a review, such as "4 out of 5". Recognizing ratings can be problematic, as there is no common standard for their notation; for instance, one site may use a 10-point numerical scale instead of Rich Snippets' default 5-point scale, while another site may use a graphical "stars" definition that usually embeds some kind of reference in the *img src* attribute. If the text matches a list of predefined regular expressions, such as:

- `4.0 out of 5.0`
- `4.0 / 5.0`

we are able to recognize the rating as well as the scale. If we cannot recognize the scale, we assume the lowest of a 5-point, 10-point, and 100-point scale, such that the rating is lower than or equal to the scale maximum. Without resorting to site-specific hints, it is expected that this approach will likely not be very robust or generalizable. At the same time, it will be possible to recognize multiple similar attributes within an entity's boundaries (e.g., two person names or two date strings), and we need to have a tie-breaking algorithm for which we currently do not have a method. At the moment, we use the naive strategy of taking the first occurrence as the most authoritative, but it is likely that there will be false positives.

Date attribute. The date of an entity can be gathered by using a series of regular expressions for common date formats. This list of regular expressions is now focused towards a range of date descriptions found in test Web pages, such as:

- `1-11-2009`
- `1 Nov 2009`
- `November 1st, 2009`

This list of date formats might be broadened to include phrases such as "3 months ago". Note that there are some ambiguities in general date formatting ("1-11-2009" might be in M-D-Y or D-M-Y notation). Google Rich Snippets does not pose any requirements to this format, so we simply retain the date as it was found on the page and leave the ambiguity to the interpreter.

4.3   Reviewness Filtering

As we have discussed, the strategy during hotspot determination must be sufficiently eager to provide a wide selection of elements to process using the methods described above. After we have analyzed the elements further, they should now be annotated with various semantical attributes. In case an element slipped by the hotspot funnel that is however clearly not a review entity, it will most likely not have attributes such as a rating, date, summary or author. We use this property to perform a calculation of a review's "reviewness" r. This measure corresponds to the *number* of semantical attributes that have been recognized, excluding the product name attribute, as that attribute is derived from the page title and therefore its recognition always succeeds. Any element not satisfying the basic requirements of a review — in our current model, this is only the presence of a product name — receives a negative reviewness. If the basic requirement is met, reviewness starts out at zero, and one point is added for every semantic attribute that was successfully bound to it. After the calculation step, there is a final filtering step. Any reviews which do not satisfy a minimal reviewness of r_{min} will be ignored. The value of this parameter must be determined during testing.

4.4   Collecting Record-Based Entities

During the main process of recognizing entities, the named entity recognizer (NER) has been run on all the reviews. In the final recognition stage, the names of Person and Organization entities are harvested from the review texts. For record-based entities (Persons and Organizations), in our current method only the names of the entities (and not their attributes, such as phone numbers, postal addresses, et cetera) are discovered. The names of these entities are simply retrieved from the NER output as we incorporate a NER tagger that supports these entity types by default.

4.5   Annotation

RDFa[2] is one of the two supported annotation styles in Google Rich Snippets; the other is Microformats[3]. The simpler Microformats style uses HTML *class* attributes populated with conventional names for certain properties, which has the advantage of being usable for Web page formatting and easy to write for humans.

---

[2] http://www.w3.org/TR/xhtml-rdfa-primer/
[3] http://microformats.org/about

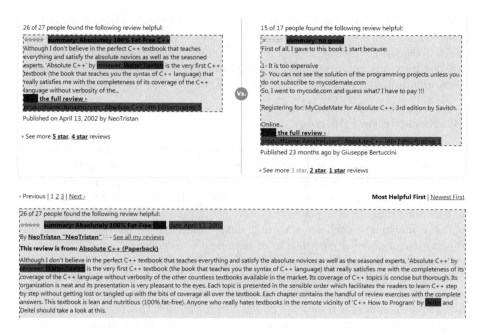

Fig. 6. Annotation of a Web page using the 'layout' annotation style. Review entities are displayed in yellow; review properties are green (and prefixed with the property name); person entities are purple; organization entities are blue.

However, these advantages are largely irrelevant for our purpose. RDFa [4] benefits from RDF, the W3C's standard for interoperable machine-readable data. RDFa is considered more flexible and semantically rich than Microformats [13]. Additionally, Rich Snippets in RDFa allow for extended functionality, such as adding URL links to Rich Snippet properties. Therefore RDFa is a better choice for meta-data annotation than Microformats.

In addition to RDFa, we found it useful to implement a "layout" annotation style where concept boundaries and attributes are displayed visually using HTML *style* attributes. This aids debugging and makes it easier to quickly assess the algorithm's output on a Web page, as is shown in Fig. 6. We recall that the attributes of an RDFa-annotated entity must remain within its boundaries (the element annotated with *typeof*). If an entity attribute was defined intrinsically, we know its textual position in the source HTML and we will rewrite an RDFa tag in place. If the attribute does not correspond to an HTML fragment within the entity (for instance when a product name is derived from the page title), we will write the RDFa tag at the bottom of the element. Google Rich Snippets supports annotating graphical ratings by placing *class* and *alt* attributes on a rating image. This feature can be used to insert rating meta-data without affecting the Web page layout, as displayed here:

```
<img class="rating" src="stars.gif" alt="4 Star Rating: Recommended" />
```

When parsing the page, Google inspects image elements marked with *class* `rating` and parses the *alt* tag in an undisclosed way. We choose not to implement this Rich Snippets feature, as using non-standard annotations outside the RDFa format is detrimental to further automatic processing of the generated document. In these cases, we do not modify the rating image and inject an additional RDFa-annotated property at the bottom of the element. Finally, after annotation, a `base href` HTML tag is injected at the top of the Web page body. This ensures that the resulting Web page can still be displayed using its original images and styling, even if the page is now served from a different location.

5 Experimental Results

Benchmark System. The approach was developed into a tool with a PHP front-end to reach it by Web[4]. It is composed by three modules implementing the three main steps discussed above. The cleaning of seriously invalid (X)HTML is achieved by the PHP's *tidy* support. For named entity recognition purposes the *Lbj-Based Named Entity Tagger* (LbjNer) [14] was used. LbjNer is now one of the best performing solutions. It reached very promising F-measure (F1) scores. For instance it obtained a F1 score of 85.74 on the MUC-7 test set[5], and 90.74 on the Reuters2003 test set[6]. One of the competitors, the Stanford NER tool, achieved a F1 score of 80.62 and 87.04 on the MUC-7 and Reuters2003 test set, respectively. The LbjNer tagger is capable of recognizing named entities of types *Person, Organization, Location,* and *Misc* in natural English text with a very impressive accuracy. It employs various statistical methods as well as heuristics. The tagger comes pre-trained on a large corpus of data extracted from Wikipedia and other well-known sources. This makes the tagger attractive for reuse in other projects such as these. A demo of the tagger is available as an on-line service [14].

Design. Overall, an important issue in designing the software was modularity and extensibility. As the work is mostly exploratory in nature, it is critical to be flexible during development, which means that the various parts of the tool should run in relative separation with few dependencies on each other. Therefore, we have split off the various stages of the algorithm into independently working classes. Where multiple strategies are used for a certain stage, such as during hotspot finding, they are implemented in a 'pluggable' fashion so that it is easy to add further heuristics that expand or focus the recognition. In Fig. 4, these stages are marked as a composite process (two vertical lines).

The class `PageAnnotator` takes care of driving the various phases of the algorithm and is useful as a starting point for reading the source code. Separate `Entity` as well as `Attribute` subclasses take care of their own parsing, so that it is tractable to extend the tool with other semantics.

---

[4] It is available at `http://annotator.lfms.nl/`

[5] `http://www.itl.nist.gov/iad/894.02/related_projects/muc/index.html`

[6] `http://www.daviddlewis.com/resources/testcollections/reuters21578/`

Where empirically established constants are used, such as the maximum tag ratio t_{max} or hotspot length limits, these are made explicit through class constants. Should it not be possible to find generally acceptable values for them, then a phase could be added in the algorithm to discover them on a per-page basis.

There are various use-cases for a tool such as demonstrated. One might be to use in an off-line fashion to annotate documents on a local computer, another might be to run as a Web service. We have implemented two "front-end" scripts, `cli.php` and `index.php` which run on the command line and a Web server respectively.

Named entity tagger. Statistical and grammar-based named entity recognition methods require natural text as an input in order to perform well. Also, the used named entity tagger *LbjNer* cannot yet handle HTML input, breaking validation of the output. Therefore, we must collect natural text first, and we should collect it from only the hotspots in the document, as these are the places where the NER tagger will work reliably.

Stripping HTML tags to generate a natural text body implies that we no longer have a 1:1 mapping between the tagger result and the original position of the tagged entities in the DOM. We will have to improvise in order to write tags back into our DOM data structure. A problem occurs when there are multiple occurrences of the recognized entity name in the original text: it becomes hard to choose which occurrence the entity points to. As a guess, we will place the entity at the first occurrence of the entity name in the DOM. This is not a perfect strategy, because we may replace a homonym instead of the right occurrence.

The LbjNer tagger has a large startup penalty due to loading of its gazetteers and statistical models. The LbjNer author has worked around this problem by running it as a daemon process controlled by a socket and an additional Perl client script. We provide a separate adapter to connect to this daemon process, which can be chosen at run-time. Since running the tagger on various hotspots separately would entail longer execution times, we coalesce the various hotspots to tag, and send these texts to the tagger in one batch. This requires a small amount of parsing in the LbjNer result interpretation.

Annotation styles. The debate between RDFa and Microformats is still very active [13], and the nature of the Web is such that often the simpler yet less powerful method gets the most traction in the community. Therefore, it is important that the annotation style is abstracted away from the recognition and processing logic. This makes it easy to add a visual annotation style, and should the marketplace decide in favor of Microformats, to annotate documents in that format instead.

Development set. We have developed the tool while testing on a number of Web pages containing product reviews, taken from popular Dutch review site *kieskeurig.nl* and the well known American shop site *amazon.com*. During the development of the methodology, we have established that a max tag ratio t_{max}

around 0.7 is a good cutoff value that invalidates recognition of most irrelevant page elements such as navigation sections, while retaining detection of most natural text hotspots. We have found that the algorithm has a tendency to over-recognize small page elements (such as simple page titles and captions) as reviews, especially in the absence of proper reviews which would lower the relative hotness of these elements in relation to the real reviews. This was resolved by setting the minimum natural text length L_{min} to 100 characters. The minimum "reviewness" r_{min} in the final filtering step was set to 2, meaning that for a review to be included in the annotation step, it must have a minimum of two recognized properties (such as rating, reviewer, summary and date). We have excluded the product name (reviewed item) from the reviewness calculation, as we almost always infer some product name from the page title.

Performance Evaluation. To assess the performance of the review recognition methodology, the tool was tested on a (non-randomized) selection of English and Dutch product review Web pages from well known E-commerce sites listed in Table 2. The tested Web pages were not included in the development set which consisted of pages from sites *amazon.com* and *kieskeurig.nl*. Model parameters had been optimized earlier empirically using the development set.

We count the actual number of reviews on the Web page manually, then present the URL to the tagger. We then review the annotated Web page for:

- the number of correct review recognitions (actual reviews which are recognized by the method);
- the number of false positives (tagger-recognized reviews that were not reviews in the source);
- and the number of false negatives (actual reviews that were missed by the method).

The results of these tests are presented in Table 2.

Table 2. Test results of review recognition. Web site languages are English, or Dutch when marked with *.

Web site	Actual reviews	Correct	False pos.	False neg.
alatest.com	*3*	1	1	2
*bol.com**	*11*	10	0	1
epinions.com	15	0	0	15
overstock.com	5	2	0	3
*pdashop.nl**	5	5	0	0

It appears that there is a large variance in performance between different Web pages, which is a result of the absence of standardization in laying out Web pages. The algorithm appears reasonably successful, but this property is certainly not ubiquitous. There is even one site, *epinions.com*, where reviews are not recognized at all. On all other sites, the results are reasonable for this first exploration of the field. False positives are almost never found; however there are some false negatives. A closer look into these false negatives suggests that we should explore more methods for finding hotspots, as some slip by the currently implemented hotspot finding heuristics. This happens on sites which do not use our listed cues for element names. Also, some of the model parameters are necessarily a compromise — a more dynamic or fuzzy approach to these parameters may be necessary to provide broader coverage.

In general the tool provides reasonable results, correctly recognizing reviews in review Web pages. We find that, for review detection on *random* (not review-specific) Web pages, our methods provide reasonable sensitivity, but not much specificity. This entails that also on Web pages that do not contain reviews, the heuristics may trigger and the algorithm may unintendedly recognize reviews. It remains a hard issue to test whether a Web page really concerns product reviews. Also of concern is the finding that many reviews do not even mention the name of the reviewed item. Therefore, heuristics for disqualifying a Web page as a review page are at this moment insufficient. This problem is not relevant when our solution is run on review Web pages solely. The required training phase of named entity recognition, as well as the recognition of element names and contents, as we have described in the previous section, possibly limits the application of our method to English Web pages. It is, however, tractable to train the NER tagger as well as revise our internal word lists in order to support other languages. We do note that our English-based name-finding heuristics have been successful on Dutch sites as well, as Web page designers tend to use English text in their DOM element names and classes. Furthermore, The LbjNer tagger is accurate at detecting names, and this property carries over rather well from English into Dutch, the other language present in tested Web pages. Therefore, our method does not perform worse on Dutch Web sites, even though the NER training set and the internal word lists are in English only.

6   Conclusions and Future Work

In this paper, we have explored named entity recognition- and heuristic-based approaches to annotating Web pages with Google Rich Snippets-compliant RDFa attributes. Heuristics used include source code analysis, pattern matching and internal word lists for discovery of entity attributes. We conclude that these approaches form a potential strategy to recognize entities on a Web page and automatically add them to the page using RDFa attributes. The methods are robust even in the face of different Web page languages. The tool that was developed performs reasonably in detecting review entities on review pages, such as *kieskeurig.nl* and *amazon.com*. At the same time, further work is needed to (1) improve the specificity of entity detection and (2) fully recognize the structure and properties of record-based entities such as persons and organizations. In particular one of the difficulties we have experienced involves recognizing the rating of a review. Although this property is not compulsory in the Rich Snippets definition, it is one of the key aspects used to display a rich snippet in Google search results. We have found that many reviews lack an explicit rating, such as a grade or a number of stars. Rich Snippets accepts a rating based on a scale of 1–5. To provide a rating for every single review, we would have to calculate a rating based on the review body text itself. This approach is known as sentiment classification. Earlier studies on various kinds of reviews show that satisfying results can be obtained when adopting sentiment classification [15,16,17,18]. Analysis and adoption of this approach might be an interesting future research direction.

References

1. Berners-Lee, T., Hendler, J., Lassila, O.: The Semantic Web. Scientific American 284, 34–43 (2001)
2. Goel, K., Guha, R.V., Hansson, O.: Introducing Rich Snippets,
   http://googlewebmastercentral.blogspot.com/2009/05/
   introducing-rich-snippets.html
3. Google: Google Webmaster Tools: About review data (2009),
   http://www.google.com/support/webmasters/bin/
   answer.py?hl=en&answer=146645
4. Adida, B., Birbeck, M.: RDFa Primer: Bridging the Human and Data Webs (2008),
   http://www.w3.org/TR/xhtml-rdfa-primer/
5. Mikheev, A., Moens, M., Grover, C.: Named Entity Recognition without gazetteers. In: Ninth Conference on European Chapter of the Association for Computational Linguistics, pp. 1–8. Association for Computational Linguistics (1999)
6. Morgan, R., Garigliano, R., Callaghan, P., Poria, S., Smith, M., Urbanowicz, A., Collingham, R., Costantino, M., Cooper, C., Group, L.: University of Durham: Description of the LOLITA System as Used in MUC-6. In: Sixth Message Understanding Conference. Morgan Kaufmann Publishers, San Francisco (1995)
7. Krupka, G.R., Hausman, K.: IsoQuest, Inc: Description of the NetOwl(TM) extractor system as used for MUC-7. In: Seventh Message Understanding Conference (1998)
8. Seomoz.org.: Search Engine Ranking Factors (2009),
   http://www.seomoz.org/article/search-ranking-factors
9. Virgilio, R.D., Torlone, R.: A Structured Approach to Data Reverse Engineering of Web Applications. In: 9th International Conference on Web Engineering, pp. 91–105. Springer, Heidelberg (2009)
10. Can, L., Qian, Z., Xiaofeng, M., Wenyin, L.: Postal Address Detection from Web Documents. In: International Workshop on Challenges in Web Information Retrieval and Integration, pp. 40–45. IEEE Computer Society, Los Alamitos (2005)
11. Yahoo!: SearchMonkey: Site Owner Overview (2009),
    http://developer.yahoo.com/searchmonkey/siteowner.html
12. Electrum: Valid HTML Statistics (2009),
    http://try.powermapper.com/demo/statsvalid.aspx
13. Tomberg, V., Laanpere, M.: RDFa versus Microformats: Exploring the Potential for Semantic Interoperability of Mash-up Personal Learning Environments. In: Second International Workshop on Mashup Personal Learning Environments, M. Jeusfeld c/o Redaktion Sun SITE, Informatik V, pp. 102–109. RWTH Aachen (2009)
14. Ratinov, L., Roth, D.: Design Challenges and Misconceptions in Named Entity Recognition. In: Thirteenth Conference on Computational Natural Language Learning, pp. 147–155. Association for Computational Linguistics (2009)

15. Turney, P.: Thumbs Up or Thumbs Down? Semantic Orientation Applied to Unsupervised Classification of Reviews. In: 40th Annual Meeting of the Association for Computational Linguistics, pp. 417–424. ACL (2002)
16. Pang, B., Lee, L., Vaithyanathan, S.: Thumbs up? Sentiment Classification using Machine Learning Techniques. In: Conference on Emprirical Methods in Natural Language Processing, pp. 79–86. ACL (2002)
17. Ye, Q., Zhang, Z., Law, R.: Sentiment Classification of Online Reviews to Travel Destinations by Supervised Machine Learning Approaches. Expert Systems with Applications 36(3), 6527–6535 (2009)
18. Kennedy, A., Inkpen, D.: Sentiment Classification of Movie Reviews Using Contextual Valence Shifters. Computational Intelligence 22(2), 110–225 (2006)

A Hybrid Approach to Constructing Tag Hierarchies

Geir Solskinnsbakk and Jon Atle Gulla

Department of Computer and Information Science,
Norwegian University of Science and Technology,
Trondheim, Norway
{geirsols,jag}@idi.ntnu.no

Abstract. Folksonomies are becoming increasingly popular. They contain large amounts of data which can be mined and utilized for many tasks like visualization, browsing, information retrieval etc. An inherent problem of folksonomies is the lack of structure. In this paper we present an unsupervised approach for generating such structure based on a combination of association rule mining and the underlying tagged material. Using the underlying tagged material we generate a semantic representation of each tag. The semantic representation of the tags is an integral component of the structure generated. The experiment presented in this paper shows promising results with tag structures that correspond well with human judgment.

1 Introduction

The collaborative effort of users tagging resources is often referred to as a *folksonomy* [1]. Generally one can say that a folksonomy consists of three entities; the *user*, the *tag*, and the *resource* [1]. Tags used in the action of tagging a resource are not necessarily bound to dictionaries or thesauri and can be created by the users themselves. As for the resources, generally anything with a URL can be tagged, web pages, images, presentations, etc. Examples of popular sites that employ tagging are among others *Delicious*[1] and *Flickr*[2]. Delicious lets users tag resources on the web, while Flickr lets users tag their own images. When a user tags a resource with a set of tags in Delicious, the combined information is called a bookmark.

Folksonomy tags do not generally have any associated structure. For visualization purposes however, tag clouds or lists of related tags can be employed and presented to users. The intention of this paper is to generate a semantic structure of tags in the folksonomy that can later support semantic information access. The idea is to combine tag structure and traditional ontologies in a unified semantic search framework.

---

[1] http://delicious.com/
[2] http://www.flickr.com/

R. Meersman et al. (Eds.): OTM 2010, Part II, LNCS 6427, pp. 975–982, 2010.

Most of the research on structuring folksonomies is based on the *tags*, *users*, and *tagged resources* alone. In our opinion, the textual content of the tagged resources themselves should also be taken into account and can give important input to the process of structuring the folksonomy. In this paper we use a combination of the *tags* and *tagged resources* to structure the folksonomy. In our research we have used Delicious as the sample data, while the general approach should be viable for any folksonomy which is based on tagging textual resources.

Our approach to generating a semantic structure of the folksonomy data builds a hierarchical structure over the tags and associates every tag in the folksonomy with a vector of semantically related terms. The structure is mainly guided by association rule mining of the tags in the bookmarks. We have then explored if there are any defining properties among the tag vectors that can help us verify the type of relation between the tags in the hierarchy. The results of our experiment seem promising with a high ratio of tag relations that are classified by the test subjects as either related or correctly related.

2   Related Work

In [2], Mika presents an approach for generating lightweight ontologies based on processing a tripartite hypergraph representation of the folksonomy. Heymann et al. [3] describe an algorithm for generating structure based on representing the tags as vectors and calculating the cosine similarities among the vectors. During hierarchy construction the tags are added to the hierarchy by considering the cosine similarity and tags are processed in order of centrality in a similarity graph. Benz et al. [4] presents an approach (extension of [3]) in which each concept is represented by one or more folksonomy tags. Zhou et al. [5] present an approach based on clustering, finding relations between clusters of tags. Specia et al. [6] describe an approach based on clustering and using external information sources (WordNet [7] and Google[3]) to assist in the structuring of the tags. Laniado et al. [8] present an approach that relies on WordNet for disambiguation and is used as a basis for structuring the tags. Schwarzkopf et al. [9] performs some experiments based on previous structuring approaches and modifies them by imposing additional requirements on similarity to filter some of the relations. In [10], Schmitz et al. derive two-dimensional views of the folksonomy data and apply association rule mining to the reduced data. Lin et al.. [11] mine association rules between pairs of tags, and structure is imposed using WordNet as a guide. Further rules are filtered based on the cosine similarity, in which the tags are represented as vectors of resources with binary weight. Our approach is similarly based on association rules for structure and cosine similarity for validation. The tag vector representation in our research is more detailed by taking into account the textual content of the documents. Further, we do not use any external knowledge sources like WordNet, since domain-specific information access normally requires vocabularies to specific for WordNet to be appropriate.

---

[3] http://www.google.com

3   Tag Vectors

We have previously done some work on extending ontologies with vectors giving a semantic representation of the concepts of the ontology and using them for information retrieval (see [12]). In line with our previous work, we are now looking at constructing similar vectors for tags in a folksonomy.

The folksonomy is a collection of triples [13] (*URL*, *tag*, *user*) where the interpretation is that the user, u_i, has tagged a resource (URL), r_j, with the tag t_k. The fact that a user has opted to tag a given resource with a specific tag means that in the user's view, the tag is a representative term/word to describe the resource. Each tag vector constructed by our approach can be interpreted as a semantic representation of the tag. The weight assigned to each term in the tag vector reflects two aspects; (1) the importance of the term with respect to the tag (internal representation) and (2) the ability the tag has to discriminate this tag from other tags (external representation). To achieve this we use the $tf \cdot idf$ measure [14]. The terms in the tag vector together with the term weights give a representation of the tag that reflects how the tag is applied by the users of the bookmarking service. Our main motivation behind these vectors is twofold; (1) we want to use them as a step in the construction of the structure to assure higher quality of the structure, and (2) we want to use the vectors for information access in a method that is compatible with the use of ontological profiles (see [12]). The definition of a tag vector is given as Definition 1.

Definition 1. *Tag Vector. Let V be the set of n terms (vocabulary) in the collection of tagged resources. $t_i \in V$ denotes term i in the set of terms. Then the tag vector for tag j is defined as the vector $T_j = [w_1, w_2, \ldots, w_n]$ where each w_i denotes the semantic relatedness weight for each term t_i with respect to tag T_j.*

4   Approach

Our approach assumes that we are dealing with a folksonomy that has been built by users tagging textual resources. The process is based on three phases; (1) *association rule mining*, (2) *hierarchy construction*, and (3) *structure confirmation* using the tag vectors.

4.1   Association Rule Mining

The first step in the process is to run association rule mining on the set of tags, using the Apriori algorithm by Agrawal and Srikant [15]. The Apriori algorithm uses prior knowledge to reduce the search space when mining for association rules. This is done by first generating the set of frequent 1-item sets (i.e. sets containing a single item). The frequent 1-item sets are used as input (prior knowledge) for generating the frequent 2-item sets, since every frequent 2-item sets must be a combination of elements from the frequent 1-item sets [16].

In our approach, we are only interested in association rules that are generated from the frequent 2-item sets, so the algorithm is terminated at this point. The reason for this is that the interpretation of rules from the frequent 2-item sets is easier than for n-item sets (for n>2).

Association rules take on the form $T_i \rightarrow T_j$, where T_i is the premise, and T_j is the consequence. This rule states that if T_i is observed, one can with a certain probability observe T_j. Within the context of bookmarking and folksonomies, this can be translated into the interpretation: Whenever tag T_i is observed, one can with a certain probability observe the tag T_j in the same bookmark. Measures that are highly important for association rules (and in fact used to filter the rules) are support and confidence. Support is the number of times an observation occurs in the data set, while confidence is the percentage of observations that contain the premise and that also contain the consequence (see Equation 1 [16]).

$$confidence(T_i \rightarrow T_j) = P(T_j|T_i) = \frac{supportCount(T_i \cup T_j)}{supportCount(T_i)} \qquad (1)$$

The data used as basis for the association rules is the bookmarking data from the folksonomy. Each set of tags used as basis in the association rule mining process consists of all tags assigned to a single resource by a single user, i.e. a single bookmark. We are employing minimum support and minimum confidence measures for the mined rules (see Section 5).

4.2   Hierarchy Construction

The first phase of our approach results in a set of association rules. Our initial interpretation is that the premise of the rule may be viewed as a child of the consequence. The motivation behind this interpretation is best described with an example. Assume two tags, A and B, and a set of bookmarks tagged with B. If a subset of the resources tagged with B also contain the full set of bookmarks tagged with A, we regard A as a specialization of B, and the rule with the highest confidence is $A \rightarrow B$. In other words, A is a subclass of B.

The construction of the hierarchy starts with an empty root node. Next we find all consequences which do not appear as premises of any rule. These are added as direct children of the root node. For each first level child, all tags that appear as premises of rules with the first level child as consequence are added as children. This process continues until there are no more children to add, or an attempt is made to add a tag that already exists in the path from the root to the current node.

4.3   Structure Verification

We now need to generate tag vectors of all the tags in the system. The first step is to collect the relevant textual content for each tag. The text relevant to a specific tag is taken to be the sum of all documents that have been allocated this tag. The first part of this phase is constructing a tag vector, which can be interpreted as a semantic description of the tag. This is done by using the textual content of the tagged resources. The textual content is then preprocessed, where we remove any markup like html, if present, remove stop words, and stem the terms using the porter stemming algorithm [17].

The next step is to generate the basic tag vectors. This is done for each tag, adding all terms remaining after preprocessing that occur in resources tagged by the tag in question. We also employ some weighting function which reflects the frequency of applying the tag to each resource. This means that if a tag has been used to tag one resource 10 times and another 3 times, the first should be more important to the tag vector than the second. We argue that the use of the tag on the first resource is in greater agreement among the users, which should be reflected in the tag vector. It might however be the case that the resource tagged 3 times has been tagged a much higher number of times in total (with other tags) than the resource that has been tagged 10 times. In light of this it could seem reasonable to add this to the equation, but in our view, we are trying to represent how the public have used each tag, and thus the tagging frequency of a resource with other tags is not that interesting. The basic weight of the terms in the tag vector at this stage is calculated according to Equation 2, where $tv_{i,j}$ is the weight of term i in the tag vector of tag j, $\alpha_{j,r}$ is the number of times tag j has been used to bookmark resource r, $f_{i,r}$ is the frequency of term i in resource r, and R_j is the set of resources tagged with tag j.

$$tv_{i,j} = \sum_{r \in R_j} \alpha_{j,r} \cdot f_{i,r} \tag{2}$$

This basic vector is a good description of the internal representation of the tag, while we also need the vector to discriminate against other tags. This is done by calculating the final weight of the terms in the vectors according to the $tf \cdot idf$ score. The calculation is shown as Equation 3, where $tfidf_{i,j}$ is the tfidf score for term i in the vector for tag j, $tv_{i,j}$ is the result of Equation 2, N is the number of tag vectors, and n_i is the number of tag vectors containing term i. Lastly the tag vectors are normalized to unit length.

$$tfidf_{i,j} = \frac{tv_{i,j}}{max(tv_{l,j})} \cdot \log \frac{N}{n_i} \tag{3}$$

The similarity between two tag vectors is found using standard cosine similarity calculations [14]. Unlike association rules, the cosine similarity does not give any direction of the relation, only a numeric value of the strength of the relation. Thus, the cosine similarity is used as a supporting tool for confirming the structures that have been built from the association rules.

4.4   Interpretation of Confidence and Cosine Similarity

Confidence. *As the confidence of a rule used as basis for a relation increases, so does the quality of the relation.* The motivation for this interpretation is that a higher confidence in theory means that the probability for the connection is higher; thus we expect to see that a high confidence will lead to a high probability for a good or correct relation.

Cosine Similarity. *The cosine similarity between two tags can give us supporting information on how two tags are related.* The motivation for this interpretation is to see whether the cosine similarity can give any information in addition to the information from the association rule that will help us interpret the relation. E.g. a high cosine similarity could point in the direction of synonyms, and a low value in the direction of no relation.

5   Preliminary Results

Our initial experiment is based on a data set from Delicious which we crawled between December 2009 and January 2010. The data set consists of 195471 bookmarks tagging resources in the English section of Wikipedia ("http://en.wikipedia.org/wiki") which were mapped to a cleaned and Part-of-Speech tagged Wikipedia dump from June 2008 [18]. This dump has been used as the textual foundation for constructing the tag vectors.

In the experiment we set a confidence threshold of 0.4, and a support threshold of 50, which left us with 1752 tags resulting in 771 association rules. The structures we chose for evaluation were chosen based on requiring the depth of the tree to be at least 3 (not counting the root). This left 40 trees and 303 relations to evaluate (for an example see Figure 1). The evaluation consisted of having 9 colleagues evaluate the relations. The relations could be described as *correct* (correct hierarchy relation), *related* (correct relation, but not hierarchical or reverse hierarchical), *equivalent* (synonym), *not related*, and *unknown* (the evaluator does not recognize the meaning of the tag(s)). On average, 31.7% of the relations in the hierarchy received the classification *related*, while 43.7% received the classification *correct*. Only 5.3 % of the relations were classified as *not related*, 13.2% as *unknown*, and 6.1% as *equivalent*. This points out to us that the approach gives a generally good quality hierarchy. One aspect that needs further attention is that relatively many (31.7%) of the relations were classified as related (correct non-taxonomic or reverse taxonomic relations). This may be due to the test subjects having different views on the relations in terms of how the relations should be modeled.

From the evaluation we also found that the cosine similarity between the tags were generally helpful in locating relations classified by the test subjects as *equivalent*, with an average score ranging from 0.78 to 0.86 (depending on parameter settings) with a stable difference of approximately 0.2 to the next highest scoring relation type. The average value of the cosine score between tags of the other relation types did not give any indication of relation type. In fact, *correct* and *related* tag relations had approximately equal cosine similarities, while *non related* relations had marginally lower scores (difference in the range 0.02-0.05).

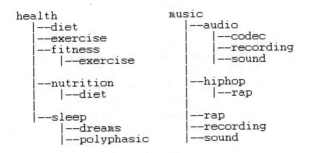

```
health                      music
  |--diet                     |--audio
  |--exercise                 |   |--codec
  |--fitness                  |   |--recording
  |    |--exercise            |   |--sound
  |                           |
  |--nutrition                |--hiphop
  |    |--diet                |   |--rap
  |                           |
  |--sleep                    |--rap
       |--dreams              |--recording
       |--polyphasic          |--sound
```

Fig. 1. Sample hierarchies from the experiment rooted at health and music (evaluated versions)

Looking at the confidence scores we found that higher confidence levels seem to produce a higher ratio of *correct* relations, a lower ration of *related* relations, and a small increase in the ratio of *non related* tag relations.

Overall the approach seems promising, although more work would be needed to improve the overall quality of the approach.

6   Conclusion

In this paper we have described an approach for creating a semantic structure based on folksonomies. The main structure is based on association rule mining of the tag set. We have also introduced the concept of tag vectors as semantic representations of the tags in the folksonomy, and how they can be used to evaluate the quality of the structure generated.

Our experiment based on a data set from delicious containing 195471 bookmarks, and the evaluation of the structure based on a minimum support count of 50, shows promising results. Looking at the combined results for the relations classified by the test subjects as *related* and *correct*, the results show that on average 75.4% of the evaluated relations were by the test subjects described as such. Only 5.3% of the relations were classified as *not related*. This seems to point in the direction that our approach based on co-tags is good for generating ontological structures based on folksonomies. The cosine similarity between tag vectors also seem to be a good tool to identify equivalent tags. We will continue to improve the approach to try to find ways of isolating and removing relations that are not correct. We will also in our future work use the semantic tag structure for information access.

Acknowledgment. This research was carried out as part of the IS_A project, project no. 176755, funded by the Norwegian Research Council under the VERDIKT program.

References

1. Vander Wal, T.: Folksonomy coinage and definition, http://vanderwal.net/folksonomy.html (accessed March 2010)
2. Mika, P.: Ontologies are us: A unified model of social networks and semantics. In: Gil, Y., Motta, E., Benjamins, V.R., Musen, M.A. (eds.) ISWC 2005. LNCS, vol. 3729, pp. 522–536. Springer, Heidelberg (2005)
3. Heymann, P., Garcia-Molina, H.: Collaborative Creation of Communal Hierarchical Taxonomies in Social Tagging Systems, InfoLab Technical Report, Stanford (2006)
4. Benz, D., Hotho, A., Stützer, S., Stumme, G.: Semantics made by you and me: Self-emerging ontologies can capture the diversity of shared knowledge. In: Proceedings of the 2nd Web Science Conference, Raleigh, NC, USA (2010)
5. Zhou, T.C., King, I.: Automobile, Car, and BMW: Horizontal and Hierarchical Approach in Social Tagging Systems. In: Conference on Information and Knowledge Management, Proceeding of the 2nd ACM Workshop on Social Web Search and Mining, Hong Kong, China (2009)
6. Specia, L., Motta, E.: Integrating Folksonomies with the Semantic Web. In: Franconi, E., et al. (eds.) ESWC 2007. LNCS (LNAI), vol. 4519, pp. 624–639. Springer, Heidelberg (2007)
7. Fellbaum, C. (ed.): WordNet: An Electronic Lexical Database. MIT Press, Cambridge (1998)
8. Laniado, D., Eynard, D., Colombetti, M.: Using WordNet to turn a folksonomy into a hierarchy of concepts. In: Proceedings of SWAP 2007, the 4th Italian Semantic Web Workshop, CEUR Workshop Proceedings, Bari, Italy, December 18-20 (2007), http://ceur-ws.org/Vol-314/51.pdf
9. Schwarzkopf, E., Heckmann, D., Dengler, D., Kröner, A.: Mining the Structure of Tag Spaces for User Modeling. In: Workshop on Data Mining for User Modeling (International Conference on User Modeling 2007) (2007)
10. Schmitz, C., Hotho, A., Jäschke, R., Stumme, G.: Mining Association Rules in Folksonomies, Data Science and Classification. In: Proc. of the 10th IFCS Conf., Studies in Classification, Data Analysis, and Knowledge Organization (2006)
11. Lin, H., Davis, J., Zhou, Y.: An Integrated Apporoach to Extracting Ontological Structures from Folksonomies. In: Arayo, L., et al. (eds.) ESWC 2009. LNCS, vol. 5554, pp. 654–668. Springer, Heidelberg (2009)
12. Solskinnsbakk, G., Gulla, J.A.: Ontological Profiles in Enterprise Search. In: Gangemi, A., Euzenat, J. (eds.) EKAW 2008. LNCS (LNAI), vol. 5268, pp. 302–317. Springer, Heidelberg (2008)
13. Heymann, P., Koutrika, G., Garcia-Molina, H.: Can Social Bookmarking Improve Web Search? In: First ACM International Conference on Web Search and Data Mining (WSDM 2008), Stanford, CA, February 11-12 (2008)
14. Baeza-Yates, R., Ribeiro-Neto, B.: Modern Information Retrieval. ACM Press, New York (1999)
15. Agrawal, R., Srikant, R.: Fast Algorithms for Mining Association Rules. In: Proceedings of the 20th International Conference on Very Large Databases (September 1994)
16. Han, J., Kamber, M.: Data Mining: Concepts and Techniques, 2nd edn. Morgan Kaufmann, San Francisco (2006)
17. Porter, M.F.: An algorithm for suffix stripping. Program 14(3), 130–137 (1980)
18. Artiles, J., Sekine, S.: Tagged and Cleaned Wikipedia (TC Wikipedia), http://nlp.cs.nyu.edu/wikipedia-data/ (accessed December 2009)

Toward a Uniform Cause-Based Approach to Inconsistency-Tolerant Database Semantics

Hendrik Decker*

Instituto Tecnológico de Informática, UPV, Valencia, Spain

Abstract. Because of extant inconsistencies in the database, answers to queries may or may not be in accordance with the intended semantics of stored data, as encoded by integrity constraints. Also updates may or may not be in accordance with the integrity constraints. Approaches to query answering usually differ from approaches to check updates for integrity preservation, even more so if they have to cope with extant inconsistencies. We present a novel, cause-based approach that improves inconsistency-tolerant query answering and integrity checking, and provides a uniform foundation for both.

1 Introduction

Each database schema provides a rudimentary ontology. Its application-specific semantics is encoded by the integrity constraints associated to the schema.

In practice, databases are rarely 100% consistent with the semantic constraints imposed on them, although most of the data may not be involved in any integrity violation. Thus, query answering should be able to provide reasonable answers to most queries even if integrity is violated. Similarly, integrity checking should be able to make reasonable decisions to accept or reject updates in the presence of extant inconsistencies, i.e., semantic integrity violations.

Consistent query answering (CQA) [1] is a popular approach to provide useful answers in inconsistent databases. However, CQA cannot be used to query integrity constraints, since, by definition, each consistent answer to each repairable constraint would indicate integrity satisfaction, even if the constraint is violated.

An inconsistency-tolerant approach to integrity checking has been introduced in [11] and further developed in [10,8]. However, although inconsistency-tolerant integrity checking methods can diagnose if an update does or does not introduce new cases of constraint violations, they cannot be used to distinguish consistent from inconsistent answers to queries.

In this paper, we present a uniform foundation of inconsistency tolerance that applies to both query answering and integrity checking. After some formal preliminaries in section 2, we introduce in section 3 the concept of "causes", i.e., minimal extracts of the database that serve to explain why an answer is given, or why a constraint is violated. Based on causes, we define in section 4 that an answer "has integrity" if it has a cause that does not overlap with any cause

---

* Supported by ERDF and Spanish grants TIN2009-14460-C03 and TIN2010-17193.

R. Meersman et al. (Eds.): OTM 2010, Part II, LNCS 6427, pp. 983–998, 2010.

of integrity violation. Also based on causes, we revise inconsistency-tolerant integrity checking in section 5, by defining that a method is inconsistency-tolerant if it only accepts updates that do not increase the amount of causes of extant integrity violation. In section 6, we generalize the cause-based approach to queries and constraints containing negation, though only for flat relational databases. In section 7, we compare the application of causes for inconsistency-tolerant query answering with consistent query answering [1], and the application of causes for inconsistency-tolerant integrity checking with previous work in the field. In section 8, we conclude with an outlook to upcoming work.

2   Preliminaries

As a formal framework and language of representation, we opt for *datalog*. Up to section 6, we limit our studies to relational databases with view definitions that may be recursive but do not contain negation.

We assume that each database consists of a set of *rules* (i.e., database clauses with non-empty body) and a set of *facts* (i.e., database clauses with empty body). Rules define views on which the evaluation of integrity constraints may recur. For each database D, we denote the well-known *completion* of D [7,14] by $comp(D)$. Further, let D^* denote the set of all ground instances of clauses in D.

We assume a finite domain of constant terms over which each variable in the language ranges. W.l.o.g., we represent the constants in the domain by natural numbers including 0.

We assume that each integrity constraint (shortly, constraint) is a denial, i.e., has the form of a conjunctive query. As it is well-known, empty answers to denial queries indicate integrity violation. For each constraint I, each instance of I is called a *case* of I, as in [11,8] (where this terminology also caters for constraints that are not in denial form, since not necessarily each instance of a constraint qualifies as a case in general). For each database D and each constraint I, let the set of cases of I that are violated in D be denoted by $\mathsf{VioCas}(D, I)$. We call each finite set of constraints an *integrity theory*.

We denote logical consequence by $\models$. By overloading, we use $=$ as identity predicate, as assignment symbol in substitutions of variables with terms, and as metalevel equality. Since "," is the conjunction operator between literals in the body of clauses, we use ";" as the delimiter between elements of sets of clauses.

Except in section 6, we do not flatten databases by materializing views, since that may lead to a loss of causal information. For example, the flattened version $\{p; r; s\}$ of the databases $D = \{p \leftarrow r; r; s\}$ and $D' = \{p \leftarrow s; r; s\}$ does not provide to identify that r is part of the cause of the truth of p in D and s is not, nor that s is part of the cause of the truth of p in D' and r is not.

We say that a formula F is a *conjunctive sentence* if F is a universally closed conjunction of literals.

For each database D and each sentence F, we write $D(F) = true$ if $comp(D) \models F$; otherwise, we write $D(F) = false$.

We say that two sets *overlap* if their intersection is not empty.

3   Causes

We are going to formalize "causes" in two steps. First, we define, for each database D and each conjunctive sentence F that is *true* in D, an "explanation base" of F in D to be a subset E of D^* such that $E(F) = true$. Second, we define a "cause" of F in D to be a minimal explanation base of F in D.

Similarly, we define the causes of an answer substitution θ of a conjunctive query $\leftarrow B$ in D to be the causes of $\forall(B\theta)$ in D, and the causes of the violation of a denial constraint $\leftarrow B$ as the causes of the answer *yes* (i.e., the identity substitution) to the query $\leftarrow violated$ in $D \cup \{violated \leftarrow B\}$, where *violated* is a distinguished 0-ary predicate that does not occur in D.

Based on causes, we will then define in section 4 that an answer to a query in a database D "has integrity" if it has a cause that does not overlap with any cause of the violation of any constraint in D. And in section 5, we will define that an integrity checking method is "inconsistency-tolerant" if only those updates that do not increase the set of causes of integrity violation are accepted.

Note that inconsistency tolerance is quite unusual in the field of database integrity. In fact, each traditional integrity checking method in the literature is absolutely intolerant against the least bit of inconsistency, since all of them insist on the total integrity of each database state, so as to soundly simplify the otherwise costly evaluation of constraints upon updates [6].

The computation of causes will be addressed in 4.2.

3.1   Explanation Bases

Definition 1.   Let D be a database, E a subset of D^*, and F a conjunctive sentence. E is called an *explanation base* of F in D if $E \models F$.

Example 1. Let $D = \{p \leftarrow q;\ p \leftarrow r;\ q;\ r;\ s\}$. Each of $E_1 = \{p \leftarrow q;\ q\}$ and $E_2 = \{p \leftarrow r;\ r\}$ is an explanation base of p in D.

The following corollary states immediate consequences of Definition 1. Part *a* says that each ground fact in a database explains itself.

Corollary 1.   Let D be a database, F a conjunctive sentence, E an explanation base of F in D and E' an extract of D.
a) For each ground fact A in D, $\{A\}$ is an explanation base of A in D.
b) If $E \subseteq E'$, then E' is an explanation base of F in D.

3.2   Causes

Part *b* of Corollary 1 says that each extract which contains an explanation base of some sentence F in some database D also is an explanation base of F in D. Thus, there may be superfluous clauses in an explanation base, i.e., the presence or absence is irrelevant for explaining the truth of F in D.

Example 2. Clearly, $E = \{p(0) \leftarrow r(0,1); \; r(0,1); \; s(2)\}$ is an explanation base of $p(0)$ in $D = \{p(x) \leftarrow r(x,y); \; r(0,0); \; r(0,1); \; r(1,1); \; s(2)\}$, but $s(2)$ in E is superfluous for explaining $p(0)$ in D.

In order to get rid of superfluous clauses, a cause of F in D is going to be defined as a minimal explanation base, i.e., one without unnecessary clauses.

Definition 2. For each database D, each conjunctive sentence F and each explanation base E of F in D, E is called a *cause* of F in D if there is no explanation base E' of F in D such that $E' \subsetneq E$.

Thus, a cause of a sentence F in a database D is an explanation base E of F in D, the elements of which are necessary, i.e., it is not possible to explain F with any extract obtained by dropping any element from E.

We are going to extend Definition 2 to answers and constraints.

Definition 3. Let D be a database.
a) For each query $\leftarrow B$, each substitution θ of the free variables in B and each cause E of $\forall(B\theta)$ in D, we say that E is a *cause of the answer* θ to $\leftarrow B$ in D.
b) For each constraint I of the form $\leftarrow B$ and each cause E of the answer *yes* to $\leftarrow violated$ in $D \cup \{violated \leftarrow B\}$, we also say that E is a *cause of the violation* of I in D.
c) Let the set of causes of the violation of I in D be denoted by $\mathsf{VioCau}(D, I)$.
d) For each integrity theory IC and each cause E of the answer *yes* to $\leftarrow violated$ in $D \cup \{violated \leftarrow B \mid \leftarrow B \in IC\}$, we also say that E is a *cause of the violation* of IC in D.
e) Let the set of causes of the violation of IC in D be denoted by $\mathsf{VioCau}(D, IC)$.

Example 3. Let $D = \{p \leftarrow q; \; p \leftarrow r,s; \; q \leftarrow s; \; r; \; s\}$ and $I = \leftarrow p$. Clearly, $\{p \leftarrow q; \; q \leftarrow s; \; s\}$ is a cause of the violation of I in D, and so is $\{p \leftarrow r,s; \; r; \; s\}$. There are no other causes of the violation of I in D.

4   Answers That Have Integrity (AHI)

In 4.1, we define that an answer to a query in a database D "has integrity" if one of its causes does not overlap with any cause of the violation of any constraint in D. We also show how to differentiate the notion of "has integrity", in a way that is not provided by CQA. In 4.2, we show how to compute answers that have integrity. Occasionally, we abbreviate "answers that have integrity" by AHI.

4.1   Defining Answers That Have Integrity

Definition 4. Let D be a database, IC an integrity theory, $\leftarrow B$ a query and θ an answer to $\leftarrow B$ in D.

a) We say that $\forall(B\theta)$ *has weak integrity* in (D, IC) if there is a cause of $\forall(B\theta)$ that does not overlap with any cause of the violation of IC.
b) We say that $\forall(B\theta)$ *has strong integrity* in (D, IC) if there is a cause of $\forall(B\theta)$ that does not overlap with any cause of the violation of any constraint in IC.

We may omit to say "in (D, IC)" if the database and the constraints are understood. Also, we may simply say that the answer has (weak, resp., strong) integrity if the query and the substitution are understood.

It is easy to see that an answer has weak integrity if it has strong integrity. Thus, we may say that an answer does not have integrity if it does not have weak integrity. In fact, the notions in parts a and b of Definition 4 are not equivalent, as shown by the following example.

Example 4. Let $D = \{r(1, 1); s(1)\}$, $IC = \{\leftarrow r(x, x); \leftarrow r(x, y), s(y)\}$. The answer $x = 1$ to the query $\leftarrow s(x)$ in D has weak integrity, since its cause $\{s(1)\}$ does not overlap with the only cause $\{r(1, 1)\}$ of the violation of IC in D. However, it does not have strong integrity, since $\{s(1)\}$ overlaps with the cause $\{r(1, 1), s(1)\}$ of the violation of the constraint $\leftarrow r(x, y), s(y)$ in IC. The answer $\{x = 1,\ y = 1\}$ to $\leftarrow r(x, y)$ in D does not have integrity, since its only cause $\{r(1, 1)\}$ overlaps with some (in fact, with each) cause of the violation of IC.

Note that, in the example above, $x = 1$ also is a consistent answer according to CQA, since the only minimal repair of the violation of IC is $D' = \{s(1)\}$, obtained by deleting $r(1, 1)$ from D. However, CQA does not provide to differentiate between weakly and strongly consistent answers, in analogy to the weak and strong integrity of answers that can be distinguished by Definition 4.

Such a differentiation is desirable, since the violation of $\leftarrow r(x, y), s(y)$, which is partially caused by the presence of $s(1)$ in D, casts doubt on the consistency of the answer $y = 1$ to the query $\leftarrow s(y)$ in D, as claimed by CQA.

Further differentiations of weak and strong integrity of answers as defined above are possible. Some of them are provided by the following definition.

Definition 5. Let D be a database, IC an integrity theory, $\leftarrow B$ a query and θ an answer to $\leftarrow B$ in D.
a) We say that $\forall(B\theta)$ *has unrelieved integrity* if each cause of $\forall(B\theta)$ does not overlap with any cause of the violation of IC in D.
b) We say that $\forall(B\theta)$ *has solid integrity* if each cause of $\forall(B\theta)$ does not overlap with any cause of the violation of any constraint in IC.

It is easy to see that each answer that has solid integrity has unrelieved integrity. Moreover, each answer that has unrelieved or solid integrity obviously has weak or, resp., strong integrity. However, the converse does not necessarily hold, i.e., the weak, resp., strong integrity of an answer is not necessarily unrelieved or, resp., solid, as shown by parts a and b of the following example.

Example 5
a) Let $D = \{p(x) \leftarrow r(x, y);\ \ p(x) \leftarrow s(x), t(x);\ \ r(1, 1);\ \ s(1);\ \ t(1)\}$ and $IC = \{\leftarrow r(x, x);\ \ \leftarrow r(x, y), s(y)\}$. Similar to Example 4, the answer $x = 1$ to the query $\leftarrow p(x)$ in D has weak but not strong integrity, since its cause $\{s(1); t(1)\}$ does not overlap with the only cause $\{r(1, 1)\}$ of the violation of IC in D but does overlap with the cause $\{r(1, 1); s(1)\}$ of the violation of $\leftarrow r(x, y), s(y)$. Yet, the weak integrity of this answer is not unrelieved since its cause $\{r(1, 1)\}$ overlaps (in fact, is identical) with the cause of the violation of IC in D.

b) Let $D = \{p(x) \leftarrow q(x, y); \ p(x) \leftarrow r(x, y); \ p(x) \leftarrow s(x), t(x); \ q(0,1); \ q(1,2);$ $r(0,0); \ s(0); \ t(0)\}$, $IC = \{\leftarrow r(x, x); \ \leftarrow r(x, y), s(y)\}$. The causes of the violations of constraints in IC are $\{r(0,0)\}$ and $\{r(0,0); \ s(0)\}$. The causes of the answer $x = 0$ to $\leftarrow p(x)$ are $\{p(0) \leftarrow q(0,1); \ q(0,1)\}$, $\{p(0) \leftarrow r(0,0); \ r(0,0)\}$, $\{p(0) \leftarrow s(0), t(0); \ s(0); \ t(0)\}$. Hence, there is a cause of $p(0)$, viz. $\{p(0) \leftarrow q(0,1); \ q(0,1)\}$, that does not overlap with any cause of the violation of any constraint in IC. Hence, $p(0)$ has strong integrity. But the integrity of that answer is not solid, since its cause $\{r(0,0)\}$ overlaps with one (in fact, with each) of the causes of the violation of some (in fact, of each) constraint in IC. As opposed to that, the strong integrity of the answer $x = 1$ to the query $\leftarrow p(x)$ in D is solid, since its only cause $\{p(1) \leftarrow q(1,2); \ q(1,2)\}$ does not overlap with any cause of the violation of any constraint in IC.

Differentiations similar to unrelieved and solid consistency of answers are not provided by CQA. For instance, the only minimal repair in the database D of Example 5b is to delete $r(0,0)$. Hence, both answers $x = 0$ and $x = 1$ to $\leftarrow p(x)$ in D are equally consistent according to CQA, while the lack of solidity of the integrity of the first and the solidity of the second is reflected by Definition 5.

4.2   Computing Answers That Have Integrity

The well-known query answering procedure of SLD resolution [12,14] provides a straightforward way to compute causes. For seeing that, let us assume, as usual, that each database clause is *range-restricted*, i.e., for each clause C, each variable in the head of C also occurs in the body of C.

Let D be a database, $\leftarrow B$ a query, R an SLD refutation of $D \cup \{\leftarrow B\}$, $i(R)$ the set of input clauses used in R, ρ the substitution computed by R, and θ the restriction of ρ to the variables in B. Thus, θ is an answer to $\leftarrow B$ in D. Further, let $i(R)\rho$ denote the set of ground clauses obtained from $i(R)$ by instantiating each clause in $i(R)$ with ρ.

Clearly, $i(R)\rho$ is an explanation base, and usually also a cause, of $B\theta$ in D. There may be SLD refutations the input clauses of which provide no cause, e.g., each refutation using $p \leftarrow p$ as input clause from $D = \{p \leftarrow p; \ p \leftarrow q; \ q\}$ for refuting $\leftarrow p$. However, by a slight generalization of the completeness theorem of SLD resolution in [14], it can be shown that each cause of each answer to $\leftarrow B$ in D can be drawn from some refutation of each SLD tree of $D \cup \{\leftarrow B\}$.

Similarly, also each cause of the violation of each constraint I and each integrity theory IC can be drawn from each refutation tree that proves the inconsistency of $D \cup \{I\}$ and, resp., $D \cup IC$.

Thus, it can be decided if an answer has integrity by matching its causes with the causes of integrity violation, according to Definitions 4 and 5.

The causes of integrity violation can be computed ahead of query time, so that the matching with causes of computed answers can be done at query time. Hence, the cost of computing AHI essentially is that of query evaluation.

In fact, the computation of AHI with SQL seems to be less complicated than computing consistent answers according to CQA. (There are essentially four different ways to compute such answers [3]. One uses techniques known from semantic query optimization. Two other approaches compute CQA from compact representations of repairs, either by conflict graphs or by extended disjunctive logic programs. Finally, repairs can actually be computed in order to decide whether an answer is *true* in each repair.)

5 Inconsistency-Tolerant Integrity Checking (ITIC)

In 5.1, we recap the definition of case-based inconsistency-tolerant integrity checking [8], henceforth abbreviated ITIC, and identify two shortcomings of that definition. In 5.2, we propose a new definition, based on causes, which overcomes the shortcomings of the old definition.

In both definitions, we characterize each integrity checking method $\mathcal{M}$ by its output upon the input of triples (D, IC, U). Each such triple consists of an "old" database state D, an integrity theory IC and an update U (a bipartite set of clauses to be inserted or, resp., deleted). U, when committed, leads to a "new", updated state, denoted by D^U. For each such triple, the output $\mathcal{M}(D, IC, U)$ takes one of the two possible values $\{sat, vio\}$, where *sat* indicates that $\mathcal{M}$ accepts U, while *vio* indicates that $\mathcal{M}$ rejects U.

5.1 Case-Based ITIC

Definition 6 below restates the definition of case-based ITIC in [8]. Informally, it characterizes an integrity checking method $\mathcal{M}$ as inconsistency-tolerant if $\mathcal{M}$ accepts an update U only if U does not introduce any new violated case, i.e., a violated instance of a constraint in the new, updated state that does not exist in the old state before the update. Thus, updates of states with extant violations of integrity are tolerable as long as they do not lead to new violations.

It has been shown in [11,10,8] that most, though not all known integrity checking methods are inconsistency-tolerant in the sense of Definition 6. As already indicated, ITIC brings about a massive extension of the practical applicability of methods for integrity maintenance. Such methods hitherto have existed only as academical ivory tower plants, since they uncompromisingly and unnecessarily require total integrity, which is rarely encountered in real-life databases.

Definition 6. *(case-based integrity checking)*
Let $\mathcal{M}$ be a method for integrity checking. $\mathcal{M}$ is called *sound* and, resp., *complete*, *for case-based ITIC* if (1) or, resp., (2) holds, for each triple (D, IC, U) of a database D, an integrity theory IC and an update U.
(1) If $\mathcal{M}(D, IC, U) = sat$ then $\mathsf{VioCas}(D^U, IC) \subseteq \mathsf{VioCas}(D, IC)$.
(2) If $\mathsf{VioCas}(D^U, IC) \subseteq \mathsf{VioCas}(D, IC)$ then $\mathcal{M}(D, IC, U) = sat$.

If a method $\mathcal{M}$ is sound for case-based ITIC, we may also say that $\mathcal{M}$ is *inconsistency-tolerant wrt. cases*, or simply that $\mathcal{M}$ is *case-based*.

Example 6. The constraint $\leftarrow r(x), s(x)$ is violated in $D = \{r(0), r(1), s(0), s(2)\}$ since the body of its case $\leftarrow r(0), s(0)$ is *true* in D. Hence, each case-based method can accept updates such as *insert* $r(3)$ and *delete* $s(0)$, or any other update that does not cause any instance other than $\leftarrow r(0), s(0)$ to be violated in the new state. However, each case-based method must reject the update $U = insert\, s(1)$ of D, since U causes the violation of the case $\leftarrow r(1), s(1)$ in D^U that has been satisfied in D.

A shortcoming of case-based inconsistency tolerance is that there are no theoretical grounds upon which it could be compared to CQA, the most well-known approach to inconsistency tolerance. In [8], there is a performance study of ITIC with comparisons to CQA. It observes that the application of ITIC prevents a consistency degradation of databases across updates while CQA does not, and that the performance of query answering in databases that apply ITIC is better than computing answers by CQA. However, the results are only supported by experiments, not by any theoretical foundation, since the theories of CQA and case-based ITIC are quite different.

The cause-based definition of ITIC in subsection 5.2 overcomes this shortcoming. Since causes serve as a common foundation of ITIC and answers that have integrity, and since the latter can be compared directly to CQA, also a more principled comparison of ITIC and CQA can be expected. However, such a study of comparison of CQA, cause-based querying of answers that have integrity, and cause-based ITIC, still remains to be done; first steps are taken in section 7.

Another shortcoming of case-based ITIC is that it does not provide a differentiation of different degrees of inconsistency tolerance.

Moreover, case-based inconsistency tolerance is dependent on the syntactic representation of constraints, as illustrated by the following example. That drawback is avoided by cause-based ITIC as presented in subsection 5.2.

Example 7. Let the constraint in example 6 be represented by $\leftarrow$ *violated* and D be augmented to D' by adding the rule *violated* $\leftarrow r(x), s(x)$. Thus, the constraint $\leftarrow$ *violated* is its own single case. If that case is violated in the old state, then, by definition, each update U whatsoever is acceptable, since no new violated case could ever be introduced by U. In particular, also the update *insert* $s(1)$ of D' is acceptable, although that update leads to an additional violated case of the original constraint in example 6.

5.2   Cause-Based ITIC

Case-based inconsistency tolerance of $\mathcal{M}$ (Def. 6) means that extant constraint violations may be tolerated as long as no new violated cases are introduced by U. That is, the output *sat* of a case-based inconsistency-tolerant method indicates that, even if some cases of constraints are violated in the old state, U is acceptable since all cases that are satisfied in the old state remain satisfied in the new state. However, if U would violate some instance of some constraint in the new state that was not violated in the old state, then U must be rejected by each method $\mathcal{M}$ the inconsistency tolerance of which is case-based.

Similarly, cause-based inconsistency tolerance of $\mathcal{M}$, as defined below, means that extant constraint violations may be tolerated as long as no new causes of integrity violation are introduced by U. That is, the output *sat* of a cause-based inconsistency-tolerant method $\mathcal{M}$ indicates that, even if there are some causes of integrity violation in the old state, U is acceptable since the set of all causes of integrity violation remains the same or decreases in the new state. However, if U would lead to a violation of integrity in the new state by some cause that did not exist in the old state, then U must be rejected by each method $\mathcal{M}$ the inconsistency tolerance of which is cause-based.

Analogous to the weak and strong integrity of answers in Definition 4, we are going to distinguish between weak and strong cause-based inconsistency tolerance. Roughly, the weak version rejects updates that change the causes of the violation of some constraint, while the strong one tolerates such updates as long as the causes of violation of the whole integrity theory are not changed. This subtle but significant difference will be illustrated by an example.

Definition 7. *(cause-based integrity checking)*
Let $\mathcal{M}$ be a method for integrity checking.
a) $\mathcal{M}$ is called *sound* and, resp., *complete*, *for weak cause-based ITIC* if (1) or, resp., (2) holds, for each triple (D, IC, U).
(1) If $\mathcal{M}(D, IC, U) = sat$ then, for each $I \in IC$, $\mathsf{VioCau}(D^U, I) \subseteq \mathsf{VioCau}(D, I)$.
(2) If, for each $I \in IC$, $\mathsf{VioCau}(D^U, I) \subseteq \mathsf{VioCau}(D, I)$ then $\mathcal{M}(D, IC, U) = sat$.
b) $\mathcal{M}$ is called *sound* and, resp., *complete*, *for strong cause-based ITIC* if (3) or, resp., (4) holds, for each triple (D, IC, U).
(3) If $\mathcal{M}(D, IC, U) = sat$ then $\mathsf{VioCau}(D^U, IC) \subseteq \mathsf{VioCau}(D, IC)$.
(4) If $\mathsf{VioCau}(D^U, IC) \subseteq \mathsf{VioCau}(D, IC)$ then $\mathcal{M}(D, IC, U) = sat$.

If a method $\mathcal{M}$ is sound for weak or strong cause-based ITIC, we may also say that $\mathcal{M}$ is *weakly* or, resp., *strongly inconsistency-tolerant wrt. causes*, or, simply, that $\mathcal{M}$ is a *weak* or, resp., *strong cause-based* method. If the difference between the weak and the strong variant does not matter, we may simply say that $\mathcal{M}$ is *cause-based*.

Note that the distinction between weak and strong cause-based methods provides a differentiation of different degrees of inconsistency tolerance that is not offered by Definition 6 of case-based ITIC.

Example 8. As we have seen in example 6, $IC = \{\leftarrow r(x), s(x)\}$ is violated in $D = \{r(0); r(1); s(0); s(2)\}$. The only cause of integrity violation in D is $\{r(0); s(0)\}$. Hence, each cause-based method can accept updates such as *insert* $r(3)$ and *delete* $s(0)$ or any other update that does not constitute a new cause of integrity violation in D. However, as in example 6, each cause-based method must reject the update $U = insert\ s(1)$ of D, since $\{r(1); s(1)\}$ is a cause of the violation of integrity in D^U but not in D.

The following result is easy to show, by applying the definitions.

Theorem 1. *Each weakly inconsistency tolerant cause-based integrity checking method is also a strongly inconsistency-tolerant cause-based method.*

Theorem 1 says that strongly inconsistency-tolerant cause-based methods accept more inconsistency than weakly tolerant ones. Thus, strong cause-based ITIC generalizes weak cause-based ITIC. In other words: if an update is accepted by a weak cause-based method, then it will also be accepted by each strong cause-based method. And, conversely, if an update is rejected by a strongly inconsistency-tolerant cause-based method, then it will also be rejected by each weakly tolerant cause-based method.

The difference between both variants of cause-based ITIC is illustrated by the following example, which shows that the converse of theorem 1 does not hold.

Example 9. Let $D = \{r(1,1)\}$, $I_1 = \leftarrow r(x,y), s(y)$, $I_2 = \leftarrow r(x,x)$, $IC = \{I_1; I_2\}$ and $U = insert\ s(1)$. Since $\mathsf{VioCau}(D, IC) = \mathsf{VioCau}(D^U, IC) = \{r(1,1)\}$, each strong cause-based method $\mathcal{M}$ that is also complete will accept U. However, $\mathsf{VioCau}(D, I_1) = \{\ \}$, while $\mathsf{VioCau}(D^U, I_1) = \{r(1,1); s(1)\}$. Hence, each weak cause-based method must reject U. Hence $\mathcal{M}$ is strongly but not weakly inconsistency-tolerant for cause-based integrity checking.

The careful reader will have noticed a swap of analogy in the the definitions of weak and strong integrity of answers, on one hand, and strong and weak cause-based ITIC, on the other. For tuples (D, IC) of databases and integrity theories, weak integrity of answers and strong inconsistency tolerance of integrity checking are both defined by properties of $\mathsf{VioCau}(D, IC)$, while strong integrity of answers and weak inconsistency tolerance of integrity checking are both defined by properties of $\mathsf{VioCau}(D, I)$, for each $I \in IC$. That is because, the stronger the inconsistency tolerance of a method is, the weaker will become the integrity of answers across updates.

5.3   Discussion of Cause-Based ITIC

Examples 6 and 8 suggest that case- and cause-based ITIC are similar. Their relationship is studied in more precise terms below. A first result is the following.

Theorem 2. *Each weak cause-based integrity checking method is case-based.*

Proof. It is easy to see that, whenever an update U of some database D would lead to the violation of some case C of some constraint I in D^U that is not violated in D, then there must also be a cause of the violation of C, hence of I, in D^U that does not exist in D. Thus, by definitions 6 and 7, each weakly cause-based method is case-based.

The inverse of theorem 2 does not hold. Example 10 below shows that not each case-based method is cause-based. That goes for both the weak and the strong variants of cause-based ITIC, since, by definition, they coincide for databases with singleton integrity theories, as in example 10.

Example 10. Let $D = \{p(x) \leftarrow q(x); \ q(a) \leftarrow r(x); \ r(a)\}$ be a database, $IC = \{\leftarrow p(x)\}$ an integrity theory, $U = insert\ r(b)$ an update and $\mathcal{M}$ a complete case-based integrity checking method. Since $\mathsf{VioCas}(D, IC) = \mathsf{VioCas}(D^U, IC) = \{\leftarrow p(a)\}$ and $\mathcal{M}$ is complete, it follows by Definition 6 that $\mathcal{M}(D, IC, U) = sat$. Yet, since $\mathsf{VioCau}(D, IC) = \{p(a) \leftarrow q(a); \ q(a) \leftarrow r(a); \ r(a)\}$, it follows from $\mathsf{VioCau}(D^U, IC) = \mathsf{VioCau}(D, IC) \cup \{\{p(a) \leftarrow q(a); \ q(a) \leftarrow r(b); \ r(b)\}\}$ that $\mathcal{M}'(D, IC, U) = vio$, for each cause-based method $\mathcal{M}'$. Hence, $\mathcal{M}$ is not cause-based.

Part a of the following result shows that weak cause-based inconsistency tolerance in theorem 2 cannot be replaced by strong cause-based inconsistency tolerance. Part b generalizes example 10.

Theorem 3

a) Each complete strongly inconsistency-tolerant cause-based method is not case-based.

b) Each complete case-based method is not strongly inconsistency-tolerant wrt. causes.

Proof

a) Let $D = \{r(a, a)\}$, $IC = \{\leftarrow r(x, y), s(y); \ \leftarrow r(x, x)\}$ and $U = insert\ s(a)$. Since $\mathsf{VioCau}(D, IC) = \mathsf{VioCau}(D^U, IC) = \{\leftarrow r(a, a)\}$, each complete strongly inconsistency-tolerant cause-based method $\mathcal{M}$ will accept U. However, note that $\mathsf{VioCas}(D, IC) = \{\leftarrow r(a, a)\}$ while $\mathsf{VioCas}(D^U, IC) = \{\leftarrow r(a, a); \ \leftarrow r(a, a), s(a)\}$. Hence, each case-based method must reject U. Hence $\mathcal{M}$ is not case-based.

b) Let $D = \{p(x, y) \leftarrow r(x), s(y); \ p(x, y) \leftarrow r(x), t(y); \ r(a); \ s(b); \ t(a); \ t(c)\}$, $IC = \{\leftarrow p(x, x)\}$ and $U = insert\ s(a)$. Clearly, the only violated case of IC in both D and D^U is $\leftarrow p(a, a)$. Hence, each complete case-based method will accept U. However, the only cause of the violation of IC in D is $\{p(a, a) \leftarrow s(a), t(a); \ r(a); \ t(a)\}$, while in D^U, $\{p(a, a) \leftarrow r(a), s(a); \ r(a); \ s(a)\}$ is an additional cause of the violation of IC. Hence, each strong cause-based method will reject U.

Theorem 3a (resp., b) shows that completeness is a sufficient condition for cause-based (resp., case-based) integrity checking methods to be not case-based (resp., not cause-based). However, it can be shown that, in both results, completeness is not a necessary condition. In fact, for the given examples of triples (D, IC, U) in the proofs of parts a and b above, also incomplete methods *may* behave like complete ones, (although they do not *have to*, as complete ones do, by definition).

As shown by example 11 below, the completeness of cause-based methods also is a sufficient (though not necessary) condition for cause-based methods to be not compositional. As defined in [10], a method $\mathcal{M}$ is *compositional* if the following implication (*) holds, for each database D, each integrity theory IC, each constraint I in IC and each update U:

$$(*) \quad \text{If} \quad \mathcal{M}(D, IC, U) = sat \quad \text{then} \quad \mathcal{M}(D, \{I\}, U) = sat$$

It has been shown in [10] that each case-based method is compositional. However, no complete cause-based method is compositional, as shown by example 11.

Example 11. Let $D = \{r(a,a)\}$ be a database, $I_1 = \leftarrow r(x,y), s(y)$ and $I_2 = \leftarrow r(a,a)$ two constraints, $IC = \{I_1; I_2\}$, $U = insert\ s(a)$ an update, and $\mathcal{M}$ be a complete cause-based method. Then, it follows that $\mathcal{M}(D, IC, U) = sat$, since the only cause of violation of integrity in D and D^U is $\{r(a,a)\}$. However, $\mathcal{M}(D, \{I_1\}, U) = vio$, since the cause $\{\leftarrow r(a,a), s(a)\}$ of the violation of I_1 in D^U does not exist in D. In fact, I_1 is satisfied in D, i.e., the set of causes of the violation of I_1 in D is empty. Hence, $\mathcal{M}$ is not compositional.

The compositionality of case-based methods and the non-compositionality of some cause-based methods seems to speak in favor of case-based over cause-based methods. However, the following result can be proved easily by applying the definitions.

Theorem 4. *Each weakly cause-based integrity checking method is compositional.*

Last, we illustrate that cause-based inconsistency-tolerant integrity checking does not suffer the problem illustrated in example 7 for case-based methods.

Example 12. In example 6, the update *insert* $s(b)$ will be rejected by each cause-based method, since it clearly leads to the additional violated cause $\{r(b); s(b)\}$ of the constraint, no matter if it is represented by $\leftarrow r(x), s(x)$, as in example 6, or by the denial $\leftarrow violated$ and the additional rule $violated \leftarrow r(x), s(x)$, as in example 7.

6   Causes for Negation

So far, we have only considered queries and denials without negative literals in their body, and causes only of positive answers to queries. In the section, the definitions and results in sections 2–5 are generalized to *general conjunctive queries* (or, simply, *general queries*), which are of the form $\leftarrow B$, where B is a conjunction of positive or negative literals, and *general denials*, i.e., constraints of the form of general queries. In upcoming work, further generalization that cover also negative answers to arbitrary first-order queries will be dealt with.

However, as opposed to sections 2–5, we do not consider here relations defined by views, i.e., each database in this section is a flat relational one.

For each flat relational database D, all causes of positive answers to queries without negation are obviously sets of ground facts in D. The following generalization of definitions 1, 2 and 3 captures also causes of answers to queries with negative literals in their body. Its essence is to allow for negative literals in explanation bases.

Definition 8. Let D be a database, E a set of ground literals such that $D(L) = true$ for each $L \in E$, F an arbitrary sentence, $\leftarrow B$ a general query, θ an answer to $\leftarrow B$ in D, and I a general denial. E is called a *general explanation base* of F in D if $E \models F$. E is called a *general cause* of F in D if there is no general explanation base E' of F in D such that $E' \subsetneq E$. E is called a *general cause* of the answer θ to $\leftarrow B$ in D if E is a general cause of $\forall(B\theta)$.

Example 13 illustrates general causes for general queries.

Example 13. Let $D = \{p(0); \ p(1); \ q(1); \ r(0,1); \ r(1,0)\}$ be a database, $B = p(x), q(y), \sim r(x,y)$ the body of a query and $I = \leftarrow p(x), \sim q(x), r(y,x)$ an integrity constraint. Clearly, $\{p(1); \ q(1); \ \sim r(1,1)\}$ is the only cause of the answer $\{x = 1, \ y = 1\}$ to $\leftarrow B$ in D, and $\{p(0); \ \sim q(0); \ r(1,0)\}$ is the only cause of the violation of I in D.

It is easy to show that the general cause of each answer θ to a general range-restricted query $\leftarrow B$ in a flat relational database is unique and precisely consists of the literals in $B\theta$. Hence, computing general causes essentially is for free.

Based on Definition 8, analogously generalized definitions and results for AHI and cause-based ITIC are straightforward, and can be left to the reader.

7   Related Work

There is yet no comprehensive analysis of commonalities and differences between cause-based inconsistency tolerance and CQA. However, each of the following paragraphs identifies a point in favor of AHI wrt. CQA.

The minimality of explanation bases required in definition 2 does not suffer from the ambivalence of the minimality of repairs in CQA.

The definitions in sections 3–5 provide for a differentiation of different degrees of consistency and integrity that is not provided by CQA.

Inconsistency can be measured in accordance with AHI, simply by counting causes, or by comparing sets of causes of the violation of constraints. A similar way to measure inconsistency in accordance with CQA could be to quantify minimal repairs, but that appears to be less simple.

By definition, an answer has integrity only if it is *true* in the given database. More precisely, if, for an answer substitution θ of a query $\leftarrow B$ in a database D, $\forall(B\theta)$ has integrity in D, then $D(\forall(B\theta)) = true$. Similarly, if the answer *no* to $\leftarrow B$ in D has integrity, then $D(\forall(\sim B)) = true$. As opposed to that, consistent answers according to CQA may be *false* in the given database. For instance, let $D = \{p\}$ be a database and $IC = \{\leftarrow p\}$ an integrity theory. The answer *yes* to the query $\leftarrow p$ in D is computed by most query answering systems. However, this answer does not have integrity and is not consistent. Yet, this answer as well as the information about its lack of integrity is given only in the framework of AHI, not in CQA. In fact, the answer to $\leftarrow p$ in D as given by CQA is *no*, since the only minimal repair is the empty database, which is different from D. Arguably, the information conveyed by the answer according to AHI (that p is *true* in D but does not have integrity) is more useful than the answer *no* according to CQA.

Answers may or may not have integrity in databases with unsatisfiable integrity theories, while each answer whatsoever is consistent by definition of CQA if integrity is unsatisfiable: each answer is vacuously *true* in each repair, since there is no repair. For instance, let $D = \{r(a), \ s(b,b)\}$ and $IC = \{\exists s(x,x); \leftarrow s(x,y)\}$, which is clearly unsatisfiable. Rewriting $\exists s(x,x)$ in denial form yields $IC' = \{\leftarrow \sim q; \ \leftarrow s(x,y)\}$ and $D' = D \cup \{q \leftarrow s(x,x)\}$. The answer $\{x = a\}$ to the query $\leftarrow r(x)$ in D' has integrity, while the answer $\{x = b\}$ to $\leftarrow s(x, x)$ does not. However, both answers are consistent by definition of CQA.

CQA does not consider that the integrity theory, rather than the database could be in need of a repair, while AHI is impartial wrt. both possibilities. For example, let $D = \{q(1, 2, 3, 1), q(2, 3, 2, 4), q(2, 1, 2, 3)\}$ and $IC = \{\leftarrow q(x, y, x, z)\}$. Clearly, none of the two answers $\{x = 3, y = 2, z = 4\}$ and $\{x = 1, y = 2, z = 3\}$ to the query $\leftarrow q(2, x, y, z)$ has integrity in D wrt. IC, since their respective cause coincides with one of the two causes $\{q(2, 3, 2, 4)\}$ and $\{q(2, 1, 2, 3)\}$ of the violation of IC in D. The answer according to CQA to the same query is *no*, since the only minimal repair of D is to delete the two tuples given as answers according to AHI. However, it might well be that IC, rather than D is in need of a repair (which can of course only be determined if the particular "real-world" meanings of q and IC are taken into account). For instance, a reasonable repair of IC could be $IC' = \{\leftarrow q(x, y, z, y)\}$. For any change of IC, all answers given to queries in D according to AHI remain the same, while answers given by CQA may change completely, such as they do in the preceding example.

Essentially, AHI in can be computed by SLD, i.e., by a query evaluation procedure that is used also for conventional query answering. As opposed to that, each of the four known approaches to compute CQA, as mentioned in section 4, appears to be more complicated.

Apart from measuring inconsistency, as mentioned above, there are several more applications of causes and AHI that come to mind. One is the related issue of modeling and monitoring the quality of information. A cause-based approach analogous to the case-based approach described in [9] is easily conceivable. Also, it should be interesting to look into explanation bases and causes for a fresh take on explanations in expert systems [2] [13]. Moreover, we have several other possible applications in mind for future research, among them the automatic enforcement of declarative integrity for concurrent transactions, which up to now has been largely left to the application programmer. In one way or the other, each of these applications is related to inconsistency tolerance [4]. Quite a different reach of possible applications of CQA is addressed, e.g., in [5]. It remains to be seen if causes could be useful also for those applications.

8   Conclusion

For databases without negation and denial integrity constraints, we have presented initial findings related to the development of a concept of causes that can explain the correctness of query answering and integrity checking in the presence of extant inconsistencies in the database.

The main contribution of this paper is to have identified a simple approach based on causes that conceptually unites the two fields of inconsistency-tolerant query answering and inconsistency-tolerant integrity checking.

So far, integrity checking has been considered to be prohibitively expensive, if not impossible, in the presence of inconsistency. That has been one of the justifications of research for inconsistency-tolerant query answering [4]. In fact, the latter has hardly ever dealt with integrity checking.

On the other hand, inconsistency-tolerant integrity checking (ITIC) as presented in [11,10,8] has shown that the efficiency of most simplification methods for integrity checking can be achieved also in the presence of extant constraint violations, and that these violations can be contained, and in fact reduced, by ITIC. However, query evaluation in ITIC had been limited to evaluating simplified constraints, without being applicable to answer general queries consistently.

The idea of the concept of causes is that an answer from an inconsistent database is correct if one the answer's causes does not overlap with any cause of integrity violation, and that integrity checking in inconsistent databases is correct if it rejects each update that would increase the causes of integrity violation.

In particular, we have presented two main results. First, we have shown that causes serve to determine whether positive answers to queries have integrity or not. Second, we have shown that causes permit to define a new concept of inconsistency-tolerant integrity checking.

By intents and purposes, the concept of answers that have integrity is strongly related to CQA. We have shown that our concept provides a differentiation of various degrees of integrity that answers may have, while CQA does not. However, a deeper study of commonalities and differences between answers that have integrity and CQA is still pending as a topic of upcoming research.

Cause-based inconsistency-tolerant integrity checking has the advantage of being independent of the representation of constraints, while a previously developed case-based concept of inconsistency-tolerant integrity checking suffers from being dependent on the representation of constraints. More similarities and differences between case- and cause-based ITIC also is the subject of future research. At this point, one of the similarities can already be anticipated: Similar to cases, it should be straightforward to also use causes as a measure of inconsistency, as described for cases in [9].

The concept of causes relies on a concept of explanation bases, the development of which has only just begun. A big challenge is its generalization to negative answers for general queries in databases involving view definitions with negation. In a follow-up paper, we intend to present an extension of explanation bases and causes that explicitly takes positive and negative information into account, in order to make causes applicable to more general settings.

References

1. Arenas, M., Bertossi, L., Chomicki, J.: Consistent query answers in inconsistent databases. In: Proc. 18th PODS, pp. 68–79. ACM Press, New York (1999)
2. Arora, T., Ramakrishnan, R., Roth, W., Seshadri, P., Srivastava, D.: Explaining program execution in deductive systems. In: Ceri, S., Tsur, S., Tanaka, K. (eds.) DOOD 1993. LNCS, vol. 760, pp. 101–119. Springer, Heidelberg (1993)
3. Bertossi, L.: Consistent query answering in databases. SIGMOD Record 35(2), 68–76 (2006)
4. Bertossi, L., Hunter, A., Schaub, T. (eds.): Inconsistency Tolerance. LNCS, vol. 3300. Springer, Heidelberg (2005)
5. Chomicki, J.: Consistent Query Answering: Five Easy Pieces. In: Schwentick, T., Suciu, D. (eds.) ICDT 2007. LNCS, vol. 4353, pp. 1–17. Springer, Heidelberg (2006)

6. Christiansen, H., Martinenghi, D.: On simplification of database integrity constraints. Fundamenta Informaticae 71(4), 371–417 (2006)
7. Clark, K.: Negation as Failure. In: Gallaire, H., Minker, J. (eds.) Logic and Data Bases, pp. 293–322. Plenum Press, New York (1978)
8. Decker, H., Martinenghi, D.: Inconsistency-tolerant Integrity Checking. To appear in IEEE Transactions of Knowledge and Data Engineering, Abstract and preprints at, http://www.computer.org/portal/web/csdl/doi/10.1109/TKDE.2010.87
9. Decker, H., Martinenghi, D.: Modeling, Measuring and Monitoring the Quality of Information. In: Heuser, C.A., Pernul, G. (eds.) ER 2009 Workshops. LNCS, vol. 5833, pp. 212–221. Springer, Heidelberg (2009)
10. Decker, H., Martinenghi, D.: Classifying integrity checking methods with regard to inconsistency tolerance. In: Proc. 10th PPDP, pp. 195–204. ACM Press, New York (2008)
11. Decker, H., Martinenghi, D.: A relaxed approach to integrity and inconsistency in databases. In: Hermann, M., Voronkov, A. (eds.) LPAR 2006. LNCS (LNAI), vol. 4246, pp. 287–301. Springer, Heidelberg (2006)
12. Kowalski, R.: Predicate Logic as a Programming Language. In: Proc. IFIP 1974, pp. 569–574 (1974)
13. Liebowitz, J. (ed.): Handbook of Applied Expert Systems. CRC Press, Boca Raton (1998)
14. Lloyd, J.: Foundations of Logic Programming, 2nd edn. Springer, Heidelberg (1987)

Identifying and Eliminating Inconsistencies in Mappings across Hierarchical Ontologies

Bhavesh Sanghvi, Neeraj Koul, and Vasant Honavar

Iowa State University,
Ames, IA 50011-1041, USA

Abstract. Many applications require the establishment of mappings between ontologies. Such mappings are established by domain experts or automated tools. Errors in mappings can introduce inconsistencies in the resulting combined ontology. We consider the problem of identifying the largest consistent subset of mappings in hierarchical ontologies. We consider mappings that assert that a concept in one ontology is a subconcept, superconcept, or equivalent concept of a concept in another ontology and show that even in this simple setting, the task of identifying the largest consistent subset is NP-hard. We explore several polynomial time algorithms for finding suboptimal solutions including a heuristic algorithm to this problem. We experimentally compare the algorithms using several synthetic as well as real-world ontologies and mappings.

1 Introduction

Many semantic web applications (e.g., building predictive models from disparate data sources, assembling composite web services using components from multiple repositories) rely on mappings to bridge the semantic gaps between disparate ontologies. Such mappings may be established by domain experts, or automated tools designed to discover such mappings from data[1, 9]. This is inherently an error prone process. Errors in mappings can make the resulting ontology inconsistent. Consider for example an ontology with a single concept (say c_a) and another ontology with a single concept (say c_b). Consider the following set of mapping between the ontologies: (1) $c_a \prec c_b$ and (2) $c_b \prec c_a$ where $\prec$ denotes *strict* subconcept relationship. Obviously both these mappings cannot simultaneously hold. To ensure the consistency of the resulting ontology, one of the two mappings has to be discarded. While in this case the ontologies were simple and mappings were straightforward, in general, because of the large number of concepts and mappings involved, it is necessary to automate the process of identifying and eliminating inconsistencies.

In this paper we consider the problem of identifying the maximum subset of consistent mappings between hierarchical ontologies. We show that this problem is NP-hardeven in the restricted setting of mappings that assert that a concept in one ontology is a subconcept, superconcept, or equivalent concept of a concept in another ontology. We introduce several polynomial time algorithms for finding suboptimal solutions to the problem. We experimentally compare the algorithms using several synthetic as well as real-world ontologies and mappings.

R. Meersman et al. (Eds.): OTM 2010, Part II, LNCS 6427, pp. 999–1008, 2010.

2   Problem Description

We first introduce notations and definitions that we use in formalizing the problem of identifying the maximum subset of consistent mappings between hierarchical ontologies.

Definition 1 (Concept and Relationships). *A concept (or a class) represents a collection of objects or individuals. We consider two types of relationships between any pair of concepts:(1) strict subconcept relation ($\prec$) and equivalence relation($\equiv$).*

Definition 2 (Ontology). *An ontology $\mathcal{O}_x$: $\langle \mathbb{C}_x, \mathbb{R}_x \rangle$ where $x \in \mathbb{N}$ is a two-tuple of a non-empty finite set of concepts $\mathbb{C}_x$ and a finite set of relationships $\mathbb{R}_x$ between those concepts.*

In our setting each ontology can be represented as a directed graph (called the *ontology graph*) where the each vertex is a set of equivalent concepts in the transitive closure of the ontology and a directed edge exists between two nodes in the graph if and only if a relationship exists between the concepts associated with two nodes (Note the edge is directed from the subconcept towards the superconcept).

Definition 3 (Ontology Graph). *The ontology graph associated with a given ontology $\mathcal{O}_x$: $\langle \mathbb{C}_x, \mathbb{R}_x \rangle$ is the graph $\mathcal{G}_{\mathcal{O}_x}$: $\langle \mathbb{V}_{\mathcal{O}_x}, \mathbb{E}_{\mathcal{O}_x} \rangle$ where $\mathbb{V}_{\mathcal{O}_x} = \{v_1^x, v_2^x \ldots\}$ is a non-empty finite set of vertices and each vertex v_i^x represents a non-empty finite set of equivalent concepts in $\mathbb{C}_x$ such that exactly one of the following conditions is true: (1) either v_i^x is a singleton set and the only concept contained in this set is not related to any other concept in $\mathbb{C}_x$ with the equivalence relation or (2) Cardinality of v_i^x is more than 1 and each concept in v_i^x is related to at least one other concept in v_i^x with the equivalence relation. $\mathbb{E}_{\mathcal{O}_x}$ is a finite set of edges such that if $\left(e_p^x = v_i^x \dashrightarrow v_j^x\right)$ then, $\exists c_{i_m}^x \in v_i^x, \exists c_{j_n}^x \in v_j^x: c_{i_m}^x \prec c_{j_n}^x \in \mathbb{R}_x$.*

Note that each concept in the ontology is associated with one and only one vertex in its associated ontology graph. In addition, if any two concepts are related through an equivalence relation they must have the same associated node in the ontology graph.

Remark 1 (Simplifying Assumption). Given an ontology $\mathcal{O}_x$: $\langle \mathbb{C}_x, \mathbb{R}_x \rangle$, it is fairly straightforward to generate the corresponding ontology graph $\mathcal{G}_{\mathcal{O}_x}$: $\langle \mathbb{V}_{\mathcal{O}_x}, \mathbb{E}_{\mathcal{O}_x} \rangle$. Note that we are actually merging all the equivalent classes in an ontology into a single vertex in the corresponding ontology graph. Since this merging is just the conceptual merging in the representation and not the actual merging of classes in the ontology, for simplicity, we will assume that the input ontologies do not contain any equivalence relationships. As a result, all the relationships contained in an ontology are subconcept relationships (hierarchical ontologies). This implies that all the vertices in the corresponding ontology graph have a single concept associated with them.

Definition 4 (Inconsistent). *An ontology $\mathcal{O}_x$: $\langle \mathbb{C}_x, \mathbb{R}_x \rangle$ is said to be inconsistent, if the transitive closure of $\mathbb{R}_x$ contains $c_i^x \prec c_i^x$.*

Each subset of relationships in $\mathbb{R}_x$ that lead to some relationship $c_i^x \prec c_i^x$ in the transitive closure of the ontology is said to be a set of **conflicting relationships**. For any inconsistent ontology there may be one or more sets of conflicting relationships and each set may contain two or more relationships that conflict as a whole.

Definition 5 (Consistent). *An ontology* $\mathcal{O}_x$: $\langle \mathbb{C}_x, \mathbb{R}_x \rangle$ *is said to be* consistent *if it is not inconsistent.*

Theorem 1. *An ontology* $\mathcal{O}_x$ *is consistent if and only if its ontology graph* $\mathcal{G}_{\mathcal{O}_x}$ *is a directed-acyclic graph (DAG).*

Proof. The proof (for the if direction) is by contradiction and follows from the fact that there is one-to-one mapping between concepts and relationships in ontology to vertices and edges in ontology graph. As such any concept associated with a vertex participating in a cycle will have a subconcept relationship with itself in the transitive closure of $\mathbb{R}_x$. The reverse direction of the statement follows in a similar way.

Definition 6 (consistent)**.** *We define function* consistent: $\mathbb{O} \longrightarrow \{\top, \bot\}$ *as:*
$$\text{consistent}\,(\mathcal{O}_x) = \begin{cases} \top & \text{if } \mathcal{G}_{\mathcal{O}_x} \text{ is DAG} \\ \bot & \text{otherwise} \end{cases}$$
Therefore, the function consistent *can be implemented using the topological ordering algorithm with a running time of* $O\,(|\mathbb{V}| + |\mathbb{E}|)$ *where* $|\mathbb{V}|$ *is the number of vertices and* $|\mathbb{E}|$ *is the number of edges in the graph [11]. Alternatively, we have a running time of* $O\,(|\mathbb{C}| + |\mathbb{R}|)$ *where* $|\mathbb{C}|$ *is the number of concepts and* $|\mathbb{R}|$ *is the number of relationships in the ontology.*

Given any two different ontologies $\mathcal{O}_x$: $\langle \mathbb{C}_x, \mathbb{R}_x \rangle$ and $\mathcal{O}_y$: $\langle \mathbb{C}_y, \mathbb{R}_y \rangle$ the Mappings define the relationships between any two concepts in the ontologies.

Definition 7 (Mapping Relationship). *Given* $\mathcal{O}_x$ *and* $\mathcal{O}_y$, *a mapping relationship* $r^{x:y}$ *is a relationship* $c_i^x \mathcal{R} c_j^y$ *where* $c_i^x \in \mathbb{C}_x$, $c_j^y \in \mathbb{C}_y$, *and (1)* $c_i^x \prec c_j^y$ *represents that* c_i^x *is subconcept of* c_j^y; *(2)* $c_i^x \succ c_j^y$ *represents that* c_i^x *is superconcept of* c_j^y *and (3)* $c_i^x \equiv c_j^y$ *represents that* c_i^x *is equivalent to* c_j^y.

Definition 8 (Mapping Set). *Given* $\mathcal{O}_x$ *and* $\mathcal{O}_y$, *a mapping set* $\mathbb{M}_{x:y}$ *is a finite set of mapping relationships.*

Given ontologies $\mathcal{O}_x$, $\mathcal{O}_y$, and mapping set $\mathbb{M}_{x:y}$, we can generate a *merged ontology* by using the relationships specified in the mapping set $\mathbb{M}_{x:y}$. We denote the *merged ontology* by $\mathcal{O}_z$: $\langle \mathbb{C}_z, \mathbb{R}_z \rangle$. In addition we use the following notations: $|\mathbb{C}| = |\mathbb{C}_x| + |\mathbb{C}_y|$, $|\mathbb{R}| = |\mathbb{R}_x| + |\mathbb{R}_y|$, and $|\mathbb{M}| = |\mathbb{M}_{x:y}|$.

This merged ontology can be represented by a graph called *mapping graph*. Given a pair of ontologies $\mathcal{O}_x$, $\mathcal{O}_y$ and a mapping set $\mathbb{M}_{x:y}$, the corresponding *mapping graph* is $\mathcal{G}_{\mathbb{M}_{x:y}}$: $\langle \mathbb{V}_{\mathbb{M}_{x:y}}, \mathbb{E}_{\mathbb{M}_{x:y}} \rangle$ where,

Table 1. Relationships in Mapping Graph

Relationship	In Mapping Graph	Edge Type
$c_i^x \prec c_j^x$	$v_i^x \dashrightarrow v_j^x$	Ontology edge
$c_i^x \prec c_j^y$	$v_i^x \longrightarrow v_j^y$	Mapping edge
$c_i^x \succ c_j^y$	$v_j^y \longrightarrow v_i^x$	Mapping edge
$c_i^x \equiv c_j^y$	$v_i^x \longleftrightarrow v_j^y$	Mapping edge

- $\mathbb{V}_{M_{x:y}}$ is finite non-empty set of vertices
- $\mathbb{E}_{M_{x:y}}$ is finite set of labeled directed edges such that each edge is one of the following:

  - an *ontology edge* corresponding to some subconcept relationship specified in either ontology.
  - an *mapping edge* corresponding to some subconcept or superconcept relationship specified in mapping set.
  - an *mapping edge* corresponding to some equivalence relationship specified in mapping set.

  Table 1 lists down how each relationship is being represented in the mapping graph.

The *mapping graph* intuitively differs from the *ontology graph* in the sense that it allows to distinguish between the edges corresponding to the relationships in the ontologies and the edges corresponding to the mapping relationships. In addition it can contain bidirectional edges corresponding to the equivalence relationships in the mapping set.

Remark 2 (Converting Mapping Graph to Ontology Graph). A mapping graph $\mathcal{G}_{M_{x:y}}$ can be easily converted to the corresponding ontology graph $\mathcal{G}_{O_{M_{x:y}}}$ by first copying all the non-mapping edges and unidirectional mapping edges to the ontology graph and then merging the vertices that are combined by the bidirectional mapping edges.

Theorem 2. *A merged ontology $\mathcal{O}_{M_{x:y}}$ is consistent if its mapping graph $\mathcal{G}_{M_{x:y}}$ is a DAG.*

Proof. This is straightforward since the mapping graph $\mathcal{G}_{M_{x:y}}$ can be converted to ontology graph $\mathcal{G}_{O_{M_{x:y}}}$ which in turn must be a DAG for the combined ontology $\mathcal{O}_{M_{x:y}}$ to be consistent as per Theorem 1.

Theorem 3. *Given consistent ontologies $\mathcal{O}_x$, $\mathcal{O}_y$, and a mapping set $M_{x:y}$, any cycle in $\mathcal{G}_{M_{x:y}}$ must contain at least two edges corresponding to the mapping relationships, that is, at least two edges in any cycle must belong to the set $\left(\mathbb{E}_{M_{x:y}} \setminus \left(\mathbb{E}_{O_x} \bigcup \mathbb{E}_{O_y} \right) \right)$. Moreover, those edges must be either ($v_i^x \longrightarrow v_j^y$ and $v_l^y \longrightarrow v_k^x$) or ($v_i^x \longrightarrow v_j^y$ and $v_k^x \longleftrightarrow v_l^y$) or ($v_i^x \longleftrightarrow v_j^y$ and $v_l^y \longrightarrow v_k^x$) or ($v_i^x \longleftrightarrow v_j^y$ and $v_k^x \longleftrightarrow v_l^y$).*

Proof outline. Since the given ontologies are consistent, they must be both DAGs by Theorem 1. Moreover, for the vertices corresponding to these DAGs to participate in a cycle in the mapping graph, there must be a path that goes from one DAG to the other DAG and back to the first DAG. Consequentially, two directed edges with opposite directions must exist between vertices in the two DAGs. Since the edges between the two DAGs are due to the mapping set, at least two of the edges in any cycle must be the mapping edges as specified above.

Remark 3. We can observe that each cycle can in turn be represented as a chain of relationships which will lead to inconsistency in the ontology. Hence, any such chain would contain at least two mapping relationships which must be either $(c_i^x \prec c_j^y$ and $c_k^x \succ c_l^y)$ or $(c_i^x \prec c_j^y$ and $c_k^x \equiv c_l^y)$ or $(c_i^x \equiv c_j^y$ and $c_k^x \succ c_l^y)$ or $(c_i^x \equiv c_j^y$ and $c_k^x \equiv c_l^y)$.

Definition 9 (Consistent Mapping Subset). *Given consistent ontologies* $\mathcal{O}_x$ *and* $\mathcal{O}_y$, *and a mapping set* $\mathbb{M}_{x:y}$, *a subset* $\mathbb{M}'_{x:y} \subseteq \mathbb{M}_{x:y}$ *is said to be a* consistent mapping subset *if* consistent $\left(\mathcal{O}_{\mathbb{M}'_{x:y}}\right) = \top$.

Definition 10 (Maximal Consistent Mapping Subset). *Given* $\mathcal{O}_x$ *and* $\mathcal{O}_y$, *and* $\mathbb{M}_{x:y}$, *a consistent mapping subset* $\mathbb{M}'_{x:y} \subseteq \mathbb{M}_{x:y}$ *is said to be a* maximal consistent mapping subset *if* $\left(\text{consistent}\left(\mathcal{O}_{\mathbb{M}'_{x:y}}\right) = \top\right)$ *and* $\forall r_p^{x:y} \in \mathbb{M}_{x:y} \setminus \mathbb{M}'_{x:y}$, $\left(\text{consistent}\left(\mathcal{O}_{\mathbb{M}''_{x:y}}\right) = \bot\right)$ *where* $\mathbb{M}''_{x:y} = \left(\mathbb{M}'_{x:y} \bigcup \{r_p^{x:y}\}\right)$

Intuitively, a consistent mapping set is maximal if adding any more mapping to it will lead to inconsistencies. Note that for any given pair of consistent ontologies and a set of mappings between them there can be, in general, multiple maximal consistent mapping subsets. Furthermore, the user might have preferences over the mappings to be retained in the solution. A simple way to specify such preferences is by assigning weights to the individual mappings.

Definition 11 (Weighted Mapping Set). *Given a pair of ontologies* $\mathcal{O}_x$ *and* $\mathcal{O}_y$, *a weighted mapping set* $\mathbb{M}_{x:y}$ *is a set of mapping relationships along with a weight function* $\omega \colon \mathbb{M}_{x:y} \longrightarrow (R_{\geq 0})$ *where* $(R_{\geq 0})$ *is the set of positive reals.*

We will often use shorthand notation $\omega^\Sigma (\mathbb{M}_{x:y})$ to represent sum of weights of all relationships in $\mathbb{M}_{x:y}$. In the rest of the paper, we will assume weighted mapping sets. If the ω function is not specified, we will assume each mapping has a unit weight.

Definition 12 (Maximum Consistent Mapping Subset). *Given a pair of ontologies* $\mathcal{O}_x$ *and* $\mathcal{O}_y$, *a weighted mapping set* $\mathbb{M}_{x:y}$, *a maximal consistent mapping subset* $\mathbb{M}'_{x:y} \subseteq \mathbb{M}_{x:y}$ *is said to be a* **maximum consistent mapping subset** *if* $\forall \mathbb{M}''_{x:y} \subseteq \mathbb{M}_{x:y} \colon \omega^\Sigma \left(\mathbb{M}'_{x:y}\right) \geq \omega^\Sigma \left(\mathbb{M}''_{x:y}\right)$ *where* $\mathbb{M}''_{x:y}$ *is a maximal consistent mapping subset.*

So a maximum consistent mapping subset is a *maximal consistent mapping subset* with the most weight. Again, for any given pair of consistent ontologies and a weighted mapping set between those two ontologies, there can be multiple maximum consistent mapping subsets.

Definition 13 (Feedback Arc Set (FAS)). *Given a directed graph* $\mathcal{G}\colon \langle \mathbb{V},\ \mathbb{A} \rangle$ *where* $\mathbb{V}$ *is the set of vertices and* $\mathbb{A}$ *is the set of directed edges (arcs), feedback arc set of* $\mathcal{G}$ *is a subset of edges,* $\mathbb{A}' \subseteq \mathbb{A}$ *such that* $\mathcal{G}'\colon \langle \mathbb{V},\ \mathbb{A} \setminus \mathbb{A}' \rangle$ *is acyclic.*

We now introduce the definition of *Minimum Feedback Arc Set in Bipartite Tournament MFASBT* [8].

Definition 14 (MFASBT). *Given a bipartite tournament graph* $\mathcal{G}\colon \langle \mathbb{X}, \mathbb{A}, \mathbb{Y} \rangle$ *where* $\mathbb{X}$ *and* $\mathbb{Y}$ *are bipartite sets of vertices and* $\mathbb{A}$ *is set of directed arcs between the bipartite and a number* $k \in \mathbb{N}$, *is there a feedback arc set of size at most* k, *that is, is there a subset* $\mathbb{A}' \subseteq \mathbb{A}$ *such that* $|\mathbb{A}'| \leq k$ *and* $\mathcal{G} \setminus \mathbb{A}'$ *is acyclic?*

2.1   Problem Formulation

We now formally introduce the problem we are trying to solve in terms of the notation and definitions introduced above.

Decision Version (McM_d)**:** Given two consistent ontologies $\mathcal{O}_x$ and $\mathcal{O}_y$, some weighted mapping set $\mathbb{M}_{x:y}$, and a number $k \in \mathbb{N}$, is there a maximal consistent mapping subset $\mathbb{M}'_{x:y} \subseteq \mathbb{M}_{x:y}$ of weight at least k? Formally, McM_d can be stated as:

Given $\mathcal{O}_x$, $\mathcal{O}_y$, $\mathbb{M}_{x:y}$, and some $k \in \mathbb{N}$, is there $\mathbb{M}'_{x:y} \subseteq \mathbb{M}_{x:y}$ such that all the following are true:

1. $\text{consistent}\left(\mathcal{O}_{\mathbb{M}'_{x:y}}\right) = \top$.
2. $\forall r_p^{x:y} \in \mathbb{M}_{x:y} \setminus \mathbb{M}'_{x:y}\colon \left(\text{consistent}\left(\mathcal{O}_{\mathbb{M}''_{x:y}}\right) = \bot\right)$ where $\mathbb{M}''_{x:y} = \left(\mathbb{M}'_{x:y} \bigcup \{r_p^{x:y}\}\right)$.
3. $\omega^{\Sigma}\left(\mathbb{M}'_{x:y}\right) \geq k$.

Optimization Version (McM)**:** Given two consistent ontologies $\mathcal{O}_x$ and $\mathcal{O}_y$, and some weighted mapping set $\mathbb{M}_{x:y}$, identify a maximum consistent mapping subset $\mathbb{M}'_{x:y} \subseteq \mathbb{M}_{x:y}$. Formally, McM can be stated as:

Given $\mathcal{O}_x$, $\mathcal{O}_y$, and $\mathbb{M}_{x:y}$, find a subset $\mathbb{M}'_{x:y} \subseteq \mathbb{M}_{x:y}$ such that all the following are true:

1. $\text{consistent}\left(\mathcal{O}_{\mathbb{M}'_{x:y}}\right) = \top$.
2. $\forall r_p^{x:y} \in \mathbb{M}_{x:y} \setminus \mathbb{M}'_{x:y}\colon \left(\text{consistent}\left(\mathcal{O}_{\mathbb{M}''_{x:y}}\right) = \bot\right)$ where $\mathbb{M}''_{x:y} = \left(\mathbb{M}'_{x:y} \bigcup \{r_p^{x:y}\}\right)$.
3. $\forall \mathbb{M}''_{x:y} \subseteq \mathbb{M}_{x:y}\colon \omega^{\Sigma}\left(\mathbb{M}'_{x:y}\right) \geq \omega^{\Sigma}\left(\mathbb{M}''_{x:y}\right)$ where $\mathbb{M}''_{x:y}$ is a maximal consistent mapping subset.

3   Eliminating Inconsistent Mappings

We first show that the decision problem McM_d is NP-complete. We then proceed to describe several efficient algorithms for finding sub-optimal solutions to the optimization version of the problem.

Theorem 4. *McM_d is NP-complete.*

Proof Outline. The complete details of the proof are omitted for lack of space but main idea of the proof to reduce problem of Minimum Feedback Arc Set in Bipartite Tournament (MFASBT) [8], a known NP-completeproblem, to a special instance of the decision problem McM_d.

Theorem 5. McM *is NP-hard.*

Proof. The proof follows from Theorem 4.

Since McM is NP-hard, we consider several sub-optimal solutions to the problem. Specifically, we relax McM by dropping the 3rd condition in its definition to obtain McM_m.

Definition 15 (McM_m). *Given a pair of consistent ontologies $\mathcal{O}_x$ and $\mathcal{O}_y$ and a mapping set $\mathbb{M}_{x:y}$, find a subset $\mathbb{M}'_{x:y} \subseteq \mathbb{M}_{x:y}$ such that all the following are true:*

1. $\mathrm{consistent}\left(\mathcal{O}_{\mathbb{M}'_{x:y}}\right) = \top$

2. $\forall r_p^{x:y} \in \mathbb{M}_{x:y} \setminus \mathbb{M}'_{x:y}: \left(\mathrm{consistent}\left(\mathcal{O}_{\mathbb{M}''_{x:y}}\right) = \bot\right)$ *where* $\mathbb{M}''_{x:y} = \left(\mathbb{M}'_{x:y} \bigcup \{r_p^{x:y}\}\right)$

We consider three polynomial time algorithms for McM_m which provide sub-optimal solutions to McM.

3.1 Naïve Approach

A simple approach to identifying a maximal consistent subset of $\mathbb{M}_{x:y}$ is to start with the set $\mathbb{M}'_{x:y}$, initially empty, and add to it mappings from $\mathbb{M}_{x:y} \setminus \mathbb{M}'_{x:y}$ one at a time, in decreasing order of their weights, as long as the combined ontology $\mathcal{O}_{\mathbb{M}'_{x:y}}$ remains consistent. The correctness of the algorithm follows by construction and a straightforward analysis shows that the running time of the algorithm is $O\big(|\mathbb{M}|\,(|\mathbb{C}| + |\mathbb{R}| + |\mathbb{M}|)\big)$ (Recall $|\mathbb{C}| = |\mathbb{C}_x| + |\mathbb{C}_y|$, $|\mathbb{R}| = |\mathbb{R}_x| + |\mathbb{R}_y|$, and $|\mathbb{M}| = |\mathbb{M}_{x:y}|$).

3.2 Biased Approach

It follows from Remark 3 that given a pair of strict partial order ontologies $\mathcal{O}_x$, $\mathcal{O}_y$ and a mapping set $\mathbb{M}_{x:y}$ the resulting combined ontology is guaranteed to be consistent if $\mathbb{M}_{x:y}$ contains only mappings relations of type $\prec$ or of type $\succ$. This is because in such a case the associated mapping graph is guaranteed to be acyclic. This observation leads to the following *biased* algorithm: Let $M_\prec$ and $M_\succ$ be the subsets of mapping relations (respectively) of type $\prec$ and $\succ$ in $\mathbb{M}_{x:y}$. We start with the subset $\mathbb{M}'_{x:y}$ initialized to one of the mapping subset that has the larger weight among $M_\prec$ and $M_\succ$. We add to $\mathbb{M}'_{x:y}$, mappings one at a time, from $\mathbb{M}_{x:y} \setminus \mathbb{M}'_{x:y}$, in decreasing order of their weights, as long as the combined ontology $\mathcal{O}_{\mathbb{M}'_{x:y}}$ remains consistent. The correctness of the algorithm follows by construction and a straightforward analysis shows that the running time of the algorithm is also $O\big(|\mathbb{M}|\,(|\mathbb{C}| + |\mathbb{R}| + |\mathbb{M}|)\big)$.

3.3   Graph-Based Approach

We proceed to describe a solution for McM_m that is inspired by an algorithm introduced by Demetrescu and Finocchi for finding a feedback arc set in a weighted directed graph [2]. We start with the mapping graph $\mathcal{G}_{\text{M}_{\text{x:y}}}$ constructed from a given pair of ontologies $\mathcal{O}_{\text{x}}$, $\mathcal{O}_{\text{y}}$ and a set of mappings $\text{M}_{\text{x:y}}$. Recall that the edges in $\mathcal{G}_{\text{M}_{\text{x:y}}}$ are of two types: (1) those corresponding to relations in $\mathcal{O}_{\text{x}}$ and $\mathcal{O}_{\text{y}}$; and (2) the edges corresponding to mappings in $\text{M}_{\text{x:y}}$. The basic idea is to identify and remove a minimal feedback arc set in $\mathcal{G}_{\text{M}_{\text{x:y}}}$ while preserving all the edges of type (1). We construct $G_{\mathcal{W}}$, a weighted version of $\mathcal{G}_{\text{M}_{\text{x:y}}}$ by assigning *infinite* weights to edges of type (1) and weights that reflect user preferences for mappings in $\text{M}_{\text{x:y}}$ to edges of type (2). The edges in a minimal feedback arc set of $G_{\mathcal{W}}$ correspond precisely to the mappings that need to be removed from $\text{M}_{\text{x:y}}$ in order to obtain a maximal consistent mapping subset of $\text{M}_{\text{x:y}}$. As computed by Demetrescu and Finocchi, the worst runtime complexity of this algorithm is $O\left(|\mathbb{V}|\,|\mathbb{E}|\right)$ which in our case turns out to be $O\left(|\mathbb{C}|\left(|\mathbb{R}|+|\mathbb{M}|\right)\right)$. Moreover this algorithm guarantees an approximation ratio bounded by the length (in terms of number of edges) of the longest simple cycle in the graph. We note that Demetrescu and Finocchi's algorithm for MFASBT works by removing edges with the minimum weight. Consequently, we need a procedure to assign weights to the edges in the Ontology Graph. To ensure that only the mapping edges are removed in our solution we assign an *infinite* weight to all the non-mapping edges. Approaches to assign weights to non-mapping edges include assigning unit weight to all non-mapping edges. The user preference of mappings can be incorporated by assigning user defined weights to the mappings.

4   Evaluation and Results

Since there are no benchmarks available for evaluating the performance of algorithms for identifying maximal consistent subsets of mappings between ontologies, we used randomly generated ontologies and mapping sets. We chose parameters of the distribution used to generate the ontologies based on a survey of real world ontologies published by Wang et. al. [15]. We say that an algorithm outperforms another if the cardinality of the solution (maximal consistent mapping subset) returned by it exceeds that of the solution returned by the other.

Our first set of experiments were designed to compare the sub-optimal solutions computed by the Naïve, Biased and Graph based approaches with each other. The graph-based approach yielded the best result on 88% of the cases; The Biased approach provided the best result in 7% of the cases; and the Naïve approach yielded the best result 5% of the cases.

Our second set of experiments focused on the execution time of the algorithms on some real world ontologies and mappings taken from [4]. The results of these experiments are shown in Table 2. Interestingly, in this case, the graph based algorithm executes significantly faster than the other two algorithms. This can

Table 2. Avg. Execution Time (in ms) for Real World Ontologies and Mappings

Ontology Name	$|\mathbb{C}|$	$|\mathbb{R}|$	$|\mathbb{M}|$	Simple Naïve	Biased	Graph-based
animals (A, B)	17	19	9	7	2	1
people+pets (A, B)	116	147	58	100	90	2
russia (C, D)	225	243	86	264	285	2
russia (1, 2)	314	327	70	336	286	3
russia (A, B)	254	275	103	374	379	3
Sport (Soccer, Event)	570	558	148	1326	1332	8
Tourism (A, B)	814	850	190	2827	2754	124

be explained by the fact that the mappings used were specified by experts and contained few inconsistencies. In such a setting the resulting mapping graph contains few cycles and the graph based algorithm is able to terminate quickly. However, the other algorithms need to check for consistency whenever they try to add a mapping to the solution set, and hence, they end up performing poorly.

Our third set of experiments were designed to compare the best of these three approaches with the brute force approach. The latter exhaustively enumerates all possible subsets of $\mathbb{M}_{x:y}$, checks each of them for consistency and outputs a maximum consistent subset. To permit exhaustive enumeration, we had to limit the cardinality of the mapping set to a maximum of 31. We found that in 97% of the cases, the heurstic solution was as good as the optimal solution. Morever, in the cases where the heuristic solution differed from the optimal, the cardinality of the set of mappings in the heuristic solution differed from the optimal solution by atmost 2.

5   Summary and Discussion

We showed that the problem of identifying the maximum subset of consistent mappings between hierarchical ontologies is NP-hard. We explored introduce several polynomial time algorithms for finding suboptimal solutions to the problem in the restricted setting of mappings that assert that a concept in one ontology is a subconcept, superconcept, or equivalent concept of a concept in another ontology. These algorithms can be extended in a natural way to deal with more expressive mappings between hierarchical ontologies e.g., those that assert the equivalence of a concept in a target ontology with a concept that is formed by *Union, Intersection* or *Difference* of two or more concepts in the source ontology. The task of specifying the mappings has been extensively studied in the semantic web, database and the ontology communities in various contexts including *ontology mapping, ontology matching, ontology alignment, ontology merging* and *ontology integration* (see survey papers [1], [3],[9], and the book [6]). The Ontology Alignment Evaluation Initiative is a coordinated international initiative that is aimed at developing a set of common metrics and benchmarks for evaluating ontology alignment methods [5]. A variety of techniques for automating the specification of mappings between ontologies have been explored. These include schema based approaches, instance based approaches or a combination of the two (see [6] for a detailed discussion of these methods). Of related interest is the work in learning from heterogeneous data sources in presence of mapping errors [12]. Ensuring consistency of mappings, specially in large ontologies, has been identified as one of the major challenges in ontology integration [14]. Barring a few exceptions ([13],[10],[7]) the problem of eliminating inconsistent mappings has received limited attention in the literature. To the best of our knowledge, the the problem of finding the maximum consistent subset of mappings has not been studied.

References

1. Choi, N., Song, I.Y., Han, H.: A survey on ontology mapping. SIGMOD Rec. 35(3), 34–41 (2006)
2. Demetrescu, C., Finocchi, I.: Combinatorial algorithms for feedback problems in directed graphs. Inf. Process. Lett. 86, 2003 (2003)
3. Doan, A., Halevy, A.Y.: Semantic-integration research in the database community. AI Mag. 26(1), 83–94 (2005)
4. Ehrig, M., Sure, Y.: Foam - a framework for ontology alignment and mapping. In: Gil, Y., Motta, E., Benjamins, V.R., Musen, M.A. (eds.) ISWC 2005. LNCS, vol. 3729. Springer, Heidelberg (2005)
5. Euzenat, J., et al.: Ontology alignment evaluation initiative (2010), http://oaei.ontologymatching.org/
6. Euzenat, J., Shvaiko, P.: Ontology Matching. Springer, Berlin (2007)
7. Falconer, S.M., Storey, M.A.D.: A cognitive support framework for ontology mapping. In: Aberer, K., Choi, K.-S., Noy, N., Allemang, D., Lee, K.-I., Nixon, L.J.B., Golbeck, J., Mika, P., Maynard, D., Mizoguchi, R., Schreiber, G., Cudré-Mauroux, P. (eds.) ASWC 2007 and ISWC 2007. LNCS, vol. 4825, pp. 114–127. Springer, Heidelberg (2007)
8. Guo, J., Hüffner, F., Moser, H.: Feedback arc set in bipartite tournaments is np-complete. Inf. Process. Lett. 102(2-3), 62–65 (2007)
9. Kalfoglou, Y., Schorlemmer, M.: Ontology mapping: the state of the art. Knowl. Eng. Rev. 18(1), 1–31 (2003)
10. Kalyanpur, A., Parsia, B., Sirin, E., Grau, B.C.: Repairing unsatisfiable concepts in owl ontologies. In: Sure, Y., Domingue, J. (eds.) ESWC 2006. LNCS, vol. 4011, pp. 170–184. Springer, Heidelberg (2006)
11. Kleinberg, J., Tardos, E.: Algorithm Design. Addison-Wesley Longman Publishing Co., Inc., Amsterdam (2005)
12. Koul, N., Honavar, V.: Learning in presence of ontology mapping errors. In: Web Intelligence (2010)
13. Meilicke, C., Stuckenschmidt, H., Tamilin, A.: Repairing ontology mappings. In: AAAI, pp. 1408–1413 (2007)
14. Shvaiko, P., Euzenat, J.: Ten challenges for ontology matching. In: Meersman, R., Tari, Z. (eds.) OTM 2008, Part II. LNCS, vol. 5332, pp. 1164–1182. Springer, Heidelberg (2008)
15. Wang, T.D., Parsia, B., Hendler, J.: A survey of the web ontology landscape. In: Cruz, I., Decker, S., Allemang, D., Preist, C., Schwabe, D., Mika, P., Uschold, M., Aroyo, L.M. (eds.) ISWC 2006. LNCS, vol. 4273, pp. 682–694. Springer, Heidelberg (2006)

Towards Evaluating GRASIM for Ontology-Based Data Matching

Yan Tang

VUB STARLab
10G731, Vrije Universiteit Brussel
Pleinlaan 2, 1050 Elesene
Brussels, Belgium
yan.tang@vub.ac.be

Abstract. The GRASIM (Graph-Aided Similarity calculation) algorithm is designed to solve the problem of ontology-based data matching. We subdivide the
matching problem into the ones of restructuring a graph (or a network) and calculating the shortest path between two sub-graphs (or sub-networks). It uses
Semantic Decision Tables (SDTs) for storing semantically rich configuration
information of the graph. This paper presents an evaluation methodology and
the evaluation results while choosing Dijkstra's algorithm to calculate the
shortest paths. The tests have been executed with an actual use case of eLearn-
ing and training in British Telecom (the Amsterdam branch).

Keywords: GRASIM algorithm, ontology-based data matching, Semantic Decision Table, DOGMA, ontology.

1 Introduction and Motivation

In the EC FP6 Prolix project[1], we have developed an ontology-based data matching
framework called ODMF to calculate competency gaps between a learning module
(such as a learning material or a course), a person's profile (such as his Curriculum
Vitae), and the descriptions of a job or a task in the human resource management
(HRM) domain. ODMF is a collection of several matching strategies, in which GRA-
SIM has been designed and implemented. Although GRASIM has been designed for
matching two data sets that are properly annotated with our competency ontology, it
is general enough for any kinds of ontologies.

This paper focuses on how to evaluate GRASIM and the evaluation results. It is
organized as follows. Section 2 is the paper background, which includes Semantic

---

[1] The EC Prolix (FP6-IST-027905, Process-Oriented Learning and Information Exchange,
http://www.prolixproject.org/) is project co-funded by the European Commis-
sion under the Sixth Framework Program. It is to align learning with business processes in
order to enable organisations to faster improve the competencies of their employees according to continuous changes of business requirements.

R. Meersman et al. (Eds.): OTM 2010, Part II, LNCS 6427, pp. 1009–1017, 2010.

Decision Table (SDT) and GRASIM. We present the evaluation methodology in section 3. Section 4 contains the evaluation results, discussions and lessons learnt. Section 5 is the related work. We conclude and illustrate our future work in section 6.

2 Background

Semantic Decision Table (SDT, [12], e.g., **Table 1**) is a decision table properly annotated with domain ontologies and modelled in the Developing Ontology-Grounded Methods and Applications (DOGMA [10]) framework.

An SDT contains a set of lexons, which are the simple binary fact types, e.g., the lexon in **Table 1** represents a fact that "an Arc has a Weight". It also contains a set of *commitments*, each of which is a rule in a given syntax, e.g., the SDT commitment in **Table 1** contains a *value range* constraint for "Weight".

Table 1. An SDT of deciding the tree arc weights used by GRASIM

Condition	1*	2	3	N		1080
Int(r)	is-a	{define, describe}	...	Has char. of	...	N/A
Cons(r1,r2)	Uniqueness	Uniqueness	...	Mandatory	...	N/A
Sub(t,t')	Yes	Yes	...	Yes	...	No
Action						
Weight = 0				*		
0 < Weight < 50		*				
Weight = 50						
50<Weight<=70						*
70<Weight<100						
Weight = 100 (∞)	*					
SDT lexon	$\langle Arc, has, is\ of, Weight \rangle$					
SDT commitment	$0 \leq Weight \leq 100$					

GRASIM

Let us use G_1 and G_2 to indicate two annotations sets. Each set contains a list of lexons. G for the complete graph (the ontology), $G_1, G_2 \subseteq G$. We decompose the procedure into three steps: 1) study G and label its arcs; 2) reorganize G and use the Dijkstra's algorithm [4] to find the shortest path P between G_1 and G_2; 3) calculate the similarity score based on P.

On step 1, we use SDTs to propose the arc weights and label the arcs. Once a user gets the proposed weights, he could check and update them if unsatisfied. Our system uses these SDTs to check the consistency of the updated weights.

Table 1 shows an SDT that contains the decisions on the ranges of the arc weights based on the interpretations of the role $Int(r)$, the constraints on the role pair $Cons(r_1, r_2)$ and the constraints between the terms, e.g., $Sub(t, t')$[2]. Users can assign each weight with a number in the given range and label the tree arcs with these weights.

---

[2] It is a condition stub indicating whether a concept presented by t is a subtype of the other one presented by t'.

<u>On step 2</u>, we choose Dijkstra's algorithm to calculate the shortest path. Let G_1 be the source graph and G_2 the target graph. $G = \langle T, R \rangle$ where T is a set of graph vertices/nodes and R is a set of graph arcs. We use "·" to indicate the source graph of T and R. A graph vertex (which is also a lexon term) is denoted as $G \cdot t$ where $G \cdot t \in G \cdot T$. A graph arc (which corresponds to a role/co-role pair) is denoted as $G \cdot r$ where $G \cdot r \in G \cdot R$.

The weight on $G \cdot r$ is the user specified weight from Step 1. If the weight is 0, then merge the two vertices. If 100, then remove the arc.

The traveral cost from $G_1 \cdot t_i$ to $G_2 \cdot t_j$ is a positive number given by the function of Dijkstra's shortest path $\alpha(G_1 \cdot t_i, G_2 \cdot t_j)$. We refer to [4] for its detailed explanation. The shortest path P from G_1 to G_2 is denoted as a positive number P_{1-2} where for all $t_i \in G_1 \cdot T$ and $t_j \in G_2 \cdot T$, $P_{1-2} \leq \alpha(G_1 \cdot t_i, G_2 \cdot t_j)$. That is to say, P_{1-2} is equal to the smallest output of $\alpha(G_1 \cdot t_i, G_2 \cdot t_j)$.

Note that an arc in a graph has two directions. We need to cacluate all the shortest paths from G_1 to G_2 and vice versa.

<u>On step 3</u>, Suppose G_1 has in total n_1 vertices and G_2 has n_2 vertices. We use the following formula to calcuate the similarity score.

$$S = \lambda \times \frac{\sum_{i=1}^{n_1} \left(1 - \dfrac{\text{sp}(G_1 \cdot t_i, G_2 \cdot t_j)}{\text{sp}'(G_1 \cdot t_i, G_2 \cdot t_j)} \right)}{n_1} + (1 - \lambda) \times \frac{\sum_{j=1}^{n_2} \left(1 - \dfrac{\text{sp}(G_2 \cdot t_i, G_1 \cdot t_j)}{\text{sp}'(G_2 \cdot t_i, G_1 \cdot t_j)} \right)}{n_2}$$

In the above formula, the function $sp(x, y)$ is the shortest path from the vertex x to y. It uses the user defined weights. The function $sp'(x, y)$ is also the shortest path from x to y, which uses the largest Integer within the weight ranges. The ter $\lambda, 0 \leq \lambda \leq 1$ is used to tune the importance of the tree traveling direction.

3 Evaluation Methodology

Our evaluation methodology adapts the methodological principles of program evaluation [9], purpose oriented evaluation [1], and utilization-focused evaluation [11]. The principles are listed as follows.

— **Enhancement.** It needs to help the engineers to improve the system functions.
— **Usefulness.** It needs to help to ensure that a system is delivering right functions.
— **Transparency.** It helps to determine what information in the process is important.
— **Evolution.** It needs to test and collect continuous feedbacks for revising a system.
— **Accomplishment.** It has a precondition analysis and post-condition analysis in order to determine whether all the functions of a system are well accomplished.
— **Judgment.** The end users must be able to judge the outcome of a system.

The above principles are at a high level. We call them "macro" evaluation items.

At a more detailed level, we design the evaluation criteria for a matching algorithm (e.g., GRASIM). They are the "micro" evaluation items (see below).

— **Performance analysis.** It is to check whether it is expensive to run an algorithm or not in order to evaluate the functional results. The principle of **Usefulness** is applied to this criterion. It also includes the algorithm analysis.

— **Advantages and disadvantages.** It is to explain the situations that an algorithm is applicable and not applicable, which can help to improve it in the future. The principles of **Evolution** and **Enhancement** are applied on this criterion.

— **End users' judgment.** It is to check whether the scores match the end users' expectations or not. It is used for evaluating whether it is delivering complete and good functional results or not. It is designed based on the principles of **Judgment** and **Accomplishment**. In particular, we use *satisfaction levels* as the measurement.

— **Difficulty levels of management.** It includes the following sub-items.

Managing required knowledge base. It is to check whether it is difficult or not for end users or engineers to manage the knowledge base in order to evaluate whether it is easily used or not. This criterion is based on the principle of **Usefulness**.

Using an algorithm. It is to check whether it is difficult or not for the engineers to manage the parameters of the algorithm. It complies with the principles of **Usefulness** and **Enhancement**.

Improving outcomes. It is to find with which factors an algorithm is delivering good functional results in order to improve the function. It is designed based on the principles of **Transparency** and **Improvement**.

Accordingly, our evaluation methodology contains the following six steps:

— Step 1 (preparation step): we scope our test case by designing a general use case.

— Step 2 (preparation step): we specify our test case in a *story*, which contains triggers, actors, scenarios, and precondition/post-condition analysis.

— Step 3: we design the test data to feed GRASIM. In particular, we need to build the ontology and the annotation sets.

— Step 4: we design a test suit for the non-technical end users. A user test suite records the **levels of relevance** between G_1 (e.g., a company value) and G_2(e.g., a learning material). It can be 1, 2, 3, 4, or 5. 1 means that they are completely irrelevant. 2 means "not very relevant (or I don't know)". Level 3 means "relevant". Level 4 means "very relevant" and level 5 means "100% relevant".

— Step 5: we compare the results generated by the algorithm with the expectations from the end users. The outcome is a report containing a list of comparisons.

— Step 6: we analyze the above report and draw the conclusions, which will be used to enhance the algorithm for the next iteration.

We observe that the similarity scores change every time when the *ontology, annotation sets*, or the *weights* in the SDTs are updated. In order to correctly interpret the relevance levels before Step 5, we should not change any of the above three items.

How to interpret them is as follows. We first get the maximum score after running a complete test. Then, we equally split it into 5 ranges; e.g., if the maximum similarity score is 0.3225, then its scale is [0, 0.3225]. For the relevance levels 5,4,3,2 and 1, the ranges are: (0.258,1), (0.193,0.258], (0.129,0.193], (0.0645, 0.129] and (0,0.0645].

If a score falls in the range, then we say it is "completely satisfied". Otherwise, we calculate the smaller bias. For instance, if the score for relevance level 4 is 0.2, then bias 1 is 0.2-0.1935 = 0.0065 and bias 2 is 0.258-0.2 = 0.058. The bias is the smaller values in {0.0065, 0.058}, therefore, 0.0065.

If the bias is less than 0.0645 (one interval), then we say that this similarity score is "satisfied". If it is more than 0.0645 and less than 0.129 (two intervals), then we say that is "not really satisfied". All the rest are "completely unsatisfied".

4 Results and Lessons Learnt

Our test data is taken from BT. We need to compare a BT *assessment capacity* with a *learning material* that are annotated with the BT competency ontology. With their help, we have executed the evaluation methodology to evaluate GRASIM.

Performance Analysis
The complete test contains 26 learning materials and 10 assessment capacities. The ontology contains 1365 lexons (382 vertex and 208 arcs).

Table 2. Similarity scores of comparing the assessment capacity „Heart" to 18 learning materials. $\lambda_1 = 0, \lambda_2 = 0.1, \lambda_3 = 0.3, \lambda_4 = 0.5, \lambda_5 = 0.7, \lambda_6 = 0.9, \lambda_7 = 1$.

ID	Learning material	$S_{\lambda 1}$	$S_{\lambda 2}$	$S_{\lambda 3}$	$S_{\lambda 4}$	$S_{\lambda 5}$	$S_{\lambda 6}$	$S_{\lambda 7}$
1	Problem solving and decision making	0.78	0.77	0.75	0.72	0.7	0.68	0.66
2	Flexibility in changing circumstances	0.49	0.48	0.44	0.41	0.38	0.34	0.33
3	Communication	0.56	0.55	0.54	0.53	0.51	0.5	0.49
4	Understanding the market	0.33	0.33	0.33	0.33	0.33	0.33	0.33
5	Self management and professionalism	0.44	0.36	0.2	0.04	0.30	0.35	0.46
6	Identifying customer needs	0.46	0.38	0.22	0.05	0.21	0.28	0.33
7	Technical organization of site	0.33	0.33	0.33	0.33	0.33	0.33	0.33
8	Identifying customers' needs …	0.49	0.48	0.44	0.41	0.38	0.34	0.33
9	Problem solving and group decision…	0.51	0.49	0.46	0.42	0.38	0.34	0.32
10	Decision making: implementation …	0.62	0.63	0.63	0.64	0.65	0.66	0.66
11	Attendance management guidance…	0.54	0.53	0.53	0.53	0.53	0.52	0.52
12	Decision making (HARVARD)	0.63	0.63	0.64	0.65	0.65	0.66	0.66
13	3 day MBA	0.51	0.53	0.56	0.59	0.62	0.65	0.66
14	Cross-selling in customer serv. call	0.77	0.75	0.69	0.63	0.58	0.52	0.49
15	Valuing ability	0.53	0.53	0.52	0.51	0.51	0.5	0.49
16	Keep it simple	0.67	0.61	0.47	0.33	0.19	0.05	-
17	Bright ideas	0.53	0.47	0.36	0.25	0.14	0.03	-
18	Communications skills web seminar	0.71	0.67	0.58	0.5	0.41	0.33	0.29

Table 2 contains a part of our test data and the results. The last columns of tests 16 and 17 contain empty values, which mean that GRASIM does not return any value. It happens when no path can be found between $G_1 \cdot t_i$ and $G_2 \cdot t_j$.

We also observe that a similarity score depends on the value of λ. It does not affect the scores (e.g., tests 4 and 7 in **Table 2**) when the shortest path value from G_1 to G_2 equals to the one from G_2 to G_1. It happens when the arc weights assigned by the SDTs are "completely balanced" in the both directions. If the weights stored in the SDTs are "well balanced", then λ does not affect the scores a lot (e.g., tests 10, 11 and 12 in **Table 2**).

Advantages and Disadvantages
The advantages of using GRASIM are as follows:

- It is easily modified by the non-technical end users. It has been proven that a business person can deal with spreadsheets and decision tables more easily than other decision support tools, e.g., decision trees (see [12]).
- It can deal with rich ontological commitments for reasoning.
- It is easy to adjust the weights.

The disadvantage is the cost. The cost in miliseconds is 23657 miliseconds when calculating the similarity between the assessment capacity "trustworthy" and the learning material "Cross-selling in a Customer Service Call". The annotation set of this learning material contains 46 lexons and the one of "trustworthy" has 56 lexons.

End Users' Judgment
We use the means introduced in section 3 to interpret the levels of relevance from the test suite. The total numbers of the scores that are completely satisfied, satisfied, not really satisfied and completely unsatisfied are 32, 81, 55 and 33.

The satisfaction rate is **56%** (the total scores of "completely satisfied" and "satisfied"). The 'tolerable' satisfaction rate is **83%** (the ones that are not "completely unsatisfied").

The satisfaction rate is not very high because there are two BT domain experts involved in this evaluation process. Expert A provides the materials for creating the ontology and the annotations for the assessment capacities and the learning materials. Expert B provides the levels of relevance for the test suite. The advantage of having two different experts is: the satisfaction rate is more convincing because the understandings or views of expert B are not biased by the ones from expert A. The disadvantage is: the differences in the understandings may result in a not-very-good satisfaction rate.

Difficulty Levels of Management
We have developed a tool called ODMatcher to help users to modify the knowledge base, e.g., modify the annotation sets of G_1 and G_2, set the arc weights in SDTs. It also contains a function to support the users with the matching process information, which can be considered as an assessment of end users' judgment.

Concerning the difficulty level of **managing the required knowledge base**, the end users need to know how to use domain ontologies to annotate the assessment capacities and the learning materials. The knowledge engineers need to be the ontology engineers so that they can assign meaningful weights. Therefore, the required management level is **professional**.

With regard to the difficulty level of **using GRASIM**, the knowledge engineers need to know how to construct SDTs. For instance, they need to know how to write the SDT commitments. Hence, the required level is **professional**.

Concerning the difficulty level of **improving the similarity scores**, we judge based on the difficulty levels of the following five tasks. The first one is to improve the *weights on the graph arcs stored in SDTs*, which implies that the knowledge engineers need to know the meaning of the weights.

The second one is to adjust the *value of λ in GRASIM*. As discussed, our ontology graph is a directed graph. λ is used to balance the results calculated from two directions. It does not affect a lot the final similarity score if the weights on the arcs in two directions are well balanced. The knowledge engineers need to know which value the most "suitable" one for λ.

The third one is to update the *structure of the domain ontology*. The knowledge engineers need to understand the domain and have the knowledge in ontology engineering. The scores more likely increase if more arcs (relations between the concepts) are introduced.

The forth one is to modify the *annotation sets*, which requires the expertise of domain experts. When the two annotation sets almost overlap, the similarity score is high. If they are disparate, then the similarity score depends heavily on the shortest distance between these two graphs. If the shortest paths are short, then the score is high. If they are long, then the score is low.

The last one is to improve the *expertise levels of expert A and expert B*. GRASIM will provide more accurate scores when they are improved.

Accordingly, the required level of improving the similarity scores is **professional**.

5 Related Work

A generic evaluation methodology for the problem of ontology-based data matching does not exist. The existing methodologies are trivial and often application specific. *Program evaluation* is the systematic collection of information about the *activities*, *characteristics* and *outcomes* of *programs* to make judgments about the program, improve program effectiveness, and inform decisions about future programming [9]. It is "the systematic assessment of the operation and/or outcomes of a program or policy, compared to a set of explicit or implicit standards as a means of contributing to the improvement of program or policy". The evaluation methods in [3, 7] are this type of evaluation methods.

Utilization-focused evaluation [11] is an approach to executing evaluations that are practical, ethical and accurate. Examples of such methods are the evaluation methods for non-experimental data [2], which show how to use non-experimental methods to evaluate social programs.

One kind of evaluation methods is called *purpose oriented evaluation methodologies* [1], which contain three subtypes of evaluation methodologies – *formative evaluation*, *pretraining evaluation* and *summative evaluation*. They are used respectively on evaluating process, the value before the implementation, and the outcome of a method/system.

The related work, which is not directly relevant to our work but often used in our life, are product evaluation, personnel evaluation, self evaluation, advocacy evaluation, policy evaluation, organizational evaluation and cluster evaluation.

Our evaluation methodology contains the best practices of the methodologies of program evaluation, utilization-focused evaluation, and purpose-oriented evaluation.

With regard to the related work of GRASIM, we argue that GRASIM is used to solve the problem of *ontology-based data matching*, which is different from the one of *ontology matching*. Ontology matching (e.g., S-Match [5]) is to solve the inconsistency problem when merging several ontologies. In our problem setting, there exists *only one* ontology. GRASIM is to find the similarities between two data sets, each of which corresponds to one part in this ontology.

We solve this problem by transferring it into the problems of finding and calculating the semantic connections between two sub-networks in a graph. In this sense, [8, 13] are the related work of measuring this kind of semantic connections. The main focus of [13] is to find and group the web pages (considered as data objects) that belong to a same or similar context. The goal of [8] is to discover data based on distance. An approach taken by the authors from [8, 13] is to draw a boundary in the search spaces because the total world is unforeseen. This open world problem is out of the scope of GRASIM.

Compared to their solutions, GRASIM has two main innovative contributions – 1) we transfer the shortest path values between two sub-networks into a similarity score; 2) we study the semantics of the arcs and vertices in the graph using SDT.

6   Conclusion and Future Work

In this paper, we have discussed the evaluation methodology for GRASIM, which is an ontology-based data matching algorithm using SDTs. It is general enough for evaluating any kinds of ontology-based data matching algorithms. It has been tested with a real-life use case in BT and confirmed to be useful for the particular enterprise.

Currently, we are applying GRASIM to some use case scenarios in the ongoing ITEA-2 DIYSE project (http://dyse.org:8080). One use case is to search for similar software components.

Note that GRASIM is not restricted to the Dijkstra's algorithm. It can also use other graph algorithms, such as *A* algorithm* (also called *heuristic search* algorithm [6]). In the future, we will study how to use SDTs to pipeline matching tasks, propose the combinations of several shortest path algorithms, take the feedbacks from the users, and automatically adjust the SDTs.

Acknowledgments. The work has been supported by the EU ITEA-2 Project 2008005 "Do-it-Yourself Smart Experiences", founded by IWT 459. It is the author's pleasure to thank the colleagues who have been involved in the EC Prolix project, especially Ellen Leenarts (mentioned as Expert A in section 4) and Hans Dirkzwager (mentioned as Expert B in section 4) from British Telecom (the Amsterdam branch). I shall also thank Peter De Baer and dr. Gang Zhao for their valuable feedbacks of GRASIM.

References

1. Bhola, H.S.: Evaluating "Literacy for development" projects, programs and campaigns: Evaluation planning, design and implementation, and utilization of evaluation results. Hamburg, Germany: UNESCO Institute for Education; DSE [German Foundation for International Development], 306 pages (1990)
2. Blundell, R., Costa Dias, M.: Evaluation methods for non-experimental data. Fiscal Studies 21(4), 427–468 (2000)
3. CDC: Developing Process Evaluation Questions, At the National Center for Chronic Disease Prevention and Health Promotion, Healthy Youth, Program Evaluation Resources (2009), http://www.cdc.gov/healthyyouth/evaluation/resources.html
4. Dijkstra, E.W.: A note on two problems in connexion with graphs. Numerische Mathematik 1, 269–271 (1959)
5. Giunchiglia, F., Shvaiko, P., Yatskevich, M.: S-Match: an Algorithm and an Implementation of Semantic Matching. In: Bussler, C.J., Davies, J., Fensel, D., Studer, R. (eds.) ESWS 2004. LNCS, vol. 3053, pp. 61–75. Springer, Heidelberg (2004) ISBN 978-3-540-21999-6
6. Hart, P.E., Nilsson, N.J., Raphael, B.: A Formal Basis for the Heuristic Determination of Minimum Cost Paths. IEEE Transactions on System Science and Cybernetics SSC -4(2) (1968)
7. Johnson-Laird, P.N., Byrne, R.M.J., Schaeken, W.: Prepositional Reasoning by Model. Psychological Review, 99(3), 418 (1992) ISSN: 0033-295X
8. Korn, F., Sidiropoulos, N., Faloutsos, C., Siegel, E., Protopapas, Z.: Fast Nearest Neighbor Search in Medical Databases. In: International Conference on Very Large Databases (VLDB), India, pp. 215–226 (1996)
9. Patton, M.Q.: Qualitative Research and Evaluation Methods, 3rd edn. Sage Publications, Inc., London (2002) ISBN 0-7619-1971-6
10. Spyns, P., Tang, Y., Meersman, R.: An Ontology Engineering Methodology for DOGMA. Journal of Applied Ontology 3(1-2), 13–39 (2008); special issue on Ontological Foundations for Conceptual Modeling, Guizzardi, G., Halpin, T. (eds.)
11. Stufflebeam, D.L., Madaus, G.F., Kellaghan, T.: Utilization-Focused Evaluation. In: Evaluation in Education and Human Services, 2nd edn., vol. 49, pp. 425–438. Springer, Netherlands (2006)
12. Tang, Y.: Semantic Decision Tables - A New, Promising and Practical Way of Organizing Your Business Semantics with Existing Decision Making Tools. LAP LAMBERT Academic Publishing AG & Co. KG, Saarbrucken (2010) ISBN 978-3-8383-3791-3
13. Venkateswaran, J., Kahveci1, T., Camoglu, O.: Finding Data Broadness Via Generalized Nearest Neighbors. In: Ioannidis, Y., Scholl, M.H., Schmidt, J.W., Matthes, F., Hatzopoulos, M., Böhm, K., Kemper, A., Grust, T., Böhm, C. (eds.) EDBT 2006. LNCS, vol. 3896, pp. 645–663. Springer, Heidelberg (2006) ISSN 0302-9743

Expressing and Managing Reactivity in the Semantic Web

Elsa Tovar[1,2] and María-Esther Vidal[1]

[1] Universidad Simón Bolívar
Caracas, Venezuela
{elsa,mvidal}@ldc.usb.ve
[2] Universidad de Carabobo, Venezuela
eltovar@uc.edu.ve

Abstract. Ontological knowledge and reasoning provide the basis to define the semantics and static properties of Web resources. However, in existing approaches data reactivity is encoded in a different formalism by using rules, and the integration of ontologies and rules is not always natural or user-friendly. In this paper we present an alternative approach to represent active knowledge in ontologies. First, the ACTION formalism, in which events are categorized as ontological concepts, is proposed. Events are used in conjunction with classes, properties and instances during reasoning tasks and query answering. ACTION ontologies are processed within the REACTIVE framework. The REACTIVE reasoning and query engine supports the discovery tasks required to identify the effects of a given set of fired events. Additionally, an optimization strategy named IMR (Intersection of Magic Rewritings) is implemented. IMR identifies the events and properties that need to be considered multiple times and constructs the minimal set of rules that will produce the required result. The expressiveness of the ACTION formalism was empirically studied as well as the performance of the optimization and evaluation strategies. Initial experimental results suggest that ACTION is more expressive than rule-based formalisms; in addition, the REACTIVE engine in conjunction with IMR strategies reduce execution time to at least 50% of the execution time of traditional strategies.

1 Introduction

Typical ontologies used in the Semantic Web are formal representations of static knowledge. They express static properties of particular domain resources. In these ontologies, we can express that a resource X is a concept C, but we cannot express that X *ceases to be concept C to become concept C'* when a specific event occurs. Statements such as X *is a concept C'* and X *is a concept C* describe static properties of X. But, X *ceases to be concept C to become concept C'* when a specific event occurs, describes an active property of X. The process of data active properties is known as reactivity processing. Existing formalisms only represent static properties, i.e., they express information about data and

R. Meersman et al. (Eds.): OTM 2010, Part II, LNCS 6427, pp. 1018–1035, 2010.

metadata that do not react when events occur; for example, classes and properties of RDF/RDFS and OWL. However, the values of resource properties may change when certain events are fired. For example, the intensity of an earthquake depends on its focal depth; thus, when the focal depth is less than 70 km, the earthquake is highly destructive and its intensity is very high. Furthermore, when the earthquake intensity increases, a natural disaster occurs and some actions need to be taken in place. From an ontological point of view, earthquake and natural disaster can be modeled as classes, intensity and focus depth are properties, and events that fire the earthquake and the natural disaster are concepts related by a subsumption relationship. However, none of the existing ontological languages are tailored to express properties or relationships between events at the same level as properties and classes; in consequence, reactivity is managed outside of ontologies and the effects of events may not always be used to infer new knowledge. In this paper, we present a framework named REACTIVE (pRocEssing of ACTIVE Ontologies) to efficiently processing reactivity. Our approach is comprised of: an ontological formalism name ACTION [25] that is able to express classes, properties and events as concepts to implement active ontologies; a formalization of active ontologies as a deductive database to construct a rule-based framework which supports reactivity using static and active knowledge during the reasoning tasks; a query processing technique to efficiently evaluate the reactive behavior of ontological data [25]; a dialect of RDFS to represent active ontologies; and an extension of SPARQL that provides operators to specify a set of events which can be fired in sequence or in parallel during the reactive processing task. We have implemented optimization and evaluation techniques for ACTION, and conducted a preliminary experimental study to analyze the expressiveness, efficiency and scalability of our proposed approach. Our initial results suggest that our approach is an alternative approach to define and process reactivity on ontologies in the Semantic Web, while the evaluation time can be reduced to at least a half the reactive processing time when the proposed optimization and evaluation techniques are executed.

This paper comprises five additional sections. The next section summarizes the related work. In section 3, our approach is described. Section 4 presents extensions of the SPARQL and RDFS languages. The experimental study is reported in section 5. Finally, in section 6, conclusions are pointed out.

2   Related Work

Existing active ontological approaches follow a hybrid representation model, where reactivity is represented by active rules which have the syntactical structure and the semantics of the event-condition-action rules or the ECA rules paradigm [21]. Different approaches that combine XML data with ECA rules to process reactivity have been proposed [1, 2, 4, 7–9, 11, 19, 23], and ontologies with ECA rules [6, 13, 22, 26]. However, in these approaches, events are not represented as part of the universe of discourse, and active knowledge is not used in conjunction with static data to infer new knowledge when reactivity is processed. Active knowledge, classes and roles are also treated independently.

Behrends et. al. [4] propose an ECA-based approach were rules are combined with algebras of processes to manage reactive behavior. This framework is comprised of a model and an architecture for ECA rules that use heterogeneous events, query, and action languages. Different parts of ECA rules are handled by specific services that implement the respective languages. Rules are specified in a markup language RuleML that expresses simple and complex events, as well as, reactive processing [5]. Active knowledge coded in rules is associated with domain ontologies, but events are not represented as part of the domain. Similarly, in [1, 6] reactive behavior is modeled by using ECA rules. Alferes et. al. propose a foundational ontology to represent the language needed to specify these ECA rules, and this formalism is used to represent reactive policies, while Bonatti et. al. define a Horn based approach to describe ECA rules and evaluation techniques to evaluate them when events are fired. In none of these ECA-based approaches, active knowledge is used in conjunction with static data during query processing or reasoning.

Fox and Gruninger [13] describe a framework to manage data changes over time. This approach consists of a logical framework for representing activities, states, and time within an ontology in First Order Logic and reasoning regarding occurrence of actions by means of intelligent agents. Although this approach categorizes static and active knowledge at the same level, it does not augment the expressive power of the formalism by using the reactive behavior represented in the active knowledge. Recently, an ontology-based information integration approach [26] was presented for distributed sources. Ontologies are used to express information about frequent changes of metadata and overlapping pieces of information in distributed and heterogeneous sources. In [18] a dynamic logic-based formalism [16] to represent a multi-version ontology reasoning system is described. In this approach different versions of an ontology are represented as spaces of the logic semantic model, and relationships between versions are modeled by sequence-based operators. In a similar way, our ontology framework ACTION could be formalized by using a dynamic logic; however, in order to efficiently manage reactivity, the REACTIVE system does not store the different spaces of an ontology. Also, REACTIVE provides tailored methods to minimize the changes required to move from one space to the next when events are fired.

To enhance the expressiveness of ontology languages, hybrid rule-based systems like SWRL, have been defined [17, 22]. In [17], Horn clause rules were added to OWL-DL. However, SWRL extends OWL with the most basic kind of Horn rules where predicates are limited to being OWL classes and properties. Relations between values of properties and events cannot be represented; thus, it is not possible to express how ontological data react to the events that affect them. Furthermore, in hybrid systems, rules are used to augment the knowledge represented in ontologies; but, neither ontologies nor rules are able to represent reactivity or use the changes induced by the reactivity to infer new knowledge.

In conclusion, although ECA rules are the most widely used approach to process reactive behavior, in general relationships between active rules and ontologies are modeled in an operational way, and active knowledge, classes and roles are treated independently. To overcome this limitation, we propose an alternative processing scenario and formalism to represent reactivity.

3   Active Ontologies

In a previous work, we presented the active ontology formalism called ACTION [25], aiming at enriching the Semantic Web with active specification to express reactive behavior. ACTION formalism represents the active ontology canonical form that models basic ontological operators such as classes and properties in addition to events, active properties and the object reactive behavior.

Definition 1. *An ACTION ontology is defined as a 7-tuple*
$Oa = < C, E, Ps, Pa, F, fr, I >$, *where:*

- C: *a set of classes or basic data types.*
- E: *a set of events.*
- Ps: *a set of static properties; each property corresponds to a function from* $C \cup E$ *to* $C \cup E$.
- Pa: *a set of active properties; each property corresponds to a function from* C *to* C.
- F: *a set of predicates representing instances of the classes, properties and events.*
- fr *a function, s.t.,* $fr : F \times Pa \times E \rightarrow F$; *fr defines the reactive behavior.*
- l: *a set of axioms that describe the properties of the ontological language.*

The set of static properties Ps is comprised of properties that may induce a hierarchy of events, or a hierarchy of classes, and there will be a deductive rule indicating that the built-in predicate *isSubEventOf* is transitive in the set of axioms I of the ACTION ontology. Similarly, there are some other rules that establish the properties of the predicates *isSubClassOf* and *isSubPropertyOf*. Thus, event, classes and properties are considered as first-class citizens and are undistinguished treated by the reasoning engine.

3.1   Motivating Example

Consider the domain of natural disasters. Natural phenomena are caused by nature, e.g., earthquakes, hurricanes and so on. Each of them has its own features, e.g., an earthquake is generated at certain depth of its foci, and it produces a seismic wave whose amplitude expresses the earthquake power; and the wind speed is the main property of a hurricane. Phenomena have different names according to the environment where they occur, e.g., hurricanes are named typhoons in the Pacific Ocean. All these concepts can be modeled by RDF/RDFS, e.g., *NaturalPhenomenon*, *Earthquake*, *Hurricane* and *Typhoon* classes can be defined. Properties such as the intensity of an earthquake and the category of a hurricane can also be expressed. Furthermore, it could be asserted that *Earthquake*, *Hurricane* and *Typhoon* are subclasses of *NaturalPhenomenon*. But, it is not possible to represent that if the depth of an earthquake foci is shallow focus, i.e., if it is less than 70 km depth, then the intensity is very high, the earthquake is very destructive, and it needs to be considered as a natural disaster of great magnitude; thus, particular actions need to be taken, e.g., evacuation scale has to be full and recovery fund needs to be equal to 1 Billion.

ACTION static and active properties can be used to differentiate between the characteristics that describe the above described reactive behavior, e.g., foci depth, earthquake intensity, evacuation scale and recovery fund. Events specify when and how the active properties are affected, e.g., if foci depth is less than 70 km depth, the earthquake intensity is very high and the events of a very destructive earthquake and natural disaster of great magnitude are fired. Finally, hierarchies of events can conceptualize subsumption relationships between events, e.g., the event very destructive earthquake is a sub-event (e1) of the event natural disaster of great magnitude (e3) - e1 and e3 are hexagons in Figure 1.

In order to support the discovery tasks required to identify the effects of a given set of fired events, we have incorporated evaluation techniques into the REACTIVE query and reasoning engine. These techniques are able to identify the minimal set of changes that need to be performed to the active properties, when some events are triggered and they may activate the same changes multiple times. To illustrate this problem consider the hierarchy of events presented in Figure 1, when events e1 and e2 are simultaneously fired, and the effects of the common super-events need to be evaluated several times (events inside the highlighted circle). Properties p1 and p2 (circles) are affected by these events, and in a similar way, all the super-properties are considered several times, (properties inside the highlighted oval). Our proposed optimization technique Intersection of Magic Rewritings (IMR), identifies the events and properties that need to be considered multiple times, and constructs the minimal set of rules that will produce the same result, but that will avoid duplicates.

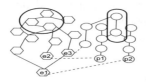

Fig. 1. An **ACTION** ontology

3.2   Active Deductive Ontology Base - ADOB

Similar to the approach presented in [24], ACTION ontologies are represented as deductive databases ADOBs. An extensional deductive database for an ACTION ontology Oa is comprised of meta-level predicates that model the knowledge explicitly represented by sets C, E, Ps, Pa, and F, while the intensional component of ADOB is composed of the rules that define the semantics of the knowledge represented in the extensional predicates and modeled by the axioms in I. We have defined a set of meta-level predicates to represent the reactive behavior of the data. Some of the meta-level predicates are as follows: *isEvent(E)* where E is a name event, the built-in predicate *isSubEventOf(E1,E2)* defines that the event name $E1$ is a sub-event of the event name $E2$, and the intensional meta-level predicate *areSubEvents(E2,E1)* is specified by a deductive rule that states that the predicate *isSubEventOf(E1,E2)* is transitive. Furthermore, the meta-level predicate *activeProperty(AP,T,D,R)* defines an active property AP in terms of its type T (not the same as rdf:type), domain D and range R; and the predicate *reactiveBehavior(AP,E1,BE,V)*, specifies the reactive behavior of an active property AP that takes the value V when an event $E1$ occurs and the Boolean expression BE holds. BE is a Boolean expression over the properties in Ps and Pa. As usual, an active ontology query is a rule $q : Q(X) \rightarrow \exists Y B(X,Y)$ where B is a conjunction of predicates. No free variables exist in the ontology, and our approach is based on the Closed-World assumption.

A model-theoretic semantics for ACTION ontology ADOB is as follows:

Definition 2. *Vocabulary: A vocabulary of an ACTION ontology consists of:*

- V_U: *a set of URI references of ontological resources.*
- V_L: *a set of literals* $V_L \subseteq V_U$.
- V_E: *a set of events* $V_E \subseteq V_U$.
- V_P: *a set of properties* $V_P \subseteq V_U$.
- V_V: *a set of variables of intensional predicate arguments.*

Definition 3. *Interpretation: Given an ontology ADOB=<AEO,AIO>, an interpretation structure of ADOB is a 8-tuple I=<D,U^I,L^I,P^I,E^I,RB^I,R^I,fr^I> where D is the set of names which interprets resources of vocabulary V and holds:*

- $U^I \subseteq D$ *is the set of URI references which interpret references in* V_U.
- $L^I \subseteq D$ *is the set of names which interpret literals in* V_L.
- P^I *is a term of* D^3 *which interprets built-in predicates of AEO. These built-in predicates express the value of a property of* V_P *for a resource of* V_U *(references of* $U^\uparrow$*).*
- E^I *is a term of D which interprets built-in predicates of AEO. These built-in predicates represent events of* V_E.
- RB^I *is a term of* D^5 *which interprets built-in predicates of AEO. These built-in predicates express value of an active property when an event occurs and a Boolean condition holds.*
- $r_i^I \subseteq D^n$, *where* r_i^I *is a formula of* D^n *and belongs to the set of intensional predicates* R^I, *n is the arity of* r_i^I. *The* r_i^I *terms represent the arguments of the intensional predicates.*
- fr^I *is a function of* D_3, *s.t.,* $fr^I : U^I \times Boolean(U^I) \times U^I \rightarrow U^I$ *which interprets the reactive behavior function in ADOB. Boolean(*U^I*) is a Boolean expression on (active or static) properties of ADOB.*

Definition 4. *Valid Instantiation: Given a function* $\mu : Vars \rightarrow D$, *where Vars is a set of variables and D is a set of constants, given R a built-in predicate, a valuation* μ *is a valid instantiation of R, iff* $\mu(R)$ *evaluates to true in ADOB.*

The interpretation of ADOB variables on I is a function μ which maps variable names of V_V to elements of D. Additionally, I interprets all terms as follows:

- $\mu(a_k) = a_k^I$, where $a_k^I \in (U^I \cup L^I \cup P^I)$.
- $\mu(p_k(a_i, a_j)) = p_k^I(\mu(a_i), \mu(a_j))$, where $p_k^I \in P^I$.

Definition 5. *Satisfiability: Given an ontology ADOB, an interpretation structure $I =< D, U^I, L^I, P^I, E^I, RB^I, R^I, fr^I >$ and function μ, a pair $< I, \mu >$ satisfies the formula φ, $< I, \mu > \models \varphi$, where:*

- *For each built-in predicate $ri \in AEO$ holds:*
  $< I, \mu > \models ri(t_1, t_2, \ldots, t_k)$ if $< \mu(t_1), \mu(t_2), \ldots, \mu(t_k) > \in R^I$.
- *For each intensional $ri(t_1, t_2, \ldots, t_n) \in AIO$, defined by a rule:*

$$ri(t_1, t_2, \ldots, t_n) :- r_1(t_1, t_2, \ldots, t_k), r_2(t_1, t_2, \ldots, t_l), \ldots, r_m(t_1, t_2, \ldots, t_j).$$

where, a pair $< I, \mu >$ satisfies rule $ri(t_1, t_2, \ldots, t_n)$, if whenever $< I, \mu >$ satisfies each predicate in rule body, $< I, \mu >$ also satisfies $ri(t_1, t_2, \ldots, t_n)$:
$< I, \mu > \models ri(t_1, \ldots, t_n)$ if $< I, \mu > \models r_1(t_1, \ldots, t_k) \wedge, \ldots, \wedge r_m(t_1, \ldots, t_j)$.

Definition 6. *Model: Given an ontology ADOB and an interpretation structure I, I is a model of ADOB iff I satisfies each predicate of ADOB.*

Definition 7. *Consistency: An ontology ADOB is consistent iff ADOB is satisfied, i.e., there is an interpretation structure I that is a model of ADOB.*

The minimal model of an ontology $ADOB =< AEO, AIO >$ corresponds to the model for which there is not other MM' such that $MM' \subset MM$.

Theorem 1. *The fixed point $d_1, \ldots, d_m$ w.r.t. the facts $h_1, \ldots, h_k$ of the extensional active ontology base AEO corresponds to the minimal model of ADOB.*

Theorem 2. *Given a deductive active ontology $ADOB =< AEO, AIO >$ and the fact isEvent(e), the result of reaching the fixed point for ADOB that is a solution for rules of the AIO w.r.t. the predicates of $AEO \cup \{isEvent(e)\}$, represents the unique minimal model MM for ADOB.*

4   The REACTIVE Architecture

REACTIVE is a rule-based framework that supports reactive processing of active ontologies. REACTIVE architecture is showed in Figure 2. Active ontologies are specified in ActRDFS an extension of RDFS, and they are translated into an Active deductive database (ADOB). ActSPARQL queries are decomposed by the Query Decomposer into a traditional SPARQL query, and an Active Query. The SPARQL query will be evaluated by an SPARQL query engine on the ontology produced as the result of processing the reactive behavior fired by the active query. Next, an Active Query Preprocessor receives the Active Query and produces an Adorned Magic Set Rules processing query in three steps. First, it aggregates sub-goals of the Active Query according to the aggregation criteria that will be presented in the next section. After, an Event Planner generates all super-events of the aggregated sub-goals. The process above implies generating not only the super-events (with no repetitions), but it also checks if the Boolean conditions of the events do not have active properties. In this case, a reordering of events must be done, due to the fact that if two events affect the same active properties only the last event must be processed. However, if there are active properties in the Boolean conditions, the IMR Query Writer must generate the Adorned Magic Set Rules according to a concurrent study producing a set of rules to process reactivity of a set of events that guarantees termination. Finally, a Rule-based engine evaluates the Adorned Magic Set Rules in conjunction with the rule-based representation of the input ontology, and produces a new static ontology. This static ontology and the SPARQL query are sent to a SPARQL engine, to produce the query answer.

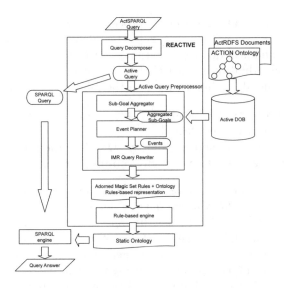

Fig. 2. The REACTIVE Architecture

4.1 Processing Explicit Reactivity and Implicit Reactivity

Throughout the times, reactivity processing has been approached in a variety of realms. Before the rising of the Semantic Web and ontologies, contexts [10] have been defined as representations of knowledge to specify how a system should behave when certain conditions hold. Under this approach, the change contexts provide a formalization to explain and predict how active properties of concept should evolve. On the other hand, dynamic modal logics [20] are formalisms aimed to represent reasoning systems that may model data reactivity. Under this approach, it is possible to reduce the problem of managing the evolution of the ontological data into a problem of managing reactive behavior.

The same as in ECA rules, change contexts, dynamic modal logics and First Order Logics [14] are oriented to processing the reactive behavior on active knowledge explicitly codified. For example, all the previous formalisms process reactivity codified as **when event wind speed increase occurs over 250 kph then the value intensity [of hurricane] must be 5**. New properties are not derived from the reactive processing of property Intensity. Nevertheless, if *Intensity* is a sub-property of *Strength* and *Strength* is a sub-property of *Power*, then both *Strength* and *Power* must also be modified in the reactivity processing. From our point of view, the reactivity processing in an ontology includes the active knowledge explicitly expressed as well as the active knowledge implicitly expressed. Hence, we define algorithm that can derived new active knowledge from ontological knowledge implicitly expressed.

4.2   Algorithm to Processing Reactivity

Algorithm 1 is a general algorithm to process reactive behavior triggered by an event E occurring on concept C [25]. This algorithm receives the minimal model MM of a canonical deductive database ADOB of an ontology Oa, and it determines the individuals in the set C that are affected by the event E and all its super-events. The algorithm is based on the following assumptions:

- if an active property AP is affected by an event E, then all the super-properties of AP are also affected.
- if an event E affects an active property AP when the property P takes the value V, then E affects AP when any sub-property of P has the value V.

To compute the minimal model MM the following predicates are evaluated: *areSubEvents(F, E), areSubProperties(AP, PA), areStatements(Ii, PA, V1), areReactiveBehavior(PA, F, P, BC, V2)*. It must be pointed out that this algorithm alters extensional knowledge but it does not alter metadata or intensional predicates. Thus, there is not possibility to generate inconsistencies between ontological Definitions and data produced during the reactive processing. The time complexity of the active algorithm is bound by the time complexity of the transitive closure [12]. Thus, the complexity of the active algorithm is $O(n^3 \times M)$, where n is the number of instances of the predicates $isSubEventOf$, and M is the number of active property predicates to be changed. The number of derived facts polynomially depends on the number and relationships of the events and the same evaluations may be fired by different events (details in [25]). Thus, this enrichment of expressiviness can negatively impact the complexity of the reasoning task implemented by the active algorithm; hence efficient query evaluation techniques are necessary. A naive solution is to follow a bottom-up evaluation. This strategy computes the minimal model and each fact is inferred once but a large number of irrelevant facts may be inferred. On the other hand, top-down evaluation only computes the relevant facts but the same fact can be inferred several times (repeated inferences). Thus, unnecessary inferences can be performed. To overcome these limitations, Magic Set techniques can be applied hence they reduce repeated and unnecessary inferences; magic predicates are introduced to represent bound arguments in the fired events; and supplementary predicates represent sideways-information-passing in the deductive database rules [3].

Our current version of the query engine algorithm is able to process a set of events that affect a particular class. Additionally, we consider that Boolean conditions associated with events can be comprised of static and active properties, i.e., there exists no restriction about the kind of properties that can be used in the Boolean conditions. This characteristic impacts on the complexity of the reactive processing task; this is because an active property $ap1$ affected by an event $e1$ could depend on the changes of another active property $ap2$ which is affected by another event $e2$, when $e1$ and $e2$ are processed simultaneously. Thus, criteria to detect when reactive processing will terminate is required. Finally, we consider that a collection of events on a particular class can be serial, i.e., events occur one after another; and parallel, i.e., events occur *at once*. In this work the IMR method presented in [25] has been extended to process reactivity in these two scenarios.

To deal with serial and parallel sets of events, we have introduced the notion of *processing schedule* that indicates the order in which events that appear in an input active query, must be processed. The rules that define the processing schedule for an active query are as follows:

- If events on class C occur in parallel, and:
  - there are no active properties in any Boolean condition associated with the events, then the order in which events appear in the processing schedule can be the same as the order in which they appear in the active query;
  - there are active properties in at least one Boolean condition associated with the events, then the events of the processing schedule have to be partially ordered. Events with static properties in their Boolean conditions must appear in any order at the beginning of processing schedule, but a subset of events with active properties must appear according to the dependencies among the active properties.
- If events on class C occur in serial mode, and:
  - there are not active properties in any Boolean conditions associated with the events, then the order in which events appear in the processing schedule and the order in which they appear in the active query are the same;
  - there are active properties in at least one Boolean condition associated with the events, then the order of the events must not be altered. If an event in the input active query depends on the change of an active property affected by another event that appears after in the input active query, then the execution of reactive processing is aborted.

Additionally, before the processing schedule is constructed, a preprocessing of the input active query can be done. This preprocessing consists on the aggregation of the query sub-goals in order to minimize the size of query, according to the following criteria:

- events that affect a class under the same mode - serial or parallel - are aggregated in only one sub-goal;
- when the set of events affect a class following the parallel mode, duplicated events are deleted from the input active query;
- otherwise, sub-goals remain the same as they were in the active query.

We present the extensions of SPARQL and RDFS to express and process reactivity. We extend the SPARQL query language with the *when* clause to specify the events that fire reactive process. Table 1 specifies the syntax of the ActSPARQL language. We illustrate the proposed extension of SPARQL with the following

---

Algorithm 1. The Reactivity Processing Algorithm

Input: Oa modeled as $ADOB =$<AEO,AIO>; $AQ=\{S1,\ldots,Sn\}$ an active query
Output: Oa resulting ontology ABOB after processing AQ

$Oa \Leftarrow \emptyset$;
for $Si = (M, \{E1, E2,, En\}, C) \in AQ$ **do**
  if M==p **then**
    $MM \Leftarrow minimal\ model\ Oa \cup \{isEvent(E1), isEvent(E2), \ldots, isEvent(En)\}$
    for $areIndividuals(I,C) \in MM$ **do**
      if $(areSupEvents(F,E)$ $\vee$ $areSubProperties(AP,PA)$ $\vee$
      $areSubProperties(P,P)$ $\vee$ $activeProperty(PA,T,D)$ $\vee$
      $areStatements(Ij,PA,V1) \vee areReactiveBehavior(PA,F,P,BC,V2)) \in$
      MM **then**
        for $areStatements(Ij,P,BC) \in MM$ **do**
          $Oa \Leftarrow Oa \cup \{statement(Ii,AP,V2)\}$
        end for
      end if
    end for
  end if
  if (M==s **then**
    for $Ei \in \{E1, E2,, En\}$ **do**
      $MM \Leftarrow minimal\ model\ Oa \cup \{isEvent(Ei)\}$
      for $areIndividuals(I,C) \in MM$ **do**
        $Oa \Leftarrow Oa \cup \{isEvent(Ei)\}$
        if $(areSupEvents(F,E)$ $\vee$ $areSubProperties(AP,PA)$ $\vee$
        $areSubProperties(P,P)$ $\vee$ $activeProperty(PA,T,D)$ $\vee$
        $areStatements(Ij,PA,V1) \vee areReactiveBehavior(PA,F,P,BC,V2)) \in$
        MM **then**
          for $areStatements(Ij,P,BC) \in MM$ **do**
            $Oa \Leftarrow Oa \cup \{statement(Ii,AP,V2)\}$
          end for
        end if
      end for
    end for
  end if
end for

Table 1. The ActSPARQL Syntax (BNF format)

<ActSPARQL query> ::= <SPARQL query><When-clause>
<When-clause>   ::= <EventBasicPattern>|
                         <EventBasicPattern><Oper><When-clause>
<Oper>   ::= SERIAL | PARALLEL
<EventBasicPattern> ::= {<BasicPattern><FILTER>}
<BasicPattern>   ::= <VAR> action:event < VAR>.
                         <VAR>action:reactiveBehavior <VAR>.
                         <VAR> action:activeProperty <VAR>.
<FILTER>   ::= Filter (<VAR> = <Class> && <VAR> = <Class>) .

query. It uses two execution modes: serial to represent events that occur is sequence, and parallel for events that occur simultaneously.

The following query retrieves *evacuation scale* of all members of *Phenomenan,
Hurricane, IndonesiaIslands* and *Earthquake* classes after is fired the execution of
the reactive processing of the events *naturalDisaster_ocurrs, wind_goes_up,
tsunamiGenerated, shallowEpicenter*, respectively. The ActSPARQL engine receives two requests. First, to execute the event *wind_goes_up* on the class *Hurricane*
after the execution of the event *naturalDisaster_ocurrs* on the class *Phenomenan*,
two sets of rules are evaluated. Second, to execute in parallel, events *tsunamiGenerated, shallowEpicenter* on classes *IndonesiaIslands* and *Earthquake*, the reactive
process evaluates one set of rules.

```
PREFIX act: < http:// facyt.uc.edu/action1.0/>
PREFIX nd: < http://funvisis.gov.ve/naturalDisaster/ >
SELECT ?rv
WHERE { ?x nd:evacuationScale ?rv }
{{{?e action:event ?o. ?ap action:reactiveBehavior ?e .?ap action:activeProperty ?c .
  Filter (?e = naturalDisaster_ocurrs && ?c=Phenomenan)  }
 SERIAL
  {?e action:event ?o.?ap action:reactiveBehavior ?e .?ap action:activeProperty ?c .
   Filter (?e = wind_goes_up && ?c=Hurricane)  } }.
{{?e action:event ?o.?ap action:reactiveBehavior ?e.?ap action:activeProperty ?c .
   Filter (?e = tsunamiGenerated && ?c=IndonesiaIslands)  } }
 PARALLEL
 {?e action:event ?o.?ap action:reactiveBehavior ?e.?ap action:activeProperty ?c .
  Filter (?e = shallowEpicenter && ?c=Earthquake)  } }}
```

The query engine interprets the active clause *when* of the query, and processes the
reactive behavior of the data in the ontology *O*. Thus, for example, if the value of
the property *evacuationScale* is *Null* before the event *tsunamiGenerated* occurs,
then the execution of the *when* clause alters the value of property *evacuationScale*
changing this value to *Full*. Once the reactive processing is evaluated on ontology
O, the engine returns ontology *O*ı; any SPARQL engine can be used to evaluate
the rest of the query.

Additionally, we propose a dialect of RDFS to express ACTION ontologies. Some of the new properties are listed in Table 2. Predicate *isSubEvent* is

Table 2. Some of the ActRDFS Property Descriptions

RDFS property	Description
(e action:event)	e is an event of ontology o
(e1 action:isSubEvent e2)	e1 is a sub-event of e2
(p rdf:type activeProperty)	p is an active Property
(p action:activeProperty e)	p is an active of event e
(bc action:BooleanExpression e)	bc is the Boolean expression of event e
(p action:changedTo v)	active property p changes to v

transitive and its semantics is implemented at the deductive database level as an implicit predicate.

5   Experimental Study

An experimental study was conducted on synthetic ontologies with three goals. First, we measure the expressive capability of ACTION formalism. Second, we measure performance the bottom-up evaluation of IMR rewritings, in contrast with, the bottom-up evaluation of of the program rewritten by using traditional Magic Sets techniques. Finally, we measure performance of the IMR method with and without the reordering of sub-goals of active queries. We report on the number of derived facts and on evaluation time.

5.1   Experiment Configuration

Dataset: The experimental study was conducted on the Lehigh University Benchmark (LUBM) [15]. We have extended the instance generator LUBM to insert active properties and events. The *univ_num* parameter (number of universities to generate) of the generator program, was used to construct the different dataset sizes. Once the instances of the repositories were generated as RDF/RDFS/XML documents, this information was translated into meta-level predicates of ADOB by means of Prologs DCG (Definite Clauses Grammars). To compare IMR (with and without the reordering of sub-goals) versus classic magic set evaluation [3], we consider a dataset with three kinds of repositories: small (information of five university), medium (twenty universities) and large (fifty universities). Ten different reactive goals (queries) were posed to each kind of repository; each of them evaluated using classic magic set evaluation and IMR. In Table 3, the generated repositories are described in terms of the number of classes, static and active properties.

Hardware and Software: The experiments were evaluated on a Solaris machine with Sparcv9 1281 MHz processor and 16GB of RAM. The proposed algorithms have been implemented in SWI-Prolog, Version 5.6.54.

Metrics: We report on the following metrics:
- Number of Derived Facts (NDF): the expressiveness of ACTION is measured as the number of derived facts from the reactive processing.

Table 3. DataSet Description

#Univ	#Class-Inst	# Prop-Inst	#ActProp-Inst	MB
5	91,408	325,429	69,441	33.5
20	414,194	1,305,736	278,876	151.0
50	978,764	4,212,872	741,150	379.9

- Total Number of Derived Facts (TNDF): the cost of reasoning and query evaluation is measured as the number of derived facts needed for the reactive processing. TNDF represents the minimal model size.
- TIME: measures the reactive processing time in seconds.

5.2   Results

In order to measure expressiveness of the ACTION formalism, we considered ten queries. Each query consists of one event affecting one class. Ten queries are posed both on lineal hierarchy - where each event has just one super-event - and on bushy hierarchy - where each event may have one up to n super-events or no super-event. Figure 3 shows the average NDF for ten queries on lineal hierarchies (panel a) and on bushy hierarchies (panel b). In Figure 4 panel a we observe that the NDF monotonically grows as the ontology depths. This is because the occurence of an event implies the occurennce of all of their super-events and, in average, the new active implicit knowledge tends to augment. While Figure 4 panel b shows that the NDF does not increase proportionally to the number of events affecting the active properties. This is because when an event is triggered not necessarilly another event from the hierarchy will be

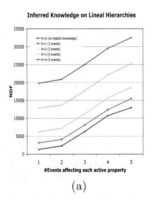

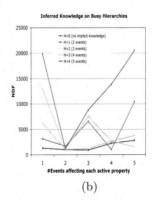

(a)   (b)

Fig. 3. Number of Derived Facts: (a) Lineal Hierarchies; (b) Bushy Hierarchies

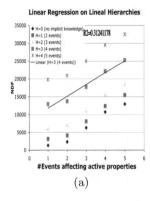
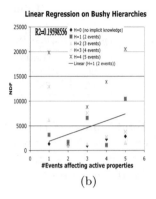

(a)   (b)

Fig. 4. Linear Regression: (a) Lineal Hierarchies (b) Bushy Hierarchies

triggered or, inversely, the new active implicit knowledge might suddenly grow when an event having many super-events is triggered.

Figure 4 shows the coefficient of determination R^2 of linear regression study on lineal and bushy hierarchies. R^2 measures the proportion of new derived facts that can be explained due to the augment of the number of events in each event hierarchy. This indicates the percentage of new derived facts is obtained as a product of processing the implicit active knowledge in event hierarchy. Results indicate that such percentage is 31% in the case of lineal hierarchies (panel a) and 19% in the case of bushy hierarchies (panel b). Eleven active properties were used in these experiments. Augmenting from 1 to 5 the number of events affecting each property means augmenting the explicit knowledge approximately 5%. If the explicit knowledge is augmented just 5%, then 31% of active knowledge on lineal hierarchies and 19% of active knowledge on bushy hierarchies is reached when processing the implicit knowledge.

We considered ten queries. Each query consists of three to nine sub-goals, one to ten events affecting one class, one to five different affected classes in the query, and one random execution scheduler per sub-goal - serial or parallel. Figure 5 shows TIME and TNDF for the bottom-up evaluation of ten input programs with Classic Magic Sets rewritings (CMS) that represent the reactive processing versus the bottom-up evaluation of the IMR rewriting of the same programs. In Figure 5 panel a we observe that non-ordering sub-goals IMR method (NOrdIMR) speeds up the tasks of reasoning and query evaluation by 55% w.r.t. CMS, while the ordering sub-goal IMR method (OrdIMR) reduces evaluation time by 72% w.r.t. CMS. Figure 5 panel b also shows that both versions of IMR outperform CMS by four orders of magnitude (TNDF). This is because IMR avoids duplicate inferences when it processes a set of events. In contrast, classic Magic Sets performs all the inferences for each event.

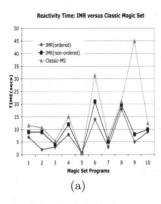

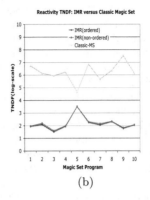

(a)   (b)

Fig. 5. Cost of ordering sub-goals IMR(ordered), non-ordering sub-goals IMR method(non-ordered), Classic Magic Sets: (a) TIME (secs); (b) TNDF(log-scale)

6   Conclusions and Future Work

ACTION ontologies extend the expressiveness of ontological languages in order to incorporate events as first-class concepts, and make use of traditional deductive reasoning tasks to manage reactivity. In order to efficiently process reactive behavior the REACTIVE architecture was proposed. This platform implements an evaluation engine to efficiently manage the reactive behavior of ontological data was developed. Results of the conducted empirical study indicate that our approach is an alternative - declarative - way to express and process reactivity. In the future we plan to integrate REACTIVE to existing SPARQL query engines.

References

1. Alferes, J.J., Amador, R., Kärger, P., Olmedilla, D.: Towards reactive semantic web policies: Advanced agent control for the semantic web. In: ISWC (Posters & Demos) (2008)
2. Bailey, J.: Transformation and reaction rules for data on the web. In: ADC 2005: Proceedings of the 16th Australasian Database Conference, Darlinghurst, Australia, pp. 17–23. Australian Computer Society, Inc. (2005)
3. Bancilhon, F., Maier, D., Sagiv, Y., Ullman, J.D.: Magic Sets and Other Strange Ways to Implement Logic Programs. In: PODS, pp. 1–15 (1986)
4. Behrends, E., Fritzen, O., May, W., Schenk, F.: Embedding Event Algebras and Process for ECA Rules for the Semantic Web. Fundam. Inform. 82(3), 237–263 (2008)
5. Biletskiy, Y., Hirtle, D., Vorochek, O.: Toward the Identification and Elimination of Semantic Conflicts for the Integration of RuleML-based Ontologies. In: CSWWS, pp. 135–142 (2006)
6. Bonatti, P.A., Kärger, P., Olmedilla, D.: Reactive policies for the semantic web. In: Aroyo, L., Antoniou, G., Hyvönen, E., ten Teije, A., Stuckenschmidt, H., Cabral, L., Tudorache, T. (eds.) ESWC 2010. LNCS, vol. 6088, pp. 76–90. Springer, Heidelberg (2010)

7. Bonifati, A., Ceri, S., Paraboschi, S.: Active rules for XML: A new paradigm for E-services. VLDB J. 10(1), 39–47 (2001)
8. Bonifati, A., Paraboschi, S.: Active XQuery. In: Web Dynamics, pp. 249–274 (2004)
9. Braga, D., Campi, A., Martinenghi, D., Raffio, A.: ActiveXQBE: A Visual Paradigm for Triggers over XML Data. In: Grust, T., Höpfner, H., Illarramendi, A., Jablonski, S., Mesiti, M., Müller, S., Patranjan, P.-L., Sattler, K.-U., Spiliopoulou, M., Wijsen, J. (eds.) EDBT 2006. LNCS, vol. 4254, pp. 865–875. Springer, Heidelberg (2006)
10. Brézillon, P.: Context in artificial intelligence: I. a survey of the literature. Computers and Artificial Intelligence 18(4) (1999)
11. Bry, F., Eckert, M., Grallert, H., Patranjan, P.-L.: Evolution of Distributed Web Data: An Application of the Reactive Language XChange. In: ICDE, pp. 1517–1518 (2007)
12. Cohen, E.: Estimating the Size of the Transitive Closure in Linear Time. In: FOCS, pp. 190–200 (1994)
13. Fox, M., Gruninger, M.: On Ontologies and Enterprise Modelling. The AI Magazine, 109–121 (1997)
14. Gruninger, M., Fox, M.: The logic of enterprise modelling (1995)
15. Guo, Y., Pan, Z., Heflin, J.: LUBM: A benchmark for OWL knowledge base systems. J. Web Sem. 3(2-3), 158–182 (2005)
16. Harel, D., Kozen, D., Tiuryn, J.: Dynamic logic. In: Handbook of Philosophical Logic, pp. 497–604. MIT Press, Cambridge (1984)
17. Horrocks, I., Patel-Schneider, P.F., Boley, H., Tabet, S., Grosof, B., Dean, M.: SWRL: A Semantic Web Rule Language Combining OWL and RuleML. W3C Member Submission (May 21, 2004), http://www.w3.org/Submission/SWRL/
18. Huang, Z., Schlobach, S., van Harmelen, F., Casellas, N., Casanovas, P.: Dynamic aspects of opjk legal ontology. In: Casanovas, P., Sartor, G., Casellas, N., Rubino, R. (eds.) Computable Models of the Law. LNCS (LNAI), vol. 4884, pp. 113–129. Springer, Heidelberg (2008)
19. Levene, M., Poulovassilis, A.: Special issue on Web dynamics. Computer Networks 50(10), 1425–1429 (2006)
20. Li, J., Tang, J., Li, Y., Luo, Q.: Rimom: A dynamic multistrategy ontology alignment framework. IEEE Transactions on Knowledge and Data Engineering 21, 1218–1232 (2009)
21. Morgenstern, M.: Active Databases as a Paradigm for Enhanced Computing Environments. In: VLDB, pp. 34–42 (1983)
22. O'Connor, M., Shankar, R., Das, A.: An Ontology-Driven Mediator for Querying Time-Oriented Biomedical Data. In: CBMS 2006: Proceedings of the 19th IEEE Symposium on Computer-Based Medical Systems, Washington, DC, USA, pp. 264–269. IEEE Computer Society, Los Alamitos (2006)
23. Poulovassilis, A., Papamarkos, G., Wood, P.T.: Event-Condition-Action Rule Languages for the Semantic web. In: Grust, T., Höpfner, H., Illarramendi, A., Jablonski, S., Mesiti, M., Müller, S., Patranjan, P.-L., Sattler, K.-U., Spiliopoulou, M., Wijsen, J. (eds.) EDBT 2006. LNCS, vol. 4254, pp. 855–864. Springer, Heidelberg (2006)
24. Ruckhaus, E., Ruiz, E., Vidal, M.: Query Evaluation and Optimization in the Semantic Web. In: TPLP (2008)
25. Tovar, E.L., Vidal, M.-E.: Magic Rewritings for Efficiently Processing Reactivity on Web Ontologies. In: OTM Conferences, vol. (2), pp. 1338–1354 (2008)
26. Xing, W., Corcho, O., Goble, C., Dikaiakos, M.: Active Ontology: An Information Integration Approach for Highly Dynamic Information Sources. In: ESWC (June 2007)

7   Appendix-Proofs

Theorem 1. Let M be the model where only the facts that are $d_1, \ldots, d_m$ and $h_1, \ldots, h_k$ are true, then any valid instantiation $\mu(R_i)$ that satisfies the body of some rule r also satisfies the head of r. Thus, if $r(a_1, \ldots, a_n)$, then the set of constants $(a_1, \ldots, a_n)$ must be in the predicate r of the intensional rules of AIO or the chosen rules of AIO are not a fixed point. But, M is a solution for the predicates of AIO. If there is no other fixed point $M' \subset M$, minimal model M is the minimal model w.r.t. the predicates of AEO.

Theorem 2. Let MM and MM' be two solutions of the fixed points for ADOB, according to *Theorem 1.* Hence, AEO is comprised of a finite number of predicates that describe reactive behavior of any active property ap when event e occurs (*reactiveBehavior(ap, e, p, v, vr)*), then if rules of AIO are computed with the *reactivebehavior* predicates, solution will converge to the unique minimal fixed point because ap only takes the value vr if p has value v, according *reactiveBehavior* predicates express. Then, MM and MM' are the same.

Onto-DIY: A Flexible and Idea Inspiring Ontology-Based Do-It-Yourself Architecture for Managing Data Semantics and Semantic Data

Yan Tang[1], Christophe Debruyne[1], and Johan Criel[2]

[1] Semantic Technology and Application Laboratory, 10G-731,
Department of Computer Science, Faculty of Science and Bioengineering
Vrije Universiteit Brussels, Pleinlaan 2, 1050 Ixelles, Brussels, Belgium
{yan.tang,christophe.debruyne}@vub.ac.be
[2] Alcatel-Lucent Bell Labs (Belgium)
Copernicuslaan 50, B-2018 Antwerpen, Belgium
johan.criel@alcatel-lucent.be

Abstract. The Do-It-Yourself (DIY) culture has been continuously articulated since mid-1920s. The goal of DIY has been gradually shifted from the solution of the "time-rich and money-poor" situation into the confirmation of personal creativities and the needs of outsourcing and social contact. This paper addresses the design of a DIY environment for managing data semantics from different intelligent components in the ITEA Do-It-Yourself Smart Experiences project (DIY-SE). In particular, it is a flexible and idea inspiring ontology-based DIY architecture named Onto-DIY. Including the DIY aspect, Onto-DIY also takes socio and community aspects into account.

Keywords: Ontology Engineering, Do-It-Yourself, Ontology, Ambient Computing, Semantic Decision Table.

1 Introduction and Motivation

The culture of Do-It-Yourself (DIY) can be traced back to the 18th century, when the art handcrafts were proposed as a means of self-expression and helping people to avoid idleness. Recently, the spirit of DIY culture has been reformed with Internet technologies, especially in the IT/ICT domain. This trend initially became visible in DIY content creation and distribution (such as Youtube[1] and Microsoft Photo Story), which is now also emerging in creating applications by providing non professional users accesses to online tools for (DIY) application creation (such as Yahoo! Pipes[2], Zoho creator[3] and Scratch[4]) and hardware assemblage (e.g., Arduino[5]).

---

[1] http://www.youtube.com
[2] http://pipes.yahoo.com
[3] http://creator.zoho.com/
[4] http://www.arduino.cc
[5] http://scratch.mit.edu/

R. Meersman et al. (Eds.): OTM 2010, Part II, LNCS 6427, pp. 1036–1043, 2010.
© Springer-Verlag Berlin Heidelberg 2010

Although these tools lower the barrier for end user creation, they still stay too difficult to use for non technical end users and do not allow them to define and use their own defined semantics. Hence, we propose a flexible and idea inspiring ontology-based architecture (called Onto-DIY), with which end users can manage data semantics for smart objects and services in a ubiquitous network.

The related works are illustrated in [2, 4, 8]. Compared to their approaches, ours tackles the challenges of managing evolving semantics and helping non-technical people to DIY their own applications.

The paper is organized as follows: the design of Onto-DIY will be discussed in section 2. We will pinpoint the problem space by introducing a naughty boy use case. Then, we will discuss three DIY aspects/problems in Onto-DIY and the solutions. Section 3 shows the implementation and some experiments of Onto-DIY. Section 4 covers the conclusion and our future work.

2 Onto-DIY

Onto-DIY allows end users to create their own applications using their own evolving semantics. We identify its challenges as below:

- *Data semantics.* The data used by the ambient components in a ubiquitous network, such as sensors and smart devices/services, need to be meaningful and semantically rich, which allows these components to communicate unambiguously with each other[6].
- *Expertise level of end users.* The DIY aspect is required not only by computer geeks and technicians, but also by non-technical end users. They should have the means to create ambient applications.
- *Inspiring end users with new DIY ideas.* Our architecture needs to support the DIY activities by continuously stirring the ideas of the end users. We consider the end users as the prosumers. They produce ideas, and consume the ideas produced by other people. When people start to share their new DIY solutions, more ideas will be inspired.
- *Evolutionary knowledge base.* The knowledge base contains two parts – an ontology base and the component information databases that are vendor specific. The ontology base needs to be increasingly enriched when new concepts are introduced by end users. When a new component, e.g., a sensor, is plugged in the network, the end users should be able to manage the new incoming sensor data and use it in their own applications.

These challenges are reflected in the Onto-DIY shown in **Fig. 1**. It involves two types of users: the *technical end users* (such as ontology engineers, knowledge engineers, geeks and professional programmers) and the *non-technical* ('ordinary') *end users*. The non-technical users use every day, the shelf smart objects and services, such as Twitter©[7], Nabaztag Bunny©[8], smart cameras, smart phones and screens as shown in

---

[6] It is also called system interoperability.
[7] http://twitter.com/
[8] http://www.nabaztag.com

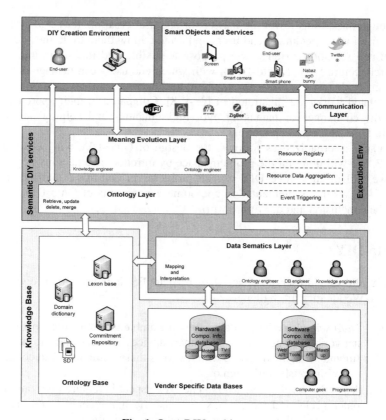

Fig. 1. Onto-DIY architecture

Fig. 1. They are used as the input and outputs of Onto-DIY and can easily be extended with new ones.

The descriptions of the inputs, outputs and new created domain specific ambient applications are stored in the knowledge base, which contains two parts:

- An *ontology base*, which consists of *lexon base* (a lexon is a binary fact type) and *commitment repository* [7] describing domain ontologies that are built from the domain dictionary, taxonomy, business process models and WordNet [5]. It also contains a set of Semantic Decision Tables (SDTs, [9]), which contains user defined semantically rich decision rules.
- Vendor/company specific *data bases* that contain the information of the *hardware, software components* and *services*.

Onto-DIY provides three categories/layers[9] of services that can be used to manipulate the knowledge base:

---

[9] Since the different layers of services are often implemented on separate servers we will the words layer will both words interchangeably in what follows.

- *Ontology layer*, which provides the basic ontological services, such as querying, retrieving, modifying and reasoning from the *ontology base*.
- *Meaning evolution layer* provides the services that allow ontology versioning. They provide the technical users with a flexible, semi-automatic means, and supplies the non-technical users with controlled, user friendly means. It is designed based on a community-driven methodology called Meaning Evolution Support Systems (MESS, [3]).
- *Data semantics layer* deals with mapping and interpreting data from the heterogeneous databases. The data storage for this layer is highly *flexible* because it stores data from various resources, such as sensor data, TV components data or software API information data. This layer allows the heterogeneous databases to be *compliant* to the Semantic Web standards, such as RDF(s) without having to change all the existing ones.

Next to these semantic oriented services, Onto-DIY provides the functionalities that are used during the *execution* of the user created ambient applications. They are, for instance, as resource (sensor, service, and device) discovery, resource connection management and event triggering mechanisms. Since this article focuses on the semantics related to DIY, we will not describe these functionalities in detail.

Naughty Boy Use Case
Mary is a housewife with a one-year old son called James. James has discovered Mary's iPhone and started banging his new toy. Mary decides to install an existing application called "naughty boy protector" from the Onto-DIY app-store.

When James starts banging Mary's phone again, the (Nabaztag) bunny, standing next to his crib, starts speaking loudly with the same intonation as his mother "Do not touch the iPhone, James!" It continues until Mary comes in and lays it flat again.

Initially, the technicians build a few software and hardware pieces. There are preinstalled ontologies (version 1.0, created by domain experts, knowledge engineers and ontology engineers), databases and condition/action rules (including ontological commitments, SDTs and rules stored/implemented in the smart objects).

One day, James starts realizing that shaking the iPhone always triggers the bunny and an angry mother. So he decides to smash the bunny. Onto-DIY gets the messages from the bunny, such as, its ears are continuously moved with force, or its switch button is tapped very rapidly. Unfortunately, the existing ubiquitous network does not know how to react. In the next subsection, we will describe how Mary can create an application (DIY her own solution) in order to react on the new situation.

After Mary will create her own application successfully, her new solution will be automatically uploaded to the community portal of Onto-DIY. New DIY ideas and concepts are shared and can now be used by other people as parts for implementing their new DIY ideas or just as an inspiration.

DIY Aspects
Before the DIY evolution process starts, the domain experts and knowledge engineers need to create the ontology of version 1.0 (the initial version) from existing legacy databases, structural data files, domain taxonomy and domain dictionaries.

The DIY process starts with the end users' *needs* of *extending* this initial group of hardware/software pieces, when the existing ubiquitous network does not contain the new functions that the users want. It may be triggered by at least one of the following requirements.

1: Mary wants to use concepts in her applications that are not defined yet in the *ontology server*.
2: Mary wants to define *rules* using her new concepts.
3: The *data semantics server* cannot find proper maps for the data information of the objects.

DIY solution to Requirement 1 – concepts are not defined
We use the *meaning evolution server* (in **Fig. 1**) to assist users with a community-based means to gradually enrich the domain ontologies. This problem can be solved by applying the methodology illustrated in [3].

DIY Solution to Requirement 2 – decision rules are not defined
The semantically rich decision rules in Onto-DIY are stored as SDTs.

Table 1. A semantic decision table that decides the actions from the smart screen and iPhone based on the conditions of bunny ear and baby crib

Condition		1	2	3	4
People move Ear		Yes	No	Yes	No
Pressure on Crib		Yes	Yes	No	No
Action					
Screen shows Message		Message1			
iPhone rings				RingTone1	
SDT Lexons					
Lexon 1	⟨Bunny, has, is of, Ear⟩				
Lexon 2	⟨Bunny, has, is of, Name⟩				
Lexon 3	⟨Ear, is moved by, move, People⟩				
Lexon 4	⟨Crib, has, is of, Name⟩				
Lexon 5	⟨Screen, shows, is shown by, Message⟩				
Lexon 6	⟨iPhone, rings with, is rang with by, RingTone⟩				
SDT Commitments					
Commitment 1	EACH Bunny has EXACT ONE name.				
Commitment 2	EACH Crib has EXACT ONE name.				
Commitment 3	EACH Screen shows AT LEAST ONE Message				
Commitment 4	Each iPhone rings with AT LEAST ONE Ring Tone.				
Instantiation of Decision Items					
People move Ear	"People" is James. "Ear" is the ear from the Bunny in the living room.				
Pressure on Crib	"Crib" is James' crib. "Pressure on Crib – Yes" means that James is in his crib.				
Screen shows Messages	"Screen" is the smart screen in the living room.				
iPhone rings	"iPhone" is Mary's iPhone. She has only one iPhone.				

An SDT is a decision table properly annotated with domain ontologies. **Table 1** shows an SDT, which contains a tabular format, SDT lexons, SDT commitments and its instantiation for our use case.

The ontology server communicates with the smart screen and the iPhone in order to execute the actions "Screen shows Message" and "iPhone rings" (**Table 1**), which are preprogrammed in the smart screen and iPhone. The concepts "Ear", "Crib", "Screen" and "iPhone" are defined in the ontologies. If they are not defined, then we can take the DIY solution to Requirement 1.

If the conditions "People move Ear – Yes" and "Pressure on Crib – Yes" are not preprogrammed, then Mary needs to ask for the help from the professional users from a *community*. Someone that is familiar with programming Nabaztag API[10] can provide the software module of "People move Ear – Yes".

iPhone	Ring Tone
iPhone2093113	RingTone1
iPhoneYan23	RingTone25
...	...

Fig. 2. From ontology (left, modeled in Object Role Modeling method [6]) to databases (right)

Message1 and RingTone1 in Table 1 are the instances that are stored in the data tables *Message* and *Ring Tone* in the database. Fig. 2 shows a data table, the schema of which is derived from the commitment "Each iPhone rings with AT LEAST ONE Ring Tone". It is where the instances of "Ring Tone" and "iPhone" are stored.

Note that every decision item in an SDT has its meaning, which is not only defined in the ontology (SDT lexons and SDT commitments in Table 1), but also in natural language (see "Instantiation of Decision Items" in Table 1). These user-friendly texts are provided to the users for helping their DIY activities.

DIY solution to Requirement 3 – data semantics is not defined
Every smart object/service in Onto-DIY is an instance of a type. Properly assigned instances are the premise of correctly firing a decision rule in an SDT.

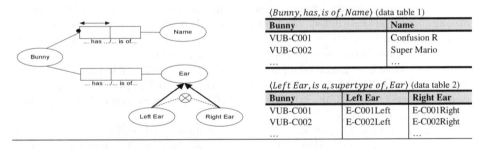

⟨*Bunny, has, is of, Name*⟩ (data table 1)

Bunny	Name
VUB-C001	Confusion R
VUB-C002	Super Mario
...	...

⟨*Left Ear, is a, supertype of, Ear*⟩ (data table 2)

Bunny	Left Ear	Right Ear
VUB-C001	E-C001Left	E-C001Right
VUB-C002	E-C002Left	E-C002Right
...		...

Fig. 3. From ontology (left) to databases (right)

Table 2. Semantic data mapping table (Message1 and RingTone1 are already instances)

SDT item	Concept in the SDT item	Mapped instance
People move Ear	Ear	VUB-C001Right
Pressure on Crib	Crib	Crib-XYZ
Screen shows Message	Screen	MAR-X-C12
Message1	Message	Message1
RingTone1	Ring Tone	RingTone1
iPhone rings	iPhone	iPhone2093113

---

[10] http://doc.nabaztag.com/api/home.html

When a user introduces new concept "Ear" and assigns proper constraints (e.g., Each Bunny has and only has 2 Ears), Onto-DIY will automatically update the existing database schemas that are illustrated in Fig. 3.

Then, the user needs to retrieve the information of the bunny ears by querying the bunny using the existing APIs (e.g. the tag of the right ear of bunny "VUB-C001" is "VUB-C001Right"). Afterwards, Onto-DIY tool set will help the user to insert new data to the new data table (see data table 2 in Fig. 3).

When Mary wants to use a new SDT, he needs to specify the firing events by linking the SDT with the instances in the databases. Take Table 1 as an example, Table 2 is the possible mapping between the decision items and the instances.

All the instances (that refer to the smart pieces like chips and sensors) from Table 2 are installed by sensor engineers/technicians. If Mary needs more instances, she will have to ask for the help from these professional people.

3   Implementation and Experiments

Smart objects and services are often developed autonomously and therefore have heterogeneous data representations within their own systems and applications.

The Onto-DIY server needs to know the communication data formats from the smart objects/services. For instance, the data format of obtaining data by querying the position of the Nabaztag's ears and the desired format (used by the SDT engine on the Onto-DIY server). We use Ω-RIDL [10] as the mapping language.

Users design and instantiate the decision rules with an SDT editor, the construction method of which can be found in [9].

When the smart bunny listener, which resides at the communication layer, gets a message from the shelf bunny, the SDT engine will process the rules, take the appropriate actions and pass the output actions to the appropriate smart object listener (e.g., an iPhone listener in our example) at the communication layer.

The tests have been executed on an Apple Mac Book with 2 GHz Intel Core 2 Duo, 2 GB 1067 MHz DDR3 memory, Mac OS X version 10.5.8. Both client and server were developed in Java JDK 5.0 and the Ω-RIDL engine was wrapped around a Web service hosted on a JBoss 5.1.0.GA application server.

The average time for performing a transformation is 15 milliseconds for 5 concepts. Currently, we are working on several other evaluations. The first one is to evaluate the quality of lifted concepts in the domain ontologies. The second one refers to the usability test of Onto-DIY, which is to evaluate how easy it is to help end users to DIY his/her smart environment.

4   Conclusion and Future Work

In this paper, we have discussed the Onto-DIY architecture, which helps users to DIY their own applications using the *evolving semantics* defined by themselves. With Onto-DIY, we can manage data semantics for smart objects and services in a ubiquitous network. *Flexible* means of building *personal semantics* are the first point that we want to make in this paper.

The second point is how we can involve both *professional* and *non-professional* end users in the DIY cycle. The former helps to provide technical supports. The latter generates the requirements of extending the applications of an existing system.

Onto-DIY helps users to continuously *inspire new DIY ideas* by showing the use cases (e.g., the naughty boy use case), existing solutions (e.g., how a case can be solved) and building blocks (e.g., the conditions and actions in an SDT), which is the third point in the paper. This paper shows an initial idea of using meaning evolution support systems for Onto-DIY and a simple algorithm. In the future, we will focus on an advanced algorithm including how to derive fact types from implicit information and explicit information in the databases. We will also continue the ongoing evaluations that have been listed in the previous section.

Acknowledgments. The work has been supported by the EU ITEA-2 Project 2008005 "Do-it-Yourself Smart Experiences", founded by IWT 459.

References

1. Brewster, C., Wilks, Y.: Ontologies, taxonomies, thesauri learning from texts. In: The Keyword Project: Unlocking Content through Computational Linguistics, Kings College, London, February 5-6 (2004)
2. Chen, H., Fenin, T., Joshi, A.: Semantic Web in Context Broker Architecture. Paper Presented at the Second IEEE International Conference on Pervasive Computing and Communications (Percom 2004), Washington, DC (2004)
3. de Moor, A., De Leenheer, P., Meersman, R.: DOGMA-MESS: A Meaning Evolution Support System for Interorganizational Ontology Engineering. In: Schärfe, H., Hitzler, P., Øhrstrøm, P. (eds.) ICCS 2006. LNCS (LNAI), vol. 4068, pp. 189–203. Springer, Heidelberg (2006)
4. Dey, A.K.: Providing architectural support for building context aware applications. Doctoral dissertation, College of Computing, Georgia Institute of Technology (2000)
5. Fellbaum, C.: WordNet: an electronic lexical database (Language, Speech, and Communication). MIT Press, Cambridge (1998) ISBN-10:026206197X, ISBN-13: 978-0262061971
6. Halpin, T.A.: Information Modeling and Relational Databases: From Conceptual Analysis to Logical Design. Morgan Kaufman Publishers, San Francisco (2001)
7. Spyns, P., Meersman, R., Jarrar, M.: Data Modeling versus Ontology Engineering. SIGMOD Record: Special Issue on Semantic Web and Data Management 31(4), 12–17 (2002)
8. Strobbe, M., Hollez, J., De Jans, G., Van Laere, O., Nelis, J., De Turck, F., Dhoedt, B., Demeester, P., Janssens, N., Pollet, T.: Design of CASP: An open enabling platform for context aware office and city services. Paper Presented at the 4th International Workshop on Managing Ubiquitous Communications and Services, Munich, Germany (2007)
9. Tang, Y., Meersman, R.: On constructing semantic decision tables. In: Wagner, R., Revell, N., Pernul, G. (eds.) DEXA 2007. LNCS, vol. 4653, pp. 34–44. Springer, Heidelberg (2007)
10. Trog, D., Tang, Y., Meersman, R.: Towards Ontological Commitments with Ω- RIDL Markup Language. In: Paschke, A., Biletskiy, Y. (eds.) RuleML 2007. LNCS, vol. 4824, pp. 92–106. Springer, Heidelberg (2007)

Save Up to 99% of Your Time in Mapping Validation*

Vincenzo Maltese, Fausto Giunchiglia, and Aliaksandr Autayeu

DISI - Università di Trento, Trento, Italy
{fausto,maltese,autayeu}@disi.unitn.it

Abstract. Identifying semantic correspondences between different vocabularies has been recognized as a fundamental step towards achieving interoperability. Several manual and automatic techniques have been recently proposed. Fully manual approaches are very precise, but extremely costly. Conversely, automatic approaches tend to fail when domain specific background knowledge is needed. Consequently, they typically require a manual validation step. Yet, when the number of computed correspondences is very large, the validation phase can be very expensive. In order to reduce the problems above, we propose to compute the minimal set of correspondences, that we call the minimal mapping, which are sufficient to compute all the other ones. We show that by concentrating on such correspondences we can save up to 99% of the manual checks required for validation.

Keywords: Interoperability, minimal mappings, mapping validation.

1 Introduction

Establishing semantic correspondences between different vocabularies is a fundamental step towards achieving interoperability among them [12]. In the recent years, several manual and semi-automatic approaches have been proposed. For instance, we can mention projects such as CARMEN[1], Renardus [15], Interconcept [12] and other similar initiatives mainly focusing on LCSH [16, 17, 18] and DDC [19].

Manual approaches clearly produce better quality results, but hardly scale in case of very large Knowledge Organization Systems, such as LCSH and DDC. On the other hand, automatic procedures can be very effective, but tend to fail when domain specific background knowledge is needed [3, 20]. Nevertheless, semantic matching techniques are nowadays considered a fundamental practice in many applications and many automatic tools are offered. A good survey is represented by [1].

Despite the progress on this topic, a lot of work still has to be done [13]. A recent study [6] has underlined that current matching tools offer poor support to users for the process of creation, validation and maintenance of the correspondences. In fact, given two schemas in input, most of the tools limit their support to the suggestion of an initial set of correspondences, called mapping or alignment, which is automatically computed by the system. In addition, when a graphical interface is provided, it typically has

---

* This paper is a variation of the paper [4] presented at the non-archival 4th Ontology Matching Workshop 2009.

[1] http://www.bibliothek.uni-regensburg.de/projects/carmen12/index.html

R. Meersman et al. (Eds.): OTM 2010, Part II, LNCS 6427, pp. 1044–1060, 2010.
© Springer-Verlag Berlin Heidelberg 2010

scalability problems as the number of nodes and correspondences grows [5]. It is rather difficult to visualize even a single ontology. Current visualization tools do not scale to more than 10,000 nodes, and only a few systems support more than 1,000 nodes [8]. The problem becomes even more challenging with matching, because it is necessary to visualize two ontologies, called the source and target ontologies, and the (potentially very big) set of semantic correspondences between them. The number of potential correspondences grows quadratically in the size of the ontologies, e.g. two ontologies with 10^3 nodes may have up to 10^6 correspondences. As a consequence, handling them turns out to be a very complex, slow and error prone task.

In this paper we present MinSMatch[2], a semantic matching tool that takes two lightweight ontologies [2], and computes the minimal mapping between them. The minimal mapping is that minimal subset of correspondences such that all the others can be efficiently computed from them, and are therefore said to be redundant. At the best of our knowledge no other tools directly compute minimal mappings. In [23, 24, 25] the authors use Distributed Description Logics (DDL) [26] to represent and reason about existing ontology mappings. They introduce a few debugging heuristics to remove correspondences which are redundant or generate inconsistencies in a given mapping [24]. However, the main problem of this approach is the complexity of DDL reasoning [25]. Our experiments demonstrate a substantial improvement both in runtime and total number of discovered correspondences w.r.t. similar matching tools. They also show that the number of correspondences in the minimal mapping is typically a very small portion of the overall set of correspondences between the two ontologies, up to 99% smaller [12]. Therefore, minimal mappings have clear advantages in visualization and user interaction. As we explain in this paper, this is particularly important to reduce the effort in mapping validation. Being aware that the matching process cannot be completely automated and leveraging on the properties of minimal mappings, we propose the specification for a new tool to interactively assist the user in the process of mapping creation and validation.

The rest of the paper is organized as follows. In section 2 we analyze the weaknesses of the current tools which intend to support mapping creation, validation and maintenance. In section 3 we present the notion of minimal mapping. In section 4 we present the MinSMatch algorithm. In section 5 we provide a detailed description of the user interaction issues in the mapping validation phase. Evaluation results are given in section 6. The last section concludes the paper by drawing some conclusions and outlining future directions.

2   Limitations of Current Matching Tools

Many automatic tools are currently available which identify the set of semantic correspondences between two different schemas [1]. However, as underlined in [13] there are still several challenges to address. In this section we focus on the problems for which we provide a substantial improvement:

- **Low performance.** Identifying semantic correspondences is a computational expensive task. In fact, tools leveraging on semantics, including MinSMatch, typically require logical reasoning support that can amount to exponential

---

[2] A more detailed description of MinSMatch can be found in [4]. MinSMatch is part of the semantic matching open source suite available at `http://semanticmatching.org/`

computation in the worst case [22]. It is therefore fundamental to develop techniques that limit as much as possible the calls to logical reasoners.

- **Lack of background knowledge.** Automatic tools tend to fail when domain specific background knowledge is needed [3, 20]. Experiments show that results are very precise when syntactic techniques (e.g. string comparison) are used, while recall rapidly degrades when semantic comparison is needed.

- **Lack of support for validation.** The problem of finding semantic correspondences between two schemas cannot be completely automated [12]. Thus, it is fundamental to provide a tool which assists the user in the task of creating, validating and maintaining a mapping in time. This should be done taking into account the interaction of the user with the current, incomplete and transitory set of established correspondences. Most of the tools currently available provide an initial set of automatically created correspondences. Unfortunately, none of them, including those offering a graphical user interface, provide an effective support for validation and maintenance [6].

- **Inadequate interaction.** Current tools are cognitively demanding. They tend to show information which is irrelevant for the decisions to take. To reduce the cognitive load, the tool should reduce the number of items that the user must at each step internally (i.e. in memory) track and process, allowing the user to concentrate on important parts of the task [6]. This can be achieved by focusing on the relevant parts of the two schemas [7], namely the subset of objects which have to be considered to take a decision. Examples of objects which influence a decision are node labels, contextual information (i.e. the path from the root to the node) and domain knowledge.

- **Scalability.** Current tools hardly scale in the number of nodes and links. Minimizing the amount of information to visualize is the only viable way to solve scalability problems. In fact, as described in [8], no tool designed to visualize ontologies scales up to 10,000 nodes. Many of them have rendering problems and object overlap (in terms of node labels and links between the nodes).

3 Minimal Mappings

Semantic matching techniques establish a set of semantic correspondences between the nodes of two vocabularies (e.g. thesauri, classifications, formal ontologies). This set is called mapping or alignment. We suggest the adoption of MinSMatch. It produces the minimal mapping between two tree-like structures that are beforehand translated into lightweight ontologies.

3.1 Lightweight Ontologies

There are different kinds of ontologies, according to the degree of formality and expressivity of the language used to describe them [10]. MinSMatch works on lightweight ontologies [2]. They are tree-like formal ontologies in which nodes are connected through subsumption in classification semantics [11]. This means that the extension of each concept is the set of documents about the label of the node and the arcs between nodes represent subset relations. For instance, the extension of the concept "animal" is the set of documents about real world animals. Note that this is the semantics implicitly used in libraries. Many types of commonly used ontologies (such as on-line catalogs, file systems, web directories and library classifications) can be translated into lightweight ontologies. For instance, [12] describes how this can be done for LCSH and NALT. Each node label is translated into a logic formula representing the meaning of the node taking into account its context, i.e. the path from the root to the node. Each atomic concept appearing in the formulas is taken from a controlled vocabulary, such as WordNet. A formal definition of lightweight ontology can be found in [4], while further information about the translation procedure can be found in [2]. Fig. 1 shows an example taken from [12]. It shows two classifications that are translated into lightweight ontologies following the procedure described in [2]. Natural language labels are shown in bold. Each formula is reported under the corresponding label. Each atomic concept (e.g. water#6) is represented by a string followed by a number representing the sense taken from a WordNet synset.

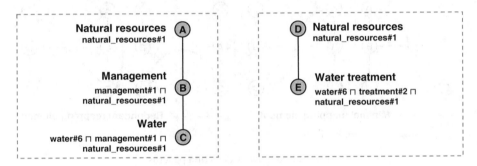

Fig. 1. Two lightweight ontologies

3.2 Minimal and Redundant Mappings

MinSMatch computes a set of semantic correspondences, called mapping elements, between two lightweight ontologies. A **_mapping element_** is defined as follows:

Definition 1 (Mapping element). Given two lightweight ontologies O_1 and O_2, a mapping element m between them is a triple $<n_1, n_2, R>$, where:

  a) $n_1 \in N_1$ is a node in O_1, called the source node;

  b) $n_2 \in N_2$ is a node in O_2, called the target node;

  c) $R \in \{\perp, \equiv, \sqsubseteq, \sqsupseteq\}$ is the strongest semantic relation holding between n_1 and n_2.

The strength of a semantic relation is established according to the partial order where disjointness precedes equivalence and more and less specific are unordered and follow equivalence. Under this ordering, MinSMatch always computes the strongest semantic relation holding between two nodes. In particular, it computes the **_minimal mapping_**, i.e. the minimal subset of mapping elements between the two ontologies such that all the others can be efficiently computed from them, and are therefore said to be redundant. The fundamental idea is that a mapping element _m'_ is redundant w.r.t. another mapping element *m* if the existence of *m'* can be asserted simply by looking at the positions of its nodes w.r.t. the nodes of *m* in their respective ontologies. The four redundancy patterns in Fig. 2, one for each semantic relation, cover all possible cases. A proof is given in [4]. The blue dashed elements are redundant w.r.t. the solid blue ones. The red solid curves show how a semantic relation propagates.

For instance, in pattern (1), the element <C, D, ⊑> is redundant w.r.t. <A, B, ⊑>. In fact, the chain of subsumptions C ⊑ A ⊑ B ⊑ D holds[3] and therefore by transitivity we can conclude that C ⊑ D. Notice that this still holds in case we substitute A ⊑ B with A ≡ B. Taking any two paths in the two ontologies, a minimal subsumption mapping element is an element with the highest node in one path whose formula is subsumed by the formula of the lowest node in the other path.

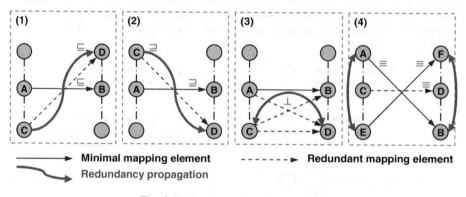

Fig. 2. Redundancy detection patterns

This can be codified in the following redundancy condition:

Definition 2 (Redundant mapping element). Given two lightweight ontologies O_1 and O_2, a mapping M and a mapping element m'∈ M with m' = <C, D, R'> between them, we say that m' is redundant in M iff one of the following holds:

(1) If R' is ⊑, ∃m∈ M with m = <A, B, R> and m ≠ m' such that R ∈ {⊑, ≡}, A ∈ path(C) and D ∈ path(B);

(2) If R' is ⊒, ∃m∈ M with m = <A, B, R> and m ≠ m' such that R ∈ {⊒, ≡}, C ∈ path(A) and B ∈ path(D);

(3) If R' is ⊥, ∃m∈ M with m = <A, B, ⊥> and m ≠ m' such that A ∈ path(C) and B ∈ path(D);

(4) If R' is ≡, conditions (1) and (2) must be satisfied.

Here path(n) is the path from the root to the node n. Note that we enforce *m ≠ m'* to exclude the trivial situation in which a mapping element is compared with itself. We prove in [4] that it captures all and only the cases of logical redundancy (of a mapping element w.r.t. another one). This definition allows abstracting from logical inference to computing the redundant elements just by looking at the positions of the nodes in

---

[3] This is because nodes in lightweight ontologies are connected through subsumption relations.

the two trees. The notion of redundancy given above is fundamental to minimize the amount of calls to the logical reasoners and to reduce the problem of lack of background knowledge. Given a mapping element $m = <A, B, \sqsupseteq>$, by looking for instance at pattern (2) in Fig. 2, we can observe that it is not necessary to compute the semantic relation holding between A and any descendant C in the sub-tree of B since we know in advance that it is $\sqsupseteq$. The minimal mapping is then defined as follows:

Definition 3 (Minimal mapping). Given two lightweight ontologies O_1 and O_2, we say that a mapping M between them is minimal iff:

a) $\nexists m \in M$ such that m is redundant (minimality condition);

b) $\nexists M' \supset M$ satisfying condition a) above (maximality condition).

A mapping element is minimal if it belongs to the minimal mapping.

Note that the conditions (a) and (b) ensure that the minimal set is the set of maximum size with no redundant elements. We also prove that for any two given lightweight ontologies, the minimal mapping always exists and it is unique [4].

Minimal mappings provide clear usability advantages. Consider the example in Fig. 3 taken from [12]. It provides the minimal mapping (the solid arrows) and the maximum number of mapping elements, that we call the ***mapping of maximum size***, between the two lightweight ontologies given in Fig. 1. Note that only the two solid ones are minimal, because all the others (the dashed ones) can be entailed from them. For instance, $A \sqsupseteq E$ follows from $A \sqsupseteq D$ for pattern (2). As we will show, the validation phase can be faster if we concentrate on the minimal mapping. The key intuition is that, if the user accepts as correct an element which is in the minimal set then all the inferred ones will be automatically validated as correct.

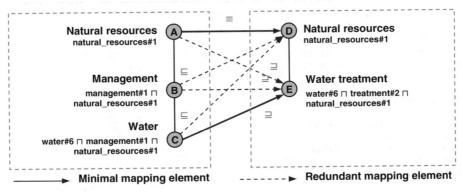

Fig. 3. The minimal and redundant mapping between two lightweight ontologies

4   The MinSMatch Algorithm

At the top level the algorithm is organized as follows:

- **Step 1, computing the minimal mapping modulo equivalence:** compute the set of disjointness and subsumption mapping elements which are *minimal* *modulo equivalence*. By this we mean that they are minimal modulo collapsing, whenever possible, two subsumption relations of opposite direction into a single equivalence mapping element;

- **Step 2, computing the minimal mapping:** collapse all the pairs of subsumption elements (of opposite direction) between the same two nodes into a single equivalence element. This will result in the *minimal mapping*;
- **Step 3, computing the mapping of maximum size:** Compute the mapping of maximum size (including minimal and redundant mapping elements). During this step the existence of a (redundant) element is computed as the result of the propagation of the elements in the minimal mapping.

The first two steps are performed at matching time, while the third is activated on user request. The following three subsections analyze the three steps above in detail.

4.1   Step 1: Computing the Minimal Mapping Modulo Equivalence

The minimal mapping is computed by a function **TreeMatch** whose pseudo-code is described in Fig. 4. M is the minimal set while T1 and T2 are the input lightweight ontologies. **TreeMatch** is called on the root nodes of T1 and T2. It is crucially dependent on the node matching functions **NodeDisjoint** (Fig. 5) and **NodeSubsumedBy** (Fig. 6) which take two nodes n1 and n2 and return a positive answer in case of disjointness or subsumption, or a negative answer if it is not the case or they are not able to establish it. Notice that these two functions hide the heaviest computational costs; in particular their computation time is exponential when the relation holds and, exponential in the worst case, but possibly much faster, when the relation does not hold. The main motivation for this is that the node matching problem should be translated into disjointness or subsumption problem in propositional DL.

```
10   node: struct of {cnode: wff; children: node[];}
20   T1,T2: tree of (node);

30   relation in {⊑, ⊒, ≡, ⊥};
40   element: struct of {source: node; target: node; rel: relation;};
50   M: list of (element);
60   boolean direction;

70   function TreeMatch(tree T1, tree T2)
80     {TreeDisjoint(root(T1),root(T2));
90      direction := true;
100     TreeSubsumedBy(root(T1),root(T2));
110     direction := false;
120     TreeSubsumedBy(root(T2),root(T1));
130     TreeEquiv();
140   };
```

Fig. 4. Pseudo-code for the tree matching function

The goal, therefore, is to compute the minimal mapping by minimizing the calls to the node matching functions and, in particular minimizing the calls where the relation will turn out to hold. We achieve this purpose by processing both trees top down. To maximize the performance of the system, **TreeMatch** has therefore been built as the sequence of three function calls: the first call to **TreeDisjoint** (line 80) computes the minimal set of disjointness mapping elements, while the second and the third call to **TreeSubsumedBy** compute the minimal set of subsumption mapping elements in the two directions modulo equivalence (lines 90-120). Notice that in the second call, **TreeSubsumedBy** is called with the input ontologies with swapped roles. These three calls correspond to Step 1 above. Line 130 in the pseudo code of **TreeMatch** implements Step 2 and it will be described in the next subsection.

TreeDisjoint (Fig. 5) is a recursive function which finds all disjointness minimal elements between the two sub-trees rooted in n1 and n2. Following the definition of redundancy, it basically searches for the first disjointness element along any pair of paths in the two input trees. Exploiting the nested recursion of **NodeTreeDisjoint** inside **TreeDisjoint**, for any node n1 in T1 (traversed top down, depth first) **NodeTreeDisjoint** visits all of T2, again top down, depth first. **NodeTreeDisjoint** (called at line 30, starting at line 60) keeps fixed the source node n1 and iterates on the whole target sub-tree below n2 till, for each path, the highest disjointness element, if any, is found. Any such disjoint element is added only if minimal (lines 90-120). The condition at line 80 is necessary and sufficient for redundancy. The idea here is to exploit the fact that any two nodes below two nodes involved in a disjointness mapping element are part of a redundant element and, therefore, to stop the recursion thus saving a lot of time expensive calls (n*m calls with n and m the number of the nodes in the two trees). Notice that this check needs to be performed on the full path. **NodeDisjoint** checks whether the formula obtained by the conjunction of the formulas associated to the nodes n1 and n2 is unsatisfiable (lines 150-170).

```
10   function TreeDisjoint(node n1, node n2)
20   {c1: node;
30    NodeTreeDisjoint(n1, n2);
40    foreach c1 in GetChildren(n1) do TreeDisjoint(c1,n2);
50   };

60   function NodeTreeDisjoint(node n1, node n2)
70   {n,c2: node;
80    foreach n in Path(Parent(n1)) do if (<n,n2,⊥> ∈ M) then return;
90    if (NodeDisjoint(n1, n2)) then
100       {AddMappingElement(<n1,n2,⊥>);
110        return;
120       };
130    foreach c2 in GetChildren(n2) do NodeTreeDisjoint(n1,c2);
140   };

150  function boolean NodeDisjoint(node n1, node n2)
160  {if (Unsatisfiable(mkConjunction(n1.cnode,n2.cnode))) then
            return true;
170   else return false; };
```

Fig. 5. Pseudo-code for the **TreeDisjoint** function

TreeSubsumedBy (Fig. 6) recursively finds all minimal mapping elements where the strongest relation between the nodes is ⊑ (or dually, ⊒ in the second call; in the following we will concentrate only on the first call).

```
10   function boolean TreeSubsumedBy(node n1, node n2)
20   {c1,c2: node; LastNodeFound: boolean;
30     if (<n1,n2,⊥> ∈ M) then return false;
40     if (!NodeSubsumedBy(n1, n2)) then
50       foreach c1 in GetChildren(n1) do TreeSubsumedBy(c1,n2);
60     else
70       {LastNodeFound := false;
80        foreach c2 in GetChildren(n2) do
90           if (TreeSubsumedBy(n1,c2)) then LastNodeFound := true;
100       if (!LastNodeFound) then AddSubsumptionMappingElement(n1,n2);
120       return true;
140      };
150    return false;
160  };

170 function boolean NodeSubsumedBy(node n1, node n2)
180 {if (Unsatisfiable(mkConjunction(n1.cnode,negate(n2.cnode)))) then
       return true;
190   else return false; };

200 function AddSubsumptionMappingElement(node n1, node n2)
210 {if (direction) then AddMappingElement(<n1,n2,⊑>);
220   else AddMappingElement(<n2,n1,⊒>); };
```

Fig. 6. Pseudo-code for the **TreeSubsumedBy** function

Notice that **TreeSubsumedBy** assumes that the minimal disjointness elements are already computed; thus, at line 30 it checks whether the mapping element between the nodes n1 and n2 is already in the minimal set. If this is the case it stops the recursion. This allows computing the stronger disjointness relation rather than subsumption when both hold (namely with an inconsistent node). Given n2, lines 40-50 implement a depth first recursion in the first tree till a subsumption is found. The test for subsumption is performed by **NodeSubsumedBy** that checks whether the formula obtained by the conjunction of the formulas associated to the node n1 and the negation of the formula for n2 is unsatisfiable (lines 170-190). Lines 60-140 implement what happens after the first subsumption is found. The key idea is that, after finding the first subsumption, **TreeSubsumedBy** keeps recursing down the second tree till it finds the last subsumption. When this happens, the resulting mapping element is added to the minimal mapping (line 100). Notice that both **NodeDisjoint** and **NodeSubsumedBy** call the function **Unsatisfiable** which embeds a call to a SAT solver.

To fully understand **TreeSubsumedBy,** the reader should check what happens in the four situations in Fig. 7. In case (a) the first iteration of the TreeSubsumedBy finds a subsumption between A and C. Since C has no children, it skips lines 80-90 and directly adds the mapping element <A, C, ⊑> to the minimal set (line 100). In case (b), since there is a child D of C the algorithm iterates on the pair A-D (lines 80-90) finding a subsumption between them. Since there are no other nodes under D, it adds the mapping element <A, D, ⊑> to the minimal set and returns true. Therefore LastNodeFound is set to true (line 90) and the mapping element between the pair A-C is recognized as redundant. Case (c) is similar. The difference is that **TreeSubsumedBy** will return false when checking the pair A-D (line 30), thanks to previous computation of minimal disjointness mapping elements, and therefore the mapping element <A, C, ⊑> is recognized as minimal. In case (d) the algorithm iterates after the second subsumption mapping element is identified. It first checks the pair A-C and iterates on A-D concluding that subsumption does not hold between them (line 40). Therefore, it recursively calls TreeSubsumedBy between B and D. In fact, since <A, C, ⊑> will be recognized as minimal, it is not worth checking <B, C, ⊑> for pattern (1). As a consequence <B, D, ⊑> is recognized as minimal together with <A, C, ⊑>.

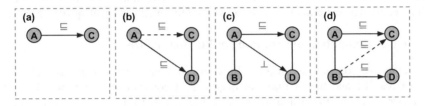

Fig. 7. Examples of applications of the **TreeSubsumedBy**

Five observations. The first is that, even if, overall, **TreeMatch** implements three loops instead of one, the wasted (linear) time is largely counterbalanced by the exponential time saved by avoiding a lot of useless calls to the SAT solver. The second is that, when the input trees T1 and T2 are two nodes, **TreeMatch** behaves as a node matching function which returns the semantic relation holding between the input nodes. The third is that the call to **TreeDisjoint** before the two calls to **TreeSubsumedBy** allows us to implement the partial order on relations defined in the previous section. In particular it allows returning only a disjointness mapping element when both disjointness and subsumption hold (see Definition 2 of mapping). The fourth is that, in the body of **TreeDisjoint**, the fact that the two sub-trees where disjointness holds are skipped is what allows not only implementing the partial order (see the previous observation) but also saving a lot of useless calls to the node matching functions (line 2). The fifth and last observation is that the implementation of **TreeMatch** crucially depends on the fact that the minimal elements of the two directions of subsumption and disjointness can be computed independently (modulo inconsistencies).

4.2 Step 2: Computing the Minimal Mapping

The output of Step 1 is the set of all disjointness and subsumption mapping elements which are minimal modulo equivalence. The final step towards computing the minimal mapping is that of collapsing any two subsumption relations, in the two directions, holding between the same two nodes into a single equivalence relation. The tricky part here is that equivalence is in the minimal set only if both subsumptions are in the minimal set. We have three possible situations:

1. None of the two subsumptions is minimal (in the sense that it has not been computed as minimal in Step 1): nothing changes and neither subsumption nor equivalence is memorized as minimal;
2. Only one of the two subsumptions is minimal while the other is not minimal (again according to Step 1): this case is solved by keeping only the subsumption

mapping as minimal. Of course, during Step 3 (see below) the necessary computations will have to be done in order to show to the user the existence of an equivalence relation between the two nodes;

3. Both subsumptions are minimal (from Step 1): in this case the two subsumptions can be deleted and substituted with a single equivalence element.

Notice that Step 3 can be computed very easily in time linear with the number of mapping elements output of Step 1: it is sufficient to check for all the subsumption elements of opposite direction between the same two nodes and to substitute them with an equivalence element. This is performed by function **TreeEquiv** in Fig. 4.

4.3 Step 3: Computing the Mapping of Maximum Size

For brevity we concentrate on the following problem: given two lightweight ontologies T1 and T2 and the of minimal mapping M compute the mapping element between two nodes n1 in T1 and n2 in T2 or the fact that no element can be computed given the current available background knowledge. Pseudo-code is given in Fig. 8.

```
10 function mapping ComputeMappingElement(node n1, node n2)
20 {isLG, isMG: boolean;
30   if ((<n1,n2,⊥> ∈ M) || IsRedundant(<n1,n2,⊥>)) then return <n1,n2,⊥>;
40   if (<n1,n2,≡> ∈ M) then return <n1,n2,≡>;
50   if ((<n1,n2,⊑> ∈ M) || IsRedundant(<n1,n2,⊑>)) then isLG := true;
60   if ((<n1,n2,⊒> ∈ M) || IsRedundant(<n1,n2,⊒>)) then isMG := true;
70   if (isLG && isMG) then return <n1,n2,≡>;
80   if (isLG) then return <n1,n2,⊑>;
90   if (isMG) then return <n1,n2,⊒>;
100  return NULL;
110 };

120 function boolean IsRedundant(mapping <n1,n2,R>)
130   {switch (R)
140     {case ⊑: if (VerifyCondition1(n1,n2)) then return true; break;
150      case ⊒: if (VerifyCondition2(n1,n2)) then return true; break;
160      case ⊥: if (VerifyCondition3(n1,n2)) then return true; break;
170      case ≡: if (VerifyCondition1(n1,n2) &&
                    VerifyCondition2(n1,n2)) then return true;
180     };
190    return false;
200 };

210 function boolean VerifyCondition1(node n1, node n2)
220   {c1,c2: node;
230    foreach c1 in Path(n1) do
240      foreach c2 in SubTree(n2) do
250         if ((<c1,c2,⊑> ∈ M) || (<c1,c2,≡> ∈ M)) then return true;
260    return false;
270 };
```

Fig. 8. Pseudo-code to compute a mapping element

ComputeMappingElement is structurally very similar to the NodeMatch function described in [27], modulo the key difference that no calls to SAT are needed. **ComputeMappingElement** always returns the strongest mapping element. The test for redundancy performed by **IsRedundant** reflects the definition of redundancy provided in Section 3 above. For lack of space, we provide below only the code which does the check for the first pattern; the others are analogous. Given for example a mapping element $<n1, n2, \sqsubseteq>$, condition 1 is verified by checking whether in M there is an element $<c1, c2, \sqsubseteq>$ or $<c1, c2, \equiv>$ with c1 ancestor of n1 and c2 descendant of n2. Notice that **ComputeMappingElement** calls **IsRedundant** at most three times and, therefore, its computation time is linear with the number of mapping elements in M.

5   Mapping Validation

Validating means taking a decision about the correctness of the correspondences suggested by the system [6]. We say that the user positively validates a correspondence, or simply accepts it, if he accepts it as correct, while we say that the user negatively validates a correspondence, or simply rejects it, if he does not accept it as correct. Both rejected and accepted correspondences have to be marked to record the decision. We use MinSMatch to compute the initial minimal mapping. Focusing on the elements in this set minimizes the work load of the user. In fact, they represent the minimum amount of information which has to be validated as it consequently results in the validation of the rest of the (redundant) elements.

5.1   Validation Sequence

The system has to suggest step by step the order of correspondences to be validated. In particular, this order must follow the partial order over the mapping elements defined in [4]. As also described in [12], the intuition is that if an element m is judged as correct during validation, all mapping elements derived by m are consequently correct. Conversely, if m is judged as incorrect we need to include in the minimal set the maximal elements from the set of mapping elements derived by m, that we call the sub-minimal elements of m, and ask the user to validate them.

For instance, for the mapping in Fig. 3, in the case $<A, D, \equiv>$ is rejected, we need to validate the maximal elements in the set $\{<A, E, \sqsupseteq>, <B, D, \sqsubseteq>, <C, D, \sqsubseteq>\}$ of elements derived by m. They are $<A, E, \sqsupseteq>$ and $<B, D, \sqsubseteq>$. The element $<C, D, \sqsubseteq>$ needs to be validated only in the case when $<B, D, \sqsubseteq>$ is further rejected. Sub-minimal elements can be efficiently computed (see next section).

Note that, for a better understanding of the correspondences, it is important to show to the user the strongest semantic relation holding between the nodes, even if it is not in the minimal set. For example, showing equivalence where only a direction of the subsumption is minimal.

5.2   User Interaction during Validation

The validation process is illustrated in Fig. 9. The minimal mapping M between the two lightweight ontologies T1 and T2 is computed by the **TreeMatch** (line 10) described in the previous section and validated by the function **Validate** (line 20). At the end of the process, M will contain only the mapping elements accepted by the user. The **Validate** function is given at lines 30-90. The validation process is carried out in a top-down fashion (lines 40-50). This is to evaluate in sequence the elements that share as much contextual information as possible. This in turn reduces the cognitive load requested to the user to take individual decisions. The presence of an element m between two nodes n1 and n2 in M is tested by the function **GetElement** (line 60). In positive case the function returns it, otherwise NULL is returned. Each element is then validated using the function **ValidateElement** (line 70), whose pseudo-code is given in Fig. 10. The process ends when all the nodes in the two trees have been processed. A possible optimization consists in stopping the process when all the elements in M have been processed.

```
10   M := TreeMatch(T1, T2);
20   Validate(M);

30   function void Validate(list of (element) M)
40   { foreach n1 in T1 do
50        foreach n2 in T2 do {
60            m := GetElement(M, n1, n2);
70            if (m != NULL) ValidateElement(m);
80        }
90   };
```

Fig. 9. The validation process of the minimal mapping M

```
10   function void ValidateElement(element m)
20   { S: list of (element);
30     if IsValid(m) AddElement(m, M);
40     else {
50        RemoveElement(m, M);
60        S := GetSubminimals(m);
70        foreach m in S do { if (!IsRedundant(m)) ValidateElement(m); }
80     }
90   };
```

Fig. 10. The validation process of a single element m

The validation of a single element m is embedded in the **ValidateElement** function. The correctness of m is established through a call to the function **IsValid** (line 30), that takes care of the communication with the user. The user can accept or reject m. If m is accepted, m is added to the set M using the function **AddElement** (line 30). Note that this is necessary when the **ValidateElement** is called on a sub-minimal element at line 70. Otherwise, if m is rejected, it is removed from M using the function **RemoveElement** (line 50) and its sub-minimal elements, computed by the function **GetSubminimals** (line 60), are recursively validated (line 70). The pseudo-code for the **GetSubminimals** function is in Fig. 11. It applies the rules for propagation suggested in [4] to identify the elements that follow an element m in the partial order.

Two observations are needed. The first is that a sub-minimal element can be redundant w.r.t. more than one element in M. In these cases we postpone their validation to the validation of the elements for which they are redundant. For instance, <A, E, ⊒> is redundant w.r.t. both <A, D, ≡> and <C, E, ⊒> in Fig. 3. Therefore, the validation of <A, E, ⊒> is postponed to the validation of <C, E, ⊒>. In other words, if <C, E, ⊒> is positively validated, then it will be superfluous asking the user to validate <A, E, ⊒>. We use the function **IsRedundant** described in [4] (line 70) for this. This also avoids validating the same element more than once. The second is that, in order to keep the strongest relation between two nodes, the following rules are enforced:

(a)   if we add to M two subsumptions of opposite directions for the same pair of nodes, we collapse them into equivalence;

(b)   if we add an equivalence between two nodes, it substitutes any subsumption previously inserted between the same nodes, but it is ignored if we already have in M a disjointness between these nodes;

(c)   if we add a disjointness between two nodes, it substitutes any other relation previously inserted in M between the same nodes.

```
10   function list of (element) GetSubminimals(element <n1,n2,R>)
20   { S: list of (element);
30     if (R == ⊑ || R == ≡) {
40       c2 := GetParent(n2);
50       if (c2 != NULL) AddElement(S, <n1,c2,⊑>);
60       else foreach c1 in GetChildren(n1) do AddElement(S, <c1,n2,⊑>);
70     }
80     if (R == ⊒ || R == ≡) {
90       c1 := GetParent(n1);
100      if (c1 != NULL) AddElement(S, <c1,n2,⊒>);
110      else foreach c2 in GetChildren(n2) do AddElement(S, <n1,c2,⊒>);
120    }
130    if (R == ⊥) {
140      foreach c2 in GetChildren(n2) do AddElement(S, <n1,c2,⊥>);
150      foreach c1 in GetChildren(n1) do AddElement(S, <c1,n2,⊥>);
160    }
170    return S;
180  };
```

Fig. 11. The function for the identification of the sub-minimal elements

6   Evaluation

We have tested MinSMatch on datasets commonly used to evaluate matching tools [21]. Their short description is in [4, 21]. Table 1 summarizes their characteristics.

Table 1. Complexity of the datasets

#	Dataset pair	Node count	Max depth	Average branching factor
1	Cornell/Washington	34/39	3/3	5.50/4.75
2	Topia/Icon	542/999	2/9	8.19/3.66
3	Source/Target	2857/6628	11/15	2.04/1.94
4	Eclass/Unspsc	3358/5293	4/4	3.18/9.09

Table 2 shows the percentage of reduction in the number of elements contained in the minimal mapping w.r.t. the mapping of maximum size. The reduction is calculated as (1-m/t), where m is the number of elements in the minimal set and t is the total number of elements in the mapping of maximum size. We have a significant reduction, in the range 68-96%.

Table 2. Mapping sizes and percentage of reduction on standard datasets

#	MinSMatch		
	Mapping of maximum size, elements (t)	Minimal mapping, elements (m)	Reduction, %
1	223	36	83.86
2	5491	243	95.57
3	282648	30956	89.05
4	39818	12754	67.97

As described in [12], we have also conducted experiments with NALT and LCSH. As reported in Table 3, these experiments show that the reduction in the number of correspondences can reach 99%. In other words, this means that by concentrating on minimal mappings we can save up to 99% of the manual checks required for mapping validation.

Table 3. Mapping sizes and percentage of reduction on NALT and LCSH

Id	Source	Branch
A	NALT	Chemistry and Physics
B	NALT	Natural Resources, Earth and Environmental Sciences
C	LCSH	Chemical Elements
D	LCSH	Chemicals
E	LCSH	Management
F	LCSH	Natural resources

Branches	Mapping of maximum size, elements (t)	Minimal mapping, elements (m)	Reduction, %
A vs. C	17716	7541	57,43
A vs. D	139121	994	99,29
A vs. E	9579	1254	86,91
B vs. F	27191	1232	95,47

Finally, we have compared MinSMatch w.r.t. the state of the art matcher S-Match [22]. Table 4 shows the reduction in computation time and calls to the logical reasoners. As it can be noticed, the reductions are substantial.

Table 4. Run time and SAT problems

#	Run Time, ms			Calls to logical reasoners (SAT)		
	S-Match	MinSMatch	Reduction, %	S-Match	MinSMatch	Reduction, %
1	472	397	15.88	3978	2273	42.86
2	141040	67125	52.40	1624374	616371	62.05
3	3593058	1847252	48.58	56808588	19246095	66.12
4	6440952	2642064	58.98	53321682	17961866	66.31

7 Conclusions and Future Work

We have discussed limitations of existing matching tools. We have observed that, once the initial mapping has been computed by the system, current tools provide poor support (or no support at all) for its validation and maintenance in time. In addition, current visualization tools are cognitively demanding, hardly scale with the increasing number of nodes and the resulting visualizations are rather messy. We have proposed the use of MinSMatch for the computation of the minimal mapping and showed that, by concentrating on the correspondences in the minimal set, the amount of manual checks necessary for validation can be reduced up to two orders of magnitude. We have also showed that by minimizing the number of calls to logical reasoners, the MinSMatch algorithm is significantly faster w.r.t. state of the art semantic matching tools and reduces the problem of lack of background knowledge.

Yet, maintaining a mapping in time is an extremely complex and still largely unexplored task. Even a trivial change of a node label can have an enormous impact on the correspondences starting or terminating in this node and all the nodes in their respective subtrees. In future we plan to further explore these problems and develop a user interface which follows the specifications provided in this paper.

Acknowledgments. The research leading to these results has received funding from the European Community's Seventh Framework Programme (FP7/2007-2013) under grant agreement n° 231126 LivingKnowledge: LivingKnowledge – Facts, Opinions and Bias in Time.

References

1. Shvaiko, P., Euzenat, J.: Ontology Matching. Springer, New York (2007)
2. Giunchiglia, F., Marchese, M., Zaihrayeu, I.: Encoding Classifications into Lightweight Ontologies. Journal of Data Semantics 8, 57–81 (2006)
3. Giunchiglia, F., Shvaiko, P., Yatskevich, M.: Discovering missing background knowledge in ontology matching. In: Proc. of ECAI 2006, pp. 382–386 (2006)
4. Giunchiglia, F., Maltese, V., Autayeu, A.: Computing minimal mappings. At the 4th Ontology Matching Workshop at the ISWC 2009 (2009)
5. Robertson, G.G., Czerwinski, M.P., Churchill, J.E.: Visualization of mappings between schemas. In: Proc. of SIGCHI Conference on Human Factors in Computing Systems (2005)
6. Falconer, S., Storey, M.: A cognitive support framework for ontology mapping. In: Aberer, K., Choi, K.-S., Noy, N., Allemang, D., Lee, K.-I., Nixon, L.J.B., Golbeck, J., Mika, P., Maynard, D., Mizoguchi, R., Schreiber, G., Cudré-Mauroux, P. (eds.) ASWC 2007 and ISWC 2007. LNCS, vol. 4825, pp. 114–127. Springer, Heidelberg (2007)
7. Halevy, A.: Why your data won't mix. ACM Queue 3(8), 50–58 (2005)
8. Katifory, A., Halatsis, C., Lepouras, G., Vassilakis, C., Giannopoulou, E.: Ontology visualization methods - a survey. ACM Comput. Surv. 39(4), Article No. 10 (2007)
9. Ranganathan, S.R.: The Colon Classification. In: Artandi, S. (ed.) Rutgers Series on Systems for the Intellectual Organization of Information, vol. IV. Graduate School of Library Science, Rutgers University, New Brunswick, NJ (1965)

10. Giunchiglia, F., Zaihrayeu, I.: Lightweight ontologies. In: LNCS, S. (ed.) Encyclopedia of Database Systems (2008)
11. Giunchiglia, F., Dutta, B., Maltese, V.: Faceted lightweight ontologies. In: Borgida, A.T., Chaudhri, V.K., Giorgini, P., Yu, E.S. (eds.) Conceptual Modeling: Foundations and Applications. LNCS, vol. 5600, pp. 36–51. Springer, Heidelberg (2009)
12. Giunchiglia, F., Soergel, D., Maltese, V., Bertacco, A.: Mapping large-scale Knowledge Organization Systems (2009)
13. Shvaiko, P., Euzenat, J.: Ten Challenges for Ontology Matching. In: Proc. of the 7th Int. Conference on Ontologies, Databases, and Applications of Semantics, ODBASE (2008)
14. Shvaiko, P., Giunchiglia, F., da Silva, P.P., McGuinness, D.L.: Web Explanations for Semantic Heterogeneity Discovery. In: Gómez-Pérez, A., Euzenat, J. (eds.) ESWC 2005. LNCS, vol. 3532, pp. 303–317. Springer, Heidelberg (2005)
15. Koch, T., Neuroth, H., Day, M.: Renardus: Cross-browsing European subject gateways via a common classification system (DDC). In: McIlwaine, I.C. (ed.) Proc. of the IFLA Satellite Meeting on Subject Retrieval in a Networked Environment, pp. 25–33 (2003)
16. Vizine-Goetz, D., Hickey, C., Houghton, A., Thompson, R.: Vocabulary Mapping for Terminology Services. Journal of Digital Information 4(4), Article No. 272 (2004)
17. Whitehead, C.: Mapping LCSH into Thesauri: the AAT Model. In: Beyond the Book: Extending MARC for Subject Access, p. 81 (1990)
18. O'Neill, E., Chan, L.: FAST (Faceted Application for Subject Technology): A Simplified LCSH-based Vocabulary. In: World Library and Information Congress: 69th IFLA General Conference and Council, Berlin, August 1-9 (2003)
19. Nicholson, D., Dawson, A., Shiri, A.: HILT: A pilot terminology mapping service with a DDC spine. Cataloging & Classification Quarterly 42(3/4), 187–200 (2006)
20. Lauser, B., Johannsen, G., Caracciolo, C., Keizer, J., van Hage, W.R., Mayr, P.: Comparing human and automatic thesaurus mapping approaches in the agricultural domain. In: Proc. Int'l Conf. on Dublin Core and Metadata Applications (2008)
21. Avesani, P., Giunchiglia, F., Yatskevich, M.: A Large Scale Taxonomy Mapping Evaluation. In: Gil, Y., Motta, E., Benjamins, V.R., Musen, M.A. (eds.) ISWC 2005. LNCS, vol. 3729, pp. 67–81. Springer, Heidelberg (2005)
22. Giunchiglia, F., Yatskevich, M., Shvaiko, P.: Semantic Matching: algorithms and implementation. Journal on Data Semantics IX (2007)
23. Stuckenschmidt, H., Serafini, L., Wache, H.: Reasoning about Ontology Mappings. In: Proc. of the ECAI 2006 Workshop on Contextual Representation and Reasoning (2006)
24. Meilicke, C., Stuckenschmidt, H., Tamilin, A.: Improving automatically created map-pings using logical reasoning. In: Proc. of the 1st International Workshop on Ontology Matching OM 2006, CEUR Workshop Proceedings, vol. 225 (2006)
25. Meilicke, C., Stuckenschmidt, H., Tamilin, A.: Reasoning support for mapping revision. Journal of Logic and Computation (2008)
26. Borgida, A., Serafini, L.: Distributed Description Logics: Assimilating Information from Peer Sources. Journal on Data Semantics, 153–184
27. Giunchiglia, F., Yatskevich, M., Shvaiko, P.: Semantic Matching: algorithms and implementation. Journal on Data Semantics IX (2007)

XML-SIM-CHANGE: Structure and Content Semantic Similarity Detection among XML Document Versions

Waraporn Viyanon and Sanjay K. Madria

Department of Computer Science
Missouri University of Science and Technology
Rolla, Missouri, USA
wvz7b@mst.edu, madrias@mst.edu

Abstract. XML documents from different sources may represent the same or similar information with respect to content and structure. Being able to integrate similar XML documents is important to query systems and search engines. However, information changes periodically, therefore, it is important to detect the changes among different versions of an XML document and use the changed information to discover semantic similarity among XML documents. In this paper, we introduce such an approach to detect XML similarity using the change detection mechanism to join XML document versions. In our approach, keys in subtrees play an important role in order to avoid unnecessary comparisons of subtrees within different XML versions of the same document. We use relational database to store XML versions and apply SQL for detecting similarities. We show that our approach is highly scalable and has better efficiency in terms of execution time and provides comparable result quality.

Keywords: XML Similarity, Change Detection, Keys, Join.

1 Introduction

XML has become the universal standard for data representation and semi-structured data exchange due to its simplicity, platform independence, and ease of processing [7]. It is evident that XML sources may have similar contents, but may be described differently using different tag names and structures such as bibliography data DBLP [19] and SIGMOD Record [1]. Integrating similar XML documents from different data sources is not only important to query systems and search engines but also benefits users to get access to more complete and useful information. In the environment of frequently changing online information, being able to quickly detect the changes between the two versions of information is important to have up-to-date integrated information.

Since XML documents encode not only structure but also store data, therefore, to measure accurate similarities among them requires measuring the content and structural similarity. A simple comparison comprises counting the number of common occurrences of XML elements or PCDATA between two XML documents is enough to find the similarity in terms of structure and content but this method can be very

R. Meersman et al. (Eds.): OTM 2010, Part II, LNCS 6427, pp. 1061–1078, 2010.

time-consuming. There exists several methods [9, 10, 11, 15, 16, 17] addressing this problem. We have also proposed an efficient method called XML-SIM [15] in order to measure semantic content and structural similarity of XML documents. This method uses information theory-based method for semantic similarity and subtree keys for comparison.

As XML documents change periodically, the change detection mechanism between two different versions can be used to perform XML join. We developed an approach called XML-CHANGE based on XRelChangeSQL [14] to discover changes between two versions using SQL which is very efficient in comparison to main memory algorithms.

In this paper, we develop a technique called XML-SIM-CHANGE by incorporating XML-CHANGE and XML-SIM to find structure and content similarity among XML documents. The differences found in the change detection phase are used to reduce the number of nodes which need to be compared between two versions. Our objective is to design, implement and evaluate the technique that can detect the similarity in terms of both content and structure of XML documents after they change using the similarity matching algorithm and the changes detected between two versions. The contributions of this paper can be summarized as follows:

1. We proposed a framework of XML-SIM-CHANGE for detecting XML document similarity after documents have changed. We defined a comparison method for subtree matching using subtree keys with the changed subtrees found during the change detection technique.
2. We performed experiments using two bibliography data sets DBLP and SIG-MOD and evaluate the framework proposed by comparing it with XML-SIM approach. Our experimental results show that our new approach of combining XML-SIM and XML-CHANGE can detect XML document similarity among versions much faster than XML-SIM and provide a comparable result quality.

2 Related Work

XML documents are considered as a collection of items represented in XML tree forms. In most XML document matching algorithms [9, 10, 11, 15, 16, 17], an XML document is fragmented into small independent items which identify entities representing the same real-world objects called subtrees. Then subtree similarities are measured between two XML documents where subtree pairs having higher similarity than a given threshold are considered as matched pairs which are finally integrated into one XML document.

XML document similarity can be categorized into (1) structural similarity and (2) content and structural similarity. The structural similarity is mostly used in document clustering and in the change detection process. Most algorithms in finding structural similarity are based on tree edit distance [5, 21]. The basic idea in all of tree edit distance algorithms is to find the cheapest sequence of edit operations that can transform one tree into another. However, tree edit distance has not been used on a large scale due to its complexity and high computational cost. To integrate XML documents both the content and structural semantic similarity are to be considered. In our previous work [17] we have outperformed LAX [10] and SLAX [11] which determine the tree similarity degree based on the mean value of the similarity degrees of matched sub-trees. The subtrees are clustered based on XML document's characteristics in terms of its depth and the number of instances contained to cluster the document into subtrees which are used to calculate the similarity. Though they outperform edit distance based-schemes, they ignore semantic information available such as "keys"; rather they rely on finding subtrees or *"clustering point"* which does not work for all types of XML data.

To identify the similarity between two elements, there are many approaches like (1) string matching, (2) edit distance and, (3) semantic similarity. These approaches are effective and widely used for measuring similarity. String matching is simple to implement but the result may miss some similar strings. As mentioned above, the tree edit distance is time-consuming and the similarity result may not be accurate in terms of semantics [3, 21]. Another approach similar to the edit distance is the Longest Common Subsequence (LCS) [2]. It finds the longest sequence of tokens common to the two strings but it may fail in identifying any kind of connection between texts. Semantic similarity methods [8, 13] have been introduced in order to capture meaning of words. The semantic measures are based on using Natural Language Processing (NLP) techniques to compute the degree of similarity between words (concepts). The similarity of two concepts is defined as the maximum of the information content of the concept that subsumes them in the taxonomy hierarchy.

In addition, keys are an essential part of database design and fundamental to data models and conceptual design. Not only semantic similarity, but using XML keys also assists in the subtree matching. XML key concept is introduced in [4]. If we could identify keys, it can help in identifying the real-world objects in XML documents, which would reduce the number of matching dramatically. Since most of the XML data is data-centric (derived from the relational data model), therefore, in such cases, it is better to exploit keys to improve performance in order to find better similarity matching subtrees. [15, 16, 17] utilized keys (subtree keys) to find subtree matches.

3 M-XRel

In our approach, to increase the scalability of XML document similarity and changes, they are stored in a relational schema using M-XRel, a modified scheme from XRel. XRel [20] is an approach for storing and retrieval of XML documents using relational databases. Most similarity detections in XML documents are focused on constructing Document Object Model (DOM) tree in order to find the similarity. The tree compari-son approach is not efficient in handling large XML documents due to the fact that the entire trees of both documents have to reside in the main memory during the compari-son process.

XRel approach uses a model-mapping approach to decompose an XML document into nodes on the basis of its tree structure and stored in relational tables according to the node type with path information from the root to each node as depicted in Figure 1a.

The basic M-XRel schema consists of the five relational schemas as in Figure 1b. They are similar to XRel's schema but two additional columns, the 'parentid' and parent 'start' region are added to 'Element' and 'Text' tables. The extra fields are to improve the efficiency of the change detection process since the relational inequality comparisons can be replaced by equality comparisons in order to detect the parents of XML leaf nodes and non-leaf nodes. The database attributes 'docID', 'pathID', 'start', 'end' and 'value' represent document identifier, simple path expression identifier, start position of a region, end position of a region, and string-value respectively. The occurrence of an element node or a leaf node is identified by its region and stored in the relations 'Element' and 'Text'. To identify each of the attribute nodes, the attribute name is stored as the suffix of the simple path expression of an attribute node and the attribute value is stored in the relation 'Attribute'. The database attribute "pathexp" in the relation Path stores simple path expressions. The ancestor-descendant relationships and the ordering between nodes can be found by 'parentid', parent 'start' region, and 'index' value as the regions define the range of nodes (elements, leaf-node and attribute values) in the XML document.

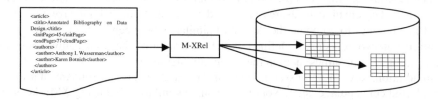

Fig. 1. (a) Generating relational tables using M-XRel

Document(docID, document)
Element(docID, pathID, start, end, index, reindex, **parentid, pstart**)
Attribute(docID, pathID, start, end, value)
Text(docID, pathID, start, end, value, **parentid, pstart**)
Path(pathID, pathexp)

Fig. 1. (b) M-XRel's schema

Table 1. M-XRel's field descriptions

Field descriptions	
docid	Document ID
Parentid	Parent's path expression ID
pstart	Parent's start value of the region
pathid	Path expression ID
pathexp	Path expressions of XML elements
start	Start value of the region
end	End value of the region
index	Forward index
reindex	Reverse index
value	Leaf node and attribute values

4 XML-SIM

In previous work [16], we have proposed XML-SIM for evaluating the similarity between XML documents. Consider two XML documents Doc_b and Doc_t as base and target documents, respectively which are stored into the relational database using M-XRel mentioned in Section 3. The following definition defines XML document tree:

Definition 1: XML Document Tree – *An XML document tree is a triple $T_i = (V, v_0, E)$, where :(i) V is the set of nodes; (ii) v_0 is the root node, and (iii) E is the set of edges in the tree T_i. Let T_b be a base document tree from a base document Doc_b and T_t be a target document tree from a target document Doc_t.*

Definition 2: Path expression – *Any node v_i can be identified its location within a tree T_i by a path expression or path signature p_{v_i}. A path expression p_{v_i} consists of a series of one or more nodes from the node set V separated by "/".* The path expressions are employed to measure semantic structure similarity.

XML-SIM algorithm consists of three phases as Figure 2: (1) subtree generation and validation, (2) key generation and subtree filter and (3) similarity detection.

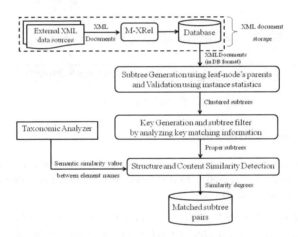

Fig. 2. XML-SIM framework

Subtree Generation and Validation

The first phase is to extract subtrees from XML documents because an XML document is considered as a collection of items. Since data in XML documents is stored at the leaf nodes, to retrieve the data, parents of leaf nodes are utilized to group related information together as a subtree. The leaf node's parent can be described in Definition 3.

Definition 3: Leaf node's Parent –*For a document tree T_i with a node set V and an edge set E, v_p is a leaf node's parent, if (i) $v_p \in V$ (ii) $(v_l, v_p) \in E$, where v_p is the parent of v_l and v_l is a leaf node.* Figure 3a shows leaf node's parents in XML document. The edges above the leaf node's parents are considered as clustering points. They will be removed to identify subtrees.

Extracted subtrees representing an independent object should contain nodes representing different information (author, title, date, etc); it should not have only one kind of information like "authors" list. The instance statistics concept based on subtree element structure [18] is applied in order to check the relationships between the leaf node's parent element and its children's leaf node elements whether they preserve a loose 1:1 relationship. The extracted subtrees are stored in the subtree relation. The clustered subtrees are categorized into two groups: simple and complex subtrees. A simple subtree is a tree having only one leaf node's parent, on the other hand, a complex subtree is a tree containing more than one leaf node's parent.

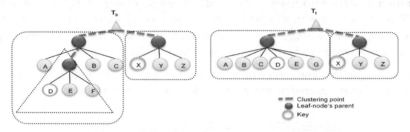

Fig. 3. (a) Subtree clustering by leaf node's parents

Subtree (docID, ppathID, pstart, pend, pathid, start, end, value, **key**, **subtreeid**)

Fig. 3. (b) Subtree relation

Key Generation and Subtree Filter

This phase is to define key(s) of subtrees. The key of a subtree is modeled as an XML attribute which is one of leaf nodes in a subtree. It has a unique value and is able to identify other attributes in its subtree.

Definition 4: Subtree key – *A subtree key is a leaf node v_{key} which has a unique value compared with any leaf nodes v_l having the same path expression $p_{v_{key}}$, where $p_{v_{key}}$ is the path expression of the node v_{key}.*

We identify the possible subtree keys for XML documents using the SQL query given in Figure 4 by retrieving unique values from the *text* relation that can be used to distinguish items from others.

```
SELECT docid, pathid, value
FROM text
GROUP BY docid, PathID, Value
HAVING Count(Value) = 1
```

Fig. 4. SQL query to identify leaf nodes as key(s)

The labels associated with the returned leaf nodes from the query in Figure 4 are considered as subtree keys. We flag "Y" the attribute "key" on the matched records (according to their docid, pathid, and value) in the *subtree* relation.

Next is a task that overlaps between detecting subtree similarity using the subtree keys and filtering subtrees. The subtree keys found are used to match subtrees by comparing the subtrees having their leaf nodes (labels) marked as "key" and having an identical value. Even though this comparison ignores the structure of the leaf nodes but its matching results can be analyzed in order to find out which subtree level is not appropriate to be compared. The matching information is analyzed by examining the number of subtree matchings with the median number of alternate keys. The intuition behind is that a complex subtree may contain a huge number of simple subtrees having alternate keys inside. This kind of complex subtrees may cause several ineffective matchings and is considered as improper subtrees. To eliminate the improper subtrees, we define a threshold calculated from the median number of the alternate subtree keys. The subtrees causing the number of multiple matchings more than the threshold value keys are eliminated.

Similarity Detection

The subtree keys found in the previous step are compared in order to find matches. The unmatched subtrees will be compared later in the third phase. This phase is to detect the right matched subtree pairs; we consider both structure and content on the base and target XML subtrees.

Notation: *For any subtree $s_i = (V_i, v_p, E_i)$ rooted by a distinct label of node v_p, let $V_l = \{v_{l1}, v_{l2}, \dots, v_{ln}\}$ be a collection of leaf nodes in s_i iff $V_l \in V_i$. Consider $P_l = \{p_{l1}, p_{l2}, \dots, p_{ln}\}$ as a collection of path expressions (defined in Definition 2) of the leaf nodes in V_l; V_l has n elements.*

All p_{lj} in the base subtree where $1 \le j \le n_b$ are compared with all p_{lk} in the target subtree where $1 \le k \le n_t$; n_b and n_t are the number of leaf nodes in the base subtree s_j and target subtree s_k respectively to determine the path semantic similarity. To be able to measure the path similarity between p_{lj} and p_{lk}, we need to compare the node labels from p_{lj} and p_{lk} first.

Definition 5: Node Label Semantic Similarity Degree (NSSD) – *For each pair of path expressions p_{lj} and p_{lk}, let $V_j = \{v_{j1}, v_{j2}, \dots, v_{jn_b}\}$ and $V_k = \{v_{k1}, v_{k2}, \dots, v_{kn_t}\}$ denote a series of nodes in p_{lj} and p_{lk} respectively. The node label semantic similarity degree is based on Jiang's and Resnik's information theory-based methods [7, 12] and defined as follows:*

$$NSSD\left(l(v_j), l(v_k)\right) = 1 - \frac{IC\left(l(v_j)\right) + IC(l(v_k)) - 2sim(l(v_j), l(v_k))}{2}. \tag{1}$$

The IC value is calculated by considering negative log of the probability:

$$IC(c) = -\log p(c). \tag{2}$$

where (i) $p(c)$ is the probability of having c in a given corpus and (ii) c is a concept in WordNet. The basic intuition behind the use of the negative likelihood is that the more probable a concept is of appearing then the less information it coveys.

The function $sim(c_1, c_2)$ is evaluated by using the subsumer $S(c_1, c_2)$ of c_1, c_2 as follows:

$$sim(c_1, c_2) = max_{c \in S(c_1,c_2)} IC(c). \qquad (3)$$

Definition 6: Path Semantic Similarity Degree (PSSD) – *A path semantic similarity degree is the ratio of summation of the average NSSD for each node v_j in the path expression p_{lj} and the number of nodes in the path expression series. It can be written in the equation below as:*

$$PSSD(p_{lj}, p_{lk}) = \frac{\sum_{j=1}^{n_b} avg(NSSD_j)}{n_b}. \qquad (4)$$

where $avg(NSSD_j)$ is computed from:

$$avg(NSSD_j) = \frac{\sum_{k=1}^{n_t}(NSSD(l(v_j), l(v_k))}{n_t}. \qquad (5)$$

Definition 7: Matched Path Pair (MPP) – *A matched path pair is selected from the maximum pair having the highest PSSD() value.*

$$MPP(p_{lj}, p_{lk}) = max_{1 \leq j \leq n_b; 1 \leq k \leq n_t} (PSSD(p_{lj}, p_{lk})). \qquad (6)$$

Definition 8: Selected Path Pair – *The selected path is the path expression having MPP() value greater than a given threshold τ_p*

At this point, all path expressions at the leaf node levels are evaluated and selected. The selected paths from Definition 8 will be used to determine the content similarity among the subtrees.

Definition 9: Subtree Similarity based on structure and content – *Each subtree $s_j(1 \leq j \leq n_b)$ is evaluated against the subtrees $s_k(1 \leq k \leq n_t)$ by comparing PCDA-TA value (content approach) based on the selected path (structure approach) to decide which subtree is the proper matched subtree pair (MSP).*

This comparison based on content and structure can be done simply using loops but it would take much more time if the number of subtrees is large. Instead of loops, we use a SQL query by defining its criteria on selected path pair and PCDATA value to retrieve subtree pairs which returns result much faster. The resulted subtree pairs based on the same leaf node's parent are intersected together in order to find the best matched subtree pair satisfying the conditions, having the same PCDATA content and similar semantic structure. We store the matched subtree pairs in a relation called matching which has the schema as Figure 5.

Matching (base_docid, base_ppathid, base_subtreeid, target_docid, target_ppathid,
        target_subtreeid)

Fig. 5. Matching relation

5 XML-SIM-CHANGE Framework

We propose a time-efficient technique for subtree similarity detection between two versions of XML documents after they change, not by running full pair-wise comparisons but by comparing the changes with the previous matching result. We first explain the framework of XML-SIM-CHANGE approach and then provide more definitions, details of each component, and the algorithm for our approach.

5.1 Overview of XML-SIM-CHANGE

This approach enables us to find the similarity using the change detection results between two versions of XML documents and the semantic similarity described in Section 4.

In Figure 6, we start the approach by comparing two XML documents, Doc_bV_1 and Doc_tV_1 which have some similar content from two heterogeneous data sources (referred as base and target data sources). Then use XML-SIM which clusters the documents into subtrees using leaf node's parents and compare the clustered subtrees using subtree keys and semantic similarity degrees which result into matched subtree pairs. The matched subtree pairs can be joined in order to integrate the XML documents together.

When one of the XML documents or both have been altered from Doc_bV_1 to Doc_bV_2 and/or from Doc_tV_1 to Doc_tV_2 after the integration, the changes are detected from their old versions by identifying deleted and inserted non-leaf nodes, and leaf node changes (delete, insert and update). We then efficiently utilize the results from XML-SIM and the changes identified to compute the similarity between the two versions of the XML documents.

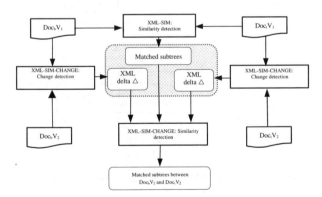

Fig. 6. Overview of XML-SIM-CHANGE approach

5.2 Finding XML Document Changes

Consider any two documents Doc_iV_1 and Doc_iV_2 from the same data source Doc_i stored in a relational database using M-XRel as discussed in Section 3 and assume that changes are detected between two XML document versions. The approach consists of three phases as shown in Figure 7: (1) finding matching subtrees, (2) detecting deleted and inserted non-leaf nodes, and (3) detecting leaf node changes. The result from these steps will output an XML delta (the changes).

Finding Matching subtrees

First, we compare subtrees s_j from the old version of an XML document and s_k from the new version of the XML document, where (i) $1 \leq j \leq n_{V1}$ and (ii) $1 \leq k \leq n_{V2}$ by matching leaf node's parents among subtree keys v_k (unique leaf node value) in $Doc_i V_1$ and $Doc_i V_2$.

Definition 10: Subtree pairs Matched by subtree Keys (SMK) – *Each subtree $s_j (1 \leq j \leq n_{V1})$ in $Doc_i V_1$ is evaluated against the subtrees $s_k (1 \leq k \leq n_{V2})$ in $Doc_i V_2$ using their subtree key defined in Definition 2. s_j and s_k are matched iff*

(i) *Their leaf node's parents have the same path expression:*
   $pathid \left(v_{p_{s_j}} \right) = pathid \left(v_{p_{s_k}} \right)$
(ii) *There exists leaf nodes designated as subtree keys and having values common in both the versions such that* $pathid \left(v_{key_{s_j}} \right) = pathid \left(v_{key_{s_k}} \right)$ *and* $value \left(v_{key_{s_j}} \right) = value \left(v_{key_{s_k}} \right).$

The definition 10 is to identify the best match between leaf node's parents and to avoid unnecessary comparisons between duplicates later. The unmatched subtrees are compared using subtree similarity degrees discussed next.

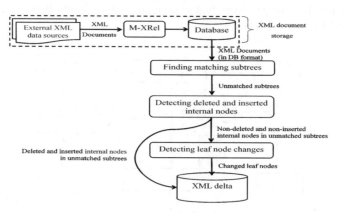

Fig. 7. Framework of finding changes between two versions

Definition 11: Subtree Similarity Degree (SSD) – *Assume n is the number of leaf nodes having the same PCDATA value and the same pathid. Let n_j represent the number of leaf nodes in subtree s_j and n_k represent the number of leaf nodes in subtree s_k.*

$$SSD(s_j, s_k) = \frac{2 \times n}{n_j + n_k} \tag{7}$$

SSDs having values greater than a defined threshold are stored in the relational database. These values will be used in the next step.

Definition 12: Subtree pairs Matched by SSD (SMS) – *The matched subtree pair of subtrees s_j and s_k is the pair that has the maximum subtree similarity degree from Definitions 11. The maximum subtree similarity degree is considered as a matched subtree.*

$$SMS[i] = \max (SSD_i(s_j, s_k)) \tag{7}$$

Once the possible matching subtrees are found, we flag corresponding matched subtrees including SMK (Subtree pairs Matched by subtree Keys) and SMS (Subtree pairs Matched by SSD) to distinguish them from unmatched subtrees.

Detecting deleted and inserted non-leaf nodes

The deleted and inserted subtrees are detected from the sets of matched subtrees using Definition 13.

Definition 13: Deleted and inserted non-leaf nodes – *Let S_1 and S_2 be the sets of all subtrees from the XML document version Doc_iV_1 and the XML document version Doc_iV_2 respectively. Assume MS_{v1} and MS_{v2} are the sets of matched subtrees $\{SMK \cup SMS\}$ from Doc_iV_1 and Doc_iV_2. Then, the set $D_{inter} = \{S_{v1} - MS_{v1}\}$ is the set of deleted non-leaf nodes and the set $I_{inter} = \{MS_{v2} - S_{v2}\}$ is the set of inserted non-leaf nodes.*

Since the leaf node's parent matching in the previous step is 100%, we can be certain that the unmatched leaf node's parents in the first version are deleted non-leaf nodes and unmatched leaf node's parents in the second version are inserted non-leaf nodes.

Detecting leaf node changes

The deleted and inserted nodes are the leaf nodes that have their parents identified as matched subtrees but their values are not matched with any leaf node values in the matched subtree. We identify deleted and inserted leaf node as defined in Definition 14.

Definition 14: Deleted and inserted leaf nodes – *Let ML_1 and ML_2 be the sets of all exactly matched leaf nodes. Let L_{v1} and L_{v2} denote the sets of all matched leaf nodes from the subtree matching step. The deleted leaf nodes can be identified by the set $D_{ln} = \{L_{v1} - ML_{v1}\}$ and the inserted nodes can be detected by the set $I_{ln} = \{L_{v2} - ML_{v2}\}$.*

The results from Definition 14 provide the updated leaf nodes. If there are leaf nodes with the same signature and have the same matching parent in the set of the deleted and inserted nodes, then those leaf nodes are considered as updated.

Definition 15: Updated leaf nodes – *Let U_{2ln} denote the set of updated nodes. U_{2ln} can be found iff there exists a leaf node $v_j \in D_{1ln}$ and $v_k \in I_{2ln}$, such that (i) $pathid(v_j) = pathid(v_k)$, (ii) $pathid\left(parent(v_j)\right) = pathid(parent(v_k))$, and (iii) $value(v_j) \neq value(v_k)$.*

From this point, it results in the XML delta Δ which are the set $\{D_{ln} \cup I_{ln} \cup U_{ln} \cup D_{inter} \cup I_{inter}\}$. The XML delta will be used in the next step.

5.3 Detecting Subtree Similarity of a New Version of XML Document

The base XML document Doc_bV_1 and target XML document Doc_tV_1 are computed to find the best matched subtree pairs (MSP) by XML-SIM. When the XML documents Doc_bV_1 and Doc_tV_1 are modified to Doc_bV_2 and Doc_tV_2 respectively, the old and new versions from the base and target XML documents are detected in order to find the change Δ of each document.

Algorithm XML-SIM-CHANGE

Input: $M_{old}\{(s_j, s_k)\}$ //Matching result from measuring the similarity of Doc_bV1 and Doc_tV1
     $\Delta = \{D_{1ln} \cup I_{2ln} \cup U_{2ln} \cup D_{1inter} \cup I_{2inter}\}$ //the change
Output: $M_{new}\{(S_{j,new}, S_{k,new})\}$ //Matching result from measuring the similarity of Doc_bV2 and Doc_tV2

//***Pre-processing***
//Clustering an XML document by the selected leaf node's parent in XML-SIM
$S_{b,v2} = \text{Cluster}(Doc_bV2);$ //$S_{b,v2}$ is the set of subtrees in Doc_bV2
$S_{t,v2} = \text{Cluster}(Doc_tV2);$ //$S_{t,v2}$ is the set of subtrees in Doc_tV2

//Matching the subtrees with the change
$S_\Delta = \text{changeMatching}(S_{b,v2}, S_{t,v2}, \Delta)$ //S_Δ is the set of subtrees having some change

//***Detecting the matching for the documents Doc_bV2 and Doc_tV2***
for each s_i having the flag as 'update' in S_Δ
 { if (matchSubtree(s_i, the set of all subtrees in M_{old})) //check for a subtree match
    update s_i to the matched subtree in M_{new};
 }
}
for each s_i having the flag as 'delete' in S_Δ
 {if (matchSubtree(s_i, the set of all subtrees in M_{old}))
    {if (flag == 'deleted internal node' && deleted node == the root of s_i)
    { delete a pair having s_j as a match from M_{new};}
    else{ Remove the deleted node from subtree in M_{new}; }
 }
}
for each s_i in Doc_bV2 having the flag as 'insert' in S_Δ
 { if (matchSubtree($s_i, S_{j,v1}$))
    { insert a pair of $(s_i, s_{j,v1})$ into the set of M_{new} };
 }
for each s_i in Doc_tV2 having the flag as 'insert' in S_Δ
 {if (matchSubtree($s_i, S_{k,v1}$))
    { insert a pair of $(s_i, s_{k,v1})$ into the set of M_{new} };
 }
Module: matchSubtree(subtree s_i, setOfSubtree S_j){
 rs = select count(*) from S_j
     where $pathid(v_{p,si}) = pathid(v_{p,sj})$ and $pathid(v_{key,si}) = pathid(v_{key,sj})$
        and $value(v_{key,si}) = value((v_{key,sj})$
 if (rs == 1){   //found a match
   return true;
 }
 return false;
}

Fig. 8. XML-SIM-CHANGE Algorithm

XML-SIM-CHANGE approach takes the matching results from XML-SIM and the change results from the previous step in order to find the new best matched pair in the new version of XML document. We split this step into two phases as (1) pre-processing and (2) checking the matched subtree pairs with changes.

Pre-processing

The new versions of both the documents are clustered into subtrees using the selected leaf node's parents after filtering subtrees obtained by XML-SIM. We then map the changes resulted from XML-CHANGE to the clustered subtrees. The mapping of the changes with the subtrees can be simply done using the region elements (the start and end attributes) defined in M-XRel.

The subtrees matched with the changes are marked accordingly as 'updated leaf node', 'deleted leaf node', inserted leaf node', 'deleted internal node', or 'inserted internal node'. These marked subtree flags identify which level of subtrees is changed.

Checking the matching with the change

In this section, we discuss how to find the similarity of the new versions of XML documents. The algorithm of XML-SIM-CHANGE is shown in Figure 8. To detect the similarity on the new versions, we start with finding a match between the subtrees marked as 'update' and the subtrees in the previous result matching. A match can be performed by comparing the path signature of the root of subtrees, the path signature of the node identified as a subtree key, and the value of subtree key. If a match is found, the subtree in the result matching is updated by its change type. Then we move on to the deleted subtrees which either have a deleted leaf node(s) or a deleted internal node(s). If a match is found between comparing the deleted subtrees with the set of subtrees in the matching, we check further whether the deleted node is the root of the subtree or it is a non-root node. If it is the root, the subtree is removed from the matching set. If it is not, only the deleted node is removed.

For the inserted nodes, we need to compare to the previous version of the compared document. If the match is found, the matched subtree pair from the previous version and the inserted subtree is added to the matching set. After processing this algorithm, the matched subtree pairs are up to date corresponding to the new versions.

6   XML-SIM-CHANGE Performance Evaluation

We observe the efficiency and effectiveness of XML-SIM-CHANGE algorithm comparing with the pure XML-SIM algorithm (since we have shown in [15] that it outperforms other comparable approaches).

6.1   Experimental Setup and Data Sets

We conduct experiments using Intel Core 2 Duo CPU 2.20GHz with 4GB of RAM running on a Windows XP Professional with Sun JDK 1.6.0_02 and an Oracle Database 10g Standard Edition. The M-XRel was used to store the XML documents on the Oracle 10g. The implementation was tested using the real data sets, Sigmod Record and DBLP, and some modification of the datasets to create new versions of the documents varied by different sizes of change. The data sets are categorized into three groups (1) Large size, (2) medium size, and (2) small size. Each group has three different percentages of changes: 25%, 50%, and 75%. For simplicity, we classify the change happening in leaf nodes or inter nodes into two groups: (1) deletion and (2) insertion since an update operation is considered here as a combination of a deletion and an insertion.

In this experiment, we use XML documents from SigmodRecord [1] referred as doc1 and DBLP [19] referred as doc2. doc1.V1 represents the XML document from doc1 before any changes and doc1.V2 represents the XML document from doc1 after changes. We assume that doc1 is not changed but doc2V1 has some changes become doc2.V2. Table 2 and Table 3 describe the dataset information. As each XML document contains a collection of items or subtrees, for this case the items from doc1 represent <article> in SigmodRecord and the items in doc2 represent <inproceedings>, <incollection>, <book>, <article>, <www>, <masterthesis>, <phdthesis>, or <proceedings> in DBLP. Doc2.V2 is represented by its size and percentage of changes for each data set.

Table 2. Controlled data sets

Document	Small document		Medium document		Large document	
	File size (KB)	# of subtrees	File size(KB)	# of subtrees	File size (KB)	# of subtrees
Doc1.V1	7	20	482	1504	482	1504
Doc1.V2*	7	20	482	1504	482	1504
Doc2.V1	12	11	679	1337	10 MB	31016

*Note: the Doc1.V1 and Doc1.V2 are the same since no change on the first document (Doc1).

Table 3. Data set descriptions for Doc2.V2

Group/Change	Data set (size-% change)	File size (KB)	# of subtrees
Large/Delete	L25D	8 MB	25997
	L50D	5 MB	9199
	L75D	3 MB	8997
Large/Insert	L25I	12MB	32944
	L50I	15MB	41074
	L75I	18MB	46092
Medium/Delete and Insert	M25	683	774
	M50	678	768
	M75	669	772
Medium/Delete only	M25D	487	564
	M50D	299	350
	M75D	114	131
Medium/Insert only	M25I	812	919
	M50I	1006	1154
	M75I	1166	1338
Small/Delete and Insert	S25	14	11
	S50	13	11
	S75	12	11

6.2 Experimental Results

We have compared XML-SIM to existing approaches in the previous papers [15, 16, 17] and showed that it outperforms XDI-CSSK and XDoI which perform better than LAX and SLAX [10, 11]. In this section, we show the results of our experiments by evaluating (1) execution time and (2) accuracy of the similarity detection. First, we evaluated the performance in terms of how fast XML-SIM-CHANGE is by comparing with the pure XML-SIM. We use 0.7 as the similarity threshold τ in both approaches. This threshold is used to evaluate the content similarity.

Figure 9 shows the performance of detecting the content and structural semantic similarity of the new version of Sigmod Record and DBLP. Figure 9(a) shows the execution time of measuring the similarity of the new version of the small datasets. Here, the pure approach XML-SIM performs better than XML-SIM-CHANGE for changes occurring in the small documents since the overhead involved in detecting the changed nodes is higher when the document size is small and therefore, it needs to compare very few subtrees and thus, the XML-SIM performed better. However, XML-SIM-CHANGE dramatically outperforms XML-SIM when the XML documents are become larger. The data points of Small-25% in Figure 9(a) show that the file size (14KB) of the document (the biggest file among the small group) significantly affects the execution time in both the approaches. In particular, in case of medium and large documents, if the new document version has less than 50% nodes changed then the execution time shows a remarkable improvement over the pure XML-SIM approach in Figure 9(c and e). Figure 9(b) shows the execution time for medium-size documents having both insertion and deletion. Since the sizes of the documents (Medium-25%, Medium-50% and Medium-75%) referred in Table 2 are almost the same, it obviously shows that the execution times for each pair in XML-SIM are unvaried. Figure 9(c) and Figure 9(e) show when nodes in the old document version have been deleted; the size of the new version becomes smaller which decrease the execution time of XML-SIM. Similarly, Figure 9(d) and 9(f) show when nodes in the old document version have been added; the size of the new version grows which affect the execution of XML-SIM. However, XML-SIM-CHANGE performs better because it gets benefit from the change results which help in avoiding unnecessary comparisons for all pairs of both XML documents. The change detection process is performed in a short period of time compared to the matching process in XML-SIM as it takes advantage of using regions stored by M-XRel in the DBMS. Thus, the new approach is much more scalable in detecting the similarity among the XML document versions which are very large in size and have both insertion and deletion of nodes.

We did measure the result quality from the matching results. The result quality of subtree matching was evaluated as $Q = Sn/An$, where Sn is the number of matched subtrees by a given approach and An is the number of actual matched subtrees. The qualities of the results from the both approaches are shown in Figure 10. The results of the both XML-SIM and XML-SIM-CHANGE approaches are the same because both utilize the same matching method. They are able to identify the matched path pair and subtree keys for both the XML documents by taking advantage from subtree keys and subtree filters. The result quality for XML-SIM-CHANGE is based on the matching subtree in the change detection phase relying mainly on leaf node value matches.

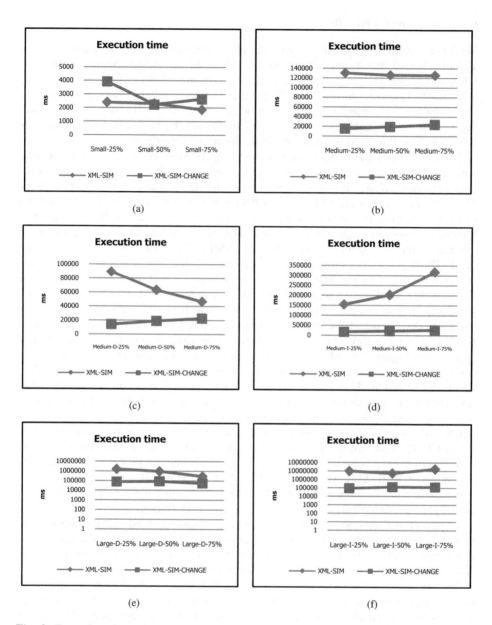

Fig. 9. Execution time of (a) small data sets with the change of insertions and deletions (b) medium data sets with the change of insertions and deletions (c) medium datasets with the change of deletions (d) medium data sets with the change of insertions (e) large datasets with the change of deletions (f) large data sets with the change of insertions

Fig. 10. Result Quality

7 Conclusions and Future Work

We have proposed a technique called XML-SIM-CHANGE for finding XML document similarity after XML documents have been changed by collaborating with the change detection method and subtree matching. This technique avoids unnecessary comparisons by taking advantage of subtree keys and subtree filters in XML-SIM by comparing only sub-trees with changes in order to find the best matched subtree pairs in the new versions. As part of our future work, we would like to consider different types of XML documents (shallow, semi-shallow, deep etc) and then apply our technique to measure the impact of different types of XML schema.

References

1. ACM SIGMOD Record in XML (n.d.), http://www.acm.org/sigmod/record/xml
2. Apostolico, A., Galil, Z.: Pattern Matching Algorithms. Oxford University Press, USA (1997)
3. Bille, P.: Tree edit distance, alignment distance and inclusion. IT Univ. of Copenhagen, Citeseer (2003)
4. Buneman, P., Davidson, S., Fan, W., Hara, C., Tan, W.: Keys for XML. Computer Networks, 473–487 (2002)
5. Chawathe, S.: Comparing hierarchical data in external memory, Citeseer, pp. 90–101(1999)
6. Christiane, F.: WordNet: An Electronic Lexical Database. MIT press Cambridge, MA (1998)
7. Extensible Markup Language (XML). In: World Wide Web Consortium (W3C), http://www.w3.org/XML/
8. Jiang, J., Conrath, D.: Semantic similarity based on corpus statistics and lexical taxonomy. Jiang, J.J., Conrath, D.W., pp. 19–33 (1997)
9. Liang, W., Yokota, H.: A path-sequence based discrimination for subtree matching in approximate XML joins. In: Proceedings of the 22nd International Conference on Data Engineering Workshops (ICDEW 2006), pp. 23–28 (2006)

10. Liang, W., Yokota, H.: LAX: An Efficient Approximate XML Join Based on Clustered Leaf Nodes for XML Data Integration. In: Jackson, M., Nelson, D., Stirk, S. (eds.) BNCOD 2005. LNCS, vol. 3567, pp. 82–97. Springer, Heidelberg (2005)
11. Liang, W., Yokota, H.: SLAX: An Improved Leaf-Clustering Based Approximate XML Join Algorithm for Integrating XML Data at Subtree Classes. IPSJ Digital Courier 2, 382–392 (2006)
12. Pirro, G., Seco, N.: Design, Implementation and Evaluation of a New Semantic Similarity Metric Combining Features and Intrinsic Information Content. In: Meersman, R., Tari, Z. (eds.) OTM 2008, Part II. LNCS, vol. 5332, pp. 1271–1288. Springer, Heidelberg (2008)
13. Resnik, P.: Using information content to evaluate semantic similarity in a taxonomy. In: Proceedings of the 14th Internaltional Joint Conference on Artificial Intelligence, pp. 448–453 (1995)
14. Sathyanarayanan, S., Sanjay, M.: XREL CHANGE SQL: A Change Detection System for Unordered XML documents. University of Missiouri-Rolla, Rolla (2005)
15. Viyanon, W., Madria, S.: A System for Detecting XML Similarity in Content and Structure Using Relational Database. In: 18th ACM International Conference on Information and Knowledge Management (ACM CIKM 2009), pp. 1197–1206 (2009)
16. Viyanon, W., Madria, S.: XML-SIM: Structure and Content Semantic Similarity Detection using Keys. In: Proceeding of the 8th International Conference on Ontologies, DataBases, and Applications of Semantics (ODBASE 2009), pp. 1183–1200 (2009)
17. Viyanon, W., Madria, S.K., Bhowmick, S.S.: XML Data Integration Based on Content and Structure Similarity Using Keys. In: Meersman, R., Tari, Z. (eds.) OTM 2008, Part I. LNCS, vol. 5331, pp. 484–493. Springer, Heidelberg (2008)
18. Weis, M.: Fuzzy Duplicate Detection on XML Data. In: Proceedings of VLDB 2005 PhD Workshop, p. 11 (2005)
19. XML Version of DBLP (n.d.), http://dblp.uni-trier.de/xml/ (retrieved May 2006)
20. Yoshikawa, M., Amagasa, T., Shimura, T., Uemura, S.: XRel: a path-based approach to storage and retrieval of XML documents using relational databases. ACM Transactions on Internet Technology 1(1), 110–141 (2001)
21. Zhang, K., Shasha, D.: Simple fast algorithms for the editing distance between trees and related problems. SIAM Journal on Computing 1245 (1989)

Ontology-Driven Possibilistic Reference Fusion

Fatiha Saïs[1], Rallou Thomopoulos[2,3], and Sébastien Destercke[3]

[1] LRI (Paris-Sud 11 Univ.) and INRIA Saclay, 2-4 rue J. Monod, F-91893 Orsay, France
[2] LIRMM (CNRS & Univ. Montpellier II), 161 rue Ada, F-34392 Montpellier cedex 5, France
[3] INRA/CIRAD, UMR1208, 2 place P. Viala, F-34060 Montpellier cedex 1, France
Fatiha.Sais@lri.fr, rallou@supagro.inra.fr,
sebastien.destercke@supagro.inra.fr

Abstract. It often happens that different references (i.e. data descriptions), possibly coming from different heterogeneous data sources, concern the same real world entity. In such cases, it is necessary: (i) to detect, through reconciliation methods, whether different data descriptions refer to the same real world entity and (ii) to fuse them into a unique representation. Here we assume the reference reconciliation is solved, and we propose a fusion method based on possibility theory, able to cope with uncertainty and with ontological knowledge. An implementation using W3C standards is provided. Rising from the fusion process, an ontology enrichment procedure is proposed to complete the global ontology.

Keywords: Data integration, Data fusion, Ontologies, Hierarchical Fuzzy Set.

1 Introduction

In a context of increasing available information, modern integration systems must be able to deal with heterogeneous information sources and more specifically to provide consistency checking mechanisms. Key issues to obtain this consistency, by providing an integrated representation of data, concern the problem of schema/data reconciliation and fusion. Schema heterogeneity is a major cause of the mismatch of data descriptions between sources. Extensive research work has been done recently (see [1] for surveys) to reconcile schemas or ontologies through mappings.

However, the homogeneity or reconciliation of the schemas does not prevent variations between the data descriptions. Data reconciliation consists in deciding whether different data descriptions, here called references, concern the same real-world entity (e.g. the same person, the same experiment, the same paper). In this paper, reconciliation is assumed to be solved (see [2] for more details). Data fusion then consists in merging the reconciled references into a single one. This is the problem considered in this paper. Performing the fusion step offers several advantages: (i) it provides the user with more consistent and detailed answers, since they gather information from multiple references; (ii) it reduces the number of returned answers and consequently makes query evaluation faster and (iii) it makes query results more user-friendly, as the result returns only one reference for each group of redundant references.

The fusion procedure should be as automated as possible, as it is likely to deal with large amounts of data. The final merged references should also take account of the

R. Meersman et al. (Eds.): OTM 2010, Part II, LNCS 6427, pp. 1079–1096, 2010.
© Springer-Verlag Berlin Heidelberg 2010

uncertainties arising from the data heterogeneity and from automatic reconciliation: variability of attribute values (e.g. the same molecule can be named *"Vitamin B2"* in one reference and *"Riboflavin"* in another), lack of data, incorrect entries, *etc.* Most of reference reconciliation systems used in data cleaning (e.g. ETL systems in data warehouses) settle for detecting the reconciliation decisions and delegate the fusion task to the user. The few fusion procedures proposed up to now do not satisfy the previous requirements, as they need human intervention to be performed and only provide one value per attribute of the fused reference [3]. Besides, these existing methods do not take account of additional domain knowledge, coming for instance from an ontology.

In this paper, we propose a fusion method that satisfies the above issues. More precisely, we have chosen to preserve as much as possible the original values of the data descriptions. Owing to the potential uncertainty in the reconciliation decisions, the certainty in the choice of relevant values cannot be guaranteed. Therefore, all the values appearing in the data descriptions are kept and are given different confidence degrees modelling the final uncertainty.

We propose to use possibility theory to model the uncertainty, as this theory allows to model explicitly the imprecision in the information and to easily take account of source reliability. It is also computationally convenient and offers a simple interpretation. We also consider that some generic information about the references is available in the form of an ontology (formalised in OWL language). After introducing notations and basics about possibility theory and ontology in Section 2, we develop the proposed approach to build fused references in Section 3. In particular, we present how various features of the data are taken into account in the fused uncertainty models, through the use of criteria and of the ontology. As we are working under an open-world assumption (i.e. not all existing values are in the ontology), we also develop a simple enrichment approach allowing to integrate new values into the ontology. Once this fusion is done, classical or fuzzy query methods [4] can be applied to them. An implementation of the proposed approach in W3C standardised languages (RDF and SPARQL) is proposed in Section 5, allowing for the proposed approach to be implemented without having to build extensions of classical languages. The method is then experimented (see Section 6) on a real dataset of the scientific publication domain on which it has obtained promising results. Finally, we discuss the interest of our approach with respect to some existing related works in Section 7.

2   Materials

In this section, we present the basic notions of possibility theory [5] and ontology [6] needed in this paper, as well as the used notations.

2.1   Possibility Theory

When the value assumed by a variable X over a (finite) domain $\mathcal{X}$ is uncertain, possibility theory can be used to model this uncertainty. In particular, it is able to model imprecision and incompleteness in the available information, a feature that classical probability is arguably unable to account for (see Walley [7] for a full discussion). The main tool of possibility theory are possibility distributions, defined as follows:

Definition 1 (Possibility distribution). *A possibility distribution π on a domain $\mathcal{X}$, is a mapping $\pi : \mathcal{X} \to [0,1]$ from $\mathcal{X}$ to the unit interval such that there is at least one element $x \in \mathcal{X}$ for which $\pi(x) = 1$.*

From a possibility distribution π, two set-functions are then defined, namely the possibility and necessity measures, such that, for any subset $A \subseteq \mathcal{X}$:

$$\Pi(A) = \sup_{x \in A} \pi(x) \qquad \text{(Possibility measure)} \qquad (1)$$

$$N(A) = 1 - \Pi(A^c) = \inf_{x \in A^c} (1 - \pi(x)). \qquad \text{(Necessity measure)} \qquad (2)$$

While necessity is a lower confidence measure indicating how much A is certain, possibility measure indicates how much A is plausible. Both measures quantify our uncertainty about the true value of variabe X. A possibility distribution π is formally equivalent [8] to a fuzzy set $\mu : \mathcal{X} \to [0,1]$ such that $\pi = \mu$.

2.2   Ontology

In this paper, we consider that we have a unique global ontology. We define an ontology by using a fragment of OWL DL, which is the description logic fragment of the Ontology Web Language recommended by the W3C.

We consider an ontology $\mathcal{O}$ as a tuple $(\mathcal{C}, \mathcal{P}, \mathcal{I}, \mathcal{D})$ composed of a set $\mathcal{C}$ of classes (unary relations), a set $\mathcal{P}$ of typed properties (binary relations), a set $\mathcal{I}$ of individuals (or concrete values) and a set $\mathcal{D}$ of data types, containing for example $rdfs : Literal$.

We consider that the ontology is also composed of a set of constraints between classes and properties (e.g. subsumption and equivalence relations) summed up in the following table:

Ontology Constraints	DL notation	OWL notation
Subsumption between classes	$C_1 \sqsubseteq C_2$	SubClassOf($C_1\ C_2$)
Class equivalence	$C_1 \equiv C_2$	EquivalentClasses($C_1\ C_2$)
Subsumption between properties	$P_1 \sqsubseteq P_2$	SubPropertyOf($P_1\ P_2$)
Domain typing of a property	$\exists P \sqsubseteq C$	Domain($P\ C$)
Range typing of a property	$\exists P^- \sqsubseteq C$	Range($P\ C$)

In OWL, two kinds of properties can be distinguished: the *abstract properties* which have classes as domain and range, and the *concrete properties* which have a class as domain and a basic data type as range (e.g. Integer, Date, rdfs:Literal).

Given two classes C_1 and C_2, we denote by $lcs(C_1, C_2)$ their least common subsumer, that is $lcs(C_1, C_2) = \{C \in \mathcal{C}|C_i \sqsubseteq C$, and $((\exists C'$ s.t. $C_i \sqsubseteq C') \Rightarrow (C \sqsubseteq C'))$, $i \in \{1, 2\}\}$.

As usually done, we consider a *Universal* class subsuming all the other classes of the ontology, to ensure that such a lcs always exists. Note that the notion of lcs can be easily extended to any number of classes. Due to the semantics of subsumption $\sqsubseteq$, if a property has a class C as domain or range, then for any class C' such that $C' \sqsubseteq C$, the same property holds with respectively C' as domain or range.

Table 1. Specification of individuals $\mathcal{I}$ through assertional statements relating data to the domain ontology

Ontology assertions	DL notation	OWL notation
Class assertion	$C(i)$	Individual($i : C$)
Data type assertion	$D(v)$	Individual($v : D$)
Abstract property assertion	$P(i_1, i_2)$	ObjectProperty(P domain($i_1 : C_1$) range($i_2 : C_2$))
Concrete property assertion	$P'(i, v)$	DataTypeProperty(P' domain($i : C$) range($v : D$))

A small part of the class hierarchy of $\mathcal{C}$ is given as an example in Figure 1. The properties are pictured by dashed Arrows from the domain class to the range class (or data type). The partial order $\sqsubseteq$ is pictured by $\rightarrow$ and describes the subsumption relation. The equivalence relation $\equiv$ is pictured by the relation $equivTo$.

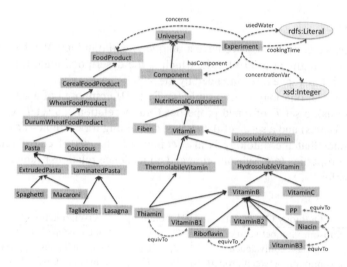

Fig. 1. A part of the domain ontology

In the sequel, we call values the following elements describing an individual i:

– Let *ObjectProperty(P domain($i : C$) range($i' : C'$))* be an abstract property assertion. The value i', referring to a class, is related to i through the property P. In this case, we thus consider hierarchical symbolic values. The hierarchical organization of values is induced by the subsumption relation and the associated ordering.
– Let *DataTypeProperty(P domain($i : C$) range($v : D$))* be a concrete property assertion. v is the value related to i through the property P. Two cases can be distinguished:

  • non-hierarchical symbolic values without referring to a class, e.g. String, Date;
  • numeric values, i.e., the range of P is a closed interval $[\underline{v}, \overline{v}]$.

Remark 1. In OWL, the intervals can be expressed by using XML data type restrictions ($xsd : minInclusive, xsd : maxInclusive$) and the OWL constructor $owl : allValuesFrom$ (see [9] for more details).

3   Reference Fusion Approach

After introducing some notations with an illustrative example and recalling how reference reconciliation is achieved, we introduce the fusion method used to merge reconciled references. To do so, we focus on one group of reconciled references. Both used criteria and ontology enrichment procedure (used in case of newly encountered hierarchical values) are detailed.

3.1   Problem Statement and Illustrative Example

We consider N different references $ref_1, \ldots, ref_N$, coming from M different sources $S_1, \ldots, S_M$, with $M \leq N$. Note that all sources and references share the same ontology. These references are individuals of a given class C and have common descriptions represented by a set $\mathbb{P} = \{P_1, \ldots, P_K\}$ of K properties. In Example 1, used thorough the paper to illustrate the fusion approach, show references that are identified as individuals of class *Experiment*, and where the the property set is $\mathbb{P} = \{$cookingTime, usedWater, hasComponent, concentrationVar$\}$.

Example 1. We consider two data sources describing experiments on vitamin rate variation during the cooking of food products. Data are summarized in Figure 2.

Source S1:

Ref.	cookingTime	usedWater	hasComponent	concentrationVar
idE11	12 mins	Distilled water	Thiamin	-53.3
idE12	12 mins	Tap water	Niacin	-45.6

Source S2:

Ref.	cookingTime	usedWater	hasComponent	concentrationVar
idE21	13 mins	Water	VitaminB6	-46
idE22	10 mins	Deionized water	Thiamine	-52.9
idE23	10 mins	Deionized water	VitaminB	-51.8

Fig. 2. Data to be reconciled concerning the impact of cooking on vitamin level in pasta

For readability reasons, we have chosen to represent data in a relational form, as it is shown in Figure 2. The OWL DL representation of source 1 data is illustrated in Figure 3 as a set of DL assertional statements on individuals (references and basic values).

We denote by $\mathcal{V}_k$ the set of possible values of the property P_k (numerical values, non-hierarchical values or hierarchical values). To simplify notations, when a property P_k has as range a class c_{P_k} of the ontology $\mathcal{O}$ (i.e. P_k is an abstract property), we denote by $\mathcal{O}_{P_k} = \{\mathcal{C}_{P_k}, \mathcal{P}_{P_k}\}$ the reduced ontology such that $\mathcal{C}_{P_k} = \{c \in \mathcal{C} | c \sqsubseteq c_{P_k}\}$ and the

Experiment(idE11); Thiamin(idVita100) ; cookingTime(idE11, "12 mins");
usedWater(idE11,"Distilled water"); hasComponent(idE11, idVita100);
concentrationVar(idE11, -53.3);
Experiment(idE12); Niacin(idVita101) ; cookingTime(idE12, "12 mins");
usedWater(idE11,"Tap water"); hasComponent(idE12, idVita101);
concentrationVar(idE12, -45.6);

Fig. 3. *Data of* Source 1 *in the form of DL assertionnal statements*

properties are limited to $C_{P_k} \times C_{P_k}$ (i.e., $\mathcal{P}_{P_k} = \mathcal{P} \cap (C_{P_k} \times C_{P_k})$). A given reference ref_n can therefore be described by a set $\{v_{n1}, \ldots, v_{nK}\}$ of K values, where v_{nK} is the value of the property P_k for reference ref_n. Note that missing data (null values) may exist.

Reconciliation Problem. The first step of reference reconciliation consists in identifying the pairs of duplicated references (i.e. that represent the same real-world entity) by the use of a dedicated algorithm (e.g. the N2R method [2]). From the set of reconciled pairs, groups of duplicated references are then built by transitive closure. The obtained groups[1] provide a partition of $\{ref_1, \ldots, ref_N\}$. In Example 1 , the pairs $\{idE11, idE22\}$, $\{idE22, idE23\}$ are considered as duplicates. The group built from these pairs is $\{idE11, idE22, idE23\}$. In the sequel, we consider that L groups denoted by $Rec_1, \ldots, Rec_L$ are obtained by reconciliation; and the set of values taken by a property P_k among a group Rec_l will be denoted by V_{lk}, with $k = 1, \ldots, K$ and $l = 1, \ldots, L$.

Fusion Problem. Once reconciled groups are obtained, references within each group must be merged so that a unique reference is associated to each group (ending up with L references). We propose to base this fusion on possibility theory. The method handles ontological knowledge whenever a property takes as value a concept of the ontology $\mathcal{O}$ (i.e. it is an abstract property). For a given group Rec_l, it consists in two main steps:

- build, for each reference $ref_n \in Rec_l$, a possibility distribution $\pi_{n,k}$ defined on V_{lk} and describing the uncertainty concerning the real value of property P_k. This steps build a possibility distribution defined over V_{lk} for each reference, ending up with $|Rec_l|$ distributions for each property;
- the $|Rec_l|$ distributions are then fused in a single one, so that to each property P_k inside a group Rec_l is associated a unique possibility distribution.

To build this model, the method is based on a small set of criteria. These criteria corresponds to information that is always available and that appears sensible to evaluate the relevance of a given value. This allows the method to be general and applicable to the great majority of situations and problems where redundant references can exist. However, in specific situations or problems, there could be additional criteria that should be considered. In such situation, one would have to integrate them in a meaningful way to the uncertainty model. We now details these criteria.

---

[1] A reference that is not duplicated forms a group by itself.

3.2   Criteria for Uncertainty Modeling and Reference Fusion

Several features contribute to the evaluation of the relevance of the property values: variability of encountered values, lack of data, abstract or concrete property, commonness of a given value, uncorrect input, etc. Therefore, several criteria will be used to build the uncertainty model. The first criterion (conceptual similarity) concerns hierarchical symbolic values and thus applies to abstract properties. It is based on the classical Wu & Palmer measure [10] (again, other measures may be more adapted for specific problems). The other criteria concern all kinds of values and were already considered and their use justified in [11], but with an had-oc construction of the uncertainty models.

Consider a given group Rec_l and a fixed property P_k. Let v be the value taken by P_k in the considered reference of the group Rec_l. The criteria are:

- *Conceptual Similarity (CS)*: measures the semantic similarity between two classes. Here, we use the Wu & Palmer measure [10]. Let c_1, c_2 be two classes, N_1, N_2 the path lengths between $lcs(c_1, c_2)$ and respectively c_1 and c_2, and N_3 the path length between $lcs(c_1, c_2)$ and the class Universal. Then, $CS(c_1, c_2)$ reads[2]:

$$CS(c_1, c_2) = \frac{2\,N_3}{N_1 + N_2 + 2\,N_3}.$$

  This criterion will be used to compare the values taken by two abstract properties, whose ranges are classes. Indeed, if one hierarchical value would have to be replaced by another one, the best replacement candidates are the one that are semantically closer to it.
- *Homogeneity (Hom)*: measures the frequency of occurrence of a given value v inside a group of reconciled references $ref_n \in Rec_l$. This criteria is chosen for the reason that the more often a value appears in a group, the more likely it is to be the right one. Homogeneity reads:

$$Hom(v) = |\{v_{nk} = v \,|\, ref_n \in Rec_l\}| / |Rec_l|.$$

- *Syntactic similarity (Sim)*: we will denote by $Sim(v, v')$ a syntactic similarity measure between two values v and v' taken by the property P_k in a group of reconciled references. There are many such measures [12], and choosing a particular measure is often dependant of the nature of the data. The argument for retaining this criteria is similar to the one of conceptual similarity (this latter one only applying to hierarchical values).
- *Data source reliability (α_m)*: we consider that a reliability value α_m is associated with each source S_m, $m = 1, \ldots, M$, measuring the confidence we have in the information coming from this source. We consider that information coming from a highly reliable source should have more impact than the one coming from a poorly reliable one, without discarding completely any of these information. This reliability can be, for instance, a function of the last update date of the source [11].
- *Global frequency (f)*: measures the frequency of a value v among all the references ref_n, $n = 1, \ldots, N$. Indeed, a value appearing numerous times is less likely to contain typographic errors, and is more reliable. It reads:

$$f(v) = |\{v_{nk} = v \,|\, n = 1, \ldots, N\}| / N$$

---

[2] Note that Conceptual Similarity between two equivalent classes is 1.

These criteria form a basis from which uncertainty can be estimated. They are significant and general enough so as to be accessible in most situations. Other criteria, more problem specific, can then be added.

3.3 Uncertainty Modeling

Three cases can occur: P_k takes hierarchical symbolic values (it is an abstract property), non-hierarchical symbolic values or numerical values (in the last two cases it is a concrete property). We mainly concentrate on the first case, the two other cases being simpler to deal with.

Symbolic Hierarchical Values (Abstract Property). We assume that all values in $\mathcal{V}_{lk}$ are present in the ontology as classes, i.e., any $v \in \mathcal{V}_{lk}$ is also in $\mathcal{C}_{P_k}$. A simple method using syntactic similarity (not taken into account here) to integrate newly encountered values is explained afterwards 4. If v is the value given by the reference, we denote by $\mathcal{V}_{lk}^v = \{v^{1,v}, \ldots, v^{|\mathcal{V}_{lk}|,v}\}$ the set of ordered values taken by the references of Rec_l, indexed with respect to their conceptual similarity with v, i.e. $i < j \Rightarrow CS(v, v^{i,v}) \leq CS(v, v^{j,v})$ (note that $v^{1,v} = v$). The order relation induced by CS values is a preorder, since multiple values can have the same Wu & Palmer measure with respect to v. For $j = 1, \ldots, |\mathcal{V}_{lk}|$, a first possibility distribution $\pi'_{n,k}$ is built as follows:

$$\pi'_{n,k}(v^{j,v}) = \tag{3}$$

$$
\begin{cases}
1 & \text{if } j = 1 \\[2mm]
\left(1 - \dfrac{f(v)}{\displaystyle\sum_{v \in \mathcal{V}_{lk}} f(v)}\right)\left(1 - \dfrac{\displaystyle\sum_{i<j} CS(v, v^{i,v})}{|\mathcal{V}_{lk}| \displaystyle\sum_{j=1} CS(v, v^{j,v})}\right) & \text{if } j>1 \text{ and } CS(v, v^{j,v}) < CS(v, v^{j-1,v}) \\[6mm]
\pi'_{n,k}(v^{j-1,v}) & \text{if } j>1 \text{ and } CS(v, v^{j,v}) = CS(v, v^{j-1,v})
\end{cases}
$$

In this distribution, the observed value is the most plausible. When the global frequency of this value v is high, other values are made less plausible (their possibility degree being inversely proportional to $f(v)$). In other words, our confidence that v is a reliable value increase with $f(v)$. The plausibility degree of other values than v are also made lower when their conceptual similarities with v are lower (note that equivalencies and equalities of conceptual similarities are treated by the last case). $\pi'_{n,k}$ thus takes account of both conceptual similarity and global frequency.

The reliability α_m of the source S_m from which the reference comes is then used in a classical discounting operation, which consists in transforming, for all $v \in \mathcal{V}_{lk}$, the distribution $\pi'_{n,k}$ into:

$$\pi_{n,k}(v) = \max(1 - \alpha_m, \pi'_{n,k}(v)).$$

This is equivalent to make the information more imprecise when it is less reliable, thus reducing its impact on the final model (original information is kept if $\alpha_m = 1$ and has no impact at all if $\alpha_m = 0$).

Example 2. We consider the subgroup of references $\{idE11, idE22, idE23\}$ from Figure 2, and the property $P_3 = hasComponent$. We also consider that $\alpha_1 = 0.9$ and $\alpha_2 = 0.8$. The set of possible values for this subgroup is $\mathcal{V}_{13}$ =*{Thiamine, Thiamin, Vitamin B}*. The hierarchical symbolic value "Thiamine" is equivalent to "Thiamin", and thus considered as being in the same equivalence class. The conceptual similarity between "Thiamin" and "Vitamin B" is such that $N_1 = 1$, $N_2 = 0$ and $N_3 = 5$ ("VitaminB" being the Least Common Subsumer), hence $CS(Thiamin, VitaminB) = {}^{10}/_{11}$. Finally, we assume that $f(\{Thiamine, Thiamin\}) = 18/123$ and that $f(\{VitaminB\}) = 2/123$, since data about experiments generally give the precise name of the tested vitamin. For the reference $\{idE23\}$, we have $\mathcal{V}_{lk}^v$ = *{Vitamin B, Thiamine, Thiamin}*, and the distribution $\pi'_{3,3}$ is such that:

$$\pi'_{3,3}(VitaminB) = 1; \quad \pi'_{3,3}(\{Thiamine, Thiamin\}) = (1 - {}^2/_{20})(1 - \frac{1}{{}^{20}/_{11}}) = 0.405$$

and we have $\pi_{3,3} = \pi'_{3,3}$, all values of $\pi'_{3,3}$ being above $1 - \alpha_1 = 0.1$. Note that a missing value would have been modelled by the distribution:
$\pi(VitaminB) = \pi(\{Thiamine, Thiamin\}) = 1$

Non Hierarchical Symbolic Values. In this case, no hierarchical proximity has to be integrated to the uncertainty model, and we consider that $\mathcal{V}_{lk}^v = \{v^{1,v}, \ldots, v^{|\mathcal{V}_{lk}|,v}\}$ is indexed and ordered according to syntactic similarity of values with v, i.e., $i < j \Rightarrow Sim(v, v^{i,v}) \le Sim(v, v^{j,v})$. The first distribution $\pi'_{n,k}$ is then computed by the same equation as Eq. (3), except that $CS(v, v^{j,v})$ is replaced by $Sim(v, v^{j,v})$, that is, for $j = 1, \ldots, |\mathcal{V}_{lk}|$,

$$\pi'_{n,k}(v^{j,v}) = \tag{4}$$

$$
\begin{cases}
1 & \text{if } j = 1 \\[2ex]
\left(1 - \dfrac{f(v)}{\sum\limits_{v \in \mathcal{V}_{lk}} f(v)}\right)\left(1 - \dfrac{\sum\limits_{i<j} Sim(v, v^{i,v})}{|\mathcal{V}_{lk}| \sum\limits_{j=1} Sim(v, v^{j,v})}\right) & \text{if } j>1 \text{ and } Sim(v, v^{j,v}) < Sim(v, v^{j-1,v}) \\[3ex]
\pi'_{n,k}(v^{j-1,v}) & \text{if } j>1 \text{ and } Sim(v, v^{j,v}) = Sim(v, v^{j-1,v})
\end{cases}
$$

The discounting operation is then applied as in the hierarchical case. Arguments justifying the uncertainty model are similar to those of the hierarchical case.

Numerical Values. Properties that take numerical values can possibly be subject to small variations between references. They can be, for example, physical measurements coming out from experiments. In general, such numerical values concern physical parameters. In these cases, assume $[v^-, v^+]$ is the interval given by the source (precise values are retrieved when $v^- = v^+$). The possibility distribution $\pi_{n,k}$ modeling the uncertainty for this property and reference is then

$$\pi_{n,p}(v) = \left\{ \begin{array}{ll} 1 & \text{if } v \in [v^-, v^+] \\ 1 - \alpha_m & \text{if } v \in [\underline{v}_k, \overline{v}_k] \setminus [v^-, v^+] \end{array} \right\}. \tag{5}$$

Other numerical values such as postal code, customer number, ID number, *etc.* are treated as symbolic values without hierarchical structure.

Missing Data. The treatment of missing data in databases is a well-known problem. In the present method, modeling the ignorance about a property value P_k for ref_n can be easily done, using the so-called vacuous (or non-iformative) possibility distribution, that is the distribution $\pi_{n,k}$ such that, for each $v \in \mathcal{V}_{lk}$, $\pi_{n,k}(v) = 1$. This distribution can then be merged with the others, with the effect of increasing the final imprecision. Note that that no additional assumptions has to be made about missing data in this method.

3.4   Fusion Method Using the Uncertainty Model

Given a group of reconciled references Rec_l, we denote by ref_{Σ_l} the single fused reference resulting from the fusion process. This fused reference will consist of K possibility distributions $\pi_{\Sigma_l,k}$ defined over spaces $\mathcal{V}_{lk}$, $k = 1, \ldots, K$ and obtained from the distributions described in Section 3.3.

There exists many rules to merge possibility distributions [13]. Here, using a simple arithmetic mean operator is a relevant choice, as it corresponds to a statistical counting and presents a natural way to integrate the homogeneity criterion in the final representation: a value will have all the more weight as it appears more frequently in the group of reconciled references. For a property P_k and a group Rec_l, the final representation $\pi_{\Sigma_l,k}$ is computed, for all $v \in \mathcal{V}_{lk}$, as follows:

$$\pi_{\Sigma_l,k}(v) = \sum_{ref_n \in Rec_l} \frac{1}{|Rec_l|} \pi_{n,k}(v) \tag{6}$$

which is then made consistent by applying the following transformation to all $v \in \mathcal{V}_{lk}$: $\pi_{\Sigma_l,k}(v) = \pi'_{\Sigma_l,k}(v)/\max_{v \in \mathcal{V}_{lk}} \pi'_{\Sigma_l,k}(v)$. Once this fusion step is achieved, we end up with L final representations, where each property value is described by a possibility distribution reflecting our uncertainty about the real value.

Example 3. Let us pursue example 2 by considering the same subgroup and the same property $A_3 = hasComponent$. As the values $Thiamin, Thiamine$ are considered as equivalent, we have $\pi'_{1,3} = \pi'_{2,3}$ (resp. the distributions induced by references $\{idE11\}$ and $\{idE22\}$). The different distributions are then

$$\pi'_{3,3}(VitaminB) = 1; \quad \pi'_{3,3}(\{Thiamine, Thiamin\}) = 0.405$$
$$\pi'_{1,3}(\{Thiamine, Thiamin\}) = 1; \quad \pi'_{1,3}(VitaminB) = 0.045.$$

However, since sources do not have the same reliability, we have, after the discounting operation, $\pi_{3,3} = \pi'_{3,3}$ and

$$\pi_{1,3}(\{Thiamine, Thiamin\}) = 1; \quad \pi_{1,3}(VitaminB) = 0.1$$
$$\pi_{2,3}(\{Thiamine, Thiamin\}) = 1; \quad \pi_{2,3}(VitaminB) = 0.2.$$

The obtained fused distribution $\pi_{\Sigma_l,3}$ (Using Eq. (6) on $\pi'_{i,3}$, $i = 1, 2, 3$) is

$$\pi_{\Sigma_l,3}(VitaminB) = \frac{0.115}{0.802} = 0.143; \quad \pi_{\Sigma_l,3}(\{Thiamine, Thiamin\}) = \frac{0.802}{0.802} = 1.$$

4   Ontology Enrichment

Up to now, we have assumed that every value of V_{lk} corresponding to an abstract property P_k was in the ontology $\mathcal{O}_{P_k}$. In practice, there are high chances that some references contain values absent from the ontology, since we work under open-world assumption. Therefore, in order to fuse the references of a group of duplicates Rec_l, we must integrate new values to the ontology. This section providesa simple method to enrich the original ontology with new values, before the fusion process.

Algorithm 1. Ontology enrichment algorithm

---

input : - V_{lk}: the set of values taken by the considered property P_k in Rec_l;
        - $\mathcal{O} = \{\mathcal{C}, \mathcal{P}, \mathcal{I}, \mathcal{D}\}$: an initial ontology;
        - th: a similarity threshold.
output: $\mathcal{O}'$: the enriched ontology.

$\mathcal{O}' \leftarrow \mathcal{O}$; $D \leftarrow subClasses(c_{P_k})$; $E \leftarrow D \cap V_{lk}$
foreach {$v \in V_{lk}$} **do**
  if $(v \notin E)$ **then**
    $bestScore \leftarrow 0$
    $bestClass \leftarrow null$
  end
  foreach {$d \in D$} **do** $S \leftarrow Sim(v, d)$
  if $(S > th \text{ and } S > bestScore)$ **then**
    $bestScore \leftarrow S$
    $bestClass \leftarrow d$
  end
  if $(bestClass \neq null)$ **then**
    $\mathcal{O}' \leftarrow addEquivalence(\mathcal{O}', v, bestClass)$
  end
  else
    if $(E \neq \emptyset)$ **then** $bestClass \leftarrow LCS(E)$ **else** $bestClass \leftarrow c_{P_k}$
    $\mathcal{O}' \leftarrow addSubClass(\mathcal{O}', v, bestClass)$
  end
end

Algorithm 1 describes the method for a set of values V_{lk}. It consists in considering that a new value is either equivalent to another one in $\mathcal{C}_{P_k}$ if it is syntactically close enough to it, or is subsumed by the least common subsumer of the values of V_{lk} in $\mathcal{C}_{P_k}$. It contains the following functions:

- $subClasses(c) = \{c' \in \mathcal{C}_{P_k} | c' \sqsubseteq c\}$ computes the set of descendants of a class c including c itself;
- $addEquivalence(O, c_1, c_2)$ adds the class c_1 in the ontology O as equivalent to the class c_2 (i.e. $c_1 \equiv c_2$);
- $addSubClass(O, c_1, c_2)$ adds the class c_1 in the ontology O as a sub-class of the class c_2 (i.e. $c_1 \sqsubseteq c_2$ and $\not\exists c_3$ s.t. $c_1 \sqsubseteq c_3 \sqsubseteq c_2$).

Example 4. Consider the subgroup made of references $\{idE11, idE22, idE23\}$ from Figure 2, and the property $P_3 = hasComponent$. We have $V_{l3} = \{Thiamine, Thiamin, Vitamin B\}$ and $E = V_{l3} \cap subClasses(A_3) = \{Thiamin, VitaminB\}$. Referring to Fig. 1, we have $LCS(E) = \{VitaminB\}$. However, assuming that *Sim(Thiamine, Thiamin)* = *0.95* and that $th = 0.9$, applying Algorithm 1 leads to declare $Thiamine \equiv Thiamin$, and to consider them as equivalent values. The ontology is thus enriched by adding the class $Thiamine$ as equivalent to the existing class $Thiamin$.

5   Implementation of the Approach

In this section we show how we implement our approach for reference fusion and querying. To implement the proposed approach, we apply a maping beween the structural specification of OWL language and the sepecification of RDF language (see [14]). We have chosen to use the semantic web languages RDF and SPARQL for respectively describing fused references and querying them.

We first give a representation of the fused references by using an extension of RDF to a fuzzy-RDF language. Then we propose a transformation of the obtained fuzzy-RDF data into plain RDF data. In section 5.3, we present the flexible querying of fused references by using SPARQL.

5.1   Fuzzy-RDF Representation of Fused Data

To represent uncertain data, Mazzieri [15] proposes an extension of RDF language into a fuzzy-RDF language, providing its syntax and semantics. The syntax extension consists in expressing RDF declarations in the form of triples *<subject, predicate, object>* by using declarations of the form $\alpha : $ *<subject predicate object>*. For each triple, a degree α in $[0, 1]$ is added, representing the truth value of the triple. Note that other representation choices are also possible, such as the syntax proposed in [16].

Using the fusion method, the obtained description of the reference Rec_l takes the form, for a value v: $\pi_{\Sigma_l, k}(v) :< Rec_l\ P_k\ v >$, where P_k is a property and v is a value in V_{lk}. Note that only one value of each equivalence class has to be stored, as the synonyms can be obtained through the ontology.

Example 5. The fused datum given in example 3 leads to the following declarations describing the possibility distribution for the value of the attribute A_3 *:hasComponent* :

$1 \ :< \ Rec_1 \ hasComponent \ "Thiamin" >$
$0.143 \ :< \ Rec_1 \ hasComponent \ "Vitamin \ B" >.$

5.2 Transformation of Fuzzy-RDF Data into Plain RDF Data

In order to guarantee the implementation of the fusion method in all platforms based on plain RDF, we propose a transformation of our fuzzy-RDF representation of the fused data into plain RDF. We use the reification mechanism (for the reification semantics, see [17]) that allows adding new elements to the descriptions of the RDF declarations, like data author, creation date,.... In our case, the reification consists in adding to the triples of the form $< \ Rec_l \ P_k \ v >$ the *possibility* property that has a resource as domain and a decimal as range.

Let ns be the namespace of the RDFS schema which we have enriched by the *possibility* property. We obtain, for each fuzzy-RDF triple of the form $\pi_{\Sigma_l,k}(v) \ :< Rec_l \ P_k \ v >$, to which an identifier $tripleID - i$ is assigned, its reified representation. For example, for the triple $1 \ :< \ Rec_l \ hasComponent \ "Thiamin" >$ we obtain the following reified representation:

```
<tripleID-1 rdf:type rdf:Statement > .
<tripleID-1 rdf:subject ns:Rec1> .
<tripleID-1  rdf:predicate ns:hasComponent> .
<tripleID-1  rdf:object "Thiamin"^^xsd:string > .
<tripleID-1  ns:possibility 1^^xsd:decimal> .
```

By applying this transformation, the fused references can be queried by using the SPARQL language without any need of extension.

5.3 Fused Reference Querying

The SPARQL syntax is close to the SQL one classicaly used in relational databases. The queries in SPARQL are evaluated on the set of triples contained in RDF data. In the following we will use *select queries*, which return a set of triples that check the constraints expressed in the WHERE clause. The SPARQL queries are evaluated on the set of fused references represented in plain RDF, by reification.

```
PREFIX rdf: <http://www.w3.org/1999/02/22-rdf-syntax-ns#>
PREFIX ns: <http://www.lri.fr/~sais/myRDFS-1/>
SELECT  ?ref ?comp ?confidence
WHERE {
?x rdf:type rdf:Statement  .
?x rdf:subject ?ref  .
?x rdf:predicate ns:hasComponent .
?x rdf:object ?comp .
?x rdf:object ?confidence .
}
ORDER BY ?confidence
LIMIT 1
```

6   Experiments

In this section we present some experiment results of the fusion method. In order to assess the quality of the method, we use a dataset that we can compare to ideal value, in this case references of articles, of conferences and of persons. First, we give a description of the dataset that we have used. Then, we present the evaluation criteria that we have considered to validate / invalidate the obtained results.

6.1   Presentation of *Cora* Dataset

The fusion method has been implemented and evaluated on the *Cora* data set related to the scientific publication domain. It has been used as a benchmark by several reference reconciliation approaches [2,18]. Cora dataset is a collection of 1295 citations of 124 different research papers in computer science. These citations have been collected from the research engine Cora specialized on scientific publications search. A reference is associated to each article, conference and author (person). An article is described by several properties: *title*, *year*, *pageFrom*, *pageTo* and *type* which takes values in {proceedings, journal, book, ...}. A person is described by his *name* and a conference is described by three properties: *confName*, *confYear* and a *city*. There are two relations (objectProperties) which link each article to its authors and to the conference where it is published.

Table 2. Cora dataset description

	Article	Conference	Person
#Groups	124	134	68
#References	1295	1292	3521
#distinct-values-per-group	[1..5]	[1..28]	[1..37]
Avg(#disctinct values-per-group)	3	8	9

We have applied the fusion method on the gold-standard of Cora dataset. It is organized as a set of 326 groups of pairwise reconciled references for the three classes: article, conference and person. In table 2, we present some statistics of the characteristics of the gold-standard: the number of renconciled reference groups, the number of references, the interval bounded by the minimum and maximum number of distinct values per group and the average of distinct values per reconciled group.

6.2   Evaluation Protocol

To evaluate the validity of the fusion method, we have compared, for a set of selected properties, the ranking of their values according to the confidence degree obtained by the fusion method with the ranking given by a humain expert.

In some application domains, the identification of the right value can be purely subjective. For example, choosing between the two painting names "*La joconde*" and "*Mona-lisa*" is not obvious, as the two names are acceptable. Nevertheless, there are some obvious criteria that allow to differentiate a right value from a wrong value, which mainly consists in features that contribute to the syntactic integrity of the values.

- Typographical errors, like *"Criptographic"* instead of *"Cryptographic"*.
- Syntactic errors that are due to the data extraction processing, like, *"for - -mulae"* instead of *"formulae"* or **Bart (1993).** *Reasoning with characteristic models"* instead of *"Reasoning with characteristic models"*.
- Missing words, like *"... free probabilistic concepts"* instead of *"... free probabilistic* **learning** *concepts"*
- Additionnal words, like **"some** *experiments with a new ..."* instead of *"experiments with a new"*

When the previous criteria do not help the expert to classify the values, the DBLP[3] browser is used to determine the right-values and the wrong ones.

The second evaluation step consists in reviewing the list of ranked values of each property and classifying them, according to the previous criteria, into two classes: the right-values and the wrong-values. In the case of the Cora dataset, there is only one right value which satisfy the defined criteria. However, in some application domains they can be several values which can correspond to the right value in case of synonymies. The expert gives a ranking of the values by putting the right-value in the top rank, i.e., before all the wrong-values. The third step consists in comparing the ranked lists of values obtained by the fusion method with those given by the expert. In this step we count:

1. *#well-ranked-RV*: the number of well-ranked right-values, that is the number of right values that appear in the top rank.
2. *#misranked-RV*: the number of misranked right-values, that is the number of cases where the right value appears after one or several wrong-values (it has a lower confidence degree).

A less strict evaluation protocol could be used: instead of considering the top rank of the value list, we can consider the top-k list of values and check if the right-value belongs to this top-k list of values or not.

6.3   Fusion Method Results

In Table 3, we give the results for the three properties which contain most of syntactic variations: *Title, ConfName* and person *Name*. We compute the precision for the right-values as the proportion of the number of well-ranked values in reconciled groups[4]:

$$Precision = \frac{\#well - ranked - right - values}{\#reconciled - groups}$$

We note that the recall value equals the precision value because of the strict evaluation protocol. Indeed, as we consider that the fusion method fails when the right-value does not appear in the top position, the recall value corresponds also to the proportion of the well-ranked right-values in the reconciled groups.

---

[3] The DBLP Computer Science Bibliography which provides bibliographic information on major computer science journals and proceedings.

[4] We have considered the reconciled groups where the size of value list is (≥ 2).

Table 3. Fusion results in terms of precision for the values of: Title, ConfName, Name

	Article-Title	Conference-Name	Person-Name
#reconciled-groups	66	66	44
#well-ranked-RV	62	49	33
#misranked-RV	4	17	11
Precision=Recall	93.9%	74.2%	75%

The results of Table 3 show that the fusion method has obtained a precision of 93.9% for the ranking of the right values of article title. It obtains also a precision of 74.2 % for the ranking of conference name and of 75% for the person names. We can notice that the precision for the conference names and for the person names are lower than the precision of article titles. This can be due to the important rate of syntactic variation in their corresponding possible values.

As it is shown in Table 2, the number of distinct values of the conference names variates between 1 to 28 values and between 1 to 37 for the person names. For the conference names, the variations are mostly caused in by abbreviations (e.g. proc./proceedings, symp./symposium), by a variety of codifications (e.g. 9th/ninth) and by extraction problems (e.g. net-works/networks). For the person names, even when only considering the English-speaking world, a name can have several different spelling forms for a variety of reasons. In the Anglo-Saxon region and most other Western countries, a personal name is usually made of a given name, an optional middle name, and a surname or family name. Hispanic names can contain two surnames. For example, in the dataset we have 11 variations for the person name *Umesh Virkumar Vazirani*: {*Umesh Vazirani*; *U. Vazirani*; *Umesh V. Vazirani*; *Vazirani U.V.*; etc.}. Hence the main difficulties arise from what we could consider as abbreviations or synonyms. We could therefore improve our results by declaring such values as synonyms in our ontology. However, the results about article title show a very good recognition rate in case of a strict evaluation protocol. We can guarantee that the results can only be better for a top-k evaluation.

By these experiments we have shown the good performances of the developed fusion approach where data are syntactically very heterogeneous.

7   Related Work

There are some studies on reference reconciliation that deal to a certain degree with reference fusion. In [3], a rule-based language is used by the administrator of the integration system to define different functions of reference fusion. Particular constructors are used to specify information on reliable data sources that are exploited in case of conflicts between values. Thus, the fusion can be achieved without considering the values coming from the other sources. Consequently, the value conflicts are not even detected. In [19], the fusion is also performed by using fusion rules that are specified by the integration system administrator. The authors propose five strategies for the resolution of conflicts between values. In [20], the authors propose a new operator FUSE BY used in SQL queries. This operator takes as arguments a set of pre-defined functions (e.g. vote, max, min) which are associated with attributes that are involved in the SQL query.

In our method, heterogeneity and conflict between redundant references is handled through the use of these criteria and of possibility theory, whereas previous methods [3] tends to ignore or bypass these features. The computation of possibility degrees is based on a combination of various criteria which are related to the value features, like frequency, but also related to data source features, like reliability. Unlike other approaches[20,19], our method does not need any extension of the query language to be able to query the fused data. Finally, the representation of the fusion result in the form of possibility distributions allows to rank values by their plausibilities and thus offers some flexibility when handling and querying the fused data. It is based on justified theoretical uncertainty treatment tools and in-depth uncertainty modeling (discounting operation, homogeneity criterion taken into account through the merging operator, etc.) allowing to model imprecision. To our knowledge, such possibilistic-based methods are new.

Also, the fusion method we propose takes into account the hierarchical organization of the vocabulary, as well as equivalence relations, provided by an ontology, which is not the case in previous studies. A cooperation between the reconciliation/fusion process and ontology completion is also firstly provided in this paper, through the ontology enrichment procedure.

A preliminary study to the present work was presented in [11]. This work did not yet take into account the ontology, and used a more had-oc construction of uncertainty models. Note that we consider crisp ontology in this paper and not fuzzy ontology [21]. Indeed, in our case, fuzzy sets are used to describe uncertainty and arise from the fusion process, not from the ontology definition. That is, even if they are defined over concepts of the ontology, they do not pertain to the ontology.

8   Conclusion

In this paper, we have proposed a method for reference fusion, driven by ontological knowledge including subsomption and equivalence relations between concepts. The fusion method allows the computation, for each candidate value of a given property, of a possibility degree. The set of values that is assigned to a property is expressed as a possibility distribution.

We have shown the applicability of our methods and illustrated them on agronomical data. By the experiments on scientific publication dataset, we have shown the efficiency of the developed fusion approach even where data are syntactically very heterogeneous. We plan in a short term to apply the fusion method on datasets of other application domains where the use of semantic knowledge is more relevant (subsumptions, synonymies, etc.).

From a methodological point of view, an assumption that we made in this study is that values encountered in the data are not necessarily declared in the ontology (open-world assumption); we proposed a method that uses the values missing in the ontology as candidates to complete the existing ontology. Another perspective is to combine this approach with methods allowing automatic detection of synonyms, which is currently under study.

References

1. Rahm, E., Bernstein, P.A.: A survey of approaches to automatic schema matching. The VLDB Journal 10(4), 334–350 (2001)
2. Saïs, F., Pernelle, N., Rousset, M.C.: Combining a logical and a numerical method for data reconciliation. J. Data Semantics 12, 66–94 (2009)
3. Papakonstantinou, Y., Abiteboul, S., Garcia-Molina, H.: Object fusion in mediator systems. In: VLDB, San Francisco, CA, USA, pp. 413–424 (1996)
4. Dubois, D., Prade, H.: Tolerant fuzzy pattern matching: an introduction. In: Bosc, P., Kacprzyk, J. (eds.) Fuzziness in Database Management Systems, pp. 42–58. Physica-Verlag, Heidelberg (1995)
5. Dubois, D., Prade, H.: Possibility Theory - An Approach to Computerized Processing of Uncertainty. Plenum Press, New York (1988)
6. Dean, M., Schreiber, G.: OWL Web Ontology Language Reference, W3C Recommendation Technical report (2004), http://www.w3.org/tr/owl-ref/
7. Walley, P.: Measures of uncertainty in expert systems. Artifical Intelligence 83, 1–58 (1996)
8. Zadeh, L.: Fuzzy sets as a basis for a theory of possibility. Fuzzy Sets and Systems 1, 3–28 (1978)
9. Motik, B., Horrocks, I.: Owl datatypes: Design and implementation. In: Sheth, A.P., Staab, S., Dean, M., Paolucci, M., Maynard, D., Finin, T., Thirunarayan, K. (eds.) ISWC 2008. LNCS, vol. 5318, pp. 307–322. Springer, Heidelberg (2008)
10. Wu, Z., Palmer, M.: Verbs semantics and lexical selection. In: Proceedings of the 32nd Annual Meeting on Association for Computational Linguistics, Morristown, NJ, USA, pp. 133–138. Association for Computational Linguistics (1994)
11. Saïs, F., Thomopoulos, R.: Reference fusion and flexible querying. In: Meersman, R., Tari, Z. (eds.) OTM 2008, Part II. LNCS, vol. 5332, pp. 1541–1549. Springer, Heidelberg (2008)
12. Cohen, W., Ravikumar, P., Fienberg, S.E.: A comparison of string metrics for matching names and records. In: Proc. of the KDD-2003 Workshop on Data Cleaning, Record Linkage, and Object Consolidation (2003)
13. Dubois, D., Prade, H.: Possibility theory in information fusion. In: Riccia, G.D., Lenz, H., Kruse, R. (eds.) Data Fusion and Perception. CISM Courses and Lectures, vol. 431, pp. 53–76. Springer, Berlin (2001)
14. W3C: Owl ontologies to rdf graphs (2007), http://www.w3.org/2007/owl/wiki/mapping-to-rdf-graphs
15. Mazzieri, M.: A fuzzy rdf semantics to represent trust metadata. In: 1st Workshop on Semantic Web. Applications and Perspectives (2004)
16. Buche, P., Dibie-Barthélemy, J., Hignette, G.: Flexible querying of fuzzy rdf annotations using fuzzy conceptual graphs. In: Eklund, P., Haemmerlé, O. (eds.) ICCS 2008. LNCS (LNAI), vol. 5113, pp. 133–146. Springer, Heidelberg (2008)
17. Hayes, P.: RDF Semantics Technical report (2004), http://www.w3.org/tr/rdf-mt/
18. Dong, X., Halevy, A., Madhavan, J.: Reference reconciliation in complex information spaces. In: Proceedings of the 2005 ACM SIGMOD International Conference on Management of Data, SIGMOD 2005, pp. 85–96. ACM Press, New York (2005)
19. Subrahmanian, V., Adali, S., Brink, A., Emery, R., Lu, J.L., Rajput, A., Rogers, T.J., Ross, R., Ward, C.: Hermes: A heterogeneous reasoning and mediator system (1995)
20. Bleiholder, J., Naumann, F.: Declarative data fusion – Syntax, semantics, and implementation. In: Eder, J., Haav, H.-M., Kalja, A., Penjam, J. (eds.) ADBIS 2005. LNCS, vol. 3631, pp. 58–73. Springer, Heidelberg (2005)
21. Calegari, S., Ciucci, D.: Integrating fuzzy logic in ontologies. In: Proc. of the 8th International Conference on Enterprise Information Systems, pp. 66–73 (2006)

Towards Duplicate Detection for Situation Awareness Based on Spatio-temporal Relations*

Norbert Baumgartner[1], Wolfgang Gottesheim[2], Stefan Mitsch[2],
Werner Retschitzegger[2], and Wieland Schwinger[2]

[1] team Communication Technology Mgt. Ltd., Goethegasse 3, 1010 Vienna, Austria
[2] Johannes Kepler University Linz, Altenbergerstr. 69, 4040 Linz, Austria

Abstract. Systems supporting situation awareness typically integrate information about a large number of real-world objects anchored in time and space provided by multiple sources. These sources are often characterized by identical, incomplete, and even contradictory information. Because of that, duplicate detection methods are of paramount importance, allowing to explore whether or not information concerns one and the same real-world object. Although many such duplicate detection methods exist, a recent survey revealed that the characteristics of situation awareness—highly dynamic and vague information, which is often available in qualitative form only—are not supported sufficiently well. This paper proposes concepts for qualitative duplicate detection to cope with these key issues of situation awareness based on spatio-temporal relations between objects.

1 Introduction

Situation awareness [17] is gaining more and more importance as a way to help human operators cope with information overload in large-scale control systems [6], like, e. g., encountered in the domain of road traffic management [26]. Systems supporting situation awareness typically deal with a *vast amount of information* about a large number of *real-world objects* anchored in *time and space* provided by *multiple sources*. These sources are often characterized by heterogeneous formats and, most crucial, contain identical, incomplete, and often even contradictory information [30]. Besides having to resolve structural heterogeneities at schema level, the data itself has to be fused into a single consistent form at instance level [8].

Characteristics of duplicates in situation awareness. As a major prerequisite for the latter task, duplicate detection methods are of paramount importance, allowing to explore whether or not information having, e. g., different origins or different observation times, concern one and the same real-world object. As was pointed out in a recent survey [5], existing duplicate detection methods, however, fail to consider the characteristics of situation awareness with respect to duplicate detection. In particular, the underlying data about real-world objects (e. g., a traffic jam) is often highly dynamic and vague. This entails that reliable numerical values are hard to obtain, thus making *qualitative*

---

* This work has been funded by the Austrian Federal Ministry of Transport, Innovation and Technology (BMVIT) under grant FIT-IT 819577.

R. Meersman et al. (Eds.): OTM 2010, Part II, LNCS 6427, pp. 1097–1107, 2010.

duplicate detection approaches better suited than quantitative ones [14]. Current quali-tative duplicate detection methods, however, are highly domain-specific, like e. g., such being proposed for detecting similar trajectories of moving objects in a road network [23], and measure similarity only with respect to a single spatial aspect, like distances between points of interest, at most taking time as additional dimension into account.

Duplicate detection on the basis of qualitative spatio-temporal relations. To over-come these limitations, we base upon the observation of Keane et al. [25], who state that humans generally tend to base their similarity judgement on (multiple) relation simi-larities, if present. Such relations can be expressed by employing relation calculi, each of them focusing on a certain spatio-temporal aspect, like mereotopology [31], orienta-tion [15], or direction [29]. These calculi are often formalized by means of Conceptual Neighborhood Graphs (CNGs, [19]), imposing constraints on the transitions between relations. By that, CNGs are an important notion for modeling continuously varying pro-cesses [28], and are adopted in, e. g., qualitative simulation [12], prediction [7], tracking moving objects [34], or agent control [16]. We propose a duplicate detection approach on the basis of similarity measures derived from relation calculi and their CNGs, com-prising *rule-based* similarity measures defined by domain experts, which are accompa-nied by *distance-based* ones. With rule-based similarity measures, domain experts can express their knowledge for detection of identical information (e. g., two objects are du-plicates, if they are in the same-type- and equal-region-relationship). Complementary, with distance-based similarity measures duplicates in incomplete and contradictory in-formation can be detected as well (e. g., two traffic jams being in VeryFar relationship from distance calculus are less likely duplicates then such being VeryClose). The applicability of this approach is demonstrated on the basis of real-world traffic data collected by the Austrian Highways Agency ASFINAG.

Structure of the paper. In the next section, we summarize the characteristics of sit-uation awareness with respect to duplicate detection by means of examples from the domain of road traffic management. In Section 3, we propose concepts for duplicate detection being applicable in presence of such characteristics. We then evaluate these concepts in Section 4. Finally, we provide an overview of related work in Section 5, before we conclude the paper in Section 6 by indicating future work.

2 Motivating Example

Road traffic management systems, being responsible for, e. g., improving traffic flow and ensuring safe driving conditions, are a typical application domain for situation awareness, aiming at assisting human operators by providing reliable qualitative in-formation, e. g., "a wrong-way driver heading towards a traffic jam". In our previous work [6] we introduced a framework[1] for building situation-aware systems on the basis of a domain-independent ontology representing qualitative information about the sys-tem under control. In the framework's ontology, *objects* and *relations* between them are aggregated into *situations*, whereas objects can either be real-world objects with

---

[1] This framework was used to build a prototype supporting human operators, thereby showing the feasibility of our approach.

a physical identity (e. g., a tunnel) or reified representations of events (e. g., a traffic jam). Information about such objects and relations stems from various sources being maintained independently, which, naturally, leads to duplicates in the form of identical, incomplete, and even contradictory information about the same real-world object. Changes of objects over time (i. e., object evolution), like, e. g., movement on a road, also lead to changes in relations between objects and make it particularly challenging to detect duplicates. In the following, we will exemplify these specific issues.

Let us suppose that a traffic jam builds up on a highway during rush hour, which may lead to a sequence of entries (cf. Fig. 1, 1–5) in the road traffic management system, originating from a call center and from a traffic flow detector. From a chronological

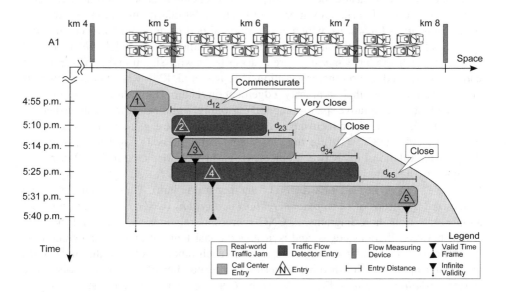

Fig. 1. Information about a traffic jam during rush hour

point of view, first of all a motorist informs the call center (entry 1). As the traffic jam's starting point is located between two flow measuring devices, it takes a while until the traffic jam has grown to an extent also observed by the traffic flow detector (entry 2). Both the traffic flow detector and the call center subsequently report updated information, as described by entries 3–5. However, motorists located at the end of the traffic jam are less and less able to observe the traffic jam's whole extent, resulting in inexact information about its starting point (entry 3), or even just in information about its end (entry 5).

In order to identify that all of these entries in fact describe one and the same real-world object, existing duplicate detection methods typically compute a *similarity measure* from *selected properties* [8]. Fig. 1 shows an exemplary similarity measure based on the distance between the end positions of traffic jam entries (e. g., d_{23}). Such duplicate detection methods, however, fail if reliable numerical values cannot be provided and if objects dynamically evolve [5], which are both important characteristics of application domains for situation awareness. For example, a "traditional" similarity measure would calculate d_{23} as the quantitative distance between the positions of entry 2 and entry 3, which is not possible if the only information available is, that these positions are *close* to each other. In the following section, we propose concepts to overcome these limitations. Please note that, since we build on our previous work [6], we assume that structural heterogeneitis between data sources have already been resolved.

3   Measuring Similarity of Qualitative Spatio-Temporal Data

A major task in duplicate detection for situation awareness, as exemplified in the previous section, is to measure the similarity of entries being anchored in time and space. In this section, we describe our approach to defining similarity measures on the basis of *spatio-temporal relations*, which are an integral part of describing objects in situations. In contrast to traditional duplicate detection methods based solely on an object's properties, such similarity measures are in accordance with Situation theory of Barwise and Perry [3][2] and exploit the observation of Keane et al. [25], who state that humans generally tend to base their similarity judgement on relation similarities, if present.

In the field of qualitative spatio-temporal reasoning, a number of well-established relation calculi, each of them focusing on a certain aspect, like e. g., mereotopology in the Region Calculus (RCC, [10]) or time in Allen's Time Intervals Algebra [1], structure the possible relationships between objects (e. g., in RCC depicted in Fig. 2, a region occupied by a traffic jam can be `Disrelated` from, `PartiallyOverlapping`, `ProperPart`, or `Equal` to a region of another traffic jam). These calculi are often formalized by means of *conceptual neighborhood graphs* (CNG, cf. [18]), resembling simple state transition diagrams. A CNG represents relations as nodes and the transitions between them as edges, and is arranged consistent with the human perception of similarity, i. e., similar relations are close to each other in a CNG, dissimilar ones are farther apart from each other in terms of the number of transitions in-between (termed *relation distance*). Fig. 2 shows the CNG of RCC, whereby the meaning of each relation is depicted inside the relation's node with circular objects. It can be seen, that the calculus contains one relation, which holds in case two objects are equal (i. e., the identity relation of RCC), three relations for describing somewhat similar objects (`ProperPart`, `PartiallyOverlapping`, and `ProperPartInverse`, because their regions in some form overlap or are contained in each other), and one relation for describing dissimilar objects (`Disrelated`, being farthest from `Equal`). Based on this, in the following we describe how to determine the similarity of entries, on the one hand, using exact definitions given by domain experts in a *rule-based* manner, and, on the other hand, by measuring *relation distances*.

3.1   Rule-Based Similarity Measure

Recently, ontology-driven situation awareness techniques [11], [2] have emerged, providing the vocabulary for describing situations with rules [6], [27]. Such approaches

---

[2] This notion makes the proposed approach applicable to a wide range of efforts in situation awareness, like e. g., to Kokar's approach [27].

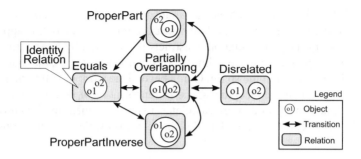

Fig. 2. Conceptual Neighborhood Graph of RCC

define the necessary pre-requisites for a rule-based duplicate detection approach, allowing domain experts to describe their knowledge about duplicates in the form of exact definitions. In the following example, the rule

$$Accident(?a) \wedge Accident(?b)$$
$$\wedge rcc : Equals(?a, ?b) \wedge allen : Equals(?a, ?b) \qquad (1)$$

defines that, for determining whether two accident entries a and b are duplicates, equality of their regions ($rcc : Equals(?a, ?b)$) as well as their temporal intervals ($allen : Equals(?a, ?b)$, i. e., valid time frames in Fig. 1) is most relevant. Such rules are suitable for detecting identical duplicates, and therefore need to be accompanied with concepts allowing the detection of duplicates in incomplete and contradictory information, as described in the following section.

3.2 Distance-Based Similarity Measure

We can use the distance between relations in a CNG to describe similarity of objects: for this, we identify an *identity relation* in each calculus that is valid if two objects are equal. This identity relation then serves as a reference point for calculating the distance to the relation being actually valid between the two objects. For example, the distance between `Disrelated` and `Equals`—being the identity relation of RCC—is 2 according to the CNG in Fig. 2, whereas `PartiallyOverlapping` and `Equals` are direct neighbors (distance 1). Therefore, if `PartiallyOverlapping` is actually valid between two objects, they are considered to be more similar than two objects being `Disrelated`[3].

Such a very basic one-dimensional computation, however, does not reliably describe the similarity of two objects being characterized by many different real-world aspects. Therefore, we combine calculi describing such different real-world aspects, like mereotopology, orientation, distance, and size from the spatial domain, as well as distance and size from the temporal domain. For combining these calculi, we base upon

---

[3] Note, that for using a CNG to determine a similarity measure, a calculus needs to be *joint exhaustively and pairwise disjoint (JEPD)*, which means that between any two objects *exactly one* of the calculus' relations is valid.

the work of Schwering [32], which uses a variant of Gärdenfors' *conceptual spaces* [22] to combine different metrics to a similarity measure for relations. In this approach, the similarity of natural-language relation constructs is measured by interpreting the conceptual space as a geometric space delimited by quality dimensions, making it possible to calculate distances within the space. Going beyond the work of Schwering, however, our approach uses such a conceptual space to represent *each relation calculus* on its own quality dimension, and thereby calculates a similarity measure for *entries representing objects*, as depicted in Fig. 3. In this figure, we show the valid relations between

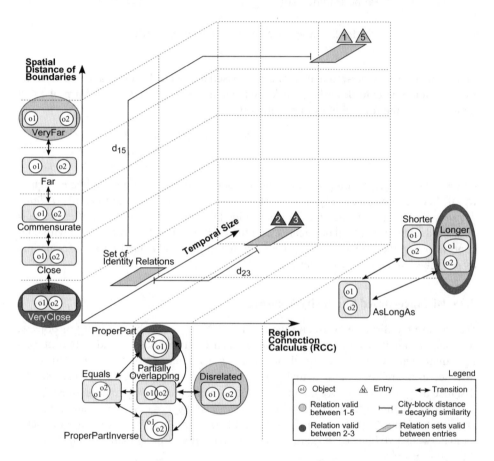

Fig. 3. Entry distances in a conceptual space

some of the entries from our motivating example. For example, the entries 1 and 5 are Disrelated in the quality dimension RCC, their spatial distance is VeryFar, and entry 1 is Longer in temporal size than entry 5. The relations valid between entry 2 and entry 3 are ProperPart, VeryClose and Longer. The fact that the relation distance defines a metric for each of the quality dimensions allows us to calculate distances between *relation sets* (like, e.g., the relation sets {Disrelated, VeryFar,

Longer}, {ProperPart, VeryClose, Longer}, and {Equals, VeryClose, AsLongAs} depicted in Fig. 3). Particularly interesting is the distance between the set of identity relations and the entries' valid relations, as we define the similarity measure of entries as a decaying function of this distance. For example, the distance d_{15} between the set of identity relations and the relations of entries 1 and 5 indicates that these entries are unlikely to be duplicates. In comparison, the distance d_{23} is smaller, indicating that the entries 2 and 3 are more likely to be duplicates. For calculating such a distance, we can use well-known metrics like Euclidian distance or city-block distance (also known as Manhattan distance) [13]. We follow the suggestion of Johannesson [24] to use the city-block distance, allowing to combine semantically separable dimensions (e. g., time and space), which are predominant in situation awareness.

Since the calculation of relation distances requires comparing every object with every other object, the proposed approach's runtime behaviour can be improved using clustering strategies that reduce the number of object comparison operations. One such strategy could cluster objects by their type, based, e. g., on type subsumption information defined in ontologies, so that only objects having the same type are compared. Other possible strategies include clustering by spatial information, since, e. g., accidents that have occurred on different roads can be assumed to be distinct and, therefore, do not require the calculation of relation distances. Additional improvements are possible by incorporating a domain expert's knowledge formalized in rules as shown in Sect. 3.1 to select only appropriate calculi and identity relations for inclusion in the conceptual space (alternatively, all available calculi could be included), thereby minimizing the number of required comparison operations. Further improvements in terms of accuracy might be achieved by integrating additional qualitative dimensions into the conceptual space and taking knowledge on correlations and subsumptions between calculi into account.

4   Evaluation

For evaluating the proposed concepts, we collaborate with our project partners[4] providing real-world data. These data are reported by multiple sources, like, e. g., traffic flow sensors, road maintenance schedules, and motorists reporting incidents to a call center. The recorded data set used for this evaluation consists of 3,563 distinct road traffic objects, comprising, among others, 778 traffic jams, 819 road works, 1,339 other obstructions, 460 accidents, and 64 weather warnings. In this early stage, we focussed on detecting duplicate traffic jams, and relied on the help of domain experts, who manually examined the recorded data set, resulting in a test data set comprising 35 duplicates among a total of 94 traffic jam messages. It has to be noted, that the presented preliminary evaluation results, although they indicate the applicability of the proposed approach, further need critical observation, as we continuously extend our test data set.

For evaluating duplicate detection we first employed duplicate detection rules specifying that two traffic jam entries are duplicates if the following condition holds:

---

[4] We are currently realizing ontology-driven situation awareness techniques for the domain of road traffic management together with our project partners Heusch/Boesefeldt, a German supplier of road traffic management systems, and the Austrian highways agency ASFINAG.

`RCC:PartiallyOverlapping` ∧ `TemporalDistance:Close`, cf. Fig. 4 (a). In contrast to that, our approach exploiting relation distances was configured with a two-dimensional conceptual space measuring distances in RCC and Allen's Time Intervals Algebra (allowing duplicates to have a distance of one to each dimension's identity relation), cf. Fig. 4 (b).

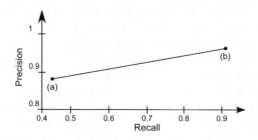

Fig. 4. Precision and recall of proposed concepts

As the evaluation reveals, duplicate detection relying on rules is only able to detect information exactly satisfying the rule, which leads, on the one hand, to high precision, but on the other hand to many missed duplicates (20, resulting in low recall). In contrast, working with similarity measures based on relation distances holds the risk of interpreting non-duplicates as duplicates (i. e., an increase in *false positives* from two to three), but enables us to detect also duplicates stemming from incomplete or contradictory information (an increase from 15 to 33 true positives, a decrease from 20 to two false negatives, resulting in higher recall). When examining the false positives in detail, we found out that they mainly stem from incomplete temporal information, resulting in entries having no ending time and thus entailing overlapping time intervals. An experienced human operator could substitute such missing temporal information with typical object evolutions, thus avoiding this issue. This observation underpins the hypothesis that object evolution characteristics—as we proposed as an optimization technique for predicting object evolutions [4]—are promising for improving duplicate detection.

5   Related Work

Relevant related work for qualitative duplicate detection in situation awareness can be found in geospatial database research, as well as in research on moving object trajectories.

The survey of Schwering [33] focuses on semantic similarity of geospatial data, thereby emphasizing the importance of appropriate similarity measures for different spatial representation models. One such similarity measure for spatial relations is proposed in [32]. However, this similarity measure is restricted to topologic and distance aspects of relations between lines and regions, and leaves the incorporation of directional relations, or non-spatial relations as further work. We generalize this work to measure similarity between arbitrary *objects* by comparing the relations between them with appropriate *identity relations*.

Similarity analysis of trajectories is an area concerned with comparing the traces of moving objects in time and space [21]. Several such methods exist, like [9], [20], and [23]. However, most of them in fact measure similarity in Euclidian space only (whereas in our domain graphs are more suitable to describe spatial information), and lack support for qualitative spatio-temporal information. The work of Hwang et al. [23] is particularly relevant for our work due to its applicability to road networks. Hwang et al. propose spatio-temporal similarity measures to detect duplicates in trajectories of moving objects. Being based on qualitative information in terms of "points of interest" and "times of interest", the method, however, is not able to consider multiple different spatial aspects, resulting in rudimentary duplicate detection only.

6   Future Work

In our future work we plan to concentrate on two major areas: on the one hand, we aim to improve the detection of inexact duplicates, and on the other hand, we will incorporate object evolution support.

Our experience shows that exact duplicates only rarely occur, therefore the detection of inexact duplicates is of major importance. Currently, our rule-based approach only supports the detection of duplicates exactly matching a rule's definition, while our relation distance-based approach can be configured with a threshold that determines whether two objects are considered to be duplicates. By relaxing our current constraint that requires relations in a calculus to be pairwise disjoint and instead allowing multiple valid relations annotated with a probability to hold simultaneously, we plan to be able to not only state that, e. g., "an accident is partially overlapping with a traffic jam", but instead express that "an accident is partially overlapping with a traffic jam with a confidence of 60%, proper part of it with a confidence of 25%, and disrelated from it with a confidence of 15%". By this, we can partially match duplicate rules and give a confidence estimate on our duplicate detection. In addition, we plan to improve the distance-based approach's runtime behaviour as indicated above by incorporating clustering strategies. We will also investigate how this approach's scalability can be assured by evaluating how adding additional dimensions can enhance accuracy without hampering runtime behaviour.

The second major area we plan to address is the consideration of object evolution in duplicate detection. As our example in Sect. 2 shows, objects are not static and, therefore, similarity between them changes over time. Based on the knowledge on possible transitions in a CNGs and by regarding object evolution characteristics as described in [4], we aim to reconstruct object histories and reason on possible evolutions.

In addition, we plan to further evaluate the proposed duplicate detection method on real-life data from the Austrian highways agency ASFINAG[5] to verify our initial findings. For this, further issues identified in our survey [5] aside from the major areas pointed out above (e. g., data stream support allowing continuous duplicate detection on live data in real time, explanations for human operators why objects are considered to be duplicates) need to be incorporated.

---

[5] www.asfinag.at

References

1. Allen, J.F.: Maintaining knowledge about temporal intervals. Communications of the ACM 26(11), 832–843 (1983)
2. Bailey-Kellogg, C., Zhao, F.: Qualitative spatial reasoning - extracting and reasoning with spatial aggregates. AI Magazine 24(4), 47–60 (2003)
3. Barwise, J., Perry, J.: Situations and Attitudes. MIT Press, Cambridge (1983)
4. Baumgartner, N., Gottesheim, W., Mitsch, S., Retschitzegger, W., Schwinger, W.: On optimization of predictions in ontology-driven situation awareness. In: Karagiannis, D., Jin, Z. (eds.) KSEM 2009. LNCS, vol. 5914, pp. 297–309. Springer, Heidelberg (2009)
5. Baumgartner, N., Gottesheim, W., Mitsch, S., Retschitzegger, W., Schwinger, W.: "Same, Same but Different"—A Survey on Duplicate Detection Methods for Situation Awareness. In: Proceedings of the 8th International Conference on Ontologies, DataBases and Applications of Semantics, Vilamoura, Portugal. Springer, Heidelberg (2009)
6. Baumgartner, N., Gottesheim, W., Mitsch, S., Retschitzegger, W., Schwinger, W.: BeAware!—situation awareness, the ontology-driven way. Accepted for publication in: International Journal of Data and Knowledge Engineering (2010)
7. Bhatt, M., Rahayu, W., Sterling, G.: Qualitative simulation: Towards a situation calculus based unifying semantics for space, time and actions. In: Proceedings of the Conference on Spatial Information Theory, Ellicottville, NY, USA (2005)
8. Bleiholder, J., Naumann, F.: Data fusion. ACM Computing Surveys 41(1) (2008)
9. Chen, L., Özsu, M.T., Oria, V.: Robust and fast similarity search for moving object trajectories. In: Proceedings of the International Conference on Management of Data, pp. 491–502. ACM, New York (2005)
10. Clarke, B.L.: A calculus of individuals based on "connection". Notre Dame Journal Formal Logic 22(3), 204–218 (1981)
11. Cohn, A.G., Renz, J.: Qualitative Spatial Representation and Reasoning. In: Handbook of Knowledge Representation, pp. 551–596. Elsevier Science Publishers Ltd., Amsterdam (2008)
12. Cui, Z., Cohn, A.G., Randell, D.A.: Qualitative simulation based on a logical formalism of space and time. In: Proceedings AAAI 1992, pp. 679–684. AAAI Press, Menlo Park (1992)
13. Deza, M.-M., Deza, E.: Dictionary of Distances. Elsevier Science Publishers Ltd., Amsterdam (2006)
14. Dylla, F., Moratz, R.: Exploiting qualitative spatial neighborhoods in the situation calculus. In: Freksa, C., Knauff, M., Krieg-Brückner, B., Nebel, B., Barkowsky, T. (eds.) Spatial Cognition IV. LNCS (LNAI), vol. 3343, pp. 304–322. Springer, Heidelberg (2005)
15. Dylla, F., Wallgrün, J.O.: On generalizing orientation information in OPRA$_m$. In: Freksa, C., Kohlhase, M., Schill, K. (eds.) KI 2006. LNCS (LNAI), vol. 4314, pp. 274–288. Springer, Heidelberg (2007)
16. Dylla, F., Wallgrün, J.O.: Qualitative spatial reasoning with conceptual neighborhoods for agent control. Journal of Intelligent Robotics Systems 48(1), 55–78 (2007)
17. Endsley, M.: Situation Awareness Analysis and Measurement. In: Theoretical Underpinnings of Situation Awareness: A Critical Review, pp. 3–33. Lawrence Erlbaum Associates, New Jersey (2000)
18. Freksa, C.: Conceptual neighborhood and its role in temporal and spatial reasoning. In: Singh, M., Travé-Massuyès, L. (eds.) Proceedings of the Imacs International Workshop on Decision Support Systems and Qualitative Reasoning, pp. 181–187 (1991)
19. Freksa, C.: Temporal reasoning based on semi-intervals. Artificial Intelligence 54(1), 199–227 (1992)

20. Frentzos, E., Gratsias, K., Theodoridis, Y.: Index-based most similar trajectory search. In: Proc. of the 23rd Int. Conf. on Data Engineering, pp. 816–825. IEEE, Los Alamitos (2007)

21. Frentzos, E., Pelekis, N., Ntoutsi, I., Theodoridis, Y.: Trajectory Database Systems. In: Mobility, Data Mining and Privacy—Geographic Knowledge Discovery, pp. 151–188. Springer, Heidelberg (2008)

22. Gärdenfors, P.: Conceptual Spaces: The Geometry of Thought. MIT Press, Cambridge (2000)

23. Hwang, J.-R., Kang, H.-Y., Li, K.-J.: Searching for similar trajectories on road networks using spatio-temporal similarity. In: Proc. of the 10th East Euro. Conf. on Adv. in Databases and Inf. Sys., Thessaloniki, Greece, pp. 282–295. Springer, Heidelberg (2006)

24. Johannesson, M.: Combining integral and separable subspaces. In: Proceedings of the 23rd Annual Conference of the Cognitive Science Society, Edinburgh, Scotland, UK, pp. 447–452. Lawrence Erlbaum Associates, Mahwah (2001)

25. Keane, M.T., Hacket, D., Davenport, J.: Similarity processing depends on the similarities present: Effects of relational prominence in similarity and analogical processing. In: Proceedings of the 23rd Annual Conference of the Cognitive Science Society, Edinburgh, Scotland, UK. Lawrence Erlbaum Associates, Mahwah (2001)

26. Kirschfink, H., Hernandez, J., Boero, M.: Intelligent traffic management models. In: Proccedings of the European Symposium on Intelligent Techniques (ESIT), Aachen, Germany, pp. 36–45 (September 2000)

27. Kokar, M.M., Matheusb, C.J., Baclawski, K.: Ontology-based situation awareness. International Journal of Information Fusion 10(1), 83–98 (2009)

28. Ligozat, G.: Towards a general characterization of conceptual neighborhoods in temporal and spatial reasoning. In: Proceedings of the AAAI 1994 Workshop on Spatial and Temporal Resoning, Seattle, WA, USA, pp. 55–59. AAAI, Menlo Park (1994)

29. Ragni, M., Wölfl, S.: Temporalizing cardinal directions: From constraint satisfaction to planning. In: Proceedings of 10th International Conference on Principles of Knowledge Representation and Reasoning, pp. 472–480. AAAI Press, Menlo Park (2006)

30. Rahm, E., Do, H.H.: Data Cleaning: Problems and Current Approaches. IEEE Data Eng. Bull. 23(4), 3–13 (2000)

31. Randell, D.A., Cui, Z., Cohn, A.G.: A spatial logic based on regions and connection. In: Proceedings of the 3rd International Conference on Knowledge Representation and Reasoning. Morgan Kaufmann, San Francisco (1992)

32. Schwering, A.: Evaluation of a semantic similarity measure for natural language spatial relations. In: Winter, S., Duckham, M., Kulik, L., Kuipers, B. (eds.) COSIT 2007. LNCS, vol. 4736, pp. 116–132. Springer, Heidelberg (2007)

33. Schwering, A.: Approaches to semantic similarity measurement for geo-spatial data: A survey. Transactions in GIS 12(1), 5–29 (2008)

34. van de Weghe, N., Maeyer, P.D.: Conceptual neighborhood diagrams for representing moving objects. In: Akoka, J., Liddle, S.W., Song, I.-Y., Bertolotto, M., Comyn-Wattiau, I., van den Heuvel, W.-J., Kolp, M., Trujillo, J., Kop, C., Mayr, H.C. (eds.) ER Workshops 2005. LNCS, vol. 3770, pp. 228–238. Springer, Heidelberg (2005)

Ontology Mapping and SPARQL Rewriting for Querying Federated RDF Data Sources
(Short Paper)

Konstantinos Makris[1], Nektarios Gioldasis[1],
Nikos Bikakis[2], and Stavros Christodoulakis[1]

[1] TUC/MUSIC Lab, Technical University of Crete, Greece
{makris,nektarios,stavros}@ced.tuc.gr
[2] KDBS Lab, National Technical University of Athens, Greece
bikakis@dblab.ntua.gr

Abstract. The web of data consists of distributed, diverse (in terms of schema adopted), and large RDF datasets. In this paper we present a SPARQL query rewriting method which can be used to achieve interoperability in semantic information retrieval and/or knowledge discovery processes over interconnected RDF data sources. Formal mappings between different overlapping ontologies are exploited in order to rewrite initial user SPARQL queries, so that they can be evaluated over different RDF data sources on different sites. The proposed environment is utilized by an ontology-based mediator system, which we have developed in order to provide data integration within the Semantic Web environment.

1 Introduction

Information access from federated resources, distributed over the internet, is extremely important for Semantic Web applications and end users. In this paper, we introduce an environment that provides transparent access to federated RDF data sources. A set of mappings between OWL ontologies is defined in order to integrate the access to the federated resources. The queries of the Semantic Web users are expressed in SPARQL over an OWL ontology. The mappings are used to transform the original SPARQL query, through rewriting, to a set of SPARQL queries which are used to access the federated RDF data sources.

We focus on the following research issues: (a) determination of the ontology mapping types, which can be used in the context of SPARQL query rewriting, (b) modeling of the mappings between a source ontology and the target ontologies, (c) rewriting of the SPARQL queries posed over a source ontology in terms of the target ontologies.

Ontology mapping in general is a task that has received tremendous attention by the Semantic Web community [6], [7], [3]. In this work we are only interested in the specification of the kinds of mappings between OWL ontologies, which can be exploited by the SPARQL query rewriting process. Despite the extensive studies, to the best of our knowledge, there is no work addressing the problem of ontology mappings in the context of SPARQL query rewriting.

R. Meersman et al. (Eds.): OTM 2010, Part II, LNCS 6427, pp. 1108–1117, 2010.

In the field of query rewriting, limited studies examine the problem of posing a SPARQL query over different RDF datasets. An approach [4] which comes closer to ours, with some of its parts based on a preliminary description of our work [8], proposes a method that exploits transformations between RDF structures (i.e. graphs) in order to perform SPARQL query rewriting. Compared to our approach, where mappings rely on Description Logic semantics, this choice seems to restrict the mappings expressivity and also the supported query types.

Paper Outline. Section 2 describes the mapping model which has been developed in order to express mappings between OWL ontologies. Sections 3 and 4 provide an overview of the SPARQL query rewriting process. Section 5 presents an illustrative query rewriting example, while Sect. 6 concludes our work.

2   Ontology Mapping Model

In order for SPARQL queries posed over a source ontology to be rewritten in terms of a target ontology, mappings between the source and target ontologies should be specified. In Fig. 1, we show the structure of two overlapping ontologies. The source ontology describes a store, while the target ontology describes a bookstore. Between these two ontologies, various kinds of mappings can be identified.

In this section we introduce a model for the expression of mappings between OWL ontologies in the context of SPARQL query rewriting. In this context, some mapping types may not be useful, and therefore not examined here, due to the lack of specific features (e.g. aggregates) in the current specification of SPARQL. Such mapping types are described in [5] and some of them could be useful for post-processing the query results but not during the query rewriting and query answering process.

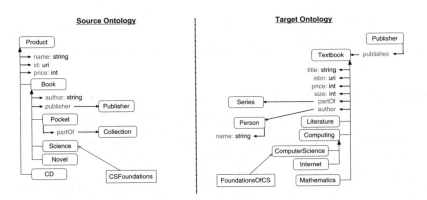

Fig. 1. Semantically Overlapping Ontologies. The rounded corner boxes represent classes. They are followed by their object/datatype properties. The rectangle boxes represent individuals. The arrows represent relationships between basic constructs.

2.1   Abstract Syntax and Semantics

The basic constructs of OWL are the classes c, the object properties op, the datatype properties dp and the individuals i. In order to define the mapping types which are useful for the rewriting process, we use Description Logics (DL). We treat OWL classes as DL concepts, OWL properties as DL roles and OWL individuals as DL individuals. Following our convension, let C, D be OWL classes (treated as atomic concepts), R, S be OWL object properties (treated as atomic roles) and K, L be OWL datatype properties (treated as atomic roles). Similarly, let a, b, c, v_{op} be individuals and v_{dp} be a data value.

An interpretation $\mathcal{I}$ consists of a non-empty set $\Delta^{\mathcal{I}}$ (the domain of the interpretation) and an interpretation function, which assigns to every atomic concept A a set $A^{\mathcal{I}} \subseteq \Delta^{\mathcal{I}}$, to every atomic role B a binary relation $B^{\mathcal{I}} \subseteq \Delta^{\mathcal{I}} \times \Delta^{\mathcal{I}}$ and to every individual k an element $k^{\mathcal{I}} \in \Delta^{\mathcal{I}}$ (based on [1]).

In Tables 1, 2 and 3 we present the set of class and property constructors that we use for the mapping definition. In these tables we introduce some new constructors (preceded with asterisk) which should not be confused with the basic DL constructors defined in [1]. In addition to the constructors, a DL knowledge base consists of common assertional axioms, i.e. inclusion ($\sqsubseteq$, $\sqsupseteq$) and equality ($\equiv$). The semantics of concept/role inclusion and equality are available in [1].

Table 1. Class constructors used in the definition of mappings

Name	Syntax	Semantics
Intersection	$C \sqcap D$	$C^{\mathcal{I}} \cap D^{\mathcal{I}}$
Union	$C \sqcup D$	$C^{\mathcal{I}} \cup D^{\mathcal{I}}$
*Class Restriction	$C.(R\ \overline{\mathbf{cp}}\ v_{op})$	$\{\alpha \in C^{\mathcal{I}} \mid \exists b.\ (\alpha, b) \in R^{\mathcal{I}} \wedge b\ \overline{\mathbf{cp}}\ v_{op}\}$
	$C.(K\ \mathbf{cp}\ v_{dp})$	$\{\alpha \in C^{\mathcal{I}} \mid \exists b.\ (\alpha, b) \in K^{\mathcal{I}} \wedge b\ \mathbf{cp}\ v_{dp}\}$
	$C.(R\ \overline{\mathbf{cp}}\ S)$	$\{\alpha \in C^{\mathcal{I}} \mid \exists b, \exists c.\ (\alpha, b) \in R^{\mathcal{I}} \wedge (\alpha, c) \in S^{\mathcal{I}} \wedge b\ \overline{\mathbf{cp}}\ c\}$
	$C.(K\ \mathbf{cp}\ L)$	$\{\alpha \in C^{\mathcal{I}} \mid \exists b, \exists c.\ (\alpha, b) \in K^{\mathcal{I}} \wedge (\alpha, c) \in L^{\mathcal{I}} \wedge b\ \mathbf{cp}\ c\}$
	$\overline{\mathbf{cp}} \in \{\neq, =\}$, $\mathbf{cp} \in \{\neq, =, \leq, \geq, <, >\}$	

Definition 1 (Class Expression). *A class expression is a class or any complex expression between two or more classes, using union or intersection operations. A class expression is denoted as CE and is defined recursively in (1). Any class expression can be restricted to the values of one or more object property expressions OPE (Definition 2) or datatype property expressions DPE (Definition 3), using the comparators $\overline{\mathbf{cp}} \in \{\neq, =\}$ and $\mathbf{cp} \in \{\neq, =, \leq, \geq, <, >\}$, respectively. Moreover, it is possible for a class expression to be restricted on a set of individuals having object/datatype property values with a specific relationship between them.*

$$CE := c \mid CE \sqcap CE \mid CE \sqcup CE \mid CE.(OPE\ \overline{\mathbf{cp}}\ v_{op}) \mid CE.(DPE\ \mathbf{cp}\ v_{dp}) \\ \mid CE.(OPE_1\ \overline{\mathbf{cp}}\ OPE_2) \mid CE.(DPE_1\ \mathbf{cp}\ DPE_2) \tag{1}$$

Table 2. Object property constructors used in the definition of mappings

Name	Syntax	Semantics
Intersection	$R \sqcap S$	$R^{\mathcal{I}} \cap S^{\mathcal{I}}$
Union	$R \sqcup S$	$R^{\mathcal{I}} \cup S^{\mathcal{I}}$
Composition	$R \circ S$	$\{(a, c) \mid \exists b.\ (a, b) \in R^{\mathcal{I}} \wedge (b, c) \in S^{\mathcal{I}}\}$
*Inverse	$inv(R)$	$\{(b, a) \mid (a, b) \in R^{\mathcal{I}}\}$
*Domain Restriction	$R.domain(C)$	$\{(a, b) \mid (a, b) \in R^{\mathcal{I}} \wedge a \in C^{\mathcal{I}}\}$
*Range Restriction	$R.range(C)$	$\{(a, b) \mid (a, b) \in R^{\mathcal{I}} \wedge b \in C^{\mathcal{I}}\}$

Definition 2 (Object Property Expression). *An object property expression is an object property or any complex expression between two or more object properties, using composition, union or intersection operations. An object property expression is denoted as OPE and is defined recursively in (2). Inverse property operations are possible to appear inside an object property expression. Any object property expression can be restricted on its domain and/or range using a class expression to define the applied restrictions.*

$$OPE := op \mid OPE \circ OPE \mid OPE \sqcap OPE \mid OPE \sqcup OPE \mid inv(OPE) \\ \mid OPE.domain(CE) \mid OPE.range(CE) \tag{2}$$

Table 3. Datatype property constructors used in the definition of mappings

Name	Syntax	Semantics
Intersection	$K \sqcap L$	$K^{\mathcal{I}} \cap L^{\mathcal{I}}$
Union	$K \sqcup L$	$K^{\mathcal{I}} \cup L^{\mathcal{I}}$
Composition	$R \circ K$	$\{(a, c) \mid \exists b.\ (a, b) \in R^{\mathcal{I}} \wedge (b, c) \in K^{\mathcal{I}}\}$
*Domain Restriction	$K.domain(C)$	$\{(a, b) \mid (a, b) \in K^{\mathcal{I}} \wedge a \in C^{\mathcal{I}}\}$
*Range Restriction	$K.range(\text{cp }v_{dp})$	$\{(a, b) \mid (a, b) \in K^{\mathcal{I}} \wedge b\ \text{cp }v_{dp}\}$
	$\text{cp} \in \{\neq, =, \leq, \geq, <, >\}$	

Definition 3 (Datatype Property Expression). *A datatype property expression is a datatype property or any complex expression between object and datatype properties using the composition operation, or between two or more datatype properties, using union or intersection operations. A datatype property expression is denoted as DPE and is defined recursively in (3). Any datatype property expression can be restricted on its domain values using a class expression to define the applied restrictions. In addition, the range values of a datatype property expression can be restricted on various data values v_{dp}, using a comparator $\text{cp} \in \{\neq, =, \leq, \geq, <, >\}$.*

$$DPE := dp \mid OPE \circ DPE \mid DPE \sqcap DPE \mid DPE \sqcup DPE \\ \mid DPE.domain(CE) \mid DPE.range(\text{cp }v_{dp}) \tag{3}$$

2.2 Ontology Mapping Types

In this section we present a rich set of 1:N cardinality mapping types, in order for mappings of these types to be used for the rewriting of a SPARQL query.

Class mapping (c_s *rel* CE_t, ***rel*** $:= \equiv \mid \sqsubseteq \mid \sqsupseteq$). A class from a source ontology s can be mapped to a class expression from a target ontology t.

Object property mapping (op_s *rel* OPE_t, ***rel*** $:= \equiv \mid \sqsubseteq \mid \sqsupseteq$). An object property from a source ontology s can be mapped to an object property expression from a target ontology t.

Datatype property mapping (dp_s *rel* DPE_t, ***rel*** $:= \equiv \mid \sqsubseteq \mid \sqsupseteq$). A datatype property from a source ontology s can be mapped to a datatype property expression from a target ontology t.

We note here that the equivalence/subsumption between two different properties or between a property and a property expression, denotes equivalence/subsumption between the domains and ranges of those properties or property expressions. The proof for the above statement is available in [9].

Individual mapping ($i_s \equiv i_t$). An individual from a source ontology s can be mapped to an individual from a target ontology t.

3 SPARQL Query Rewriting Overview

Query rewriting is done by exploiting a predefined set of mappings which is based on the different mapping types described in Sect. 2.2. The SPARQL query rewriting process lies in the query's graph pattern rewriting. The rewritten query is produced by replacing the rewritten graph pattern to the initial query's graph pattern. Consequently the rewriting process is independent of the query type (i.e. SELECT, CONSTRUCT, ASK, DESCRIBE) and the SPARQL solution sequence modifiers (i.e. ORDER BY, DISTINCT, REDUCED, LIMIT, OFFSET).

Graph pattern operators (AND, UNION, OPTIONAL, FILTER) remain the same during the rewriting process. Variables, literal constants, operators and built-in functions appearing in a FILTER expression, remain also the same. We use 1:1 cardinality mappings for the rewriting of IRIs which may appear inside a FILTER expression.

Since a graph pattern consists basically of triple patterns, the most important part of a SPARQL query rewriting is the triple pattern rewriting. Triple patterns may refer either to data (e.g. relationships between instances) or schema (e.g. relationships between classes and/or properties) information. Due to the inability in handling all the different triple pattern types in the same manner, we distinguish triple patterns into Data Triple Patterns (Definition 4) and Schema Triple Patterns (Definition 5). Triple patterns having a variable on their predicate part are not taken into consideration, since they can deal either with data or schema info.

Let L be the set of literals, V the set of variables, I the set of IRIs, I_{RDF} the set containing the IRIs of the RDF vocabulary, I_{RDFS} the set containing the IRIs of the RDF Schema vocabulary and I_{OWL} the set containing the IRIs of the OWL vocabulary.

Definition 4 (Data Triple Pattern). *The triple patterns that only apply to data and not schema info are considered to be Data Triple Patterns, e.g. (?x, rdf:type, src:Product). A tuple $t \in DTP$ (Data Triple Pattern set - shown in (4)) is a Data Triple Pattern.*

$$DTP = (I' \cup L \cup V) \times (I' \cup \{rdf : type, owl : sameAs\}) \times (I' \cup L \cup V) \qquad (4)$$

$$I' = I - I_{RDF} - I_{RDFS} - I_{OWL} \qquad (5)$$

Definition 5 (Schema Triple Pattern). *The triple patterns that only apply to schema and not data info are considered to be Schema Triple Patterns, e.g. (?x, rdfs:subClassOf, src:Product). A tuple $t \in STP$ (Schema Triple Pattern set - shown in (6)) is a Schema Triple Pattern.*

$$STP = \big((I \cup L \cup V) \times I \times (I \cup L \cup V)\big) - DTP \qquad (6)$$

Since a triple pattern consists of three parts (subject, predicate, object), in order to rewrite it we have to follow a three-step procedure by exploiting mappings for each triple pattern's part. The rewriting procedure follows a strict order. Firstly, the triple pattern is rewritten using the mapping which has been specified for its predicate part, resulting to a graph pattern which may contain one or more triple patterns. Then, the resulted graph pattern is rewritten triple pattern by triple pattern, using the mappings of the triple patterns' object parts. Finally, the same procedure is repeated for the triple patterns' subject parts. Variables, blank nodes, literal constants and RDF/RDFS/OWL IRIs which may appear in a triple pattern part do not affect the rewriting procedure. This means that the variables of the initial query appear also in the rewritten query.

We note that the rewriting of a triple pattern, is not dependent on mapping relationships (i.e. equivalence, subsumption). These relationships, affect only the evaluation results of the rewritten query over the target ontology. The complete set of functions that perform triple pattern rewriting, the algorithms that perform graph pattern rewriting, as well as a set of examples is available in [9].

4   Data Triple Pattern Rewriting

In this section, we provide an overview of the set of functions that perform Data Triple Pattern rewriting based on a set of mappings. These functions are actually rewriting steps in the process of Data Triple Pattern rewriting. We have formally shown [9] that each rewriting step that is performed, in order to rewrite a triple pattern, is semantics preserving, in the sense that it preserves the mapping semantics. The complete set of functions, including those that perform Schema Triple Pattern rewriting, as well as a set of examples is available in [9].

Let $\mathcal{D}_y^x$ be the function that produces the resulted form of a Data Triple Pattern, after being rewritten by $x \in \{s, p, o\}$ (subject, predicate, object). The subscript $y \in \{c, op, dp, i\}$ shows the type of x (e.g. class, object property, etc.). The function $\mathcal{D}$ takes as arguments a Data Triple Pattern t, as well as a mapping μ. In what follows, we use the subscripts s and t to denote that a class, a property or an individual belongs to the source or target ontology, respectively.

4.1 Rewriting by Triple Pattern's Predicate Part

In order to rewrite a Data Triple Pattern by its predicate part only property mappings can be used, since a class or an individual cannot appear on a triple pattern's predicate part.

Rewriting based on object property mapping. Let op_s be an object property from the source ontology which is mapped to an object property expression from the target. Having a Data Triple Pattern $t = (subject, op_s, object)$ with op_s in its predicate part and anything in its subject and object parts, we can rewrite it by its predicate part, using a predefined mapping μ and the function (7).

$$
\mathcal{D}_{op}^p(t, \mu) = \begin{cases}
(subject, op_t, object) & \text{if } \mu:\ op_s \to op_t \\[2mm]
\begin{aligned}&\mathcal{D}_{op}^p(t_1, \mu_1) \text{ AND}\\ &\mathcal{D}_{op}^p(t_2, \mu_2)\end{aligned} & \begin{aligned}&\text{if } \mu:\ op_s \to op_{t1} \sqcap op_{t2},\\ &\text{where } t_1 = (subject, op_{t1}, object),\\ &t_2 = (subject, op_{t2}, object),\\ &\mu_1:\ op_{t1} \equiv OPE_{t1},\ \mu_2:\ op_{t2} \equiv OPE_{t2}\end{aligned} \\[2mm]
\mathcal{D}_{op}^p(t_1, \mu_1) & \begin{aligned}&\text{if } \mu:\ op_s \to inv(op_t),\\ &\text{where } t_1 = (object, op_t, subject)\\ &\text{and } \mu_1:\ op_t \equiv OPE_t\end{aligned}
\end{cases} \quad (7)
$$

Rewriting based on datatype property mapping. Let dp_s be a datatype property from the source ontology which is mapped to a datatype property expression from the target. Having a Data Triple Pattern $t = (subject, dp_s, object)$ with dp_s in its predicate part and anything in its subject and object parts, we can rewrite it by its predicate part, using a predefined mapping μ and the function (8).

$$
\mathcal{D}_{dp}^p(t, \mu) = \begin{cases}
(subject, dp_t, object) & \text{if } \mu:\ dp_s \to dp_t \\[2mm]
\begin{aligned}&\mathcal{D}_{op}^p(t_1, \mu_1) \text{ AND}\\ &\mathcal{D}_{dp}^p(t_2, \mu_2)\end{aligned} & \begin{aligned}&\text{if } \mu:\ dp_s \to op_t \circ dp_t,\\ &\text{where } t_1 = (subject, op_t, ?var),\\ &t_2 = (?var, dp_t, object),\\ &\mu_1:\ op_t \equiv OPE_t,\ \mu_2:\ dp_t \equiv DPE_t\end{aligned} \\[2mm]
\begin{aligned}&\mathcal{D}_{dp}^p(t_1, \mu_1)\\ &\text{FILTER}(object\ \mathsf{cp}\ v_{dp})\end{aligned} & \begin{aligned}&\text{if } \mu:\ dp_s \to dp_t.range(\mathsf{cp}\ v_{dp}),\\ &\text{where } \mathsf{cp} \in \{\neq, =, \leq, \geq, <, >\},\\ &v_{dp} = data\ value,\\ &\text{and } t_1 = (subject, dp_t, object),\\ &\mu_1:\ dp_t \equiv DPE_t\end{aligned}
\end{cases} \quad (8)
$$

4.2   Rewriting by Triple Pattern's Object Part

When a property appears on the object part of a triple pattern, we conclude that the triple pattern deals with schema info, as there is no way for a non RDF/RDFS/OWL IRI to appear at the same time in the triple pattern's predicate part. Similarly, in case that a class appears on a triple pattern's object part, the only factor which can be used to determine the triple pattern's type (Data or Schema Triple Pattern), is whether the RDF property $rdf : type$ appears on the predicate part or not. Thus, the only cases mentioned for the rewriting of a Data Triple Pattern by its object part concern individuals, as well as classes with the precondition that the RDF property $rdf : type$ appears on the triple pattern's predicate part at the same time.

Rewriting based on class mapping. Let c_s be a class from the source ontology which is mapped to a class expression from the target ontology. Having a Data Triple Pattern $t = (subject, rdf : type, c_s)$ with the class c_s in its object part, the RDF property $rdf : type$ in its predicate and anything in its subject part, we can rewrite it by its object part, using a predefined mapping μ and the function (9).

$$
\mathcal{D}_c^o(t,\mu) = \begin{cases} (subject, rdf : type, c_t) & \text{if } \mu : \ c_s \to c_t \\[2mm] \mathcal{D}_c^o(t_1, \mu_1) \text{ UNION} & \text{if } \mu : \ c_s \to c_{t1} \sqcup c_{t2}, \\ \mathcal{D}_c^o(t_2, \mu_2) & \text{where } t_1 = (subject, rdf : type, c_{t1}), \\ & t_2 = (subject, rdf : type, c_{t2}), \\ & \mu_1 : \ c_{t1} \equiv CE_{t1}, \mu_2 : \ c_{t2} \equiv CE_{t2} \\[2mm] \mathcal{D}_c^o(t_1, \mu_1) \text{ AND} & \text{if } \mu : \ c_s \to c_t.(dp_t \ \text{cp} \ v_{dp}), \\ \mathcal{D}_{dp}^p(t_2, \mu_2) & \text{where } \text{cp} \in \{\neq, =, \leq, \geq, <, >\}, \\ \text{FILTER}(?var \ \text{cp} \ v_{dp}) & v_{dp} = data\ value, \\ & t_1 = (subject, rdf : type, c_t), \\ & t_2 = (subject, dp_t, ?var), \\ & \mu_1 : \ c_t \equiv CE_t, \mu_2 : \ dp_t \equiv DPE_t \end{cases} \tag{9}
$$

Rewriting based on individual mapping. Let i_s be an individual from the source ontology which is mapped to an individual i_t from the target ontology. Having a Data Triple Pattern $t = (subject, predicate, i_s)$ with i_s in its object part and anything in its predicate and subject parts, we can rewrite it by its object part, using a predefined mapping μ and the function (10).

$$
\mathcal{D}_i^o(t,\mu) = (subject, predicate, i_t) \quad \text{if } \mu : \ i_s \equiv i_t \tag{10}
$$

4.3   Rewriting by Triple Pattern's Subject Part

Generally, when a class or property appears on the subject part of a triple pattern we conclude that the triple pattern involves schema info, as there is no way for a non RDF/RDFS/OWL IRI to appear at the same time in the triple pattern's predicate part. Thus, the only case mentioned for the rewriting of a Data Triple Pattern by its subject part concerns individuals.

Rewriting based on individual mapping. Let i_s be an individual from the source ontology which is mapped to an individual i_t from the target ontology. Having a Data Triple Pattern $t = (i_s, predicate, object)$ with i_s in its subject part and anything in its predicate and object parts, we can rewrite it by its subject part, using a predefined mapping μ and the function (11).

$$\mathcal{D}_i^s(t, \mu) = (i_t, predicate, object) \quad \text{if } \mu: \ i_s \equiv i_t \tag{11}$$

5   Query Rewriting Example

Consider the query posed over the source ontology of Fig. 1: "Return at most 20 titles of pocket-sized scientific books and optionally their authors. The results should be formed in ascending order based on the title value.". The SPARQL syntax of the source query is shown below:

```
@PREFIX src: <http://www.ontologies.com/SourceOntology.owl#>.
@PREFIX rdf: <http://www.w3.org/1999/02/22-rdf-syntax-ns#>.
SELECT ?name ?author
WHERE{ ?x src:name ?name. ?x rdf:type src:Science.
       ?x rdf:type src:Pocket. OPTIONAL{?x src:author ?author}
} ORDER BY ?name LIMIT 20
```

Let the available predefined mappings be m_1, m_2, m_3 and m_4 (presented below). For their representation we use the abstract syntax presented in Sect. 2.2.

$$m_1: \ src:name \ \sqsupseteq \ trg:title, \ m_2: \ src:author \ \equiv \ trg:author \ \circ \ trg:name,$$
$$m_3: \ src:Science \ \equiv \ trg:ComputerScience \ \sqcup \ trg:Mathematics,$$
$$m_4: \ src:Pocket \ \equiv \ trg:Textbook.(trg:size \leq 14)$$

In order to rewrite the initial query's graph pattern GP, every triple pattern of GP should be rewritten by its predicate, object and subject part, as described in Sect. 3. The rewriting procedure is shown in Fig. 2. Firstly, the initial graph pattern is rewritten triple pattern by triple pattern using the mappings of the triple patterns' predicate parts. Triple patterns containing an RDF/RDFS/OWL property on their predicate part do not result in modifications.

Similarly, the resulted graph pattern GP_p is rewritten triple pattern by triple pattern using the mappings of the triple patterns' object parts. Triple patterns

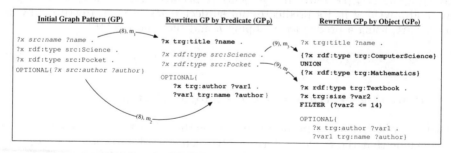

Fig. 2. Triple pattern rewriting by predicate and object part. The parameters upon the arrows denote the rewriting function and the mapping used by the rewriting process.

containing variables on their object part do not result in modifications. The same procedure is repeated for the resulted graph pattern GP_o, using the mappings of the triple patterns' subject parts. However, the graph pattern remains the same since every triple pattern of GP_o contains a variable in its subject part.

Finally, the rewritten SPARQL query, in terms of the target ontology of Fig. 1, is provided by replacing the initial query's graph pattern GP with GP_o.

6   Conclusion

In this paper we presented a method that exploits ontology mappings in order to rewrite SPARQL queries posed over a source ontology, in terms of a target ontology. For this purpose, we also introduced a formal model for describing ontology mappings which can be used in the rewriting process. The proposed SPARQL query rewriting method has been implemented as part of an ontology-based mediator system developed in the TUC/MUSIC Lab.

Our current research focuses on evaluating the system performance, exploiting advanced reasoning techniques during the query rewriting, and developing methodologies for the optimization of the query mediation process. Moreover, this work is going to be integrated with our XS2OWL [10] and SPARQL2XQuery [2] frameworks, in order to allow access to heterogeneous web repositories.

References

1. Baader, F., Calvanese, D., McGuinness, D., Nardi, D., Patel-Schneider, P.: The Description Logic Handbook. Cambridge University Press, Cambridge (2003)
2. Bikakis, N., Gioldasis, N., Tsinaraki, C., Christodoulakis, S.: Querying xml data with sparql. In: Bhowmick, S.S., Küng, J., Wagner, R. (eds.) DEXA 2009. LNCS, vol. 5690, pp. 372–381. Springer, Heidelberg (2009)
3. Choi, N., Song, I.Y., Han, H.: A survey on ontology mapping. SIGMOD Record 35(3), 34–41 (2006)
4. Correndo, G., Salvadores, M., Millard, I., Glaser, H., Shadbolt, N.: Sparql query rewriting for implementing data integration over linked data. In: 1st International Workshop on Data Semantics (2010)
5. Euzenat, J., Polleres, A., Scharffe, F.: Processing ontology alignments with sparql. In: CISIS. pp. 913–917 (2008)
6. Euzenat, J., Shvaiko, P.: Ontology Matching. Springer, Heidelberg (2007)
7. Kalfoglou, Y., Schorlemmer, W.M.: Ontology mapping: The state of the art. In: Semantic Interoperability and Integration. Dagstuhl Seminar Proceedings (2005)
8. Makris, K., Bikakis, N., Gioldasis, N., Tsinaraki, C., Christodoulakis, S.: Towards a mediator based on owl and sparql. In: Lytras, M.D., Damiani, E., Carroll, J.M., Tennyson, R.D., Avison, D., Naeve, A., Dale, A., Lefrere, P., Tan, F., Sipior, J., Vossen, G. (eds.) WSKS 2009. LNCS, vol. 5736, pp. 326–335. Springer, Heidelberg (2009)
9. Makris, K., Gioldasis, N., Bikakis, N., Christodoulakis, S.: Sparql rewriting for query mediation over mapped ontologies. Tech. rep., Technical University of Crete (2010), http://www.music.tuc.gr/reports/SPARQLREWRITING.PDF
10. Tsinaraki, C., Christodoulakis, S.: Interoperability of xml schema applications with owl domain knowledge and semantic web tools. In: Meersman, R., Tari, Z. (eds.) OTM 2007, Part I. LNCS, vol. 4803, pp. 850–869. Springer, Heidelberg (2007)

A Semantic Similarity Framework Exploiting Multiple Parts-of Speech

Giuseppe Pirró* and Jérôme Euzenat

INRIA Grenoble Rhône-Alpes & LIG, Montbonnot, France
{Giuseppe.Pirro,Jerome.Euzenat}@inrialpes.fr

Abstract. Semantic similarity between words aims at establishing resemblance by interpreting the meaning of the words being compared. The Semantic Web can benefit from semantic similarity in several ways: ontology alignment and merging, automatic ontology construction, semantic-search, to cite a few. Current approaches mostly focus on computing similarity between nouns. The aim of this paper is to define a framework to compute semantic similarity even for other grammar categories such as verbs, adverbs and adjectives. The framework has been implemented on top of WordNet. Extensive experiments confirmed the suitability of this approach in the task of solving English tests.

Keywords: Semantic Similarity, Feature Based Similarity, Ontologies, Synonymy detection.

1   Introduction

Similarity gives an estimation of to what extent two or more objects (e.g., words) are alike. It is especially useful when there is only a partial knowledge between the objects being compared and is one of the pillar of important processes such as memory, categorization, decision making, problem solving, and reasoning [17]. The origin of similarity studies has to be found in psychology and cognitive science where different models have been postulated. Similarity found its way different different areas ranging from databases [6] to distributed systems [3]. The Semantic Web is one of the most active community in which similarity is extensively used. Similarity helps to compute mappings between different ontologies [13], repair ontology mappings [10] or compute similarity between ontologies. In information retrieval, similarity is used to complement the vector-space model [21] while in natural language processing it is useful, for instance, in word sense disambiguation [7]. In artificial intelligence, there have been defined several ways of computing similarity, even if two main branches can be identified. On one hand, knowledge-base methods exploit some semantic artefacts (e.g., Word-Net) encoding human knowledge; here similarity is computed by investigating how the two entities being compared are arranged in the considered structure.

---

* This work was carried out during the tenure of an ERCIM "Alain Bensoussan" Fellowship Programme.

R. Meersman et al. (Eds.): OTM 2010, Part II, LNCS 6427, pp. 1118–1125, 2010.

A striking observation is that existing distance or similarity measures are only applicable to the hierarchical relations, which makes them only applicable to some syntactic categories (e.g., nouns and verbs). On the other hand, statistic-based methods such as PMI-IR [19], NGD [1] or LSA [2] assess similarity by analyzing the co-occurrences of the two words being compared in large corpora (e.g., documents indexed by a search engine).

The main contribution of this paper is the definition of a general framework for computing semantic similarity between words that can be nouns, verbs, adjectives or adverbs defined in WordNet [11]. The framework exploits relations both within and across different parts-of-speech. As will be explained later, a feature model to represent words is presented, which stems from our previous work on similarity[12]. By using this framework all the existing similarity measures can be augmented to work with multiple parts-of-speech as well. To have an insight, if one were calculating the similarity between *democratic* and *liberal*, using existing methods it would not be possible. However, if we observe that *democratic* and *liberal* are related to *democracy* and *liberty* in the WordNet *noun* taxonomy we can compute their similarity. We adopt WordNet as reference ontology since it it provides the most comprehensive representation of lexical knowledge ontologically encoded. The applications of this work can be several, among which word similarity, synonymy recognition, document summarization and clustering, ontology mapping and automatic thesauri construction.

The remainder of this paper is organized as follows. Section 2 provides some background on WordNet. Section 3 briefly describes some similarity measures both knowledge-based and statistic-based. Section 4 presents the similarity framework and the logical path toward its definition. Section 5 discusses the evaluation of the framework while Section 6 concludes the paper.

2   Background on WordNet

The WordNet ontology O is a graph, where nodes represent concepts and edges encode relations between concepts. There are several semantic relations that connect nodes, referred to as *synsets* i.e., sets of similar entities. WordNet gives synset definitions of four different parts-of-speech, that is, *nouns, verbs, adjectives* and *adverbs*. However, only nouns and verbs are arranged in a taxonomic structure; adjectives and adverbs are defined both in terms of relations with the same part of speech and with the noun and verb taxonomies. Each synset (S) definition, in WordNet has the following form:

$$S_x = < id, W, R, g >   \tag{1}$$

where id is a unique identifier, the set W contains pairs of the form $W = < w, n >$, where w is a word in the synset and n is the *sense number* for this word. Moreover, the set R contains pairs of the form $r = < s_r, id_r, pos >$ where s_r is the type of semantic relation that relates the given synset with the target synset id_r and pos is the part of speech of id_r. Finally, g is the gloss for the synset, which is a description in natural language. The set R is different depending on the part-of speech considered.

2.1 Features

To better understand the reasoning that motivates the present work, the notion of feature has to be introduced. An object *feature* (a word in our case) can be seen as a property of the object. In the case of *nouns* and *verbs*, words in the hierarchy inherit all the feature of their superordinate even if they can have their own specific features. As an example, in the WordNet noun taxonomy, since *car* and *bicycle* both serve to transport people or objects, in other words they are both types of vehicles, they share all features pertaining to *vehicle*. However, each word has also its specific features as *steering wheel* for *car* and *pedal* for *bicycle*. Again, in the verb taxonomy, the verb *dress* inherits all the features of its superordinate i.e., *wrap up*.

Since this work aims at exploiting the relations between parts-of-speech, the notion of feature has to be extended to also encompass relations across parts-of-speech. In this setting, the features of the adjective *active*, for instance, include its relations in the noun taxonomy with *action* as well. We will discuss in more detail such reasoning later in Section 4. For the time being, the main intuition is that in this work the feature-based model postulated by Tversky, will be projected in the information-theoretical model introduced by Resnik for the purpose of computing similarity taking into account multiple parts-of speech.

3 Related Work

This section describes some well-known similarity measures along with two of the most prominent statistic-based approaches, that is, PMI-IR, and Normalized Google Distance (NGD).

Information Theoretic Approaches. Information theoretic approaches to semantic similarity employ the notion of Information Content (IC), which quantifies the informativeness of concepts. IC values are obtained by associating probabilities to each concept in an ontology on the basis of its occurrences in large text corpora. In the specific case of hierarchical ontologies, these probabilities are cumulative as we travel up from specific concepts to more abstract ones. This means that every occurrence of a concept in a given corpus is also counted as an occurrence of each class containing it. Resnik [15] was the first to leverage IC for the purpose of semantic similarity. Resnik's formula to compute similarity states that similarity depends on the amount of information two concepts share, which is given by the Most Specific Common Abstraction (*msca*), that is, the concept that subsumes the two concepts being compared. Starting from Resnik's work two other similarity measures were proposed. The first, by Jiang and Conrath [5] and the second by Lin [9]. Both measures leverage IC-values calculated in the same manner as proposed by Resnik. The improvement with these measures is that they correct some problems with Resnik's similarity measure by considering the IC of the two concepts as well.

Ontology Based Approaches. As for ontology based approaches, the work by Rada et al. [14] is similar to the Resnik measure since it also computes the *msca* between two concepts, but instead of considering the IC as the value of similarity, it considers the number of links that were needed to attain the *msca*. Obviously, the less the number of links separating the concepts the more similar they are. The work by Hirst et al. is similar to the previous one but it uses a wider set of relations in the ontology (e.g., part-of) coupled with rules restricting the way concepts are transversed [4].

Hybrid Approaches. Hybrid approaches usually combine multiple information sources. Li et al. [8] proposed to combine structural semantic information in a nonlinear model. The authors empirically defined a similarity measure that uses shortest path length, depth and local density in a taxonomy. In [22] the *OSS* semantic distance function, combining *a-priori* scores of concepts with concept distance, is proposed.

Statistic-Based Approaches. PMI-IR [19] is a unsupervised learning algorithm for recognizing synonyms, based on statistical data acquired by querying a Web search engine. PMI-IR uses Pointwise Mutual Information (PMI) and Information Retrieval (IR) to measure the similarity of pairs of words. NGD [1] is a measure of semantic relatedness, which is computed by considering the number of hits, for a set of keywords, returned by the Google search engine. The intuition is that words with the same or similar meanings are close in terms of Google distance whereas words not related in meaning are distant.

4 A General Framework for Computing Similarity

This section describes the framework devised to compute semantic similarity. The main idea is to complement each synset definition with information that can be inferred following its relations with the same or other parts-of-speech.

4.1 The General Similarity Framework

We can see a WordNet synset definition for a word along with the relations with other synsets as the definition of its features (see Section 2.1). For instance, the WordNet definition of the adjective *democratic* includes both relations with other adjectives (with same part of speech) and a relation with the noun *democracy*. We exploit the feature based model proposed by Tversky [20], which states that similarity depends from the presence/absence of certain qualitative features. According to the feature-based model, the similarity of a concept c_1 to a concept c_2 is a function of the features common to c_1 and c_2, those in c_1 but not in c_2 and those in c_2 but not in c_1. In our case, each definition, in terms of synset, has to take into account features that can be derived both from the same and related parts-of speech. Thus, in our previous example, the features of the adjective *democratic*, should also encompass the features derived from the noun *democracy*.

This consideration is particularly useful if one were computing the semantic similarity with another adjective e.g., *liberal* since *liberal*, on its turn, is related to the noun definition of *liberality*. Without this enrichment, existing approaches would fail in computing semantic similarity, since adjectives are not arranged in a taxonomy differently from names or verbs.

In more detail, the cornerstone of the proposed similarity framework is the *msca* in the IC domain, which reflects the information shared by two concepts c_1 and c_2 and that, in a feature-based formulation of similarity, can be seen as the intersection of features from c_1 and c_2. Starting from this assumption, it is immediate to infer that the set of features specific to c_1 (resp. c_2) is given by $IC(c_1) - IC(msca)$ (resp. $IC(c_2) - IC(msca)$) in the information content formulation. A more comprehensive discussion about the mapping between features and IC is provided in our previous paper [12]. Once the IC of the two concepts and that of the msca are available, one can exploit existing IC-based similarity measures to compute similarity. At this point, what is needed is a method to compute the IC of words by taking into account relations both with the the same and other parts of speech.

4.2   Information Content Mapping to Features

Similarity measures based on IC, usually obtain IC-values by parsing large text corpora and counting occurrences of words as discussed in Section 3. This has two main disadvantages; on one hand it requires time and on the other hand it may be corpus dependent. In [18] a new way of obtaining IC-values directly from a taxonomic structure, called intrinsic Information Content *iIC* is discussed. We extend the idea of *iIC* to adjectives and adverbs by taking into account their relations with nouns and verbs. As discussed before, adjectives and adverbs are related to nouns and verbs by semantic relations enabling to assess features of each synset, in terms of IC, that can be exploited to compute semantic similarity. In particular, for each adjective and adverb synset, the multi part-of-speech IC (IC_m) for each synset S is defined as follows:

$$IC_m(S) = \sum_{j=1}^{m} \frac{\sum_{k=1}^{n} iIC(c_k \in C_{R_j})}{|C_{R_j}|}.$$ (2)

This formula takes into account all the m kinds of relations that connect a given adjective or adverb synset S with nouns and verbs. In particular, for all the synsets at the other end of a particular relation (i.e., each $c_k \in C_{R_j}$) the average iIC is computed. This enables to take into account the expressiveness of an adjective or adverb in terms of its relations with nouns and verbs.

At this point, each IC-based similarity measure can be rewritten by using the IC_m definition described in equation (2). It is important to point out that the similarity measures considered in our evaluation were originally formulated to work only with noun definitions apart from the Resnik measure, which has been evaluated on verbs as well [16]. However, in this evaluation, IC values were obtained in the classical manner, that is, by word counting.

5   Evaluation

This section discusses the evaluation of the proposed framework to compute semantic similarity using different parts-of-speech. In particular, three existing similarity measures (described in Section 3) based in IC have been rewritten according to the proposed framework. For the evaluation, we implemented the Similarity Based English Test Solver (SB-ETS), which is useful in the task of meaning recognition and synonymy detection. Given a base word and four choices, SB-ETS returns the most similar word. For each of the four considered datasets, the percentage of correct answers (P) has been calculated.

5.1   English Vocabulary Test Evaluation

The similarity measures have been evaluated against PMI-IR and NGD for which we considered two different search engines i.e., Google (G) and Yahoo (Y). This can give an insight of how much these approaches depends on the search algorithm implemented by the search engine an the amount of data the search engine indexes. For PMI-IR, we considered the best results obtained by using three different types of score described in [19]. We performed evaluations by also adopting tagging, stemming and elimination of stopwords in the case of sentences. As a tagger we used the JMontyTagger[1] whereas a basic stemmer has been implemented. The results obtained for each of the considered similarity measures along with the time elapsed for each evaluation are reported in Table 1 (with tagging) and Table 2 (without tagging). In the column *Na* it is indicated the number of tests for which it has not been computed the result since the words were not found in WordNet. Table 3 reports the results for statistic-based approaches. As can be observed, the evaluations performed after tagging the words being compared, apart from the VOA dataset, are poorer as compared to those in which tagging was not performed. This result may depend on the performance of the tagger used. In the case of not tagging, all the parts-of-speech of a given word have been considered and the higher similarity score has been taken. Performance of similarity measures are different depending on the considered test.

Table 1. Results for similarity measures with tagging

	VOA			TOEFL			Sat			GRE			GMAT			D5		
	P	Na	t(s)	P	Na	t(s)	P	Na	t(s)	P	F	t(s)	P	Na	t(s)	P	Na	t(s)
Res	0.6	0	18	0.6	1	5	0.9	0	11	0.5	2	4	0.6	2	5	0.5	11	161
J&C	0.6	0	18	0.5	1	3	0.8	0	8	0.4	2	3	0.6	2	3	0.5	11	181
Lin	0.6	0	18	0.6	1	4	0.9	0	8	0.5	2	3	0.6	2	3	0.5	11	244

For instance, the VOA test seems to be the most difficult; here the precision of similarity measures range from 0.5 for the Resnik measure to 0.6 for the

[1] http://web.media.mit.edu/~hugo/montylingua/

Table 2. Results for similarity measures without tagging

	VOA			TOEFL			Sat			GRE			GMAT			D5		
	P	Na	t(s)	P	Na	t(s)	P	Na	t(s)	P	F	t(s)	P	Na	t(s)	P	Na	t(s)
Res	0.5	0	43	0.8	0	9	0.8	0	12	0.9	0	5	0.9	0	5	0.6	24	184
J&C	0.6	0	41	0.6	0	7	0.8	0	11	0.8	0	6	0.9	0	5	0.7	24	186
Lin	0.5	0	47	0.8	0	7	0.8	0	11	0.9	0	6	0.9	0	5	0.7	24	208

Table 3. Results for statistic-based methods

	VOA			TOEFL			Sat			GRE			GMAT			D5		
	P	Na	t(s)	P	Na	t(s)	P	Na	t(s)	P	F	t(s)	P	Na	t(s)	P	Na	t(s)
PMI-IR-G	0.5	0	82	0.6	0	80	0.7	0	68	0.6	0	95	0.8	0	64	0.5	0	3024
NGD-G	0.6	0	85	0.5	0	85	0.3	0	70	0.6	0	61	0.5	0	70	0.4	0	2134
PMI-IR-Y	0.4	0	287	0.5	0	243	0.6	0	254	0.7	0	262	0.7	0	290	0.5	0	4778
NGD-Y	0.4	0	380	0.5	0	373	0.4	0	289	0.5	0	248	0.5	0	261	0.4	0	2754

J&C measure in the case of not tagging. In the case of tagging, it is 0.6 for all measures. Similarity measures perform better in the GMAT test where the value of 0.9 in precision is reached. In the D5 dataset, which includes 300 tests, the Lin measure performs better than the other.

Statistic based approaches are overcame by similarity measure in all tests. PMI-IR exploiting Google performs better than the other statistic approaches. The advantage of all these approaches is the wider coverage in terminology; in fact the number of not answered tests is equal to 0 in each case whereas. On the other had, for similarity measures the number of tests not answered is 24 in D5. Another interesting comparison between similarity measures and statistic-based approaches can be done in terms of time elapsed. Similarity measures are clearly faster than statistic-based approaches. In the D5 test, which is the largest, the time elapsed for all the 300 tests ranges from 184 secs for the Resnik measure to 4788 secs for the NGD exploiting Yahoo as search engine. This indicates that in several applications such as document clustering or text similarity, statistic-based approaches become hardly usable.

6   Concluding Remarks and Future Work

This paper described a framework to compute similarity between words belonging to different parts-of-speech. To have an insight of how the framework performs we considered automatic scoring of English tests, such as the well known TOEFL. An extensive evaluation followed by a comparison with statistic-based approaches showed the suitability of the framework. As future work, the main direction is that of investigating similarity measures between words belonging to different parts of speech as for instance the noun *car* and the verb *run*. Besides, other interesting applications could be text summarization or plagiarism detection.

References

1. Cilibrasi, R.L., Vitanyi, P.M.B.: The google similarity distance. IEEE TKDE 19(3), 370–383 (2007)
2. Deerwester, S.C., Dumais, S.T., Landauer, T.K., Furnas, G.W., Harshman, R.A.: Indexing by latent semantic analysis. JASIS 41(6), 391–407 (1990)
3. Hai, C., Hanhua, J.: Semrex: Efficient search in semantic overlay for literature retrieval. FGCS 24(6), 475–488 (2008)
4. Hirst, G., St-Onge, D.: Lexical Chains as Representations of Context for the Detection and Correction of Malapropisms. In: WordNet: An Electronic Lexical Database. MIT Press, Cambridge (1998)
5. Jiang, J., Conrath, D.: Semantic similarity based on corpus statistics and lexical taxonomy. In: Proc. ROCLING X (1997)
6. Kashyap, V., Sheth, A.: Schematic and semantic similarities between database objects: A context-based approach. VLDB Journal 5, 276–304 (1996)
7. Leacock, C., Chodorow, M., Miller, G.A.: Using corpus statistics and wordnet relations for sense identification. Computational Linguistics 24(1), 147–165 (1998)
8. Li, Y., Bandar, A., McLean, D.: An approach for measuring semantic similarity between words using multiple information sources. IEEE TKDE 15(4), 871–882 (2003)
9. Lin, D.: An information-theoretic definition of similarity. In: Proc. of Conf. on Machine Learning, pp. 296–304 (1998)
10. Meilicke, C., Stuckenschmidt, H., Tamilin, A.: Repairing ontology mappings. In: AAAI, pp. 1408–1413 (2007)
11. Miller, G.: Wordnet an on-line lexical database. International Journal of Lexicography 3(4), 235–312 (1990)
12. Pirrò, G.: A semantic similarity metric combining features and intrinsic information content. Data Knowl. Eng. 68(11), 1289–1308 (2009)
13. Pirrò, G., Ruffolo, M., Talia, D.: Secco: On building semantic links in peer to peer networks. Journal on Data Semantics XII, 1–36 (2008)
14. Rada, R., Mili, H., Bicknell, M., Blettner, E.: Development and application of a metric on semantic nets. IEEE Transactions on Systems, Man, and Cybernetics 19, 17–30 (1989)
15. Resnik, P.: Information content to evaluate semantic similarity in a taxonomy. In: Proc. of IJCAI 1995, pp. 448–453 (1995)
16. Resnik, P., Diab, M.: Measuring verb similarity. In: Proceedings of the 22nd Annual Conference of the Cognitive Science Society, pp. 399–404 (2000)
17. Schaeffer, B., Wallace, R.: Semantic similarity and the comparison of word meanings. J. Experiential Psychology 82, 343–346 (1969)
18. Seco, N., Veale, T., Hayes, J.: An intrinsic information content metric for semantic similarity in wordnet. In: Proc. of ECAI 2004, pp. 1089–1090 (2004)
19. Turney, P.D.: Mining the web for synonyms: Pmi-ir versus lsa on toefl. In: Flach, P.A., De Raedt, L. (eds.) ECML 2001. LNCS (LNAI), vol. 2167, pp. 491–502. Springer, Heidelberg (2001)
20. Tversky, A.: Features of similarity. Psychological Review 84(2), 327–352 (1977)
21. Varelas, G., Voutsakis, E., Raftopoulou, P., Petrakis, E.G., Milios, E.E.: Semantic similarity methods in wordnet and their application to information retrieval on the web. In: WIDM, pp. 10–16. ACM, New York (2005)
22. Zuber, V.S., Faltings, B.: Oss: A semantic similarity function based on hierarchical ontologies. In: IJCAI, pp. 551–556 (2007)

Biomedical Publication Knowledge Acquisition, Processing and Dissemination with CORAAL

Vít Nováček and Siegfried Handschuh

Digital Enterprise Research Institute (DERI)
National University of Ireland, Galway
IDA Business Park, Lower Dangan, Galway, Ireland
vit.novacek@deri.org

Abstract. The paper presents CORAAL, a novel solution for life science publication search that exploits knowledge locked within unstructured publication texts (apart of possessing the traditional full text functionalities). In contrast to most related state of the art solutions, CORAAL integrally addresses acquisition (i.e., extraction), processing (i.e., integration and extension) and dissemination (i.e., convenient exposure) of the publication knowledge. After detailing the motivations of our research, we outline the representation and processing framework that allows CORAAL to tackle the rather noisy and sparse automatically extracted knowledge. The architecture and core features of the CORAAL prototype itself are described then. Most importantly, we report on an extensive evaluation of the CORAAL tool performed with an assistance of actual sample users. The evaluation illustrates the practical benefits brought by our solution already in the early research prototype stage.

1 Introduction

The ever-growing number of resources available on the Internet has lead to a rising importance of the information overload problem in the last decade [1]. We have an instant access to immense amounts of content, however, we are lacking proper means for how to make sense out of it – one is very seldom able to efficiently retrieve and integrate the relevant pieces of information within the oceans of candidate answers. The problem is pertinent to virtually any type of content available on the Internet, yet there are certain domains where solutions coping with information overload are demanded more critically than elsewhere.

A prominent example of such a domain are life sciences, which is the application area targeted by our paper. Biomedical researchers and practitioners rely on accurate and complete information from relevant resources (e.g., scientific publications or patient records) in order to make delicate decisions that potentially affect human health or even life. However, it is often impossible to get truly

R. Meersman et al. (Eds.): OTM 2010, Part II, LNCS 6427, pp. 1126–1144, 2010.

accurate and complete information nowadays, as it is scattered among vast and dynamically growing amounts of scarcely relevant resources[1].

The current solutions for biomedical publication search (e.g., PubMed, cf. http://www.ncbi.nlm.nih.gov/pubmed/) are able to efficiently retrieve resources based on particular key-words, but this is often insufficient for getting accurate and complete enough answers straightaway. Imagine for instance a junior researcher compiling a survey on various types of leukemia. The researcher wants to state and motivate in the survey that *acute granulocytic leukemia* is different from *T-cell leukemia*. Although such a statement might be obvious for a life scientist, one should support it in the survey by a citation of a published paper. Our researcher may be a bit inexperienced in oncology and may not know the proper reference from the top of their head. Using the PubMed search service, it is easy to find articles that contain both leukemia names. Unfortunately, there are more than 500 such results. It is tedious or even impossible to go through all of them to discover those actually supporting that *acute granulocytic leukemia* is different from *T-cell leukemia*.

For getting relevant information from large amounts of resources in an integral manner without needing to manually process them, a corresponding automated solution must exploit also the meaning of the resources' content [3]. In particular, the meaning[2] associated with the biomedical resources has to be:

1. *acquired* by means of manual content annotation or automated extraction;
2. *processed* in order to refine and augment the acquired knowledge and also to link related pieces of knowledge possibly dispersed among multiple resources;
3. *disseminated* to the users, allowing them to search for accurate and complete answers and browse the results more efficiently.

Solutions tackling the particular phases exist. Acquisition of actionable biomedical knowledge is targeted for instance by [4] (knowledge extraction from texts by means of NLP) or by [5] (machine-assisted ontology-based annotation of biomedical data). Regarding processing of the acquired knowledge, various state of the art solutions for ontology integration or reasoning are applicable (see for instance [6] and the related part of [7], respectively). The last phase—dissemination of knowledge associated with biomedical content—is being addressed mostly by various knowledge-based extensions of traditional search engines (see for instance [8] or [9]). To the best of our knowledge, there is no framework that tackles all the phases in an integral manner, though.

This paper presents a solution that complements the current state of the art by coherently addressing all the three phases of knowledge acquisition, processing and dissemination that are necessary in order to make use of the oceans of life

---

[1] For instance, Medline, a comprehensive source of life sciences and biomedical bibliographic information (cf. http://medline.cos.com/) hosted over 18 million resources in 2009. It has a growth rate of 0.5 million items per year, which represents around 1,300 new resources per day [2]. For many practical user queries, only few documents among thousands of returned ones actually contain relevant answers, though.

[2] Or knowledge; these two terms are used interchangeably in the following.

science publications more efficiently. Section 2 outlines our novel framework for representation and processing of loosely structured noisy knowledge that is characteristic to the targeted use case. Section 3 presents the architecture and core features of CORAAL, a knowledge-based life science publication search engine, which integrally tackles the knowledge acquisition, processing and dissemination problems, building on the groundwork outlined in Section 2. An extensive evaluation involving both quantitative and qualitative analysis performed with an assistance of actual CORAAL users is reported in Section 4 (this part provides the primary contribution of the paper w.r.t. our formerly published work). Related work and conclusions are presented in Section 5 and 6, respectively.

2 Groundwork

In order to be able to target the knowledge acquisition, processing and dissemination in an integral and efficient manner, one has to utilise a knowledge representation framework with several specific features. First of all, it should be tailored to automatically extracted knowledge (manual annotation of the publication knowledge is practically impossible in large scale, which can, however, be remedied by automatic extraction of knowledge from the article texts by ontology learning techniques [10]). Such knowledge is often rather sparse, noisy and uncertain, though. Apart of reflecting these features, the representation framework of choice should straightforwardly support contexts, namely at least the provenance of acquired knowledge (to link it to the corresponding source articles). Furthermore, robust aggregation of the extracted statements based on relevance of corresponding resources is necessary, as we might need to integrate the noisy extracted knowledge with presumably more accurate manually designed domain ontologies (if available). This can be very useful for increasing the overall precision of the knowledge base powering the enhanced publication search. From the dissemination perspective, the processed knowledge has to be accessible by means of intuitive (i.e., nearly natural language) query answering, since we target users with little or no technical expertise. The query evaluation should also be approximate in order to provide useful answers in a reasonable amount of time even for queries partially evaluated on a lot of noisy data.

Approaches like [11–13] provide particular solutions apt for coping with the challenges separately, however, to the best of our knowledge there is no off-the-shelf framework integrally tackling the challenges on a well-founded basis. Therefore we have devised our own approach that provides for:

– An alternative conception of semantics, based on the formal notions of relationships and similarities between entities grounded in natural language. Such semantics is better suited to noisy, dynamic and uncertain knowledge extracted from publications than the standard, but rather brittle and heavyweight logics-based approaches. The clearly defined mapping between the computational knowledge representation and the domain of natural language also very naturally allows for querying and answer presentation involving mostly natural language expressions. This allows lay users to interact with the framework almost instantly in quite an intuitive manner.

- Approximate anytime services for knowledge aggregation, querying and general reasoning (e.g., materialisation of knowledge bases according to rules provides by users). The services are based on similarity functions and relevance-based ranking of entities that makes use of the link structure present within the stored knowledge (in a direct analogy to the ranking algorithms for the web resources).
- A straightforward efficient implementation of both knowledge storage and processing using relational databases.

Despite of proposing an alternative, light-weight notion of semantics different from the current (Semantic Web) standards that mostly utilise rather brittle logics, our framework still builds on a basic subject-predicate-object triple model. This ensures a backwards compatibility with the standard RDF [14] data format, thus maintaining interoperability with many extant applications and knowledge bases. In addition to the core triple representation, we introduce positive or negative certainty measures and additional arities of the uncertain relationships that are meant to capture various user-defined types of context (e.g., provenance). We represent the relationships corresponding to particular entities as single mathematical objects and define dual notions of distance and similarity on their sets.

The similarities provide for approximate retrieval of entities and for other, more complex light-weight reasoning services (e.g., analogical extension or rule-based closures). The reasoning can be performed in an anytime manner for large knowledge bases, which means that it is possible to programmatically adjust the completeness/efficiency trade-off (i.e., one can either have complete, but possibly largely irrelevant set of solutions in a long time, or incomplete, but rather relevant set in a relatively short time). The anytime reasoning makes use of an entity relevance measure that is derived from the relationships between entities in a knowledge base in an analogy to HITS [15], a classical information retrieval method for ranking of linked resources. Essentially, only most relevant entities in a knowledge base are processed at time within the anytime reasoning, producing some results quickly and postponing the less relevant content for being processed later (when/if a sufficient time is available).

The approach outlined here has been implemented in the form of a software library called EUREEKA, which is powering the back-end services of the CORAAL prototype that forms the primary focus of this paper. Readers interested in the theoretical and implementation details of the EUREEKA groundwork are referred to [16].

3   CORAAL

In the following we introduce the basic features of the CORAAL system. Section 3.1 provides an overview of CORAAL in terms of mapping the essential requirements to particular architecture components. In Section 3.2 we describe what we did in order to extract, process, and expose the full text, metadata and knowledge associated with a sample publication set currently represented within CORAAL.

3.1 Overview of the Solution

In order to provide comprehensive search capabilities in CORAAL, we augment the standard (full-text) publication search with novel services that enable knowledge-based search. By knowledge-based search we mean the ability to query for and browse statements that capture relations between entities in the retrieved source articles. CORAAL is composed of several interconnected modules that: (1) extract asserted publication metadata together with the knowledge implicitly present in the corresponding texts; (2) integrate the emergent content with existing domain knowledge; (3) display the content via a multiple-perspective search&browse interface. This combines the fine-grained publication search with convenient and effortless large-scale exploitation of the unstructured knowledge locked within the texts.

Table 1. Mapping requirements to the architecture components of CORAAL

Requirement	Addressed by	Comments
Extended publication search	KONNEX framework	See [17]
Automated knowledge extraction	A custom NLP module	See Section 3.2 and [16]
Emergent knowledge processing	EUREEKA framework	See Section 2 and [16]
Publication knowledge dissemination	A faceted search&browse interface	See Section 3.2

Table 1 maps the major requirements that have motivated our work to the particular components of the CORAAL architecture. The CORAAL implementation integrates the KONNEX [17] and EUREEKA [16] frameworks in a single back-end platform that can be easily deployed on an ordinary server. A front-end layer to the back-end extraction and processing services is implemented using the state of the art Exhibit interface for faceted browsing of structured data (cf. `http://www.simile-widgets.org/exhibit/`). The front-end accepts queries in the form of key-words or in a simple lay-oriented query language, and exposes the results for convenient browsing along various facets of the data (see Sections 3.2 and 4 for examples). The faceted browsing allows users to quickly focus to relevant answers only. Among other things, this provides for a remedy for the noise possibly still remaining in the automatically extracted data after the processing.

3.2 Knowledge Acquisition, Processing and Dissemination

The current CORAAL repository represents 11,761 Elsevier journal articles related to cancer research and treatment (access to the articles in an annotated XML format was provided to us during the Elsevier Grand Challenge competition we participated in, see `http://www.elseviergrandchallenge.com/winners.html` for details). In particular, we processed cancer-related articles from a selection of Elsevier journals focusing on oncology, genetics, pharmacology, biochemistry, general biology, cell research and clinical medicine.

After parsing the input articles, the metadata and structural annotations were incorporated and interlinked by KONNEX. First we eliminated possible duplicate metadata annotations using a string-based similarity heuristic. Each article was then represented as a comprehensive RDF graph consisting of its shallow metadata, such as title, authors and references. The references were anchored in citation contexts (i.e., the paragraphs they occur in), and represented as individual graphs allowing for incremental enrichment over time. The article's full-text information was managed using multiple Lucene indices (cf. `http://lucene.apache.org/`), whereas the graphs were integrated and linked within a KONNEX RDF repository.

While KONNEX catered for the raw publication text and metadata, exploitation of the publication knowledge locked in the natural language texts was tackled by our EUREEKA framework for emergent (e.g., automatically extracted) knowledge acquisition and processing [16]. In particular, we applied the framework to: (i) automatic extraction of machine-readable knowledge from particular life science article texts; (ii) integration, refinement, and extension of the extracted knowledge within one large emergent knowledge base; (iii) exposing the processed knowledge linked to its article-based provenance via a query-answering layer gluing the back-end and the faceted browsing CORAAL module.

For the initial knowledge extraction, we used a heuristics based on natural language processing (NLP)—stemming essentially from [18, 19]—to process chunk-parsed texts into subject-predicate-object-score quads. The scores were derived from overall and document-level frequencies of subject, object and predicate terms. The extracted quads encoded three major types of ontological relations between concepts: (i) taxonomical—*type*—relationships; (ii) concept difference (i.e., negative *type* relationships); (iii) "facet" relations derived from verb frames in the input texts (e.g., *has part*, *involves*, or *occurs in*). Over 27,000 variants of the latter relation type were extracted. We imposed a taxonomy on them, considering the head verb of the phrase as a more generic relation (e.g., *involves expression of* was assumed to be a type of *involves*). Also, several artificial relation types were introduced to restrict the semantics of some of the most frequent relations: a (positive) *type* was considered transitive and anti-symmetric, and *same as* was set transitive and symmetric. Similarly, *part of* was assumed transitive and being inverse of *has part*.

The quads were processed as follows in the knowledge processing pipeline:

(I) Addition – The extracted quads were incrementally added into an growing knowledge base K, applying soft aggregation of the compact entity representations corresponding to the particular imported statements. To take into account the basic domain semantics (i.e., synonymy relations and core taxonomy of K), we used the EMTREE (`http://www.embase.com/emtree/`) and NCI (`http://nciterms.nci.nih.gov`) thesauri as seed models for the extracted knowledge incorporation and reconciliation. Note that any other resource that is available in or can be converted to the RDF format may be incorporated into CORAAL for similar purposes (this holds for instance for most of the OBO Foundry life science ontologies, cf. `http://www.obofoundry.org`).

(II) Closure – After the addition of new facts into K, we computed its materialisation according to imported RDFS entailment rules (c.f. `http://www.w3.org/TR/rdf-schema/`).

(III) Extension – the extracted concepts were analogically extended using similar stored knowledge.

To give an example of the knowledge extraction and processing, let us consider a text sample ... *The rate of T-cell leukemia, acute granulocytic leukemia and other hematologic disorders in the studied sample was about three times higher than average.* .... From such a text, CORAAL can extract (via its EUREEKA module) the following quads: (T-cell leukemia, is a, leukemia, 1.0), (T-cell leukemia, is a, acute granulocytic leukemia, -0.6), (T-cell leukemia, is a, hematologic disorder, -0.6). There is an obvious mistake in the extracted knowledge – *T-cell leukemia* actually is a *hematologic disorder.* According to the NCI thesaurus, we can, however, infer the following quad: (leukemia, is a, hematologic disorder, 1.0). Using the statement, the mistake in the extracted knowledge can be resolved to (T-cell leukemia, is a, hematologic disorder, 0.73) (using the soft aggregation service of the EUREEKA module). Such a statement is already correct despite of the slightly lower certainty.

The knowledge base extracted and processed by EUREEKA has been exposed via a query-answering module in CORAAL. Answers to queries are sorted according to their relevance scores and similarity to the query (see [16] for details on the knowledge processing and querying implementation). The module currently supports queries in the following form: $t \mid s : (NOT\ )?p : o(\ AND\ s : (NOT\ )?p : o)^*$, where NOT and AND stands for negation and conjunction, respectively (the ? and * wildcards mean zero or one and zero or more occurrences of the preceding symbols, respectively, | stands for OR). s, o, p may be either a variable—anything starting with the ? character or even the ? character alone—or a lexical expression. t may be lexical expressions only.

A query that can easily solve the search problem we have mentioned in the introduction can be typed into CORAAL using a convenient query builder portrayed in Figure 1. It includes a context-sensitive auto-completion capability;

Fig. 1. Knowledge-based query construction

if one decides on, e.g., a particular subject, only relations (properties) actually associated with that subject in the knowledge base are displayed. The query being constructed in the builder corresponds to the syntax specified above and is meant to search for all documents containing (either explicitly or implicitly) the statement that *acute granulocytic leukemia is not a T-cell leukemia* (the negation is reflected by the NOT box ticked in Figure 1).

The screenshot in Figure 2 shows the highest ranked answer to the query constructed in the builder, proving that the two types of leukemia are not the same. The source article of the statement (displayed as an inline summary in the following screenshot) is the desired reference supporting the claim. The particular types of contextual information associated with result statements in CORAAL are: (i) *source* provenance – articles relevant to the statement, which can be expanded into an inline summary (as shown in Figure 2) or explored in detail after clicking on the respective publication title; (ii) *context* provenance – domain of life sciences that the statement relates to (determined according to the main topic of the journal that contained the articles the statement was extracted from); (iii) *certainty* – a number describing how certain the system is that the statement holds and is relevant to the query (values between 0 and 1; derived from the absolute value of the respective statement degree and from the actual similarity of the statement to the query); (iv) *inferred* – a boolean value determining whether the statement was inferred or not (the latter indicating it was directly extracted).

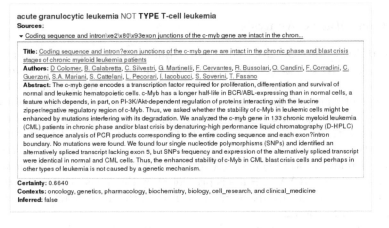

Fig. 2. Query answer detail

Further examples of actual practical queries are given in the next section. The tool itself can be accessed at `http://coraal.deri.ie:8080/coraal/`. A quick-start document and a demo video illustrating core capabilities of CORAAL are provided at `http://smile.deri.ie/projects/egc/quickstart`, `http://resources.smile.deri.ie/coraal/videos/coraal_web.mp4`, respectively.

4   Evaluation

We have recently finished an extensive evaluation of the CORAAL prototype. With an assistance of an expert evaluation committee[3], we assessed issues deemed to be most important by the committee regarding applicability of the framework within their field: (1) ease of use, real-time response; (2) quality of answers (users want to have as many correct results entailed by the incorporated articles and thesauri as possible); (3) appropriateness of the result ranking (users want to find the relevant results on the top); (4) practical relevance of the answers and of the documents retrieved (users want the tool to be useful in practice, i.e., to offer not only reasonably ranked and correct, but also unapparent and practically useful results).

Ease of use was addressed by the simple queries close to natural language, guided query builder and faceted browsing described in the previous section. The response is actually not an issue – results are presented within units of seconds in CORAAL (up to 90% of the lag owing to the HTML rendering overhead, not to the query processing itself). The remaining issues are addressed in the following sections. First we evaluated the answer quality and ranking appropriateness by quantitative measures in Section 4.1. Section 4.2 presents more qualitative analysis of the practical relevance of CORAAL results then.

4.1   Quantitative Analysis

Methodology and Setup. The answer quality and ranking appropriateness were mapped to two tasks. First of them was assessing the correctness (i.e., precision) and completeness (i.e., recall) of the statements returned as answers to significant queries. To compute the measures, we used a manually created gold standard comprising the knowledge that was associated by the evaluation committee with the queries according to their experience and to an analysis of the literature processed by CORAAL. The second task consisted of assessing the number of relevant statements as a function of their rank among the answers. The rank of the CORAAL results is presented by the measure of entity relevance derived from the relationships between entities in the underlying knowledge base, as outlined in Section 2.

For the former task, general conjunctive queries with variables were used. The latter task was evaluated using names of significant entities as mere term queries – such results in effect provided statements assumed to be related to the query entities based on the fitness, similarity and relevance in direct correspondence to the notions outlined in Section 2 and elaborated in [16]. This allowed for a straightforward analysis of the result ranking.

The actual significance of queries and entities to be used for the evaluation was determined as follows. First we picked 100 random entity names and generated 100 random queries based on the extracted content. We let the evaluation

---

[3] Cancer researchers and oncological clinical practitioners affiliated with the Masaryk Memorial Cancer Institute in Brno, Czech Republic.

committee assess the significance of respective concept and statement queries by marks in the 1-5 range (from best to worst) and used an average mark then.

We used the following best-scoring queries: (1) $Q_1 \equiv$? : type : breast cancer, (2) $Q_2 \equiv$? : part of : immunization, (3) $Q_3 \equiv$? : NOT type : chronic neutrophilic leukemia, (4) $Q_4 \equiv$ rapid antigen testing : part of : ? AND ? : type : clinical study, (5) $Q_5 \equiv$? : as : complementary method AND ? : NOT type : polymerase chain reaction.

The most relevant entities used were: (1) $E_1 \equiv$ myelodysplastic syndrome, (2) $E_2 \equiv$ p53, (3) $E_3 \equiv$ BAC clones, (4) $E_4 \equiv$ primary cilia, (5) $E_5 \equiv$ colorectal cancer.

For a base-line comparison, we employed the open source edition of Open-Link Virtuoso (cf. http://tinyurl.com/cf8ga2), a triple store with a database back-end supporting rule-based RDFS inference and querying[4]. The content fed to EUREEKA was transformed to crisp RDFS statements, omitting the unsupported negative statements and provenance arguments before import to the base-line. EUREEKA queries were mapped to statements with unique entity identifiers and then translated to the corresponding SPARQL equivalents to be executed using the base-line.

Table 2. Summary of the quantitative results

Approach	Correctness and completeness						Relevance per answer ranks				
	P	R	F	P_{nn}	R_{nn}	F_{nn}	1-10	11-50	51-100	101-200	201-...
EUREEKA	0.719	0.583	0.586	0.532	0.305	0.310	0.780	0.668	0.430	0.227	0.091
BASE	0.169	0.053	0.067	0.281	0.088	0.111	0.300	0.229	0.293	0.172	0.188

Results. The quantitative evaluation results are summed up in Table 2. P, R, F columns contain precision, recall and F-measure, respectively, averaged across the results of all evaluated queries. $X_{nn}, X \in \{P, R, F\}$ relate to average results of non-negative queries only (Q_1, Q_2, Q_4). Particular P, R values were computed as $P = \frac{c_r}{a_r}, R = \frac{c_r}{c_a}$, where c_r, a_r is a number of *relevant* and all answer entities returned, respectively. c_a is the number of all entities relevant to the query, as entailed by the documents in the CORAAL corpus (determined by the evaluation committee by means of manual analysis of full-text search results related to the entities occurring in the evaluated queries). The columns in the right hand part of Table 2 contain average values $\frac{s_r}{sz}$, where s_r, sz is the number of *relevant* and all statements in a given rank range, respectively. The average goes across results corresponding to E_{1-5} query entities. The *relevance* was determined by

---

[4] Alternatives [11, 20] capable of either arbitrary meta-knowledge, or explicit trust representation in RDF were considered, too. However, the respective implementations allow neither for soft aggregation of emergent entities, nor for inherent exploitation of certainty in approximate answering of queries close to natural language. They can only expose the certainty and/or meta-knowledge via extended SPARQL queries. Therefore their capabilities are essentially equal to the "plain" Virtuoso RDF store base-line regarding our use case, while Virtuoso handles the relatively large amount of data more efficiently, presumably due to more mature data management engine.

unequivocal agreement of the evaluation committee. Results with certainty lower
than 0.5 were disregarded (i.e., a statement was considered as a false positive if
and only if it was deemed irrelevant and its absolute certainty value was 0.5 or
more).

Regarding *correctness and completeness*, our approach offers almost three-
times better results in terms of F-measure than the base-line. That holds for the
negation-free queries supported by both frameworks. Obviously, the difference is
even bigger for generic queries having no base-line results in two out of five cases.
The increase in EUREEKA's precision was directly due to its two novel features
unsupported by the base-line: (i) relevance-based aggregation of the initially
extracted input; (ii) explicitly presented certainty of the results allowing for
disregarding presumably uncertain ones. The increase in recall was caused by
the approximate query evaluation that included also some correct results from
answers with fitness lower than 1 (similar behaviour is not directly supported
in the base-line). The relevance of answers appears to be a clearly decreasing
function depending on the rank in EUREEKA. However, no similar pattern can
be seen for the base-line.

The absolute EUREEKA results may still be considered rather poor (F-
measure around 0.3), but the evaluation committee unequivocally considered the
ability of EUREEKA to perform purely automatically as an acceptable trade-off
for the presence of some noise in the not-entirely-complete results. In conclusion,
the evaluation with sample users confirmed that the innovative principles of the
proposed approach lead to a better applicability in the current use case, when
compared to a base-line state of the art solution.

4.2   Qualitative Analysis

Methodology and Setup. The qualitative evaluation consisted of three parts:
(1) measuring the relevance of the knowledge related to interesting terms; (2) determining the relevance of the query answers (i.e., the returned instances of variables in queries) and of the documents retrieved within the answers; (3) assessing
the usefulness of CORAAL for realistic knowledge-based search tasks in comparison with state of the art tools. In each of the parts, three members of the
evaluation expert committee participated.

For the first two parts, the experts jointly created a list of 10 terms and
queries that were interesting for their daily working agenda after browsing the
knowledge available in CORAAL. The terms were: $E_0 \equiv$ testis, $E_1 \equiv$ caspase
cascade, $E_2 \equiv$ growth factor receptor, $E_3 \equiv$ clotrimazole, $E_4 \equiv$ biological half-life, $E_5 \equiv$ colonic carcinoma, $E_6 \equiv$ therapy, $E_7 \equiv$ apoptotic
cell death, $E_8 \equiv$ oncogene myc, $E_9 \equiv$ estrogen receptor 1.

Consequently, the queries were: $Q_0 \equiv$ post-treatment mortality rates
: LINK : ?, $Q_1 \equiv$ NOT ? : TYPE : acetylsalicylic acid AND NOT antipyretic agent : TYPE :?, $Q_2 \equiv$?: has part : TNF-induced apoptosis,
$Q_3 \equiv$ jaw malformation : LINK :?, $Q_4 \equiv$?: TYPE : inhibitor, $Q_5 \equiv$?
: TYPE : data, $Q_6 \equiv$?: TYPE : diagnostic, therapeutic, and research
equipment AND ? : TYPE : electromagnetic radiation, $Q_7 \equiv$ NOT ? :

TYPE : gene, $Q_8 \equiv$ NOT ? : TYPE : DNA-binding, $Q_9 \equiv$ NOT ? : TYPE : thermal injury.

For the evaluation, each of the answer statements (for the mere term-based queries), instances and retrieved documents (for the queries with variables) was independently associated with a relevance measure by each of the participating expert evaluators (the number of the results being evaluated was limited to at most 100, taken from the top of the result list, to reduce the load of the evaluators). The relevance was generally meant to express usefulness of the particular result for the daily practice of the experts. Typically, a highly relevant result should not only be a correct, but also non-trivial, unapparent and applicable piece of knowledge. Following this definition of relevance, the evaluators assigned marks from 1 to 5 to each result, where 1 stood for clearly relevant, 2 for relevant, 3 for somehow relevant, 4 for rather nonrelevant and 5 for absolutely irrelevant or incorrect. The three independent relevance marks by the three evaluators were averaged for each result to reflect a more objective aggregate expert opinion. We analysed the number of relevant answers per query and the average relevance of all answers then.

The third part of the qualitative evaluation—usefulness assessment of CO-RAAL—employed five tasks assigned to each evaluator. The sets of tasks were different for each evaluator, jointly selected by the two remaining evaluators to ensure blind testing. The selection was based on a set of 100 queries and corresponding results. The five most informative and relevant query/result elements according to the unequivocal agreement of the two evaluators were used as a basis for the tasks presented to the third evaluator.

The tasks were to retrieve publications containing a knowledge about a statement or to confirm whether two entities are related in a particular way. The tasks themselves were as follows (split into three sets corresponding to the three evaluators):

- task set 1:
    T1.1: *"Find out whether multidrug resistance protein 1 is related to microtubule associated proteins and identify the respective literature sources."*
    T1.2: *"What is both type of therapeutic function and immune procedure? Identify also the publication sources containing the respective knowledge."*
    T1.3: *"Find publications that refer to Rac accumulation by transfected cells."*
    T1.4: *"Are cathepsins a part of the apoptosis pathway? Identify 3-5 publications most relevant to the corresponding knowledge."*
    T1.5: *"Can protein overproduction be related to transfected cells? What type of relationship can it be if the answer is yes? Identify also the related publication sources."*
- task set 2:
    T2.1: *"Are the cPGES and mPGES-1 enzymes different from each other? Find the publications providing details regarding the answer to the question."*
    T2.2: *"Find publications dealing with post-treatment mortality rates in relation to pharmacologic substances."*

T2.3: *"Find publications describing use of fluorescent fusion proteins as a part of laser therapy."*

T2.4: *"Can a nonsteroid antiinflammatory agent be a type of antipyretic agent? Find publications supporting the answer to the question."*

T2.5: *"Find publications mentioning protein components as parts of the Golgi matrix."*

– task set 3:

T3.1: *"Which publications deal with genetic data in relation to vaccination?"*

T3.2: *"Can annexins be related to active caspase staining flow?"*

T3.3: *"Is endonuclease a type of DNA-binding? Identify also publications supporting the answer."*

T3.4: *"Find resources describing the process of the endothelial monocyte activating polypeptide II fragment generation from pEMAP II."*

T3.5: *"Is IgA production type of strong protective immune response? Identify publication sources supporting the respective knowledge."*

For each task, the evaluators were supposed to find the answers both with CORAAL and with a standard tool they use for publication search (e.g., Google, PubMed or ScienceDirect). We measured the time (in minutes) spent when solving the task with both tools and the rate of the task accomplishment. The rate was computed as $\frac{\sum_{found}}{\sum_{all}}$, where $\sum_{all}$ and $\sum_{found}$ were the numbers of relevant articles processed by CORAAL and the number of articles actually found by a user, respectively. For the base-line, we took into account only the articles found by users that had been incorporated into CORAAL, too. Apart of measuring the accomplishment time and rate, the evaluators were asked how did they solve particular tasks. Additional interviews were conducted in order to get more general feedback from the users.

Results. Table 3 presents two types of evaluation results: the relevance of knowledge related to interesting terms, and the relevance of answers to queries (the **KR** and **QA** parts of the table, respectively). The query answer relevance evaluation distinguishes between two aspects of the answers: (i) entities returned among the answer statements as query variable instances; (ii) documents retrieved as provenance of the answer statements (the *answers* and *documents* column spans in Table 3, respectively). The $\sum_{all}$ columns contain the absolute number of results (statements, query variable instances or retrieved documents) for each term (E_0-E_9) or query (Q_0-Q_9). The $\sum_{rel}$ and m_{rel} columns contain the relative frequency (or percentage divided by 100) of relevant results and the mean result relevance, respectively. The results were considered relevant if their aggregate mark assigned by the evaluators was at most 3 (i.e., somehow relevant). Note that only the relevant results were included in the computation of the $\sum_{rel}$ values (i.e., if there was 100 results, but only 7 of them with relevance at most 3, the corresponding $\sum_{rel}$ value was 0.07), while the m_{rel} values were computed among all the results returned.

We can clearly see that the numbers of relevant (i.e., non-trivial, unapparent, interesting and applicable) results is lower than the numbers of correct results

Table 3. Summary of the qualitative results of query answering

KR	$\sum_{all}$	$\sum_{rel}$	m_{rel}	QA	answers			documents		
					$\sum_{all}$	$\sum_{rel}$	m_{rel}	$\sum_{all}$	$\sum_{rel}$	m_{rel}
E_0	100	0.07	4.333	Q_0	9	0.111	4.593	1	0	4.333
E_1	13	0	4	Q_1	1	1	2.667	4	0.75	2.833
E_2	100	0.38	3.46	Q_2	1	0	4.667	1	1	2.333
E_3	46	0.413	3.341	Q_3	2	0.5	2.5	2	1	2.333
E_4	10	0	4.5	Q_4	10	1	1.3	9	0.667	2.741
E_5	100	0.57	3.095	Q_5	22	0.591	2.848	2	0	4.333
E_6	100	0.07	4.28	Q_6	11	0.091	4.697	2	0	4.167
E_7	36	0.333	3.481	Q_7	14	0	3.786	3	0.333	3.333
E_8	83	0.301	3.418	Q_8	11	0.182	4.061	1	0	4
E_9	100	0.75	2.857	Q_9	1	0	3.667	2	0.5	3.667
avg	68.8	0.289	3.677	avg	8.2	0.348	3.479	2.7	0.425	3.407

presented in Table 2 before. Around 28.9% of statements related to the terms selected by the evaluators were deemed to be relevant in average. The result is slightly better for answers in the form of query variable instances – 34.8%. The document retrieval scored best – in average, 42.5% of the resulting articles were deemed to be relevant to the query (and to the users, too).

One can conclude that apart of certain amount of outright noise confirmed in the results by the quantitative evaluation in Section 4.1, there is also quite a large number of irrelevant answers provided by CORAAL. However, our goal was not to cope with the irrelevance as such – we did not employ any measures at all for specifically filtering knowledge that might be irrelevant according to the expert biomedical users (we used only generic extraction, soft aggregation, refinement and ranking of processed statements). Moreover, CORAAL allows users to quickly focus on the results that are actually relevant for them, therefore the relatively low number of relevant answers is not necessarily harmful to the usefulness of our tool, as elaborated in the following analysis of the third part of qualitative evaluation.

Table 4 provides an overview of the usefulness assessment of CORAAL within realistic tasks selected by and presented to the evaluation committee members. The *Acc.* and *Time* columns represent the accomplishment rate and time spent in minutes, respectively, concerning the particular tasks (T1.1-T1.5, T2.1-T2.5, T3.1-T3.5). The accomplishment rate is the number of results (i.e., publications and/or entities) found by a user, divided by the maximal number of relevant results that can actually be found with CORAAL or with a base-line application.

The average rate of task accomplishment with CORAAL was about two and half times higher than with the base-line tool. The average duration per task is longer for CORAAL. However, one has to realise that one third of the tasks was deemed to be impossible to solve in any reasonable time with the base-line, and three more tasks did not yield the correct results. On the other hand, only one task was deemed to be impossible to be solved with CORAAL (with an equal number of three tasks without any correct results in addition). These results support our assumption that for tasks involving more expressive search, CORAAL performs better than the classical key-word publication search tools like Google, PubMed or ScienceDirect.

Table 4. Summary of the CORAAL usefulness results

TASK	CORAAL		BASE-LINE	
	Acc.	Time	Acc.	Time
T1.1	1	25	0.333	10
T1.2	1	10	0	N/A
T1.3	0.25	5	0	5
T1.4	0.6	2	0.2	2
T1.5	0	5	0.2	3
T2.1	1	5	1	5
T2.2	1	3	0	N/A
T2.3	0	5	0	N/A
T2.4	0	N/A	0.25	1
T2.5	0	5	0	1
T3.1	1	3	1	5
T3.2	1	6	0	N/A
T3.3	1	3	0	3
T3.4	1	10	1	3
T3.5	1	3	0	N/A
avg	0.657	6.429	0.266	3.8

The presence of noise and irrelevant answers in the results was not perceived as a major obstacle in accomplishing the tasks, as the evaluators were always able to focus very quickly on the piece of knowledge they were looking for (mainly due to the faceted browsing features of CORAAL). They were also quite synchronised when spontaneously commenting on the CORAAL's helpful features facilitating the solution of the evaluation tasks. All the three participating evaluators independently stated that the biggest strength of CORAAL lies in a transparent presentation of the statements associated with the search terms and/or queries, which allows for quick focusing on the resources of interest. This was considered as a great advantage over the normally used standard tools, as it reduced the need for reading through sometimes immense amounts of largely irrelevant resources when trying to get answers to more complex queries.

Despite the overall satisfaction with the CORAAL performance, couple of negative issues was identified, too (the issues were either explicitly raised by the evaluators, or derived from their performance during the usefulness evaluation). The faceted browsing was considered useful in general, however, it was suggested to provide additional means for searching in the particular facet boxes if they contain large numbers of elements. Also, more user-friendliness was demanded (with no actual specification). The relevance of this demand was further supported by the observation of the evaluators' performance when solving the tasks. In spite of having the same introduction into CORAAL—a 10 minute informal lecture about the tool, followed by 5 minutes of simple query and search examples—they were behaving quite differently. One evaluator (responsible for the tasks T1.x) was very diligent, although he was not using the query language and the capabilities of CORAAL to their full potential. This led to slightly more time spent with the tasks and to two results that were only partial. Another evaluator (tasks T2.x) was basically asking queries in CORAAL as if he were using Google, and only then browsed the resulting statements in order to get to the answers. This did not work for all the tasks, though, and he often gave up after not finding the result immediately the "simple way". The last user (tasks T3.x) was mostly using CORAAL to its full potential, discovering all results.

The observation of the evaluators' behaviour led us to two main conclusions: (1) The querying should be made even more intuitive and compelling for the users. It should be motivating for them to use expressive queries without extensive explanations of the advantages. A possible way how to address this issue is an incorporation of a query answering module or controlled natural language interfaces in order to allow for expressive queries similar to the normal communication means of the users. (2) To assist the users who will still be considering CORAAL as yet another Google-like thing (and thus possibly missing some answers they might be able to get via more expressive search), we should provide extensive, yet concise summaries of knowledge that might be indirectly related to the results of plain term search. This way we would be able to deliver the more expressive knowledge even to users that are not explicitly asking for it (but might be interested in it, nonetheless). A substantial re-design of the user interface would be quite likely necessary, though. These aspects are to be addressed within the further development of the CORAAL tool, aiming at improving the user experience and delivering industry-strength solutions.

5   Related Work

Regarding the knowledge representation and processing groundwork of CO-RAAL outlined in Section 2, the work [11] proposes generic framework for representing contextual features like certainty or provenance in RDF. These features are considered rather as "annotations" of RDF triples and thus can be merely queried for. It is impossible to use the certainty as a first class citizens already in the phase of knowledge processing (e.g., robust entity integration and/or inference), unless one builds an ad hoc application tackling that on the top of [11]. Uncertainty incorporation into the knowledge representation is tackled for instance by fuzzy extensions of logical knowledge representation [12], however, the solution does not address a straightforward representation of contextual features or dynamics. Moreover, any logics-based approach is generally not able to infer many meaningful and/or interesting conclusions from the rather sparse and noisy emergent inputs [21], which renders logical inference inadequate for a complete accomplishment of our goals (i.e., integral tackling of the automated acquisition, processing and dissemination of life science publication knowledge).

FindUR [22], Melisa [23] and GoPubMed [8] are ontology-based interfaces to a traditional publication full-text search (represented by the state of the art applications like ScienceDirect or PubMed that tackle only key word-based full text search, though). GoPubMed allows for effective restriction and intelligent visualisation of the query results. FindUR and Melisa support focusing the queries on particular topics based on an ontology (FindUR uses a Description Logic—cf. http://dl.kr.org/—ontology built from scratch, while Melisa employs a custom ontology based on MeSH, cf. http://www.nlm.nih.gov/mesh/).

GoPubMed dynamically extracts parts of the Gene Ontology (cf. http://www.geneontology.org/) relevant to the query, which are then used for restriction and a sophisticated visualisation of the classical PubMed search results. Nevertheless, none of the tools mentioned so far offers seamless and readily applicable combination of automated publication knowledge acquisition, processing and dissemination by means of querying and browsing. Textpresso [9] is quite similar to CORAAL concerning searching for automatically extracted relations between concepts in particular chunks of text. However, the system relies on underlying ontologies and their instance sets, which have to be provided manually for every domain, whereas CORAAL can operate even without any available ontology. Moreover, CORAAL includes far more full-text publications and concepts.

6   Conclusions and Future Work

With CORAAL, we have integrally addressed the acquisition, processing and dissemination of knowledge locked within the unstructured text of life science publications. We are able to extract and integrate emergent knowledge and metadata from a large number of publications, as well as augment and refine the extracted content (possibly using extant manually created domain ontologies and/or vocabularies providing as seed models). CORAAL also allows for a convenient dissemination of the knowledge associated with the processed publications via intuitive searching and faceted browsing interface. The presented extensive evaluation performed with the help of actual users proved that: (i) CORAAL is able to perform better than related state of the art approaches; (ii) it provides clearly identifiable benefits for users already at the current research prototype stage.

However, we still have to tackle several challenges in order to fully realise the potential of CORAAL. First of all, we intend to work on improving the intuitiveness of the current querying interfaces, as well as on providing more concise, interactive and relevant answer summaries (as discussed in detail in the end of Section 4). In a rather long term perspective, we want to utilise the wisdom of the crowds by supporting intuitive and unobtrusive community-based curation of the emergent knowledge processed within CORAAL. We will also investigate a distributed version of EUREEKA (the knowledge extraction and processing back-end of CORAAL) to allow for scaling up to arbitrarily large numbers of publications.

Acknowledgments. This work has been supported by the 'Líon II' project funded by SFI under Grant No. SFI/08/CE/I1380. We acknowledge much appreciated help from Tudor Groza, who developed the user interface and publication (meta)data processing framework for CORAAL. We would like to thank to Elsevier, B.V. representatives for the data and support provided within the Grand Challenge competition. Eventually, we are very grateful to our evaluators from the Masaryk Memorial Cancer Institute.

References

1. Flew, T.: New Media: An Indroduction. Oxford University Press, Australia (2008)
2. Tsujii, J.: Refine and pathtext, which combines text mining with pathways. Keynote at Semantic Enrichment of the Scientific Literature 2009 (SESL 2009) (March 2009)
3. Goble, C.: State of the nation in data integration. In: Proceedings of the WWW2007/HCLSDI Workshop. ACM Press, New York (2007)
4. Rebholz-schuhmann, D., Kirsch, H., Arregui, M., Gaudan, S., Riethoven, M., Stoehr, P.: Ebimed–text crunching to gather facts for proteins from medline. Bioinformatics 23 (2007)
5. Jonquet, C., Musen, M.A., Shah, N.: A system for ontology-based annotation of biomedical data. In: Bairoch, A., Cohen-Boulakia, S., Froidevaux, C. (eds.) DILS 2008. LNCS (LNBI), vol. 5109, pp. 144–152. Springer, Heidelberg (2008)
6. Alasoud, A., Haarslev, V., Shiri, N.: A hybrid approach for ontology integration. In: Proceedings of the 31st VLDB Conference, Very Large Data Base Endowment (2005)
7. Staab, S., Studer, R. (eds.): Handbook on Ontologies. International Handbooks on Information Systems. Springer, Heidelberg (2004)
8. Dietze, H., et al.: Gopubmed: Exploring pubmed with ontological background knowledge. In: Ontologies and Text Mining for Life Sciences, IBFI (2008)
9. Müller, H.M., Kenny, E.E., Sternberg, P.W.: Textpresso: an ontology-based information retrieval and extraction system for biological literature. PLoS Biology 2(11) (2004)
10. Buitelaar, P., Cimiano, P.: Ontology Learning and Population. IOS Press, Amsterdam (2008)
11. Schueler, B., Sizov, S., Staab, S., Tran, D.T.: Querying for meta knowledge. In: Proceedings of WWW 2008. ACM Press, New York (2008)
12. Bobillo, F., Straccia, U.: fuzzyDL: An expressive fuzzy description logic reasoner. In: Proceedings of FUZZ 2008 (2008)
13. Oren, E., Guéret, C., Schlobach, S.: Anytime query answering in RDF through evolutionary algorithms. In: Sheth, A.P., Staab, S., Dean, M., Paolucci, M., Maynard, D., Finin, T., Thirunarayan, K. (eds.) ISWC 2008. LNCS, vol. 5318, pp. 98–113. Springer, Heidelberg (2008)
14. Manola, F., Miller, E.: RDF Primer (2004), http://www.w3.org/TR/rdf-primer/ (November 2008)
15. Kleinberg, J.: Authoritative sources in a hyperlinked environment. Journal of the ACM 46(5) (1999)
16. Nováček, V.: EUREEKA! Towards a Practical Emergent Knowledge Processing. PhD thesis, Digital Enterprise Research Institute (DERI), National University of Ireland Galway (2010), http://140.203.154.209/~vit/resources/2010/pubs/phd-thesis.pdf (June 2010)
17. Groza, T., Handschuh, S., Moeller, K., Decker, S.: KonneXSALT: First steps towards a semantic claim federation infrastructure. In: Bechhofer, S., Hauswirth, M., Hoffmann, J., Koubarakis, M. (eds.) ESWC 2008. LNCS, vol. 5021, pp. 80–94. Springer, Heidelberg (2008)
18. Maedche, A., Staab, S.: Discovering conceptual relations from text. In: Proceedings of ECAI 2000. IOS Press, Amsterdam (2000)
19. Voelker, J., Vrandecic, D., Sure, Y., Hotho, A.: Learning disjointness. In: Franconi, E., Kifer, M., May, W. (eds.) ESWC 2007. LNCS, vol. 4519, pp. 175–189. Springer, Heidelberg (2007)

20. Hartig, O.: Querying Trust in RDF Data with tSPARQL. In: Aroyo, L., Traverso, P., Ciravegna, F., Cimiano, P., Heath, T., Hyvönen, E., Mizoguchi, R., Oren, E., Sabou, M., Simperl, E. (eds.) ESWC 2009. LNCS, vol. 5554, pp. 5–20. Springer, Heidelberg (2009)
21. Bechhofer, S., et al.: Tackling the ontology acquisition bottleneck: An experiment in ontology re-engineering (2003), http://tinyurl.com/96w7ms (April 2008)
22. McGuinness, D.L.: Ontology-enhanced search for primary care medical literature. In: Proceedings of the Medical Concept Representation and Natural Language Processing Conference, pp. 16–19 (1999)
23. Abasolo, J.M., Gómez, M.: M.: Melisa: An ontology-based agent for information retrieval in medicine. In: Proceedings of the First International Workshop on the Semantic Web (SemWeb 2000), pp. 73–82 (2000)

Assessing Iterations of an Automated Ontology Evaluation Procedure

Peter Spyns

Vrije Universiteit Brussel - STAR Lab, Pleinlaan 2 Gebouw G-10, B-1050 Brussel - Belgium
Tel.: +32-2-629.1237; Fax: +32-2-629.3819
Peter.Spyns@vub.ac.be

Abstract. Evaluation of ontologies is increasingly becoming important as the number of available ontologies is steadily growing. Ontology evaluation is a labour intensive and laborious job. Hence, the need grows to come up with automated methods for ontology evaluation. In this paper, we report on experiments using a light-weight automated ontology evaluation procedure (called EvaLexon) developed earlier. The experiments are meant to test if the automated procedure can detect an improvement (or deterioration) in the quality of an ontology miner's output. Four research questions have been formulated on how to compare two rounds of ontology mining and how to assess the potential differences in quality between the rounds. The entire set-up and software infrastructure remain identical during the two rounds of ontology mining and evaluation. The main difference between the two rounds is the upfront manual removal by two human experts separately of irrelevant passages from the text corpus. Ideally, the EvaLexon procedure evaluates the ontology mining results in a similar way as the human experts do. The experiments show that the automated evaluation procedure is sensitive enough to detect a deterioration of the miner output quality. However, this sensitivity cannot be reliably qualified as similar to the behaviour of human experts as the latter seem to disagree themselves largely on which passages (and triples) are relevant or not. Novel ways of organising community-based ontology evaluation might be an interesting avenue to explore in order to cope with disagreements between evaluating experts.

1 Introduction and Background

Following the growing importance of ontologies for information systems interoperability and overall business semantics in the context of the semantic web (now also more and more called the Web3.0), the need gradually arises to assess ontologies irrespectively of the way they have been created, adapted or extended. How can ontology engineers in the course of building and adapting an ontology [29] get an idea whether their modifications are actual improvements or not compared to a previous version ? Another context that involves ontology assessment is that of experimenting with various ontology mining methods: how to determine when one method performs better than another?

R. Meersman et al. (Eds.): OTM 2010, Part II, LNCS 6427, pp. 1145–1159, 2010.

One possible way would be to define on beforehand a set of competence questions [15] (with according answers) and test whether or not modifications in the ontology miner results in "deviating" answers when applying the questions to the modified ontology. But ontologies can be assessed or evaluated from many angles [6]. In many cases, human experts are still needed, which constitutes a crucial bottleneck. In addition, more often than not, a gold standard (or reference) is not available.

A way out is to use the corpus[1] itself as the basis for an automatically constructed gold standard if one wants to avoid involving human experts who are costly and rapidly bored by tedious evaluation exercises. Hence, we limit ourselves to a method that automatically measures to which extent ontological material includes the important domain notions [28] to avoid the need for humans to manually define a gold standard of any sort (e.g., the answers to competency questions) or to validate the output of an ontology miner by hand. In this paper, quality of an ontology refers to the degree with which "lexical triples" delivered by an ontology miner [25] cover the important notions and relationships conveyed in a text corpus.

From corpus linguistics, the notion of a well balanced and representative corpus (i.e. supposed to represent all the linguistic phenomena of importance) is widely accepted. For ontology mining purposes, the same notion applies. A representative corpus then comprises all the important and relevant notions and relationships of a domain. Experts find it more easy and less tedious to agree on a set of representative texts (and select passages) in natural language that should constitute the representative corpus than to validate machine generated formal(ised) output. Nevertheless, it still remains necessary to assess the quality of the ontology mining results automatically (in the idea of reducing the need for human intervention as much as possible). And to test whether or not an automated evaluation procedure is able to detect to an extent comparable to human experts an improvement (or deterioration) in the quality of an ontology miner's output over multiple rounds of ontology mining.

When discussing the results of prior evaluation experiments [26], one of the human experts involved had suggested to cut away manually irrelevant parts of the text corpus before inputting it to the ontology miner. Even though the amount of text to be processed decreases (which might compromise the statistical calculations), the hypothesis was that important terms would be detected more distinctively. As - except for a rough manual cutting away of sections deemed irrelevant - nothing else in the set-up of the experiment is changed, a comparison with the results obtained earlier is possible (a set-up similar to software regression testing[2]).

This endeavour to automate the evaluation of ontology learning fits in a broader ontology engineering methodology [29] based on the DOGMA framework [7, 18, 19, 27] as developed at VUB STAR Lab[3].

---

[1] Of course, this only applies to situations in which a corpus is available.

[2] Software engineering regression testing is about testing adapted pieces of software by means of the same carefully chosen data set to verify if software changes (e.g., a bug fix) do not result in unintended side-effects, i.e. the newly modified code still complies with its specified requirements and the unmodified code is not been affected by the modifiying activity.

[3] www.starlab.vub.ac.be

The remainder of this paper is organised as follows. The next section presents the material (section 2). The method and four major research questions are elaborated on in section 3. Subsequently, we discuss the experiments and try to answer the four research questions in the subsections 4.1, 4.2, 4.3 and 4.4. Some additional test findings are presented in section 4.5. Section 5 contains comments on the results of the evaluation experiments. Related work is outlined in section 6. Indications for future research are given in section 7, and some final remarks (section 8) conclude this paper.

2 Material

The *memory-based shallow parser for English*, being developed at CNTS Antwerp and ILK Tilburg [3][4], has been used. It is an unsupervised parser that has been trained on a large general purpose language model. No additional training sessions (= supervised) on specific corpora are needed. Hence, the distinction between learning and test corpus has become irrelevant for our purposes. Semantic relations that match predefined syntactic patterns have been extracted from the shallow parser output. Additional statistics and clustering techniques using normalised frequencies and probabilities of occurrence are calculated to separate noise (i.e. false combinations generated) from genuine results. The unsupervised memory-based shallow parser together with the additional statistical modules constitute the ontology miner. More details can be found in [22, 23]. Processing a corpus with the ontology miner results in a set of lexical triples.

An *automated evaluation procedure* (called EvaLexon) has been set up [24–26, 28]. It makes use of a gold standard that is created automatically for the text corpus. To create such a reference, we have combined various insights from quantitative linguistics, a statistical formula to compare two proportions (i.e. a technical corpus vs. a neutral corpus), with the traditional IE evaluation metrics (recall and precision).

The technical *corpus* is constituted by the *privacy directive* (English version) 95/46/EC of 18/12/2000, which EU member states have to adopt and transform into local legislation. This document is the sole official legal reference text for the domain. The text has been lemmatised. The *Wall Street Journal (WSJ) corpus* (a collection - 1290K words - of English newspaper articles) serves as a corpus representing the general language that is to be contrasted with the specific technical vocabulary of the directive. The WSJ is not really a neutral corpus (the articles are about economic topics). It is easily available and a standard in corpus linguistics.

A *triplet* is considered relevant if it is composed by at least two terms statistically relevant, i.e. belonging to the automatically created gold standard. We did not use a stopword list, as this list might change with the nature of the corpus, and as a preposition can be potentially relevant since they are included in the triplets automatically generated. A triplet score (expressed as an averaged percentage) indicates how many characters of the three triplet parts resulting from ontology mining are matched by words of the gold standard. E.g., the triplet $< rule, establish, national\_competent\_body >$ receives a score of 89 as only 'competent' is not included in the gold standard with a 95% confidence level $(91 = ((4/4)*100 + (11/11)*100 + (17/23)*100)/3)$[5].

---

[4] See http://ilk.kub.nl for a demo version.

[5] A slight imprecision occurs due to the underscores that are not always accounted for.

3   Methods

As an ontology is supposed to represent the most relevant concepts and relationships of a domain of discourse or application domain, all the terms lexicalising these concepts and relationships should be retrieved from a corpus of texts about the application domain concerned when building an ontology for that domain. The key question is thus how to determine in an automated way how well the important terms of a corpus have been retrieved and combined into relevant triples. Only triples to which the automatic evaluation procedure attributes a score higher than 65 are considered to be relevant and representative for the domain.

Two privacy experts have been involved. The first one is a privacy knowledge engineer and the second one a privacy data commissioner. They have been asked to assess the outcomes of the ontology miner, i.e. the triples, in two test rounds, During the second round, these experts have manually removed sections and passages deemed irrelevant or superfluous from the corpus - see Table 3 for an excerpt. In addition, they have been asked to assess again the triples from the first round and the new triples from the second round. The second round took place almost an entire year after the first one to avoid learning effects. Assessing a triple meant tagging it with a '+' (= triple is relevant for the domain) or a '-' (= triple is not relevant for the domain). Values of 66 and higher resp. lower attributed by the EvaLexon procedure correspond to a '+' resp. '-' given by an expert.

Table 1. Privacy excerpt with retained (boldface: expert1; italics: expert2) and removed (regular) text passages by both

CHAPTER II GENERAL RULES ON THE LAWFULNESS OF THE PROCESSING OF PERSONAL DATA
Article 5
Member States shall, within the limits of the provisions of this Chapter, determine more precisely the conditions under which the processing of personal data is lawful.
SECTION I PRINCIPLES RELATING TO DATA
Article 6
1. Member States shall provide that **personal data must be:**
(a) **processed fairly and lawfully;**
(b) **collected for specified, explicit and legitimate purposes and not further processed in a way incompatible with those purposes. Further processing of data for historical, statistical or scientific purposes shall not be considered as incompatible provided that Member States provide appropriate safeguards;**

One can clearly see that expert1 has removed (much) more text parts (all the titles, and the entire article 5) than expert2 who has removed the body of article 5. For the latter, the titles can contain relevant domain notions. Most probably, this difference in expert opinion will be reflected in results produced by the ontology miner.

These two "cleaned" versions of the directive have been concatenated and fed into the ontology miner for the second test round. A side effect is that words in the common parts obtain a higher statistical weight. So the same process has been done twice: once for the original document, and once for the concatenation of two "cleaned" versions of the basic document. In fact, the experts only evaluated the results of the ontology mining process; they were unaware of the subsequent automated evaluation procedure and its scores - see Figure 1.

The basic hypothesis is that, if the irrelevant passages are eliminated (in a quick and dirty way) before automated processing, relevant triples will be detected more easily by the ontology miner. Consequently, a good automated procedure to evaluate ontology mining results should be sensitive enough to detect this difference (if applicable) between the resulting sets of triples. And its scoring behaviour should correspond more or less with how the human experts assess the mining results. Consequently we address the following research questions:

Q1 as a result of the manual upfront removal of passages deemed superfluous and/or irrelevant by the human experts, does the ontology miner produce a set of triples different from the set of triples produced during the first test round (with the original non modified document) ? (subsection 4.1)

Q2 are the triples resulting from the second test round with the ontology miner considered better, worse or of equal quality by the privacy experts ? (subsection 4.2)

Q3 is the automated evaluation procedure (EvaLexon) sensitive enough to this change, i.e. are the evaluation scores for the second round different from the ones of the first test round ? (subsection 4.3)

Q4 are the scores of the EvaLexon procedure for the second test round triples in line with with the judgement of the human experts (better, worse or equal) ? (subsection 4.4)

These research questions have been translated in the following steps (and tests) to be undertaken (see also Figure 1):

- compare the miner behaviour on both texts (test 1)
- assess manually the miner results (of both rounds) by the experts (test 2 and test 3)
- compute the EvaLexon evaluation scores on both sets of data (test 4)
- assess manually the EvaLexon scores (two rounds) by the experts (test 5 and test 6)

Kappa-tests will be performed when appropriate to indicate to which extent two sets of outcomes exhibit a similar behaviour in relation to chance. Kappa-tests are mostly used to calculate whether or not a real outcome corresponds (or differs) from the expected outcome by mere chance or not. Important to note is that we have shown previously [25] that involving human experts in an ontology evaluation task is not obvious potentially resulting in flaws affecting the quality of the evaluation experiment. Hence, some additional tests (subsection 4.5) are performed as a work around or a supplementary validation stage.

4   Tests and Results

4.1   Q1: Does Upfront Removal of Irrelevant Passages Make a Difference ?

The original privacy directive contains 12591 words. One experts has reduced the directive to 3620 while the other expert has reduced it to 4443 words. In both cases, this represents a very substantial reduction. One can hypothesize that such a reduction will surely and seriously influence the quantity and quality of the resulting triples.

The first round of ontology mining resulted in 1115 triples, while the second round led to 525 triples. In total, there are 1193 unique triples over the two rounds. Already regarding the number of triples produced, there is thus a significant difference.

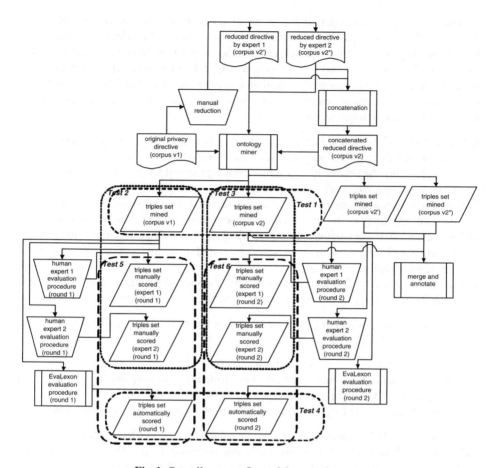

Fig. 1. Overall process flow of the experiments

Table 2. Triples resulting from ontology mining on the original vs. the concatenated reduced corpus [Test 1]

triplets mined	corpus v2 +	corpus v2 -	
corpus v1 +	449	666	1115
corpus v1 -	78	?	?
	527	?	?

Table 2 shows the number of common triples: 449. 78 new triples have been produced during the second round, while 666 triples did not show up anymore. As it is impossible to determine the true negatives (i.e. triples not produced by the miner in both rounds), a kappa-value cannot be computed. However, from the numbers alone, one can easily deduce that the behaviour of the miner on the two corpora is clearly distinct.

When looking into the two "cleaned" versions and the original document, the differences are very striking: one expert has completely removed all 72 clauses starting with "whereas", which is a traditional way in legal texts to introduce the setting of the law. The other expert has only kept 16 of these "whereas" clauses after having carefully deleted from every one of these clauses the word "whereas". In addition, from the 16 remaining clauses not only entire sentences have been removed but also chunks of sentences. Not only are the sentences very "legalese" (long and of a complex nature) but sometimes, after deletions, they are turned into sequences of juxta-positioned chunks. These chunks may be processed differently by the ontology miner than when they are part of a well formed sentence. On a few occasions, this expert slightly rephrases chunks as to turn them into a well formed sentence. He also keeps all the titles and numbers of the articles of the directive but not the section titles and numbers and additional explanatory labels as does the other expert. Hence, it is not such a big surprise that some new triples are produced during the second round. On the other hand, the number of new triples is not that high (slightly less than 7%), contrary to the amount of triples no longer produced (almost 60%).

4.2   Q2: Does Upfront Removal of Irrelevant Passages Make a Positive Difference According to the Experts ?

To try to approximate the number of true negatives, a workaround has been adopted. The 78 new triples of the second round can be considered as being not retained during the first test round. Likewise the 666 triples only resulting from the first test round are the negative cases of the second round. These latter have been evaluated by the experts in both rounds. The 78 have only been evaluated during the second round by the experts, so for these we have assumed a similar behaviour by both the experts. Although most likely the number of negatives is (much ?) larger in both cases, the current numbers can give some indication. Note that only the cases when both experts shared the same opinion have been taken into account.

Table 3. Agreement miner - experts' intersection (first round) [Test 2]

triplets mined	experts +	experts -	
corpus v1 +	112	463	575
corpus v1 -	3	51	54
	115	514	629

Table 4. Agreement miner - experts' intersection (second round) [Test 3]

triplets mined	experts +	experts -	
corpus v2 +	41	312	353
corpus v2 -	24	481	505
	65	793	858

A comparison between the two rounds (see Tables 3 and 4) shows that the number of correct triples in the second round has decreased quite proportionally to the reduction rate of the original corpus text. However, the precision (proportion of correct triples on the total of triples produced), goes down (112/575 (19%) vs. 41/353 (11%)).

Note that the actual number of negative cases remains unknown. As the experts did not first independently produce a list of triples themselves, it is impossible to calculate the amount of wrongly missed triples (= false negatives). In addition, the current way of assessing the miner's results introduces a bias in the evaluation procedure (called "leading the witness" - cf. [12]): the experts only judge what the miner has produced ignoring potential misses. Some indication can be deduced as the two rounds of ontology mining have generated two partially different sets of triples - cf. supra. But even then, there is no guarantee that all the negative cases have been examined. Hence, recall cannot be computed and no kappa scores are given. However, it seems reasonable to state that upfront removal of passages by the two experts did not result in more relevant triples having been mined, but rather in a decrease of precision. This is very probably attributable to the experts having "cleaned" the original document in a rather complementary way resulting in only 41 triples being considered correct by both experts. The same explanation could hold for the much higher number of triples rejected by both experts and the ontology miner when comparing Tables 3 and 4.

4.3   Q3: Does the Behaviour of the Automated Evaluation Procedure Change as a Result of the Modification of the Input Text ?

On basis of the data contained by Table 5, the resulting kappa value stands for a rather weak degree of similarity beyond chance in the behaviour of the automated evaluation procedure over the two test rounds. This means that the manipulation of the input text has an influence on the results of the EvaLexon procedure, although not to such an extent that the two sets of evaluated triples are completely different, which would have been very surprising. So, a core of triples evaluated as correct ones is maintained over the two rounds (some 33% or 173). One would expect these triples to originate from the parts of the corpus retained by both experts. 81 triples (15,5%) are considered correct in the second round in opposition to the first round. As the automated evaluation procedure uses the modified corpus to build its gold standard, it is normal that also a different behaviour occurs as to attributing scores to triples.

Table 5. Intra EvaLexon agreement: $\kappa = 0,248264$ [Test 4]

triplets evaluated	corpus v2 +	corpus v2 -	
corpus v1 +	173	117	290
corpus v1 -	81	154	235
	254	271	525

4.4   Q4: Does the Scoring Behaviour of the Automated Evaluation Procedure Show Any Correspondence to the Human Experts' Tagging Behaviour?

The next evident question to answer is whether or not the scores of the EvaLexon procedure are in line with the way the human experts themselves assess the triples of the second round, compared with the scores and assessment of the first round.

Note that, again, we only consider these cases where the two privacy experts share the same opinion, which seriously reduces the number of triples to be taken into account. In addition, as we examine this time the EvaLexon behaviour 54 resp. 505 negatives triples of Table 3 resp. Table 4 are not considered. These triples (78 including the 54) have not been processed by the EvaLexon procedure during the first round. In a similar vein, the 666 (including the 505) have not been evaluated automatically during the second round.

Table 6. Agreement EvaLexon - experts' intersection (first round): $\kappa = 0,043935$ [Test 5]

triplets evaluated	experts v1 +	experts v1 -	
corpus v1 +	67	243	310
corpus v1 -	45	220	265
	112	463	575

Table 7. Agreement EvaLexon - experts' intersection (second round): $\kappa = 0,002973$ [Test6]

triplets evaluated	experts v2 +	experts v2 -	
corpus v2 +	20	150	170
corpus v2 -	21	162	183
	41	312	353

The two kappa values are very low - see Table 6 and Table 7. This leads to a conclusion that in both examined cases the human tagging and automated scoring behaviour are similar by chance.

Table 8. Precision and recall of EvaLexon scores - experts' intersection

EvaLexon	round 1	round 2
precision	67/310 (21,61%)	20/170 (11,76%)
recall	67/112 (59,82%)	20/41 (48,78%)

Table 8 provides evidence of deterioration of the quality of the triples of the second round. This seems to be a rather paradoxical statement that, although the EvaLexon procedure detects a deterioration, no correspondence with the ratings of the experts can be established on another basis than chance, even though the experts themselves judge the results of the second round as worse (by approximately 10%). Also note that, according to the experts, the precision decreased with more or less 9% in the second round of ontology mining. Again, a possible explanation for this deterioration could be the divergence between text selections of the two experts. The two "cleaned" versions of the document have become less representative for the entire domain. Hence, also the gold standard, built automatically using the "cleaned" texts, has probably become less representative for the domain: less words are classified as relevant (their z-value is no longer high enough[6]), and subsequently less triples are scored as relevant. This means that cleaning the document upfront is not helpful, but has a negative effect instead. Unfortunately, the automated evaluation procedure does not resemble expert behaviour in a reliable way. However, in the context of automated ontology engineering, it might be enough to have a rough indication of the overall trend (better triples, worse triples) by means of a fast and light weight imperfect evaluation procedure than to have a heavy fine-grained almost humanly behaving procedure ?

4.5   Additional Tests

In an earlier experiment [25], we have shown that the intra and inter rater agreements are rather low, and we wanted to find how this influences the current experiment. Therefore,

---

[6] A z-value indicates how typical a word is for a technical corpus compared to a neutral corpus as a result of a statistical calculation to compare two proportions.

Table 9. Agreement EvaLexon (first round) - experts intersection (second round): $\kappa = 0,03227$

triplets evaluated	experts v2 +	experts v2 -	
corpus v1 +	38	387	425
corpus v1 -	24	397	421
	62	784	846

Table 10. Agreement EvaLexon (second round) - experts intersection (first round): $\kappa = 0,13304$

triplets evaluated	experts v1 +	experts v1 -	
corpus v2 +	27	61	88
corpus v2 -	22	99	121
	49	160	209

we have simulated the situation of a perfect intra rater agreement over the two test rounds by applying their assesments (both experts agreeing) of the first round to the resulting triple set of the second round (where possible) and vice versa.

From the comparison of Table 9 with Table 6 and Table 10 with Table 7 one can only infer that the behaviour of the automated evaluation procedure resembles the human experts' behaviour by chance. In that sense, the behaviour over the two test rounds remains stable, albeit that the kappa score of Table 10 exhibits some weak agreement.

Table 11. Agreement EvaLexon (original text) - expert 1: $\kappa = 0,150695$

triplets evaluated	expert1v1 +	expert1v1 -	
corpus v1 +	247	382	629
corpus v1 -	113	373	486
	360	755	1115

Table 12. Agreement EvaLexon (modified text) - expert 1: $\kappa = 0,154184$

triplets evaluated	expert1v2 +	expert1v2 -	
corpus v2 +	94	116	210
corpus v2 -	70	167	237
	164	283	447

In addition, as a previous experiment [25] has clearly proven that one of the raters himself behaved in an inconsistent way over the two test rounds, we have checked for each expert separately to which extent the automated procedure agrees with the expert.

Tables 11 and 12 show that the EvaLexon procedure shows a weak similar behaviour as expert 1. The agreement between expert 2 and the EvaLexon procedure is, again, due to chance. Hence, the conclusions of the previous experiment are confirmed, namely that the two experts do not rate consistently over the two rounds.

Table 13. Agreement EvaLexon (original text) - expert 2: $\kappa = -0,075909$

triplets evaluated	expert2v1 +	expert2v1 -	
corpus v1 +	206	423	629
corpus v1 -	198	288	486
	404	711	1115

Table 14. Agreement EvaLexon (modified text) - expert 2: $\kappa = 0,010841$

triplets evaluated	expert2v2 +	expert2v2 -	
corpus v2 +	82	128	210
corpus v2 -	90	147	237
	172	275	447

In order to check whether or not the intra rater agreement is also in this experiment low, we have compared the results of the automated evaluation procedure with the behaviour of an expert using the original text and his own "cleaned" version.

Table 15. Agreement EvaLexon (text modified by expert 1) - expert 1: $\kappa = 0,041813$

triplets evaluated	expert1v1 +	expert1v1 -	
corpus v2' +	55	123	178
corpus v2' -	58	158	216
	113	281	394

Table 16. Agreement EvaLexon (text modified by expert 2) - expert 2: $\kappa = -0,0041641$

triplets evaluated	expert2v1 +	expert2v1 -	
corpus v2" +	25	99	124
corpus v2" -	48	152	200
	73	251	324

The kappa scores of Tables 15 and 16 show that only an agreement by chance can be detected. When comparing them with the kappa scores of Table 11 resp. Table 13, surprisingly the kappa score of expert1 drops. Even expert1 might be more consistent in his rating behaviour, he might have removed the "wrong" parts of the text.

Table 17. Precision and recall of EvaLexon scores - experts separately

EvaLexon	expert 1 on corpus v2'	expert 2 on corpus v2"
precision	55/178 (30,89%)	25/124 (20,16%)
recall	55/113 (48,67%)	25/73 (34,24%)

Nevertheless, Table 17 shows higher precision and lower recall scores for expert1, also when compared to Table 3. It looks as if expert2 "contaminates" expert1. In sum, removing parts of the text before automated processing turns out to be not a good idea.

5 Discussion

When referring to the research questions formulated in section 3, the following answers can be provided as based on the findings of section 4.

A1 Reducing the text material (by removing by hand irrelevant parts) does lead to a smaller different set of triples being produced by an unsupervised ontology miner.

A2 Upfront removal of irrelevant passages actually results in a set of less relevant triples. Precision goes down by 8%.

A3 The EvaLexon procedure, the automated evaluation procedure, is sensitive to the change in set-up.

A4 For the automated evaluation procedure, upfront manual removal of passages deemed irrelevant results in an loss of precision and recall (both around 10%). EvaLexon scores weakly resemble the evaluation behaviour of expert 1.

Although the automated evaluation procedure is able to assess that upfront removal of textual material by experts has a negative influence on the results of subsequent ontology mining, the procedure apparently does not behave in the same way as human experts evaluating the same output of the ontology miner. This could be due to the fact that the experts have removed different parts of the text, which reflects their different views on the domain and ontology. This outcome supports earlier findings on the inconsistent behaviour of the experts (low intra and inter rater agreement scores). Another possibility would be to revise the EvaLexon procedure itself that might lack sophistication. Other methods to establish a machine reference standard on the basis of a text corpus could be explored. However, EvaLexon was originally meant as a light weight procedure, ease to use by standard knowledge engineers, that gives an overall indication of the quality of triples resulting from ontology mining.

An important point of discussion remains whether or not the experts should exhibit a high degree of inter rater agreement. In the context of ontology engineering it is important that stakeholders of diverse backgrounds and with different goals participate. Inevitably, this entails that these experts show a behaviour much more prone to differences when rating outcomes of ontology mining. Calculating traditional inter rater agreement scores may no longer be sufficient as such a score relies on the fact that experts fundamentally share a common background, expertise and purpose, which is thus not necessarily the case in the context of ontology engineering. A very practical consequence could be that, when applied to ontology engineering, an acceptable inter rater kappa score might range e.g. between 0.5 and 0 (instead of the usual 1 and 0). Introducing community-based methods, such as [8], might prove useful. Hence, the need still remains to perform a larger validation experiment involving other domains and more human experts. In that sense, the contradiction raised in a previous experiment still stands[7].

6   Related Work

Previous reports on our work contain additional details on the unsupervised miner [22], its application to a bio-medical corpus and a qualitative evaluation [23]. The method and previous quantitative experiments have been presented in [25, 26, 28]. Various researchers are working on different ways to evaluate an ontology from various perspectives. Good overviews of the recent state of the art that also contain a comparison of the characteristics of the various methods are [2, 4–6, 10, 13, 16, 21], the most recent one being [1]. One recent approach focusses on pragmatic aspects [11]. As stated in the introduction, we only considered the question if the lexicalised relevant notions and relationships of a corpus are included in the set of triples resulting from ontology mining. To some degree our approach can be related to work of *Dellschaft* [9] or *Zavitsanos* et al. [30]. Both compare a learnt ontology with a reference standard ontology. The former one makes additional use of the hierarchy to calculate similarities between a new ontology and a reference standard ontology. The reference ontology however has

---

[7] An automated evaluation procedure is needed to replace (or alleviate the burden for) human experts, while these are still crucially needed to assess and canonise first automated evaluation procedures.

been created by a single ontology engineer. In addition, no domain experts have been involved in the evaluation process. The latter one uses a corpus as a direct point of comparison. However, this method implies that the concept instances (also of the reference standard ontology) are annotated in the (new) source corpus text. This condition might be difficult to transpose to any source corpus of any ontology being learnt and automatically evaluated.

7 Future Work

The infrastructure and outcomes from this and previous experiments will allows us to organise new experiments more rapidly. A challenging research avenue is how to "represent" or "calculate" by numerical scores stakeholders' disagreement on which are the relevant domain concepts and relationships to be contained in an ontology. Investigating community-based techniques - perhaps an adapted version of the Delphimethod [17] - would be interesting.

After having used rather simple methods for the automatic evaluation procedure in order to obtain expertise on the possible pitfalls of the entire process, it is now appropriate to use more sophisticated methods (e.g., the weirdness metric [14]) to establish a reference standard. It would also be interesting to perform a test using a state of the art term extractors (e.g., [20]), or the method of Zavitsanos [30] to avoid problems with lexical matching. On the the other hand, aspects for evaluation as presented by Gangemi [13] could be additionally taken into account. Anyhow, in order to define a broadly validated reference for automated evaluation exercises requires many more experiments in many different domains with various evaluation methods.

8 Conclusion

The initial research questions have been partially answered: no, upfront removal of irrelevant text passages did not result in better triples. Yes, the automated evaluation procedure was able to detect a deterioration of the quality of the set of triples, but its agreement in this with the human experts seems to be merely a coincidence, most probably reflecting the initial difference in opinions of the human experts themselves. Hence, it becomes unavoidable to investigate and experiment with (new ?) methods to capture and express degrees of (dis)agreement for the purpose of automated evaluation of ontology mining .

Acknowledgments

We are particularly indebted to dr. Marie-Laure Reinberger (at the time at the Universiteit Antwerpen - CNTS), who has produced the privacy triplets as well as a lemmatised version of the WSJ, to dr. Giles Hogben (at the time at the EU Joint Research Centre IPSC, Italy) and to drs. John Borking (Borking Consultancy, The Netherlands). Both acted as the privacy domain experts.

References

1. Almeida, M.: A proposal to evaluate ontology content. Journal of Applied Ontology 4, 245–265 (2009)
2. Brank, J., Grobelnik, M., Mladenić, D.: Ontology evaluation. SEKT Deliverable #D1.6.1, Jozef Stefan Institute, Prague (2005)
3. Buchholz, S., Veenstra, J., Daelemans, W.: Cascaded grammatical relation assignment. In: Proceedings of EMNLP/VLC 1999. PrintPartners Ipskamp (1999)
4. Buitelaar, P., Cimiano, P. (eds.): Ontology Learning and Population: Bridging the Gap between Text and Knowledge. Frontiers in Artificial Intelligence and Applications, vol. 167. IOS Press, Amsterdam (2008)
5. Buitelaar, P., Cimiano, P., Magnini, B. (eds.): Ontology Learning from Text: Methods, Applications and Evaluation. IOS Press, Amsterdam (2005)
6. Burton-Jones, A., Storey, V., Sugumaran, V.: A semiotic metrics suite for assessing the quality of ontologies. Data and Knowledge Engineering 55(1), 84–102 (2005)
7. De Leenheer, P., Christiaens, S., Meersman, R.: Business semantics management: a case study for competency-centric HRM. Journal of Computers For Industry (2009)
8. de Moor, A., De Leenheer, P., Meersman, R.: DOGMA-MESS: A meaning evolution support system for interorganizational ontology engineering. In: Schärfe, H., Hitzler, P., Øhrstrøm, P. (eds.) ICCS 2006. LNCS (LNAI), vol. 4068, pp. 189–203. Springer, Heidelberg (2006)
9. Dellschaft, K., Staab, S.: On how to perform a gold standard based evaluation of ontology learning. In: Cruz, I., Decker, S., Allemang, D., Preist, C., Schwabe, D., Mika, P., Uschold, M., Aroyo, L.M. (eds.) ISWC 2006. LNCS, vol. 4273, pp. 228–241. Springer, Heidelberg (2006)
10. Dellschaft, K., Staab, S.: Strategies for the Evaluation of Ontology Learning. In: Ontology Learning and Population: Bridging the Gap between Text and Knowledge. IOS Press, Amsterdam (2008)
11. Dividino, R., Romanelli, M., Sonntag, D.: Semiotic-based ontology evaluation tool (s-ontoeval). In: Calzolari, N., Choukri, K., Maegaard, B., Mariani, J., Odijk, J., Piperidis, S., Tapias, D. (eds.) Proceedings of the Sixth International Language Resources and Evaluation (LREC 2008), Paris. European Language Resources Association (2008)
12. Friedman, C., Hripcsak, G.: Evaluating natural language processors in the clinical domain. Methods of Information in Medicine 37(1-2), 334–344 (1998)
13. Gangemi, A., Catenacci, C., Ciaramita, M., Gil, R., Lehmann, J.: Ontology evaluation and validation: an integrated formal model for the quality diagnostic task. Technical report (2005), http://www.loa-cnr.it/Publications.html
14. Gillam, L., Tariq, M.: Ontology via terminology? In: Ibekwe-San Juan, F., Lainé Cruzel, S. (eds.) Proceedings of the Workshop on Terminology, Ontology and Knowledge Representation (2004),
http://www.univ-lyon3.fr/partagedessavoirs/
termino2004/programgb.htm
15. Grueninger, M., Fox, M.: Methodology for the design and evaluation of ontologies. In: Skuce, D. (ed.) IJCAI 1995 Workshop on Basic Ontological Issues in Knowledge Sharing (1995)
16. Hartmann, J., Spyns, P., Maynard, D., Cuel, R., Carmen Suarez de Figueroa, M., Sure, Y.: Methods for ontology evaluation. KnowledgeWeb Deliverable #D1.2.3 (2005)
17. Linstone, H.A., Turoff, M. (eds.): The Delphi Method: Techniques and Applications (2002)
18. Meersman, R.: The use of lexicons and other computer-linguistic tools in semantics, design and cooperation of database systems. In: Zhang, Y., Rusinkiewicz, M., Kambayashi, Y. (eds.) The Proceedings of the Second International Symposium on Cooperative Database Systems for Advanced Applications (CODAS 1999), pp. 1–14. Springer, Heidelberg (1999)

19. Meersman, R.: Ontologies and databases: More than a fleeting resemblance. In: d'Atri, A., Missikoff, M. (eds.) OES/SEO 2001 Rome Workshop. Luiss Publications (2001)
20. Navigli, R., Velardi, P.: Learning domain ontologies from document warehouses and dedicated web sites. Computational Linguistics 30(2), 151–179 (2004)
21. Obrst, L., Ashpole, B., Ceusters, W., Mani, I., Ray, S., Smith, B.: Semantic Web: Revolutionizing Knowledge Discovery in the Life Sciences. In: The Evaluation of Ontologies: Toward Improved Semantic Interoperability, pp. 139–158. Springer, Heidelberg (2007)
22. Reinberger, M.-L., Spyns, P.: Unsupervised text mining for the learning of DOGMA-inspired ontologies. In: Buitelaar, P., Cimiano, P., Magnini, B. (eds.) Ontology Learning from Text: Methods, Applications and Evaluation, pp. 29–43. IOS Press, Amsterdam (2005)
23. Reinberger, M.-L., Spyns, P., Pretorius, A.J., Daelemans, W.: Automatic initiation of an ontology. In: Meersman, R., Tari, Z., et al. (eds.) OTM 2004. LNCS, vol. 3290, pp. 600–617. Springer, Heidelberg (2004)
24. Spyns, P.: Validating EvaLexon: validating a tool for evaluating automatically lexical triples mined from texts. Technical Report x6, STAR Lab, Brussel (2007)
25. Spyns, P.: Evaluating automatically a text miner for ontologies: a catch-22 situation? In: Meersman, R., Tari, Z., Herrero, P., et al. (eds.) OTM 2008, Part II. LNCS, vol. 5332, pp. 1403–1421. Springer, Heidelberg (2008)
26. Spyns, P., Hogben, G.: Validating an automated evaluation procedure for ontology triples in the privacy domain. In: Moens, M.-F., Spyns, P. (eds.) Proceedings of the 18th Annual Conference on Legal Knowledge and Information Systems (JURIX 2005), pp. 127–136. IOS Press, Amsterdam (2005)
27. Spyns, P., Meersman, R., Jarrar, M.: Data modelling versus ontology engineering. SIGMOD Record Special Issue 31(4), 12–17 (2002)
28. Spyns, P., Reinberger, M.-L.: Lexically evaluating ontology triples automatically generated from text. In: Gómez-Pérez, A., Euzenat, J. (eds.) ESWC 2005. LNCS, vol. 3532, pp. 563–577. Springer, Heidelberg (2005)
29. Spyns, P., Tang, Y., Meersman, R.: An ontology engineering methodology for DOGMA. Journal of Applied Ontology 3, 13–39 (2008)
30. Zavitsanos, E., Paliouras, G., Vouros, G.: A distributional approach to evaluating ontology learning methods using a gold standard. In: Proceedings of the Third ECAI Ontology Learning and Population Workshop (2008)

OMIT: Domain Ontology and Knowledge Acquisition in MicroRNA Target Prediction

(Short Paper)

Christopher Townsend[1], Jingshan Huang[1,*], Dejing Dou[2], Shivraj Dalvi[1],
Patrick J. Hayes[3], Lei He[4], Wen-chang Lin[5], Haishan Liu[2], Robert Rudnick[1],
Hardik Shah[1], Hao Sun[6], Xiaowei Wang[7], and Ming Tan[8,**]

[1] School of Computer and Information Sciences
University of South Alabama, Mobile, AL 36688, U.S.A.
huang@usouthal.edu
http://cis.usouthal.edu/~huang/
[2] Computer and Information Science Department
University of Oregon, Eugene, OR 97403, U.S.A.
[3] Florida Institute for Human and Machine Cognition
Pensacola, FL 32502, U.S.A.
[4] College of Science and Technology
Armstrong Atlantic State University, Savannah, GA 31419, U.S.A.
[5] Institute of Biomedical Sciences
Academia Sinica, Taipei, Taiwan
[6] Department of Chemical Pathology
Chinese University of Hong Kong, Hong Kong, China
[7] Department of Radiation Oncology
Washington University School of Medicine, St. Louis, MO 63108, U.S.A.
[8] Mitchell Cancer Institute
University of South Alabama, Mobile, AL 36688, U.S.A.
mtan@usouthal.edu
http://southalabama.edu/~tan/

Abstract. The identification and characterization of important roles microRNAs (miRNAs) played in human cancer is an increasingly active area in medical informatics. In particular, the prediction of miRNA target genes remains a challenging task to cancer researchers. Current efforts have focused on manual knowledge acquisition from existing miRNA databases, which is time-consuming, error-prone, and subject to biologists' limited prior knowledge. Therefore, an effective knowledge acquisition has been inhibited. We propose a computing framework based on the Ontology for MicroRNA Target Prediction (OMIT), **the very first** ontology in miRNA domain. With such formal knowledge representation, it is thus possible to facilitate knowledge discovery and sharing from existing sources. Consequently, the framework aims to assist biologists in unraveling important roles of miRNAs in human cancer, and thus to help clinicians in making sound decisions when treating cancer patients.

---

* Corresponding Author.
** Corresponding Author.

R. Meersman et al. (Eds.): OTM 2010, Part II, LNCS 6427, pp. 1160–1167, 2010.

1   Introduction

Healthcare is a typical area where advances in computing have resulted in numerous improvements. In particular, the identification and characterization of the important roles microRNAs (miRNAs) play in human cancer is an increasingly active area. MiRNAs are a class of small non-coding RNAs capable of regulating gene expression. They have been demonstrated to be involved in diverse biological functions [13,18], and miRNAs' expression profiling has identified them associated with clinical diagnosis and prognosis of several major tumor types [8,15,21]. Unfortunately, the prediction of the relationship between miRNAs and their target genes still remains a challenging task [4,6].

Ontologies are formal, declarative knowledge representation models, playing a key role in defining formal semantics in traditional knowledge engineering. We propose an innovative computing framework (Figure 1) based on the Ontology for MicroRNA Target Prediction (OMIT) to handle the aforementioned challenge. The OMIT is a domain-specific ontology upon which it is possible to facilitate knowledge discovery and sharing from existing sources. As a result, the long-term research objective of the OMIT framework is **to assist biologists in unraveling important roles of miRNAs in human cancer, and thus to help clinicians in making sound decisions when treating patients.**

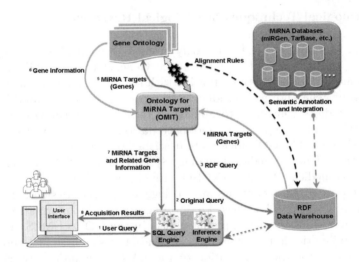

Fig. 1. OMIT System Framework

2   Background and Related Research

2.1   Background Knowledge of Ontologies

Ontology is a computational model of some portion or domain of the world [19]. The model describes the semantics of the terms used in the domain. Ontology is often captured in some form of a semantic network, i.e., a graph whose nodes are concepts or individual objects and whose arcs represent relationships or associations among the concepts. The semantic network is augmented by properties and attributes, constraints, functions, and rules, which govern the behavior of the concepts. In brief, an ontology consists of a finite set of concepts (also known as "terms" or "classes"), along with these concepts' properties and relationships. In addition, most real-world ontologies have very few or no instances, i.e., they only have the aforementioned graphical structure (also known as "schema"). **Ontology Heterogeneity** is an inherent characteristic of ontologies developed by different parties for the same (or similar) domains. The heterogeneous semantics may occur in two ways. (1) Different ontologies could use different terminologies to describe the same conceptual model. That is, different terms could be used for the same concept, or alternatively, an identical term could be adopted for different concepts. (2) Even if two different ontologies use the same terminology, which itself is almost impossible in the real world, concepts' associated properties and the relationships among concepts are most likely to be different. **Ontology Matching** is short for "Ontology Schema Matching", also known as "Ontology Alignment," or "Ontology Mapping." It is the process of determining correspondences between concepts from heterogeneous ontologies (often designed by distributed parties).

2.2   Ontological Techniques in Biological Research

Ontological techniques have been widely applied to medical and biological research. The most successful example is the Gene Ontology (GO) project [3], which is a major bioinformatics initiative with the aim of standardizing the representation of gene and gene product attributes across species and databases. The GO provides a controlled vocabulary of terms for describing gene product characteristics and gene product annotation data, as well as tools to access and process such data. The GO's focus is to describe how gene products behave in a cellular context. Unified Medical Language System (UMLS) [22] and the National Center for Biomedical Ontology (NCBO) [10] are two other successful examples in applying ontological techniques into biological research. Besides, efforts have been carried out for ontology-based data integration in bioinformatics.

[1] discusses the issue of mapping concepts in the GO to UMLS. This study reveals the difficulties in the integration of vocabularies created in different manners, and allows for the exploitation of the UMLS semantic network to link disparate genes to clinical outcomes. The authors in [2] adopt the global gene expression profiling to identify the molecular pathways and processes affected upon toxicant exposure. Their work demonstrates that the GO mapping can identify both known and novel molecular changes in the mouse liver. [24] develops a computational approach to analyze the annotation of sets of molecules. The authors reveal trends and enrichment of proteins of particular functions within high-throughput datasets at a higher sensitivity than perusal of endpoint annotations. B. Smith et al. [20] describe a strategy, the Open Biomedical Ontologies (OBO) Foundry initiative, whose long-term goal is that the data

generated through biomedical research should form a single, consistent, cumulatively expanding and algorithmically tractable whole.

3   Methodologies

3.1   Task 1: Domain-Specific Ontology

In order to develop a conceptual model that encompasses the required elements to properly describe medical informatics (especially in human cancer), it is essential to explore and abstract the miRNA data to the semantic level. The design of the OMIT will rely on two resources: existing miRNA databases and domain knowledge from cancer biologists. Besides cancer biology experts in the project team, there are six labs from around the world, (1) Yousef Lab in Israel, (2) DIANA Lab in Greece, (3) Sun Lab in Hong Kong, China, (4) Segal Lab in Israel, (5) Lin Lab in Taiwan, and (6) Wang Lab in St. Louis, MO, that have committed to actively participate in the project by providing original data sets and undertaking an in-depth analysis of integrated data and the query that follows.

3.2   Task 2: Annotation on Source Databases

Semantic annotation is the process of tagging source files with predefined metadata, which usually consists of a set of ontological concepts. We adopt a "deep" annotation that takes two steps. (1) To annotate the source database schemas, resulting in a set of mapping rules specified in the RIF-PRD format between OMIT concepts and elements from source database schemas. (2) To annotate data sets from each source, and the annotated data sets will be published in the resource description framework (RDF) [17]. Being a structure based on the directed acyclic graph model, the RDF defines statements about resources and their relationships in triples. Such generic structure allows structured and semi-structured data to be mixed, exposed, and shared across different applications, and the data interoperability is thus made easier to handle. The annotation outcomes will become the input to the next phase, i.e., data integration.

3.3   Task 3: Centralized RDF Data Warehouse

Instead of a traditional relational data warehouse, we propose to create a centralized RDF data warehouse for the data integration, which better fits the project objective. The first, and the most critical, step is to specify the correspondence between source databases and the global schema. We propose to adopt a "Globle-As-View (GAV)-like" approach. Our approach is similar to the traditional GAV approach [7] in that the global schema is regarded as a view over source databases, and expressed in terms of source database schemas. On the other hand, our approach differs from the traditional GAV approach in that we include not only a global schema, but also aggregated, global data sets as well. As a result, user query will be composed according to the concepts in the global schema, and the query answering will be based on the centralized data sets with an unfolding strategy.

3.4   Task 4: Query and Search in a Unified Style

When presenting a miRNA of interest, its potential targets can be retrieved from existing miRNA databases. Additional information will be further acquired from the GO, which is critical to fully understand the biological functions of the miRNA of interest. The OMIT system aims to provide users a single search/query engine that takes their needs in a nonprocedural specification format. Such search/query is *unified*, that is, although source miRNA databases are geographically distributed and usually heterogeneous among each other, the OMIT system presents users (biologists) a *uniform* view of such heterogeneous data, along with integrated information from the GO.

4   The OMIT Ontology

4.1   Design Methodology

As mentioned in Section 3, the OMIT ontology design relies on two resources: existing miRNA databases and domain knowledge from cancer biologists. Besides, unlike most existing biomedical ontologies that were developed through a top-down approach, our design methodology is a combination of both top-down and bottom-up approaches. On one hand, existing miRNA databases provide us with a general guideline (top-down) regarding which concepts are of most importance to cancer biologists, as well as these concepts' properties and their relationships among each other; on the other hand, domain experts, together with ontology engineers, can fine tune the conceptual model (bottom-up) by an in-depth analysis of typical instances in miRNA domain, e.g., *miR-21, miR-125a, miR-125b,* and *let-7,* etc.

There are currently different formats in describing an ontology based on different logics: Web Ontology Language (OWL) [14], Open Biological and Biomedical Ontologies (OBO) [11], Knowledge Interchange Format (KIF) [5], and Open Knowledge Base Connectivity (OKBC) [12]. We choose the OWL format, a standard recommended by the World Wide Web Consortium (W3C) [23]. OWL is designed for use by applications that need to process the content of information instead of just presenting it to humans. As a result, OWL facilitates greater machine interpretability of Web contents. The first version OMIT ontology has been added into NCBO BioPortal [9]. The link to access the OMIT ontology is: http://bioportal.bioontology.org/ontologies/42873.

4.2   The Alignment between the OMIT and the GO

An initial version of the OMIT ontology was designed using Protégé 4.0 [16], with 320 concepts in total, many of which are closely related to three sub-ontologies in the GO, i.e., BiologicalProcess, CellularComponent, and MolecularFunction:

- Some OMIT concepts are directly extended from GO concepts. E.g., OMIT concept *GeneExpression* is designed to describe miRNAs' regulation of gene expression. This concept is inherited from concept *gene expression* in the BiologicalProcess ontology. This way, subclasses of *gene expression*, such as *negative regulation of gene expression*, are then accessible in the OMIT for describing the negative gene regulation of miRNAs in question.

– Some OMIT concepts are equivalent to (or similar to) GO concepts. For example, OMIT concept *PathologicalEvent* and its subclasses are designed to describe biological processes that are disturbed when a cell becomes cancerous. Although not immediately inherited from any specific GO concepts, these OMIT concepts do match up with certain concepts in the BiologicalProcess ontology. OMIT concepts *TargetGene* and *Protein* are two other examples, which correspond to individual genes and individual gene products, respectively, in the GO.

4.3   Software Implementation

The back end of the OMIT system is implemented in the C# language, following an object-oriented approach. A class diagram is demonstrated in the left portion of Figure 2. We represent each OWL entity of interest, i.e., concepts, object properties, and data properties, as its own class. Our *OWLOntology* class constitutes the external interface to this data structure, and it stores each entity in a private hash table for quick lookup by name.

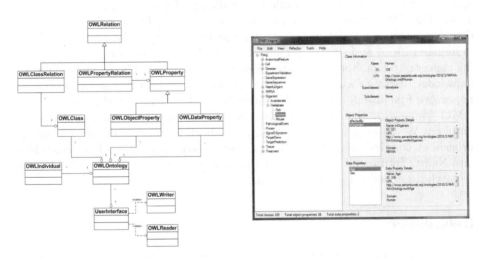

Fig. 2. OMIT Software Class Diagram and GUI Design

We have developed our own parser for OWL ontology files based on the built-in XML parsing capabilities in C#. The right portion of Figure 2 shows a friendly GUI when running our code on the OMIT ontology. In addition, we have deployed the project website (Figure 3) at http://omit.cis.usouthal.edu/, which features an interactive online discussion forum in addition to other materials, e.g., publications, software and tools, and data sets, etc.

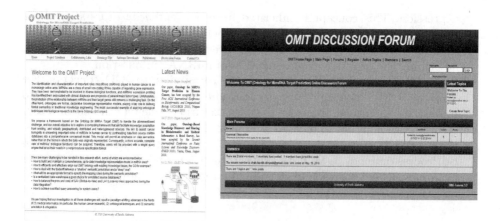

Fig. 3. Project Website Homepage and Interactive Online Discussion Forum

5   Conclusions

We propose an innovative computing framework based on the miRNA-domain-specific ontology, OMIT, to handle the challenge of predicting miRNAs' target genes. The OMIT framework is designed upon *the very first* ontology in miRNA domain. It will assist biologists in better discovering important roles of miRNAs in human cancer, and thus help clinicians in making sound decisions when treating cancer patients. Such long-term research goal will be achieved via facilitating knowledge discovery and sharing from existing sources. In this work-in-progress paper, we first discuss proposed approaches and anticipated challenges in the OMIT framework; then our efforts have focused on the development of a domain ontology. We adopt a unique combination of both top-down and bottom-up approaches when designing the OMIT ontology, whose first version has been added into NCBO BioPortal. Future investigation will be carried out according to the research tasks defined in the framework.

References

1. Castano, S., Ferrara, A., Montanelli, S.: H-MATCH: An Algorithm for Dynamically Matching Ontologies in Peer-based Systems. In: Proc. the first VLDB International Workshop on Semantic Web and Databases, SWDB 2003 (2003)
2. Currie, R., Bombail, V., Oliver, J., Moore, D., Lim, F., Gwilliam, V., Kimber, I., Chipman, K., Moggs, J., Orphanides, G.: Gene ontology mapping as an unbiased method for identifying molecular pathways and processes affected by toxicant exposure: application to acute effects caused by the rodent non-genotoxic carcinogen diethylhexylphthalate. Journal of Toxicological Sciences 86, 453–469 (2005)
3. Gene Ontology Website (August 2010),
   http://www.geneontology.org/index.shtml

4. Hsu, S., Chu, C., Tsou, A., Chen, S., Chen, H., Hsu, P., Wong, Y., Chen, Y., Chen, G., Huang, H.: miRNAMap 2.0: genomic maps of microRNAs in metazoan genomes. Nucleic Acids Research 36(D), 165–169 (2008)
5. KIF (August 2010), http://logic.stanford.edu/kif/
6. Kim, S., Nam, J., Lee, W., Zhang, B.: miTarget: microRNA target gene prediction using a support vector machine. BMC Bioinformatics 7(411) (2006)
7. Lenzerini, M.: Data Integration: A Theoretical Perspective. In: Proc. the Twenty-first ACM SIGMOD-SIGACT-SIGART Symposium on Principles of Database Systems (PODS 2002) (June 2002)
8. Nakajima, G., Hayashi, K., Xi, Y., Kudo, K., Uchida, K., Takasaki, K., Ju, J.: Noncoding microRNAs hsa-let-7g and hsa-miR-181b are associated with chemoresponse to S-1 in colon cancer. Cancer Genomics and Proteomics 3, 317–324 (2006)
9. NCBO BioPortal (August 2010), http://bioportal.bioontology.org/
10. NCBO Website (August 2010), http://www.bioontology.org/
11. OBO (August 2010), http://www.obofoundry.org/
12. OKBC (August 2010), http://www.ai.sri.com/~okbc/
13. Olsen, P., Ambros, V.: The lin-4 regulatory RNA controls developmental timing in Caenorhabditis elegans by blocking LIN-14 protein synthesis after the initiation of translation. Dev. Biology 216, 671–680 (1999)
14. OWL (August 2010), http://www.w3.org/TR/owl-features/
15. Pradervand, S., Weber, J., Thomas, J., Bueno, M., Wirapati, P., Lefort, K., Dotto, G., Harshman, K.: Impact of normalization on miRNA microarray expression profiling. RNA 15, 493–501 (2009)
16. Protégé Website (August 2010), http://protege.stanford.edu/
17. RDF Website (August 2010), http://www.w3.org/RDF/
18. Reinhart, B., Slack, F., Basson, M., Pasquinelli, A., Bettinger, J., Rougvie, A., Ruvkun, G.: The 21-nucleotide let-7 RNA regulates developmental timing in Caenorhabditis elegans. Nature 403, 901–906 (2000)
19. Singh, M., Huhns, M.: Service-Oriented Computing - Semantics, Processes, Agents, 1st edn. Wiley, Chichester (2005)
20. Smith, B., Ashburner, M., Rosse, C., Bard, J., Bug, W., Ceusters, W., Goldberg, L., Eilbeck, K., Ireland, A., Mungall, C., Leontis, N., Rocca-Serra, P., Ruttenberg, A., Sansone, S., Scheuermann, R., Shah, N., Whetzel, P., Lewis, S.: The OBO foundry: coordinated evolution of ontologies to support biomedical data integration. Nature Biotechnology 25(11), 1251–1255 (2007)
21. Sorrentino, A., Liu, C., Addario, A., Peschle, C., Scambia, G., Ferlini, C.: Role of microRNAs in drug-resistant ovarian cancer cells. Gynecologic Oncology 111, 478–486 (2008)
22. UMLS (August 2010), http://www.nlm.nih.gov/research/umls/
23. W3C (The World Wide Web Consortium) (August 2010), http://www.w3.org/
24. Wolting, C., McGlade, C., Tritchler, D.: Cluster analysis of protein array results via similarity of Gene Ontology annotation. BMC Bioinformatics 7(338) (2006)

Author Index

Printing: Mercedes-Druck, Berlin
Binding: Stein+Lehmann, Berlin